Communications
in Computer and Information Science   466

Alla Kravets   Maxim Shcherbakov
Marina Kultsova   Tadashi Iijima (Eds.)

Knowledge-Based Software Engineering

11th Joint Conference, JCKBSE 2014
Volgograd, Russia, September 17-20, 2014
Proceedings

 Springer

Volume Editors

Alla Kravets
Volgograd State Technical University, Russia
E-mail: agk@gde.ru

Maxim Shcherbakov
Volgograd State Technical University, Russia
E-mail: maxim.shcherbakov@gmail.com

Marina Kultsova
Volgograd State Technical University, Russia
E-mail: siemens2006@yandex.ru

Tadashi Iijima
Keio University, Yokohama, Japan
E-mail: iijima@ae.keio.ac.jp

ISSN 1865-0929   e-ISSN 1865-0937
ISBN 978-3-319-11853-6   e-ISBN 978-3-319-11854-3
DOI 10.1007/978-3-319-11854-3
Springer Cham Heidelberg New York Dordrecht London

Library of Congress Control Number: 2014949225

Typesetting: Camera-ready by author, data conversion by Scientific Publishing Services, Chennai, India

Printed on acid-free paper

Springer is part of Springer Science+Business Media (www.springer.com)

Preface

This volume contains the proceedings of the 11th Joint Conference on Knowledge-Based Software Engineering.

The Conference on Knowledge-Based Software Engineering (JCKBSE) was founded in 1994 by leading scientists of software engineering in Japan. The main objective of the JCKBSE series of biannual conferences is to bring together researchers and practitioners to share ideas on the foundations, techniques, tools, and applications of knowledge-based software engineering theory and practice.

The JCKBSE 2014 continues the JCKBSE conferences held in Pereslavl-Zalesskii (1994), Sozopol (1996), Smolenice (1998), Brno (2000), Maribor (2002), Bratislava (2002), Protvino (2004), Tallinn (2006), Piraeus (2008), Kaunas (2010), and Rhodes (2012).

July 2014

Alla Kravets
Tadashi Iijima
Marina Kultsova
Maxim Shcherbakov

Organization

General Chair

Dmitriy Novikov

Co-chairs

Alla Kravets
Tadashi Iijima

Steering Committee:

Vadim Stefanuk
Christo Dichev
Shuichiro Yamamoto

Pavol Navrat
Atsushi Ohnishi

Program Committee:

Alexey Kizim
Michalis Skordoulis
Marina Kultsova
Dmitriy Korobkin
Maxim Shcherbakov
Olga Berestneva
Satyadhyan Chickerur
Maria Dascalu
Hirohisa Aman
Peter Blanchfield
Constanta-Nicoleta Bodea
Adriaan Brebels
Germanas Budnikas
Nataliya Dyeyeva
Nuno Escudeiro
Paula Escudeiro
Yoshiaki Fukazawa
Oleksandr Gaydatov
Georgiy Gerkushenko
Pavel Grigorenko

Marcin Grzegorzek
Wolfram Hardt
Charaf Hassan
Atsuo Hazeyama
Tran Loc Hung
Tiko Iyamu
Kenji Kaijiri
Shigeo Kaneda
Michael Koniordos
Fumihiro Kumeno
Christos Malliarakis
Henrique Mamede
Jean-Charles Marty
Ann Matokhina
Saeko Matsuura
Mehran Misaghi
David Moffat
Alin Moldoveanu
Peter Mozelius
Takehiko Murakawa

Table of Contents

Methodology and Tools for Knowledge Discovery and Data Mining

Methods and Tools for Software Engineering Education

Knowledge Technologies for Semantic Web and Ontology Engineering

Knowledge-Based Methods and Tools for Testing, Verification and Validation, Maintenance and Evolution

Natural Language Processing, Image Analysis and Recognition

Knowledge-Based Methods and Applications in Information Security, Robotics and Navigation

Decision Support Methods for Software Engineering

Architecture of Knowledge-Based Systems, Including Intelligent Agents and Softbots

Automating Software Design and Synthesis

Knowledge Management for Business Processes, Work-Flows and Enterprise Modeling

Knowledge-Based Methods and Applications in Bio Science, Medicine and Justice

Knowledge-Based Requirements Engineering, Domain Analysis and Modeling

Intelligent User Interfaces and Human-Machine Interaction

Lean Software Engineering

Program Understanding, Programming Knowledge, Modeling Programs and Programmers

Knowledge Discovery in the SCADA Databases Used for the Municipal Power Supply System

Valery Kamaev[1], Alexey Finogeev[2], Anton Finogeev[2], and Sergey Shevchenko[3]

[1] Volgograd State Technical University, Volgograd, Russia
kamaev@cad.vstu.ru
[2] Penza State University, Penza, Russia
alexeyfinogeev@gmail.com, fanton3@yandex.ru
[3] National Technical University "Kharkiv Polytechnic Institute", Kharkiv, Ukraina
sv_shevchenko@mail.ru

Abstract. This scientific paper delves into the problems related to the development of intellectual data analysis system that could support decision making to manage municipal power supply services. The management problems of municipal power supply system have been specified taking into consideration modern tendencies shown by new technologies that allow for an increase in the energy efficiency. The analysis findings of the system problems related to the integrated computer-aided control of the power supply for the city have been given. The consideration was given to the hierarchy-level management decomposition model. The objective task targeted at an increase in the energy efficiency to minimize expenditures and energy losses during the generation and transportation of energy carriers to the Consumer, the optimization of power consumption at the prescribed level of the reliability of pipelines and networks and the satisfaction of Consumers has been defined. To optimize the support of the decision making a new approach to the monitoring of engineering systems and technological processes related to the energy consumption and transportation using the technologies of geospatial analysis and Knowledge Discovery in databases (KDD) has been proposed. The data acquisition for analytical problems is realized in the wireless heterogeneous medium, which includes soft-touch VPN segments of ZigBee technology realizing the 6LoWPAN standard over the IEEE 802.15.4 standard and also the segments of the networks of cellular communications. JBoss Application Server is used as a server-based platform for the operation of the tools used for the retrieval of data collected from sensor nodes, PLC and energy consumption record devices. The KDD tools are developed using Java Enterprise Edition platform and Spring and ORM Hibernate technologies. To structure very large data arrays we proposed to organize data in the form of hyper tables and to use the Compute Unified Device Architecture technology.

Keywords: Knowledge discovery in databases, intelligent data analysis, decision-making support, power supply, energy efficiency, energy consumption, ZigBee, sensor network, hyper table, CUDA, Hibernate ORM, analytical data processing.

A. Kravets et al. (Eds.): JCKBSE 2014, CCIS 466, pp. 1–14, 2014.
© Springer International Publishing Switzerland 2014

1   Introduction

An efficient and high-quality power supply for industrial companies is one of the main vectors of the development of the economy and successful advance of the contemporary society. The studies of the management processes of municipal power supply services that include electrical, thermal, water and gas supply engineering systems showed that the body of problems solved at different stages of decision-making can be considered in terms of system-synergetic approach [1].

The managerial structure used for the municipal power supply systems can be represented by the distribution of dedicated hierarchy –level control functions that form the clusters of problems according to the periodicity of their solution, functional content and the level of their importance. The managerial decision-making support is based on the realization of integrated methods used for the acquisition of many different data during the monitoring of the main facilities of municipal power supply system and technological processes. A theoretical statement of the problem related to an increase in the managerial efficiency takes into consideration the following features, in particular:

— realizing the strategy of optimal balancing for the solution of two problems: self-organization of efficient structures used for the off-line control and centralized coordination of the subsystems belonging to a lower level of the hierarchy;
— taking into consideration local priorities for the decision-making with regard to individual control subsystems;
— establishing optimal vertical links between the hierarchy levels of the subsystems of upper levels using the appropriate control actions;
— establish optimal horizontal links between subsystems one level using the exchange of structured information;
— optimization management functions of subsystems with different properties hierarchy of priority in accordance decision-making support.

2   Problems of the Management Automation by Municipal Power Supply Systems

Let's consider the problems faced by the developers of computer-aided decision-making support and control systems intended for the flow control services of the companies that maintain power supply networks [2].

1. Data "opacity" problem. It is known that most analytical information systems store their data and the results of work in the form, which is not appropriate for the use by other systems. The "opacity' of data protocols and formats does not allow the specialists of the company to transfer data to a different software environment or demands from specialists to apply every effort. Actually the company experiences "informational dependence" on the developer of a specific software product that may result in the disastrous consequences when the developer stops his engineering support.

2. Data mismatch problem. On the one part this problem is caused by the fact that power supply companies use different hardware, software and proprietary protocols for the data acquisition and processing. A proprietary character of the internal protocols of data exchange does not allow for the arrangement of data interrelation between the systems of different producers. For example, more than 60 types of heat computers with internal data exchange protocols are nowadays produced for municipal heat supply systems, which prevents the use of universal thermal energy control and record system for heat and hot water supply systems [3]. To solve this problem the technologies of integrated interface are used for the automated control of objects and technological processes [4] based on OPC (OLE for process control) standards. Though the introduction of appropriate standards into the SCADA systems for the acquisition of on-line (OPC data access) and archival (OPC Historical Data Access) data provided by industrial automatic systems is rather promising a lot of equipment and software still fails to use OPC technologies.

On the other part, the fact that the same data are required for the solution of the problems by different organizations that keep record of their own databases and use different software systems also presents a problem [5]. Moreover, the databases and programs present the same figures in different formats. For example, the section length of a heat network pipeline is used for hydraulic computations, thermal losses computations, accounting records of depreciation charges, repair scheduling, and the specification of the alienation zone in cadastral plans, etc. If the servicing company introduces changes into the section length due to the pipeline repair this will result in the disagreement of this figure in the databases of different organizations involved in the appropriate record-keeping. The synchronization of data in all databases requires considerable effort, labor time and appropriate expenses and very often this process is impossible to control. Therefore, it is impossible to provide reliable information data arrays, and this affects the efficiency and quality of engineering, technical and managerial decision making.

3. Information flow mismatch problem. Today engineering, technical, technological and organizational problems are solved using the transport telecommunication environment for the data exchange. Network technologies are called to solve the second problem of data disagreement in different organizations. However, lack of the uniform strategy for the use of network technologies, availability of multitude of telecommunication solutions, hardware and providers of network services result in the disagreement of information flows due to the implementation of different telecommunication solutions by companies.

4. Branch-specific data record problem [6]. This problem is related to the fact that municipal companies supplying energy of a different type (power supply, heat supply, water supply and gas supply) belong to different trade managerial proprietors that are mutually interrelated only at the level of mutual settlements of accounts. A comprehensive solution of this problem requires the introduction of the uniform SCADA system for all energy saving companies in the city, the arrangement of multidimensional "cloudy" storage of common data and the creation of the uniform transportation environment for the data exchange. A uniform monitoring and flow control system of engineering network facilities allows for the realization of the coordinated

management of the industrial and technological processes of municipal power supply services. It also provides the consistency of the operation of all appropriate links, trouble-free operation of auxiliary, maintenance and trouble repair services.

These problems and lack of uniform strategy for their solution so much needed for the municipal power supply system does not allow people involved in decision making to see the entire patters of the processes that occur in the common municipal system of engineering communications, which reduces the managerial efficiency on the whole.

3   Arrangements Made to Provide the Operation of Intelligent Analysis System

The dispatch systems SCADA are used to take measurements, collect data and analyze the parameters of energy carriers, process parameters used for their generation, transportation, consumption and utilization [7]. The purpose of the development of a comprehensive decision-making support and monitoring system for the municipal power supply system is to reach the power effectiveness through an increase in the power efficiency of power supply companies [8, reduction of power losses during the transportation of energy carriers, and the optimization of energy consumption in public and domestic buildings taking into consideration the meteorological information, information on building operation modes, the behavior of end users, etc.

The system used for the intelligent analysis and knowledge discovery in the stored data can operate under the condition of taking the following measures:

1.   Mounting energy consumption record devices with built-in OPC servers for engineering network facilities and end users;

2.   C Creating the wireless transport medium with sensor and cellular segments for the data acquisition [9];

3.   Providing the data collection using sensor units and cellular modems with automation devices via OPC servers;

4.   "Sinking" the data obtained from different sources into the multidimensional "cloudy" storage system supporting simultaneously consolidation, "refinement", normalization and transformation operations;

5.   Preparing analyzed   data samples (including learning samples for forecast models), retrieving them from storages and other sources by different slices to transmit them to hypercubes for analytical processing;

6.   Synthesizing forecast models for the purpose of iterative selection of the best model to forecast energy consumption at different facilities depending on the factors available for short-term and long-term periods [10,11];

7.   Visualizing forecast results on digital cartographic map (DCM) that provides an opportunity for the display of the figures and performances of energy consumption, energy losses and energy efficiency in numerical and graphic forms using color-differentiation circuits;

8.   Computing energy consumption parameters for different categories of consumers according to the forecast results

9.   Transmitting the forecast results, energy consumption parameters in the form of structured reports, diagrams, and color circuits of DMP to dispatchers, energy managers and the managers of services and companies to work out measures that would allow for an increase in energy effectiveness;

10.   Transfer the forecast results, the parameters of energy consumption in the form of structured reports, graphs, color schemes, DMP (dispatchers, energy managers, service managers and companies) to develop activities to improve energy efficiency;

11.   Computer-aided control of the energy consumption and on-line correction of forecast parameters according to the real factors for the purpose of the iteration adjustment of forecast models and repeated forecasting [12].

4   Heterogeneous Wireless Medium for the Sensor Data Collection

Heterogeneous wireless medium for the collection of the sensor data to provide the operation of the system used for the intelligent analysis and knowledge discovery includes the following components:

1.   Segments of ZigBee sensory networks with units connected to industrial automation devices, different sensors, fire alarm and burglar systems controlled by a segment coordinator;

2.   Segments of Bluetooth networks [13] with units connected to industrial automation devices, different sensors, fire alarm and burglar systems controlled by master devices;

3.   Cellular communication networks for the collection of data from remote objects if there is no opportunity to create own VPN circuits or it is not reasonable to do that from the economic standpoint;

4.   Satellite network for the transport monitoring of company's vehicles and tracking mobile means used by the personnel for the communication;

5.   WiFi and Ethernet segments of power supply facilities and dispatch centers;

6.   Internet segment for remote access to the information resources of SCADA systems and monitoring systems.

To provide appropriate urban communication range it is recommended to use the following methods of data acquisition:

1. Placing and using the GSM/GPRS modems to retranslate data via the cellular network. The information can be transmitted by GSM-systems in the form of SMS-messages, via the modem connection (CSD), through the transmission of tone ringing (DTMF mode) and also in the GPRS mode of batch messages. The OPC server or PLC with intergrated modems are installed in the engineering network facilities and provide the acquisition, storage and processing of primary data provided by different measuring devices with the transmission of data to the dispatcher server through the

GSM/GPRS channels. However, the drawbacks of similar systems are low noise immunity, easy suppression of the GSM-channel, unstable operation of the GSM network, exposure of the network to different attacks, dependence on the operation of cellular network, and financial dependence on the service provider.

2. Placing and using the sensor-based units of the Zigbee network (Fig. 1) for engineering communication facilities with the possibility of the data acquisition and their transmission through the central network coordinator to the dispatcher server [14] using the following equipment::
    (a) External antennas with a high gain factor;
    (b) Low-power intermediate relays of the sensor network that can be installed:
        (i) on tall buildings and posts of power transmission lines;
        (ii) on external metering terminals of underground heat pipelines with the wire leakage control system that are arranged at a space of 300 meters from each other according to the specifications. In this case the repeater performs two functions: the frame relaying and leakage detection and localization.

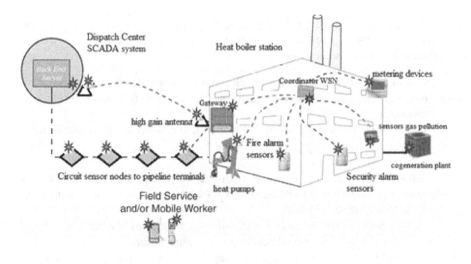

Fig. 1. Sensor network cluster for heating points

The wireless sensor-based network can perfectly be used for SCADA systems to support the decision-making [15]. Such a network serves as an infrastructure for the collection of data provided by different measurement devices. This allows the dispatchers not only to perform monitoring and to read and analyze on-line and archive data, but also to transmit control actions to actuating mechanisms. The advantage of such a system consists in the possibility of the use of energy-saving modes when sensory units are mainly in the sleeping mode and turn on just to read the data and transmit them to dispatcher server. The use of a virtual corporate network for the data acquisition is also of great importance both from the financial point of view and from the point of view of providing the information security for the corporate computer-aided system that exercises control of technological processes for municipal power supply.

An interesting solution will be the arrangement of the relays of sensory network on external ground-based terminals that are connected to the leakage control system in contemporary heat mains. Contemporary heat-carrier transfer mains use double tubes with the internal heat insulation material and wired on-line remote control system (ORC). The connection to the wires of the ORC system is done using the instrument terminals that are connected to pipe conductors and are taken out to the surface. Intermediate terminals are arranges at a space of 300 meters according to specifications. The terminals can be used to provide data transfer from cluster-type sensory and other segments through the train of sensory units to dispatcher stations.

In the general case it is necessary to use all types of accessible wireless networks [16] to create the transport medium for the data acquisition and transmission from the monitoring facilities of the municipal power supply system that are distributed across the large city territory. This allows for an increase in the reliability due to the reservation of communication channels. Figure 2 shows the segment of such a heterogeneous wireless network for the data collection in the dispatch SCADA system used for the computer-aided control of municipal networks [17].

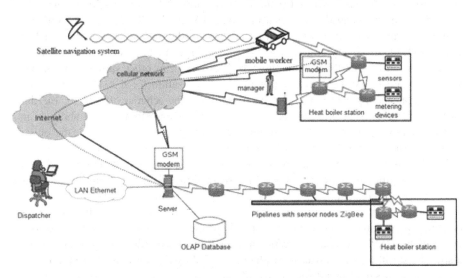

Fig. 2. The wireless network segment for data collection of heating supply system

5   Data Analysis and Knowledge Discovery Tools in SCADA Databases Used for the Municipal Power Supply

SCADA systems receive on-line and archive data from OPC servers through the sensory network units or cellular modems and transmit them to the data preparation subsystem and their "immersion" into the multidimensional storage system.

As the number of monitoring objects and records in the multidimensional storage system increases the intelligent data analysis system will sooner or later encounter efficiency problems. These problems can be related to the improperly designed architecture system or can be caused by external restrictions. The latter can be presented by insufficient facilities of application servers or database servers, and nonoptimal structure of the databases. The first problem is solved through the addition of the servers to the cluster and the second problem is solved through the optimization of the data storage scheme, the transcription of the code of the intelligent analysis application, the segmentation of complicated relational inquiries, etc.

To increase the sampling efficiency of data slices from the multidimensional storage system we propose the data storage method, which is based on the combination of the industrial SQL storage system and distributed no relational data array storage system. This is the option for the solution of the problem related to the storage efficiency and scalability, because it is based on a simpler info logical data model. For this purpose the system of intelligent analysis in combination with the Oracle data manager uses the distributed no relational Cassandra system for caching the slices of multidimensional storage; this provides a significant increase in the data sampling rate, and improves its fault-tolerance and scalability.

The data scheme is described using the structures of hash tables, trees, etc. The Cassandra system using the Java platform includes the distributed hash system, providing thus the linear scalability with an increase in the data level. The data analysis and knowledge discovery system uses the data storage model in the form of the hyper table based on the family of columns, which differs from other similar systems that store data in a key/value pack. The hierarchy organization for the storage of caches with several nesting levels has also been realized. The scheme offered for the data storage and processing is attributed to the category of the storages that show an increased immunity to malfunctions because the data are self-replicated in the cluster "cloud" of the units of the distributed network.

The specificity of the operation of non relational database during the data acquisition from engineering power supply network facilities is that the data deletion and data change are not required. The data are only replenished as a rule in large blocks during the inquiry of OPC (OLE for Process Control) servers. Each individual record of the non relational component corresponds to the cached slice from the relational Oracle database. To optimize the efficiency the initial Cassandra code was changed in a special assembly, which uses data blocks of 32Mb reducing thus their number and increasing their sampling rate and retrieval rate.

The tools used for the intelligent data analysis and knowledge discovery operate on the side of the cloud of "servers" and are developed using Java Enterprise Edition (J2EE) platform complemented by the multilayer platform used for the development of corporate Spring Framework applications and the technology of the object-relational mapping (ORM) Hibernate.

The object-relational adapter (ORM) Hibernate is used to provide the flexibility of inquiries and the storage –related operation transparency. Particularly Hibernate uses the Cassandra system as the intermediate layer (level-two cache) between the intelligent analysis application and the relational database. Thanks to such an approach we managed to combine the advantages of relational and non relational data storage systems and increase the data analysis efficiency. In this system the Hibernate library used for the solution of object-relational design problems solves the problem of associations of Java classes with database tables and Java data types with SQL data types and provides also tools for automatic generation and updating hype table columns, and also for the arrangement of inquiries and processing of the obtained data.

The data analysis and knowledge discovery system used the JBoss Application server with the public source code as a server platform. HTTPS и AMF (Adobe Media Format) protocols were selected to exchange data between the client applications and the servers and call to remote server procedures of the business-logic. The user's interface is realized using the Adobe Flex platform, which allows for the description of XLM-based interfaces designed for the storage and transmission of the structured data to mobile client applications. The client applications used for the visualization of structured data together with DCM employ the ActionScript technology.

The data analysis and knowledge discovery system has a three-level architecture, which includes the following layers, in particular (1) the presentation layer, application server layer (2) and (3) the data layer (Fig.3).

Presentation Layer. The personnel of power supply companies starts working with the system by opening the master portal through the HTTPS enquiry to the application server JBoss from the standard browser. After the authorization the user can chose the appropriate application for the operation. Afterwards the server transmits the page with JavaScript patches and Adobe Flex client applications. A flex client continues the operation with the server via the AMF protocol by means of the HTTPS Protocol.

Application Server Layer. The application server receives inquiries from the clients, performs the appropriate data-related operations and transmits the response data to the client. The application server acts both as the Web-server and intelligent data analysis server. It interacts with other servers via the API interface based on the Enterprise Java Beans (EJB) technology. The server performs computations using algorithms that require high processing power (aggregation, forecasting, and scenario analysis). To speed up computations when working with large data arrays the CUDA (Compute Unified Device Architecture) technology was realized, which allows for the data processing using a graphic video processor.

Data Layer. The data layer was realized using the Oracle DBMS server. The distributed tables of the Oracle DB keep both achieve and on-line data obtained from OPC servers of industrial controllers and other automation devices. Instrumental Data Feeds work in the multidimensional data layer and solve problems related to the intellectual data analysis and knowledge discovery [16]. This layer also uses the non relational (NoSQL) data storage system (Cassandra), which acts as the level-two cache for the ORM Hibernate and interacts with the application servers and Agent-Feeds.

Three main modules of data processing work at these layers:

1. Module SDF (Sensor Data Flow). It is used for the integration of new sensory data streams from connected objects of monitoring in multidimensional database.

2. Module EEMDPMD (Energy Efficiency Manager Dashboard). It is intended to prepare and generate reports and analytical graphs about changes in the parameters of urban energy efficiency.
3. Module ECLBPLB (Energy Consumption & Losses Breakdown). It is the tools for intellectual analysis of the sensor data include such components as:

    (a) Module of extraction of analyzed data slices from the hypercube;
    (b) Multidimensional data visualizer;
    (c) Aggregation mode editor.

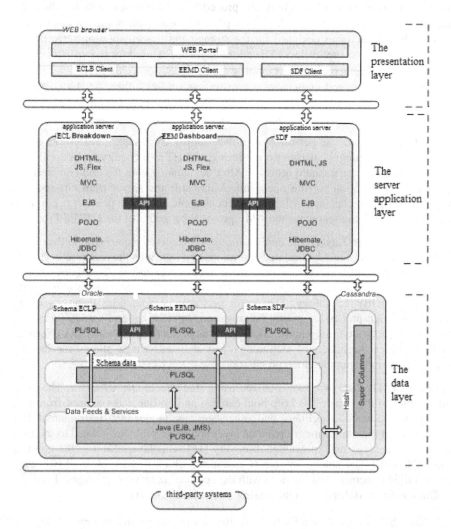

Fig. 3. Fragment of the intellectual analysis system architecture

The multidimensional data visualizer allows for the presentation of the data for the analysis and the analysis data in the form of the structured hyper table. The hyper table combines the functionality of the classic table with a tree-like structure and the elements of structured data (knowledge) control and presentation on time scales. Actually, the hyper table presents an approach to the visualization of the results of intellectual analysis. It allows for the observation of a change in archive, current and forecast values of power efficiency indexes in the form of structured knowledge in time by shifting a courser on the time scale. To update data kept in the storage the data values contained in the hyper table are changed in real time for each selected interval, which is prescribed in compliance with the selected forecast horizon or the time horizon for the scenario analysis.

The aggregation mode editor is required to support the realization of the mechanism of multilevel aggregation during the selection of data for their presentation in the hyper table. The aggregation mode editor prescribes the type and content of the hyper table of archive and current indices and forecast energy indexes and defines visible value columns, amount and character of data pooling levels, color notations, etc. The editor includes its own set of instruments required for the operation of the set of aggregation parameters.

The data sources are placed on geographically spaced engineering communication facilities of the municipal power supply system, therefore the decision-making support and monitoring system should provide the users with geospatial analysis tools. The tools are realized by special analysis subsystem, which is realized on the ArcGIS 9 platform that operates with DCM downloaded from the standard Google Map и Yandex Map geo services, coordinate data from the relational database with the description of the objects of monitoring, data slices from the multidimensional storage and the intellectual analysis data from the hyper table. This instrument gives the users additional opportunities and ease of the visualization of spatially distributed information on the objects of monitoring and provides an opportunity to display on DCM the results of intellectual and spatial analysis in the form of plots, diagrams, tables and color differentiated cartographic zones.

To process large data arrays big companies use computational clusters consisting of the thousands of server sites and programs solutions to distribute problems between the sites on the basis of the model used for the programming of distributed computations (Map-Reduce). It is not economically appropriate to use such cluster structures for the municipal energy supply companies. Therefore the unified architecture of the computing device (CUDA) was implemented for the analytical processing of multidimensional storage data and the hyper table. According to the CUDA technology the processing of large data arrays is performed in real time in many graphic videocard processors Nvidia Quadro FX 5800 4GB (240 processors) based on the model of distributed computations (Map-Reduce) for cluster-type computer systems. The principle of similar computations is based on map functions and contraction (reduce) functions used for the functional programming.

At the first level of the main server runs distribution of input data between server nodes in the cluster network. At the second level server node data distributes between cores GPU. The role of the master server performs CPU node. Results of the function of each node processor accepted, aggregated and transmitted to a higher level from the operating unit to the master node of the cluster, where they are included in the full list. Set of libraries solves the problem of load distribution on the compute nodes of the server cluster. Toolkit that implements the Mapping function, preprocesses the input sensor data and generates a multiple pairs of "key-value", which, after groupings transferred to the toolkit Reduce function, which does work on groups of data pairs, retrieving data from them.

Let's consider the method of solving the problem of sensory data in the urban heating system. Suppose we have obtained from the database of archival data slice with thermal accounting devices for the last year. Need to find out which objects urban heating networks have a maximum energy consumption. In the first step the input list is received the master node of the cluster and distributed among the remaining nodes. In the second step, each node performs a predetermined Reduce function display on his part of the list, generating a pair, whose key is the name of the object, and the value - a value of energy consumption. Mapping operation work independently of each other and can be performed in parallel by all nodes in the cluster. The next step includes the master node on the resulting key key-value pairs and distributes the group with the same keys between nodes to perform the Reduce operation.

In reduce step all nodes in parallel perform a given function, which adds all the values for the input list, thus creating a single pair with the name of the monitoring object as the key and the number of occurrences of names in the original list as the value. After that, the master node receives data from the operating units and generates a result list, in which the records with the highest value and are the desired objects.

6   Conclusion

According to the system-synergetic approach the decision-making support and monitoring system functioning is based on the considered formalized strategies of the management of municipal power supply services on the basis of data collected from the engineering communication facilities. During the monitoring system design the level of the formalization of the management problem is defined by the availability of information on the technological processes of generation, transportation, consumption and utilization of energy carriers and also on the configuration of engineering networks and characteristics of individual objects of the power supply system. The development of the unified multidimensional storage system and system software will allow for the quality improvement, reduction of performance time and the cost of the realization of managerial decisions related to the satisfaction of needs of the population in energy resources.

At the present time some components of the monitoring system are realized by the heat supply service in the city of Kuznetsk, Penza region (Russia), in particular the municipal company "Gorteploset" and by the energy supply service in the city of Kharkov (Ukraine), in particular the Scientific Production Association "KHARTEP" and "INTEP". In particular a push was given to the consideration of issues related to the management hierarchy organization in the power and heat engineering, the formation of the composition and content of management problems at individual levels, coordination and harmonization of decision-making processes at different levels, increased control efficiency, development and implementation of information and telecommunication technologies for the acquisition and processing of the large arrays of sensor-based data.

The use of the decision-making support system for the power supply on the basis of the integration of the SCADA systems of different services into the unified system, the data integration in the multidimensional "cloudy" storage, the introduction of KDD and Data Mining for the monitoring of technological processes of energy generation, transportation, consumption and utilization guarantees the reduction of energy losses and the achievement of energy effectiveness.

References

1. Finogeev, A.G.: Simulation and research system and synergetic processes in information environments: Monograph, Penza state university, 223 (2004)
2. Kamaev, V., Shcherbakov, M., Brebels, A.: Intelligent automation control system for energy conservation. Public Education 2(2), 227–231 (2011)
3. Finogeev, A.G., Maslov, V.A., Finogeev, A.A., Bogatyrev, V.E.: Monitoring and decision support system of urban heat supply based on heterogeneous wireless networks. News of the Volgograd State Technical University. Series. Actual Management Problems, Computing and Informatics in Technical Systems Volgograd University 3 (10), 73–81 (2011)
4. Kamaev, V.A., Lezhebokov, V.V.: Development and application of models of automated information management system to the problem of condition monitoring. Journal of Computer and Information Technology (9), 18–22 (2009)
5. Pakhomov, P.I., Nemtinov, V.A.: Technology support management decision-making utilities. Mashinostroyeniye, 124(2009)
6. Finogeev, A.G., Bozhday, A.S., Bogatirev, V.E.: Formalization of the principles and methodology of decision support based on the monitoring of engineering communications Housing. Scientific and Practical Journal. Public Education (2(86)) Part 2 (2011); An International Conference on Information Technologies in Education, Science and Business, The May session, Ukraine, Crimea, Yalta Gursuf, June 20-30, pp. 210–214. (2011)
7. Introduction to Industrial Control Networks. IEEE Communications Surveys and Tutorials (2012)
8. ISO 50001:2011 Energy management systems – Requirements with guidance for use (2011)
9. Finogeev, A.G., Finogeev, A.A.: Mobile sensor networks for decision support. In: Proceedings of the Scientific and Practical Conference on Innovations in the Development of Information and Communication Technologies (INFO 2009), Russia, Sochi, October 1-10, pp. 146–149 (2009)
10. Shevchenko, S.V., Kamaev, V.A., Manev, R.I.: Application of fuzzy production rules and neural networks for forecasting electricity consumption in the region. In: Proceedings VolgTU, vol. 10(14), pp. 108–112 (2012)
11. Shcherbakov, M., Kamaev, V., Shcherbakova, N.: Automated electric energy consumption forecasting system based on decision tree approach. In: IFAC Conference on Manufacturing Modelling, Management, and Control, S.-Petersburg State Univ., S.-Petersburg National Research Univ. of Information Technologies, Mechanics, and Optics, Saint-Petersburg, Russia, pp. 1061–1066 (2013)

12. Owoeye, D., Shcherbakov, M., Kamaev, V.: A photovoltaic output backcast and forecast method based on cloud cover and historical data. In: Proceedings of the 6th IASTED Asian Conference on Power and Energy Systems, AsiaPES, pp. 28–31 (2013)
13. Maslov, V.A., Finogeev, A.A., Finogeev, A.G.: Identification technique and event management of mobile devices based on the technology Bluetooth. In: Proceedings of Higher Education (Volga region). - Penza, Ed. PSU 2008, vol. (1), pp. 108–120 (2008)
14. Finogeev, A.G., Dilman, V.B., Finogeev, A.A., Maslov, V.A.: Operational remote monitoring in the urban heating system based on wireless sensor networks. Journal News of the Higher Educational Institutions. Volga Region. Engineering, Penza University 3, 27–36 (2010)
15. Akimov, A.A., Bogatirev, V.E., Finogeev, A.G.: Decision support system based on wireless sensor networks using data mining. In: Proceedings of the International Symposium on Reliability and Quality, Penza, Volga House of Knowledge, pp. 113–115 (2010)
16. Finogeev, A.G.: Wireless data transmission technology for the creation of control systems and information support persona. All-competitive selection of an overview and analytical articles on priority. Information Systems, 51,
    http://window.edu.ru/window/library?Prid=56177
17. Bershadsky, A.M.; Finogeev, A.G.; Bozhday, A.S. Development and modeling of heterogeneous infrastructures for information support of monitoring. News of higher educational institutions. Volga region. Engineering. Penza Univ PSU (1), 36–45 (2012)
18. Jarovenko, V., Fomenko, S.: Freeagent-development platform for multi-agent systems. News of the Volgograd State Technical University. Series. Actual Management Problems, Computing and Informatics in Technical Systems. -Volgograd University 4, 164–166 (2012)

Architecture and Self-learning Concept of Knowledge-Based Systems by Use Monitoring of Internet Network[*]

Evgeny Alekseyevich Leonov[**], Vladimir Ivanovich Averchenkov,
Andrey Vladimirovich Averchenkov, Yury Mikhaylovich Kazakov,
and Yury Alekseyevich Leonov

Bryansk State Technical University, Bryansk, Russia
johnleonov@gmail.com

Abstract. This article discusses an approach to building systems based on the knowledge with ability to extend their own domain knowledge through obtaining information in the Internet. In that approach proposed to use infinity loop in which the system automatically learns to find good quality documents within a knowledge area represented in Internet using ontology and expert preferences and on next step extend this ontology by extracting knowledge from retrieved documents. Such approach would let to create a system capable of continuously increase their own knowledge by exploring documents in the Internet and solve problems using current state of the knowledge area.

Keywords: knowledge based systems, ontology learning, internet monitoring, self-learning systems, metasearch.

1   Introduction

Modern intelligent systems based on knowledge are widely used in various fields of knowledge [1,2]. Knowledge base of such systems mostly represented as domain ontology which using let formalizing expert knowledge. Developing an ontology is time-consuming process that cannot be performed by only a domain expert itself and require involving knowledge engineers capable formalize the expert experience and observed precedents in unified structured knowledge base. To ensure that used ontology is objective also may need to involve wide communities of experts within domain, at that with growing ontology volume also increase complexity of providing its consistency.

Due to the labor-intensive of creating ontologies currently being active developing of various methods for their automatic generation [3,4,5]. As a result, there was a completely detached direction of research for automatic extensions of ontologies that called – "ontology learning". Most of methods within this direction are based on using production rules, lexical patterns, statistical analysis of the text, as well as a various

---

[*] The reported study was supported by RFBR, research project No. 13-01-90351.
[**] Corresponding author.

A. Kravets et al. (Eds.): JCKBSE 2014, CCIS 466, pp. 15–26, 2014.

methods of artificial intelligence, and most of that used natural language text as source data [6].

In some articles indicates that source for text can be Internet [7], and web documents as a source of natural language text [8], but most of the proposed methods for automatically expanding ontologies are not applicable to web documents in their original form. Documents in analyzing collection must be semantically similar with a given subject area, otherwise ontology built on it have not enough references between concepts and being contradictory. In this regard, the documents used for learning ontologies should be of high quality and text extracted from them being plain text written in natural language only that do not contain unnecessary information, but issues of converting, filtering web documents and preparing text for analyze are neglected when design of intelligent systems with ability of automatic extraction ontologies.

2   Filling Document Repository Strategy

For efficient application of ontology's learning methods that use natural language text as source, not only need a high quality of individual documents, but also needs a high quality of all their collection. It should have high precision at lowest sufficient recall for solves target mission of intelligent system. To achieve high level of precision and needed completeness can be selected different strategies for filling documents collections.

With extensive strategy, system can employ simplified search procedure with using web spiders [9] and download all documents available by links for accumulating maximum source information, but such approach reduce precision vastly. Thereby on next step need using strict conditions of selection collected documents and reject most of them by filtering procedure. Main drawback of this approach is need for amounts of computing resources and wide bandwidth communication channel. In addition, when applying extensive strategy, need pay special attention to optimization of existing analysis methods, since the original collection of documents can be huge, and using complex analyze method has high computing price. However, using that strategy make system is self-contained and does not require access to third-party search documents services. One of advantages of that approach is the possibility of using methods that required universal document set with highly connected documents. Using this strategy is useful when building applications that require mandatory full coverage all over the Internet.

Within intensive strategy proposed to use external search engines that let to receive documents with already known high relevance, and quality of received excerpts mostly depends on services used and accuracy of transmitted requests. These documents can also be filtered and collection of them expanded by including documents that are linked with the most relevant sources. Using this strategy allows you to deploy intelligent systems based on information from the Internet with limited computational resources and communication channels that is the most common one for their use. However, using metasearch for collecting documents does not allow assessing quality of documents by methods based on analyzing links between them (eg , PageRank [10]), and produce statistical analysis methods were based on absolute completeness of the sample. This disadvantage can be overcomes by using of direct estimates based on semantic and content of documents. Application of sufficiently sophisticated analytical methods with limited volume of collection condition does not entail sharp increasing requirements for computing resources used platforms. In this regard, using of intensive strategy of collecting information for design knowledge based intelligent systems is the most justified.

3   Using Intelligent Agents for Automation Meta-Search Process

When using metasearch for filling storage of documents is necessary to provide maximum level of automation metasearch. Since experience shows that users who are not being a specialists in information retrieval cannot arrange search descriptor that provides high precision of received excerpts with highest coverage of knowledge domain, as well as providing operability and tuning subsystems for interacting with external information search engines.

For provide autonomous work of subsystems metasearch propose to use intelligent agents capable independently finding external search services, explore their options and customizing itself to interact with them. Schematic diagram of the intelligent agent metasearch presented in figure 1.

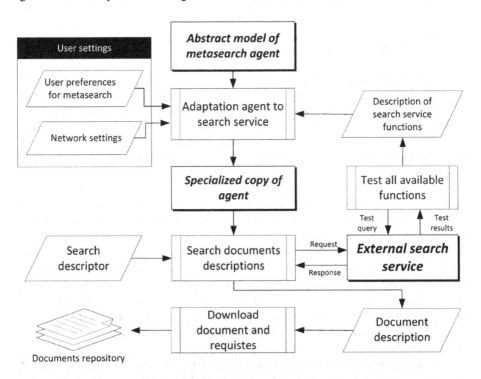

Fig. 1. Schema of interaction inteligent agent with external search services

Initial data for agent consist of search descriptor's queries expressed in internal language. For realizing such an agent, is necessary that it has universal methods of interaction with any search services. For that needed to separate description of services that describe all it distinctive features from agent implementation. Detection of search services based on testing web form's text fields and comparison returned page after submitting form with data entered in text field. After detecting a new service, agent must configures to use that service, for that it send various test queries in order to investigate structure of page with search results and produce rules for parsing results. After agent adjusting to work with external service fully complete, then all received test's results are saves.

Agent has its own format of description its internal language and functionality. Before interact with an external search service, agent conduct adaptation it capabilities to service by shutting down realized interaction algorithms that makes it inapplicable for the service. For sending query agent made translation from internal query language to language of external search engine. Configuring metasearch agents may produce on basis of complete descriptions of search engines, which prepare an expert in information retrieval. In that case, agent functionality significantly increase because automatic detection and configuration on search services can be detected only basic functionality of external systems. More detailed mechanisms of metasearch agent work described in the prior publications [11].

4   Intelligent System Concept

Using intelligent metasearch agents let creating flexible mechanisms of filling document repositories in specified knowledge domain. On basis of these mechanisms can be design systems that can generate by itself search tasks bases on prepared ontology. Conceptual diagram of such system (fig. 2) shall have procedures for generation query from ontologies prepared by domain expert, then these queries sent to a third-party universal search engines, and for each received document should be rank its quality.

Informative documents with high degree of similarity with a given subject area should be saved in document repository, that can be used to construct different views of the information contained in the documents, as well as discover new knowledge and extending existing ontology.

System based on the proposed principle can continuously accumulate information, actualizing domain knowledge from the Internet. Solutions offered by intelligent system may go beyond competencies of basic ontology authors, which implies the qualitatively new applying systems of this kind, because they will not only reproduce existing knowledge of expert or developer, but also independently self-learn new knowledge by using information from the Internet. Consider in detail the specific procedures of the presented concept.

To realize proposed ideas are very important aspect is providing high quality of documents stored in repository, because in case of their insufficient proximity of domain knowledge, ontology turn into weakly connected and its further extension would not be appropriate and could lead into complete failure of whole system.

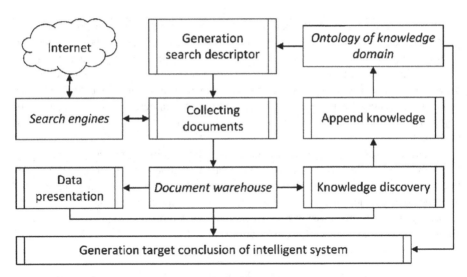

Fig. 2. Concept architecture of internet based intelligent system

5   Self-learning Metasearch Algorithm with Active Control

In order to improve quality of collected documents propose to apply self-learning metasearch algorithm with active control (fig. 3). To form query that can be send to an external universal search system uses base of production rules, source data for which are ontology's concepts and references.

Simplified ontology can be representing as a directed graph described by the following tuple

$$O = \langle E, R, I \rangle, \tag{1}$$

where E – set of ontology's entities (graph's nodes), R – set of references between entities (graph's edges), I – predicate incidence between node and edges

$$I(e, r) = \{0, 1\}, e \in E, r \in R. \tag{2}$$

In addition, each reference can be characterized by a whole set of properties using for notes semantic meaning of entities' relationship, full list of which is depending on type of intelligent system and methods of forming target conclusion in it. For proposed algorithm, most important property is combinatory power of reference, that is, whether it is unique to given node, or it may have many references of this type. It should also be noted, that specific format of representation ontology on abstract level is unimportant and classical concepts such as classes, concepts, terms, properties, attributes, items – may be described as a specific ontology notes inherited from general class and only have differing reference type among themselves. As a result, references can be described as follows:

$$r = \{t, P, l, w, f, c\}, \tag{3}$$

where t – reference type, P – set of reference property that uses for production target conclusion of system, l – lexical equivalent of reference that can be used as a part of query in production rules, w – reference weight, f – theoretical frequency (probability) of reference existing, c – combinatory power ($c \in N$), characterized essentially maximum count of references specified type that may have one node. If c = 0 then count of references for node is undefined and may be endless. For example, most of object's properties have c = 1, whereas for subsumption relationship c often is equal to zero.

Weight of reference w indicates strength of relationship, ie semantic proximity of ontology's nodes. Probability f indicates detection accuracy of reference, that is, confidence of system that relationship is exists. Probability f can be equal to one, only for reference with nodes in base ontology defined by expert. Subsystem of automatic extracting ontology must assign rank of each added references, which indicates probability of objective existence for this relationship.

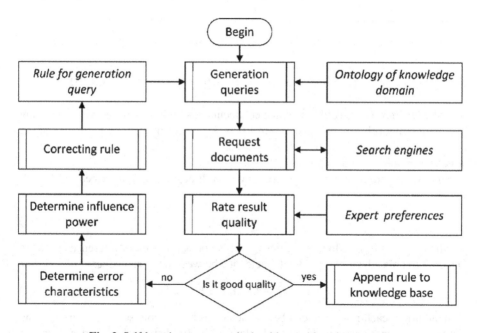

Fig. 3. Self-learning meta-search algorithms with active control

Production rules used to generate search queries may have following general form:

$$p_Q = \{S(r), L(P_{ex}, i), A: e, r \rightarrow Q_s, Q(Q_s, T_c(c))\}, \qquad (4)$$

where p_Q – identifier of production rule for considered subgraph of ontology O, $S(r)$ – class of reference r, for which rule can be applied ; $L(P_{ex}, i)$ – predicate of activation rule that define whether is reference between considering nodes and whether they meet specified conditions P_{ex}; $A: e, r \rightarrow Q_s$ – production core in which convert nodes e and references r in part query Q_s; $Q(Q_s, T_c(c))$ – postcondition in which produce insertion subquery Q_s in query Q.

Activation conditions depends on used values of P_{ex}, that contain follow elements:

$$P_{ex} = \{E_n, T_n, w, f, T_c(c)\}, \tag{5}$$

where E_n – set of entity types for which rule can be activated; T_n – set of reference types, which must be linked entities; w – weight threshold of semantic relationship for activation rule; f – probability threshold of relationship existing; $T_c(c)$ – combinatory power type $(T_c(1) = 1 \vee T_c(c) = 0 \wedge c \neq 1, 0$ – multiple, 1 – unique). In addition, for each type of combinatory power using their own production rules, as well as this parameter determines how insert generated subquery in whole query and operation type of search engine language. As a result, when generating queries to search engines involves only those entities that have strong semantic relationship.

Each rule generate set of subqueries from matching to it entities and references.

$$p_Q: O_s \rightarrow Q_s. \tag{6}$$

Combining that subqueries together can be create more complex and precision query for search engine. When query is combining by $Q(Q_s, T_c(c))$ function, if reference is unique the query is specifies otherwise searching range will be expend. Recursion deep of production inference and references type used for generation query depend on results received from search engine.

Each generated subquery sent to search engine that return set of documents with a setting depth of excerpts results. For each received document rates its information content and degree of similarity with knowledge domain that depend on the specified expert preferences [12].

For rate document, previously carried out identification of semantically meaningful part of document and transfer it in natural language. [13]. Then calculates necessary criteria for determine quality of document. If quality of document below threshold set by expert, then such query and rule on which basis it was built must be corrected. To do this, in first step needed to determine nature of existing error, depending on which, should be define procedure for correction rule.

After determining nature of occurred error, determines its influence strength on result. If given result has critical displacement from expected results rule can be completely rejected that mean it not applicable for this type of ontologies. Depending on nature of error rules may are not corrects, and used only for other ontology region.

6   Features of Application Ontology Learning Methods

Research in automate definition ontologies problems held a long time. Today appears some isolated directions in approaches that solving this problem. To extract new terms and relations can be used methods based on the frequency characteristics of texts [14, 15]. Methods of this type are based on calculating frequency of words usage in documents. For identify new concepts using closeness of usage words in texts and their interchangeability, as well as using TF*IDF and F-measure. These methods have poor results of detection reference type between concepts.

Detached direction of research were become variety of methods based on using of patterns [16, 17]. This type of methods can be separated by using pattern type on: simple text patterns, syntactic and lexical patterns or it combination. When using lexical patterns, text has been morphological and syntactic analysis in result of which all text is represented as a directed graph. Nodes of this graph are various parts of speech, and acts are relationships between individual members of sentence. Using template allow to detect relationship between members of sentence and construct on its base corresponding semantic reference in ontology between concepts that used in analyzed sentence. This approach is most easily may realized by applications. However, result quality of application this method depends entirely on correctness of defined templates and their completeness in knowledge base.

Developed methods for learning ontologies often based on methods that are common for data mining and have similar steps with methodology of knowledge discovery [18]. In addition, when ontology extracted may need to verify its integrity and consistency and in this direction also been carried out many researches.

All of these methods and approaches to extend ontology can be used in intelligent systems that capable self-learn on basis of information from the Internet. However, if ontology learning based on web documents, raises specific issues about dependability of source and accuracy of detection semantic relationship. Therefore, all methods applied for learning ontologies should be modified in such way that they return not only detected concepts and references, but also can determine the strength of relationship and probability of its existence.

It should also be noted, that use of templates for proposed conception is seen as most successful due to it have possibility of secondary using syntactic patterns for reverse conversion ontology's nodes to queries for expand ontology for unrelated concepts.

So if we have a template is used to detect specific structure of lexical items L, that rule for conversion can be simplify represented as a function of converting block of text to part of graph in ontology:

$$P: L, w_1, w_2 \rightarrow r, e_1, e_2 , \tag{7}$$

where P lexical-semantic pattern; L – set of constant lexemes is used for detection reference r; w_1, w_2 – words in text that matches with pattern and which define ontology's concepts e_1, e_2. Otherwise we can say that set of lexemes L, characterize reference r between concepts e_1 and e_2 which represent in text by words w_1 and w_2 respectively. Then if ontology have concept e_1 that have not discovered or defined reference or there is a need to expand existing set of references, then we can create a production rule to generate query using for that words which is present as concept in ontology and lexemes that characterize required reference:

$$p_Q(e_1, \{L, t\}) = \{S, L(P_{ex}, i), A: e_1, r \rightarrow Q_s \ni \{e_1, L\}, Q\}, e_1 \in O \land r \notin O , \tag{8}$$

$\{L, t\}$ – related pair of lexeme's set and required reference type ($t \in r$); O – ontology of knowledge domain. Function for search that using query can return documents containing parts of the text that matched with a given pattern P.

$$F_{SE}: Q_S \rightarrow D \ni \{L, w_1, w_2\} \in P \tag{9}$$

Further, because $F_{SE}: p_Q(e_1, \{L, t\}) \to \{L, w_1, w_2\} \in P \to \{r, e_1, e_2\} \in O$, if we determine for each type of reference the set of characterized it lexemes $\{L, t\}$, using rule P as a base, then it will allows with high degree of probability extend part of ontology that exactly required. Likewise, if we are interested in discovering or extending existing set of references between nodes of ontology, we can use them to create a query containing lexemes that characterizing required relationship. This method can be used to increase a coefficient characterizing probability of existing reference or refute existing reference in resolving inconsistencies of ontology.

7   Architecture of Web-Based Intelligent Systems

Based on proposed concept of intelligent systems can be designed software systems with different architectures. For engineering domain-specific analytical systems based on knowledge of the Internet are offer to use multiagent [19] architecture (fig. 4), which has the following working principles and main components.

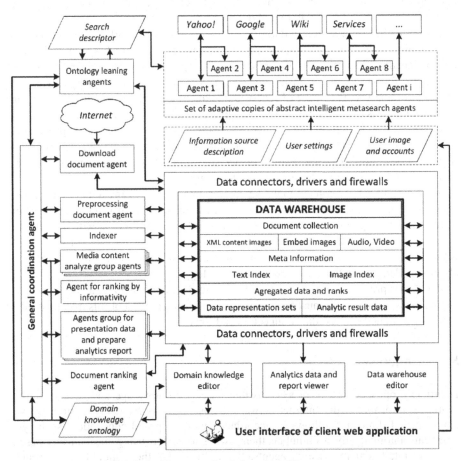

Fig. 4. Architecture of web-based intelligent system

Source data for the system begins to work are:

- initial description of information sources, list of which can be further extended automatically by the system;
- user settings, which contain information about preferences of user for determining quality and features of collected documents, Internet network settings, data warehouse parameters, general metasearch settings and other parameters of the system;
- digital user image and user accounts that system should be use when collecting information from network;
- initial domain ontology that can be further expanded on the basis of information from the Internet. Filling source data processed via web-based user interface and independent subsystem for editing base ontology.

The main means of control agents is general coordination agent. Its responsibility include formation of tasks to other agents and their groups, distributing load between parts of system, conflict resolution and reconciliation of conflicting actions of agents, balancing between steps of processing documents for formation continuous analyzing document process and maintain required volume of storage data.

Accumulating information in data warehouse produced by working together ontology learning agent, set of adapted copies of intelligent metasearch agents and agent for downloading documents. Main of them is ontology learning agent, its responsibility include formation search tasks created on base of existing ontology, formation requests for analyze and rating of received documents, as well as essentially learning ontology on basis of documents with high rank.

In system's architecture may also include many autonomous agents that processing different stages of analyzing document contents, as well as forming target conclusion in case of designing advising systems or decision support systems or agents that prepare analytical reports and presenting data for analytical systems.

Also, system should contain many agents for data preprocessing among which are: agents for converting data formats, agents for filtering semantically significant part of web documents, agents that convert various format to uniform format with using natural language text, media content analyze group agents, agents for rate normativity of documents and other agents for ranking. Part of these agents may use information about knowledge area that stored in domain ontology.

All agents presented in system should have no direct access to data store, because all changes produced in it must be coordinated with each other. For this may be used a specially designed drivers, data connectors and firewalls.

8   Conclusion

In article proposed concept of systems that based on knowledge and used as initial source of information the Internet network. Those systems are using to store knowledge special domain ontology. In accordance with proposed conception, such systems can automatically accumulate their own knowledge using mechanisms based on using intelligent metasearch agents. Search tasks for them should be generated automatically on basis of existing ontologies, which also be enriched by knowledge available in received from search engines documents. This infinity loop allow automatically and continuously renovate system knowledge about knowledge domain, and thus provide high quality of target solutions.

Particular attention is focused on describing procedures for automation creating search descriptor on basis of specific domain ontologies, as well as automation metasearch subsystems, which is an important aspect in proposed concept of intelligent systems. On basis of the considered algorithms and principles of designing intelligent systems has been offered a typical architecture that use multi-agent approach, in which described all main items and relationship between them.

The proposed architecture and the concept of designing self-learning systems based on knowledge, is a step towards creation of self-learning autonomous intelligent systems. It using will allow solves a wide range of specific problems in various fields of knowledge, using for that knowledge accumulated by humanity in the Internet, which is not able to obtain any domain expert.

References

1. Uschold, M., Gruninger, M.: Ontologies: Principles, Methods, and Applications. Knowledge Engineering Review 11 (1996)
2. Wouters, B., Deridder, D., Van Paesschen, E.: The Use of Ontologies as a Backbone for Use Case Management. In: European Conference on Object-Oriented Programming (ECOOP 2000), Workshop: Objects and Classifications, a Natural Convergence (2000)
3. Bisson, G., Nédellec, C., Cañamero, L.: Designing clustering methods for ontology building– the Mo'K workbench. In: Proceedings of the ECAI 2000 Workshop on Ontology Learning, Berlin, Germany (2000)
4. Cimiano, P., Staab, S.: Learning concept hierarchies from text with a guided agglomerative clustering algorithm. In: Proceedings of the ICML 2005 Workshop on Learning and Extending Lexical Ontologies with Machine Learning Methods (OntoML 2005), Bonn, Germany (2005)
5. Gómez-Pérez, A., Manzano-Macho, D.: A survey of ontology learning methods and techniques. Deliverable 1.5, OntoWeb Project (2003)
6. Agichtein, E., Gravano, L.: Snowball: Extracting relations from large plain-text collections. In: Proceedings of the 5th ACM International Conference on Digital Libraries (2000)
7. Brin, S.: Extracting patterns and relations from the World Wide Web. In WebDB Workshop at the 6th International Conference on Extending Database Technology (EDBT 1998) (1998)
8. Agirre, E., Ansa, O., Hovy, E., Martinez, D.: Enriching very large ontologies using the WWW. In: Proceedings of the ECAI 2000 Workshop on Ontology Learning, Berlin, Germany (2000)
9. Page, L., Brin, S., Motwani, R., Winograd, T.: The PageRank Citation Ranking: Bringing Order to the Web. Bringing Order to the Web. Technical Report. Stanford InfoLab (1999)
10. Brin, S., Page, L.: The Anatomy of a Large-Scale Hypertextual Web Search Engine. In: Computer Network and ISDN Systems. Computer Science Department, Stanford University, Stanford (1998)

11. Averchenkov, V.I., Leonov, E.A.: Mathematics model of uniform multiagent metasearch subsystem (in Russian). Vestnik Bryansk State Technical University 2(30), 101–110 (2011)
12. Averchenkov, V.I., Leonov, E.A., Averchenkov, A.V.: Formalization of Information Monitoring Process in Internet Network for Creating Data Warehouse in Specified Knowledge Domain (in Russian). Herald of Computer and Information Technologies 1, 38–45 (2012)
13. Averchenkov, V.I., Leonov, E.A.: Analyzing structure of web documents for filtering unique and semantically significant information purpose in information retrieval aspect (in Russian). In: Izvestia Volgograd State Technical University. Actual Control Problems in Computer Engineering and Computer Science in Technical Systems, vol. 11(84), pp. 30–35. Volgograd (2011)
14. Maedche, A., Volz, R.: The ontology Extraction & Maintenance Framework TextTo-Onto. In: ICDM 2001: The 2001 IEEE International Conference on Data Mining Workshop on Integrating Data Mining and Knowledge Management (2001)
15. Heinrich, G., Kindermann, J., Lauth, C., Paaß, G., Sanchez-Monzon, J.: Investigating word correlation at different scopes – a latent topic approach. In: Proceedings of the Workshop on Learning and Extending Lexical Ontologies by using Machine Learning (OntoML 2005), Bonn, Germany (2005)
16. Cimiano, P., Staab, S.: Learning concept hierarchies from text with a guided agglomerative clustering algorithm. In: Proceedings of the ICML 2005 Workshop on Learning and Extending Lexical Ontologies with Machine Learning Methods (OntoML 2005), Bonn, Germany (2005)
17. Thelen, M., Riloff, E.: A bootstrapping method for learning semantic lexicons using extraction pattern contexts. In: Proceedings of the 2002 Conference on Empirical Methods in Natural Language Processing (EMNLP 2002), Philadelphia, USA (2002)
18. Witschel, H.F.: Using decision trees and text mining techniques for extending taxonomies. In: Proceedings of the Workshop on Learning and Extending Lexical Ontologies by using Machine Learning (OntoML 2005), Bonn, Germany (2005)
19. Niazi, M., Hussain, A.: Agent-based computing from multi-agent systems to agent-based models: a visual survey. Scientometrics 89(2), 479–499 (2011)

An Experience of Optimization Approach Application to Improve the Urban Passenger Transport Structure

Elena Georgievna Krushel, Ilya Victorovich Stepanchenko,
Alexander Eduardovich Panfilov, and Elena Dmitrievna Berisheva

Kamyshin Technological Institute of the Volgograd State Technical University,
Kamyshin, Russia
stilvi@mail.ru

Abstract. The results of the private passenger transport structure parameter estimation are presented (i.e. the transport vehicle number at each route path, payment, and passenger flow prediction) in order to achieve the concordance between the partially conflicting interests of transport vehicle owners, municipal governance, route motion controllers, and passengers as participants of the whole transport system operation. The problem is formulated in the terms of the multi-objective optimization. The two methods of objective vector scalarization are applied and compared. The first method is based on the vector components weighting approach while another method follows the Tchebycheff's equalization ideas. The transport system parameter values determined via application of both methods are similar. The optimization and simulation results show that the profit of the transport owners can be increased up to 20% and at the same time common private transport vehicle number can be reduced at least twice without passenger service worsening.

Keywords: Urban passengers' transport, passengers' flow, decision method, simulation, multi-objective optimization.

1 Introduction

The municipal governance decision making is concerning social groups of different citizens the interests of which sometimes do not coincide. The citizens' relation to the accepted decisions is usually asymmetric. The groups (even in the case of their small number) which treat such decisions as contrary to their interests should sharply criticize the governance while the concordant citizens demonstrate the decisions approval rarely. The necessary and useful presence of opposition to almost every decision raises the problem to quantitatively estimate the governance decision effectiveness due to which the discussion with the opponents should be objective and convincing.

One of such estimation receipt (concerning the problem of municipal participation in the urban passenger system control) is discussed below. The interest of the municipal governance in investigating this problem is explained by the disadvantages of the existing chaotic passenger system operation leading to the transport units owners' self-wills in the questions of the route path and motion intense choice. Such mode of operation leads to the unjustified competition between the transport units owners, to

A. Kravets et al. (Eds.): JCKBSE 2014, CCIS 466, pp. 27–39, 2014.

the essential worsening of the ecology situation around the highways, to the growth of the traffic jam frequency and also to the decrease of the owners' profits because of the units' incomplete filling.

The known results of the alternative approaches to the traffic control [1,2,3,4] show that the partial arrangement of the urban transport control system is useful (i.e. the two-level control of transport system application the upper level of it being presented by single route path units joining up while the lower level corresponds to the unique transport unit subjected to the route chief or the route unit owner).

Although this variant seemed to be advisable the municipal governance decision makers have taken into account the possibilities of a certain citizen group negative reaction to the transport system control reformation. Therefore the report authors were engaged in working-out recommendations concerning the following transport system parameters:

1. The number of transport units operating at each route path.
2. The time intervals between the transport units arriving at every stop of each route path.
3. The municipal budget tax reception from the owners of every route path.
4. The estimation of a reasonable fare after implementing a new control structure.

The necessary research was carried out in 3 stages.

The 1st stage embraced a passenger flow estimation obtained after real-time flow measurements at each main stop in the peak load periods.

The subject of the 2nd stage was the choice of an approach allowing the acquisition of the enumerated questions, quantitative reasoning as well as a simulation model development in accordance with the chosen approach.

At the 3rd stage the set of computation experiments was carried out and the quantitative estimations of the transport system control parameters were submitted to the municipality for further discussion and decision making.

The overview of the 2nd and 3rd stage research is presented below.

2   The Choice of Approach to Develop a Simulation Model

The usual way consists in the expert group calling for the transport flow imitation model carrying out. But because of the unavoidable differences between each experts' decision making style it is desirable to support the expert group work by decisions depending only on objective external data and chosen criteria (such decisions would not depend on the individual decision making styles).

The chosen approach for the decision objectification was based on the optimization model application [5]. Such approach allows estimating wanted parameter boundary values corresponding to the utmost usage of the whole restriction system reserves for chosen criterion extreme value achievement. The additional advantage of the optimization approach lies in the possibility of obtaining criterion and technical-economic indicator dependence on the restriction system parameters. Particularly in the concerned problem such parameters relate to the variants of the municipal participation in urban transport system control.

3   The Optimization Model Brief Description

The subject of the optimization technique application is as follows:

1. To receive the estimation of transport unit reasonable number at every route path.
2. To determine the passenger fare at every route path.
3. To estimate the expected profit values at every route path (for the purposes of the municipal budget tax reception prediction).

The optimization criteria list should be chosen to achieve the concordance between following partially distinct interests of the citizen different social groups:

— *from the municipal governance point of view* – to achieve predictability and an accepted level of the budget tax reception from the transport system operation; to prevent the transport unit owner competition for the profitable route path reception; to prevent citizens negative estimating the transport system operation mode;
— *from the point of view of the route path owners* – to achieve a high level of profit;
— *from the point of view of unique transport unit users* – to have the high level of salaries depending on the profit falling on one transport unit;
— *from the point of view of the route motion controllers* – to achieve the transport unit number decrease in order to receive the accepted value of the motion rate and to reduce the probabilities of the transport jams forthcoming;
— *from the point of view of passengers* – to ensure acceptable time interval values between the transport unit arrival at the stops with free seats; a low fare.

According to the multi-objectiveness of the problem the 5 following variants of units per hour operation number and fare values at each route path were computed:

1. Variant 1 corresponding to the achievement of the maximum summarized hour profit of the whole transport unit operation. This variant conforms to the municipal and the whole city interests because of the high level of city budget tax filling.
2. Variant 2 corresponding to the achievement of the maximum hour profit per transport unit for every transport subsystem. This variant conforms to unique transport unit user interests.
3. Variant 3 corresponding to the achievement of the minimal number of transport units per hour at the whole route paths. This variant conforms to the route motion controller interests.
4. Variant 4 corresponding to the minimum value of the weighted (by the number per hour of units at the routes) passenger fare. This variant conforms to the passengers' interests.
5. Variant 5 corresponding to the minimum value of maximal (between all route paths) fare. This variant conforms to the route owners because it leads to smoothing the profit inequalities at the different route paths.

Therefore the urban transport operation would be described by the sequence of indicators to be considered as vector criterion components: {Q_1: summarized profit per hour; Q_2: the profit per single transport unit; Q_3: the total transport units number per hour; Q_4:

weighted mean fare; Q_5: maximal (between all route paths) fare. The essence of each i-th variant consists in the Q_i-th indicator's optimizing, $i = 1,..., 5$, the result being conformed to the corresponding social group interests. The optimal value of Q_i-th indicator is designated below as Q_i^*. The values of the remaining indicators Q_j, $j = 1,..., 5$, $j \neq i$ commonly should achieve the values not only different from the optimal values but they also perhaps would be unacceptable for the other social groups.

Two approaches were applied to compromise the conflicting interests.

The 1st approach consists in the following two scalarization techniques:

— Finding a decision which brings weighted deviations of the normalized indicators from their optimal values to minimum.

$$\hat{Q} = \sum_{k=1}^{5} \alpha_k \cdot \frac{|Q_k - Q_k^*|}{\max(Q_k^*; Q_k)} \tag{1}$$

— The weights α_k of each indicator are determined according to the number of citizens which are interested in the corresponding indicator improvement;
— The application of Tchebycheff's equalization ideas [7] of minimizing the common right-hand bound w of the normalized indicator deviations from their optimal values:

$$\alpha_k \cdot \frac{|Q_k - Q_k^*|}{\max(Q_k^*; Q_k)} \leq w, \quad w \rightarrow \min, \forall k = 1,..,5 \tag{2}$$

Since the indicators Q_k, $k = 1,..., 5$, are not fully contradictable the dependence of the decisions on α_k, was expected to be weak (which was confirmed in the computation experiments).

The 2nd approach follows variant 1 but certain modes of the municipal participation in the transport system control are provided for the different citizen group interest accounting.

The variants 1..5 and the compromising variant criteria are optimized on the same restriction set with two blocks.

Block 1 contains the restrictions which are obligatory for all variants:

— The passenger income flow securing under the peak load hours (the value of income flow is supposed to depend on the fare);
— Accounting either free seat mean value in the transport unit after the unit's entry into the considered transport network section or the unit's seat places after passenger get off at the transport stop;
— The compliance with the prescribed bounds of transport units per hour number at each route path;
— The achievement of urban transport self-repayment operation.

Block 2 contains the restrictions related to the following modes of municipal participation in the transport system control:

— The fixing of an equal fare for every route path;
— The fixing of a total (across all route paths) number of transport units per hour;
— The fixing of different route path profit equalization maximal admissible error.

Computations with restrictions of block 1correspond to an almost marketable transport system mode of operation. Those including block 2 correspond to the refusal from two-level control system (unique unit – route path units join) and to the introduction of the 3rd (upper) level for coordination of the route path joins preventing the conflicts between interests of different social groups.

4   Optimization Main Features

The transport network structure was interpreted as oriented graph the nodes of which correspond to main stops while arcs correspond to highway sections between the stops. The nodes were numerated arbitrary and each arc was designated by its entry and exit node numbers.

Each variant mentioned above relates to the class of single-criterion optimization problems. The formalization of these problems was carried out in the nonlinear mathematic theory terms with nonlinearities present both in the criteria and restriction system. The criterion of each variant is quadratic and includes the products of the sought variables (i.e. the fare values and transport unit numbers per hour at each route path). Because of the criterion non-convexity the decision uniqueness is not guaranteed and the set of saddle points ripples and ridges can occur. Since it was necessary to estimate not only the criterion value but also the values of the sought variables the convergence of the mathematical programming algorithm was extremely slow. The generalized reduced gradient method [8,9,10] was chosen to solve the optimization problem. In spite of the known non-convex optimization problem decision difficulties the computational technique was found to be suitable for the purposes of a small city transport system optimization.

5   Simulation Results Examples

The practical results were obtained for the transport system structure optimization of one of the Volga region small cities.

The problem dimension characteristics: the sought variable number – 200; the number of explicit constraints for the sought variables – 100; the number of simple constraints (boundary values) for the sought variables – 400.

The optimization technique was applied to compare different variants of the city transport network mode of operation including the following:

1. Variants of municipal and private transport system joining up.
2. Different suppositions about the free seats at each arc of the transport network graph-scheme.
3. Different kinds of transport units applied at the route paths.
4. Variants of several stops dislocation.

The examples considered below relate to the optimization problem solution with separate and compromise criteria as well as to different variants of municipality influence on the urban transport system operation. The latter corresponds to the inclusion of several restrictions from block 2 in addition to the restrictions of block 1 afterwards the corresponding problem is considered as the parametric one. Therefore the results of computer experiments were obtained in the form of chosen variables and indicators dependence on the varying parameters of the restriction system and the criterion. Such form of result presentation is suitable for the expert analysis and municipal decision makers' treatment.

1. The varying parameter is the fare being established equal for every route paths.
2. The varying parameter is the total unit number operating per hour.
3. The varying parameter is the accuracy of different route path profit equalization.

5.1   The Comments to the Separate Criteria Optimization Results

Table 1 presents the results of the separate criteria optimization in respect of block 1 restriction system. The optimal value of each separate criterion is assumed as 100%; the remaining indicators in the row corresponding to the separate criterion are determined in the percentages of extreme value that could be achieved if the appropriate indicator should be designed as the optimization criterion. For example the minimization of the total transport unit number leads to making the total profit at the level of 6% from its value which would be achieved at the variant of its maximization.

Table 1. The separate criteria optimization results

Indicators Criteria	Total profit	The profit per transport unit	The total transport unit number	The weighted mean fare	The maximal (between all route paths) fare
1	2	3	4	5	6
Total profit (to be maximized)	100%	34%	628%	1079%	1233%
The profit per transport unit (to be maximized)	51%	100%	108%	899%	1097%
The total transport units number (to be minimized)	6%	12%	100%	1296%	1274%
The weighted mean fare (to be minimized)	0%	0%	288%	100%	107%
The maximal (between all route paths) fare (to be minimized)	0%	0%	293%	107%	100%

Although the computations are useful to forecast the after-effects of the corresponding criterion choice all variants shown in table 1 are unacceptable.

1. The tendency of the maximal municipal budget tax revenues (row 1 of table 1) leads to the route paths abrupt differentiation according the profit values. The main part of total profit would be made at the route paths possessing minor matches with other route paths at the transport network sections with intensive passenger flow. This circumstance leads to the utmost growth of such route paths transport unit number at profitable network sections with negative effect of almost whole passenger flow capture. The rest of profit would be obtained by the route paths with intensive passenger flow at the terminal network sections. The majority of the route paths would be unprofitable. The total transport unit number would exceed the existing number which is now considered by experts as overvalued. The weighted fare would exceed more than twice the existing value. Therefore this variant can be acceptable nor for transport organizations, nor for the motion controllers, nor for the passengers.

2. The orientation towards the transport unit owner interests (row 2 of table 1) leads to abrupt reduction of transport unit number up to the minimum bound of admissible values at the majority of the route paths. The weighted fare would rise in 2.5 times (comparable to the value existing now) with the variation from 0.8 to 3.4 times of existing fare between the different transport paths. The total profit would be reduced twice as compared with variant 1 and about 20% of the route paths would be unprofitable. The rest of the route paths would make profits with essential variety. This variant contradicts to the interests of the transport organization as well as the whole city.

3. The orientation towards the route motion control (row 3 of table 1) leads to reduction of transport unit number up to the minimum bounds at all route paths. Therefore the passenger waiting time at the stops would rise as well as the fares (average value would be 3.7 times more of the current fare with the minor variety between different route paths). Half of the route paths would be unprofitable and the total profit of the transport organization would be reduced to the 6% level of variant 1. This variant contradicts to the interests of the transport organization as well as the whole city.

4. The orientation towards the passenger interests (row 4 of table 1) leads to the loss of transport system profitability. The municipal compensation of the transport system costs can be achieved while the weighted value of the fare would be decreased to 30% of the existing value with the variety from 27% to 34% of the existing payment at the different route paths. This variant is attractive not only for the passengers but also for the route motion controllers. However the variant cannot be accepted because of its contradiction to the business interests.

5. The orientation towards the fare equalization between different route paths (row 5 of table 1) leads to the after-effects similar to variant 4 with reduction of the fare variety range (from 29% to 31% of the current fare at different route paths).

5.2   The Comments on the Tradeoff Optimization Criteria Application

The above-said analysis of the separate criteria optimization after-effects shows that the two-level structure of the transport system control is unsuitable to achieve a concordance between different social groups interested in the transport system mode of operation. The vector criterion scalarization variants are discussed below (the results are shown in the table 2).

Table 2. The comparison of the vector criterion scalarization variants

Criteria \ Indicators	Tchebycheff's equalization, different weights of the criterion components	Tchebycheff's equalization, equal weights of the criterion components	Convolution of indicators, different weights of the criterion components	Convolution of indicators, equal weights of the criterion components	Criterion: total profit while the fare is fixed at the current level	Criterion: total profit while the fare is fixed at the 130% of current level
1	2	3	4	5	6	7
Total profit	40%	31%	36%	34%	31%	40%
The profit per transport unit	29%	28%	34%	32%	29%	41%
The total transport unit number	297%	237%	228%	229%	233%	210%
The weighted mean fare	375%	331%	371%	360%	347%	452%
The maximal (between all route paths) fare	640%	353%	395%	359%	319%	415%

The table columns present the indicator values (i.e. the vector criterion components listed in the 1st column) in the percentages of the potentially achieved values (i.e. extreme values shown in the table 1). Two scalarization variants were examined: 1st –Tchebycheff's equalization (2) both with different and equal weights α_k, $k = 1,...,$ 5 (columns 2, 3 of table 2), 2nd – the convolution of the indicators deviation from their optimal values (1) also both with different and equal weights α_k, $k = 1,..,$ 5 (columns 4, 5 of table 2). The results were compared with the indicators values attainable as the effect of the total hour profit provided the trip payment would be fixed (column 6) or 30% raised (column 7) with respect to the fare existing now.

The indicator values were found to be similar and acceptable in every variant. Thus Tchebycheff's equalization with different weights (column 2) leads to the 8% raise of the existing trip payment. But the same profit value is attainable by the fixed payment profit maximization only with major payment raise (30% more than existing value, column 7). Tchebycheff's equalization with equal weights (column 3) leads to the profit value at the level coinciding with the maximal profit attainable in the condition of fare fixed at the existing value (column 6). But the Tchebycheff variant is preferable not only because of the fare reduction (5% less than existing value) but mainly because of the possibility of the existing total transport unit number twofold reduction.

The optimization of the indicators convolution with different weights (column 4) leads to the minor (5%) profit raise comparable with the maximal profit attainable in the condition of fare fixed at the existing value (column 6). But the convolution variant reception would lead to the 2.5 times reduction of the transport unit number while the trip payment would rise slightly (by 10%). The optimization results of the indicator convolution with different weight results (column 5) are comparable with the variant of Tchebycheff's equalization with equal weights (column 3)

In all cases the final choice should be executed by the expert group.

5.3   The Comments on the Results of Block 2 Restrictions Included in Addition to the Restrictions of Block 1

The compromise between the different social groups partially conflicting interests may be achieved not only by the vector criterion scalarization approach but also by the optimization problem decisions with separate criteria $Q_1,.., Q_5$ in the case of addition of non-obligatory block 2 restrictions to the obligatory restrictions of block 1. Non-obligatory restrictions are considered as models of the different variants of municipal participation in the transport system control. The dependences of each criterion on the non-obligatory restriction rigidity were examined; three examples shown below relate to the problem of the transport organization total hour profit maximization.

Fig. 1 illustrates the dependence of the total profit (in percentages of the maximal value attainable on the restriction set of block 1 only) on the fare being fixed by the municipal governance equal for all route paths. The upper curve corresponds to the absence of the different route paths profits equalization demand. The lower curve was computed for the case of rigid demand for the profit equalization accuracy (no more than 5% deviation from weighted middle profit with weights proportional to the transport unit numbers on the different route paths). Both of dependencies possess the maxima corresponding to the optimal balance between the transport organizations passenger service propositions and passenger trip requests depending on the fare value setting.

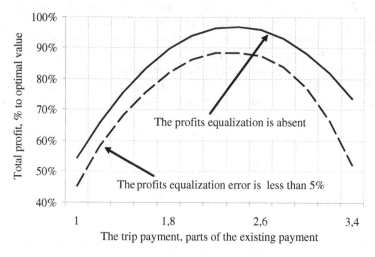

Fig. 1. The dependence of the total profit from the fixing trip payment

The experts would be interested in the payments values on the left side of the maximum point. In the absence of profit equalization demand the retention of the existing fare value leads to the undesirable 50% losses of the total profit. The inclusion of this demand can smooth the negative effects: the 30% raise of fare would be accepted by the citizens perhaps without active protests and also the transport organization total profit would be decreased slowly at the level acceptable for the transport system workers.

The profits equalization demand inclusion leads to 10% profit loss (comparably with the absence of equalization demand) while the fare varies in the range to the left of the maximum point. Taking into account the objective inaccuracy of the passenger flow estimation such losses seem to be inconsiderable.

The computations show that the replacement of the route paths individual fares settled by the transport organization owners independently with the common payment settled by the municipality provides no noticeable influence on the total profit. This result is valid only for the small cities with compact transport network and slight differences between different route path mileages.

Fig. 2 illustrates the dependence of the total profit (in percentages of the maximal value attainable on the restrictions set of block 1 only) from the total transport units number being fixed by the municipality. The upper curve (as in fig. 1) corresponds to the absence of demand for the different route paths profits equalization. The lower one was computed for the case of the rigid demand for the profits equalization accuracy (no more than 5% deviation from the weighted middle profit provided the weights being proportional to the transport unit numbers on different route paths).

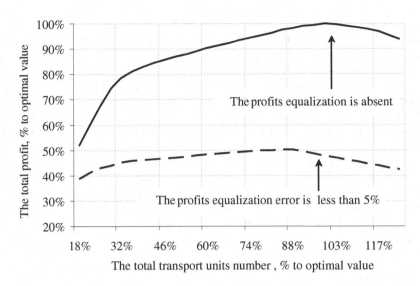

Fig. 2. The dependence of the total profit from the fixing number of transport units

It is possible to notice that the demand of the profit equalization leads to the useful effect: the dependence of the total profit value on the total transport unit number is weak. Therefore the transport organizations owners would accept (without opposition) the municipality decision on the twofold reduction of the total transport unit number. In the absence of the profits equalization demand the undesirable tendency of the transport unit number raise at the route paths: at the point of profit maximum this value exceeds the existing number by 20%.

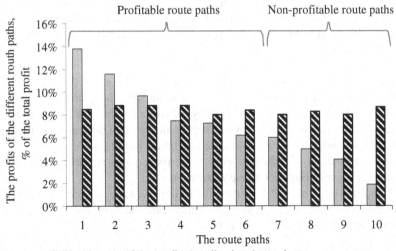

Fig. 3. The profits distribution between the different route paths

Fig.3 illustrates the comparison of different route path profits under the conditions of fare fixed at the existing level. In the absence of the profits equalization demand the rigid differentiation of the route paths would be expected according to its profitability (light-solid colored columns of diagram, fig.3). At the route paths with slight passenger flow at the terminal transport network sections as well as at the route paths with long sections coinciding with other route paths the profit values are expected at the level of 4 times less than at the profitable route paths (i.e. at the route paths either with intensive passenger flow at the terminal transport network sections or with the short sections coinciding with other route paths).

Including rigid demand for profit equalization accuracy (no more than 5%) leads to the route paths leveling (dark-stroked columns of diagram, fig.3) but the total profit would be decreased by 50% if the trip payment would be fixed at the existing level. Taking into account the minor part of transport system contribution in the whole city budget taxes such a decrease is acceptable for the sake of effective passenger service at each route path.

6   Conclusion

1. The computation experiments with the transport system optimization model show that the two-level control system structure (i.e. the structure with lower level corresponding to the unique transport unit owners and upper level corresponding to the unit owners of the distinct route path join) is insufficient since such structure cannot assure the achievement of a compromise between different social groups interested in the transport system mode of operation. Including the third (upper) level is reasonable for the purposes of the transport organizations effective coordination preventing the different social group conflicts.

2. The developed optimization model allowed to estimate the efficiency of the different municipality participation in the transport system control as well as to forecast the after-effects of transport system reformation. The results were accepted by the municipality governance.

3. The computations main results are as follows:
   (a) The transport units existing number can be reduced not less than twice without worsening the passenger service. At the same time the profits of the distinct route paths would rise not less than by 20% comparable with the existing values. The reduction of the transport unit number would decrease the motion intensity and improve the ecology state around the highways.
   (b) The introduction of different fares at the route paths is unreasonable for the small cities with compact transport network.
   (c) Including the demand for profit equalization between different route paths is recommended in order not to unjustifiably raise the fares and also to retain the transport system existing route paths.

Acknowledgements. The article was based on work supported by grants of Russian Foundation for Basic Research Povolzhie No. 13-07-97033, No. 14-07-97011.

References

1. Romanova, N.A.: Problemy i perspektivy razvitija transportnoj infrastruktury goroda: municipal'nyj podhod. Problemy sovremennoj Jekonomiki Evrazijskij Mezhdunarodnyj Nauchno-analiticheskij Zhurnal 1(21), 230–234 (2007) (in Russian)
2. Low, N., Astle, R.: Path dependence in urban transport: An institutional analysis of urban passenger transport in Melbourne,1956–2006. Transport Policy 16(2), 47–58 (2009)
3. Goldman, T., Gorham, R.: Sustainable urban transport: Four innovative directions. Technology in Society 28, 261–273 (2006)
4. Trentini, A., Malhene, N.: Flow Management of Passengers and Goods Coexisting in the Urban Environment: Conceptual and Operational Points of View. Procedia - Social and Behavioral Sciences 39, 807–817 (2012)
5. Polak, E.: Computational Methods in Optimization: A Unified Approach. In: Bellman, R. (ed.) Mathematics in Science and Engineering, vol. 77, Academic Press, New York (1971)
6. Primak, M.E.: Convergence of modified method of Chebyshev centers for solving problems of convex programming. Cybernetics 13, 738–741 (1977)
7. Jameson, A.: Gradient Based Optimization Methods. MAE Technical, Report No. 2057, Princeton University (1995)
8. Frank, M., Wolfe, P.: An algorithm for quadratic programming. Naval Res. Logis. Quart. 3, 95–110 (1956)
9. Fukushima, M.: A modified Frank-Wolfe algorithm for solving the traffic assignment problem. Transportation Research Part B: Methodological 18(2), 169–177 (1984)
10. Bertsekas, D.: Nonlinear Programming, p. 222. Athena Scientific, Athena (2003)

Cognitive Techniques of Knowledge Formation

Elena Rusyaeva

Institute of Control Sciences, Moscow, Russia
rusyaeva@ipu.ru, eur5@mail.ru

Abstract. We presented sequentially stages of studying the cognitive processes and obtaining scientific knowledge: from traditional social to individual cognitive techniques. Given comparative tables of knowledge levels, subjects' goal tasks during the transition to each level and types of mental entities themselves. Cognitive techniques, "tools" of the cognitive process are stated.

Keywords: levels of complexity, cognitive process, mental types of subjects, cognitive techniques.

1 Introduction

Earlier, in science, in the heyday of its rationalistic bases and approaches to the study, the accumulation of new knowledge, starting with the "Gold" for it XIX-th century, the emphasis was on the social aspect. I.e., the notion of science as a specialized cognitive activity of scientists and their communities put at the forefront a general social character of formation, storage and broadcasting of scientific data and methods for their production / finding. Then came and stuck in conceptually general philosophical terms, the notion of "positivism" - from the French. positive. Since the time of Comte in the history of philosophy under a positivism understood specific philosophical trend that formed in 1830. and preserve its influence to our time, having three historical stages - the "first" ("classical") positivism, "second"- empiriocriticism and "third" - neopositivism. With the name of Comte the two main principles of the XIX century science are linked: 1) recognition of the relativity of all "positive" (factual) knowledge; 2) the desire for accumulation and synthesis of new knowledge through the systematization and classification of "scientific facts". [1] Moreover, some settings of the positivist program survived to our time, albeit in a much reduced form. Modern post-positivism is based on the investigation of the laws of historical development of scientific theories and methods, partly why it has not lost its influence up to the present day.

But as it known, science today formed in super sociocultural system, with a huge potential for self-organization. For now occurring processes can not be explained by the classical causality. In the philosophical aspect the attention of major scientists recently aimed specifically at the methodological implications of scientific work, because there is still not enough structural "transparency" of the knowledge and the system structure definition can not be traced. That is why attention is drawn to the basics of human activity in general, the methodology itself is now treated as a

A. Kravets et al. (Eds.): JCKBSE 2014, CCIS 466, pp. 40–48, 2014.

science of the activity organization [2]. Attempt to systematize the foundations of scientific activity deserves attention. But it is worth to consider the dialectical dichotomy of social and individual in the formation of new, primarily scientific knowledge

2   Social and Individual in Science

It is worth noting that classic, traditional scientific knowledge was formed as a kind of social knowledge base, the so-called objective knowledge. The scientific research itself is seen as a subjective process - as an activity to obtain new scientific knowledge by separate individual - a scientist, researcher or a group, a team that is, in turn, the subject of scientific methodology – the methodology of scientific research. And, as emphasized in [2,3], scientific knowledge does not exist outside of cognitive activity of individuals, but the latter can learn something (explore) only insofar as the master collectively generated, objectified knowledge systems passed down from one generation to the other scientists [2].

So, it turns out that traditionally, mainly filters to scientific knowledge of the world were constructed , where in scientific terms determined that new knowledge, which is almost always identified with the scientific.

But times have changed and now the emphasis is on the individual, as opposed to the previously predominating social scientific paradigm. Moreover, the emphasis from the social to the individual shifted periodically in human history, and science as a social and cultural subsystem has not escaped this fate. So, nowadays the most popular and relevant research techniques have become individual cognition. Accordingly, the interest towards cognitive techniques is raised, techniques activating expansive (conceptual) thinking are practiced. New mode of research is technology of knowledge generation and means to "push" and intensify this process.

The problem is that the moment of generation of new knowledge, that is, the "mechanism" of knowledge, sort of "slipped" by scientific interests. Study of the generation technology seemed not so interesting occupation as construction of general metaphysical constructions (major philosophical plans). Although some moments were thoroughly investigated (eg, dialectical "withdrawal" in Hegel), but the study integrity of the cognition process lacked.

Therefore it is important to note that to date in dealing with cognitive problems there is a 5-levels concept of complexity [5]. Note that, although individually each level has been studied and like many times discussed in philosophy, science, but there was no seeing the whole picture at all. As they say now, "puzzle" did not converge, which is why it took a new synthesis of existing knowledge on the subject, a holistic approach.

In this paper we consider the immanent (internal) mechanisms, motives, stimulating different types of cognitive processes in correlation with levels of difficulty in solving cognitive tasks specified in [5]. Moreover, in our understanding of five difficulty levels correlate with our understanding of semantic-genetic theory of A.A. Pelipenko [4]. It was he who created the theory, in which he described the evolution of cultural and historical subjects, stressing that culture system (whole civilization) defines the space of meanings, and outside of it sublevels there's no knowledge available. And outside the psycho-mental, individual characteristics of people knowledge isn't generated.

3   Five Levels of Difficulty in Solving Cognitive Tasks

Detailed description of the five levels of difficulty in solving cognitive tasks is given in [5]. But since in this study we are talking about dealing with precisely the scientific cognitive task in order to obtain / gain new knowledge, we emphasize the importance of the condition. The process of cognition is individual, like any conscious activity of each person. After all, as there is no abstract person in general [2], and there is no knowledge beyond the psycho-mental, individual characteristics of people. Yes, all cognitive constructs are fully drawn in the socio-cultural environment. But the beginning of this process is inseparable from the individual consciousness. This is the first and very important statement. That's why, trying to identify some general patterns in the individual cognitive process, we do not want, on the one hand, the "sliding" of process' excessive descriptive detail. On the other hand, it is obvious that phases must be rated as very structure of the cognitive process. To do this, in the future, it is intended to compare the cultural and anthropological types of man described in detail in [4] with a possible solution for each cognitive level [5]. Here we present only the mental types, according to semantic-genetic theory [4].

Under the levels of difficulty in solving cognitive tasks we mean the following:

1.   At the first level of difficulty unknown problems are usually solved, but with the proviso that the way to this decision is precisely known. That is why the problem of this level of complexity is usually trivial, that to scientific knowledge is also quite important. For example, it is necessary to compile a catalog, directory, make a scientific review of research in a particular subject area. To do this we need to iterate over a large volume of material and create a archive of the available information. This is the level of the initial stage of studying a certain subject area. It uses basic research skills of collecting and processing information already available on the subject. This level is called the base.

2.   The second level of difficulty includes problems to solve which it is necessary to try all possible solutions from a set. Nontriviality moment in such problems is to determine the "snatching" generalizing, "the stick" property of the set and its variants, enumerated by the researcher. That is, there is some systematization performed while learning available data. This is a level of logical operations, classifications, initial ordering and finding generic-specific definitions.

3.   In solving the problems of the third level of difficulty there is some randomization busting, and its essence is to transfer the researcher's focus of attention to the rarely "visited" meaning (representations) loci space. So, we can overcome the knowledge inertia and find a not obvious solution to the problem, while remaining within the current system of ideas. This is a level of dialectical withdrawals. The mechanism itself to visualize the circuit is shown on Figure 1, and as an example will serve the process of semantic mediation of binary oppositions, ie, mediation of antinomical poles meanings of semantic inversion loop. This is the key to solving problems of this level of complexity.

4.   In contrast, when solving a cognitive task of the fourth level of complexity the researcher needs to move from the current system to a fundamentally new ideas. Moreover, the transition to a fundamentally new system of representations in solving the problem of the fourth level of complexity is carried out discursively. For example, the transition to the new scientific paradigm in terms of Kuhn. This is the level of so-called hypothetical- deductive reasoning (analysis).

5.   Cognitive task of the fifth level of difficulty can be solved only through outdiscursive (extra-linguistic), ie direct knowledge (intuition and / or insight). Sometimes it is called a literal information "reading". But it is the destiny of geniuses or "devoted", although the role of intuition in scientific knowledge is very high. In the scientific picture of the world, in our opinion, this kind of level can be correlated with a certain version of "going beyond." There is, for example, a certain conviction of mathematicians (representatives of "strong version" sciences [2,3]) that better is go beyond sets that in this mathematical abstraction you can see what we do not see in our reality. This is one of the "methods of hope" because of this "going beyond" may have certain fundamental, root importance for the practical reality, perhaps in the future. This connection acts imperative as an important "mythologem" for scientists.

Table 1. Correlation of levels of difficulty with immanent goals and motivations of subjects to transition to a new cognitive level

Levels of difficulty	Immanent goals and motivation of subjects to move to another level of cognitive				
	I *To learn more about this subject area*	*II* *To learn how to structure, organize and classify knowledge*	*III* *To find something new, not previously studied in this subject area*	*IV* *To create a new system of ideas in science, new industry, science*	*V* *to perceive holistically (not fragmented) new knowledge*
V **The level of "direct knowledge"**					direct knowledge (intuition and / or insight) as a new subject area

Table 1. (*continued*)

IV **Level of** **hypothetical** **-deductive** **reasoning** **(analysis)**				Hypotheti cal-deductive analysis is applicable to go to another knowledge paradigm (a new perspective on the problem)	
III **Level of** **dialectical** **withdrawals**			"Dialecti cal withdrawal", translating the focus of attention in the rarely visited sense loci		
II **logical** **operations,** **classification** **s and** **generic-** **specific** **definitions**		"Snatchin g" rod phenomena properties, classification , classification of information			
I **Primary,** **basic**	Initial study of a certain subject area. Trivial information enumeration				

4   Dialectical Withdrawal as an Example of the Cognitive Process

Let's take a closer look to a type of cognitive process, namely, the dialectic withdrawal. By itself, this particular mechanism of knowledge is not just considered in philosophical and scientific research. Especially a lot of attention paid to it description by G.Gegel in "Science of Logic." But at the same time, brilliantly insighted this move of cognitive dynamics, Hegel didn't saw, perhaps, even more precisely, not wishing to synthesize all stages of movement of human thought, going directly to the evolution of the Spirit as a kind of transcendental idealist (prohibitive) design.

Diagram of the "dialectical withdrawal" process can be illustrated by the example of binary semantic oppositions (antinomies) withdrawal, shown on Figure 1.

The median area is mental mediation, ie, is the moment of consciousness when, roughly speaking, people in their own understanding can calm down and stop, not "tossing" (inversion) more from extreme to extreme (by inversion loop). This is area of mediation or "withdrawal" of contradictions. Moreover, different cultural and mental types that withdrawal is achieved in different ways. More types of transitions for different cultural and mental subjects are discussed in [4]. In this research paper, we present only an outline of the overall process.

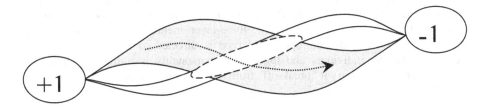

Fig. 1. Scheme of "dialectical removal" in the case of binary oppositions (antinomies)

Fig. 1 shows the inversion loop, where it is shown as one of the binary opposition – point +1 to the point – 1 can move, relatively speaking, thought, "tossing" between antonymous, opposite sense until mediated in the "middle" of mediation zone. Some consciousness paradigms tend to be contrails, then take one extreme position or the other, "skipping" the middle. But mature personal consciousness still tend to define in the mediation area. This, incidentally, is one of the important criteria for cultural and mental differences of subjects.

Examples of semantic antinomical "poles" may be as follows:

+1. Speech and language; - 1. Text, discourse. The middle zone - this is *Dialogue* as a means of mediation, that is, the possibility of mediation, removing semantic contradictions.

+1. Individual; - 1. Social. The middle zone of mediation - *The Social Contract*.

So, schematically presenting (Fig. 1) the withdrawal of dialectical process as contrails semantic loop (SL), we can substitute different semantic dichotomy and find their options for mediation.

5   Mental Types of Subjects or Cultural-Anthropological Human Types, According to Theory of A.A. Pelipenko

In details, as we said above, cultural and anthropological types of subjects, their appearance at different times in different metacultural systems are described in [4].

We only give some definitions and explanations to it, in Fig. 2 we schematically represent the dominant for today mediation logocentric type of cognitive process inherent to logotcentric and personality. We explain that mental types of subjects formed in different cultural and historical epochs do not disappear, but coexist as if in parallel in different eras. Moreover, some features like laminated and exist in a mixed form, so in some situations, people may behave as Archaic (eg, at home, in the family), and in other circumstances show features of logocentric and even personality. Base for allocation of these types of agents is hemispheric asymmetry of the human brain.

So, let's briefly explain: emergence of the human subject, according semantc-genetic theory is associated with the appearance of archaic with right hemispheric dominance. Palliative forms we do not consider in detail, and further history, in the era of mythos-ritual system domination appears a generic individual. Next a new type of mental constitution is formed and takes the dominant position, based on the dominance of the left hemisphere of her subject-carrier - logocentric. In the era of dualist Revolution (so-called "axial age" according to Jaspers, during the first millennium BC) had another cultural anthropological type - personality. This type is a carrier of most complexly organized, three-layer mentality type - personality. Personality as a cultural- anthropological type is directed to exit the logocentric system. Unlike the individual and logocentric, personality is unfinished, transient type: throughout its history it "break-off" from the logocentric framework.

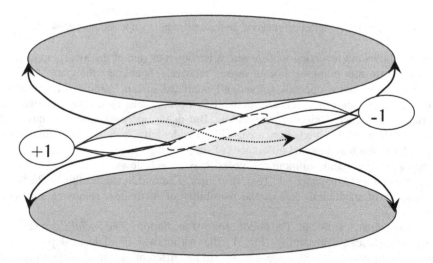

Fig. 2. Dominant mediation paradigm scheme for cognitive process, characteristic of logocentric epoch

Let us explain what is depicted in Figure 2 conditionally cognitive process, where the main principle is mediation domination over inversion. It characterizes primarily logocentric type of mentality and personality, characteristic for Western local cultural system. The problem is that the crisis of the system is precisely characterizes the absence of multi-directional (chaos) thought iterations. Figuratively speaking, the cognitive capabilities of logocentric reached its conditional horizontal "ceiling" and continue now almost endless circular motion. Example-explanation: +1. male; - 1. female. Mediation area - Family with all the possible variations on this theme.

At the end of XX - beginning of XXI century replacing the "people of the Word" - logocentrics come "people of the Number" - new naturalness carriers - the mental constitution, based on hemispheric dominance. New naturalness person - the carrier of the next level of mental complexity. Mental sphere becomes a qualitatively more autonomous and self-sufficient system. General evolutionary front passes through another phase of consolidation and is now localized in the mental sphere of man, and the man of the element of the system becomes a system in the system, emphasizes A.A. Pelipenko in his study [4]. Individual now dominates social.

Some comparatives of the levels of difficulty and types of mental subjects. If we conditionally compare mental types of subjects and levels of difficulty in dealing with cognitive tasks, we can come to the following conclusions. Probably all types of mental subjects can solve the problems of the first level of difficulty. Problems arise when solving cognitive tasks of the second and third level of complexity. In our opinion, to the archaic it is already difficult to solve the problems of the second level of complexity, and the individual and logocentric are pretty easy cope with the tasks of the second level. An individual may have difficulty in solving problems of the third level of complexity. Obviously, without cognitive techniques training, the individual will not solve tasks of dialectical withdrawal Logocentric can also meet the difficulties, because his cognitive abilities also require constant "training" to the inversion of the paradigm of mediation to move safely. Personality is quite capable of dealing with the problem as the third and fourth levels, cognitive training will help quickly overcome cognitive levels. But now for the emerging of "new natural" (not quite a good definition, but there is no other) with some offset to the right-hemisphere revenge, it is possible for the task forces will be the fifth level of complexity Although, the same moments of "inspiration" may well "come down" and on the individual and on logocentric. Another question is whether they can adequately convey to others the knowing descended on them. But all these issues require further conceptual elaboration.

In conclusion we can say that, of course, the degree of heuristic of current systematization time will tell. But in modern science increasingly important become conceptual approaches and individual characteristics of cognitive processes.

6   Conclusion

Thus, in summary of the study, we can name three cognitive techniques, which helps to activate the transition to the next educational level:

1. First - it's logical operations and classification of generic concepts (corresponding to the second cognitive level in our classification).
2. Second is activation of dialectical withdrawal - mediation (third cognitive level)
3. Third - the hypothetical-deductive analysis (fourth cognitive level).

The objective of this study was only detection, correlation and classification of cognitive techniques in individual cognitive process in the formation of scientific knowledge. We are interested, first of all, the genesis of knowledge generation, as further work is underway to establish methods of intensification of this process. Indeed, as stated above, if the individual parts of the process of knowledge were described by many researchers, since even philosophers of the first millennium BC, the holistic vision, and especially understanding of the cognitive process as a whole and was not created. Due to A.A.Pelipenko's cultural theory and extensive research work of modern scientists, especially mathematicians there is an opportunity to see and describe the problem in its entirety. But it is the task of the fourth level of complexity in our classification. In the meantime, this paper solves the problem of the second level of difficulty: gives the classification, mapping, as well as calls and organize themselves cognitive techniques, giving only a few possible definitions. In the future we plan to perform in-depth studies of the language of science and the creation of an adequate language tool for obtaining new knowledge.

References

1. New Encyclopedia of Philosophy (2010), http://iph.ras.ru/elib/2350.html
2. Novikov, A., Novikov, D.: Research Methodology: From Philosophy of Science to Research Design, p. 130. CRC Press, Leiden (2013)
3. Novikov, D.: Control Methodology, p. 76. Nova Science Publishers, New York (2013)
4. Pelipenko, A.A.: Learning the culture, ch. 1. Culture and meaning - M.: Rospen, p. 608 (2012)
5. Saltykov, S.A., Sidelnikov, Y.V., Rusyaeva, E.Y.: Properties of methods for solving complex problems. Economic Strategy 7, 98–103 (2013)

Concept of Complex Infrastructure Territory for Solving Problems of Integration Intersectoral Statistics

Alexander Bershadsky, Alexander Bozhday,
Irina Burukina, Pavel Gudkov, and Alexey Gudkov

CAD Dept. Penza State University, Russia
bam@pnzgu.ru, bozhday@yandex.ru, burukina@rambler.ru,
{p.a.gudkov,alexei.gudkov}@gmail.com

Abstract. The article discusses the promising approach to solving the problems of system integration and the use of fragmented sectoral statistics within a unified intersectoral monitoring system. The approach is based on a new concept of the complex infrastructure of the territory (CIT), which is a set of anthropogenic, technogenic and natural geographic systems forming a single integrity within the selected spatial and temporal scale. It is proposed a four-level model as a formalized description of the CIT, including abstract mathematical, logical, spatial and physical levels. As part of the abstract mathematical level, it is discussed new kinds of operations on hypergraphs - dynamic restructuring hyperedges structure and installing multiple layers structure hyperedges. Moreover, the article considers the technology development universal monitoring systems by integrating arsenal of advanced information technology (OLAP, Data Mining, GIS).

Keywords: complex infrastructure of the territory, intersectoral databases, statistics, monitoring, online analytical process, hypergraph.

1   Introduction

Analysis of the current status of the various socio-economic sectors reveals a number of general system properties with the fundamental importance for information support of management processes. These properties include:

- mainly the strategic nature of the management and planning;
- yearly frequency of collection sectoral report statistics;
- possibility of spatial georeferencing for sectoral statistics;
- similar requirements to the results of information-analytical activities to support management decision-making;
- a similar class of hardware used for the collection and processing sectoral statistics.

Such similarity causes a number of common problems associated with the collection, storage and processing sectoral data. Solving these problems in different sectoral

A. Kravets et al. (Eds.): JCKBSE 2014, CCIS 466, pp. 49–60, 2014.

departments happens often in many different ways. Head governing organizations, engaging analytics work their subordinate hierarchies, produce the collection and analysis sectoral statistics separate from each other way without trying to implement correlation forms of primary reporting and not taking into account the current conditions and trends adjacent socio-economic systems (SES).

This leads to the general problem of intersectoral incompatibility of formats and methods of data processing, which is especially critical in the current requirements to electronic document management processes.

This leads to the general problem of intersectoral incompatibility of formats and methods of data processing, which is especially critical in the current requirements to electronic document management processes. For example, a united intersectoral databases necessary to implement E-Government technologies.

It can be concluded that the present approach permits only state the total current status SES achieved during the reporting period. Many important issues concerning intersectoral interactions remain out of sight. This results in the loss of many causal relationships that can lead to incorrect estimates of the current situation, erroneous forecasts and inefficient decision-making.

Obviously, any local SES is an open system and is part of the overall infrastructure (which is more extensive on the territorial and thematic coverage). Administrative and economic boundaries SES can not prevent explicit or indirect effects from the adjacent infrastructure subsystems. In other words, the infrastructure of human activity within the selected territorial scope is a single system and many causal laws should look across the entire infrastructure.

Thus, the problem of system integration and the use of fragmented sectoral statistics within a single intersectoral multidimensional database is particularly relevant and importance.

2   Background and Related Works

For terminological identification system unity of various socio-economic sectors, we propose to use the notion of a complex infrastructure of the territory (CIT) (Bozhday 2009, Bershadsky and Bozhday 2010). It is defined as a set of anthropogenic, technogenic and natural geographic systems, which are system integrity within the selected spatial and temporal scale. The concept of the inextricable link between the natural and anthropogenic systems has been discussed by scientists in the various scientific disciplines (geography, geoecology, sociology, computer science, nonlinear dynamics, synergy, etc.). There are two concepts which closest to CIT – geosystem (GS) (Michailoff 1973, Armand, D. 1975, Armand, A. 1975, Sochaeva 1975, Christopherson 1997) and natural-technical system (NTS) (Oldack 1981, Armand, A. 1988, Christopherson 1997, Mainzer 2010). The concept of CIT assumes paramount emphasis on the informational component of socio-economic infrastructure processes that distinguishes it from GS and NTS concepts. This is particularly important for problems of informatization management, support decision-makers, and the related information and analytical studies. Integrated physical infrastructure is provided by the spatial reference of all the subsystems of the infrastructure to a single site in a single coordinate system. Border of CIT is determined based on the socio-economic (infrastructure) aspects. CIT complexity is estimated based on information complexity of appropriate infrastructure.

For information support and monitoring of natural and anthropogenic systems use a variety of modern information technologies. Particularly noteworthy is work in the form of Spatial Decision Support System (SDSS) on the integration of geographic information technologies and decision support systems (Sprague and Carlson 1982, Dragicevic 2008). Sharing software among GIS, OLAP and Data Mining (Thomsen, 1997, Fayyad, 1996, Larose, 2005) allows you to create an effective means of monitoring, proven to support decision-making in both the technical and socio-economic spheres (Son et al. 1998, Bedard et al. 2003, Scotch and Parmanto 2005, Bapna and Gangopadhyay 2005, Hernandez et al. 2004).

Nevertheless, using these techniques do not solve all the problems. Often, specific requirements for data formats, results visualization and analytic functions require strict configuration of monitoring systems for a particular subject area. It is not possible to use them to analyze the intersectoral interactions. Often developers use component of GIS, OLAP and DataMining as standalone software products from different manufacturers, which causes additional difficulties in their integration at the level of hardware and software platforms and data formats.

3   The Concept of Complex Infrastructure of the Territory

We offer the following main structural components of CIT: section of the territory, infrastructure layer, the information space. Section of the territory is the area of the earth surface, accommodating all the material basis CIT subsystems and limited their spatial extension.

Classification of socio-economic functions in relation to the territorial, information and organizational aspects, allows to define the notion of infrastructure layer. Infrastructure layer is thematically detached sphere of human activity, which is inseparably connected with the corresponding section of the territory, interacts with other layers of CIT and the environment, has its own substantive information structure and controls. Typical infrastructure layers are:

— various social and socio-economic sectors (such as education, health, economics, etc.);
— manufacturing sectors as the basis of the existence of socio-economic sectors;
— sectors of human interaction with the natural resources and natural systems.

Each layer may contain a large number of subsystems with an extensive network of relationships with other subsystems of the layers.

CIT information space formed of three interrelated types of information sets: own information (describing the internal state of CIT: structure, functions, objectives, spatial and temporal characteristics, key states); external information (information about the state of the environment that are external to the boundaries CIT); control information (information about the control decisions).

As a result, it is possible to identify a number of basic principles for the concept of intersectoral monitoring CIT:

1. Principle of thematic invariance to the monitoring sphere. Methods of monitoring and management of processes within the various layers of the infrastructure are invariant through the use of a single model to describe the entire infrastructure. Therefore CIT regarded as indivisible integrity of the system, not as a set of separate thematic layers.
2. The principle of openness and interdependence CIT infrastructure layers. Single information space of CIT, accommodating information processes each sector, provides a holistic intersectoral study of extensive environment of human activity.
3. The principle of the inextricable link with the territory. The border of infrastructure is determined by the spread of corresponding section of the territory which is an integrating factor. This provides a system unity of the entire set of investigated CIT processes.

4   Multi-level Mathematical Model of CIT

The real-time monitoring of CIT requires a flexible mathematical model that takes into account the specificities of different points of view, criteria and control purposes. Also, such the model should be formalized criteria management decisions and templates fetch data from intersectoral database. To ensure these requirements the model must account four different aspects:

1. System-wide aspect. CIT should be considered with infological perspective taking into account the heterogeneous structure of information and organizational links between sectoral subsystems.
2. Logical aspect. CIT should be considered from the viewpoint of the datalogical relationship between sectoral databases.
3. Spatial aspect. CIT should be considered in light of its enclosing space-geographic environment and the corresponding coordinate data bindings.
4. Physical aspect. CIT should be considered from the perspective of hardware and software platforms, protocols, rights of access to information, telecommunications which are used in its sectoral subsystems.

These aspects allow to form a multi-level mathematical model in which there are four levels: abstract level, logical level, spatial level, physical level.

On the abstract level CIT is represented as single description that includes all the structural elements and dynamics of relationships between them. To describe the abstract level model is proposed to use a hypergraph (Zykov 1974, Barany 2005, Bollobas 2001). Its hyperedge structure formed as a result of the CIT elements classification depending on the specific tasks of monitoring (fig. 1).

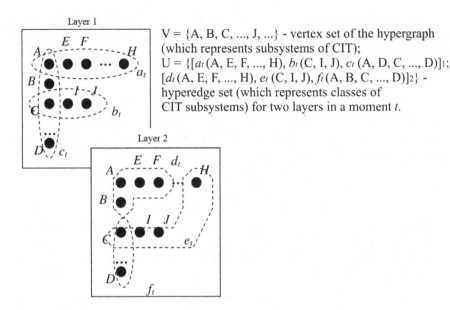

V = {A, B, C, ..., J, ...} - vertex set of the hypergraph (which represents subsystems of CIT);
U = {[a_t(A, E, F, ..., H), b_t(C, I, J), c_t(A, D, C, ..., D)]₁; [d_t(A, E, F, ..., H), e_t(C, I, J), f_t(A, B, C, ..., D)]₂} - hyperedge set (which represents classes of CIT subsystems) for two layers in a moment t.

Fig. 1. Model of abstract mathematical level (example with two layers of hyperedges)

We define a hypergraph *AMG* as a model of abstract mathematical level. It consists of two sets and predicate:

$$AMG = (V, U, P) \tag{1}$$

Set *V* describes the structure of a hypergraph in terms of vertices:

$$V = \{v_{i,(x,y)}\}, i = 1,2,\dots, N \tag{2}$$

where *N* - the total number of vertices corresponding to the number of CIT elements; *(x, y)* - weight vertex tuple, defining the spatial reference CIT element (spatial coordinates).

Set *U* has a variable cardinality and describes a multilayer structure of hyperedges:

$$U = \{u_j\}_f; j = 1, 2, \dots, K_t; f = 1, 2, \dots, F_t \tag{3}$$

where K_t - number of hyperedges at time t in the layer *f*; F_t – the number of layers. Order of interaction elements can vary significantly and, therefore, the cardinality of the *U* is variable.

Predicate *P* - determines incidence of vertices and hyperedges of each layer. *P* is defined on the set of all pairs $(v \in V, u \in U)$. Truth domain of predicate *P* is the set *R* of variable cardinality $B_t \neq$ const:

$$F(P) = \{(v, u) \mid P(v, u)_r\} \tag{4}$$

where: $v \in V, u \in U, r \in R = \{1, 2, \dots, Bt\}$.

Considered a set-theoretic representation of abstract mathematical model allows to determine the matrix representation of this model. It is useful for creating software for monitoring of CIT. Matrix representation (the incidence matrix) of the hypergraph on a layer hyperedges f, will have the form:

$$M_f = \| m_{ij} \|_{N \times Kt, f} \tag{5}$$

where: $m_{ij} = 1$, if $(v_i, u_j) \in F(P)$ or $m_{ij} = 0$, if $(v_i, u_j) \notin F(P)$, $(v \in V, u \in U)$.

In some cases it is more convenient to use the connectedness matrix of the hypergraph (eq. 6), which reflects the pairwise connectivity relations through incident hyperedges:

$$M_c = \| m_{ij} \|_{N \times N} \tag{6}$$

where: $m_{ij} = 1$, if $(v_i, v_j) \; \exists \, u_k$, $(v_i, u_k) \in F(P)$ or $m_{ij} = 0$, if $(v_i, v_j) \; \neg(\exists \, u_k)$, $(v_i, u_k) \in F(P)$, $(v \in V, u \in U)$

Full matrix representation of the hypergraph is a set of incidence matrices for each layer of hyperedges:

$$M = \{M_f\}, f = 1, 2, ..., F_t \tag{7}$$

Thus, we propose to expand the hypergraph properties such features as dynamic restructuring hyperedges and multi-layer structure of hyperedges.

For accounting and analysis information exchange between the CIT subsystems it is necessary to convert full heterogeneous model (eq.1) in a strictly rank structure. Classes of CIT subsystems (hyperedges) that have been identified on the abstract mathematical level, are combined into logical domains. The entire set of domains makes a single information model in the form of a multidimensional cube where each domain corresponds to a measurement axis (fig. 2).

Set-theoretic representation of the logical model *DM* is as follows:

$$DM = (D, Pd)_f \tag{8}$$

where D – set of domains formed on base of the current structure of the *AMG* hyperedges layer f:

$$D = \{d_i\}, i = 1, 2, ..., K_t \tag{9}$$

Pd – predicate defined on the set of all pairs (d_i, d_j), where $i \neq j$, $i = 1, 2, ..., K_i$; $j = 1, 2, ..., K_t$. Its truth detects cross-domain communication between domains d_i and d_j.

The main purposes of the logical model is:

— strict classification of CIT elements and their data arrays;
— definition of the hierarchical structure of organizations involved in monitoring;
— removing the problems of heterogeneity and decentralization of data.

However, the logical model does not account for spatial dynamics of information flows. Therefore, we introduce a spatial level model that allows the use of geographic information technologies apparatus.

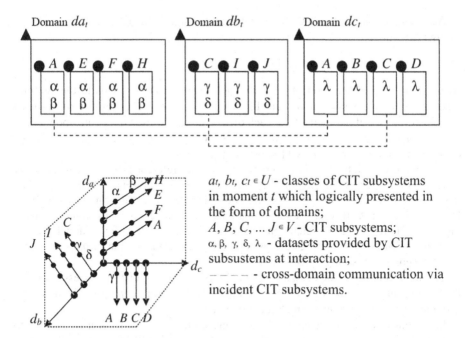

Fig. 2. Model of the logical level and the corresponding multidimensional cube

Each domain logical level is assigned to an object of spatial level with a georeference. Due to such spatial reference, we can uniquely associate a logical domain and all its contents (CIT subsystems and its inherent information) with other related socio-economic systems and other layers of the territorial infrastructure. Domain georeference is made to the digital cartographic basis of territory that corresponding to CIT. Thus, the model of spatial level describes georeferenced data flows by means of the theory of graphs (fig. 3).

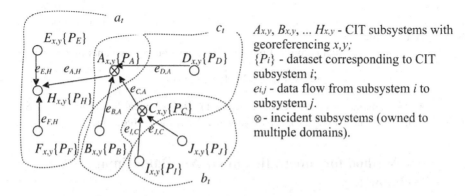

Fig. 3. Model of CIT on the spatial level

According to the set-theoretic representation, the spatial model of CIT level has the following form:

$$ISG = (V', U') \tag{10}$$

where $V' = \{v'_{i,(x,y)}(P_i)\}$ – set of vertices, each of which corresponds to the georefe-rencing (x, y) and some set of data P_i; $i = 1, 2, ..., N$ – the number of vertices; $U' = \{u'_j(e)\}$ – set of directed edges, each of which has a weight of e, corresponding to the volume of data transmitted between the incident vertices; $j = 1, 2, ..., M$ – number of edges (interactions between CIT subsystems).

ISG graph is weighted, directed graph with spatial reference. Its vertices represent CIT subsystems and their territorial position. Its edges represent data flow between the CIT subsystems. In fig. 3 ISG graph is divided into three subgraphs: at: A, E, F, H; bt: C, I, J; ct: A, B, C, D. These subgraphs represent the domain structure of the logic level model and rank heterogeneous vertices of the abstract level model. Vertic-es A and C play the role of "gateways" and allow the transmission of data flows be-tween heterogeneous subgraphs.

The main feature of the spatial level model is gridding statistics processed during the monitoring. So we can process information without departing from space-geographical environment to which it corresponds.

In the transition from the spatial level model to the physical level it is possible to consider physical communications between CIT subsystems. For example, objects of physical level may be associated with the telecommunications network nodes, keep-ing its logic domain affiliation. Proposed at the logical level incident subsystems es-tablish the procedure for cross-domain locking of segments of the physical network.

Set-theoretic representation of the physical model is as follows:

$$PhG = (V'', U'') \tag{11}$$

where: $V'' = \{v''_i(W_i)\}$ - set of vertices, each of which simulates a hardware and soft-ware platform of CIT subsystems; $i = 1, 2, ..., N$ – the number of vertices; W_i – set of data provided by the node v''_i; $U'' = \{u''_j(h)\}$ - set of directed edges, each of which has a weight of h, according to the characteristics of the communication link between incident CIT subsystems; $j = 1, 2, ..., M$ – number of edges (communication links between CIT elements).

Thus, the multi-level mathematical model of CIT has the follow generalized form:

$$CM = (AMG, DM, ISG, PhG) \tag{12}$$

where: *AMG* – abstract level model of CIT (eq. 1); *DM* – logical level model (eq. 8); *ISG* – spatial level model (eq. 10); *PhG* – physical level model (eq. 11).

5   The Method for Integration of OLAP, DataMining, GIS Technologies

To ensure the thematic invariance and territorial scalability of the CIT monitoring process we propose a method for integration of OLAP, DataMining and GIS technologies, in which the corresponding subsystems interact as shown in fig. 4: building intersectoral multidimensional database implemented is by means of statistical and OLAP-analysis subsystems, then constructing abstract level model (based on the criteria defined by the decision maker). The resulting model is used as a template for the formation of multi-dimensional data sampling which is transmitted to subsequent analysis into DataMining and GIS subsystems.

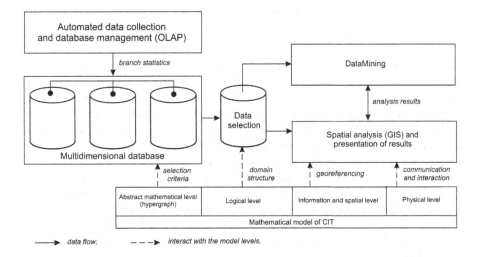

Fig. 4. Scheme of the integrating OLAP, DataMining, GIS technologies

Thus, the proposed method provides a substantial increase in productivity (on average 40-50% , Bozhday 2009) in the data analysis in comparison with conventional OLAP systems through the use of compact data samples (in-memory) which operatively reflect the dynamics of criteria and viewpoints on management decisions. The proposed method of integration OLAP, DataMining and GIS technologies defines a block diagram of a CIT monitoring system (fig. 5). Its features and scientific innovation which are:

— invariance structure to a specific field of monitoring or socio-economic problems of management;
— providing possibilities to integrate advanced technologies (OLAP, DataMining, GIS) into a single monitoring system;
— convenience of territorial scale the monitoring system.

When implementing the method of integrating OLAP, DataMining, GIS technologies, particular importance is the subsystem of the mathematical modeling that focused on three main objectives:

1. determination of the number (F) and the composition of selection criteria for data sampling from a multidimensional database (k_f, $f = 1, 2, \ldots, F$);
2. generation hypergraph model using obtained criteria k_f;

3. perform modeling procedures using the obtained hypergraph.

Thus generated hypergraph AMG:

$$AMG = (V, U, P); V = \{v_i\}, i = 1, 2, ..., N;$$

$$U = \{u_j\}_f; j = 1, 2, ..., KS_f; f = 1, 2, ..., F; KS_f \leq |u_{jf}|;$$

$$\mu_f = [Z_{max}(k_f) - Z_{min}(k_f)]/KS_f \qquad (13)$$

$$D_j = [(Z_{min}(k_f) + \mu_f \times (j - 1)) \div (Z_{min}(k_f) + \mu_f \times j)] \qquad (14)$$

where: KS_f – classification complexity factor for each f-th criterion among of selected (this factor is defined by the user and determines the number of classes of monitoring objects for each criterion k_f); $|u_{jf}|$ – cardinality of the set of vertices that incident of hyperedge u_{jf}; $Z_{max}(k_f)$, $Z_{min}(k_f)$ – the maximum and minimum from set of values corresponding to the criterion k_f; μ_f – pitch that determines the objects values range in the criteria set $Z(k_f)$; D_j – objects values range in the criteria set $Z(k_f)$.

Equations (13) and (14) define a linear way of classifying of monitoring objects according to the criterion k_f. However, the problem of the criteria distribution of vertices by hyperedges is brought to the problem of cluster analysis if the distribution of values is highly nonlinear and the number of objects (vertices of the hypergraph) is sufficiently large. In this case, we can take pair-group method using arithmetic averages (Ivazian, Buchstaber, Enukov etc. 1989) (for example, by way of building the dendrograms).

6   Conclusion

Thus, we propose the following main results which have scientific novelty and practical significance:

1. Notion of a complex infrastructure of the territory (CIT) as a combination of anthropogenic, technogenic and natural geographic systems which are controlled system integrity within the selected space-time scale. In contrast to existing concepts reflecting the relationship between natural and human systems, the primary importance of the notion of CIT has information component in the socio-economic infrastructure processes. It has a special significance for problems of management informatization and support for decision-makers.
2. CIT monitoring concept based on the principles of thematic invariance to the monitoring spheres, openness and interdependence of the various socio-economic sectors and their relationship with the territorial aspect.
3. Approach to solving scientific and practical problems of system integration of fragmented sectoral statistics within a single intersectoral multidimensional database.
4. Multi-level mathematical model of CIT with new kinds of operations on hypergraphs: dynamic restructuring of the hyperedge structure and assignment multiple layers in the hyperedge structure. These properties allow to formalize and take into

account (in real-time of monitoring) specifics of various viewpoints, criteria and management objectives.

5. The method for integration of OLAP, DataMining, GIS technologies which provides the ability to create and use an intersectoral multidimensional database as well as thematic and spatial invariance of the monitoring. This method determines a block diagram of a typical system for intersectoral monitoring of CIT.

References

1. Armand, A.: Information models of natural systems, p. 126. Nauka Press, Moscow (1975)
2. Armand, A.: Self-organization and self-regulation of geosystems, p. 261. Nauka Press, Moscow (1988)
3. Armand, D.: The science of landscape (Fundamentals of the theory and logical-mathematical methods), p. 288. Mysl Press, Moscow (1975)
4. Bapna, S., Gangopadhyay, A.: A Web-Based GIS for Analyzing Commercial Motor Vehicle Crashes. Information Resources Management Journal 18(3), 1–12 (2005)
5. Barany, I.: Applications of Graph and Hypergraph Theory in Geometry. Combinatorial and Computational Geometry 52, 31–50 (2005)
6. Bedard, Y., et al.: Integrating GIS components with knowledge discovery technology for environmental health decision support. Int. J. Med. Inf. 70(1), 79–94 (2003)
7. Bedard, Y.: JMAP Spatial OLAP: Innovative technology to support intuitive and interactive exploration and analysis of spatio-temporal multidimensional data, K. Technologies. Edito: Montreal, PQ. pp. 1–14 (2005)
8. Bershadsky, A., Bozhday, A.: The concept of monitoring the complex infrastructure of the territory. Penza State University Press, Penza (2010)
9. Bollobas, B.: Random graphs. Cambridge University Press, Cambridge (2001)
10. Bozhday, A.: A Complex Infrastructure of a Territory: Methods and Models of an Informational Monitoring. Information Technologies (9), 57–63 (2009) ISSN 1684-6400
11. Christopherson, R.: Geosystems: An Introduction to Physical Geography, 3rd edn. Prentice Hall, Upper Saddle River (1997)
12. Dragicevic, S.: Modeling and Visualization for Spatial Decision Support. CaGIS 35(2) (2008)
13. Fayyad, U.: Data Mining and Knowledge Discovery: Making Sense Out of Data. IEEE Expert: Intelligent Systems and Their Applications 11(5), 20–25 (1996)
14. Hernandez, V., Gohring, W., Hopmann, C.: Sustainable Decision Support for Environmental Problems in Developing Countries: Applying Multi-Criteria Spatial Analysis on the Nicaragua Development Gateway in niDG. In: IEEE Workshop on e-Environment, San Jose, pp. 136–150 (2004)
15. Ivazian, S., Buchstaber, V., Enukov, I., Meshalkin, L.: Applied Statistics: Classification and reduction of dimensionality. Finance and Statistics Press, Moscow (1989)
16. Mainzer, K.: Causality in Natural, Technical, and Social Systems (2010), http://journals.cambridge.org/abstract_S1062798710000244
17. Michailoff, Y.: Theoretical problems of geography. Riga, p. 41 (1973)
18. Munn, R.: Global environmental monitoring system: SCOPE Report. Toronto (3), 130 (1973)
19. Larose, D.: Discovering Knowledge in Data: An Introduction to Data Mining, p. 222. John Wiley & Sons, Inc. (2005)

20. Oldack, P.: Equilibrium nature and formation of consumer queries, p. 88. Novosibirsk State University Press (1981)
21. Scotch, M., Parmanto, B.: Development of SOVAT: A Numerical-Spatial Decision Support System for Community Health Assessment Research. International Journal of Medical Informatics (2005)
22. Sochava, V.: Doctrine of the geosystems, p. 546. Nauka Press, Moscow (1975)
23. Solncev, V., Ermakov, Y.: Quantitative methods for studying the nature. Questions of Geography Journal (98), 69 (1975)
24. Son, E.-J., et al.: A spatial data mining method by clustering analysis. In: Proceedings of the Sixth ACM International Symposium on Advances in Geographic Information Systems, Washington, D.C (1998)
25. Sprague, R., Carlson, E.: Building effective Decision Support Systems. Prentice-Hall, Inc., Englewood Cliffs (1982)
26. Thomsen, E.: OLAP Solutions: Building Multidimensional Information Systems. John Wiley & Sons, New York (1997)
27. Zykov, A.: Hypergraphs. Advances of Mathematical Sciences Journal 6 (180) (1974)

Data Processing Algorithm for Parallel Computing

Igor Barabanov, Elizaveta Barabanova, Natalia Maltseva, and Irina Kvyatkovskaya

Astrakhan State Technical University, Tatishcheva 16 Street, Astrakhan, Russia
igorussia@list.ru, elizavetaalexb@yandex.ru, maltsevans@mail.ru,
i.kvyatkovskaya@astu.org

Abstract. The algorithm of parallel data processing for the organization of parallel computing is suggested for consideration. The developed algorithm of parallel data channels identification is intended for use in switching schemes which are applied to communicate microprocessors solving a complex problem. This algorithm allows to increase commutation speed of data twice in comparison with existing methods that in its turn increases the general productivity of the computing system. Besides, positive property of algorithm in relation to parallel calculations is combination of the new data processing with transfer the results on already conducted operations. It is proved by means of the imitating modeling that secures a gain in productivity of the multiprocessor system using the developed algorithm.

Keywords: a parallel computing, the parallel identification, the algorithm, an imitating modeling, a switching system, a multiprocessor system.

1 Introduction

It is required to solve in real time many tasks necessary for the needs of practice, in other case a very large amount of computations are required for their solving. Parallel computing is computing, which can be implemented on a multiprocessor system using the simultaneous implementation of many actions generated by the process of the solution of one or many tasks. The main goal of parallel computing is the time reduction for solving the task.

Currently, there is plurality of great ways to build architectures for multiprocessor systems, but their weak point is a way of organizing relations between the processors of the system. It affects the data exchange rate and performance of the whole system.

One of the ways to increase the computing speed is the use of parallel processing algorithms. Therefore, the development of new processing algorithm for parallel computing is an actual problem. [1]

Traditionally the producers of the commutation equipment use in the function of the commutating sphere such topologies as the bus-line, the shared memory and the matrix switch, multistage structures. One of the popular commutation solutions for the high-performance computing systems is InfiniBand. But it main disadvantage is size limitation. There are researching of multistage switching systems with parallel processing, but they operate in the single mode of switching when checking available communication channels and transmitting of information are at different times. [3]

A. Kravets et al. (Eds.): JCKBSE 2014, CCIS 466, pp. 61–69, 2014.

The subject of our research is multistage switching structure implementing parallel processing of information and transmitting of information at the same time   to solve the problems that require a very large amount of computations.

The object of the research is parallel information processing algorithm for parallel computing.

2   Classification of Switchboard Management Methods

The method of management has a great impact on structure of switching systems (SS). Management of switching system is the complex of measures, necessary for their realization in structure of any network and maintenance of functioning of this network.

All SS can be divided into systems with the centralized or decentralized control depending on the principles of control.

The SS control is transfer of all its elements to certain states for establishment of demanded connection. If a switching element of system is the key, then it can be in two states – is closed and opened. It is necessary to establish in a demanded state everything or part of switching elements for connection installation between an entrance and an exit of the switchboard. This process is described by some algorithm. The systems with the centralized control have a uniform central control unit which operates work all systems. The systems with the decentralized control have a set of local control units at each cell of switching. Information on necessary connection is transferred from a system entrance to switching elements consistently: from already adjusted element to another, yet to not adjust. The control unit adjusts the switching element and transfers it to a control unit of the following switching element when it received this information.

Advantages of the SS with the centralized control of elements:

   — the smallest complexity;
   — fast implementation of control,
   — shortcomings:
   — lack of autonomy;
   — existence of the big memory, which volume   is defined by dimension of SS generally. [2]

The most part of the control unit (CU) is distributed on elements of switching system in case of the decentralized management of switching system. As a result of SS together with a control unit performs tuning on the basis of identical multiterminal networks. These multiterminal networks functionally unite some number of switching points and logical schemes of CU.

Systems with the decentralized control are more perspective from the point of view of their realization in the form of integrated circuit. Using enough simple local control units allows to use possibilities of integration of elements in a bigger measure and to improve characteristics of process of the SS control, as need to collect all information in the central unit and then to distribute it on all switching elements disappears. But such systems aren't favorable at a large number of entrances and witching cells, as big hardware expenses are required.

Advantages of the SS with the decentralized control:

— big autonomy;
— small number (in an ideal total absence) adjusting tires;
— lack of external memory for storage of adjusting information. [3]

The main disadvantage SS with the decentralized control of elements is the large number of operating tires.

3   The Structure of Multistage Parallel Identification of Free Data Channels SS

We can consider switchboards with the centralized control. As the actuation device it can be used to use the microcontroller.

If the SS has 2048 inputs and 2048 outputs, and must consist of five cascades, the input and the output cascades of the system will have 128 blocks with dimensions of 16x64 and 64x16 correspondingly. The second and the fourth cascades will consist of 64 switching blocks with dimensions of 128x128. The intermediate cascade of the system consists of 256 blocks with dimensions of 128x128.The controllers (c) are connected to the outputs of SS, they are all connected by the basic bus-line, designed for the exchange of information, and are connected to the CU. (Fig. 1).

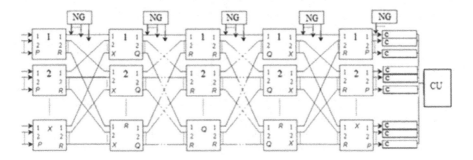

Fig. 1. The block diagram of the multistage SS with the parallel identification of free channels

The CU provides functioning of the SS with the parallel identification of the data channels. The automated device with the unconditional logic can be chosen as a control device. Name Generator (NG) is a device that allows at some time to supply to the appropriate input of the commutation cell the name of the output line of the switching block, to which this commutation cell is connected. [4]

4   The Simulation of the Parallel Identification Algorithm

4.1   The Parallel Identification of Free Data Channels Algorithm

Parallel identification method consists in the searching for free channels in SS. A searching is produced in the external device with respect to the switching field (in avr-microcontrollers). As a result the values of numbers of switching cells through which connection will be established are determined.

A parallel identifier is a complex of intermediate communication links namespaces, that is multi-bit codes of the intermediate lines along the way information from input to output. In addition, parallel identifier is also assigned a specific communication channel before its switching.

We consider the proposed algorithm of parallel identification of free channels implementing parallel processing of information and transmitting of information at the same time. This is the main advantage of our research. The algorithm of parallel identification of data channels is presented in fig. 2.

The searching of free data channels algorithm is realized in the microcontroller, is written in language Si programming. This algorithm allows to find free channels given in multilink SS with odd number of cascades (the number of cascades is set at the beginning of the program). Entrance values of this algorithm are number of an entrance to SS and exit number. The algorithm analyzes free cells of switching and gives out the parallel identifier which contains numbers of exits from intermediate blocks of system. This identifier unambiguously defines a way through SS. If it is necessary to connect the 7th entrance to the 12th exit of system and at this SS has 5 cascades (three intermediate),then the program, gives out result in the form of numbers of switching blocks and exits from these blocks, having analyzed free ways.

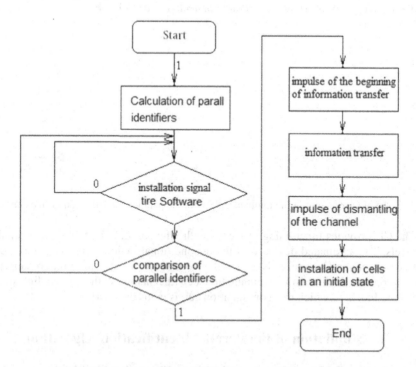

Fig. 2. The algorithm of parallel identification of data channels

The algorithm lays a way via all first blocks of system as SS isn't occupied yet. During the further work of algorithm the part of cells of switching will be occupied in information transfer and the way will be laid via other blocks of switching.

4.2   Realization of the Parallel Identification of Data Channels Algorithm in Microcontroller

Further we will create model of the microcontroller and will check a correctness of work of algorithm by means of the logical analyzer.

Now there are some programs simulators of operation of the electronic devices, one of such – Proteus 7.2.

For check of correctness algorithm functioning of search free communication channels in the ATmega128 microcontroller we will carry out modeling of operation of the device in the program Proteus 7.2 simulator. This simulator allows to debug work of the scheme without assembly of the real device and to check operability of the offered algorithm (fig. 3).

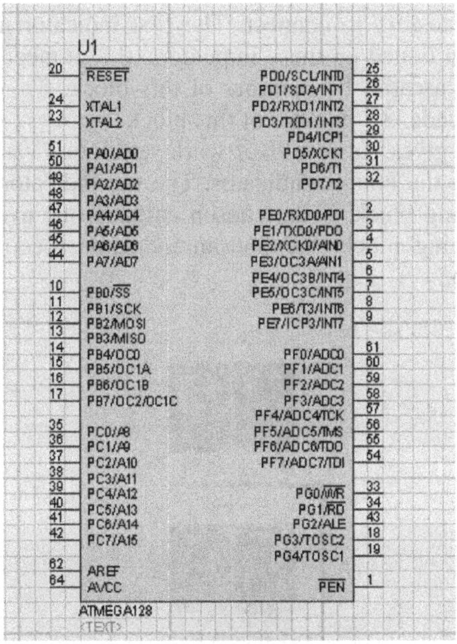

Fig. 3. ATmega128 microcontroller

The window appears at program start in which it is possible to choose type of the microcontroller and to connect the additional devices necessary for check of action of algorithm.

We choose the ATmega128 microcontroller. The first three entrances of the microcontroller are intended for record in a hexadecimal numeral system of numbers of an entrance and an exit of SS between which it is necessary to lay connection.

The following conclusion is intended for giving of an impulse of permission of the beginning of work of the program of search. The Gentbl impulse allows to update data files. This impulse in real SS moves from CU. PE exits are intended further for connection of the microcontroller to the general control unit.

The algorithm of operation of the microcontroller or search of free communication channels was written in the Si language and then by means of the compiler CodeVer-sionAVR V≥1.35 was transformed to the program for a controller insertion.

After a microcontroller insertion we connect indicators to exits and entrances of the device and we check a correctness of work of the program.

For insertion of the microcontroller we count number of switching blocks in each cascade at observance of criterion of Paul. We accept that SS has 2048 entrances and 2048 exits and consists of 5 links. Thus, entrance and output links of system have on 128 blocks dimension 16x64 and 64x16 respectively. The second and fourth links consist of 64 switching blocks dimension 128x128. The intermediate link of system has 256 switching blocks dimension 128x128.

When developing SS with other parameters minor changes are made to algorithm of search of free channels of data. [5]

The second and third indicator specify (in a hexadecimal numeral system), what entrance and what block of the entrance cascade with what exit and what block of the output cascade it is necessary to connect. The first indicator in figures from 0 to 3 defines type of the data issued on these indicators: 0 – number of an entrance of the block of the entrance cascade, 1 – number of this block. 2 – exit number from the block of the output cascade, 3 – number of this block.

The microcontroller gives out results of work serially on cascades. Number of the cascade is specified on the bottom indicator. The top indicator shows number of an entrance to the switching block of the chosen cascade, the average indicator shows number of this switching block, the bottom indicator specifies an exit from the switching block (fig. 4).

Fig. 4. Operation of the microcontroller

For example, in figure 4 it is shown that in the second cascade are involved 1A an entrance to E8 the switching block and 1A an exit from this block. After transfer to a decimal numeral system we will receive the 26th entrance to 232 switching block and the 26th exit from this block.

4.3   Comparison of the Parallel Identification SS with Single and Consecutive SS

In fig. 5 graphic dependences of probability of expectation of a package are presented to turns from package length at number of busy exits - 80% for SS with the consecutive principle of establishment of connections, SS with a single mode of switching and SS with the parallel principle of establishment of connections. Modeling was carried out in specially developed program. [6] Results of modeling are presented in table 1.

Table 1. Average values of probability of expectation of packages in turn

Package length	Size of the buffer, cell	Size of the buffer, cell	Size of the buffer, cell
15	0,35	0,74	0,67
30	0,54	0,82	0,77
45	0,71	0,88	0,86
60	0,72	0,89	0,86

The error of modeling is 5%. It is displayed on the schedules.

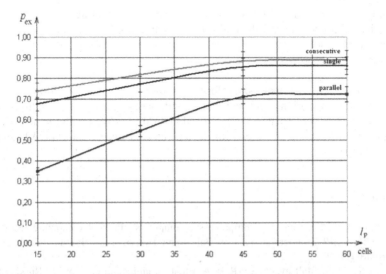

Fig. 5. Dependence of probability of expectation of a package in turn from package length at number of busy exits of 80%

Analyzing the constructed schedules it is possible to draw a conclusion that with a length of package lp = 60 cells the probability of expectation of a package in turn when using a method of parallel processing is 20% less in comparison with SS using consecutive algorithm of establishment of connections, and 18% less in comparison with SS working in a single mode of switching.

According to a single mode of switching of SS functions in three stages: first stage - scheme control; the second stage - information transfer; third stage dismantling of communication channels. At a stage of process of establishment of connections search of free intermediate ways is carried out, at the second stage there is a transfer of useful information on the adjusted communication channels. Thus the new stage of establishment of connections can begin only after the end of process of transfer by all devices. This mode is acceptable not for all systems of telecommunications, but only for those cases where the moments of receipt of packages aren't casual and known in advance.

Therefore, using of a method of parallel information processing in SS allows to serve arriving packages quicker that is positive property of system in case the traffic sensitive to delays is transferred, and also allows to lower significantly requirements to the extent of buffer memory of the switchboard.

5   Conclusion

Many tasks require a computing with plenty of operations that take extensive resources of the modern technology, while it requires to solve them that the result was obtained for the smallest possible time, or even strictly limited. Evident way to increase the speed of computation it would be application more than one computing device, and several working together to solve a problem. This approach is known as parallel computing. [7]

An important problem in constructing the parallel computing is to build a system which might be released the realization of parallel information processing. This problem can be solved by using the proposed method of parallel information processing in a multiprocessor system.

The advantage of our research is using the parallel identification of free data channels method in SS. The method performs parallel processing of information and transmitting of information at the same time, and increases a speed of multiprocessor systems in general. Performance the proposed algorithm proved with the help simulation program Proteus 7.2. As a control device selected microcontroller ATmega128 AVR family firm Atmel.

References

1. Abramov, A.: Computing on multiprocessor computers.: Parallel computing technology based OPENMP/ Monograph, p. 149. Publishing House of the Polytechnic Univ., St. Petersburg (2012)
2. Barabanova, E.A., Maltseva, N.S.: (RU): A patent for an invention. 2359313 Russian Federa-tion, the IPC G06F 7/00, a three-cascade switching system, - No 2007107780/09; reg.01.03.2007. Bull. Number 17 (June 20, 2009)

3. Kutuzov, D., Utesheva, A.: Switching Element for Parallel Spatial Systems: International Si-berian Conference on Control and Communications (SIBCON-2011), Proceedings. - Kras-noyarsk: The Institute of Electrical and Electronics Engineers (IEEE). Russia Siberia Sec-tion of the IEEE Siberian Federal University. The Tomsk IEEE Chapter & Student Branch. The IEEE GOLD Affinity Group SIBCON, September 15-16, pp. 60 – 62 (2011)
4. Barabanova, E.A., Maltseva, N.S., Barabanov, I.O.: The algorithms for parallel information processing in multistage commutation systems for high performance computing systems and communication systems. In: Third International Conference on High Performance Computing, HPC-UA 2013, pp. 39–44 (2013)
5. Barabanova, E.A., Maltseva, N.S.: The algorithms of processing of parallel commutation systems: Vestnik. Astrachan. State. tehn. Univ. Ser.: Management, Computer Engineering and Computer Science: Astrakhan Astrakhan State Technical University Publishing House 1, 150–156 (2011)
6. Barabanova E.A., Maltseva, N.S.: ASTU holder.2008611841 Certificate of official registration of computer programs FIPS Russia: The simulation program structure and algorithm of switching systems. - No 2008611147 appl. 20.03.2008, publ. from (April 14, 2008)
7. Akhmedov, D., Yelubayev, S., Bopeyev, T., Abdoldina, F., Muratov, D., Povetkin, R.: Research on performance dependence of cluster computing system based on GPU accelerators on architecture and number of cluster nodes. In: Third International Conference on High Performance Computing, HPC-UA 2013, pp. 1–13 (2013)

Analysis of User Profiles in Social Networks

Alexander A. Chumak, Sergei S. Ukustov, and Alla G. Kravets

Volgograd State Technical University Russia, 400005, Volgograd, Lenin Avenue, 28
saintgluk@gmail.com, sergey@ukstv.me, agk@gde.ru

Abstract. Virtual social networks play an important role in modern life, they allow you to talk to people with different views and interests, to hold conferences, publish news, personal and public information. This paper describes the analysis virtual social network profiles largest Russian social network «Vkontakte». The study aims to identify the areas of interest of the user. We identify the interests of some users and compared them with the interests of their friends and consider the extent to which their interests coincide.

Keywords: the social network, analysis of the profiles, comparative analysis.

1   Introduction

Virtual social networks play an important role in the modern life, they have become so important in people's lives that currently more than 60% of the Russian population use Internet to access to social networks such as «VKontakte», «Twitter», «Odnoklassniki». These social networks allow people to communicate with people who have different views and interests, to hold conferences, publish news, share information, post personal and public information.

Nowadays there is a fierce competition on the Internet for the provision of more accurate information about users, their interests, desires, needs, etc. Search engines, such as «Google», «Yandex» collect and analyze data in order to provide a more accurate information retrieval. On the other hand, there are no public tools, which are available for analyzing profiles in social networks.

Systems for analysis of the profiles in social networks could significantly help administrators of the communities in social networks to accept applications to join the community on the special selected measure. Sales representatives on the internet find those people who are interested in their products. This system could be used in commercial projects to build or to determine the areas of the user's profiles interests in social networks.

We tried to search for systems like ours, but we couldn't find the analogue or something which is close to the analysis of user profiles in social networks. This system has no analogs and it's greatly important in the field of studying user profiles in social networks. So we had the idea of analyzing profiles and we decided to analyze the users in a social network «VKontakte» in Ukraine. The main aim of this work is to verify the possibility of analyzing the social network users. And to develop a system that could determine the selected network user opinion about the annexation of Crimea to Russia.

A. Kravets et al. (Eds.): JCKBSE 2014, CCIS 466, pp. 70–76, 2014.

2   Subject Area Analysis

We selected a social network «VKontakte», as this social network is the most popular in Russia, but it is also widely used abroad. «VKontakte» is one of the largest social networks in RuNet, it is the first most popular website in Belarus, Russia, and the second in Ukraine and Kazakhstan, and in the world, it takes 21st place. [2]

This social network is actively expanding and attracts new users from all over the world, this year social network «VKotakte» set a new record for attendance in the night, and it is 60 million users.

3   Data Collection

One of the criteria for choosing a social network «VKontakte» was its API (Application programming interface). This social network supports a wide variety of API methods to work on WEB - sites, Standalone - applications, iOS and Android - applications. In this article, we will use the Standalone application.

Standalone application supports client-based authentication protocol OAuth 2.0 [3]. After passing the authorization a pass key is generated, with wich you can work and get the data from user pages «VKontakte».

All methods of API «VKontakte» in response return JSON structure in the form:

```
response: {
count: 1,
items: [{
id: 2943,
first_name: 'Vasya',
last_name: 'Babich',
screen_name: 'antanubis',
photo:
'http://cs307805.vk.me/v307805943/343d/kWYZkr7tCFk.jpg'
}
}
```

For data collection, it was decided to get all users living in Ukraine. To do this API method «users.search» has been used. The method returns a list of users in accordance with the specified search criteria. [3] One of the main criteria for this method is a «city» - City ID. In response to this request, we obtain a list of user IDs, which match our search criteria.

City ID can be obtained by using the API method «database.getCities», which returns a list of cities. The main parameters for this method is «country_id» - country identifier [3], the identifier of the country of Ukraine is two.

The newest API method, which collects all the necessary information, is getting records from the wall of users after being obtained through the search criteria above method . «wall.get» - returns a list of records from the wall or from the user community. [3] We already know the user IDs, so we need to fill only option «owner_id» - the user ID or the community, from the wall of which is necessary to obtain records. [3] On the formed request, the server «VKontakte» send structured JSON, which contains a list of entries from the wall of the specified user. One of the parameters of the JSON's response will contain «text», which will contain the record on the wall that we need to handle further.

Using all the methods listed above, we can create a file that contains records from the walls of users, who live in Ukraine and who referred the tag «Crimea».

4   Text Preprocessing

Before moving to the next step, we need to break a sentence into words, and to parse the words, for this we use a parser called MaltParser.

MaltParser is a system for data-driven dependency parsing, which can be used to induce a parsing model from treebank data and to parse new data using an induced model [5].

Parsing in linguistics and computer science – is the process of comparison of the linear sequence of tokens (words, tokens) of the natural or formal language with its formal grammar. The result is usually a parse tree (syntax tree). It's usually used in conjunction with lexical analysis [6].

5   Naive Bayesian Classifier

Classification describes a reference structure, which divides the space of all possible output data on a set of classes (they are also called categories or concepts), which (usually) do not overlay each other. Classification algorithms allow to identify objects automatically which belong to a particular class.

The job of the classifier is to assign a concept for a sample: and it is everything he does. To know which concept is to be assigned to a particular sample, the classifier reads the training set TrainingSet – a sample set Instances, which is already assigned to a concept. After downloading these samples classifier trains, or learns to compare concepts and Instances, taking it as a basis of a set of destination TrainingSet. The method of training the classifier depends on each type of classifier. [3]

We use naive Bayesian classifier as a mean of assessing relevance to a particular record received from the wall member. Naive Bayesian classifier is good because it provides a certain rank, which is called conditional probability X, with the condition Y, which will tell you what is the probability of observing events X, providing that we have seen the event Y. In particular, this classifier uses as an input information the following data:

The probability of observing the concept X in the general case, it is called the prior probability and is denoted $P(X)$.

— The probability of observing the sample Y, if we randomly select a sample of those who have been assigned to the concept X; this probability is also called the likelihood and is denoted $P(Y \mid X)$.
— The probability of observing a sample Y in the general case, it was still called the evidence and denoted $P(Y)$.

The most important part of the classifier – is the calculation of the probability that the observed sample Y belongs to concept X; this probability is called posterior probability and denoted $P(X \mid Y)$. Computation of posterior probabilities is performed according to the following formula (called Bayes' theorem):

$$P(X \mid Y) = P (Y \mid X) P (X) / P (Y) \qquad (1)$$

We use naive Bayesian classifier to classify text from the walls of social network users to determine the probability that this text belongs to one of the embodiment signs. Therefore, we will use only the ability that allows us to compute relevance score, which is exactly in line with our objectives.

6   Training Naive Bayesian Classifier

Having prepared the text after semantic processing, we can start to train a naive Bayes classifier. Firstly, we need to identify the main categories into which we can divide our text:

— «Good» - classification which is responsible for the text that says that the user supports the accession of the Crimea to Russia;
— «Bad» - classification which is responsible for the text that says that the user doesn't support the accession of the Crimea to Russia;
— «Unknown» - classification which is responsible for the text, which contains information about the Crimea, but does not belong to a theme of annexation.

Once we have decided on the classifications, we need to create a table for training naive Bayesian classifier for each classification of 100 examples (Table 1).

Table 1. Comparison of signs correspondences classification

Symptom	Classification
Putin signed a contract and officially took Crimea and Sevastopol to Russia. Our friends! Crimea is RUSSIA!	Good
While there are Crimean Tatars in Crimea, no Russian will be here. Deal with it!	Bad
Minister of Youth and Sports of Ukraine Dmitry Bulatov announced that Crimean clubs received an offer to act in the Russian league.	Unknown

Classifier stores all encountered signs, as well as the likelihood that the feature is associated with a particular classification. Examples are presented to the classifier one by one. After each example, classifier updates its data by calculating the probability that the text of this category contains a particular word. After the training, we obtain a set of probabilities (see Section Table 2).

Table 2. Probability of belonging words Category

Sign	Unknown	Good	Bad
against	0,23	0,15	0,6
sign	0,15	0,44	0,08
and	1	1.1	0.91
youth	0,46	0,25	0,24
constitute	0,31	0,37	0,22
spring	0,37	0,01	0,01
people	0,15	0,14	0,14

This table shows, that after learning, associations with different categories of signs are getting stronger or weaker. The word «against» is more likely to «bad», the word «sign» is more likely to «good», and the word «spring» – is «unknown». Ambiguous signs, such as the word «and» have similar probabilities for the three categories (the word «and» is found in almost any document, regardless of its subject matter). Trained classifier - is just a list of symptoms with associated probabilities gathered together. Unlike some other classification methods, there is no need to store the original data as training.

7   Mathematical Software for the Analyzing Profiles in Social Networks

The purpose of this method is to determine the ratio of the text to one of the appropriate category. For this we use the formula (1) of the naive Bayes classifier:

$$P(Category \mid Text) = P(Text \mid Category) \times P(Category) \tag{2}$$

where, P(Category) – is the probability of hitting submitted text entry in this category, it is calculated by the formula

$$P(Category) = number\ of\ texts\ in\ this\ category\ /\ total\ number\ of\ texts \tag{3}$$

The final probability values are compared with each other and a maximum value is the result.

8   Design of the System

Figure 1 shows the architecture of the application which consists of the three main components:

— VKontakte server - provides information about the users;
— Model training – a trained model of the naive Bayesian classifier;
— Application module - basic module, which connects the GUI with algorithmic module that communicates with the server «VKontakte» and training model to produce a result.

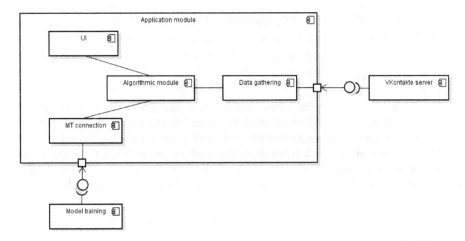

Fig. 1. Module application architecture analysis profiles in social networks

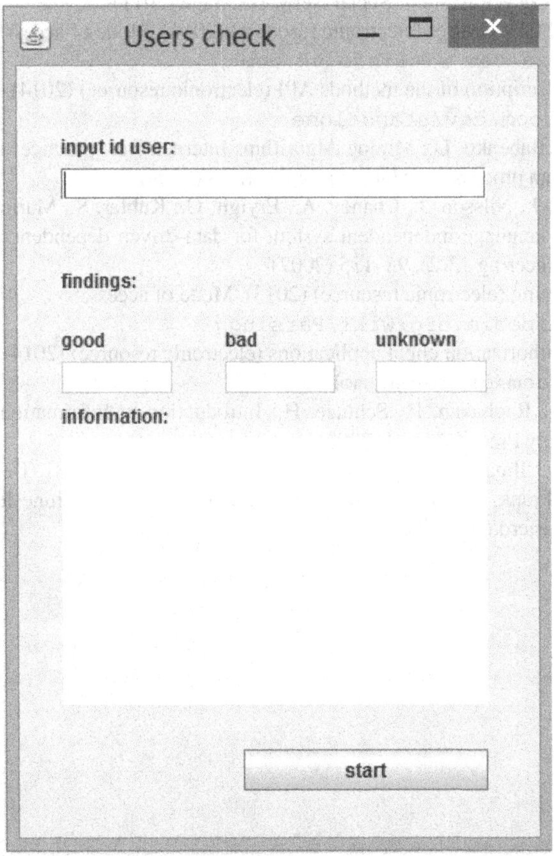

Fig. 2. The main application window analysis profiles in social networks

Figure 2 demonstrates the main application window of the analyzing of the profiles in social networks.

9 Conclusion

Authors aimed to analyze the users' profiles in a social network «VKontakte» in Ukraine and Russia to develop a system that could determine the selected network user opinion about the annexation of Crimea by Russian Federation. To achieve this goal the methods of data collection, data processing, training and application of machine learning were used. Authors considered an algorithm to determine an opinion on the annexation of the Crimea to Russia. We developed a desktop application for using in practice.

References

1. Barnett, G.A.: Encyclopedia of Social Networks. Sage (2011)
2. Alexa Top 500 Global Sites (electronic resource) (2014), Mode of access: http://alexa.com/siteinfo/vk.com
3. VKontakte: Description of the methods API (electronic resource) (2014), Mode of access: http://vk.com/dev/standalone
4. Marmanis, H., Babenko, D.: Mining Algorithms Internet. Best practices in data collection, analysis and data processing. Manning Publications (2009)
5. Nivre, J., Hall, J., Nilsson, J., Chanev, A., Eryigit, G., Kübler, S., Marinov, S., Marsi, E.: MaltParser: A language-independent system for data-driven dependency parsing. Natural Language Engineering 13(2), 95–135 (2007)
6. Wikipedia: parsing (electronic resource) (2013), Mode of access: http://wikipedia.org/wiki/Parsing
7. VKontakte: Authorization client applications (electronic resource) (2014), Mode of access: http://vk.com/dev/auth_mobile
8. Manning, C.D., Raghavan, P., Schütze, H.: Introduction to Information Retrieval. Cambridge University Press (April 1, 2009)
9. Rajaraman, A., Ullman, J.: Mining of Massive Datasets, pp. 437–481 (December 2011)
10. Witten, L.H., Frank, E., Hall, M.A.: Data mining: practical machine learning tools and techniques, Amsterdam, p. 560 (2005)

Understanding of Class Diagrams Based on Cognitive Linguistics for Japanese Students

Shigeo Kaneda, Akio Ida, and Takamasa Sakai

Faculty of Science and Engineering,
Doshisha University, Kyoto, 610–0321, Japan
skaneda@mail.doshisha.ac.jp

Abstract. This paper demonstrates that the structure of a *class diagram* reflects the cognitive structure of English based on *cognitive linguistics*. Native English speaking students of software engineering are expected to easily utilize class diagrams because no impedance mismatch exists between their mother language and class diagrams. On the other hand, since the cognitive structures of Japanese are quite different, class diagrams are hard to understand for Japanese students of software engineering. To overcome this impedance mismatch, this paper argues that Japanese students must understand the correspondence between *seven English sentence patterns* and class diagrams. The cognitive view shows that *Is-a* and *Has-a* relationships are necessary and sufficient as specially prepared relationships. Our proposed cognitive linguistics views result in essential and applicative understanding of class diagrams for Japanese students.

Keywords: Object Oriented, Requirement Analysis, English seven sentence patterns, A class diagram, cognitive linguistics, English, Japanese, Relationship.

1   Introduction

A *class diagram* is a major tool for domain modeling in requirement analysis, and the model is usually described by the mother language of the analysts. Since class diagrams were originally developed by English speakers in the United States and the United Kingdom, their structure is deeply affected by English cognitive structures. English speaking students are expected to understand and utilize class diagrams based on English cognitive structures.

On the other hand, Japanese software engineering students and engineers often find it difficult to utilize class diagrams. This paper assumes that one major reason for this difficulty is the impedance mismatch between the English cognitive structures of class diagrams and the cognitive structures of Japanese. Japanese students have to overcome this mismatch. If they recognize the differences of the cognitive structures between Japanese and class diagrams, using them will become more convenient.

A. Kravets et al. (Eds.): JCKBSE 2014, CCIS 466, pp. 77–86, 2014.

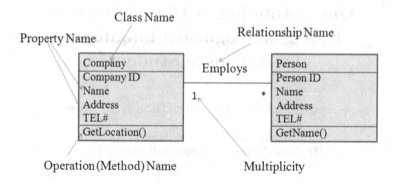

Fig. 1. An Example of a Class Diagram

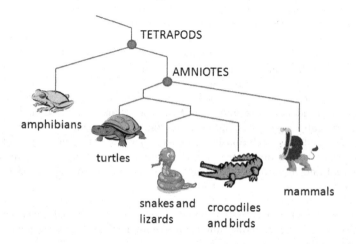

Fig. 2. Tree of Lives

To resolve the above problem, this paper proposes the application of *cognitive linguistics* [Kawakami96] [Langacker02] [Lakoff90]. Class diagram structures are explained using *seven English sentence patterns* and cognitive linguistics. By clearly understanding the cognitive structures of class diagrams, Japanese software engineering students will benefit.

The rest of our paper is organized as follows. Section 2 describes questions about class diagrams, and Section 3 discusses their parts of speech. Section 4 clarifies the relation between seven English sentence patterns and class diagrams. Section 5 outlines the process to convert to Japanese specification descriptions, and Section 6 concludes this paper.

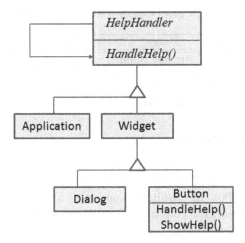

Fig. 3. Chain of Responsibility Pattern

2   Object Oriented Approach and Cognitive Linguistics

2.1   Difficulty Using Class Diagrams for Japanese

When Japanese students of software engineering start to study *object-oriented approaches*, the first question is "What is an *object?*" Fig. 1 shows an example of a class diagram. Some Japanese textbooks argue that "An object is a concept." Most students are confused by this explanation. They can vaguely understand that a "person" and a "company" are objects (classes). However, they have no way of telling whether "debts" or "sand" are objects[1].

Other questions posed by textbooks include "What is an Is-a relationship?" and "Why do we make an exception in favor of Is-a and Has-a relationships?" Fig. 2 shows a tree of life that explains Is-a relationships. Mammals is a lower concept under a higher concept called Amniotes. Most Japanese students misunderstand that the higher side of Is-a relationships is more general and abstract. However, Fig. 3 betrays their expectations and shows the well-known *Chain of Responsibility* pattern proposed by GOF[Gamma94]. In this pattern, an *abstract class* HelpHandler is the higher concept of an Application class, which is huge and general. On the other hand, HelpHandler is a specified and small concept that is odd based on the Japanese understanding of Is-a relationships shown in Fig. 2.

In the above situation, Japanese students and software engineers feel less confident in their self-made class diagrams. They have no guidelines to decide whether a written class diagram is correct and rarely draw conceptual class diagrams in the requirement analysis process of large-scale system developments.

---

[1] Japanese language makes no distinction between countable and un-countable nouns. The difference between an action verb and a state verbs is also ambiguous.

Table 1. Class Diagram and Part of Speech

Part of Speech	Usage	UML Class Diagram
Noun	Countable Noun	Class
	Un-countable Noun	Property or Property Value
Verb	Action Verb	Method (Operation)
	State Verb	Relationship

2.2 Cognitive Linguistics

To solve the above questions, this paper focuses on cognitive linguistics, which was developed by George P. Lakoff and Ronald W. Langacker [Kawakami96] [Langacker02] [Lakoff90]. In cognitive linguistics, a single word has only one *core image*. For instance, the core image of the preposition "for" is "exchange." Examine the following sentence:

"The train is bound for Tokyo."

In this case, catching the train and arrival at Tokyo are exchanged. Tokyo station is the final destination in the above sentence. This train never changes its destination. On the other hand, the core image of the preposition "to" is "direction." Thus, the following sentence doesn't guarantee arrival at Tokyo because the train may stop next to Tokyo station:

"The train is bound to Tokyo."

Even though the difference between the above two sentences may be trivial for native English speakers, it is not trivial for most Japanese students.

3 Class Diagram from View of Cognitive Linguistics[Kaneda12a][Kaneda12b]

Japanese cognitive psychologist Mutsumi Imai argues that un-countable nouns (material nouns) are not included in *objects*[Imai10]. Objects are countable nouns. This viewpoint simply indicates the relation between English and an object (Table 1). Class names are countable nouns, and relationship names are state verbs. Property names are un-countable nouns, and methods (operations) are action verbs. Even though Table 1 may be implicitly trivial for English speakers, it is beyond the scope of Japanese textbooks and the understanding of Japanese students.

Marked and *unmarked* are also important concepts of cognitive linguistics. For instance, "mickey" is marked, and "mouse" (a kind of animal, not the surname of Mickey Mouse) is unmarked. A class is a *set*. A class name is a name of a set. For instance, John, Alice, and Taro are marked; they are instance names.

Table 2. Seven Sentence Patters(*S*:subject,   *V*:verb,   *O*:object,   *A*:adverbial, *C*:complement)

Sentence No	Sentence Pattern	Example
1st	$S+V$	The sun (S) is shining (V).
2nd	$S+V+O$	That lecture (S) bored (V) me (O).
3rd	$S+V+C$	Your dinner (S) seems (V) ready (C).
4th	$S+V+A$	My office (S) is (V) in the next building (A).
5th	$S+V+O+O$	I (S) must send (V) my parents (O) an anniversary card (O).
6th	$S+V+O+C$	Most students (S) have found (V) her (O) reasonably helpful (C).
7th	$S+V+O+A$	You (S) can put (V) the dish (O) on the table (A).

On the other hand, children is unmarked because it is a class name candidate. To draw a class diagram, the given specification description should be generalized. Marked names should be converted into unmarked and general names.

4   Seven English Sentence Patterns and Class Diagram [Kaneda14]

4.1   Seven English Sentence Patterns

This section clarifies that the structure of a class diagram matches the cognitive structure of English. We selected *seven English sentence patterns* to study English cognitive structures for Japanese students. Table 2 shows seven English sentence patterns that are designed for non-native English speakers. *Five English sentence patterns* are also quite popular in Japan. These patterns are old and are no longer used in the United Kingdom.

All seven English sentence patterns have necessary and sufficient elements. For instance, subject (S), verb (V), and object (O) are the essential elements in the $S+V+O$ pattern. The connections among these essential elements are very strong. O cannot be removed from the $S+V$ parts, for example. Any English sentence can be classified into one of the seven sentence patterns. If seven English sentence patterns can be translated into class diagrams, the essential elements of any English sentence can be converted into class diagrams. Also, the strong connection among the elements provides robustness for class diagrams, even if the business procedures change in the application domain. The following paragraphs show the relations between seven English sentence patterns and UML class diagrams.

1st Sentence Pattern (ex. The Sun Is Shining)

The verb is intransitive with no object. This verb doesn't become a relationship. It becomes an operation (method) of a class.

2nd Sentence Pattern (ex. That Lecture Bored Me)

It has a typical S(subject) $+ V$(verb) $+ O$(object) pattern. Cognitive linguistics argues that S controls O in English. This is the energy flow from S to O. If V is a state verb, then it becomes the relationship between the S and O classes. For instance, the verb "bore" has a relationship name. The subject "lecture" puts energy into object "me". This controllability between S and O equals the functional dependency of relational databases.

3rd Sentence Pattern (ex. Your Dinner Seems Ready)

The verbs of the 3rd sentence patterns are restricted to "to be," "become," "look," and "seem," for instance. Most verbs can be replaced by a "to be verb." This sentence pattern corresponds to an Is-a relationship or a property value. The Is-a relationship semantically implies "define" or "presume." For this example, the "ready" state is a property value of the class "dinner."

4th Sentence Pattern (ex. My Office Is in the Next Building)

This verb has an *adverbial*. This pattern's adverbial has a preposition. If the adverbial part is removed, the remaining sentence "My office is" is strange. Semantically, for this sentence the adverbial is essential, and its important aspect is that it is a *locative case*. Locative is a grammatical case that indicates a place. An adverbial becomes a class name or a property value in this sentence pattern. For this example, the "office" class has a property "location," and the property value is the "next building."

5th Sentence Pattern (ex. I Must Send my Parents an Anniversary Card)

In this sentence pattern, the verb has two words without prepositions. In this case, cognitive linguistics shows that two types of static relationships can be selected: Is-a and Has-a. Such sentences often have an action verb, such as "give," "pass," "send," "teach," "tell," "bring," "lend," "read," "sell," and "show." The core image of these verbs is "moving something from one position to another."

In this sentence pattern, the verb is an action verb. If the resultant object state in the real world is persistent, the relationships between the two words can be expressed by Is-a or Has-a relationships. In this example, a Has-a relationship is suggested. My parents have an anniversary card. Action verb "send" is converted to state verb "have."

6th Sentence Pattern (ex. Most Students Have Found Her Reasonably Helpful)

In this sentence pattern, the verb also has two words without prepositions. The verb is not a state verb. However, the resultant object state in the real world is static. Thus, an Is-a relationship or a property value is suggested. In this example, the girl has a "character" property and the property value is "helpful."

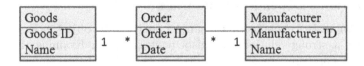

Fig. 4. An example of "Mono (Object)-Koto (Action)-Mono (Object)" Pattern

7th Sentence Pattern (ex. You Can Put the Dish on the Table)
The adverbial part, which is essential and cannot be removed, is a locative case. The verb is an action verb. However, the resultant object state in the real world s static. In this example, the location of the dish is on the table, and an Is-a relationship or a property value is suggested.

As mentioned above, each sentence of the seven English sentence patterns includes the essential elements of English sentences. The relation among these elements doesn't change even if the superficial business flows are modified. A class diagram expresses a *static structure* in the target domain. Even if a sentence has an action verb, the generated state of the real world should be expressed in the class diagram in as far as the result of the action lasts for a finite period of time.

Is-a and Has-a relationships are necessary and sufficient as specially prepared relationships from the view of cognitive linguistics. This is one reason that textbooks make exceptions in favor of them.

4.2   Mono (Object)-Koto (Action) -Mono (Object) Pattern

Figure 4 shows an example of the Mono (object)-Koto (action)-Mono (object) pattern, which is well-known and specially treated in Japan. Many Japanese textbooks teach that an action (*Order* in Fig. 4) changes into an object. This pattern expresses the following sentence:

"The company ordered the goods to the manufacturer."

The subject of this sentence is "company;" however, the term "company" is not shown in Fig. 4. If students mistakenly believe that one side of a relationship should be a subject, they will have difficulty understanding Fig. 4, because neither the right- nor the left-hand classes are subjects.

The above sentence is the 7th sentence pattern. Thus, the locative case is essential and cannot be removed. *Manufacturer* is a locative case and becomes a class. Also, object "goods" in the sentence becomes a class. Finally, "order" becomes a *relationship class.*

In the above sentence, the value of subject "the company" is fixed in so far as the requirement analysis is limited to the client company. Thus, this "company" class is not necessary in a class diagram. Fig. 4 can be easily understood if the analyst knows the 7th sentence pattern and the locative case.

4.3   Functional Dependency and Class

Cognitive linguistics explains that a subject controls the object in English. This means that a strong relationship exists between them. Examine this sample sentence: "A company employs a person." In this case, if the company name is decided, the names of the employees are determined automatically. The energy flow between the subject and the object closely resembles functional dependency.

However, the dependency of relationships is not persistent in class diagrams. For instance, assume that a company employs a person for the summer season. The class diagram has an "employs" relationship between the "company" and "person" classes. This relationship is valid during the summer season for this employee. But the number of employees is not just one. Another person is employed for the winter season, for instance. The class diagram represents both cases. The time dependency is removed from the class diagram.

On the other hand, there are persistent functional dependencies in objects. For instance, a class "company" has such properties as company ID, address, and telephone number. In this case, these properties come up to this world when the company instance is born. The properties also have values as long as the company instance is alive. If the company instance goes out of this world, its properties and values are also removed. This behavior shows that an object is normalized and its structure is a *third normal form* of relational databases.

5   Rewriting of Japanese Simple Sentences

5.1   Necessity of Rewriting

As mentioned above, subjects control objects in English sentences. The relationship of a class diagram should have functional dependency. However, verbs in Japanese usually don't have such an energy flow. For instance, note the following Japanese sentence:

"Fuji-san ga mieru."

This sentence means that we can see Mt. Fuji. However, its nuance is quite different. An extremely loose translation of the Japanese nuance is "Mt. Fuji can be seen, but the existence of a particular watcher is not mentioned." There is no energy flow in this Japanese sentence.

Japanese sentences often avoid non-living subjects. For instance, a literal translation of the following sentence is odd:

"This table has four legs."

In Japanese, a non-living "table" cannot generate actions. The following is a Japanese translation of the above sentence:

"Tsukue niwa 4 hon no ashi ga aru."

An extremely free translation of the nuance is "Four legs are provided with a table. The legs exist from the time when we found the table." Since this sentence has no energy flow, it should be rewritten in the style of: "This table has four legs."

5.2   Class Diagram Creation from Specification Descriptions

To draw a class diagram, Japanese specification descriptions must be converted into simple sentences, and the resultant simple sentences must be translated into quasi-English versions of Japanese simple sentences having energy flow. This rewriting is time consuming, but it enables accurate and easy transformation from Japanese specification sentences to class diagrams. The following is an outline of the sentence transformation:

STEP 1: Simple Sentence Generation
  The Japanese specification descriptions are converted into simple sentences with only one verb.
STEP 2: Energy Flow Generation
  Since Japanese simple sentences usually have no energy flow, they must be rewritten into quasi-English Japanese simple sentences that do have energy flow.
STEP 3: Generalization
  If the nouns in simple sentences are marked, the marked nouns should be rewritten as unmarked nouns, which are the candidates of the class names.
STEP 4: Class Generation
  Each simple sentence is converted into a class diagram. In this conversion, seven English sentence patterns and functional dependency assist students create a class diagram.

6   Conclusion

This paper demonstrates that a class diagram's structure reflects the cognitive structure of English. Native English speaking students are expected to completely exploit class diagrams. On the other hand, since Japanese's cognitive structure is quite different, class diagrams are hard to understand for Japanese students. To resolve this problem, we argued that they should be understood from the viewpoint of cognitive linguistics. Japanese students have to study the correspondences between seven English sentence patterns and class diagrams. The following are the major results of the paper:

1. Class names, property names, relationship names, and operation (method) names correspond to countable nouns, un-countable nouns, state verbs, and action verbs, respectively.
2. Each of seven English sentence patterns exactly corresponds to some part of a class diagram. The elements of each pattern are essential and indivisible. A class diagram is robust and insulated from the influence of superficial business flow changes.

3. Is-a and Has-a relationships are necessary and sufficient. Is-a relationships imply "regard" and "define," not only hierarchical higher and lower relationships.
4. Subjects in English sentences control their objects. On the contrary, a subject in a Japanese sentence does not control. Thus, Japanese specification description should be rewritten into quasi-English style sentences in Japanese. This is an important process for class diagram creation.
5. The Mono (object)-Koto (action)-Mono (object) patterns, well-known in Japan, can be understand as a typical pattern in which the original sentence's adverbial part has a locative case.
6. An object's structure is a third normal form of relational database theory. The relationships between classes also have functional dependency. This is a good guideline for class diagram creation.

The authors express our deep appreciation to the late Dr. Satoru Ikehara, a former professor at Tottori University, who provided an opportunity to harvest the fruitful results of cognitive linguistics.

References

[Kawakami96]   Kawakami, S.: An Introduction to Cognitive Linguistics (In Japanese), Kenkyusha, Tokyo (1996)

[Langacker02]   Langacker, R.W.: Concept, Image and Symbol, 2nd edn. Mouton de Gruyter, Berliln (2002)

[Lakoff90]   Lakoff, G.: Women, Fire, and Dangerous Things: What Categories Reveal About the Mind, Univ. of Chicago Pr (T), Reprint Version (1990)

[Gamma94]   Gamma, E., Johnson, R.H.R., Vissides, J.: Design Patterns: Elements of Reusable Object-Oriented Software. Addison-Wesley Professional (1994)

[Imai10]   Imai, M.: Language and Thinking. Iwanami Shoten (2010) (in Japanese)

[Kaneda12a]   Kaneda, S., Seko, T.: Understanding of Class-diagram based on Cognitive Grammar (In Japanese), Technical-report, SIG-KBSE, IEICE of Japan 111(396), pp. 61–66 (January 2012)

[Kaneda12b]   Kaneda, S.: Understanding of Object-oriented approach based on cognitive grammar (In Japanese), Department Bulletin Paper, Graduate School of Policy and Management, Doshisha University, 13(2), 21–45 (March 2012)

[Kaneda14]   Kaneda, S., Ida, A., Sakai, T.: Guidelines for Class Diagram Design based on English Sentence Patterns and Functional Dependency (In Japanese). Technical-report, SIG-KBSE, IEICE of Japan (to appear, March 2014)

Adaptive Testing Model
and Algorithms for Learning Management System

Dmitry Litovkin, Irina Zhukova, Marina Kultsova,
Natalia Sadovnikova, and Alexander Dvoryankin

Volgograd State Technical University, Volgograd, Russia
litd@mail.ru

Abstract. Skill gap analysis is one of the most important problems in learning management. Using the computerized adaptive testing provides the effective way to solve this problem and allows adapting the test to the examinee's ability level. This paper presents an adaptive testing model that integrates hierarchy of knowledge and skills of subject domain and difficulty of the test items. This combination of testing features allows using the presented model for criterion-referenced testing. The following algorithms on the base of adaptive testing model have been developed: starting point selection, item selection, test termination criterion, skill gap assessment. Implementation of these algorithms in the learning management system allows testing the student's knowledge and skills in specific subject domain purposefully and consider the different ability levels. Developed adaptive testing model and algorithms are applied for testing the basic knowledge and skill gaps in subject domain of variables declaration in C programming language.

Keywords: computerized adaptive testing, criterion-referenced testing, learning management system, skill gap analysis.

1   Introduction

In the process of learning management one of important problems is to assess student knowledge. To solve this problem, testing is commonly used, in particular computer testing [1]. Computer tests are used to assess knowledge in various subject areas [2,3,4,5]. There are fixed and adaptive tests.

Fixed tests are the tests that provide a fixed sequence of tasks imposed in the testing process. Adaptive tests are the tests that involve a change in sequence of tests in the testing process, taking into account the responses of the student to previously received test items [6].

Adaptive tests have several advantages over fixed tests [6,7]. These tests are usually shorter than fixed ones because they are focused on the student's ability level. Thus, during the test, neither students with a high ability level can receive simple test items, nor students with low ability level can receive sophisticated tasks.

Most of adaptive tests are norm-referenced, i.e. allow ranking students upon the ability level within a single atomic theme [8]. Basically the creation of such tests is

A. Kravets et al. (Eds.): JCKBSE 2014, CCIS 466, pp. 87–99, 2014.

based on the models of Item Response Theory (IRT) [9,10]. According to IRT the set of test items are ranked by difficulty. The next test item is selected according to the expected student ability level and the item difficulty.

Other class of adaptive tests are criterion-oriented tests. Such tests in the testing process can determine the level of achievement by student of specific section in given subject area. In compiling this type of tests the domain concepts are taken into consideration. The purpose of the testing process is to determine what knowledge and skills a student possesses after studying the concepts of the domain [11,12,13]. It helps to solve the problem of analyzing the students' skill gaps. The general ability level of the student in this case plays a secondary role. For example, there may be students that have the same ability level, but possess a different set of skills. There are approaches to the creation of such tests, based on the theory of IRT and Bayesian method [14,15,16]. However, the question of reducing the number of test items received by student in these approaches is still open.

In this paper, we propose an approach to development of adaptive criterion-based test using combination of IRT and method of hierarchical analysis of domain concepts. This approach will reduce the number of test items offered in the testing process, as each test item will be used to assess several skills of the student.

2   Concept of Adaptive Testing

To reduce the number of offered tasks it should be taken into account that the domain skills are interconnected and form a hierarchy. Target skills are at the top of the hierarchy. They are subdivided into simpler skills. At the bottom level of the hierarchy one can observe the most simple, indivisible skills. We assume that:

— if the student does not possess the bottom level skill, he therefore is devoid of the skill to top-level fully;
— if the student possesses top-level skill, he is therefore capable of all of the associated lower-level skills.

To assess each of the skills we shall use a single test item. Having presented it and estimating the correct answer on a "correct-incorrect" scale, we appreciate the skill to scale "possesses-does not possess". Considering combination of the skill, presentation and assessment of one test item can lead to assessment of several related skills. This reduces the number of the administered items. However, the reduction of items number is not always possible. Therefore, to reduce the number of test items in addition to skills hierarchy consideration, it is proposed to further utilize the difficulty of test items. The difficulty of the next test item should correspond to the student ability level. This will help to eliminate setting knowingly simple or complex test items and assess several skills with one test item.

The process of adaptive testing in accordance with the proposed approach is presented in Fig. 1. The process is iterative. At each iteration, we select a test item, which (after the answer to it) makes it possible to assess several related skills. To do this, we take into account the test item difficulty (represented in the repository of test items), the ability level (represented in the student model) and skills' relatedness (represented in the domain model). Testing is terminated when all the skills are estimated. At the final stage out of the set of estimated skills we select only those that the student does not possess.

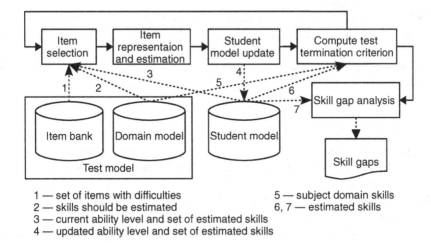

1 — set of items with difficulties
2 — skills should be estimated
3 — current ability level and set of estimated skills
4 — updated ability level and set of estimated skills

5 — subject domain skills
6, 7 — estimated skills

Fig. 1. Scheme of adaptive testing process

To implement the proposed concept the following models and algorithms were developed:

1. Adaptive test model in which the test items have difficulty and are associated with skills (knowledge) of subject domain. At that the skills (knowledge) of subject domain are hierarchical.
2. Student model, which represents the current ability level and the skills that student possesses or not.
3. Adaptive testing algorithm, providing the selection of such test items, which assess several related skills. Test item selection should be carried out on the base of the hierarchy of skills, the current student ability level and the difficulty of the test items.

3   Adaptive Test Model

According to the proposed concept of adaptive testing a test model integrates the repository of test items and the domain model, as shown in Fig. 2. The domain model is viewed as the hierarchy of skills and knowledge. Each test item is associated with the skill (knowledge) in the model, which helps to assess this skill. Thus, the test is a set of task items and a set of skills (knowledge) associated with these items:

$$TEST = \{QB, DOMAN\_MODEL, ASS\_SET\},$$

where QB – repository of test items, i.e. $QB = \{Q_1, Q_2, \ldots, Q_n\}$, where Q_i – test item, n – total number of test items;

$DOMAIN\_MODEL$ – domain model, represented the subject domain where knowledge and skills are tested;

ASS_SET – a set of association relations between test items and skills (knowledge).

In our model the test items meet the following requirements: 1) they should be ranked in terms of difficulty, and 2) the correct answer to the test item should be assessed on a dichotomous scale of "correct-incorrect". Accordingly, the test item has the following definition:

$$Q_i = \{DESC, DIFFIC\},$$

where $DESC$ - description of test item, which includes the type of items (open answer item, closed answer item, etc.), formulation, variants of correct answers, the estimation procedure of the test item (assessment test item should be expressed in the scale of "correct-incorrect");

$DIFFIC$ – the difficulty of the test item in the range [-5, 5] according to Item Response Theory.

To assess the hierarchy of skills (knowledge) let's define the domain model in the form of directed acyclic graph:

$$DOMAIN\_MODEL = \{SK\_SET, AGGR\_SET\},$$

where SK_SET – set of skills (knowledge) of subject domain, i.e. $SK\_SET = \{SK_1, SK_{12}, \ldots, SK_n\}$, where SK_j – skill (knowledge) of subject domain, n – the total number of domain skills;

$AGGR\_SET$ – a set of directional aggregation relations among skills (knowledge), i.e. $AGGR\ (SK_i, SK_j) -> \{0, 1\}$, 1 - if to possess the skill SK_i one needs to be able to have the skill SK_j; 0 - otherwise.

Derivation of skills graph should be performed in accordance with the following conditions.

1. In the graph the source-vertexes correspond to the target domain skills. The leaves of the graph set basic indivisible skills and knowledge.
2. Child nodes for a certain skill SK_j are skills and knowledge that are required for possession of parent skill SK_j.
3. If student is not capable of at least one child skill, it is considered that the student can not fully possess parent skill.
4. If a student has all child skills, he would not necessarily possess parent skill. For example, parent skill requires the right combination of child skills.
5. Several parent skills may depend on a child one.
6. If student possesses a parent skill, he also possesses all the child ones.

To assess the skills and knowledge they need to be associated with test items. For this it is given in our model a set of associations ASS_SET between test items and domain skills (knowledge). The association relation is defined as $ASS\ (Q_i, SK_j) \rightarrow \{0, 1\}$, where 1 - if to successfully respond to the test item Q_i one must possess the skill (knowledge) SK_j; 0 – otherwise.

According to specified aggregation relations between skills, as well as association relations between skills and items, one should note the following features.

1. Between skill and test item one can observe relation of 1:1, i.e. each skill is associated with one test item, and each test item is associated with a single skill.
2. The task formulation associated with parent skill, should depend on the test item involving child skills.

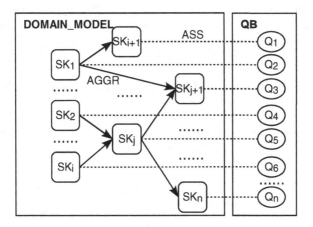

Fig. 2. Fragment of adaptive test model (three level)

Thus, the proposed test model takes into account the difficulty of the test items, and makes it possible to associate test items with domain skills. The skills themselves form a hierarchy represented as a directed acyclic graph.

4   Student Model

During testing in a student model we should fix upon the skills that student possesses or does not. Additionally, the model should represent the current student's ability level, in accordance with which the next test item is selected. Therefore, the student model is described as follows:

$$STUDENT\_MODEL\ =\ \{\ LEVEL, LB\_SK\_SET, GRAP\_SK\},$$

where $LEVEL$ – student's ability level on a scale of [-5, 5] according to IRT;

LB_SK_SET – set of labels for skills of SK_SET, i.e. $LB\_SK\_SET = \{LB\_SK_1, LB\_SK_2, ..., LB\_SK_n\}$, where LB_SK_j – label for skill SK_j; the label can have one of three values "undefined", "possesses" and "does not possess";

GRAP_SK – minimal set of unrelated skills, which a student does not possess.

Thus, the proposed model represents the student's ability level, and also includes assessments of his skills.

5   Skill Gap Analysis on the Base of Adaptive Testing

According to the proposed models the skill gaps analysis is reduced to the following tasks.

Task 1. Generate such sequence of test items from test items repository QB, that would lead to the estimation of all skills SK_SET and generate the set of labels LB_SK_SET. Thereby only a part of repository of test items should be used.

Task 2. Based on the skill assessments (LB_SK_SET) form a minimal set of unrelated skills, which the student does not possess ($GRAP\_SK$). At the same time the skills should refer to the lower levels of the hierarchy of skills of $MODEL\_DOMAIN$.

Below are the algorithms for solving these tasks.

5.1   Algorithm of Student's Skill Estimation on the Base of Adaptive Testing

This algorithm solves the problem of generation a sequence of test items to assess student skills. Input of the algorithm are the test model $TEST$ and the student model $STUDENT\_MODEL$.   Steps of the algorithm are shown in Fig. 3.

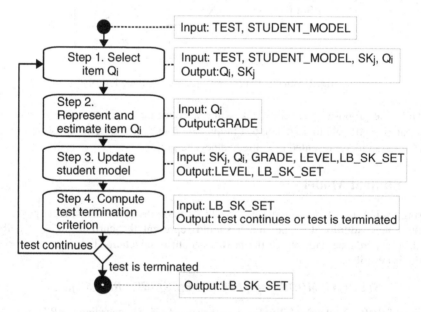

Fig. 3. Adaptive testing algorithm (activity diagram)

Feature of the algorithm is that in one iteration there can be estimated several domain skills in response to one test item, that reduces the number of test items. Furthermore, let us consider the details of steps of test item selection and the student model update, because these steps provide the specified feature of the algorithm.

Next Item Selection Algorithm. The input data of the algorithm are: SK_j - skill that has been assessed at the previous iteration; LB_SK_SET - current assessments for all skills; $LEVEL$ - the current student's ability level; $DOMAIN\_MODEL$ - graph of skills and knowledge for the subject domain; set of the test items of QB that have not been represented yet.

The algorithm consists of the following steps.

Step 1. Form set of skills $SK\_ANALYSIS$, which is necessary to assess at the current moment. There are 3 situations that arise during the testing process.

Situation 1. The test has just begun and no skills have been assessed so far. In this case, the set $SK\_ANALYSIS$ is equal to the original SK_SET.

Situation 2. It is previously determined that the student does not possess the skill SK_j (the student failed on the test item related to skill SK_j). To determine the membership of skill SK_j to set $GRAP\_SK$, it is necessary that its child skills are labeled as "possesses" or "does not possess". If a child skill is labeled as "undefined", it should be assessed. In this case, the set $SK\_ANALYSIS$ is composed of descendant skills for SK_j, which have label LB_SK = "$undefined$".

Situation 3. It is previously determined that the student possesses the skill SK_j (the student responded to the item associated with the skill SK_j). As a result, all the descendant skill are labeled as "possesses" and they don't need to undergo further analysis. In this case, the set $SK\_ANALYSIS$ is composed of domain skills, which have not been assessed so far, i.e. have label LB_SK = "$undefined$".

Step 2. Generate set of test items Q_SET for assessment of skills from $SK\_ANALYSIS$. Set Q_SET is formed on the base of association relationships between skills and test   items.

Step 3. Retain the test items in set Q_SET, which correspond to student's ability level ($LEVEL$). To make the test item neither too easy nor too difficult, it should correspond to the student's ability level. In this case, according to IRT the probability of correct response to the test item is 50%. A verb "correspond" is defined as the minimum difference between the difficulty of test item and student's ability level.

Step 4. Retain the task items in set Q_SET, which allow to assess as many as possible skills after response to them. For this we use the following measure of the test item Q_i:

$$LB\_COUNT\ (Q_i) = LB\_ANCESTOR\ (SK_j) + LB\_DESCENDANT\ (SK_j) + 1,$$

where SK_j – skill associated with test item Q_i;

$LB\_ANCESTOR (SK_j)$ - the number of ancestor skills that are rejected in the case of the incorrect response to the test item Q_i;

$LB\_DESCENDANT (SK_j)$ - the number of descendant skills that will be in the case of the correct response to the test item Q_i.

Step 5. If the set Q_SET contains several test items, then one should randomly select any of them. For the selected task item Q_i there should be determined the associated skill SK_j.

As a result, the output of the algorithm is next test item Q_i and associated skill SK_j.

Thus, the algorithm selects the next test item that assesses several skills concurrently. To do this, one should take into account relatedness of skills, the difficulty of test items and the current student's ability level.

Algorithm for Student Model Update. The input data for the update algorithm are: SK_j - current skill under analysis; Q_i - the represented test item (it is associated with the skill SK_j) with the difficulty $DIFFIC$; $GRADE$ - assessment of response to test item Q_i; $LEVEL$ - the current ability level.

The algorithm consists of the following steps.

Step 1. Update the student's ability level. New student's ability level is defined by the difficulty of the test item and correctness of response. If response to the test item is correct, then the student's ability level is higher than item difficulty, otherwise it is lower. Moreover, in case of the correct answer student's ability level should not decrease, and in case of the incorrect answer it should not increase. To update the ability level the following rules are used.

1. If a student answered correctly ($GRADE$ = "correct") and $DIFFIC + DELTA >= LEVEL$, then the new student's ability level increases and becomes $DIFFIC + DELTA$, where $DELTA$ – tuned parameter of the algorithm.
2. If a student did not answer correctly ($GRADE$ = "incorrect") and $DIFFIC - DELTA <= LEVEL$, then the new student's ability level decreases and becomes $DIFFIC - DELTA$.

Step 2. Update assessments of domain skills. Depending on the correctness of the response to the test item Q_i the skill SK_j and related skills are assessed. As a result the set of labels for skills (LB_SK_SET) are updated. In accordance with the previous assumptions formulated by defining the subject domain graph, the update of labels performs using the following rules.

1. If the response is correct ($GRADE$ = "correct"), then one should assume that the student possesses this skill, i.e. LB_SK_j = "possesses" . For all descendants SK_j, which are labelled as "undefined" set the label "possess".
2. If the answer is not correct ($GRADE$ = "incorrect"), then assume that the student does not possess this skill, i.e. LB_SK_j = "does not possess" . For all ancestors SK_j, which are labelled as "undefined" set the label "does not possess".

As a result, the output of the algorithm is the new student's ability level ($LEVEL$) and updated skill labels (LB_SK_SET).

Thus, the algorithm depending on the answer to the test item allows   to assess several related skills of domain knowledge and to compute the new ability level of the student.

5.2   Skill Gap Analysis Algorithm

This algorithm solves the problem of forming a minimal set of unrelated skills, which the student does not possess. The input data for the algorithm is the skill assessments, i.e. LB_SK_SET.

The algorithm consists of the following steps.

Step 1. On the basis of labels LB_SK_SET perform the set $GRAP\_SK$ of skills that are not possessed by the student.

Step 2. Remove from set $GRAP\_SK$ all skills that have child skills labeled as «does not possess». As a result all parent skills that are not possessed by the student should remove from set of $GRAP\_SK$.

The output of the algorithm is the set $GRAP\_SK$, that contains the minimum number of unrelated skills, which are not possessed by the student. Thus, we obtain the skills that the student has to master primarily.

6   Adaptive Test Example

The proposed models and algorithms were applied to testing knowledge and skills of students in the field of programming in C language. In particular, we analyzed the skills and knowledge to work with variables of basic data type.

The process of preparing and testing includes the following steps.

1. Preparation for the testing.
   (a) Development of hierarchy of domain skills and the test item repository.
   (b) The initialization of the student model before the testing.
2. Testing and skill gap analysis.
   (a) Administering the test and assessing the domain skills.
   (b) Formation of minimum set of skills that are not possessed by the student.

6.1   Development of Skill Hierarchy and Test Item Repository

In accordance with previously described test model the subject domain is defined by a graph which is shown in Fig. 4. The student's ability in this subject domain are assessed by two target skills SK_1 and SK_2. To analyze gaps in student skills in more detail, skills SK_1 and SK_2 are decomposed into simpler skills SK_3, SK_4, SK_5 and SK_6. Thus, the domain is characterized by hierarchy consisting of skills $SK\_SET = \{SK_1, SK_2, SK_3, SK_4, SK_5, SK_6\}$, where SK_1 – declaration of variables, SK_2 - construction of semantic variable names, SK_3 – selection of relevant data types for variables, SK_4 – interpretation/understanding of source code with declaring variables, SK_5 – knowledge of data types, SK_6 – knowledge of rules for constructing variable names.

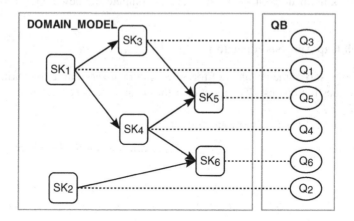

Fig. 4. Test model for subject domain «Use of basic data types in C programming language»

With each skill a test item is related, that assesses it. Therefore, repository of test items contains the task items $QB = \{Q_1, Q_2, Q_3, Q_4, Q_5, Q_6\}$. It should be noted that for a given domain, test item is not a single question but a set of them as shown in Table 1. This is due to the fact that it is impossible to make a single test item, the correct answer to which could be interpreted as possession skill. To confirm the skill it is necessary to responds to all the questions correctly from the set. To reject the skill it is enough to responds to one question incorrectly. Difficulty of the test item in this case is already assessed for the whole item set. Table 2 shows the difficulty of test items for a given subject domain.

Table 1. Subset of questions for item Q_6

№	Question formulation	Answer choices	Question type	Correct answer
1	Identify correct integer types	1) unsigned char 2) long int 3) long double 4) byte	multiple choice	1), 2)
2	Choose data types for variable that can store positive rational numbers	1) unsigned int 2) unsigned float 3) double 4) long double	multiple choice	3), 4)

Table 2. Item difficulties

Item	Q_1	Q_2	Q_3	Q_4	Q_5	Q_6
Difficulty	3	-1	0	0	-1	-3

6.2 Initializing the Student Model Before Testing

Before testing it is necessary to specify the presupposed ability level of the student. Let us define the average level of student knowledge, i.e. $LEVEL = 0$. His skills have not been assessed yet, so labels are defined as $LB\_SK\_SET = \{$"undefined", "undefined", "undefined", "undefined", "undefined", "undefined"$\}$. Gaps in the student's knowledge have not yet been discovered so far, so set $GRAP\_SK$ is empty.

6.3 Administering a Test and Assessing Skills Domain

For the given repository QB, student's ability level ($LEVEL$) and graph of domain skills $DOMAIN\_MODLE$, the proposed algorithm of adaptive testing at each iteration will generate test items in accordance with the Table 3.

Table 3. Trace of adaptive testing algorithm

	Iteration 1	Iteration 2	Iteration 3	Iteration 4
Step 1. Select item Q_i	Q_4 (DIFFIC = 0, LB_COUNT $(Q_4) = 4$)	Q_5 (DIFFIC = -1, LB_COUNT $(Q_5) = 3$)	Q_3 (DIFFIC = 0, LB_COUNT $(Q_3) = 1$)	Q_2 (DIFFIC = -1, LB_COUNT $(Q_2) = 2$)
Step 2. Represent and estimate item Q_i	GRADE = "incorrect"	GRADE = "correct"	GRADE = "incorrect"	GRADE = "correct"
Step 3. Update student model	LEVEL = -1, $LB\_SK_4=$ "does not possess", $LB\_SK_1 =$ "does not possess "	LEVEL = 0, $LB\_SK_5 =$ "possesses"	LEVEL = -1, $LB\_SK_3=$ "does not possess"	LEVEL = 0, $LB\_SK_2 =$ "possesses", $LB\_SK_6=$ "possesses"
Step 4. Compute test termination criterion	test continues	test continues	test continues	test is terminated

According to the submitted trace a sequence of test items was Q_4, Q_5, Q_3 and Q_2. At that all the skills were assessed, i.e. LB_SK_SET = {"does not possess", "possesses", "does not possess", "does not possess", "possesses", "possesses"}. Thus, the sequence of the submitted test items is less than the total number of test items in the repository. Reduction of the number of task items is achieved by the fact that in response to test item Q_4 two related skills SK_1 and SK_4 were assessed, and in response to test item Q_2 - SK_2 and SK_6 skills were assessed.

6.4 Formation of a Minimum Set of Skills That a Student Does Not Possess

According to obtained labels LB_SK_SET the student does not possess the skills SK_1, SK_3 and SK_4. This set is redundant, since it contains parent skills. In accordance with the proposed algorithm of skill gap analysis we exclude skill SK_1, because it is the parent of SK_3 and SK_4. We get a set $GRAP\_SK$ = $\{SK_3, SK_4\}$, which contains unrelated skills of the lowest level of the hierarchy.

Thus, the results of testing determine that the student should primarily learn to 1) choose the right data types for storing the given information and 2) understand of the source code with the declaring variables.

7 Conclusion

The paper presents the concept of adaptive testing, which makes it possible to reduce the number of the administered test items by taking into account the hierarchy of knowledge and skills of the subject area, the student's ability level and the difficulty of the test items. To implement the proposed concept the following tasks were put forward.

1. The test model was developed, which takes into account the hierarchy of skills and the difficulty of the subject area of the test items. Domain hierarchy is determined by acyclic graph of arbitrary form that provides ample opportunities to represent different subject areas.
2. The student model was developed, which represents the student's ability level and his skills' assessment. This model can be used to identify gaps in the student's skills. In particular, it provides a minimum set of skills that a student does not possess, and which he must master primarily.
3. The algorithm of adaptive testing was developed, which reduces the number of test items generated in the process of student testing. This property is ensured by the fact that the response to the test item allows estimating several related skills. In the presented algorithm the selection of such test items is administered on the basis of the student's ability level, test item difficulty and hierarchy of domain skills.

Later the developed models and algorithms are to be implemented as a module of adaptive testing in LMS Moodle [17]. We plan to use adaptive testing module to analyze gaps in knowledge and skills of the first and second year students of Volgograd State Technical University within the discipline of "Programming in C".

This paper presents the results of research carried out under the RFBR grant 13-07-00219 "Intelligent support of strategic planning based on the integration of cognitive and ontological models".

References

1. Thissen, D., Mislevy, R.J.: Testing Algorithms. In: Wainer, H. (ed.) Computerized Adaptive Testing: A Primer. Lawrence Erlbaum Associates, Mahwah (2000)
2. Ortigosa, A., Paredes, P., Rodriguez, P.: AH-questionnaire: An adaptive hierarchical questionnaire for learning styles. Computers & Education 54(4), 999–1005 (2010)
3. Van Der Maas, H.L.J., Wagenmakers, E.-J.: A Psychometric Analysis of Chess Expertise. The American Journal of Psychology 118, 29–60 (2005)
4. Klinkenberg, S., Straatemeier, M., Van der Maas, H.L.J.: Computer adaptive practice of Maths ability using a new item response model for on the fly ability and difficulty estimation. Computers & Education 57(2), 1813–1824 (2011)
5. Stark, S., Chernyshenko, O.S., Drasgow, F., White, L.A.: Adaptive Testing With Multidimensional Pairwise Preference Items Improving the Efficiency of Personality and Other Noncognitive Assessments. Organizational Research Methods 15(3), 463–487 (2012)
6. Papanastasiou, E.: Computer-adaptive testing in science education. In: Proc. of the 6th Int. Conf. on Computer Based Learning in Science, pp. 965–971 (2003)
7. Van der Linden, W.J., Glas, C.A.W.: Computerized Adaptive Testing: Theory and Practice. Kluwer Academic Publishers, Netherlands (2000)
8. Huang, S.X.: A Content-Balanced Adaptive Testing Algorithm for Computer-Based Training Systems. In: Lesgold, A.M., Frasson, C., Gauthier, G. (eds.) ITS 1996. LNCS, vol. 1086, pp. 306–314. Springer, Heidelberg (1996)
9. Van der Linden, W., Hambleton, R.: Handbook of Modern Item Response Theory. Springer, New York (1997)
10. Baker, F.: The Basics of Item Response Theory. ERIC Clearinghouse on Assessment and Evaluation, University of Maryland, College Park, MD (2001)
11. McCalla, G.I., Greer, J.E.: Granularity-Based Reasoning and Belief Revision in Student Models. In: Greer, J.E., McCalla, G. (eds.) Student Modeling: The Key to Individualized Knowledge-Based Instruction, vol. 125, pp. 39–62. Springer (1994)
12. Kumar, A.N.: Using Enhanced Concept Map for Student Modeling in Programming Tutors. In: FLAIRS Conference, pp. 527–532. AAAI Press (2006)
13. Anohina, A., Graudina, V., Grundspenkis, J.: Using Concept Maps in Adaptive Knowledge Assessment. In: Advances in Information Systems Development, pp. 469–479 (2007)
14. Guzmán, E., Conejo, R.: Simultaneous evaluation of multiple topics in SIETTE. In: Cerri, S.A., Gouardéres, G., Paraguaçu, F. (eds.) ITS 2002. LNCS, vol. 2363, pp. 739–748. Springer, Heidelberg (2002)
15. Guzmán, E., Conejo, R.: A Model for Student Knowledge Diagnosis Through Adaptive Testing. In: Lester, J.C., Vicari, R.M., Paraguaçu, F. (eds.) ITS 2004. LNCS, vol. 3220, pp. 12–21. Springer, Heidelberg (2004)
16. Dang, H.F., Kamaev, V.A., Shabalina, O.A.: Sreda razrabotki algoritmov adaptivnogo testirovanija. Informatizacija i Svjaz' 2, 107–110 (2013)
17. Moodle - Open-source learning platform, https://moodle.org/

Models of Supporting Continuing Education of Specialists for High-Tech Sector

Tatiana Glotova[1], Mikhail Deev[1], Igor Krevskiy[2], Sergey Matukin[2],
Elena Sheremeteva[1], Yuri Shlenov[2], and Maria Shlenova[2]

[1] CAD Dept. Penza State University, Russia
{penzado,tatyana}@pnzgu.ru
[2] Russian State University for Innovation Technologies and Business, Russia
{itbu58,garryk63}@gmail.com

Abstract. The concept of continuing education for professionals for high-tech sectors is topical, especially for software engineering education. Processes of continuing training professionals, creation and development of educational programs, support for e-learning resources are closely tied and require complex automation to provide quality and relevant education. We develop the models for life cycle of specialist, e-learning resources and educational programs. Prototype of CALS-system is developed on the basis of these models. For online synchronization of the developed models it is needed networking environment for creating community of universities and industry. Federal state education standards and professional standards in information technologies have different ontologies now and the networking environment will help to improve information interaction and understanding of high-tech sector labor market and universities. The networking environment includes not only the issues of education, assessment and counseling, but scientific activities (joint research and development) and commercialization of university research results.

Keywords: continuing education, high-tech sector, software engineering education, e-learning resources, networking environment.

1 Introduction

The concept of continuous education for professionals for high-tech sectors is topical, especially for software engineering education, because it is necessary to be adapted to the rapidly changing technologies and software. So, it is important to improve skills regularly as well as to receive relevant knowledge for working in the rapidly developing areas of industry. The quick obsolescence of information needs constant updates of teaching methods and tools, which is impossible without using the modern information technology. Within the literature the university model in Australia - university of the future - is presented in [1]. They have summarized the drivers of change into five key trends: democratization of knowledge and access: contestability of markets and funding; digital technologies; global mobility; integration with industry. Universities will need to build significantly deeper relationships with industry in the decade

A. Kravets et al. (Eds.): JCKBSE 2014, CCIS 466, pp. 100–112, 2014.

ahead — to differentiate teaching and learning programs, support the funding and application of research, and reinforce the role of universities as drivers of innovation and growth[1]. However, the issues of designing an information system have not been considered.

The issue of reuse Learning objects (Los) are considered in [2]. The authors describe workflow for LOs lifecycle that can support LOs reuse and enable to define a set of metrics for cost. However, connection between lifecycles of specialist, e-learning resources and educational programs hasn't been considered.

Processes of continuous training professionals, creation and development of educational programs, support for e-learning resources, that required for teaching are interlinked and require complex automation to provide quality and relevant education. We have analysed the life cycle of continuous training. We also developed the models of life cycle specialist, e-learning resources and educational programs. A prototype of CALS- system supporting e-learning resources and their source objects using a content management system is developed on the basis of these models.

For online synchronization of the developed models development of the networking environment for creating community of universities and enterprises is needed, which integrates possibilities of modern information and communication technologies. Federal state education standards and professional standards in information technologies have different ontology now and the networking environment will help to improve information interaction and understanding of high-tech sector labor market and universities. The networking environment includes not only the issues of education, assessment and counseling, but scientific activities (joint research and development) and university research results commercialization.

This article gives an analysis of the life cycle of continuing training of specialists for high-tech sector is made and the models of life cycle specialist, e-learning resources and educational programs as UML state machines are proposed. Developed models are considered in relation to each other in the process of continuing education using information technologies. Synchronization of the developed models needs for realization of continuing education.Then we propose decision of this problem using networking environment for creating community of universities and enterprises, which would integrate possibilities of modern information and communication technologies. Implementation issues - prototype of the system for life cycle support of electronic learning resources and prototype of the networking environment – are considerate for conclusion.

2   Models of Specialist and Educational Programs Life Cycles

The Federal Law N 273-FZ "On Education in the Russian Federation" refers to continuing education (lifelong education). The education system creates conditions for continuing education through the implementation of major educational programs and a variety of additional educational programs, enabling simultaneous development of several educational programs, as well as taking into consideration existing education, qualifications, experience of practice in education. All educational professional programs of universities in Russia must comply with the federal state educational standards. At formation of the federal state educational standards it is taken into account provisions the relevant professional standards [3].

New professional standard specifications in the field of information technologies are developed in Russia by Information & Computer Technologies Industry Association (APKIT) [4]. In 2013 APKIT developed the following professional standards: Programmer, Head of Software Development, Master of Information Systems, Head of Projects in the IT field, Tester in the IT field, Software Architect, Database Administrator, Manager of Information Technology, IT Product Manager, System Analyst, Content Manager [4].

Computer Science Curricula 2013[5] is said of commitment to life-long learning for graduates of a computer science program. They should realize that the computing field advances at a rapid pace. Specific languages and technology platforms change over time. Therefore, graduates need to realize, that they must continue to learn and adapt their skills throughout their careers. To develop this ability, students should be exposed to multiple programming languages, tools, and technologies as well as the fundamental underlying principles throughout their education. It is important to engage the broader computer science education community in a dialog to better understand new opportunities, local needs, and to identify successful models of computing curriculum – whether established or novel [5].

Engineering education and real-world demands on engineers have in recent years drifted apart. To solve this problem leading engineering schools in the world formed the CDIO Initiative [6]. CDIO is based on a commonly shared premise that engineering graduates should be able to: Conceive – Design — Implement — Operate complex value-added engineering systems in a modern team-based engineering environment to create systems and products. CDIO is developed with input from academics, industry, engineers, and students. The 12 CDIO Standards address program philosophy, curriculum development design-build experiences and workspaces, new methods of teaching and learning, faculty development, and assessment and evaluation CDIO is currently in use in university aerospace, applied physics, electrical engineering, and mechanical engineering departments [6].

IMS Global Learning Consortium [7] is concerned with establishing interoperability for learning systems and learning content and the enterprise integration of these capabilities. IMS GLC has approved and published some 20 standards that are the most widely used learning technology standards in the world. Widely-used IMS GLC standards include meta-data, content packaging, common cartridge, enterprise services, question & test, sequencing, competencies, access for all, ePortfolio, learner information, tools interoperability, resource list, sharable state persistence, vocabulary definition, and learning design. These standards have been used widely in higher education, K-12 education, and corporate education in regions around the globe [8].

Processes of continuing training of specialists, creation and development of educational programs, support for e-learning resources, required in training, are closely linked and require complex automation to provide quality and relevant education [9].

We consider the life cycle of specialist training in the high tech sector of the economy from the perspective of lifelong education. The model of specialist life cycle is shown as a state machine using UML state diagram [10]. Figure 1 shows that a specialist has two states during his life cycle: "Learning» and «Performance of job duties". From the initial state specialist goes into the "Learning", and to the execution of job duties may commence only after obtaining the required level of general education and professional competences. Indeed professionals can take in-service training of their core activities, but perform the duties that require certain competencies they can only after graduation.

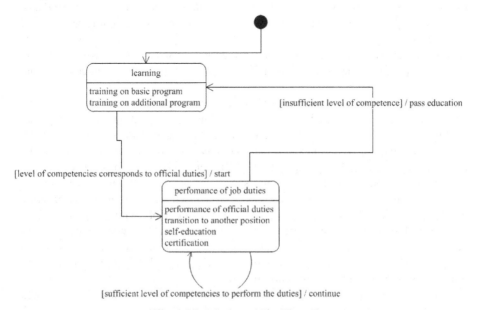

Fig. 1. Model of specialist life cycle

State " Learning " has the following actions: training in basic educational programs of higher education - Bachelor, Specialist, Master, and additional training in professional educational programs - training, retraining. In the field of software engineering basic training is usually given at a university, highly qualified professionals work in the specified field using the defined programming languages and the tools. It is regularly need improving skills and further training, such as mastering new software products or their new versions. Getting a new position or changing kind of activity often requires retraining. For example, APKIT professional standard [4] of head of projects in the IT field recommends for advanced training in project management. Software architect compared with the programmer should have the competence to use modern Computer-Aided Software Engineering tools - CASE-tools. A head of software development should have competence of Version control software in accordance with the rules and the selected version control system.

The state "Performance of job duties" has the following actions and transitions: performance of job duties, the transition to another position; certification for the position or category; self-education. Automaton transitions show the need for completing the course in the case of an insufficient level of competence required position or category and transition to execution of job duties after training. It should be noted that the specialist life cycle corresponds to iterative development model.

Training on basic and additional educational programs (EP) should be organized to provide cycle training of specialists having the competencies required to perform the job functions. Each educational program extends its life cycle, which also corresponds to the iterative development model (Figure 2). Educational program in accordance with the developed model can be in two states: "Creation or Evolution Program" -- in accordance with the iterative development model it is no difference between the creation of entirely new programs and programs created on the basis of already existing - and "Implementation of the EP" when directly educational process is being by EP.

Main actions of the program state "Creating - evolution EP» are an analysis of the needs and requirements of the program, program planning, program development (creation of educational resources, including e-learning resources, organization of information learning environment), and the creation of evaluation tools for the program. In the state of implementation of EP performed the choice of technology training, the organization of educational space and accommodation for participants, providing training, assessment of participants, feedback - evaluation of the program by their participants and employers. If EP ceases to comply with the requirements (educational standards have changed, there is obsolescence of knowledge, such as information technology or changed versions of the software, etc.), the program becomes uncompetitive and its modification is necessary. In this case there is a transition to state of creation (evolution) program. With high probability, this transition will require implementation actions "Creating (evolution) e-learning resources." It should be noted that there might be multiple versions of EP, for example, for users with different levels of initial training. This feature is taken into account in the information modeling when developing of the automated system.

Various learning technologies are used during the implementation of educational programs, including popular distance learning programs using modern information and communication technologies and the ELR. It should be noted that currently the ELR are used in traditional learning technology, so one of the state activity "Creation (evolution) of the educational program" is the development of e-learning resources [9, 11].

If a specialist it is required to possess a new professional competence to perform his job duties, it can get them passing training or retraining in the corresponding EP in case it has implemented (training is running). In order to the educational program is in the state it requires to prepare all necessary e-learning resources. If lifecycles of the professionals, the educational programs and the e-learning resources are not consistent, that it is almost impossible to ensure the quality and relevance of professional training.

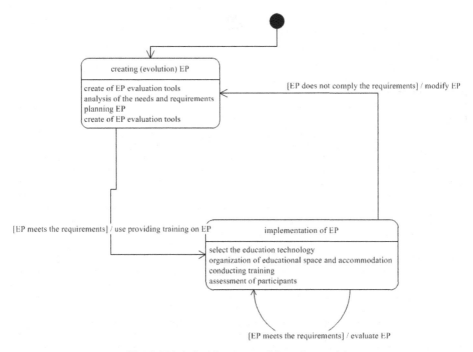

Fig. 2. Educational programs life cycles model

3   Models of E-Learning Resources Life Cycle

Nowdays to provide links between the educational system and the labor market it is necessary to organize a comprehensive system of training, retraining, advanced training, consulting support of specialists and to solve problem of mass development, updating of electronic educational resources, using modern information technology. Mass development and customization of electronic learning resources require continuous improvement by using models of the software life cycle.

Electronic educational resources (e-learning resources, ELR) – are an educational resource represented in digital form and included structure, subject content and metadata about them. ELR may include data, information, and software necessary for its use in the learning process [12]. The life cycle of electronic educational resources - the development of electronic educational resources, ranging from idea and ending with decommissioning [13].

Currently e-learning resources are used in distance learning technologies and classical learning technologies. Development of educational programs may need a large amount of e-learning resources in various fields, disciplines, subjects and difficulty levels. In this regard, much attention is paid to minimizing the cost of providing support throughout the lifecycle of the e-learning resources. In [14] the life-cycle model of e-learning resources is proposed as state machine (Figure 3).

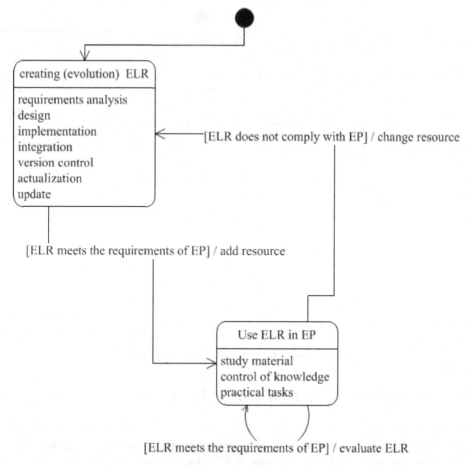

Fig. 3. E-learning resources life cycles models

Life cycle model of e-learning resources has two actions: creation (evolution) and the use of the e-learning resources in the educational program. The state "Creating (evolution) of e-learning resources" performs the following steps: requirements analysis, e-learning resources design, implementation, integration objects, version control, modification and updating e-learning resources. The state «Using ELR in EP" has the following actions: learning the material of e-learning resources, control of knowledge on ELR material, practical tasks on ELR and other material. If e-learning resources do not correspond to the educational program, which uses it, change of e-learning resources is required, i.e. transition occurs to the evolution of e-learning resources. Necessary to clarify those e-learning resources consists of objects that are also educational resources, such as pictures, diagrams, source code, which also passes through their life cycles. Hence it is necessary to have the action of integration and support of objects versions. One of the requirements to work with the ELR is the storage requirement of the initial (original) version of the educational object, which is used in the development of an information model of e-learning resources.

Creating e-learning resource passes six states: Analysis – Design – Implementation - Integration- Version control - Checking. State "Analysis" includes content analysis methodical analysis, in terms of technical implementation. State "Design e-learning resources" has actions: structure determination, design of objects, the definition of storage formats and selection of implementing tools for its objects. It should be noted that in the analysis and design states that are closely related to each other joint actions are needed as by educators (teachers, trainers), and by programmers who are responsible for the technical implementation of e-learning resources. The "Implementation" includes the following main actions: representation of objects in the specified format, saving objects. If a representation of the object in a specified format by specifies implementation tool is not possible, return occurs to the state of design. After the implementation of all objects for e-learning resource, transition occurs in the state of integration of objects. Version control of e-learning resources is performed in case of successful integration, for example, verification should be implemented between the version of the textbook and the version of the test cases. State "Checking" includes the following basic actions: checking the relevance e-learning resources (primarily educational standards compliance), check the relevance of incoming objects, publication e-learning resources. Upon successful checking e-learning resources is ready for use, otherwise just updating requires e-learning resources or separate objects within its structure (the transition to the analysis).

An important property of an educational object is the possibility of multiple uses. Thus, the dynamic fragment designed for e-learning resources on one discipline can often - directly or with small modifications - be used in e-learning resources on other disciplines. As an example, animated videos showing stack principles of ISO / OSI and TCP / IP. They will be useful in almost any e-learning resources on technologies of computer networks, Internet, building the corporate information systems, etc. for a wide range of areas, from computer to purely humanitarian, as well as in a lot of additional education programs.

4   The Networking Environment for Creating Community of Universities and Industry

For online synchronization of the developed models it is needed networking environment for creating community of universities and industry. Currently federal state education standards and professional standards in information technologies have different models of ontology [15] and the networking environment will help to improve information interaction and understanding of high-tech sector labor market and universities. The networking environment includes not only the issues of education, assessment and counseling, but scientific activities (joint research and development) and commercialization of university research results.

In [16] the networking environment provides common social networking features in communication, as well as specialized functions for the professional community. The network environment is intended for the following groups of users: teachers, employers, researchers, students, graduate, participants of joint projects, investors, experts, innovation managers, knowledge brokers [17]. UML case diagrams are developed for the analysis functions required for all user groups, the main user roles and opportunities available to them by the information environment are considered.

University teachers and supervisors can perform: automated preparation of educational programs and curricula to meet the requirements of standards of higher education and professional standards, construction and analysis of the matrix of competencies and covering their disciplines, analysis and coordination of interdisciplinary connections; analysis of satisfaction questionnaires of employers. Thus universities and educational institutions will be able to take into account local needs and requirements of companies quickly.

An employer can fill out the questionnaire to make assessment of professional competencies of its candidates - graduates of educational institutions - and can use all the features to view and analyze the questionnaire results and compare competences of state educational standards of and professional standards. The relationships between the competences of professional and state educational standards are not fully automatically determined due to mismatched ontological models. Interactive forms for automated identifying such linkages are developed which are filled with experts in these areas, who have experience in creating and coordination of curricula and educational programs with the federal state educational standards. Thus, industry will affect to the content of the educational programs offered by educational institutions more efficiently. The employer can also use functions such as communication, sending and receiving bids, placement vacancies, staff recruitment, view score of graduates, in house personnel reserve of innovative industries (Figure 4).

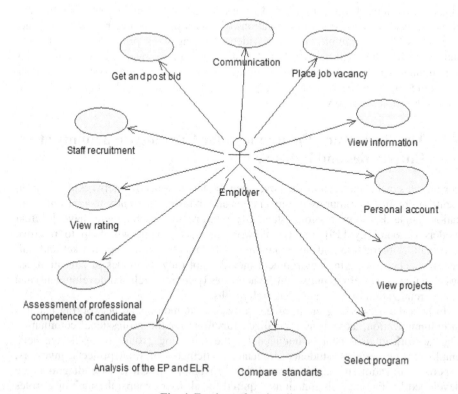

Fig. 4. Employer functionality

The network environment provides the set of functions for students and researchers, participants of joint projects and development. They are shown in the UML use cases diagram of participant, member of the professional community (Figure 5): accommodation resume and portfolio, placing the project on the portal, the formation of the project team, the introduction to the project team, working with a business plan and regulatory documents, event organization, participated in the event and the competition, posting multimedia information, job search. The learning function can be realized through the interaction with the network electronic University (NEU) using distance learning technologies and providing educational environment for continuing training. Member may apply for training on the selected program and undergo training or retraining in the network environment.

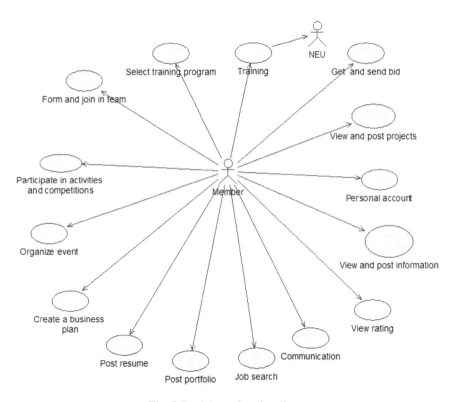

Fig. 5. Participant functionality

The sets of functions for expert and innovation manager are shown in Figure 6 and Figure 7.

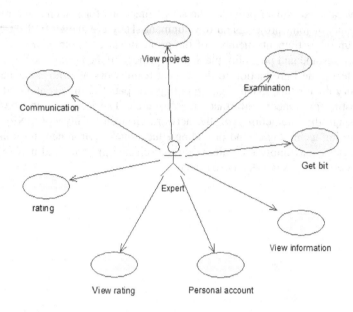

Fig. 6. Expert functionality

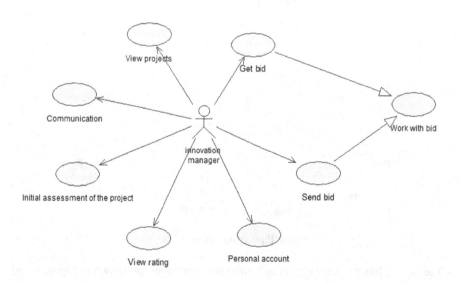

Fig. 7. Innovation manager functionality

Investors, experts, innovation managers, knowledge brokers have to take part in the developed networking environment to improve efficiency of joint research and to commercialize university research results.

5   Conclusion

We have done the analysis of the life cycle processes of continuing education for professionals for high-tech sector and have developed the models of specialist life cycle, e-learning resources and educational programs life cycles. A prototype of CALS- system supporting e-learning resources and their source objects has been developed on the basis of these models. The working prototype includes repository of finished electronic educational resources and their initial objects, versioning means and the formation of sets of electronic educational resources.

The networking environment information system for online interaction of universities and industry is developed for synchronization of the specialist life cycle, e-learning resources and educational programs life cycles models. The network environment is intended for the following groups of users: teachers, employers, researchers, students, graduate, participants of joint s projects, investors, experts, innovation managers, brokers of knowledge. The main user roles and opportunities available to them by the information system are considered. UML case diagrams for employer, participant of joint projects, expert, and innovation manager are shown in Figures 4-7. The proposed approach will help to improve the cooperation of educational institutions and employers and accelerate the development of updated educational programs and e-learning resources.

The prototype of information system for the implementation of the networking environment of universities and enterprises are realized using PHP, MySQL, Ajax, JavaScript, CSS and HTML. The results of the research will be used to support the learning process in continuing education of specialists for high-tech sectors.

The article was published in the framework of the project "Theoretical and methodological basis of modeling and forecasting of innovative development of the university and its effective participation in the development of high-tech sectors of the economy through the development of the virtual clusters interaction environment" (State task of Ministry of Education and Science of the Russian Federation № 2014/272).

References

1. Ernst & Young University of the future (2012)
2. Sampson, D.G., Zervas, P.: A Workflow for Learning Objects Lifecycle and Reuse: Towards Evaluating Cost Effective Reuse. Educational Technology & Society 14(4), 64–76 (2011)
3. The Federal Law N 273-FZ On Education in the Russian Federation
4. Professional standards in the IT,
   http://www.apkit.ru/committees/education/meetings/standarts.php
5. Computer Science Curricula (2013), http://www.acm.org/education/CS2013-final-report.pdf
6. Worldwide CDIO Initiative, http://www.cdio.org/faq
7. IMS, http://www.imsglobal.org/search.html

8. IMS Interoperability Standards,
   http://www.imsglobal.org/specifications.html
9. Krevskiy, I.G.: Innovative Models Provide Training Using Distance Learning Technologies. Innovation Management (3), 222–231 (2008)
10. Krevskiy, I.G., Glotova, T.V., Deev, M.V.: Models of Support The Life Cycle of Continuous Training of Specialists. Fundamental Research 10(5), 991–995 (2013)
11. Finogeev, A.G., Maslov, V.A., Finogeev, A.A.: Architecture of virtual learning environment with support for wireless access to information resources. Distance and Virtual Learning (6), 76–97 (2010)
12. GOST 52653-Information and communication technologies in education. Terms and Definitions Gost 52653 (2006)
13. GOST P 52656- Information and communication technologies in education. Educational Internet Portals Federal Level. General requirements (2006)
14. Krevskiy, I.G., Glotova, T.V., Deev, M.V.: Design The System For Support The Life Cycle of Electronic Educational Resources. Modern Problems of Science and Education (5) (2013), http://www.science-education.ru/111-10148
15. Glotova, T.V., Sheremeteva, E.G., Koshkina, J.G., Meljakova, E.S.: Design Information and Analytical Support System of Educational Process of School and University in Informatics and Information and Communication Technology. In: XXI Scientific and Technical Conference, Telematika, pp. 115-116 (2013),
   http://tm.ifmo.ru/tm2013/db/doc/get_thes.php?id=74
16. Krevskiy, I.G., Glotova, T.V., Matyukin, S.V., Sheremeteva, E.G.: Prototype of Environment for The Implementation of the Networking of Universities, Enterprises and Innovators. Modern problems of science and education 6 (2013),
   http://www.science-education.ru/113-10672
17. Shlenov, J.V., Kostrykin, D.S.: The Role of Knowledge Brokers in The Innovation Organizations. Innovations (10), 112–117 (2009)

Students' Satisfaction from Their Educational Context through DREEM and LOT-R

Michalis Skordoulis[1], Miltiadis Chalikias[2], and Michalis Koniordos[3]

[1] Laboratory of Management Information Systems
and New Technologies, Department of Business Administration,
School of Business and Economics, Technological Education Institute of Piraeus,
250 Thivon & Petrou Ralli Av., 12244 Egaleo, Greece
mskordoulis@gmail.com
[2] Laboratory of Applied Economic Statistics
and Operations Research Department of Business Administration,
School of Business and Economics, Technological Education Institute of Piraeus,
250 Thivon & Petrou Ralli Av., 12244 Egaleo, Greece
mchalikias@hotmail.com
[3] Department of Business Administration, School of Business and Economics,
Technological Education Institute of Piraeus, 250 Thivon & Petrou Ralli Av.,
12244 Egaleo, Greece
laertis@teipir.gr

Abstract. Quality is a matter of vital importance in today's higher education. Along with it, students' satisfaction from their educational context is equally important. Students' satisfaction from their educational context is a very important element of the total quality in higher education. This paper concerns the satisfaction of the Technological Education Institute (T.E.I.) of Piraeus Business Administration Department students. Data from 100 students' answers to DREEM and LOT-R questionnaires have been statistically analyzed. Factor analysis has been operated as well as a regression analysis to certain of the factors resulted from the previous factor analysis. The results were interesting since the understanding of the factors concerning the students' satisfaction became feasible.

Keywords: Students' satisfaction, DREEM, LOT-R, factor analysis.

1 Introduction

The matter of quality in education becomes more and more important nowadays. Quality has become matter of vital importance in today's higher education. Students' satisfaction from their educational context is a very important element of the total quality in higher education.

Quality in education is a constant effort to approach the excellent results; it is what makes learning a pleasant process and has to do with the use of methods for effective learning, the continuous effort for improving the educational process by encouraging people for teamwork and, with the participation of all those involved in the operation of an educational organization (Zavlanos, 2003).

A. Kravets et al. (Eds.): JCKBSE 2014, CCIS 466, pp. 113–122, 2014.

2   Theoretical Framework

2.1   The Quality in Education

Lots of scientists have tried to define quality. Crosby (1979) defines quality as "the identification with the customer's requirements" while Juran (1988) defines it as "the product or service harmonization with the purpose or intended use".

In order to improve the courses quality, teachers should pay attention not only to their research activities but also to the way of their teaching. Furthermore teachers should give great importance to obtain information about the degree of their students' satisfaction. The introduction of teamwork, the various ways to motivate the students, the continuous improvement of processes, the improving of the curriculum, the improving of the pedagogical training of teachers as well as the use of information technology in teaching are some ways for high-quality education (Zavlanos, 2003).

In the Greek higher education, quality is ensured by the provisions of 4009/2011 and 4076/2012 laws. These laws provide that each University and Technological Education Institute is responsible for the quality assurance and the continuous improvement of the teaching and research quality. For this purpose in each Higher Education Institution is established a Quality Assurance Unit.

According to the law 3374/2005 the Authority for Quality and Certification in Higher Education is established. The purpose of this Authority is to support institutions of higher education to perform procedures aimed at ensuring and improving quality, informing the state and foundations for modern international developments related issues and promote research in this area.

2.2   Students' Satisfaction

At a first glance, students' satisfaction is easy to be defined. Nevertheless, there are hundreds of scientific articles that attempt to define it, to quantify it and to measure the impact of it (Letcher & Neves, 2010). According to Oliver & DeSarbo (1989), students' satisfaction has to do with their subjective judgment on various results and experiences from their educational context. Oliver (1980) argued that given that satisfaction is based on experience, students' satisfaction is influenced by the constantly changing experiences into an educational context.

Many studies have been conducted with the aim of discovering the factors associated with student satisfaction in an educational institution.

According to Hearn (1985), the two main factors that affect students' satisfaction is whether a course is interesting or not, as well as the way of teaching.

Another factor that is correlated with students' satisfaction is the environment in which they study (Miles et al, 2012).

Participation in the activities of the institution, the curriculum as well as the usefulness of the courses for the professional life of students, are, according to Bean and Bradley (1986), factors related to the overall students' satisfaction.

Other studies demonstrated that the academic profile of satisfied students was more positive than that of the less satisfied ones (Morstain, 1977). There is still a large number of factors affecting students' satisfaction of an educational institute, such as the interaction of teachers with students (Umbach & Porter, 2002), the advisory staff and the pattern of courses (Hameed & Amjad, 2011) as well as the students' career opportunities (Letcher & Neves, 2010).

Most of the satisfaction types could characterized as multicriterial and colud be measured by methods such as MUSA (Drosos et al., 2011). As shown, factors associated with students' satisfaction are multicriterial and are different for each person and educational institute (Lee et al., 2000).

3   Research Framework

The assessment of the quality into an education institute is of great importance. Through measuring the satisfaction of students it becomes possible to assess the quality of the education institute to a significant degree, to reveal both the strengths and weaknesses in its operation and finally, to take the appropriate measures to improve its quality through eliminating the weaknesses and reinforcing the strengths of it. A total of 100 students of the T.E.I. of Piraeus Business Administration Department participated in the research.

For this study, three questionnaires were used in combination. In the first questionnaire, students were asked to answer general questions as the semester in which they enrolled, their age and whether they consider themselves as good students or not. The second questionnaire is the students' satisfaction measure DREEM (adapted to the science of administration) and the third one is the individuals' attitude and optimism/pessimism measure LOT-R. The collected data were statistically analyzed.

The DREEM (Dundee Ready Education Environment Measure) method was developed by the University of Dundee and was designed primarily for undergraduate health professions schools. Overall, it consists of 50 questions (Dimoliatis et al, 2010). Through the analysis of DREEM results becomes possible to identify the strengths and weaknesses of the evaluated educational framework (Agamolaei & Fazel, 2010). Thus, the results of DREEM can be a very useful tool for those running the courses and are in charge of the curricula in order to maintain a high quality education (Tontus, 2010). The LOT-R (Life Orientation Test - Revised) method is a quick way to measure optimism predisposition (Burke et al, 2000).

Initially, a chi-square test was conducted for the responses given to DREEM and LOT-R in order to find if there is a correlation between them and the responses given to the first general questionnaire. A Kruskal-Wallis test that checks the equality of the means of two or more populations was performed. Furthermore, a Mann-Whitney test that shows whether any of the independent variables tend to get a higher price than another was applied. Moreover a factor analysis for the DREEM and LOT-R responses was conducted. Finally, a regression analysis between the DREEM and the LOT-R factors derived from the factor analysis was conducted.

4   Data Processing – Results Analysis

4.1   Demographics of the Sample

The students asked to answer the questionnaires aged between 19 and 23 years old. A 72% of them were women and a 28% were men. The educational semester in which they were registered was between the 5th and the 9th (studies normally last eight semesters and can be extended for four). A 44% of the students wished to study in this department. Finally, a 33% of them considered themselves as good students.

4.2   Chi-square Test of Independence

As mentioned above, a chi-square test of independence was conducted for the DREEM and LOT-R responses in order to find if there is a correlation between them and the demographics resulted from the responses in the general questionnaire. The results of this test are presented in tables 1 and 2.

Table 1. Correlations between the responses in DREEM and the students' demographics

Question	Correlation with
1. I am encouraged to participate during teaching sessions	Age, semester, desire to work in business
2. The course organisers are knowledgeable	Age, semester, desire to work in business
3. There is a good support system for registrars who get stressed	-
4. I am too tired to enjoy the course	Age, semester
5. Learning strategies which worked for me before continue to work for me now	Age, semester
6. The course organisers espouse a patient centred approach to consulting	Self-evaluation
7. The teaching is often stimulating	Age
8. The course organisers ridicule the registrars	Semester
9. The course organisers are authoritarian	Age, semester
10. I am confident about my passing this year	Age, desire to work in business, self-evaluation
11. The atmosphere is relaxed during consultation teaching	Age, semester
12. This course is well timetabled	Age, semester, self-evaluation
13. The teaching is registrar centred	Age, semester
14. I am rarely bored on this course	Age, self-evaluation
15. I have good friends on this course	Students' sex, age, semester, self-evaluation
16. The teaching helps to develop my competence	Age, semester, desire to work in business
17. Cheating is a problem on this course	Age
18. The course organisers have good communication skills with students	Desire to work in business

Table 1. (*continued*)

19. My social life is good	Self-evaluation
20. The teaching is well focused	Age, semester, desire to work in business
21. I feel I am being well prepared for my profession	Age, semester, desire to work in business, self-evaluation
22. The teaching helps to develop my confidence	Age, semester, desire to work in business, self-evaluation
23. The atmosphere is relaxed during lectures	Age, semester
24. The teaching time is put to good use	Age, semester
25. The teaching over emphasizes factual learning	Age, semester
26. Last year's work has been a good preparation for this year's work	Age, semester, desire to work in business
27. I am able to memorise all I need	Age, semester
28. I seldom feel lonely	Self-evaluation
29. The course organisers are good at providing feedback to registrars	Age, semester, desire to work in business
30. There are opportunities for me to develop interpersonal skills	Age, desire to study in the department
31. I have learnt a lot about empathy in my profession	Desire to work in business
32. The course organisers provide constructive criticism here	Age, semester, desire to work in business
33. I feel comfortable in teaching sessions socially	Self-evaluation
34. The atmosphere is relaxed during seminars/tutorials	Age, semester, origin, self-evaluation
35. I find the experience disappointing	Age, desire to study in the department, desire to work in business, self-evaluation
36. I am able to concentrate well	Age, semester
37. The course organisers give clear examples	Age, semester, origin, desire to study in the department, desire to work in business
38. I am clear about the learning objectives of the course	Age, semester
39. The course organisers get angry in teaching sessions	Semester
40. The course organisers are well prepared for their teaching sessions	Age, semester
41. My problem solving skills are being well developed here	Age, semester

Table 1. (*continued*)

42. The enjoyment outweighs the stress of the course	Age, semester, desire to work in business, self-evaluation
43. The atmosphere motivates me as a learner	Age, semester
44. The teaching encourages me to be an active learner	Age, semester
45. Much of what I have to learn seems relevant to a career in business	Age, semester, origin
46. My accommodation is pleasant	Self-evaluation
47. Long term learning is emphasized over short term learning	Age, semester
48. The teaching is too teacher centred	Age, semester
49. I feel able to ask the questions I want	Age, semester, desire to work in business, self-evaluation
50. The registrars irritate the course organisers	Age, semester

Table 2. Correlations between the responses in LOT-R and the students' demographics

Question	Correlation with
1. In uncertain times, I usually expect the best	-
2. It's easy for me to relax	Self-evaluation
3. If something can go wrong for me, it will	Desire to study in the department
4. I'm always optimistic about my future	Age, semester,
5. I enjoy my friends a lot	Semester, Self-evaluation
6. It's important for me to keep busy	Self-evaluation
7. I hardly ever expect things to go my way	-
8. I don't get upset too easily	Age, semester
9. I rarely count on good things happening to me	Desire to work in business
10. Overall, I expect more good things to happen to me than bad	-

4.3   Kruskal-Wallis Test

This test checks the equality of means of two or more populations or otherwise, if the samples examined derive from one or more populations. The test for the medians of the responses in questionnaires and students' semester showed that almost all of the answers to DREEM have different a median with the semester, while this happens only for the 8th LOT-R question.

4.4   Mann-Whitney Test

The test's results analysis showed that the students' sex and the answers to DREEM and LOT-R are distributed identically, except for a single case concerning the 8th question in LOT-R.

Moreover the test has shown that generally there is an equal distribution between the answers to DREEM and LOT-R and the students' desire to study in the department.

Finally, the test has shown a 48% equal distribution for the answers to DREEM and students' desire to work in business, while, concerning the LOT-R answers and students' desire to work in business, this distribution is equal in all cases except for the 9th question.

4.5   Factor Analysis

Factor analysis is the process of finding common factors in a group of variables. In this factor analysis Varimax rotation was used, a rotation that minimizes the number of variables that have large weight and makes them more interpretable factors. Factor analysis goal is to have large correlations among the variables. Thus the correlation coefficients and the partial correlation coefficients are calculated. Then the relative magnitude of the correlation coefficients should be compared with the partial correlation coefficients. The measure that gives the value of this comparison is the Kaiser-Meyer-Olkin test. The accepted values for Kaiser-Meyer-Olkin test are higher than 0.75. Indeed, both the values for DREEM and LOT-R are acceptable. Another way to assess the appropriateness of the factor analysis model is Bartlett test of sphericity. The test results reject the existence of chi-square statistical significance, which means that the variables are correlated to each other and the current factor analysis model is appropriate.

Table 3. Kaiser-Meyer-Olkin and Bartlett Tests results for DREEM

	DREEM	LOT-R
Kaiser-Meyer-Olkin Measure of Sampling Adequacy.	0.860	0.645
Bartlett's Test of Sphericity	0.000	0.000

The number of factors in whose DREEM and LOT-R questions will be categorized will be decided after the Scree Plots analysis according to Kaisers' rule.

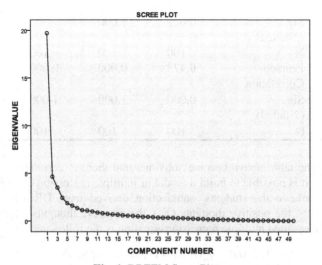

Fig. 1. DREEM Scree Plot

Depending on the fig.1 analysis, DREEM questions will be categorized into five factors. These factors are the process of learning, the environment of the institute, the social life within it, the students' opinion about their teachers, and finally, the students' opinion about their fellow students.

According to the same process LOT-R questions will be categorized into three factors. These factors are the students' positive thoughts, their negative thoughts, and the use of their time.

4.6   Regression Analysis

Regression analysis checks the correlation between two or more variables in order to predict the price of one by the price of the other variable. In the current multiple regression model, the dependent variable is the student satisfaction resulting from DREEM as independent variables LOT-R factors.

Table 4. Pearson's correlation coefficient values

		Students' satisfaction	Positive thoughts	Negative thoughts	Use of time
Students' satisfaction	Pearson Correlation	1	-0.341	0.228	0.473
	Sig. (2-tailed)		0.001	0.022	0.000
	N	100	100	100	100
Positive thoughts	Pearson Correlation	-0.341	1	0.000	0.000
	Sig. (2-tailed)	0.001		1.000	1.000
	N	100	100	100	100
Negative thoughts	Pearson Correlation	0.228	0,000	1	0.000
	Sig. (2-tailed)	0.022	1,000		1.000
	N	100	100	100	100
Use of time	Pearson Correlation	0.473	0.000	0.000	1
	Sig. (2-tailed)	0.000	1.000	1.000	
	N	100	100	100	100

Analyzing the table above becomes obvious that there is correlation between the variables; thus it is possible to build a model of multiple regression considering as the independent variable the students' satisfaction derived from DREEM (Y) and as the independents, the positive thoughts (X_1), the negative thoughts (X_2) and the use time (X_3). The resulted multiple regression equation is the following:

$$Y = 182,460 + 9,316X_1 - 11,905X_2 - 7,826X_3 \qquad (1)$$

The normal distribution diagram shows the proper adaption of the current multiple regression model.

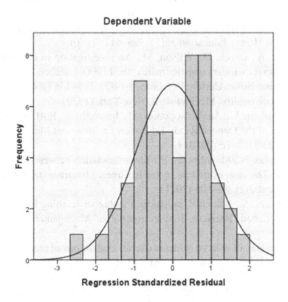

Fig. 2. Normal distribution diagram

Anova's p-value which equals to 0 also certifies the proper adaption of the current multiple regression model. Finally the models' proper adaption is confirmed by the R squared and Durbin-Watson coefficients.

5   Conclusion – Results Interpretation

Factor analysis made it possible to understand the satisfaction of students from their educational context. More specifically, the factors of satisfaction derived from DREEM and LOT-R questionnaires are the process of learning, the environment of the institute, the social life within it, the students' opinion about their teachers, the students' opinion about their fellow students, the students' positive thoughts, their negative thoughts and, the use of their time. Analyzing the importance of each of these factors in the students' satisfaction would be very interesting.

Through the chi-square test of independence analysis became feasible to understand how students' responses were affected by various personal details of them. Regression analysis provided the opportunity to understand the correlation between some of the factors that resulted from the factor analysis of DREEM and LOT-R questionnaires.

Finally, the used method and the performed analyzes in the current study could form a basis for the development of a general method for measuring the satisfaction in educational institutions concerning all the fields of studies.

References

1. Agamolaei, T., Fazel, I.: Medical students' perceptions of the educational environment at an Iranian Medical Sciences University. BMC Medical Education 10(87), 1–7 (2010)
2. Bean, J., Bradley, R.: Untangling the satisfaction - performance relationship for college students. Journal of Higher Education 36(1), 393–412 (1986)
3. Burke, K., Joyner, A., Czech, D., Wilson, M.: An investigation of concurrent validity between two optimism/pessimism questionnaires: the Life Orientation Test - Revised and the Optimism/Pessimism Scale. Current Psychology 19(2), 129–136 (2000)
4. Crosby, P.: Let's talk quality. McGraw-Hill, New York (1979)
5. Dimoliatis, I., Vasilaki, E., Anastassopouols, P., Ioanndis, J., Roff, S.: Validation of the Greek Translation of the Dundee Ready Education Environment Measure (DREEM). Education for Health 23(1), 1–16 (2010)
6. Drosos, D., Tsotsolas, N., Manolintzas, P.: The relationship between customer satisfaction and market share: The case of mobile sector in Greece. International Journal of Engineering and Management 3(2), 87–105 (2011)
7. Hameed, A., Amjaad, S.: Students' satisfaction in higher learning institutes: a case study of Comsats Abbottabad, Pakistan. Iranian Journal of Management Studies 4(1), 63–77 (2011)
8. Hearn, J.: Determinants of college students overall evaluations of their academic programs. Research in Higher Education Journal 23(4), 413–437 (1985)
9. Juran, J.: Juran on planning for quality. The Free Press, U.S.A (1988)
10. Lee, G., Jolly, N., Kench, P., Gelonesy, B.: Factors related to student satisfaction with university. University of Sidney Faculty of Health Sciences, Sidney (2000)
11. Letcher, W., Neves, J.: Determinants of undergraduate business student satisfaction. Research in Higher Education Journal 6(1), 1–26 (2010)
12. Miles, S., Swift, L., Leinster, J.: The Dundee Ready Education Environment Measure (DREEM): A review of its adoption and use. Medical Teacher 34(1), 620–634 (2012)
13. Morstain, R.: Analysis of students' satisfaction with their academic program. Journal of Higher Education 48(1), 1–16 (1977)
14. Oliver, R.: A cognitive model of the antecedents and consequences of satisfaction decisions. Journal of Marketing Research 17(1), 460–469 (1980)
15. Oliver, R., DeSarbo, S.: Processing satisfaction response in consumption: A suggested framework and response proposition. Journal of Consumer Satisfaction, Dissatisfaction, and Complaining Behavior 5(1), 1–16 (1989)
16. Tontus, O.: DREEM; dreams of the educational environment as its effect on education result of 11 Medical Faculties of Turkey. Journal of Experimental and Clinical Medicine Deneysel ve Klinik Tıp Dergisi 27(1), 104–108 (2010)
17. Umbach, P., Porter, S.: How do academic departments impact student satisfaction; understanding the contextual effects of departments. Research in Higher Education Journal 43(2), 209–234 (2002)
18. Zavlanos, M.: Total quality in education. Stamoulis Publications, Athens (2003) (in Greek)

Methods and Tools for Software Development to Improve the Effectiveness of Engineering Education in the Direction of "Mechatronics" Using Grid-Computing Technologies

Alexander Bolshakov, Victor Glaskov, Igor Egorov, Vladimir Lobanov, Larisa Perova, and Svetlana Pchelintseva

Saratov State Technical University, Saratov, Russia

1 Introduction

One important indicator of high quality educational services is the use of electronic information in universities and educational environments (ILE) to support the learning process, which is the competitive advantage of the educational institutions of engineering education. The creation of such systems is caused by the high level of development of modern information and communication technologies and associated with the new requirements of state educational standards that meet international. Educational information environment improve accessibility, visibility and quality of teaching and methodological materials in the classroom and independent work of students, moreover, are getting educational services remotely.

Peculiarity application of educational and methodical material related to the choice of technology and platform for the implementation of a learning environment contains a number of standard services on the location of educational and methodical materials, the organization of interaction of students and teachers, knowledge control, etc. The specificity of training (bachelors, masters and PhD students) a variety of scientific directions different areas of expertise , including directions of scientific and technical skills acquisition involves solving complex problems and / or large-scale problems , computationally intensive , it requires appropriate facilities, equipment and technology.

Increasing the efficiency of computer systems associated with the technologies that suggest a conversion to alternative models of computation. These include technology distributed computing [1], based on cluster systems massive-parallel organization functioning on the basis of public servers and microprocessors , as well as the organization and implementation of parallel computing in remote access via the Internet . In particular, one of these technologies is the grid- system [2 , 3], representing a geographically distributed infrastructure that integrates many different types of resources (processors, and long-term memory , storage, and network database), access to a user can be obtained from any point, regardless of their location. Grid- technologies require collective, shared mode access to resources and related services within the globally distributed virtual organizations composed of companies and individuals, sharing common resources [4, 5].

A. Kravets et al. (Eds.): JCKBSE 2014, CCIS 466, pp. 123–133, 2014.

Development of grid-technologies in educational institutions opens up opportunities for learning (education) and for basic research. In Russia, there are examples of grid in universities. In Tambov State Technical University chair of "Distributing Computing Systems", based on the substruction of laboratory grid-technologies similar laboratory operates at the Moscow Physical-Technical Institute at the Faculty of Information Technology.

2   Characteristics Source Environment

One of the virtual project -based organizations OurGrid, created in 2004 in the Brazilian university Universidade Federal de Campina Grande, became SGTU n.a. Y.A. Gagarin, as a regional center for research and distance education. Here the project , implemented with technical and financial support HP created grid- node allows to solve complex and / or large-scale problems that require a large amount of computation , as well as a new approach to distance education as well as to implement practical and coursework work in disciplines that require large computing power [6].

2.1   Creating a Learning Environment Using Distributed Grid-Computing

Created and implemented system of distance education based on technological complex, using grid- computing, is a cross -platform system where the unifying role of the educational environment performs MS SharePoint Learning Kit 1.2, for complex and / or high-speed computing software is used OurGrid. For remote access to learning resources, learning management, and monitoring of progress of students used a software tool Class Server.

Grid- node constituting the core technology is a software-hardware complex Server 4640 HP Integrity Itanium 2 × 4 , 8Gb, operating system Linux Red Hat AS 4.0 and software OurGrid 3.2.

The pilot project includes courses on software engineering and design of industrial robots for students majoring in "Information Systems and Technology", "Information systems in the media industry", "Software computing systems", "Robotic systems and complexes" and direction "Mechatronics and Robotics" [7].

2.2   Structure Computing of Grid-Node

As a grid-system   selected free scientific infrastructure OurGrid, which is designed to solve problems of the class BoT (Bag of Tasks), ie tasks which can be executed in parallel independently from each other. OurGrid system consists of three parts:

• grid- machines that perform tasks solution parts , - Grid User Machine (GUM). They installed the software (software) interface- GUM (UserAgent). To ensure the security of the means of closing layer of operating system resources built up layer SWAN, including virtual machine Xen, run levels , check the integrity of the configuration;
• machine Peer - resource managers who register lists of available machines GUM and give them on-demand calculations leading accounting statistics on mutual use of

resources with other machines Peer. They also serve to communicate with the whole network grid. Installed software - Peer;

• user workstations from which triggered problems for distributed computing . Installed software - MyGrid. Broker MyGrid plan provides for starting jobs to perform monitoring tasks running , restart other GUM problem if previous failed.

System components OurGrid, so are three components: software MyGrid, Peer and User Agents. Peer Software and MyGrid performed only under Linux, but the interface User Agent can be installed on the platforms Windows and Linux.

3. Application of Grid-Technologies for Solving Problems of Mechatronics and Robotics

Most tasks mechatronics and robotics range of disciplines including mechanics and drives robots, information, electronic and computing devices robots, artificial intelligence techniques, the management of complex mechatronic systems, modeling and study of robotic systems have high computational complexity and often require high performance computing resources.

Feature of many algorithms for solving robotic tasks is the ability to parallelize the computational process, in particular, genetic algorithms, representing a means of finding the global minimum of a function of several variables used, for example, for training neural networks, methods of pattern recognition, artificial intelligence methods, etc. In addition, parallel calculating accelerate receiving solutions and in a case when a task does not involve parallelization, for example, while the simulation and selection of the optimum parameters and study the behavior of systems for varying the parameters and initial data. The use of distributed computing, thus substantially increases the speed of the result.

As part of a project to create an educational environment solved the task of a multi-link manipulator path planning, one of which is a sub solution for the inverse kinematics of the manipulator additional nodal points, which requires large computational resources and time.

3   The Peculiarity a Solution of the Inverse Problem Kinematics of the Situation

Decision robotic tasks such as technical operations, involves the use of manipulation systems, representing the totality of movable articulated units, providing a predetermined position and orientation in space of the gripper arm. Each joint of the manipulator is a kinematic pair, i.e., a compound of two adjoining units that allow their relative motion. In this part of the degrees of freedom is fixed by defining a class pair. Most often grips used kinematic pairs fifth grade in accordance with the number of communication conditions imposed on the relative motion (Fig. 1).

Position rigid body in space relative to a coordinate system is characterized by six independent parameters - degrees of freedom, three of which are the Cartesian coordinates that define the position and the other three - rotation angles that define the orientation of a rigid body in space. Therefore, to ensure the specified position and orientation of the gripper with respect to the base coordinate system, if and only six units linked kinematic pairs fifth grade (Fig. 1).

This condition can uniquely determine the displacement and / or angles in the joints depending on the position and orientation of the gripping device. Increase in the number of joints of the manipulator robot increases manipulative properties, which is very important, for example, avoiding obstacles. However, the manipulator becomes kinematically redundant (Fig. 2), which greatly complicates the management process. Therefore, existing manipulators have, more often, six joints. As a general rule, apply rotational joints that allow you to manage and position and orientation of the gripper.

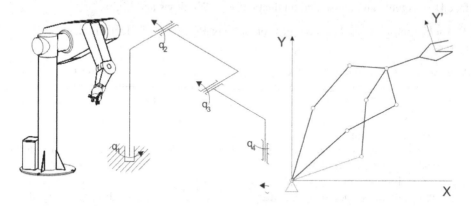

Fig. 1. Robot manipulator with six degrees of rotational mobility

Fig. 2. Example kinematically redundant manipulator

One of the main problems for kinematically redundant manipulators is to determine the value of angles joints in which are called generalized coordinates, depending on the desired position and orientation of the capture device, namely the solution of the inverse kinematics problem. Solution of the inverse kinematics problem is complicated by the ambiguity of a multilink manipulator its configuration, providing the desired position of the gripping device. From a mathematical point of view inverse kinematic problem, like many other inverse problems, is flawed, because it allows for multiple or no solutions. Analytical solution the inverse kinematic problem exists only for some constructions of non-redundant manipulators that allow dividing mobility degree of the so -called transport and orienting. For manipulators with kinematic redundancy analytical solution does not exist. Therefore for the determination, it is necessary to apply numerical methods which give an approximate solution. In this case the error solutions should not exceed the permissible limits and must be observed design constraints.

In the mathematical formulation of the numerical solution of inverse kinematic problem manipulator reduces to finding the global minimum of a scalar objective function of the generalized coordinates with inequality constraints. Since the result of the decision depends on the random initial approximation, then warrant that the obtained values of the generalized coordinates will meet the criteria of accuracy and given constraints in the general case impossible. Repeated search the solutions inverse kinematic problem for best results significantly accelerated by parallelizing the solution process between multiple computers, thus increasing the probability of finding the desired solution.

Algorithm the search solutions inverse kinematic problem using grid-system comprises the following steps:

Identification of ranges of acceptable change of generalized coordinates and a set of initial approximations, using a random number generator with uniform distribution on each of the computers in the system. The multiple solution the inverse kinematic problem with given initial approximations and selecting the best solution from the set obtained on individual computers. Number of values in a set determined the acceptable time solution of the problem on the same computer.

Set of solutions must be of sufficient volume to increase the probability of obtaining a result that meets the specified accuracy. The number of computers (GUM), on which will start out a numerical solution the inverse kinematic problem, which required obtaining the exact solution of inverse kinematic problem, can be defined by the user. If the number of free computers smaller than a predetermined process solutions the inverse kinematic problem runs on existing machines a number of times. From the resulting set of solutions that meet the criteria of accuracy, is chosen an option that requires the least change of generalized coordinates, relative to the values corresponding to the previous configuration of the manipulator, i.e., providing a more economical movement when moving from one hotspot to another.

3.1   Features and Functions of Learning Environment

The distant learning system based on the principle consistent structural organization that uses phased presentation of educational material with the relevant verification tasks, taking into account the requirements for remote automated learning systems. Training material is available in HTML- format and contains theoretical material on the methods of software development trajectories and solution of the direct and inverse kinematics of the manipulator and practical tasks, the implementation of which is based on a specially developed Java- applet located on HTML- pages.

The system has a set of kinematics of manipulators, which are characterized by design parameters and constraints. Practice includes the following elements: kinematics; interactive three-dimensional model of the manipulator with the objects in the work area; numerical characteristics of the job: the size of the manipulator links; kinematic constraints in kinematic pairs by mobility; number of degrees of freedom manipulator, for which the student has to calculate the coefficients of the approximating polynomials; Cartesian coordinates of the starting and ending points of the trajectory; the passage of the trajectory of the manipulator; velocity and acceleration at the start and end points of the trajectory; restrictions (objects in the work area of the manipulator) to movements in the vicinity of the starting and ending points of the objects in the work area of the manipulator); degree approximating polynomial (polynomials).

When forming the programmed trajectory are calculated and entered in the form of the coefficients of the approximating polynomials and formed the spatial trajectory of the gripping device manipulator. This provides the opportunity to see the configuration of the manipulator at each point of the developed trajectory. Stipulation is considered satisfied in full, if the following conditions: correct-formed matrix of homogeneous transformations; correctly selected point of care and approach; generalized coordinates of the motion generated by the trajectory of change within the kinematic constraints for degrees of freedom; no passage through the manipulator forbidden region of space, i.e., the manipulator does not hurt the surrounding objects (Figs. 2 and 3).

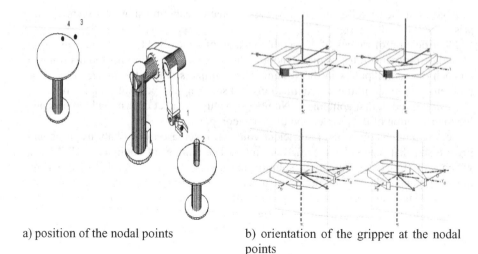

a) position of the nodal points

b) orientation of the gripper at the nodal points

Fig. 3. Position and orientation of the gripper at the nodal points

The system allows the user to visually view the interactive three-dimensional model of the manipulator. In solving the direct kinematics problem for a given generalized coordinates the distant learning system displays the corresponding configuration of the manipulator and the coordinate system formed by the system and the resulting user that when the correct solution should coincide. For more information about the result of the decision provides a visualization of the manipulator workspace for solving inverse kinematics and trajectory planning.

After entering of the coefficients the polynomial approximant for a given degree of mobility the system completes the polynomials by means the remaining degrees of in mobility and builds dependencies family (user and system-generated) generalized coordinates, velocities and accelerations of time.

3.2   The Structure of the Learning System

The system consists of a set of software components that combine various platforms and technologies.

To implement the functions of authorizing users, keeping statistics on the results of their work assignments , receiving reports on the performance is used a software tool Class Server, providing a platform for learning management and monitoring of student performance. Class Server system allows you to organize an educational portal with the possibility of publishing educational materials (theoretical information, tasks) reference database users (students and teachers), the general organization of electronic library, etc.

In the diagram shows the structure of the format of educational material - LRM (Learning Resource Material), supported by Class Server. This material includes a set of web pages (directory) containing the Web- content and file in XML (Index.xml) metadata descriptions. Format LRM, in particular, allows you to format nesting in task for students for send the tasks, to use questions with multiple variants answer and

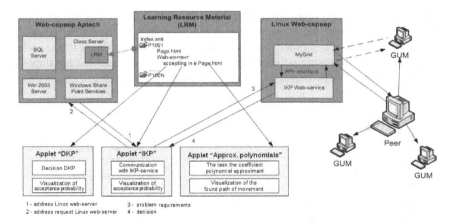

Fig. 4. The organizational and functional diagram of the system

questions, which require your input in the fields, as well as other methods of formatting tests to assess teacher tasks both manually and automatically using Class Server.

Modules for direct kinematics problem and input the coefficients of the approximating polynomials are solved on the client side and the results visualized using the library Java3D. Decision the inverse kinematic problem generally ambiguous and requires busting several options in choosing the optimal solutions according to some criterion. To expedite the process of obtaining the result carried parallelization process solutions using grid-system (OurGrid).

To link the applet with module for solving the inverse kinematics problem is used web- service EDSWebServise accommodating inverse kinematics problem to solve in the grid- system and returns the results to the applet. This web- service accepts the terms of the problem of inverse kinematics applet splits them into independent parts and sends machines to perform GUM, which receives from the machine Peer. To perform these independent parts for machine GUM sent executable. Results of work in the form of files returned to the inverse kinematics servlet selected the best option and sent the inverse kinematics applet, in which the imaging solutions. After the assignment results are recorded in the database on the basis of Class Server service access CSDataService through the API.

4 Stages of Solving the Problem of Trajectory Planning in the Learning System

The training course includes the study of theoretical material and the solution of practical problems for the planning program trajectories robot manipulator.

Planning trajectories manipulator is associated forming control laws drives each joint of the robot motion to transfer an object from the start point to the end point. To do this, the student should be able to solve the direct and inverse kinematics of the position. Solution of the direct and inverse kinematics determines the position and orientation of the working body of the manipulator arm and the configuration given by the displacements and rotation angles in the joints. To solve the problem of planning the position and orientation selected in two additional points intended path of movement and defines the configuration of the manipulator at specified points by solving inverse kinematic problem is determined laws of angles (bias) in the joints, counting ratios approximating polynomials subject to the restrictions that are imposed on the motion path.

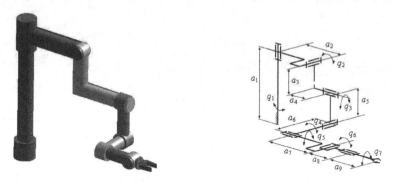

Fig. 5. Kinematic scheme and 3D-model of the manipulator

For a given kinematic scheme and 3D-model of the robot manipulator (Fig. 5) is required to form a programmed trajectory using a planning method generalized coordinates.

4.1 Solution of the Direct Kinematics Problem

Solution of the direct kinematics problem is to determine the position and orientation of the gripper arm for given generalized coordinates (angles of rotation of the joints), and as a result, in the finding the path of movement of the object under given joint trajectory. The initial data is the kinematics scheme, design parameters and values of the generalized coordinates that define the configuration of the manipulator.

Sequence of elementary transformations on the values of the displacements and / or turns on a generalized coordinate or design parameter value generates the resulting transformation matrix that determines the position and orientation of the working body of the manipulator. Comparison of the resulting matrix with the matrix formed by the system allows evaluating the result of the decision.

4.2 Solution of the Inverse Kinematics Problem

In the next step, using visual information about the workspace of the manipulator, restrictions, location of start and end point of the trajectory, you must enter the position and orientation of the gripper arm for additional nodal points. Subsidiary points, namely the exit point and approach point are given in the vicinity of the start and end points of the trajectory.

For these points is performed to solve the inverse kinematics problem, i.e., determined values of the generalized coordinates corresponding to the position and orientation of the working body at the exit point and approach point. The inverse problem of kinematics for kinematically redundant manipulator (7 units) can be solved with the assistance of the system grid-node. This step may require multiple solutions inverse kinematic problem and re-enter the nodal points.

4.3   Determination of the Coefficients of the Approximating Polynomials

To determine the changes law the correct generalized point is necessary to calculate the coefficients of the approximating polynomials. The initial data are the values of the generalized coordinates at the branching point, including the results of the solutions in the previous step inverse kinematic problem initial and final velocity and acceleration, traveling time on the path sections, kind of approximation.

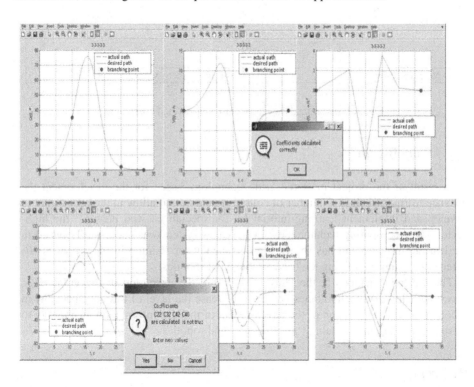

Fig. 6. Joint trajectory, velocity, acceleration for a given degree of mobility on the screen form

The appropriate applet after entering coefficients builds joint trajectory for all degrees of mobility and space trajectory of movement of the manipulator. Next, are determined the coefficients of the approximating polynomials for one degree of mobility which is given appropriate variant. The system compares the values entered coefficients and plotted in position, velocity and acceleration for a given generalized coordinates, and also forms the spatial path of the gripper manipulator (Fig. 6 - 8).

Graphs provide any other information on the continuity of the joint trajectory, velocity, acceleration and a formed space trajectory.

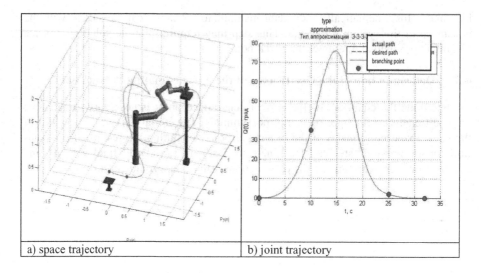

| a) space trajectory | b) joint trajectory |

Fig. 7. Programmed trajectory with well-defined coefficient

5   Conclusion

As a result of the project mastered grid- technology based for the development the distance learning shell in a number of course of study, that allow in the near future to develop and implement learning-tutorial kit for specialists, who possess the high-performance computing technologies. The created system was successfully tested in the learning process and has shown high efficiency for training in the use of distributed computing for solving the basic problems of robotics.

The created methods at the University during the execution of the grant HP's, which is using grid-technologies helped to increase the level of training specialist in robotic school and direction of the development of modern information technology to solve problems in the domain of mechatronics and robotics.

References

1. Toporkov, V.V.: Models of distributed computing. In: Toporkov, V.M. (ed.) FIZMATLIT 2004, pp. 285–320 (2004)
2. Kovalenko, V.N., Korjagin, D.A.: Grid Resource Organization, http://www.gridclub.ru/library/publication.2004-11-29.9287628406/view
3. Yagoubi, B., Slimani, Y.: Task Load Balancing Strategy for Grid Computing. Journal of Computer Science 3(3), 186–194 (2007)
4. Chinchilla, M., Arnaltes, S., Burgos, J.C.: Control of permanent magnet generators applied to variable-speed wind-energy systems connected to the grid. IEEE Transactions on Energy Conversion 21(1), 130–135 (2006)

5. Churbanov, A.G., Pavlov, A.N., Vabishchevich, P.N.: Operator-splitting methods for the incompressible Navier-Stokes equations on non-staggered grids. Part 1: First-order schemes. Int. J. Numer. Methods Fluids 21, 617–640 (1995)
6. Bolshakov, A., Dolinina, O., Lavrov, A.: Improvement of Quality of Preparation of Engineers in Robotics by using of Grid Technologies. In: Proc. ICEE 2007, Dep.de Engenharia Quimica, p. 184 (September 2007)
7. Dolinina, O., Kintsel, D.: New Approach to Distance Learning with Using of Grid-computing. In: Proc. ICEE 2007, Dep.de Engenharia Quimica, p. 255 (September 2007)

The Calculation Procedure of Competence Completeness

Irina Sibikina[1], Irina Kvyatkovskaya[2], Irina Kosmacheva[1], and Yuliya Lezhnina[2]

[1] Astrakhan State Technical University, Department of Information Security, Russia
isibikina@bk.ru, ikosmacheva@mail.ru
[2] Astrakhan State Technical University, Department of Information Technology, Russia
I.Kvyatkovskaya@astu.org, lejninau@mail.ru

Abstract. The paper presents the procedure, allowing to make an assessment of the student's competence completeness during the training. To solve this goal it is offered to create an integrated criterion on the basis of additive transformation. The choice of the method to create an integral criterion on the basis of the carried-out analysis of existing methods, with reference to this problem, is reasonable. Calculating procedure is developed and formulas for calculation of various characteristics of competence accumulation in process of time and accordingly competence losses in comparison with the maximum possible level of its formation are presented. To see it clearly, there are diagrams of competence formation level are provided in the article in process of time and in conformity with studying new disciplines. Here is considered the possibility of this procedure application for the various mark-rating systems, used in institutions of high education.

Keywords: competence assessment, competence model, integral criterion, disciplines significance.

1 Introduction

Today, training of specialists is carried out by the new standards, main requirement of these standards is formation of a necessary set of competences by specialists. Many researchers confirm efficiency of the competence-based approach in the system of higher professional education (HPE) [1-3, etc.]. The competence-based approach in HPE system today is one of the most actual ways of creating a new educational strategy. Many countries reorganise the higher professional education system according to "Bologna" type [4]. The researchers, dealing with this problem appeal to competences and competency as to leading criteria of the modern higher school graduate readiness to unstable work conditions and social sphere of life. If traditional "qualification" of the specialist meant functional compliance between requirements of a workplace and the education purposes, and preparation was led to assimilation by the pupil of more or less standard set of knowledge and skills, than "competence" assumes the person to develop the ability to orientate in a variety of difficult and unpredictable work situations. To have idea of the activity consequences, and also to be responsible for them [1]. The new competence methodology of development of federal state educational standards (FSES) of the higher professional education (HPE)

A. Kravets et al. (Eds.): JCKBSE 2014, CCIS 466, pp. 134–143, 2014.
© Springer International Publishing Switzerland 2014

was developed within the confines of Bologna Process. After introduction in the Russian education system of the new FSES based on formation by students of the necessary list of competences, and also after the appearence of such documents as «The strategy of the higher professional education modernisation» and «The conception the higher professional education modernisation» [5,6] there appeared a number of questions, connected with an assessment of these competences.

For the first time England began to develop the question of competences and competency in 50-60 years of the XX century as the answer to the concrete order of the professional sphere. Various scientists gave definitions of ideas of competence and competency and today there are a lot of such concepts. However, the general for all definitions is its understanding as properties of the personality, potential ability of the individual to cope with various tasks, as set of knowledge and skills, necessary for realization of the concrete professional activity. So, the concept "competence" should be perceived in a complex, as the structure composed from various parts. There is a natural question arising: is it possible to teach competences? Foreign researchers are not categorical, answering it. So, L. Spencer and S. Spencer [7] consider the question of competences formation in type of iceberg model, where knowledge and skills, compile its visible part, but personal features and motives are hidden «under a sea level» as they are very difficult to develop them in the course of studying. S. Parry [8] distinguishes "soft" and "tough" competences. «Tough» competences belong to professional and specific features (knowledge and abilities), whereas "soft" – to personal features, values and styles. Though he also recognises that "soft" competences influence activity performance, he does not include them in competence definition, because, in his opinion, they can be hardly developed in the course of studying. According to the new requirements of Russia FSES HPE each higher educational institution should have adequate means for an assessment of the competences being formed by students in the course of studying. Therefore the purpose of this article is development of the calculation procedure of the formation level of the student's competence.

2   Materials and Methods

2.1   The Analysis of the Existing Methods of Creating an Integral Criterion

The student competence at studying period in higher education institution is gained by means of the disciplines, having been already studied [9]. Disciplines have various importance degrees for the competence, received by means of the entropy approach [9-11] and expressed by numeral value. Besides the extent of discipline studying by a student is characterized by the integral mark gathered by the student on this discipline. The characteristic of the discipline studying extent may be:

1. the rating gathered by the student on this discipline;
2. the results of the Internet exam, revealing assimilation of the discipline didactic units;
3. the examination results on the discipline;
4. the average integrated mark on the discipline;

The problem of the competence formation level definition is a problem of decision-making, with the fixed number of the criteria expressed by means of objective functions. Therefore decision-making process can be reduced to the vector optimization objective.There are some methods of the solution of the of multi-criteria optimization problems:

- the method of the main criterion allocation;
- the lexicographic optimization method;
- the methods of the clotting of the vector criterion into the scalar one.

In the allocation method of the main criterion the person making decision appoints one main criterion, the others are deduced in a raw of restrictions, i.e. there are borders specified within which these criteria can be. The lack of the method is obvious: there is no sense to carry out deep system research if all criteria, except one, are not considered. It is obvious that in the solution of the competence assessment problem this method is unacceptable. In the lexicographic optimization method, it is supposed that the criteria making vector criterion B, can be ordered on the basis of the absolute preference relation. This method is unacceptable for the solution of the competence assessment problem. This results from the fact that process of criteria ordering which make vector criterion, is not possible owing to the task specifics (competence depends on a lot of disciplines and it's impossible to neglect any of them and furthermore to choose one and to make competence assessment by one of them in force of competence definition).

2.2   The Methods of the Clotting of the Vector Criterion into the Scalar One

The main problem of this approach is creating of the function f, called convolution. This problem breaks up to four objectives:

1. The justification of convolution admissibility.
2. The criteria normalization for their comparison.
3. Accounting of the criteria priorities (importance).
4. Creating the convolution function, allowing to solve an optimization problem.

2.3   Substantiation of the Convolution Admissibility

Substantiation of the convolution admissibility demands confirmation that considered efficiency indicators are homogeneous. It is known that the efficiency indicators are divided into three groups:

- the productivity indicators;
- the resource-intensiveness indicators;
- the efficiency indicators;

Generally, is allowed to convolve the indicators entering into the generalized indicator for each group separately. The indicators convolution from different groups can lead to the loss of physical sense of such criterion. In the problem of competence assessment, efficiency indicators are the marks collected by the student in disciplines, forming competence. These marks are homogeneous, and belong to the productivity indicators; therefore the application of the convolution is admissible.

2.4   Accounting of the Criteria Priorities

Accounting of the criteria priorities is carried out in the majority of clotting methods by a setting up a vector of the criteria importance indexes. Definition of the criteria importance indexes, as well as in the case with indicators, causes serious difficulties and is reduced to use of formal procedures, or to application of the expert estimates. In result of the criteria priorities normalization and accounting, of the new vector assessment is formed. This received vector assessment is subject to transformation with use of the convolution function.

Earlier the structure of competence formation in the form of the graph has been constructed. The calculation procedure of extent of the each discipline influence on competence formation has been received by means of the entropy approach [9]. The calculation of this characteristic has been based on data of the disciplines influence degree on the competence formation, received from experts. The *choice of the convolution method* depends on the indicators character and system estimation goals. There some types of convolution are known. Most often additive and multiplicative convolution of the vector criterion components are used.

2.5   Additive Convolution of the Vector Criterion Components

Additive convolution of the vector criterion components is a representation of the generalized scalar criterion in the form of the sum of the balanced normalized particular criteria. Multiplicative convolution of the vector criterion components is representation of the generalised scalar criterion in the form of creation. The choice between convolutions is defined by degree of importance of absolute or relative changes of values of particular criteria respectively.

2.6   Competence Assessment by Means of the Integral Criterion Construction on the Basis of the Additive Transformation

It is appropriate to use the additive convolution in the competence assessment objective. It is justified by the fact, that the distinctive property of the additive convolution is that the maximum competence assessment with its help is received by those graduates who have more criteria values of which are close to maximum (under identical averages received by all graduates).

Let $B = (b_{D_1}, b_{D_2}, ... b_{D_n})$ - vector criterion – marks at all disciplines forming competence, b_{D_i} - scalar criterion – a mark gathered by the student in discipline D_i, μ_{D_i} - discipline importance degree. For the competence assessment, the additive convolution of the generalised criterion is taken, then the mathematical model of an assessment of the competence formation level will be written so:

$$\begin{cases} B_K = \sum_{i=1}^{n} \mu_{D_i} \cdot b_{D_i} \\ \sum_{i=1}^{n} \mu_{D_i} = 1 \\ \mu_{D_i} \in [0,1] \\ b_{D_i} \in [0,1] \end{cases} \qquad (1)$$

where B_K - K competence assessment, μ_{D_i} - degree of the D_i discipline importance , b_{D_i} - mark in the discipline D_i according to the mark-rating system (MRS) working in higher education institution; b –maximum mark, n- quantity of the disciplines forming competence. The procedure of the competence formation level calculation gives final result after studying of all disciplines, forming competence. However in the course of competence formation, it is very important to monitor and forecast a possible competence assessment at any stage of studying with the following correction of the studying process. Therefore, the procedure of calculating the characteristics of competence level in the process of its formation is offered.

2.7   The Procedure of Calculating the Competence Level Current Characteristics

This procedure consists of the following stages:

- contribution calculation of each discipline to competence;
- calculation of the greatest possible assessment for competence at present time(in marks, according to MRS);
- calculation of the current assessment for competence at present time (in marks MRS agrees);
- calculation of the greatest possible contribution to competence at present time (as a percentage);
- calculation of competence losses at present time (as a percentage).

Discipline contribution D_i in competence

$$B_{K_{D_i}} = \mu_{D_i} \cdot b_{D_i} \qquad (2)$$

where b_{D_i} mark on discipline, μ_{D_i} -weight factor of discipline influence on competence. Respectively maximum and minimum possible contribution of discipline to competence is calculated by formulas:

$$B_{K_{\max D_i}} = \mu_{D_i} \cdot b_{\max D_i} \qquad (3)$$

$$B_{K_{\min D_i}} = \mu_{D_i} \cdot b_{\min D_i} \qquad (4)$$

where $b_{\max D_i}$ - greatest possible mark and $b_{\min D_i}$ - minimum possible mark, for estimation of trainees knowledge on a scale of MRS accepted in HIGHER EDUCATION INSTITUTION. Then maximum and minimum possible assessment of competence time is calculated at present time by formulas:

$$B_{K_{\max}} = \sum_{i=1}^{K} B_{K_{\max D_i}} \tag{5}$$

$$B_{K_{\min}} = \sum_{i=1}^{K} B_{K_{\min D_i}} \tag{6}$$

This assessment will be calculated in marks of that MRS in which teachers put down marks on the disciplines forming this competence. Current assessment of competence is calculated by formula (7) and also measured in marks of MRS accepted in higher education institution for an assessment of disciplines:

$$B_{K_{curr}} = \sum_{i=1}^{K} B_{K_{D_i}} . \tag{7}$$

where K–is quantity of the disciplines forming competence, studied at present time.

In various MRS there are respectively different scales for an assessment of disciplines assimilation level therefore it is expedient to lead the received values to a range [0; 1] and to receive a percentage ratio of competence formation level. The current contribution of all disciplines studied at present time for competence formation is found by means of expression:

$$I_{K_{curr}} = \frac{B_{K_{curr}}}{b_{\max}} \tag{8}$$

Value $I_{K_{max}} \in [0,1]$. The greatest possible contribution to competence of the disciplines studied at present time is calculated by formula:

$$I_{K_{\max}} = \sum_{i=1}^{K} \mu_{D_i} \tag{9}$$

Minimum possible contribution to competence of the disciplines studied at present time is calculated by formula:

$$I_{K_{\min}} = \frac{B_{K_{\min}}}{b_{\max}} \tag{10}$$

Competence losses at present time concerning its maximum level are calculated by means of expression:

$$\delta_{K_{curr}} = I_{K_{\max}} - I_{K_{curr}} \tag{11}$$

And the greatest possible number of losses meaning the minimum contribution to competence formation can be calculated by formula:

$$\delta_{K_{max}} = \frac{b_{max} - b_{curr}}{b_{max}} \tag{12}$$

where b_{max}, b_{min} – respectively minimum and maximum mark, higher education institution MRS.

Let's show on example characteristics calculation of level formations competences according to example, presented in fig. 1. The smallest mark according to the mark and rating system used in higher education institution – 3, the greatest – 5.

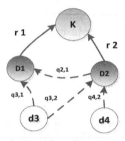

Fig. 1. Competence model

Order of disciplines studying, according to graph model is as follows: d_4 and $d_3 \rightarrow D_2 \rightarrow D_1$. Weight coefficients influences of these disciplines, marks on disciplines and a contribution of each discipline to competences are provided in the table 1.

Table 1. Characteristics of the disciplines forming competence

Disciplines	Weight factors	Mark on discipline	Contribution of each discipline to competence
D_i	μ_{D_i}	b_{D_i}	$B_{K_{D_i}} = \mu_{D_i} \cdot b_{D_i}$
d4	0,09	3	0,27
d3	0,29	4	1,16
D2	0,25	4	1
D1	0,37	5	1,85

On the diagram (fig. 2) it is possible to see, that the greatest contribution to competence formation at available marks is brought by discipline D1, the smallest contribution - by discipline d4.

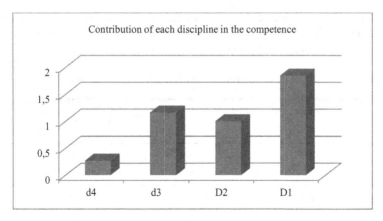

Fig. 2. Contribution of disciplines to competence

Let's calculate the greatest possible, minimum possible and current assessment of competence accumulation (table 2).

Table 2. Current characteristics of competence accumulation

The studied disciplines	The current characteristics of competence accumulation (in marks)		
	$B_{K_{max}} = \sum_{i=1}^{K} B_{K_{maxD_i}}$	$B_{K_{min}} = \sum_{i=1}^{K} B_{K_{minD_i}}$	$B_{K_{curr}} = \sum_{i=1}^{K} B_{K_{D_i}}$
d4	0,45	0,27	0,27
d4 and d3	1,9	1,14	1,43
d4, d3, D2	3,15	1,89	2,43
d4, d3, D2D1	5	3	4,28

On the diagram (Fig. 3) competence accumulation is shown after studying of each discipline, forming competence in comparison with minimum and maximum possible accumulation.

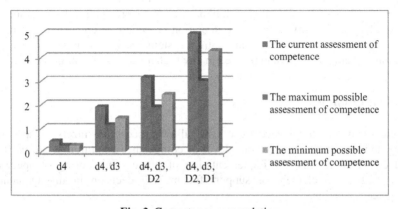

Fig. 3. Competence accumulation

In various MRS, different scales exist respectively for an assessment of disciplines assimilation level therefore it is expedient to lead the received values to a range [0; 1] and to receive a percentage ratio of competence formation level (table 3).

Table 3. Characteristics of competence accumulation after studying of disciplines

	$I_{K_{max}} = \sum_{i=1}^{K} \mu_{D_i} \cdot 100\%$	$I_{K_{min}} = \dfrac{B_{K_{min}}}{B_{K_{max\,c}}} \cdot 100\%$	$I_{K_{curr}} = \dfrac{B_{K_{curr}}}{B_{K_{max}}} \cdot 100\%$
d4	9 %	5,4 %	5,4 %
d4 and d3	38 %	22,8 %	28,6 %
d4, d3, D2	63 %	37,8 %	48,6 %
d4, d3, D2, D1	100 %	60 %	85,6 %

Respectively competence losses after studying of each discipline in comparison with the greatest possible level are given in table 4.

Table 4. Competence losses

The studied disciplines	$\delta_{K_{curr}} = I_{K_{max}} - I_{K_{curr}}$
d4	3,6 %
d4 and d3	9,4 %
d4, d3, D2	14,4 %
d4, d3, D2, D1	14,4 %

3   Discussion

Thus, for calculation of competence formation level of the offered procedure, it is necessary to have competence model (i.e. the list of all disciplines, which form it), influence weight of each discipline on competence formation and the marks gathered by the student in each of disciplines. By means of the offered formulas it is possible to calculate the current level of competence formation and the greatest possible level on this period of time. Besides this technique allows to predict level of competence formation having the current results. Calculation procedure of competence formation level is versatile for any mark and rating system used in a higher educational institution and consequently can be used in any higher education institution.

4   Conclusion

The assessment of competence losses will allow process organizers of specialists training and also the faculty to trace level of competence condition at present time. This factor is necessary for implementation of process monitoring of specialists training and is an element of support for making decision in management of competence formation.

References

1. Hartley, R., Kinshuk, K.R., Okamoto, T., Spector, J.M.: The Education and Train-ing of Learning Technologists: A Competences Approach. Educational Technology Society 13(2), 206–216 (2010)
2. Lystras, M.D.: Competencies Management: Integrating semantic web and technology enhanced learning approaches for effective knowledge management. Journal of Knowledge Management 12(6), 1–5 (2008)
3. Azjmuhamedov, I.M., Sibikina, I.V.: Determining the significance of competence of a specialist on information security. Journal of Computer and Information Technologies 7, 54-5 (2011)
4. About the Bologna Process,
   http://www.ond.vlaanderen.be/hogeronderwijs/bologna/about/
5. The strategy of modernisation of the content of General education,
   http://www.gouo.ru/pinskiy/books/strateg.pdf/
6. The concept of modernisation of russian education for the period up to 2010,
   http://archive.kremlin.ru/text/docs/2002/04/57884.shtml/
7. Spencer, L.M., Spencer, S.M.: Competence at work: models for superior performance, p. 118. John Wiley, New York (1993)
8. Parry, S.B.: The quest for competencies: competency studies can help you make HR decision, but the results are only as good as the study. Training 33, 48–56 (1996)
9. Kvyatkovskaya, I.Y., Sibikin, A.I.V., Berezhnov, G.V.: Procedure of the System Characteristics Competence Graph Model Calculation. World Applied Sciences Journal (Information Technologies in Modern Industry,& Education Society) 24, 111–116 (2013)
10. Borda, M.: Fundamentals in Information Theory and Coding, p. 487. Springer, Heidelberg (2011)
11. Volkenshtein, M.V.: Entropy and information, p. 325. Nauka, Moskow (2006)

Mastering Programming Skills
with the Use of Adaptive Learning Games

Ofut Ogar[1], Olga Shabalina[1], Alexander Davtyan[2], and Alexey Kizim[1]

[1] Volgograd State Technical University, Volgograd, Russian Federation
ofuriti4u@yahoo.com, o.a.shabalina@gmail.com, kizim@mail.ru
[2] Moscow Institute of Physics and Technology, Moscow, Russian Federation
agvs@mail.ru

Abstract. Adaptive learning game studies experienced rapid growth due to its learning benefits and popularity among younger generations. Computer programming is considered a challenging subject by learners and teachers, as a result of poor motivation towards its studies. It is important to know how adaptive educational games can help to enhance our student's motivation and learning perceptions towards Programming skills. This paper discusses the concept of using educational games as learning medium by applying the following techniques: motivation, intervention, collaboration etc with an agent based approach to reinforce and improve the students' abilities in the concepts of programming. We present a platform whereby instructional content and methods are customized to individual students to guide/facilitate learning and mastering of programming concepts.

Keywords: Adaptive learning games, programming activity, motivation.

1 Introduction

Computer programming is the underlying framework of software development and has fundamentally changed the way many individuals and organizations work. This course is being taught in tertiary institutions where they form a core area of study for undergraduate and postgraduate programmes related to computer science, software engineering and other IT related disciplines.

Student's achievement and competitiveness are determined by the level of programming skills acquired during their studies. However, teaching and learning programming subject is never an easy task as mentioned by many studies [1, 2, 3]. This is due to complexity of the subjects that require understanding of abstract concepts, logical thinking as well as problem solving as well as high level of abstraction [4]. Students found programming to be a boring subject, lecturers explanations are difficult to understand, teaching method that is not interesting, and not enough exercises or practices during class lesson [5].

On this paper we focus specifically on highlighting the benefits of using adaptive learning games to address the challenges in learning programming. Previous studies have found that using educational games as a learning approach can enhance student's

A. Kravets et al. (Eds.): JCKBSE 2014, CCIS 466, pp. 144–155, 2014.

learning of various learning domain: namely cognitive, affective as well as psycho-motor skills [6].Some examples of the application of digital games in different know-ledge domains within computer sciences such as software engineering and data structures can now be found in several works [7,8,9]. Our study would suggest a new approach of overcoming the difficulties or barriers for programming educational process by using interactive characteristics of adaptive educational games.

The following structure will cover problems with teaching programming, followed by characteristics of adaptive learning games, improving programming skills using adaptive learning game, designing the learning environment, designing the adaptive learning game environment, and lastly conclusion, and further work.

2   Problems with Teaching Programming

Programming is not an easy subject to be studied because it includes problem solving skills and effective strategies for program design and implementation. From an examination of current research in this field, it can be postulated that one reason computer program instruction seldom result in the successful transfer of problem solving skills lies on the lack of understanding about good instructional approach in this direction [10]. We attribute the difficulties of programming to poor teaching approach among younger generations.

Research by [11] on why programming students failed, revealed among others, incompetent students as well as incompetent lecturers. Among reasons stated by students are: i) did not understand lecturer's explanations, ii) did not finish course tutorial iii) copying from friends and iv) did not even try to answer questions from main text books. In a preliminary research done by the authors we reported that students found programming a boring subject, lecturers explanations are difficult to understand, teaching method that is not interesting, and not enough exercises or practices during class lesson [5]. Students also think that they need more practicing time to effectively master the subject.

A critical consideration of the above study shows a low motivation to the study of programming; we can also deduce that there is high motivation to learn by playing games to promote practice. It is on this background that we suggest adaptive learning games as the way forward towards improving programming skill. Motivation is a key concept in many theories of learning. Katzeff [12] stressed that motivation is a critical factor for instructional design, and for learning to occur the learner must be motivated to learn.

Another problem with teaching programming is that Students often have great difficulties in understanding all the issues relating to the execution of a program. Rahman, and du Boulay [13] stated that it takes quite a long time to learn the relation between a program on the page and the mechanism it describes. Learners have a problem of understanding that every instruction is executed in the state that it has been created by previous instruction. But an adaptive educational game with high interactive and intervention features can simplify the language so that all the program transformation can be visible.

3   Characteristics of Adaptive Learning Game

When we talk about Adaptive learning technology, we are usually looking at a system that gathers information about its students and then uses the information stored in the students' profiles to customize the content delivered to learners and/or the activities they must perform [14]. In adaptive learning game environment the learner interact with content presented on screen; the system adjusts what is presented based on the learner's input, responses, and navigation to questions. In this kind of learning system adjustments are designed to assist learners individually, accessing their skill and knowledge levels, and presenting information and interactions to help them build from those levels.

Adaptive learning games should have features and functions that work together to provide not only the learning content, but also instructional support as the learner progresses through the adaptive learning process:

- Motivation. Interactive educational games are good examples of adaptive learning technology. The learner makes progress based on previous choices and performance within the game. Games can also motivate learners to continue with rewards of attending advanced level.
- Feedback and Assessment Mechanism. Adaptive learning games continuously access the learner's progress as the games goes on, and also provides feedback through interactions with the learner. The gaming feedback could be wrong and correct moves response during game play, suggesting available resources for more practice.
- Adapt to Different Abilities .Adaptive learning game have the ability to immediately change instructional pattern following the learner's knowledge and performance. As each learner makes progress in the learning task, the system would be able to automatically determine what the learner is mastering or still struggling with and adjust instructions.

Using adaptive learning games for enhancing the learning of programming is just one way of helping learners who may need some assistance in specific areas of programming. The leaning the learning content can be individualized to meet the learner's needs in order to advance their knowledge and skills

4   Adaptive Learning Game as a Way of Training Programming Skills

The first step to create an adaptive educational game environment is to create several different activities, indicate for each of the learning goals involved and then group these activities into activities groups [15]. Activity is the basic unit of adaptive learning game structure and indicates a programming task to be performed. Following this methodology we divided the whole game world into two tiers, Agents and Pyramid. The Agents have the ability to instruct, guide, motivate, and express emotions during game play, and can immediately change instructional pattern following the learner's knowledge and performance. The Pyramid is the part of the game that represents a programming activity presented to the learner. Every programming activity in the pyramid has several targeted learning goals. These programming concepts learning goals include; class declaration, variable declaration, method signature, condition statement etc. The groups of activity in the game environment are made of a set of programming activities with the same learning goal. In order to train skills in a game context the game process should be organized in such a way that learning and game tasks will be fulfilled in parallel [16].

The Programming pyramid game (adaptive learning game) gathers information about learner's actions, the progress in programming activities, the achievement of learning goals and the use of tools such as hints, assistance and solution. Furthermore, data that concerns the programming activity, time spent on a programming activity, the total number of the times the agents intervene on a programming activity, the number of attempts made on programming activity, and the progress of learning goals, are saved in different data base record according to the student's names. All these data record would be used to create the learner's model and also to adjust on learners abilities.

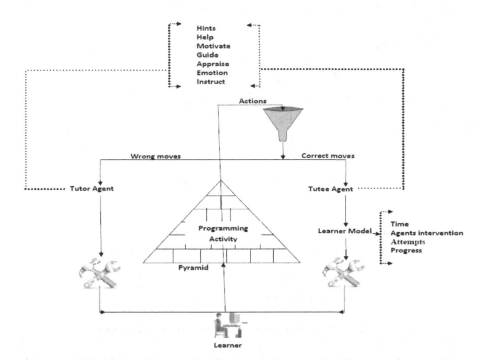

Fig. 1. The Programming Pyramid Game design showing the adaptive learning flow of various activities

The adjustments are made after a successful separation of correct and wrong moves during the game play to help the learner perfect his/her programming skills.

5   Designing the Adaptive Learning Game Environment

In this session we present a full description of our idea of adaptive learning game known as the programming pyramid game. The game would be designed particularly for learning programming languages applying the adaptive learning game features and functions mentioned above. The game is a one player game and the goal of the player is to demolish the pyramid puzzle completely at every game level.

The game consists of two pedagogical agents namely; Tutor Agent (TrA) and Tutee Agent (TeA). The TrA is engineered to interact directly with a learner and explicitly guide him/her through the learning domain. This kind of pedagogical agents are applicable in teaching components and user interfaces. They encourage the learner by providing feedback within the learning environment.

While the main agent (TrA) is engaged in tracking the learner's activities and inferring learner state, the TeA initiate interactions with the learner at the appropriate times and in appropriate manners. For instance, we want to enable an agent to intervene proactively when the learner appears to be confused or stuck. This kind of intervention would be better handled by TeA because of the type of interaction (Learner-learner interaction) that exists between them [17].

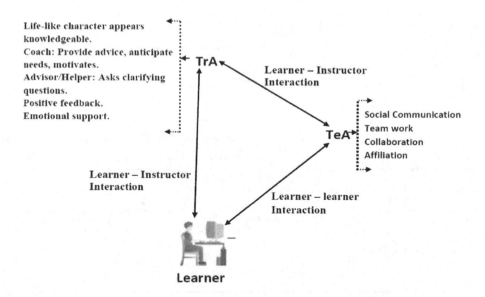

Fig. 2. Agents interaction relationship in programming pyramid game

The interactivity in the game is been performed by both agents. The agents interact with the learner following his/her performance during game play. The agents adjust its emotion and motivation at every point of intervention in order to meet the learner's need. The social interaction between the agents and learner is represented either in verbal (Voice) or non-verbal (dialog box) form.

6   Implementation Adaptive Learning Game

Pyramid programming game is designed in 2D/3D for single player with a very simple and understandable interface. The game is used for the leaning of the following programming languages: Java, C#, PHP, JavaScript, Python, Scala and Ruby. The game levels for each programming language consists of learning topics of that particular programming language from introductory to advance level with increasing difficulties.

The game has the following structural characteristics integrated in it:

Pyramid. The Pyramid is the part of the game that presents the programming activity to the learner in form of puzzle. Every programming activity in the pyramid has several targeted learning goals which can only be achieved by choosing the right combinations.

Tutor and Tutee Agents. Are pedagogical agents with the ability to instruct, guide, motivate, and express emotions during game play, and can immediately change instructional pattern based on the learner's knowledge and performance. The game is designed in such a way that all the technical hints at each stage are passed to the tutor and tutee method as argument.

Objectives and Goals. The learner is expected to successfully demolish the pyramid. To completely demolish the pyramid, the learner must construct a correct combination of available programming syntax before he/she runs out of time.

Feedback. Feedback was also considered as one of the most important characteristic features of the game design, like instructions, help, and hints. Instructions and help for each programming activities were added, as well some general instructions, in order to help the learner navigate through the game and learn to use it. The agents also provide immediate feedback upon the learner's actions. For example, in the case of wrong combination, an appropriate and encouraging message with hints or advice is presented by an agent.

Challenge and Obstacles. The learners have a limited number of lives and a specific period of time to solve a puzzle on the pyramid. For the learner to gain maximum points he/she has to make a correct combination without using any of the feedback tools. As the game progresses, the difficulty of puzzle increases, especially in the case when the learner answers correctly, and decreases or remain the same when the answer is wrong.

We also provided the following options: "Help", "Retry", "Pause", "Adjust game sound", "Scores" and "Exit". The screenshots below show a game play interactions between a learner named Ogar and the agents.

The first screen of "Pyramid Programming Game" is showing the list of existing users, and asking a new player to enter his/her name (See figure 3).The existing users are those who have played the game previously, their information is saved against their names in order to continue from where the learner stop previously. This kind of information is been used to create the leaner's model.

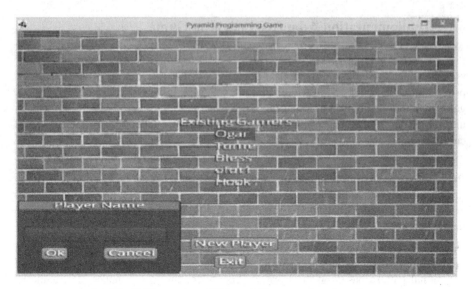

Fig. 3. First screen of "Pyramid Programming Game"

The next screen presents a list of programming languages that can be learnt. The game is used for the training of multiple programming languages. At the beginning the learner can choose any programing language from the available list on the screen (See Figure 4).

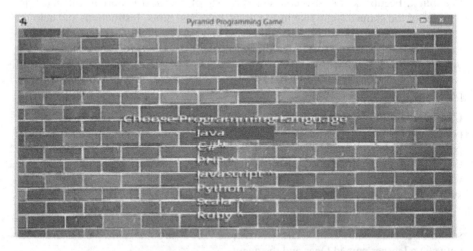

Fig. 4. Screen showing list of programming languages that can be learnt

After choosing a programming language, the learner is presented the list of topics to be learnt under that particular language as the game level/ stages. The learner can only move to the next level after he/she has successfully completed the current stage. The game stages or levels are arranged in an increasing order of difficulties but with an interesting learning goals (Figure 5).

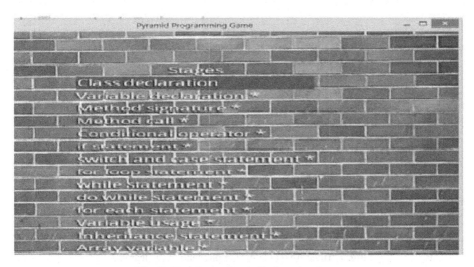

Fig. 5. Stage/game levels for learning Java

At the beginning of every stage or game level the TrA as the main agent presents a brief introduction that could help to guide the learner during the game play (Figure 6).

Fig. 6. Tutor Agent (TrA) introducing the learning content

The sub pedagogical agent TeA appears on the screen to praise the learner after a successful move during the game play. The TeA helps to motivate and encourage the learner after every attempt (Figure 7).

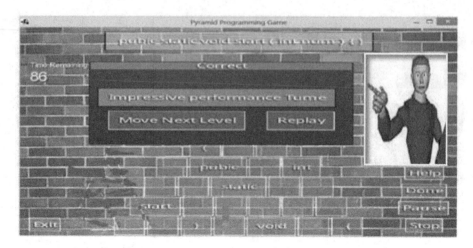

Fig. 7. Tutee Agent (TeA) complementing the learner

The TeA provides advice/hint to the learner (Ogar) after a wrong move in order to motivate and encourage the learner to stay focus (Figure 8).

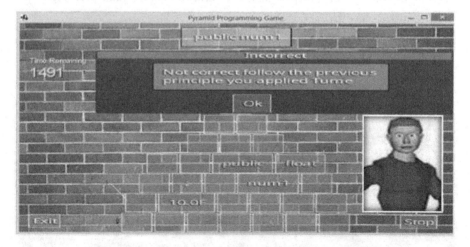

Fig. 8. Tutee Agent (TeA) providing advising the learner

After a repeated unsuccessful attempts the TeA referred the learner to the Tutor Agent for more tutorials on the subject to enable learning succeed (Figure 9).

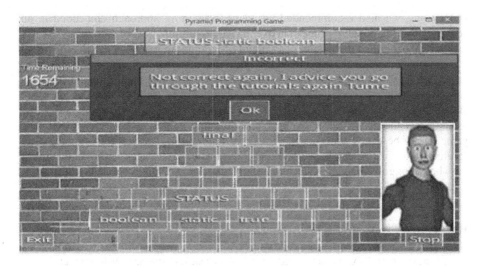

Fig. 9. Tutee Agent (TeA) referring the learner to Tutor Agent

The TrA can provide help to the learner at any point in the game when the learner is stuck. This the kind of assistance can only be offer on request by the learner (Figure 10).

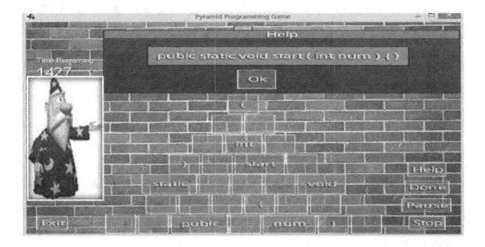

Fig. 10. Tutor Agent (TrA) providing help to the learner

7   Conclusion and Further Work

In the context of this paper, we present an adaptive learning game as a tool for supporting the teaching of programming concept. We did not only attribute the difficulties of learning programming to poor instructional approaches by younger generations, we also recommended an adaptive learning approach embedded in an adaptive learning game in order to help enhance programming skills.

We also explained the design of Pyramid programming game, an adaptive learning game using pedagogical agents to support the learner with hints, motivation and guidance. The combination of the above characteristics with game features could create an adaptive learning environment to provide individualized tutoring that can motivate and engage the learning.

Currently the prototype of pyramid programming game has been developed. The game has to be tested with real data and for this reason a research is ongoing. The results from this research will be properly analyzed to access the potential of the above suggested adaptive techniques for designing a game-based learning environment.

References

1. Rajaravivarma, R.A.: Games-based approach for teaching the introductory programming course. Inroads SIGCSE Bulletin 37(4), 98–102 (2005)
2. Chang, W.-C., Chou, Y.-M.: Introductory C Programming Language Learning with Game-Based Digital Learning. Paper Presented at the Proceedings ICWL (2008)
3. Eagle, M., Barnes, T.: Experimental evaluation of an educational game for improved learning in introductory computing. ACM SIGCSE Bulletin, 321–325 (2009)
4. Shabalina, O., Vorobkalov, P., Kataev, A., Tarasenko, A.: Game based approach in IT education. International Book Series. Information Science and Computing 12, 63–70 (2009)
5. Roslina, I., Nazli, Y.: Development and effectiveness of educational games for learning introductory programming. CTL Research Report, UTM, Malaysia, Skudai, Johor (2009)
6. Garris, R., Ahlers, R., Driskell, J.E.: Games, Motivation, and Learning: A Research and Practice Model. Simulation and Gaming 33(4), 441–467 (2002)
7. Gorriz, C., Medina, C.: Engaging girls with computers through software games. Communications of the ACM 43(1), 4249 (2000)
8. Becker, K.: Teaching with Games: The Minesweeper and Asteroids Experience. Journal of Computing in Small Colleges 17(2), 22–32 (2001)
9. Lawrence, R.: Teaching data structures using competitive games. IEEE Transactions on Education 47(4), 459–466 (2004)
10. Tholander., J., Karlgren, K., Ramberg, R.: Cognitive Apprenticeship in Training for Conceptual Modeling http://www.dsv.su.se/klas/Publications/webnet98.pdf (accessed July 15, 2003)
11. Zarina, S., Alis@Alias, M., Hanawi, S.A., Arsad, A.: Faktor-faktor Kegagalan. Pandangan Pelajar (2005)
12. Katzeff, C.: The design of interactive media for learners in an organizational setting – the state of the art. In: Proc. NordiCHI 2000, Stockholm, October 23-25 (2000)
13. Rahman, S.S.A., du Boulay, B.: Learning programming via worked-examples: Relation of learning styles to cognitive load. Computers in Human Behavior 30, 286–298 (2014)
14. Brusilovsky, P.: Adaptive Educational Systems on the World-Wide-Web: A Review of Available Technologies. In: WWW-Based Tutoring Workshop at 4th International Conference on Intelligent Tutoring Systems, San Antonio (1998)

15. Carro, R.M., Breda, A.M., Castillo, G., Bajuelos, A.L.: A Methodology for Developing Adaptive Educational-Game Environments. In: De Bra, P., Brusilovsky, P., Conejo, R. (eds.) AH 2002. LNCS, vol. 2347, pp. 90–99. Springer, Heidelberg (2002)
16. Shabalina, O., Vorobkalov, P., Kataev, A., Davtyan, A., Blanchfield, P.: Development of Computer games for Training Programming Skills. In: 6th European Conference on Games Based Learning, October 4-5, pp. 460–471. The University College Cork And Waterford Institute of technology, Ireland (2012)
17. Ofut, O.T., Shabalina, O.A.: Digital Educational Games: Adopting Pedagogical Agent to Inter Leaner's Motivation and Emotional State. In: 7th European Conference on Game-Based Learning, Porto, Portugal, October 3-4, vol. II, pp. 546–552. Instituto Superior de Engtnharia do Porto, Porto (2013)

Knowledge Based Models and Software Tools for Learning Management in Open Learning Network

Anton Anikin, Marina Kultsova, Irina Zhukova,
Natalia Sadovnikova, and Dmitry Litovkin

Volgograd State Technical University, Volgograd, Russia
anton@anikin.name

Abstract. Nowadays there is a wide variety of open informational and learning resources on the Internet, in local universities networks and other locations that can be used for the e-learning. These resources of the heterogeneous nature with different level of complexity and comprehension of knowledge content can satisfy the requirements of different learning groups and individuals. The problem is to find resources that achieve the learning objectives, current background and other requirements of the learner out of a great number of available resources, and to provide the learner a way to achieve required learning outcomes. This paper presents an ontology-based approach to create the personal collections of learning resources. To manage the learning process the set of ontologies (ontologies of learning course domain, electronic learning resources, learner's profile and personal collections) is elaborated as well as the ontology reasoning rules and algorithms for retrieval and integration of distributed learning resources into personal collections. In the framework of considered approach the software architecture and web application for creating the personal collections of learning resources have been developed. Suggested approach was applied to create personal collections for the course Programming Languages. C++ in Volgograd State Technical University.

Keywords: Semantic Web, Ontology, OWL-DL, E-learning, Adaptive learning.

1 State of the Art

The modern education technologies become student-centered, oriented toward student's learning outcomes, their background and other requirements [7], [12]. So, the Learning Management concept is defined as a capacity to design pedagogic strategies that achieve learning outcomes for students [13]. According to this approach the Learning Management Design Process (LMDP) includes the eight Learning Management Questions organised into three design phases — defining the learning outcomes, defining the learning strategies and resources, and estimating the achievements. There are many available Learning Management Systems (LMS) (Moodle, Edmodo, Blackboard and many others) that

A. Kravets et al. (Eds.): JCKBSE 2014, CCIS 466, pp. 156–171, 2014.

support this approach. Such systems provide the ability to create and deliver specialized learning content, monitor students participation and assess their achievements and completion of the required courses. The creation of the learning content is a laborious process. The content created with LMS is usually oriented toward some learning groups, not individuals. Personification and adaptivity increases the laboriousness of creating this content. Also this content is usually available for using only within this LMS and not available for reusing by course authors in other LMS. There are many open learning resources on the Internet, in local universities networks, other locations that can be used for the e-learning. These resources have different level of complexity and comprehension of learning content, use different forms of their representation and can satisfy the requirements of different learning groups and individuals. At the same time using these resources can decrease the costs of the learning course authoring. Creation of new learning content as open and available for sharing and reusing can have the same problems and advantages.

So the Open Learning Network approach [9,10] joins the advantages of Learning Management Systems and Personal Learning Environment approach (where the learner collects and organizes the learning content himself). Open Learning Network allows to use the open learning content, to support the learning process with learning outcomes defined by the university and learner, to take into account the personal learner characteristics. The main problem is to find the resources that achieve the learning outcomes and other requirements and to use it in the best way for management of learning process. The general web search engines can be used for retrieval of learning and informational resources on the Internet. But they are not designed for search of the learning resources taking proper account of their specific properties including relations with the learning outcomes. The efficiency of learning resources retrieval can be improved using resources metadata annotation on the base of the appropriate metadata standards (DCMI, LOM and others, ALOCOM Framework [15]).

Using the Semantic Web solutions became the next step to improve the efficiency of learning resources retrieval. Common metadata vocabularies (ontologies) and maps between vocabularies allows document creators to know how to mark up their documents (or annotate existing documents). So automated agents can use the information in the supplied metadata to perform tasks for users of the semantic web using this data. Also the ontology as a knowledge representation model allows to use reasoning rules to acquire a new knowledge, new relations between the concepts. This data can be used for semantic interpretation and learning content retrieval. So the ontology-based models are used to describe the data domain, learning objects, learner properties (Sosnovsky, S., Dolog, P., Henze, N., Brusilovsky, P., Nejdl, W. [2,4,6,14], Pukkhem, N. [11], projects ELENA [8], CREAM [5] etc.)

Thus the use of the ontology-based approach seems to be promising for the learning resources retrieval and allows to describe the properties of the objects and subjects of the learning process (learner, learning course domain, learning resources) on the base of common domain concepts. It also allows to automate the learning resources retrieval using the ontology reasoning. The problem is to develop the ontology-based models, algorithms and tools to support the learning resources retrieval and integration considering the current and outcome learner knowledge field and competencies.

2   Ontology-Based Approach for the Electronic Learning Resources Retrieval and Integration

The approach proposed by authors in [1,17,18] supposes to use the ontologies for modelling the learning course data domain, the learner profile. the learning resources and the personal collection of the learning resources. The data domain of learning course is described by competencies (knowledge, skills, abilities) which the student should acquire as a result of the learning process within the learning course or some part of it. The knowledge field is presented as a set of knowledge domain concepts and relations between concepts.

The learner profile is described using the current and outcome competencies (knowledge, skills, abilities) of the learner which are defined on the same domain. It also includes individual learner properties such as preferred languages, current and outcome knowledge level/comprehension etc.

The learning resources are annotated with competencies (knowledge, skills, abilities) which the learner can get using this resource, and prerequisite competencies, which he should have before using this resource. These properties are defined on the same domain along with some specific properties (resource name, authors, resource location and type, language, knowledge level, didactic role etc.). Annotated in this way learning resources can be collected into open repositories for further use.

The personal collection is a result of the learning resources retrieval and integration that can be used in the learning management. This is a set of the learning resources retrieved according to the learner profile, learner's current and outcome competencies and other requirements. It also includes relations between the resources that define the order of using the resources in learning.

The metaontology for retrieval and integration of learning resources into the personal collections (Fig. 1) is developed to integrate and manage the domain ontologies. The proposed approach includes the stages below (Fig. 2):

1. Creation or modification of the specific learning course ontology (2) based on the learning course ontology (1) using ontology editor or special-purpose software. The created ontology can be stored in the domain ontologies repository for sharing and reusing.
2. Annotating the learning resources using the learning resource ontology (4) and specific learning course ontology (3). Creating the open learning resources repository (5) using general ontology editor or special-purpose software.
3. Creating or updating the learner profile (8) using the learner profile ontology (7), specific learning course ontology (6) and general ontology editor

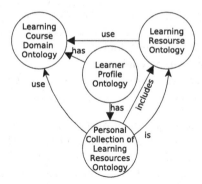

Fig. 1. The metaontology for the learning resources retrieval and integration into the personal collections

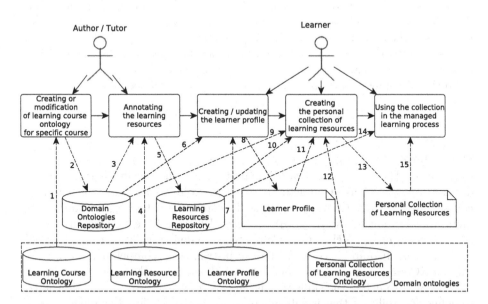

Fig. 2. Creating the personal collections of learning resources using ontologies

or special-purpose software. The current and outcome competencies can be defined by learner as well as on the base of the history of interaction the learner with system in the learning process and assessment results.

4. Creating the personal collection of learning resources (13) using the specific learning course ontology (9), learning resources repository (10), learner profile (11), personal collection ontology (12) based on the ontology reasoning rules and ontology reasoning engine.

5. Use of the created personal collection (15) integrating the retrieved resources (14) in the learning process.

So, the four domain ontologies mentioned above allow to describe any learning course, learning resource, learner profile and personal collection of learning resources which are defined on the common domain. They can be used to create learning resources repository, retrieve and integrate learning resources into personal learning collection for individual learners.

3 Knowledge Representation Models

3.1 Learning Course Domain Ontology

The ontological model for representing the subject domain of learning course provides the complete description of the knowledge field of the learning course. It represents the structure of the data domain, relations between the concepts of the data domain (hierarchical relations, meronymy, association), synonyms for the concepts of the data domain and their representation with different languages. It allows to describe different levels of competencies, knowledge, skills and abilities, as well as hierarchical relations between these elements.

So the Learning course domain ontology (Fig. 3) is defined as follows:

$$O_{DD} = < C_{DD}, Inst_{DD}, R_{DD}, I_{DD} >, \tag{1}$$

where C_{DD} — finite set of concepts of the Learning course domain ontology, $C_{DD} = \{c_{DD1}, c_{DD2}, c_{DD3}, c_{DD4}, c_{DD5}, c_{DD6}, c_{DD7}, c_{DD8}, c_{DD9}, c_{DD10}, c_{DD11}, c_{DD12}\}$, c_{DD1} — class DataDomain to define the specific learning course domain, c_{DD2} — class Competence to define competencies for the learning course, c_{DD3} — class Concept to define the concepts of the learning course domain, that is subclass of c_{DD2}, c_{DD4} — class UCompetence to define universal competencies, c_{DD5} — class ONKCompetence to define scientific competencies, c_{DD7} — class ICompetence to define the instrumental competencies, c_{DD8} — class SLKCompetence to define social, personal and cultural competencies, c_{DD9} — class Skill to define the skills that is subclass of c_{DD2}, c_{DD10} — class Ability to define the abilities, that is subclass of c_{DD2}, c_{DD11} — class Language, c_{DD12} — class Complexity to define the level of mastering competencies;

$Inst_{DD}$ — finite set of competencies, concepts of the learning course domain, skills and abilities that are exemplars of classes C_{DD}; $Inst_{DD} = \{i_{DD1}, i_{DD2}, ..., i_{DDj}, ..., i_{DDn}\}$;

R_{DD} — finite set of relations of learning course ontology; R_{DD} = $\{r_{DD1}, r_{DD2}, r_{DD3}, r_{DD4}, r_{DD5}, r_{DD6}, r_{DD7}, r_{DD8}, r_{DD9}\}$; r_{DD1} — relation hasLanguage, r_{DD2} — relation hasComplexity, r_{DD3} — relation includes, r_{DD4} — relation hasHierarchicalRelation, r_{DD5} — relation dependsOn, r_{DD6} — relation isSynonym, r_{DD7} — relation is, r_{DD8} — relation hasTitle, r_{DD9} — relation hasCompetence;

$I_{DD} = \varnothing$ — interpretation rules.

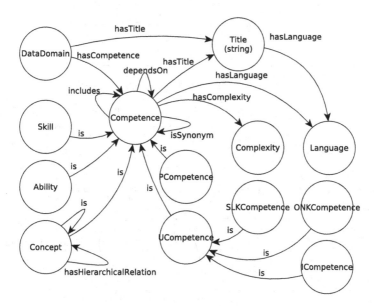

Fig. 3. Learning course domain ontology

The proposed domain ontology of learning course allows to describe subject domains of specific learning courses with competencies of different types, as well as course skills and abilities.

3.2 Learning Resource Ontology

The ontological model of learning resources represents the learning resources regardless of their representation form, location, didactic role. Such representation allows to create the repositories of learning resources based on their annotations. The description of learning resource includes the language and the learning outcomes in form of outcome competencies in addition to the properties referred above. These competencies are defined on the base of knowledge, skills, abilities and complexity level of learning resources using the common ontology domain with the learning course model. So the Learning resource ontology (Fig. 4) is defined as follows:

$$O_{ELR} =< C_{ELR}, Inst_{ELR}, R_{ELR}, I_{ELR} >, \qquad (2)$$

where C_{ELR} — finite set of concepts of Learning resource ontology;

$Inst_{ELR}$ — set of exemplars of classes C_{ELR} that are annotated learning resources, that can be organized into repositories of learning resources;

R_{ELR} — finite set of relations of Learning resource ontology;

$I_{ELR} = \varnothing$.

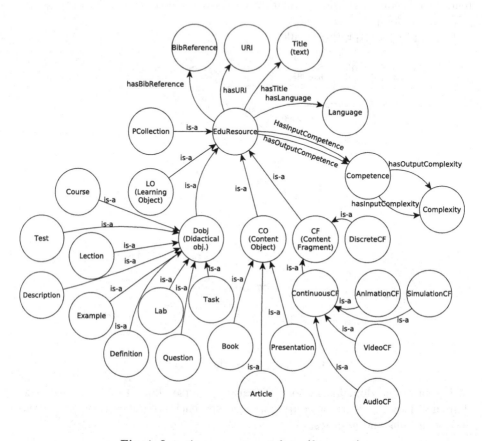

Fig. 4. Learning resource ontology (fragment)

Thus the ontology of learning resource represents the learning resources of different nature (of different didactic types, different form of representation etc.) and annotate they with the competencies which are defined in the ontology of learning course. Such ontological representation allows creating repositories of learning resources for sharing, reusing and retrieval of resources for specified learners. Description of the prerequisite and outcome competencies are used for creation of the learning collections for specified learners and definition of the learning sequences within the collections.

3.3   Learner Profile Ontology

The ontological model of learner profile represents the personal properties of learner: preferred language; the current knowledge field for the current learning course, including the knowledge level for the different structure elements of the course; mastering level for different competencies of the learning course; learning outcomes defined as outcome competencies of the current learning course.

The Learner profile ontology (Fig. 5) is defined as follows:

$$O_L = <C_L, Inst_L, R_L, I_L>, \tag{3}$$

where C_L — finite set of concepts of Learner profile ontology;

$Inst_L$ — set of exemplars of classes C_L of the Learner profile ontology;

R_L — finite set of relations of Learner profile ontology;

$I_L = \varnothing$.

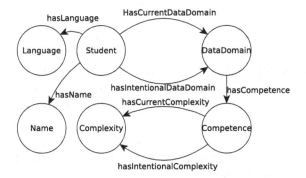

Fig. 5. Learner profile ontology

The competencies are defined on the common domain of learning course ontology, therefore the learner profile ontology allows to perform the learning resources retrieval according to the learning outcomes and create the personal collections of the retrieved learning resources.

3.4   Personal Learning Collection Ontology

The ontological model of personal learning collection describes the personal electronic learning collection as a set of the learning resources retrieved based on the learner profile. In addition this model includes the relations between the learning resources which define the order of learning, that allows manage the learning process.

Thus the Personal learning collection ontology (Fig. 6) is defined as follows:

$$O_{COL} = <C_{COL}, Inst_{COL}, R_{COL}, I_{COL}>, \tag{4}$$

where C_{COL} — finite set of concepts of Personal learning collection ontology;

$Inst_{COL}$ — set of exemplars of classes C_{COL} including created personal collections that can be stored in the repository of personal collections;

R_{COL} — finite set of relations of Personal learning collection ontology;

I_{COL} — finite set of reasoning rules for creating the collection, described in the section 4 below.

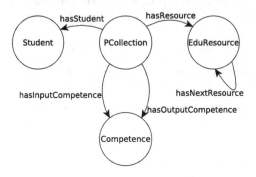

Fig. 6. Personal learning collection ontology

So the ontology of personal learning collection includes the concepts and relations, that allows to compose the learning resources into the collection using the appropriate reasoning rules for retrieve of the learning resource and creation the collection.

3.5 Metaontology for Retrieval and Integration of the Distributed Learning Resources

The metaontology for the learning resources retrieval and integration into the personal learning collections (Fig. 1) integrates all the 4 ontologies described above and defines the relations between them.

The proposed model provides the consistency and integration of resource descriptions, data domain of the learning course, learner profile and personal electronic learning collection. It is possible due to use of the common ontology domain for defining and reusing the following components:

- current and outcome competencies defined as a knowledge (in form of terms — concepts of the data domain), skills and abilities;
- language for presentation and perception of the information;
- complexity level of learning resources and mastering level of competencies.

They provide the modularity and extensibility, support of the accumulation, sharing and reusing the knowledge of the learning courses data domain and electronic learning resources. All the ontologies are implemented using OWL-DL language.

The ontologies discussed above allow to perform the adaptive retrieval of learning resources and create the personal learning collections for support and management of the learning process. The reasoning rules for these tasks are considered below.

4 Ontology-Based Rules and Algorithms for Creating the Personal Collections of Learning Resources

To create the personal collection of learning resources, the learning resources with annotations stored in the learning resources repository should be retrieved. The retrieved resources should correspond to the learner preferences such as language, learning outcomes and current knowledge level. In some cases, when there are no appropriate learning resources that comply both with outcomes and current knowledge level, the additional learning resources should be retrieved in order to fill in the gaps in prerequisite knowledge. All these tasks are implemented using the ontology reasoning rules that sequentially define the subsets of learning resources within the set of resources in the repository. Finally the relations between the learning resources in the collection should be defined to allow managing the learning process using these resources.

To represent the ontology reasoning rules for learning resources retrieval and integration we used SWRL language. SWRL extends the OWL-DL and is based on first-order predicate calculus that allows to represent the reasoning rules as a set of Horn clauses.

4.1 Ontology Reasoning Rules for Parametric Search of the Learning Resources

The SWRL-rule for learning resources retrieval based on the preferred language and learning resources has the following form:

$$COL : hasStudent(?c, ?u) \land L : hasLanguage(?u, ?l) \land$$
$$\land ELR : hasLanguage(?r, ?l) \rightarrow$$
$$\rightarrow COL : hasResourceByLanguage(?c, ?r), \quad (5)$$

where ?c, ?u, ?l, ?r – SWRL variables,

$COL : hasStudent, L : hasLanguage, ELR : hasLanguage,$
$COL : hasResourceByLanguage$ — ontology relations with ontology prefixes.

The SWRL-rule for learning resources retrieval based on the outcome competencies and resolving the synonymy problem has the form:

$$COL : hasStudent(?c, ?u) \land L : hasIntentionalDataDomain(?u, ?d) \land$$
$$\land DD : hasCompetence(?d, ?cmp1) \land ELR : hasOutputCompetence(?r, ?cmp2) \land$$
$$\land DD : is(?cmp2, ?cmp) \land DD : is(?cmp1, ?cmp) \rightarrow$$
$$\rightarrow COL : hasResourceByIntentionalcompetencies(?c, ?r). \quad (6)$$

So, the rules (5, 6) define the subset of learning resources that comply with the learner's language and outcome competencies.

4.2 Ontology Reasoning Rules for the Learning Resources Retrieval Based on the Target Knowledge Field of the Learner

The SWRL-rules for learning resources retrieval based on the target knowledge field of the learner is presented below:

$$COL : hasStudent(?c, ?u) \wedge$$
$$\wedge COL : hasResourceByIntentionalcompetencies(?c, ?r) \wedge$$
$$\wedge L : hasIntentionalDataDomain(?u, ?d) \wedge DD : hasCompetence(?d, ?cmp1) \wedge$$
$$\wedge ELR : hasOutputCompetence(?r, ?cmp2) \wedge DD : is(?cmp2, ?cmp) \wedge$$
$$\wedge DD : is(?cmp1, ?cmp) \wedge L : hasIntentionalComplexity(?cmp1, ?level) \wedge$$
$$\wedge ELR : hasOutputComplexity(?cmp2, ?level) \rightarrow$$
$$\rightarrow COL : hasResourceByOutputDomain(?c, ?r). \quad (7)$$

Two additional rules to retrieve the resources with complexity level to one level less than learner level are defined similarly to rule (7). These rules define the subset of learning resources which correspond to the learner's outcome competencies and complexity levels.

4.3 Algorithm for Additional Learning Resources Retrieval Based on the Current Knowledge Field of the Learner

The set of learning resources obtained using the relation $COL : hasResourceByOutputDomain$ can cover (full or partially) the set of the learner's outcome competencies. All these learning resources should be examined for the compliance their prerequisite competencies with the current competencies of learner. In case when the learner has not enough competencies, to resolve this issue the additional learning resources should be included into the personal collection using the algorithm, that is described below.

1. Include in the final personal collection the resources which were retrieved previously: $COL : hasResourceByOutputDomain(?c, ?r) \rightarrow$
   $\rightarrow COL : hasResource(?c, ?r)$
2. Define collection set R_0 as a set of resources required for getting the outcome competencies.
3. Define the set of learner's outcome competencies CMP_0 with corresponding levels L_0.
4. While there are competencies $?cmp$ for which corresponding competencies $?cmp2$ in the current knowledge field of learner with level not less than required have not found, for retrieval of additional learning resources, no more than $N = 3$ times do:

4.1. Define set of prerequisite competencies ?cmp, defined with relation $ELR : hasOutputCompetence(?r, ?cmp1) \wedge DD : is(?cmp1, ?cmp)$ for every learning resource for that relation $COL : hasResource(?c, ?r)$ is true.

4.2. For competencies ?cmp2, for which corresponding competencies in the current learner's knowledge field are not found with level not less than required:

4.2.1. Add the competence ?cmp2 to the outcome learner's knowledge field with corresponding level setting relations:
$DD : hasCompetence(?d1, ?cmp2)$,
where $L : hasIntentionalDataDomain(?u, ?d1)$
and $L : hasIntentionalComplexity(?cmp2, ?level)$,
where $ELR : hasInputComplexity(?cmp1, ?level)$.

4.3. Apply the rules (6,7) and the rule defined in the first step of the algorithm to retrieve additional learning resources.

5. Find the difference R_1 of the sets of learning resources defined with relation $COL : hasResource(?c, ?r)$ and the set R_0.

6. Define subset R_2 of the set R_1 of auxiliary learning resources for which:
   - prerequisite competencies are different or have complexity level that's different from the competencies of current knowledge field of learner;
   - competencies are not output competencies of the sets of resources R_0 and R_1.

According to proposed algorithm the set R_0 of learning resources is created that allows to gain the outcome competencies of learner. Also the set R_1 of additional learning resources is created that allows to fill in the gap in the current knowledge field of the learner. Finally subset R_2 of the auxiliary learning resources is created that allows to gain the additional competencies.

4.4 Rules for Creating the Personal Collection of Learning Resources

The personal collection of learning resources is the sets R_0 and R_1 (defined with relation $COL : hasResource$) of learning resources and the set R_2 of auxiliary learning resources with logical relations between the resources defined with the rule:

$$COL : hasResource(?c, ?r1) \wedge COL : hasResource(?c, ?r2) \wedge$$
$$\wedge ELR : hasOutputCompetence(?r1, ?cmp1) \wedge$$
$$\wedge ELR : hasInputCompetence(?r2, ?cmp2) \wedge DD : is(?cmp1, ?cmp) \wedge$$
$$\wedge DD : is(?cmp2, ?cmp) \rightarrow COL : hasNextResource(?r1, ?r2). \quad (8)$$

The presented algorithm and set of reasoning rules allow to create the personal collection of learning resources in accordance with the learning outcomes, current knowledge level and other preferences of learner. The collection includes relations between the learning resources to manage the learning process.

5 Software Tools for Retrieval and Integration of the Learning Resources

To automate the creation of personal collections of learning resources the software architecture was designed. Software architecture for learning resources retrieval and integration into personal learning collection (Fig. 7) includes interface, logical and data levels.

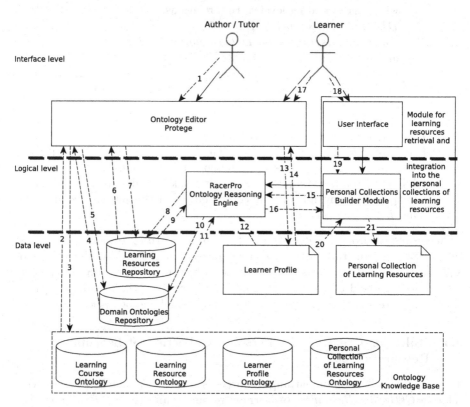

Fig. 7. Software architecture for creating the personal learning collections

Interface level provides creating the domain ontologies of learning courses, learning resources annotations and learner profile using ontology editor. The logical level includes the personal collections builder and third-party ontology reasoning engine RacerPro. The data level contains 4 ontologies described below, repositories for domain ontologies and annotated learning resources, learner profiles and personal collections of learning resources.

In the Fig. 7: 1 — author knowledge about the learning course, learning resources and learner; 2,3 — specific learning course ontology (in OWL); 4,5 — learning course ontologies created or modified by the tutor; 6,7 — learning

resources annotations created or modified by the tutor; 8 — RacerPro request
for the learning resources annotations; 9 — learning resources annotations (in
OWL); 10 — RacerPro request for specific learning course ontology; 11 — specific
learning course ontology (in OWL); 12 — learner profile for RacerPro reasoning;
13,14 — learner profile created or modified by the tutor or learner; 15 — reasoning request (in nRQL); 16 — reasoning results (the ersources and relations of the
collection, in nRQL); 17 — information about learner; 18 — information about
learner profile; 19 — information about learner profile's URL and request for
creating the personal collection; 20 — learner profile (in OWL); 21 — personal
collection of learning resources (in HTML).

The personal collection builder was implemented using C# as a client-server
application. The server side employs RacerPro reasoning engine, client side uses
nRQL language for the ontology requests. The builder provides creation of the
personal learning collections using repository of the ontology-based annotations
of resources, ontology of learning course domain and learner profile. The personal learning collection is represented as an HTML-document in the built-in
browser. It contains the set of links to the learning resources that are structured
according to the structure of the learning course domain and linked according
to the recommended sequence of learning. The system testing was performed
in the framework of learning the course "Programming Languages. C++" in
the Volgograd State Technical University. A comparative analysis of collections
created using proposed approach and tools with resources which tutor advised,
showed about 83 percents of intersection of sets of resources. Therefore it can
be argued that the presented approach and developed software are an effective
tools to support and manage the learning process.

As compared with known analogs [3], [16], the proposed software tool allows
to use the external resources annotated with open ontology-based schema for
creation of personal learning collections. Moreover, the learner profile contains
more wide set of properties that allows to improve the quality of created collections.

6 Summary

The concept of learning management in the open learning network was proposed
on the base of learning resources retrieval and creating the personal learning
collections using ontology-based approach. The ontological model for knowledge
representation was developed including ontologies of learning course domain,
learning resource, learner's profile and personal learning collection. The last one
includes the ontology reasoning rules for creating the personal learning collection. Also the algorithm for additional learning resources retrieval was proposed.
The software architecture and tool for creating the personal learning collections
were designed and implemented within framework of proposed knowledge-based
approach with employment of the object-oriented analysis and C# language.

In future work the software tools for creating the learning course ontologies
and annotating the learning resources are to be developed, as well as the ontologies for other university courses. The repository of learning resources is to be

more filled up for the domain of software engineering to provide the creation of personal collections for variety of learning courses.

This paper presents the results of research carried out under the RFBR grant 13-07-00219 "Intelligent support of strategic planning based on the integration of cognitive and ontological models".

References

1. Anikin, A.V., Dvoryankin, A.M., Zhukova, I.G., Kultsova, M.B.: Modeli i instrumentalnye sredstva integracii raspredelennykh resursov v otkrytykh obrazovatelnykh setyakh. In: Informacionnye Tekhnologii v Obrazovanii, Tekhnike i Medicine, p. 16. VSTU, Volgograd (2009)
2. Brusilovsky, P.: Adaptive Hypermedia for Education and Training. In: Durlach, P., Lesgold, A. (eds.) Adaptive Technologies for Training and Education, pp. 46–68. Cambridge University Press, Cambridge (2012)
3. Baza i generator obrazovatel'nykh resursov (2014), http://bigor.bmstu.ru
4. Dolog, P., Henze, N., Nejdl, W., Sintek, M.: Personalization in distributed e-learning environments. In: Proceedings of the 13th International World Wide Web Conference on Alternate Track Papers and Posters (WWW Alt. 2004), pp. 170–179. ACM, New York (2004)
5. Handschuh, S., Staab, S., Maedche, A.: CREAM: creating relational metadata with a component-based, ontology-driven annotation framework. In: K-CAP 2001: Proceedings of the 1st International Conference on Knowledge Capture, pp. 76–83. ACM, New York (2001)
6. Henze, N., Dolog, P., Nejdl, W.: Reasoning and Ontologies for Personalized E-Learning in the Semantic Web. Educational Technology and Society 7(4), 82–97 (2004)
7. Kravets, A.: E-Learning practice-oriented training in physics: the competence formation. In: Kravets, A.G., Titova, O.V., Shabalina, O.A. (eds.) e-Learning 2013: Proceedings of the IADIS International Conference, Section I, Prague, Czech Republic, July 24-26, pp. 351–356. IADIS Press (2013)
8. Miklos, Z.: ELENA: Creating a Smart Space for Learning. In: Proceeding of: MMGPS, IST Workshop on Metadata Management in Grid and P2P Systems: Models, Services and Architectures, London, December 16 (2003)
9. McAndrew, P., Cropper, K.: Open Learning Network: the evidence of OER impact. In: Open Ed 2010: The Seventh Annual Open Education Conference, Barcelona, Spain, November 2-4 (2010)
10. Mott, J.: Envisioning the Post-LMS Era: The Open Learning Network. Educause Quarterly 33(1), 1–9 (2010)
11. Pukkhem, N.: Ontology-based Semantic Approach for Learning Object Recommendation. International Journal on Information Technology 3(4), 12 (2013)
12. Shabalina, O.A.: Kompetentnostno-orientirovannaja model' processa obuchenija. In: Shabalina, O.A. (ed.) Informacija i Svjaz 2013 vol. 2, pp. 171–174 (2013)
13. Smith, R., Lynch, D.: Rethinking Teacher Education: Teacher education in the knowledge age. AACLM Press, Sydney (2010) ISBN 9781471604621
14. Sosnovsky, S., Dolog, P., Henze, N., Brusilovsky, P., Nejdl, W.: Translation of overlay models of student knowledge for relative domains based on domain ontology mapping. In: Luckin, R., Koedinger, K.R., Greer, J. (eds.) Proceedings of 13th International Conference on Artificial Intelligent in Education, AI-ED 2007, Marina Del Rey, CA, July 9-13, pp. 289–296. IOS (2007)

15. Verbert, K., Duval, E.: Evaluating the ALOCOM Approach for Scalable Content Repurposing. In: Second European Conference on Technology Enhanced Learning - Creating New Learning Experiences on a Global Scale, Crete, Greece, September 17-20 (2007)
16. Yu, Z., Nakamura, Y., Jang, S., Kajita, S., Mase, K.: Ontology-Based Semantic Recommendation for Context-Aware E-Learning. In: Indulska, J., Ma, J., Yang, L.T., Ungerer, T., Cao, J. (eds.) UIC 2007. LNCS, vol. 4611, pp. 898–907. Springer, Heidelberg (2007)
17. Zhukova, I.G., Dvoryankin, A.M., Siplivaya, M.B., Anikin, A.V.: Poisk i integraciya raznorodnyh raspredelyonnyh obrazovatelnyh resursov na osnove ontologicheskikh modelei. Izvestiya VolgGTU 2(2), 34–36 (2007)
18. Zhukova, I.G., Kultsova, M.B., Anikin, A.V.: Modeli i instrumentalnye sredstva integracii raspredelennykh resursov v otkrytykh obrazovatelnykh setyakh. Izvestiya VolgGTU 9(11), 91–94 (2010)

Intelligent Support of Decision Making in Human Resource Management Using Case-Based Reasoning and Ontology

Irina Zhukova, Marina Kultsova, Mikhail Navrotsky,
and Alexander Dvoryankin

Volgograd State Technical University, Volgograd, Russia
poas@vstu.ru

Abstract. In this paper a knowledge-based approach to the support of decision making in human resource management is proposed, which is a promising way to increase the efficiency of human resource management on the operational and managerial levels. Analysis of the domain of human recourse management shows that the appropriate support of decision making can be implemented using contemporary technologies of artificial intelligence such as case-based reasoning and ontology. In the paper the problems of knowledge and case representation are considered, as well as the algorithm of case retrieval. A prototype of intelligent decision support system in human resource management was implemented in framework of proposed approach to the integration of case-based reasoning and ontology.

Keywords: human resource management, human resource intelligent decision support system, case-based reasoning, ontology.

1 Introduction

The modern economy raises a number of fundamental problems, the most important of which is the most efficient use of personnel potential. Human resource management (HRM) is a core of enterprise management system and is considered one of the main criteria of its economic success. Human resource management is the management function in organization which is typically responsible for a number of activities, including employee attraction, selection, training, assessment, and rewarding. The human resource management system (HRMS) is used to automate this function.

The problem of increasing the efficiency of the human resource management system in the enterprises is associated primarily with the introduction of effective methods for evaluation of employee performance. We need to have the effective mechanisms for selection of the most efficient methods of employee performance estimation, as well as for improvement of the quality of decisions made by the enterprise head.

The possible approach to solving this problem is a development of intelligent decision support system in human resource management (HRIDSS) based on relevant contemporary technologies of artificial intelligence. Analysis of the domain

A. Kravets et al. (Eds.): JCKBSE 2014, CCIS 466, pp. 172–184, 2014.

of human resource management shows that the appropriate support of decision making can be implemented using case-based reasoning (CBR) and ontology, and this paper is devoted to problems of development of HRIDSS on the base of coupling CBR with ontology.

2   State of the Art

Human resources are important and very valuable asset for organizations and enterprises. HRM system is a key element of effective management of enterprises, it is based on the integrated and interrelated approaches to managing the human resources [1]. Activities in HRM system include a lot of unstructured processes such as employee performance evaluation, training, motivation and maintenance, etc. Therefore, the problem of increasing the efficiency of the human resource management system could be solved with the application of knowledge-based approach that means the development of automated systems for intelligent support of decision making.

Researches in HR IDSS are classified into four categories according to HRM main activities: staffing, training and development, motivation and administration [1], [2]. The most of HR IDSS are developed for the specific HRM subject domains, these systems use a variety of intelligent techniques, such as data mining, neural network, fuzzy logic, inference on ontologies, rule- and case-based reasoning, etc. for support of various tasks of human resource management [7], [8].

There are a few approaches of different focus to applying ontologies in the HR domain, ontology-based method is a new and promising approach to manage knowledge in HR, to integrate multiple data resources, and to facilitate consideration of complex relations between the concepts of subject domain.

A lot of ontologies in HR management have been developed over the last decade [3], such as: ProPer Ontology on skills management; KOWIEN Ontology [4] on competence and skills management; Knowledge Nets [5] on national and international classifications for jobs and branches; ePeople – ontology on skills, skill profiles of employees and job skill requirements; LIP Ontology for on-demand learning support; CommOnCV ontology on competencies from CV descriptions; TOVE (Toronto Virtual Enterprise Ontologies) – an integrated ontologies for the modeling of commercial and public enterprises; PROTON (PROTO-Ontology) upper-level ontology for a number of tasks in different domains; and COKE [6] – a three-level ontology containing a top-level HR ontology (representing employees and their social groups), a middle-level Business Process ontology and a lower-level knowledge Objects ontology which are related to organizational entities; ontology for operational management of the enterprise business processes [8].

Our researches are focused on the problems of integration of CBR and ontology, and development of CBR-based decision making process supported with ontology in the field of human resource management.

3   Ontological Knowledge Representation Model

In this paper we propose an integrated approach to the evaluation of employee performance, which takes into account the key performance indicators (KPI) of the staff as well as the personal properties of employee and features of his work [9]. This approach is relevant for enterprises with well-defined objectives, well-structured business processes, limited set of quantitative key performance indicators and additional qualitative parameters. We applied given approach for the evaluation of employees performance in the retail chains. The following main factors of staff performance were defined as a result of system analysis:

1. Enterprise objectives – sales budget achievement, conversion growth;
2. Key performance indicators (KPI) – individual sales target, individual sales target achieved, sales budget achieved, average sales per transaction, average items per transaction, total of transactions, etc.;
3. Additional parameters (the personal properties of employee and features of his work) – sales growth dynamics, customer satisfaction, work experience, team work skills, etc.;
4. Problems arising in everyday work of staff – financial, organizational and customer service problems;
5. Recommendations (stimulating rewards), which can be assigned to eliminate or mitigate the problems and improve the staff performance – promotion, training, cash/vacation bonuses, health benefits, disciplinary actions, etc.;
6. Dependencies between attributes defined above;
7. Rules for assessing the staff performance, as well as rules for the appointment of recommendations.

The decision making process in employee performance evaluation and staff management includes the following steps: (a) analysis of the performance indicators; (b) identification of employee's problems; (c) evaluation of employee performance; (d) development of managerial decisions (recommendations) to eliminate or mitigate the problems and improve the staff performance; (e) generating the final report. In decision making manager takes into account the objective indicators of employee performance as well as own experience and knowledge gained in solving similar problems in the past. The following hierarchy of domain concepts was defined:

1. Performance indicators;
   (a) Financial indicators;
      i. Sales budget;
      ii. Conversion rate;
      iii. Average sales budget;
      iv. Average sales per transaction;
      v. Average items per transaction;
      vi. Sales budget achievement;
      vii. Individual sales target;
      viii. Individual sales target achieved;

      ix. Transaction amount;

      x. Transaction value;

     xi. Total of checks/transactions;

    xii. Sales Growth Dynamics;

  (b) Personal indicators;

      i. Education;

     ii. Work experience;

    iii. Competence;

    iv. Communication skills;

     v. Team skills;

    vi. Leader skills;

  (c) Additional indicators;

      i. Annual leave;

     ii. Sick leave;

    iii. Threshold items per transaction;

    iv. Threshold average sales per transaction;

2. Employee's problems;

  (a) Financial problems;

      i. Failure to achieve individual target;

     ii. Failure to achieve sales indicators;

    iii. Lack of positive dynamics in sales growth;

    iv. Lack of positive dynamics in sales indicators;

  (b) Customer service problems;

      i. Number of customer complaints;

     ii. Customers outflow;

  (c) Organization problems;

      i. Delays;

     ii. Delayed completion of assignments;

3. Recommendations;

  (a) Motivators;

      i. Appreciation;

     ii. Commendation;

    iii. Praise;

    iv. Additional cash bonus;

     v. Additional days of leave;

    vi. Additional health insurance;

   vii. Additional dental insurance;

  viii. Employee motivation for promotion;

    ix. Offer of training;

     x. Pay rise;

    xi. Promotion;

  (b) Training;

      i. Individual training;

     ii. Group training;

    iii. Workshop attendance;

    iv. Work with a partner/colleague;

      v. Work with a supervisor;
     vi. Work with customers;
  (c) Certification;
      i. Assessment by company regulations;
     ii. Assessment by sales groups;
    iii. Assessment by sales brands;
  (d) Disciplinary action;
      i. Verbal warning;
     ii. Written warning;
    iii. Fine;
    iv. Suspension;
     v. Step down;
    vi. Termination of employment contract;
4. Efficiency;
  (a) Current work efficiency of employee;
  (b) Decisions efficiency.

Hence, the analysis of domain knowledge allowed to reveal their main features: (a) description of a decision making problem has a complex and variable structure with multiple logical relations between components; (b) both qualitative and quantitative parameters are taken into account; (c) knowledge about previously solved problems which are similar to the current one is actively used while decision making. Therefore ontological knowledge representation model and case-based reasoning can be considered as an appropriate AI technologies for the intelligent support of decision making in evaluation of employee performance.

In this paper the concept of integration of case-based reasoning and ontology developed by authors in [10] was implemented for given subject domain. According to this concept ontology describes general concepts and rules of domain, case representation model and contains case base. Ontology as case representation model describes case as a set of individuals and relations. Ontology as domain knowledge base describes domain knowledge as DL rules, using procedures of knowledge inferring. Ontology as case base stores cases as a part of domain knowledge.

The ontology model which satisfies these requirements is represented as follows:

$$Onto = < DomainOnto; CaseStructure >, \tag{1}$$

where $DomainOnto$ – domain ontology; $CaseStructure$ – case structure.

The domain ontology contains concepts and relations of the problem domain and specific components for supporting CBR.

$$DomainOnto = \{OB, ATT, DAT, AR, RR, PROB, REC, REL\}, \tag{2}$$

where $OB = \{OB_1, OB_2, ..., OB_n\}$ – set of enterprise objectives;
    $ATT = \{ATT_1 \cup ATT_2 \cup ... \cup ATT_n\}$ – set of attributes which are used for problem description, each subset ATT_i corresponds to objective OB_i;

DAT – set of ontology domains, which define the space of attribute values;

AR – set of adaptation rules; RR – set of revision rules;

$PROB = \{PROB_1 \cup PROB_2 \cup ... \cup PROB_n\}$ – set of employee's problems, each subset $PROB_i$ corresponds to attribute ATT_i;

$REC = \{REC_1 \cup REC_2 \cup ... \cup REC_n\}$ – set of recommendations, each subset REC_i corresponds to problem $PROB_i$;

$REL = \{REL_1, REL_2, ..., REL_k\}$ – set of relations between ontology concepts.

Structural object-oriented model was selected as a case representation model. This approach is useful at the concerned domain to obtain satisfactory results. Case description consists of four main parts:

$$CaseStructure = \{P, S(P), Ef(S(P)), CREL\}, \tag{3}$$

where P – problem description (case index), $S(P)$ – solution description, $Ef(S(P))$ – set of qualitative assessments of solution efficiency, $CREL = \{CREL_1, CREL_2, ..., CREL_8\}$ – set of case relations. Set $CREL$ contains the following relations: $CREL_1$ – relation $hasFinanchialIndicators$, $CREL_2$ – relation $hasPersonalIndicators$, $CREL_3$ – relation $hasAdditionalIndicators$, $CREL_4$ – relation $hasSolution$, $CREL_5$ – relation $hasEfficiency$, $CREL_6$ – relation $Manage$, $CREL_7$ – relation has, $CREL_8$ – relation $is\ a$.

Problem description consists of three descriptors which represent the main groups of key indicators:

$$P = \{FI, PI, AI\}, \tag{4}$$

where $FI = \{FI_1 \cup FI_2 \cup ... \cup FI_n\}$ – set of financial indicators; $PI = \{PI_1 \cup PI_2 \cup ... \cup PI_m\}$ – set of personal indicators; $AI = \{AI_1 \cup AI_2 \cup ... \cup AI_l\}$ – set of additional indicators (sets of couples "attribute - value").

Definition of case solution consists of two descriptors:

$$S(P) = \{EP, R\}, \tag{5}$$

where EP – description of employee's problems, R – description of HRM method.

Description of employee's problems consists of three descriptors, representing the problem types:

$$EP = \{FP, OP, CSP\}, \tag{6}$$

where FP – set of financial problems; OP – set of organization problems; CSP – set of custom service problems (sets of couples "attribute - value").

Description of HRM method includes four descriptors representing the types of managerial decisions (recommendations):

$$R = \{MOT, TR, CER, DA\}, \tag{7}$$

where MOT – set of motivators; TR – set of trainings; CER – set of certifications; DA – set of disciplinary actions (sets of couples "attribute - value").

Assessments of efficiency of case solution $\{Ef\}$ are determined by Harrington scale [11]: {very high, high, medium, low, very low}.

Structures of case index and case solution based on proposed case representation model are presented in Fig. 1 and Fig. 2.

In Fig. 3 the ontological representation of case structure is shown. The case
structure is defined using developed hierarchy of ontology classes and properties.
The complex case description in form of semantic net is defined on the base of
the object properties in hierarchy of properties. The parametric case description
is defined on the base of the data properties in ontology which allow to associate
with each node of semantic net a set of parameters.

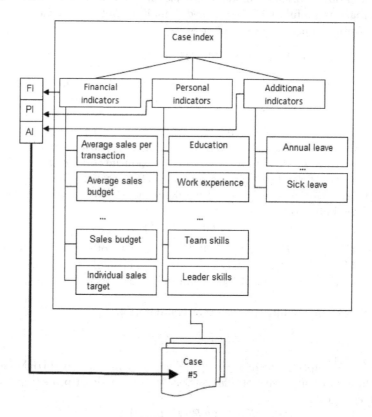

Fig. 1. Case index structure

Thus the developed case representation model based on ontological representation of domain knowledge permits to implement CBR process effectively. We
have developed OWL ontology using ontology editor Protégé 3.5 [16]. The ontology consists of 45 classes, 235 individuals, 32 properties (object properties
and data properties), case base contains 84 real word cases of HR management.
Ontological knowledge base can be extended if necessary.

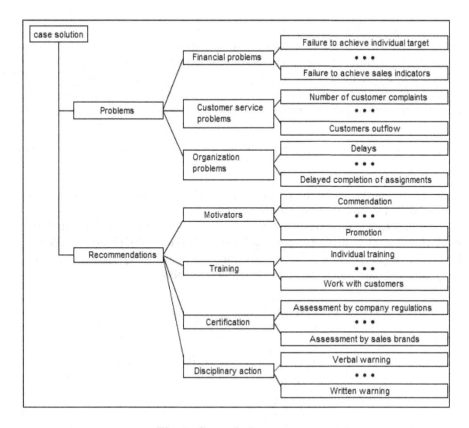

Fig. 2. Case solution structure

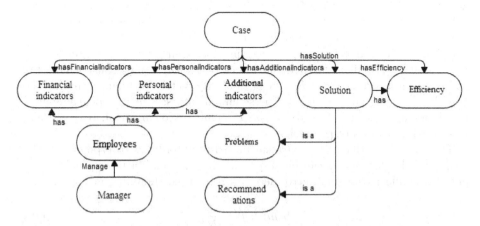

Fig. 3. Ontological representation of case structure

4   Reasoning Mechanism

The proposed ontological knowledge representation model allows supporting all stages of CBR-cycle, but currently we have implemented ontology-based case retrieval. Algorithms of case adaptation and revision are to be developed in future work. So we discuss the developed retrieve algorithm in more detail.

Typically, case retrieve algorithms are based on calculation of a global similarity metric which is determined as follows [12]:

$$S(c_1, c_2) = \sum_{i=1}^{n} w_i S_i(c_1, c_2), \tag{8}$$

where S_i similarity metric by i-th descriptor; W_i – weighting coefficients, they defined using preferences of decision maker.

According to the developed ontological case representation model the CBR-query (Q) is a set of financial, personal and additional key indicators, reflecting the employee effectiveness. The global similarity metric $G(Q, CaseIn)$ between query (Q) and case index $(CaseIn)$ is defined as follows:

$$G(Q, CaseIn) = W_F \sum_{i=1}^{n} wf_i \cdot SimF_i(QF_i, CaseIn_i) +$$

$$+ W_P \sum_{i=1}^{m} wp_j \cdot SimP_j(QP_j, CaseIn_j) +$$

$$+ W_A \sum_{i=1}^{l} wa_k \cdot SimA_k(QA_k, CaseIn_k), \tag{9}$$

where Q – CBR-query; $CaseIn$ – case index; W_F – weighting coefficient, which defines the importance of financial indicators group $\{F_i\}$ for decision maker; W_P – weighting coefficient of personal indicators $\{P_j\}$; W_A – weighting coefficient of additional indicators $\{A_k\}$; wf_i – weighting coefficient of financial indicator F_i; wp_j – weighting coefficient of personal indicator P_j; wa_k – weighting coefficient of additional indicator A_k; $SimF_i$ – local similarity metric for financial indicators; $SimP_j$ – local similarity metric for personal indicators; $SimA_k$ – local similarity metric for additional indicators; n, m, l – numbers of financial, personal and additional indicators respectively.

The local similarity metrics are calculated in accordance to type of case descriptors. The descriptors can be of quantitative and qualitative types. To compute the similarity for qualitative descriptors we used Hamming metric []:

$$Sim(x, y) = \frac{n}{N}, \tag{10}$$

where n – the number of matching descriptors, N – the total number of descriptors being compared which define the samples x and y.

Since for each descriptor comparison is carried out separately, that the metric is calculated as follows:

$$Sim(x, y) = \begin{cases} 1, if\ x = y, \\ 0, if\ x \neq y. \end{cases} \tag{11}$$

The similarity for quantitative descriptors is computed as:

$$Sim(x, y) = 1 - \frac{|x - y|}{norm}, \tag{12}$$

where x and y – descriptor values for query and case, $norm$ – normalization constant which is defined for each descriptor.

The values of weighting coefficients and normalization constants are fixed by experts and then are corrected experimentally.

The retrieval of case which is most similar to the query is reduced to the problem of defining the similarity of ontology fragments, representing query and case index, this problem can be solved using nearest neighbor algorithm (NN algorithm) [13], [14]. We have modified this algorithm in order to improve the efficiency of retrieval. The modification consists in introducing the procedure of prior classification of cases. Cases from case base are classified by the descriptor which has the most informative value for retrieval, and thus the search space is reduced. At that it is assumed that all descriptors can possess the finite set of discrete values.

The developed two-phase retrieve algorithm consists in general of the following steps:

1. Perform the procedure of prior case classification and form the subsets of cases.
   (a) Select classification descriptor.
       i. Define the indicator group with maximum value of weighting coefficient. If there are a few indicator groups with the same weighting coefficients, then the indicator group is chosen at random.
       ii. In selected indicator group define the indicator with minimum number of discrete values. If there are a few indicators with the same number of discrete values, then select the indicator with maximum weighting coefficient. If there are a few indicators with the same weighting coefficients, then the indicator is chosen at random.
   (b) Divide the set of cases using the selected classification descriptor into subclasses.
   (c) If for each formed subset all cases have the same values of classification descriptor, then the classification has successfully completed. If for each formed subset all cases have the same values of classification descriptor, then the classification has successfully completed. Otherwise define new classification descriptor and continue classification.
2. Generate the CBR-query Q.
3. Define the value of classification descriptor in Q.
4. Select the appropriate subset of cases $\{CaseClassification\}$.

5. For each case $Case_i$ of subset $\{CaseClassification\}$ do:
   (a) Compute the local similarity metrics Sim for each indicator groups using formulas (11) and (12).
   (b) Compute the global similarity metric G using formula (9).
6. Define the cases with maximum value of global similarity metric G.

Numerical experiments were performed to evaluate the efficiency of developed algorithm, at that classification was performed by financial indicator "Threshold items per transaction". The results of the numerical experiments are presented in Table 1.

Table 1. Results of numerical experiments

	Experiment 1	Experiment 2
Retrieve algorithm	NN retrieve algorithm	
Similarity metrics	Hybrid similarity metric	
Prior cases classification	no	yes
Number of cases in case base	84	
Number cases in test sample	42	
Absolute number of correct solutions	32	38
Relative number of correct solutions (%)	76	90

Thus it was experimentally proved that application of case classification procedure prior to executing the NNretrieve algorithm increases the number of correct solutions by 14%. Hence it can be claimed that the given two-phase algorithm, based on proposed local and global similarity metrics, is effective and efficient and therefore it can be used for case retrieval in HRIDSS.

5   Intelligent Decision Support System in Human Resource Management

The proposed ontology-based approach to the case retrieval was implemented in a research prototype of intelligent decision support system in human resource management.

The system evaluates the work of employees and generates recommendations to improve their performance, it operates in the following modes: input of indicators; analysis of indicators; generation of recommendations; statistics analysis; generation of reports; ontology editing. The general architecture of the system is shown in Fig. 4 (1 – parameters of the report; 2 – personal data; 3 – analysis results; 4 – request; 5 – solutions; 6 – personal data for analysis; 7 – ontology; 8 – cases).

The CBR-based process of employee performance evaluation in the system consists of two stages. At the first stage the set of employee's problems is generated on the base of key performance indicators. At the second stage the recommendations to improve employee efficiency are formulated. The following additional functionality is implemented in the system: ontology editing, databases management, data analysis and results visualisation.

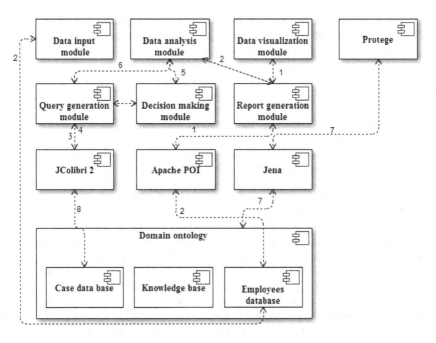

Fig. 4. The general architecture of HRIDSS (components diagram)

CBR cycle was implemented using CBR Framework jColibri 2 [15]. The data storage was implemented in OWL format using framework Apache Jena [17] for management. This variant provides the opportunities for efficient use of standard reasoning mechanisms of description logic (DL) for optimal implementation of CBR cycle.

System testing was performed using the case base which contains the results of staff performance analysis in retail chain L'Étoile in Volgograd during the period of 2010-2012 years. The system decisions coincided with expert decisions on average by 85 percents, it allows to draw a conclusion about the effectiveness of developed research prototype of HRIDSS.

6   Summary

The ontological knowledge representation model was designed in domain of human resource management. The case representation model and ontological knowledge base were developed according to proposed approach to coupling CBR with ontology. The two-phase case retrieve algorithm was designed and implemented within the framework of research prototype of intelligent decision support system in human resource management. The developed prototype of HRIDSS allows improving the quality of managerial decisions in given subject domain.

This paper presents the results of research carried out under the RFBR grant
13-07-00219 "Intelligent support of strategic planning based on the integration
of cognitive and ontological models".

References

1. Denisi, Griffin: Human resource management, 2nd edn. Houghton Mufflin Company, USA (2005)
2. Armstrong, M.: Armstrong's Handbook of Human Resource Management Practice (Google eBook), p. 800. Kogan Page Publishers (2012)
3. Ramli, R., Noah, S.A., Yusof, M.M.: Ontological-based model for human resource decision support system (HRDSS). In: Meersman, R., Dillon, T., Herrero, P. (eds.) OTM 2010. LNCS, vol. 6428, pp. 585–594. Springer, Heidelberg (2010)
4. Dittmann, L., Zelewski, S.: Ontology-based skills management (2004)
5. Bizer, C., et al.: The impact of semantic web technologies on job recruitment processes. In: Wirtschaftsinformatik 2005, pp. 1367–1381 (2005)
6. Gualtieri, A., Ruffolo, M.: An ontology-based framework for representing organizational Knowledge. In: Proceedings of I-KNOW 2005 (2005)
7. Jindal, D., Singla, R.: Decision support system in human resource management (study of HR intelligent techniques). International Journal of Research in IT, Management and Engineering (IJRIME) 1(4), 108–121 (2011) ISSN-2249-1619
8. Chernjahovskaja, L.R.: Podderzhka prinjatija reshenij pri strategicheskom upravlenii predprijatiem na osnove inzhenerij znanij Ufa, AN RB, Gilem, 128 s (2010)
9. Parmenter, D.: Key Performance Indicators (KPI): Developing, Implementing, and Using Winning KPIs, 2nd edn., p. 320. John Wiley & Sons Inc. (2010)
10. Wriggers, P., Siplivaya, M., Zhukova, I., Kapysh, A., Kultsov, A.: Integration of a case-based reasoning and an ontological knowledge base in the system of intelligent support of finite element analysis. CAMES 14, 753–765 (2007)
11. Dementieva, T.A.: Metody ocenki urovnya innovacionnogo potenciala personala na promyshlennyx predpriyatiyax, ekonomika promyshlennosti, 3, s.125–s.129 (2009)
12. Kryukov K. V., Pronina V. A., Pankova L. A., Shipilina L. B.: Mery semanticheskoj blizosti v ontologiyax, Problemy' upravleniya, 2–14 (2010)
13. Varshavskij, P.R., Eremeev, A.P.: Modelirovanie rassuzhdenij na osnove precedentov v intellektualnyx sistemax podderzhki prinyatiya reshenij, Iskusstvenny'j intellekt i prinyatie reshenij, s.45–s.47 (2009)
14. Mitchell, T.M.: Machine Learning. McGraw-Hill Companies Inc., Singapore (1997)
15. jColibri: CBR Framework jColibri 2.1 Tutorial (2014),
    http://gaia.fdi.ucm.es/research/colibri/jcolibri/documentation
16. Protégé 3.5 Tutorial (2014),
    http://protege.stanford.edu/doc/users.html#tutorials
17. Semantic Web Framework Jena (2014),
    http://jena.sourceforge.net/tools.html

Topological Structure for Building Ontology of Energy-Information Method Circuits

Yuliya Lezhnina, Tatyana Khomenko, and Viktoriya Zaripova

Astrakhan Civil Engineering Institute, Department of CAD Systems, Russia
{lejninau,t_v_homenko}@mail.ru, vtempus2@gmail.com

Abstract. The method of constructing the knowledge space is considered. This allowed to structuring of data and knowledge about the objects of design. It is necessary to have for all analogues not just similar, but a unified description equally reflects the essence of the different processes to analyze the different physical processes. Received ontology physical and technical effects, allowing solving the problem of synthesis of technical systems using energy-information method circuits. There proposed to use the apparatus of General topology for structuring ontology of energy-information method circuits in this paper. This approach enables to prove the existence of formalized solution of the problem of synthesis of energy-information method circuits. Informal presentation of topological space as pseudo cell complex, allows us to consider intra chain and inter chain physical differences as insignificant, and distinguish the class of problems.

Keywords: knowledge space, ontology, physical and technical effect, energy-information method circuits, the synthesis of technical systems.

1 Introduction

Functioning of technical systems represents as a complex interaction of a set of various physical effects. The principle of action of technical system presents as the structured set of various effects by the physical nature that provides performance by system of the set function. At the same the processes proceeding in a chain of one physical nature, linked by processes in a chain of other physical nature through one of a set between chain physics and technology effects (PTE).

Catalogs of physical and technical effects, chemical and technical, biotechnical and others effects have been form for tentative classification and application [1, 2]. Attempts to systematize the description of technically significant effects made by many researchers. Recently, based on these researches information systems of support of engineer-inventor's activity used of knowledge bases of physical effects in which physical knowledge is present especially providing more their convenient search and use are created [3]. In [4] it offered to use power information models of circuits of different physical nature based on the phenomenological equations of nonequilibrium thermodynamics. In [5] the generalized theory of converters, which based on the principle of conservation of energy and the principle of reciprocity, is suggest. In [6] attempt of

A. Kravets et al. (Eds.): JCKBSE 2014, CCIS 466, pp. 185–194, 2014.

development of the universal all-system device of modeling based on similarity of mathematical descriptions of processes of different physical nature is made.

For the analysis of various processes by the physical nature, it is necessary to have the uniform description, which is equally capturing the essence of various processes for all analogs. For this purpose, it is necessary to carry out structuring data and knowledge of objects of design [7, 8]. Structuredness of the effect's description and existence in it the formalized part are conditions for realization of synthesis algorithms of the principles of action, and also the mechanisms of information search possessing essentially more ample opportunities in comparison with traditional procedures of search in the name and keywords [9, 10].

This work is devoted to development and research of means of representation of knowledge at the solution of a problem of synthesis of circuits of different physical nature. Creation of ontology of subject domain is chose as means of formalization [11]. Formally, the ontology can be consider as a set of vertex, which submit the scientific and technical characteristics connected by the hierarchical relations. Creation of full and detailed ontology is a labor-consuming task. The solution of this task in many respects is define by as far as the developer of ontology will be equipped with methods and technologies of its formation. It is offer to use the device of the general topology for structurization of ontology of subject domain energy-information method of circuits (EIMC). This work solves the problem of the existence of formal justification for solving the problem of synthesis of energy-information method circuits. For justification of existence of the solution of a problem of synthesis, the device of the general topology is used.

2   Solution

For systematization of knowledge and creation of knowledge space of energy-information method of design of technical systems on information environment of a content imbeds to the model of topological space. Creation of topology of EIMC carried out according to the developed technique. Creation of topology of EIMC carried out according to the developed technique.

Step 1. Transformation of knowledge in knowledge space S by means of the offered operational definitions.

The basic concepts are consider as elements of a final set of M. The discrete metrics $\rho=\{0,$ if $x=y;$ $1,$ if $x{\neq}y\}$ is entered. The ρ metrics is considered in a context of a semantic metrics [12] $\rho:=$ "semantic close" also characterizes force of thematic associative link between analyzed concepts, and it possesses properties, characteristic for a metrics. Result of the entered metrics it split up a set of elements into the L classes of knowledge [13].

Definition 1. Set of classes of the splitting σ under condition $\sigma(l){\cap}\sigma(l)=\varnothing$ with $l{\neq}l'$ where $\sigma(l) \subseteq M$- a subset of elements of the set belonging to a class of knowledge of L is call as knowledge space S of methods of design of technical systems.

Definition 2. Set $x=\{x_l\}$ as point of knowledge space P is called the option of a certain combination of representatives of classes $\sigma(l)$, $x_l \in \sigma(l)$.

According to the entered definitions, space of knowledge is a set of the isolated points, each of which represents a certain set of concepts for realization of knowledge. It is possible to simplify process of the analysis of combinations order due to research of local areas of knowledge space possessing a certain structural property.

Step 2. Use of the operational device of topology for the translation of various methods of design of technical systems in space of knowledge with topological structure [14].

Definition 3. Let P^F is set of classes of splitting $\sigma(1)$ knowledge space of S:

class K: = "basic objects: the minimum system of forming initial concepts",

class K': = "objects-actions: the expanded system of concepts reflecting interrelations between basic objects",

class K'': = "objects-constructs: the resultant system of concepts reflecting interrelations between objects actions", and

class Λ: = "basic operations, the minimum system of necessary operations over concepts".

Collect of subset $\tau_p = \{U\}$ of set P^F, each of which is open and keep properties:

1. $\varnothing, P^F \in \tau_{p^F}$;

2. $\forall \{\tau_{p^F}\} \bigcup_{i=1,n} \{\tau_{p^F}\}_i \in \tau_{p^F}$;

3. $\forall \{\tau_{p^F}\} \bigcap_{i=1,n} \{\tau_{p^F}\}_i \in \tau_{p^F}$,

then collect of subset τ_p called as topology on P^F.

Definition 4. Set of open sets $Bz_p = \{B_P\}$ of topological space of $T(P^F, \tau_p)$ of knowledge of methodologies of design of technical systems is call as base of topology.

Let us consider:

— subset $\Omega^B \subset P^F$ as topological space $T(\Omega^B, \tau_{\Omega b})$, has been described of system open subset of set M, base $Bz_{\Omega b} = \{B_{\Omega b}\} \subset Bz_p$ and topological on: $\tau_{\Omega b} = \{V : V = U \cap \Omega^B, U \in \tau_p\}$, has been induced from P^F;

— subset $\Omega^G \subset P^F$ as topological space $T(\Omega^G, \tau_{\Omega g})$, has been described of system open subset of set M, base $Bz_{\Omega g} = \{B_{\Omega g}\} \subset Bz_p$ and topological on: $\tau_{\Omega g} = \{V : V = U \cap \Omega^G, U \in \tau_p\}$, has been induced from P^F.

We use transformation $i : \Omega^B \subset P^F$ and $j : \Omega^G \subset P^F$, satisfying conditions of an investment of topological spaces (Ω^B, Ω^G in P^F). Space Ω^G и Ω^B «are allocated» for their analysis. As, communication of two topological spaces remains by means of the P^F natural represent in Ω^B and Ω^G, thus from Ω^B and Ω^G the same element from P^F is compared to each element. Therefore, the space of $T(\Omega^G, \tau_{\Omega g})$ of knowledge of a method of design of technical systems is formulated in terms of topology of $T(\Omega^B, \tau_{\Omega b})$ that allows considering recurrence of structure of space of knowledge at its construction.

Step 3. Informal representation of topological space by a pseudo-cellular complex $T_G(P^F, \tau_p)$.

We will consider topological spaces of $T(\Omega^B, \tau_{\Omega b})$ and $T(\Omega^G, \tau_{\Omega g})$, each of which contains the topology constructed on classes of splittings such that $\sigma^B(1) \cup \sigma^G(1) = \sigma(1)$

We will notice that everyone $\sigma^B(l)$, $\sigma^G(l)$ at l=1...4 form a polygon KK′K″Λ. We will call K, K′, K″, Λ equivalent in the accessory to $\sigma^B(l)$ or $\sigma^G(l)$ of energy-information method of design. The polygon KK′K″Λ is homeomorphic the circle with border KK′K″Λ and the projective plane can describe a rectangle differently as a circle at which opposite points of its border are stuck together. Having executed "suitable" gluing together, we will receive the new set that is informally representing topological space of $T(P^F, \tau_p)$ of knowledge of energy-information method of design of technical systems by a cellular complex with association disjoint sets Ω^B and Ω^G, called by cages.

Step 4. Representation of a pseudo-cage $^j\Omega_i$ of a pseudo-cellular complex $T_G(P^F,\tau_p)$ as a topology of the task solution of system analysis in design methods.

According to [14]:

1. reflection f,g:X→Y are called as gomotopny (g ~ f) if there is a homotopy ϕ_t (family of continuous reflections ϕ_r:X→Y, r∈{0,1}, "continuously depending on parameters") such, as ϕ_0=f and ϕ_1=g. The homotopy specifies the equivalence relation between continuous reflection X→Y;
2. topological spaces X And $^!$X are called homotopically equivalent if there are such continuous reflection f:X→$^!$X and g: $^!$X→X that their compositions f ∘ g and g ∘ f are gomotopny to identical reflections. Thus reflections f and g are called as homotopic equivalence;
3. if topological spaces X and $^!$X homotopically equivalent, sets P(A,X) and P(A,$^!$X) are in natural mutual unambiguous compliance, as well as sets P(X,A) and P($^!$X,A).

In the analysis of a content of methods of design of technical systems, we will draw an analogy to the presented definitions, demanding their informal performance.

Considering sets K is "basic objects", and set K″ is "objects – constructs" as topological spaces, respectively K and $^!$K, we will speak about them to "homotopic equivalence" as there are such "continuous reflections" and that their compositions have an appearance: f ∘ f$^!$ and f$^!$ ∘ f. As topological spaces K and $^!$K "homotopically are equivalent", we consider that for topological space Λ of "basic operations" sets couples P(K,Λ) and P($^!$K,Λ) are in natural biunique compliance, as well as sets couples P(Λ,K) and P(Λ,$^!$K). This identification is natural on To in the following sense. Let space $^!$K and reflection f: K→K$^!$be set. Then there is a reflection P($^!$K,Λ)→P(K,Λ) at which reflection g$^!$: $^!$K →Λ compare to reflection g= g$^!$ ∘ f:K→Λ. Similarly, reflection P($^!$K,$^!$Λ)→P(K,$^!$Λ) had been define. Besides, composition with reflections Λ→$^!$Λ and $^!$Λ→Λ, entering definition of "homotopic equivalence" (Λ≈$^!$Λ), define identifications P(K,Λ)→P(K,$^!$Λ) and P($^!$K,Λ)→P($^!$K,$^!$Λ) therefore as a result we receive the chart which causes "topological structure" solutions of a system analysis task (fig. 1).

Definition: The topology of solving the problem of system analysis is oriented graph showing the routing of information flows to solve the problem.

The received chart is commutative, that is, all admissible combinations of ways on her shooters lead to the same result. Movement from a cage (K,Λ) in a cage ($^!$K,$^!$Λ) corresponds to existence of the solution of a problem of synthesis. The return streams cause solution of analysis task.

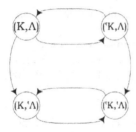

Fig. 1. Topological of a system analysis problem

3   Creation of Space of Knowledge for the Solution of a Problem of Synthesis of Technical Systems

We will apply above-mentioned stages to creation of knowledge space. The problem of creation of full and irrefragable ontology of subject domain of a power-information method of circuits in this paper is not solved. We will be limited to consideration of a problem of synthesis of circuits of a certain physical nature.

At the first stage, the classification problem is solved. Thus in dialogue with the expert the meaningful analysis of subject domain, its elements and communications between them is carried out. Based on expert knowledge in elements space of different physical nature decide on the relation of semantic similarity of elements. It is necessary for further formation of sets of basic objects, basic operations, objects-actions and objects-constructs. The entered metrics ρ on M is used for splitting a set into classes [12]: $K:$ = "basic objects: the minimum system of forming initial concepts", $K':$ = "objects-actions: the expanded system of concepts reflecting interrelations between basic objects", $K'':$ = "objects-constructs: the resultant system of concepts reflecting interrelations between objects actions", $\Lambda:$ = "basic operations, the minimum system of necessary operations over concepts".

At the following stage are found: the set of basic concepts K = {P is impulse, U is tension, Q is charge, I is current, R is resistance, G is conductivity, W is rigidity, C is capacity, L is inductance, a D is deduktivnost, coefficient of PTE}; set of objects actions of K'={I·L=P, U·C=Q, I·R=U, Q·R=P, I'·R=U', K_{in}·B_{in}=B_{out}, K_{in}·B_{in}=P_{out}, K_{in}·B_{in1}· B_{in2} =B_{out}} which represents a set of criteria of EIMC and interchain PTE; set of objects constructs of K''={chain, interchain PTE}; set of the basic operations Λ={·,=} (Table 1).

Let P^F is set of classes of splitting $\sigma(1)$ knowledge space of S:

— class K is "basic objects",
— class K' is "objects – actions",
— class K'' is "objects – constructs", and
— class Λ is "basic operations".

It is obvious that for any concept of energy-information method of design of technical systems there are such open sets from $B_p \in \tau_p$ that the conditions $x \in B_p$ is satisfied. Such sets treat a set K′ of basic objects and Λ of basic operations. Then set of subsets τ_p is called as topology on P^F.

Further, we will carry out group of basic concepts on: set of influence's values, set of reaction's values, set of parameters, set of PTE coefficients. We will note that association of values and parameters by means of basic operations allows to receive criteria of EIMC.

Table 1. Partitioning elements of knowledge into classes K′, K′, K″, Λ

Set of objects-builder K″	Set of operations objects K′	Set of basic concepts of momentum K	Set of basic operations Λ
Set of different physical chain	6 criteria of energy-information method of circuits: $Q \cdot W = U$ $U \cdot G = I$ $I \cdot L = P$ $P \cdot D = I$ $I \cdot R = U$ $U \cdot C = Q$	impulse P, voltage U, charge Q, current I, resistance R, conductance G, stiffness W, capacitance C, inductance L, deductive D	$\Lambda = \{ \cdot, = \}$
Set of inter chain physical and technical effects	Structure of physical and technical effects: $K_{in} \cdot B_{in} = B_{out}$, $K_{in} \cdot B_{in} = P_{out}$, $K_{in} \cdot B_{in1} \cdot B_{in2} = B_{out}$	U, I, N, P, L, D, C, Q, W, R, K_{in} – coefficients of physical and technical effects	$\Lambda = \{ \cdot, = \}$

Association of entrance and output sizes by means of coefficient of PTE allows forming interchain effects. As entrances of PTE can act both influence sizes, and reaction size. The set of basic operations is formed because of the analysis of mathematical representation of criteria of EIMC. The analysis of existing physical and technical effects shows that the parameters defining the physical principle of action of system as a way out can be observed. Such structurization allows describing formally the principle of combining of different physical nature circuits by means of the physical and tech-nical effects transforming values of one physical nature to values of other physical nature (Fig. 2).

Transformation of output values of i-chain in entrance values of (i+1)-chain is made also by means of the chosen basic operations (table 1). Structurization of knowledge space of energy-information method of circuits allowed receiving three-level hierarchy of classes of ontology. The ontology describes communications between elements of knowledge space. Ontology filling with the facts is given in fig. 3.

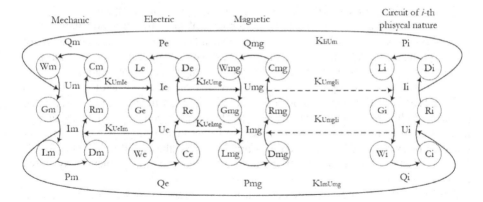

Fig. 2. Bond diagram for *n* of circuits of different physical nature

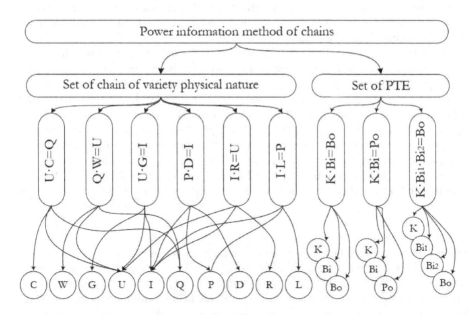

Fig. 3. Fragment of ontology of energy-information method of circuits

4   Discussion

It is obvious that essential distinction of the physical nature inter chain and intra chain dependences becomes not essential when forming structure of ontology using the General topology. The received ontology is reflected in informal representation of topology-ical knowledge space of EIMC by a pseudo-cellular complex. Distinction physical nature of inter chain and intra chain dependences is known. Application of stages of formalization, in particular informal representation of topological space by a pseudo-cellular complex, allows to consider these distinctions as insignificant and to define conditions of solved problems, to allocate a class of solved problems. Application of the requested method allows to get rid of the specification complicating perception of ontology.

Using the device of topology, we will show that the received ontology allows to solve a problem of synthesis of technical solutions. We will define topology of the problem's solution of the system analysis as the focused count reflecting routing of information streams at the solution of a task. Whether this topology is a basis of identification of existence of the solution of a problem of synthesis and is intended for diagnostic of EIMC for the purpose of the answer to a question the problem of synthesis is solved.

For use of the entered topology concept, it is necessary to consider couple $P(A,X)$. We will appoint basic objects $A:=K$ as an element A, basic operations $X:=\Lambda$ as an element X. Then "deformation" of one of elements of this couple when fixing the second element allows passing to objects-actions $P(K, \Lambda) \rightarrow P(K, {}^!\Lambda)$ and, similarly, to objects-constructs $P(K, {}^!\Lambda) \rightarrow P({}^!K, {}^!\Lambda)$. As the chart of topology is commutative, all admissible combinations of ways on her shooters lead to the same result. Alleged transitions are possible at existence of the following binary relations: $\rho 1$ = "configuration", $\rho 2$ = "streamlining", $\rho 3$ = "structure".

In EIMC in the capacity of $\rho 1$ it is possible to consider procedure of selection of basic elements, according to the specification. As a result, the truncated set of the elements participating in a problem of synthesis turns out. In the capacity of $\rho 2$ rules of obtaining one parameters and values from others are considered. In EIMC criteria and PTE turn out. In the capacity of $\rho 3$ rules of use of PTE and receiving circuits act. The set of technical solutions is result. Thus, $\rho 1$, $\rho 2$, $\rho 3$ allow to move the chosen entrance values in the output variable. That testifies to the solution of a problem of synthesis. The entered relations $\rho 1$, $\rho 2$, $\rho 3$ allow to move to the following level of hierarchy (fig. 3).

To confirm that the resulting methodology is operable we used database "Passport physical and technical effects", developed under requirements of EIMC. This automated system is designed for the synthesis of physical principle of elements of control systems and can be used in the early stage in the design of technical devices. Information PTE as passports and their morphological matrices entered into the automated system. Was composed task for synthesis using electrokinetic effects.

As a result, a variety of options of physical principle of actions of sensing elements was obtained. Were selected 10 solutions from the variety, which satisfying the user in the aggregate operational characteristics such as reliability, sensitivity, price, etc. (Figure 4). In receiving the best set of alternatives was manually searched analogues and prototypes. Analogs were found for some variants of physical principle of actions, such as "The electrokinetic converter» Copyright testimony number 866428 (decision number 3), "The electrokinetic angular acceleration sensor" by RF patent number 2018851 C1 (decision number 6), "Electrokinetic sensor" copyright certificate number 232556 (decision number 9)," Electrokinetic converter" Patent for useful model number 63526 (Decision 10).

Fig. 4. 10 selected solutions

5 Conclusion

At synthesis the structure of elements and the rule of their connection among themselves is supposed set. For final models of technical systems, there is a trivial solution of an objective. The trivial method of the decision consists in search of all schemes containing one element, with check of, whether there is among them the scheme realizing an objective, then in search of all schemes containing two elements, etc. However, the trivial method demands a large number of steps and therefore is ineffective. In addition, use of the fastest computers only insignificantly expands limits of its applicability. However, use of ontology allows simplifying a task of the developer of technical systems based on energy-information method of circuits [15]. The introduced method allows to receive demanded ontology and to prove approachability of the solution of a problem of synthesis for energy-information method of circuits.

We will note that the problem of synthesis has some various decisions and, naturally, there is a problem of a choice among them the best. At such approach, the parameter characterizing quality of a technical solution is entered. It can be number of elements, cost, sensitivity of elements, reliability etc. Therefore, the received structure of ontology has to allow expansion for providing a choice of the optimum decision.

References

1. Zaripova, V.: Elaboration of automated system for supporting and training of creative thinking and designing for engineers (INTELLECT - PRO). In: 2nd Advanced Research in Scientific Areas, ARSA (2012),
   http://www.arsa-conf.com/archive/?vid=1&aid=2&kid=60101-45
2. Zaripova, V.: Automatization of engineering activity on the stage of concept design of sensors' elements, CAI "Intellect Pro".Softwareregistrationlicence No2006613930
3. Lunev, A., Petrova, I., Zaripova, V.: Competency-based models of learning for engineers: a comparison. Journal: CEEE European Journal of Engineering Education 38(5), 543–555 (2013)
4. Irina, P., Viktoriya, Z.: Systems of teaching engineering work on base of internet technologies. International Journal Information Technologies and Knowledge 1, 37–43 (2007)
5. Kharkevich, A.A.:Izbrannyetrudy. T.1 –Teoriyaelektroakusticheskikhpreobrazovatelei. Volnovyeprotsessy. Nauka, Moscow (1973) (in Rus.)
6. Volkova, V.N., Voronkov, V.A., Denisov, A.A.: Teoriyasistemimetodysistemnogoanaliza v upravleniiisvyazi. Radio isvyaz', Moscow (1983) (in Rus.)
7. Zaripova, V.M., Petrova,I.Y.: Model razvitiyasredstvavtomatizatsiiinnovatsionnykhprotsessov (Computer Aided Innovation - CAI). Prikaspiiskiizhurnal: upravlenieivysokietekhnologii. 3, 111–130 (2012) (in Rus.)
8. Khomenko, T.V.: Sistemnyepodkhody k analizuizmeritel'nykhustroistv. VestnikAstrakhanskogogosudarstvennogotekhnicheskogouniversiteta. Seriya: Upravlenie, vychislitel'nayatekhnikaiinformatika 1, 88–93 (2009) (in Rus.)
9. Oleg, P., Tatyana, K., Oleg, G.: Technical Solutions for Conceptual Design Search Automation. World Applied Sciences Journal (Information Technologies in Modern Industry, Education & Society) 24, 138–144 (2013)
10. Alla, K., Andrei, K., Aleksander, K.: Intelligent Multi-Agent Systems Generation. World Applied Sciences Journal (Information Technologies in Modern Industry, Education & Society) 24, 98–104 (2013)
11. Irina, K., Valery, S., Gennady, B., Yulia, L.: Modified Algorithm of Information Retrieval Based on Graph Model and Latent Semantic Analysis. World Applied Sciences Journal (Information Technologies in Modern Industry, Education & Society) 24, 250–255 (2013)
12. Vasilev, Y.S., Kozlov, V.N., Maslennikov, A.S.: Kompetentnostnye modeli znanii i soderzhaniya vysshego obrazovaniya. Nauchno-tekhnicheskie vedomosti SPbGPU 66, 7–9 (2008)
13. Digital society laboratory, http://www.digsolab.ru
14. Fomenko, A.T.: Differentsial'naya geometriya i topologiya. Dopolnitel'nye glavy. Izhevskaya tipografiya, Izhevsk (1999) (in Rus.)
15. Vladimir, B., Alla, K., Valery, K.: Development of an Automated System to Improve the Efficiency of the Oil Pipeline Construction Management. World Applied Sciences Journal 24, 24–30 (2013)

Intelligent Decision Support System
for River Floodplain Management

Peter Wriggers[1], Marina Kultsova[2], Alexander Kapysh[2], Anton Kultsov[2],
and Irina Zhukova[2]

[1] Leibniz University Hannover, Hannover, Germany
wriggers@ikm.uni-hannover.de
[2] Volgograd State Technical University, Volgograd, Russia
poas@vstu.ru

Abstract. Decision making in river floodplain management is a complex process that involves many stakeholders and experts. Since stakeholders and experts often pursue mutually exclusive objectives and are often geographically distributed, decision making process takes a long time and not as optimal as it should be. Use of intelligent decision support system (IDSS) allows to decrease the duration of decision making process and to improve the quality and efficiency of decisions. In this paper we present the knowledge-based system for intelligent support of decision making in river floodplain management. This system integrates the case based reasoning (CBR), qualitative reasoning (QR) and ontological knowledge base. Proposed knowledge representation model is formally represented by the OWL DL ontology. For this model we give the descriptions of case retrieval, adaptation and revising algorithms. Designed and implemented CBR-based IDSS for river floodplain management uses object-oriented analysis and Java2 technology.

Keywords: intelligent decision support system, case-based reasoning, qualitative reasoning, ontology, river floodplain management.

1 Introduction

Global change and human induced actions can affect very negatively the fluvial ecosystems. Erosion, loss of organic matter, contamination, sealing, compaction, subsidence, salinisation, loss of biodiversity, vulnerability to floods and landslides are just a few of the hazards that can severely damage fluvial ecosystems and induce severe damage on the filter and transport functions of soils, on the water quality and on the overall ecology of the ecosystems. Prediction, risk assessment and management of these hazards requires a better understanding of the key biogeochemical processes in the fluvial ecosystems and anticipation of the consequences of global change at different scales. The integrated management of fluvial ecosystems to improve floodplain functioning is available on the base of contemporary knowledge based approaches and software tools for support of decision making.

A. Kravets et al. (Eds.): JCKBSE 2014, CCIS 466, pp. 195–213, 2014.

This paper is devoted to the problems of development of intelligent decision support system in floodplain management of Biosphere Reserve Elbe River Landscape in Lower Saxony using case-based reasoning, qualitative reasoning and ontology. Presented IDSS jRamwass was designed and implemented in the framework of EU Project RAMWASS [1].

2   State of the Art

The main component of the conceptual framework for risk-based management of a fluvial ecosystem (and other environmental systems, in general) is an environmental decision support system (EDSS) [2], [3]. It is envisioned that the required DSS should not only estimate management strategies based on todays situation in the ecosystem but also (a) identify the causes of degradation and their actual and future status, (b) improve the existing risk-assessment methodology, (c) develop preventive approach, (d) identify mitigation and remediation measures, (e) provide operational management tools and services and (f) provide knowledge base for the evolution and the implementation of community polices.

The DSS technology was implemented on a number of successful applications in environmental domain, for example, water resources management [4], [5]; waste management [6]; environmental management [3]; flood-risk management [7] and other fields [8], [9]. One of the advanced areas of decision support in environmental field is the use of artificial intelligence technologies and the development of intelligent EDSS [10], [11], [8], [9]. The current trend in the development of IDSS is an integration of different models of knowledge representation and reasoning mechanisms that allows improving the quality and efficiency of the obtained decisions. The works [12], [9], [13], [14], [15] are devoted to study and implementation of relevant integration mechanisms. Our researches are concentrated on the development of CBR-based decision making process supported with QR and ontology in the field of floodplain water management.

3   Domain Knowledge Acquisition and Formalization

The Elbe Riverland covers the area within the borders of the UNESCO Biosphere Reserve Elbe River Landscape in Lower Saxony reaching from Elbe-km 472.5 near Schnackenburg to Elbe-km 569 near Lauenburg. Altitude varies from 5 to 109 m NN. The overall area of the biosphere reserve comprises some 56,760 hectares. It is an important European landscape characterized by regular flooding and agricultural land use, especially after diking the Elbe marshes since medieval times. The area is sparcely populated and nearly no industrialization took place along the Elbe banks mainly because the river had formed the political border between West and East Germany for about 50 years.

The Elbe river landscapes are rather diversified providing excellent environmental conditions for the preservation of rare plant and faunal species. A quite different land use mosaic currently characterizes the floodplains. The landscapes high value for nature conservation is reflected by large areas being designated as Natura 2000 sites according to the European Unions Habitats Directive and Birds Directive. Therefore, management of the floodplains has to take into account not only EUs demands concerning the management and development of a favorable conservation status of the concerned habitat types (like alluvial forests, riparian mixed forests or alluvial meadows of river valleys) and species like beaver (castor fiber) or otter (lutra lutra), but has to deal with conflicting interests between these aims as well. On both sides of the river Elbe dike forelands exist, forming active floodplains. The today's dike line restrains non-flood-affected marshes from the recent floodplains, which cover just 15 percents of the total alluvial area. Both, floodplains and diked marshes, stretch across the glacial valley and are cut through by small tributaries of the Elbe River. Within the marshes sediments of moraines arise, so-called Geest islands or heathlands. Characteristic elements are also dunes deposited parallel to tributaries or at the edges of the glacial valley and heathlands [16].

A decision making in management of Elbe River floodplain is a complex non-algorithmic problem; it involves a lot of stakeholders and experts. Since stakeholders and experts often pursue mutually exclusive objectives and are geographically distributed, decision making process takes a long time and not as optimal as it should be. Use of intelligent decision support system allows to decrease the time for decision making and to improve the quality and efficiency of decisions. The first step in IDSS development is an identification of main stakeholders and their aims. More then 20 stakeholders were identified for Elba test areas by experts, including Administration of the Elbe river biosphere reserve (ABRE), Environmental Ministry of Lower Saxony, Municipalities with areas in the Elbe floodplains, Nature Conservation Associations, etc. These stakeholders have different points of view on the problem and propose mutually exclusive and often inconsistent alternatives. The next step is an identification of global aim and subaims of decision making. The global aim was identified as a conservation and development of the Elbe river floodplains in a state, that the claims of water management, flood protection, agriculture, fishery, nature conservation, tourism and navigation are answered at the best possible rate. The following hierarchy of aims was defined:

1. Flood protection;
   (a) Improvement of runoff conditions by clearing the floodplain from trees and bushes, deepening and/or widening of the runoff system;
   (b) Improvement of ice removal by deepening of the river bed and/or avoidance of obstacles in the high water bed, e.g. bridge piers and trees/bushes;
   (c) Creation of new retention areas, land use planning;
   (d) Strengthening of technical flood protection measures, e.g. heightening and/or broadening of dikes, heightening of walls, strengthening of the upper dike layer against currents and ice drift, countermeasures against water voles, clearing of trees and bushes near the dike line;
   (e) Reduction of financial expenses for flood protection;
2. Agriculture;
   (a) Conservation of floodplain soils and vegetation in a state that profit-yielding agricultural production, which is conformable to law, if possible;

(b) Socioeconomic aims;
3. Fishery;
    (a) Improvement of fish population density [kg/river km];
    (b) Improvement of fish population diversity [species/river km];
4. Nature conservation / ecology;
    (a) Conservation of a flood regime of the Elbe river being typical for this natural area;
    (b) Conservation of a mosaic of habitats being typical for floodplains and of the animal and plant species depending on these habitats;
    (c) Socioeconomic aims;
5. Tourism;
    (a) Use of as large floodplain areas and of as large sections of the Elbe river as possible for recreation purposes;
    (b) Socioeconomic aims;
6. Navigation;
    (a) Definition of design ship sizes and design navigation criteria;
    (b) Offering a sufficiently deep navigation channel;
    (c) Offering a sufficiently wide navigation channel;
    (d) Minimisation of the number of days with low water levels;
    (e) Minimisation of the number of days with ice blockage.

The top level of this hierarchy represents the main aspects of the decision making problem. For aims and subaims listed above the following priorities were defined by experts: first priority - flood protection in case of extreme flood events if life or properties of people are acutely threatened; second priority - (a) flood protection in case of regular flood events, (b) reduction of risks for farmers concerning contaminant input, (c) conservation and development of (semi-) natural situation, (d) optimization of offers for tourists. Also a set of possible control actions on the ecosystem was identified which correspond to hierarchy of aims.

The attributes for description of subaims and actions along with the possible values of the attributes were identified during consultation with experts. These attributes can be classified by their nature and origin. By nature all attributes can be classified as quantitative, qualitative and descriptive, by origin - as measured, calculated, on-line and predefined. The values of the on-line attributes are measured by sensors in real time, predefined attributes are valued from information about ecosystem in whole(e.g. map of animals distribution, information about legal prescriptions). Fragment of description of actions, attributes and attribute values for the subaim "Strong technical flood protection measures" is presented in Table 1.

The analysis of elicited domain knowledge allowed to reveal their main features: (a) description of a decision making problem has a complex and variable structure; (b) components of the problem and solution descriptions can significantly differ in their importance; (c) there are multiple logical relations between components of problem description; (d) both qualitative and quantitative parameters, which should be interpreted in a context-dependent way (not by absolute value), are taken into account; (e) knowledge about previously solved problems which are similar to the current one is actively used while decision making.

Table 1. Fragment of problem description

Subaim: Strong technical flood protection measures				
Subaim attributes	Attribute values	Control actions	Effect permanence	Seasonality
Height of dikes	*Good:* $H > 0, 7m$ *Middle:* $0, 2m \leqslant H \leqslant 0, 7m$ *Bad:* $H < 0, 2m$	Increase height of dikes	Long-term	Ice-free period
Width and slope angles of dikes	*Good:* inner and outer slope angle greater or equal 1:3 *Middle:* inner slope in between 1:3 and 1:1,5; outer slope in between 1:3 and 1:2 *Bad:* inner slope less than 1:1,5; outer slope less than 1:2	Increase width of dikes	Long-term	Ice-free period
Strength of the upper dike layer (revetment) against currents and ice drift	*Good:* grass layer with dense cover; at bottleneck situations dike enforced with revetment/paving *Bad:* grass layer with sparse cover; at bottleneck situations no revetment	Sow grass	Short- to middle-term	Spring, summer, autumn
		Change grazing or mowing frequency	Short- to middle-term	Spring, summer, autumn
		Exchange grass layer for concrete or paving layer	Short- to middle-term	Spring, summer, autumn
Damage of dikes by animals or mechanical impacts	*Good:* no damages at the dike line per meter dike length *Middle:* small number of damages at the dike line per meter dike length *Bad:* Many damages at the dike line per meter dike length	Fix smaller damages	Short- to middle-term	After flooding season
		Implement measures to avoid new damages	Short- to middle-term	After flooding season
		Rebuild the dike	Long-term	After flooding season

Based on these conclusions, ontological knowledge representation model, case-based reasoning and qualitative reasoning can be considered as an appropriate AI technologies for the intelligent decision making in floodplain management. While CBR is a leading reasoning mechanism, QR and ontology carry out the knowledge-based support of the main stages of CBR.

4 Concept of CBR-Based Decision Making

The processes involved in CBR can be represented by a schematic cycle. Aamodt and Plaza [17] have described CBR typically as a cyclical process comprising the four REs: retrieve the most similar case(s); reuse the case(s) to attempt to solve the problem; revise the proposed solution if necessary, and retain the new solution as a part of a new case. A new problem is matched against cases in the case base and one or more similar cases are retrieved. A solution suggested by the matching cases is then reused and tested for success. Unless the retrieved case is a close match the solution will probably have to be revised producing a new case that can be retained.

CBR approach is aimed for avoidance of first order knowledge use for problem solving, so support of CBR with ontology and other reasoning mechanism such as QR could be interpreted as disloyalty to grounding principles of CBR. But it is not completely correct and ontologies and QR are used in various ways to make accurate and useful CBR possible [18]. Generally case base does not comprise all knowledge required for correct solution of a new problem, but ontology allows to formalize domain knowledge and to reuse it for problem solving. Also ontology allows achieving semantic interoperability between case descriptions from different sources. Ontology could define framework for case description which allows simplifying case retrieving stage of CBR process. And finally it is recognized that general domain knowledge is necessary at the case adaptation stage. The case revision stage can be supported with qualitative reasoning on the base of qualitative model of case. This model captures qualitative dependencies between components of case solution and case index, and allows assessing proposed solution in terms of behaviour of case index attributes.

Employment of ontology coupled with a CBR process is possible in few ways [12], [9], we implemented a model which allows to use ontology for supporting all stages of CBR process:

- ontology defines case representation model and sets of parameters for case description with their possible values. Ontology contains information about the aims of stakeholders, aim attributes and their possible values. Ontology defines foundation for case description, and it can be used as a knowledge base for subsystem of automated case formulation;
- if the user has defined case index incompletely, ontology can be applied at the stage of case retrieval for redefinition of the case. Also the algorithm of similarity measure calculation depends heavily on the case representation model, which is defined by ontology;
- ontology is used at the stage of case adaptation to make decision about alternative values of parameters if adaptation algorithm has proposed a few equivalent choices, for example, a few possible values for one attribute;
- ontology contains qualitative model of case and consistency rules which can be used at the stage of case revision. Consistency rules define infeasible combinations of parameter values for different aspects of case description.

The general scheme of the integration of CBR and ontology is shown in Fig. 1. Ontology as a case representation model describes case as a set of individuals and relations. Ontology as a domain knowledge base represents domain knowledge in form of DL-rules which are used by procedures of knowledge inferring. Ontology as a case base stores cases as a part of domain knowledge. And finally, ontology stores case qualitative model as a set of individuals and relations. This scheme extends the approach to intelligent support of finite element analysis developed by the authors in works [19], [20], [21].

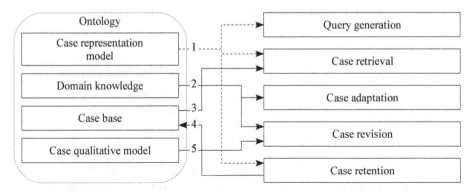

Fig. 1. General schema of integration of CBR, QR and ontology

In Fig. 1 we used the following notation: 1 - case structure, 2 - formalized domain knowledge, 3 - stored case, 4 - new case, 5 - qualitative simulation results. Modified CBR-cycle supported with QR and ontology is presented in Fig. 2.

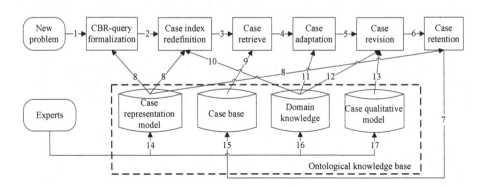

Fig. 2. Modified CBR-cycle supported with QR and ontology

In Fig. 2: 1 - problem description, 2 - CBR-query, 3 - case index, 4 - retrieved cases, 5 - adapted solution, 6 - revised solution, 7 - new case, 8 - case structure, 9 - stored cases, 10 - expert rules, 11 - adaptation rules, 12 - consistency rules, 13 - qualitative simulation results, 14 - domain conceptualization, 15 - case descriptions, 16 - general domain knowledge, 17 - qualitative dependencies between components of case description.

So according to the proposed concept the CBR process is strongly supported with ontology and qualitative reasoning at all stages, such "knowledge-intensive" approach allows to improve the accuracy and correctness of the obtained CBR-solutions.

5   Ontological Knowledge Representation Model

The ontological knowledge representation model on the one hand should have extensive descriptive capabilities to represent domain knowledge of different nature. On the other hand it should provide opportunities for easy knowledge processing and implementing the case-based, rules-based and qualitative reasoning. The following ontology model satisfies these requirements:

$$ONT = <DO, CS, QM>, \tag{1}$$

where DO – domain ontology, CS – case structure, QM – case qualitative model.

The domain ontology contains concepts and relations of the problem domain and specific components for supporting CBR and QR:

$$DO = \{OB, ATT, DAT, ACT, CR, AR, QD, REL\}, \tag{2}$$

where $OB = \{OB_1, OB_2, ..., OB_n\}$ – set of stakeholders' objectives;

$ATT = \{ATT_1 \cup ATT_2 \cup ... \cup ATT_n\}$ – set of attributes which are used for problem description, each subset ATT_i corresponds to objective OB_i;

DAT – set of ontology domains, which define the space of attribute values;

CR – set of consistency rules; AR – set of adaptation rules;

$ACT = \{ACT_1 \cup ACT_2 \cup ... \cup ACT_n\}$ – set of actions, each subset ACT_i corresponds to objective OB_i;

QD – set of qualitative dependencies between attribute values, $QD : ATT \times ATT \rightarrow \{I+, I-, P+, P-, \varnothing\}$, where $I+$ – positive direct influences, $I-$ – negative direct influences, $P+$ – positive indirect influences, $P-$ – negative indirect influences;

$REL = \{REL_1, REL_2, ..., REL_k\}$ – set of relations between ontology concepts.

The case description consists of three main parts:

$$CS = \{P, S(P), CREL\}, \tag{3}$$

where P – problem description (also can be referred as a case index);

$S(P)$ – problem solution description as a set of actions which were applied;

$CREL = \{CREL_1, CREL_2, ..., CREL_8\}$ – set of case relations. Set $CREL$ contains the following relations:

$CREL_1$ – relation $hasInitialState$,

$CREL_2$ – relation $hasActionSet$,

$CREL_3$ – relation $hasResultState$,

$CREL_4$ – relation $hasCausalState$,

$CREL_5$ – relation $hasEffectiveState$,

$CREL_6$ – relation $hasAssessmentSet$,

$CREL_7$ – relation $hasCertainAction$,
$CREL_8$ – relation $hasCertainAssessment$.
The problem description is defined as:

$$P = \{DI, DR\}, \tag{4}$$

where DI – description of initial state, DR – description of result state after action application.

$$DI = \{SI, ASSI, PREF\}, \tag{5}$$

where SI – description of case in initial state (set of couples "attribute - value");
$ASSI = \{ASSI_1, ASSI_2, ..., ASSI_n\}$ – set of qualitative assessments of initial state from the different points of view, each of the assessments $ASSI_i$ corresponds with objective OB_i;
$PREF = \{PREF_1, PREF_2, ..., PREF_n\}$ – set of preferences of decision maker, $PREF_i$ is an assessment of significance of objective OB_i for decision maker.

$$DR = \{SR, ASSR\}, \tag{6}$$

where SR – description of case in result state (set of couples "attribute - value");
$ASSR = \{ASSR_1, ASSRI_2, ..., ASSR_n\}$ – set of qualitative assessments of result state from the different points of view, each of the assessments $ASSR_i$ corresponds with objective OB_i.
The problem solution description is defined as:

$$S(P) = \{Action_1, Action_2, ..., Action_m\}, \tag{7}$$

where $Action_j$ – specific action.
The case qualitative model captures qualitative dependencies between components of case solution and case index and is defined as follows [22]:

$$QM = \{BBC, AC\}, \tag{8}$$

where BBC – set of QM model primitives; AC – set of compound components composed of the primitives.

$$BBC = \{SB, BB, AB\}, \tag{9}$$

where SB – set of structural primitives; BB – set of primitives describing behaviour of the model; AB – set of premises defining the applicability of compound components of model.

$$SB = \{SE, SC\}, \tag{10}$$

where $SE \subset (OB \cup ATT \cup ACT)$ – entity hierarchy reflecting the concept hierarchy of the problem domain; SC – set of relations between entities.

$$BB = \{QU, QS, D\}, \tag{11}$$

where $QU \subset ATT$ – set of quantities; $QS \subset DAT$ – set of quantity spaces; $D \subset QD$ – set of causal relations between quantities, D has the following range of values $\{I+, I-, P+, P-\}$.

$$AC = \{SF, PF, SC\}, \tag{12}$$

where SF – set of static model fragments; PF – set of process model fragments; SC – set of simulation scenarios.

The knowledge representation model described above was designed and implemented as OWL DL ontology. Developed hierarchy of ontology classes and properties is used to define the case description. The object properties in hierarchy of properties allow to define the complex case description in form of semantic net. The data properties in ontology allow to associate with each node of semantic net a set of parameters and thus define the parametric case description.

The fragment of ontological representation of case structure is presented in Fig. 3.

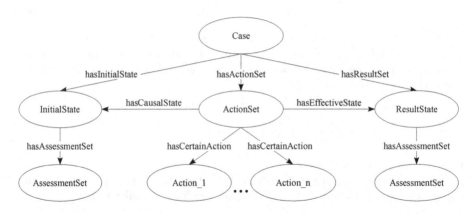

Fig. 3. Fragment of ontological representation of case structure

Ontology classes and properties are of two types - basic and extensible. Extensible classes and properties can be inherited and define the case structure for specific decision making problem. Thus, using different ontologies with the same structure we can represent cases for different decision making problems.

The case in the context of considered subject domain is a decision making situation for reach of the river bank line and the adjacent area (e.g. flood and the elimination of its consequences) which occurred in the past. For this situation the following information is known: a description of the problem situation; its assessment in terms of aspects of decision making and priorities of decision makers; a description of the taken measures (control actions) and their results; assessment of the resulting state of the ecosystem.

The fragment of ontological representation of real-world case in the framework of proposed case representation model is shown in Fig. 4.

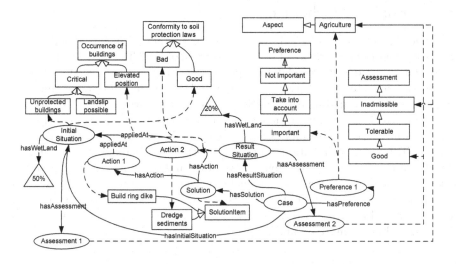

Fig. 4. Fragment of ontological representation of case

In terms of the proposed ontological model, qualitative model is represented as follows. Elements of BBC define the taxonomy used for building the case description. Elements of SB define the concepts of the problem domain connected with case description: case, initial state, action, assessments of states, aspects; as well as relations between these concepts. Elements of BB define the set of quantities with their domains, in other words, elements of BB use the taxonomy defined by components SI and SR of the ontological model:

$$BB = SI \cup SR. \tag{13}$$

SF defines the affiliation of the quantities with the set of stakeholders objectives of case description along with interdependence between the quantities:

$$SF : QU \rightarrow OB, QU \times QU \rightarrow \{I+, I-, P+, P-, \varnothing\}. \tag{14}$$

PF defines causal relations between the quantities and the actions or other quantities:

$$PF : (A \cup QU) \times QU \rightarrow \{I+, I-, P+, P-, \varnothing\}. \tag{15}$$

Qualitative simulation Sc produces result state for the initial state after the action application - $Sc : S(DI) \rightarrow DR$.

Qualitative modeling and simulation were performed with use of Garp3 system [22].

The developed ontology consists of more then 300 named classes and 50 properties (object, datatype and annotation properties), case base contains 40 real-word cases.

6   Reasoning Mechanism

The following algorithms were developed to operate on the suggested ontological knowledge representation model in the framework of the CBR mechanism implementation: CBR-query formulation support algorithm; case retrieval algorithm which uses class (concept)-based similarity (CBS) computation algorithm and property (slot)-based similarity (SBS) computation algorithm; case adaptation algorithm which uses domain knowledge in form of DL rules; case revising algorithm which uses the results of qualitative simulation on the case qualitative model. CBR-query formulation support algorithm allows reducing the amount of the routine work needed to input information and enforcing knowledge representation model integrity as well as redefining the case index with use of general domain knowledge in form of DL rules. Developed case retrieval, adaptation and revision algorithms are based on "knowledge-intensive" approach so we discuss these algorithms in more detail.

6.1   Case Retrieval Algorithms

The case retrieval algorithm which is the key part of the CBR reasoner is based on the global similarity metric Sim :

$$Sim = \left[\sum W_i \cdot S_i^2 \right]^{1/2},\qquad(16)$$

where S_i – similarity metric by i-th descriptor; W_i – weighting coefficients, they defined using preferences of decision maker.

Each descriptor can be of one of following types: real number, interval, date, list, taxonomy, qualitative variable. To compute the similarity for real numbers we used the following formula:

$$S_N = 1 - \frac{\left| p'_{iC} - p'_{iQ} \right|}{100},\qquad(17)$$

where p'_{iC} and p'_{iQ} – values of i-th parameter for case and query normalized to [0;100] interval.

The similarity for intervals is computed as:

$$S_R\left(C,Q\right) = \frac{2 \cdot Inter}{L_C + L_Q},\qquad(18)$$

where L_C – length of C-interval, L_Q – length of Q-interval, $Inter$ – length of C and Q intersection.

To compute the similarity for dates, we employed the principle of division of calendar year at the seasons with length GS, short-term periods with length PS and medium-term periods with length PM, and proposed the following similarity metric:

$$S_D\left(D_C, D_Q\right) = \begin{cases} DV_1, if\ |D_C - D_Q| \leq PS, \\ DV_2, if\ PS < |D_C - D_Q| \leq PM, \\ DV_3, if\ D_C\ and\ D_Q \in GS_i, \end{cases}\qquad(19)$$

where D_C – value of case descriptor, D_Q – value of corresponding query descriptor, DV_1, DV_2, DV_3 – expert constants.

To compute the similarity for lists the following metric is used:

$$S_E(D_C, D_Q) = \begin{cases} 1, if\ D_C = D_Q, \\ 0, if\ D_C \neq D_Q. \end{cases} \tag{20}$$

To compute the similarity for taxonomies and qualitative variables which are represented as a taxonomy in ontology we used the vector space model (VSM). Within this model each individual of ontology i is represented by a n-dimensional vector c_i, components of this vector correspond to ontology concepts C_j. If the individual i is subsumed by a concept C_j, the corresponding vector component is assigned 1, otherwise 0. CBS is then computed using the well-known cosine measure [23] (the cosine of the angle between the vectors of individuals):

$$CBS = \frac{c_1 * c_2}{\|c_1\| * \|c_2\|}, \tag{21}$$

where c_1, c_2 vectors which represent individuals i_1, i_2 respectively.

To compute the similarity for descriptors connected with case individual by object properties we developed the modified SBS algorithm (slot based similarity). This algorithm is based on graph representation of case and CBR-query, and definition of similarity as a maximum common subgraph of these two graphs. In order to calculate SBS, the recursive depth-first search is performed which begins from root node. The main idea of modified SBS algorithm is to find not general matching between components of cases but maximal projection of stored case components into components of query. The modified SBS algorithm differs from the known ones [17], [24] by method of computing the average slot based similarity. SBS takes into consideration not only similarity between graph nodes but also similarity between edges. SBS is computed using only already matched components of query and stored case by following formula:

$$SBS(i_1, i_2) = \frac{CBS(i_1, i_2)}{1 + k_2/k_1} + \frac{\sum_{r_2 \in R_2}^{r_1 \in R_1} \max_{i_{1,2} \in r_{1,2}(i_{1,2})} \left(CBS(r_1, r_2) \cdot SBS\left(i_1^-, i_2^-\right)\right)}{(1 + k_1/k_2) \cdot (N + M)}, \tag{22}$$

where R_1 and R_2 – sets of ontology relations for individuals i_1 and i_2; $r_1(i_1)$ – set of individuals connected with individuals i_1 by relation r_1; N – number of matched nodes; M – number of unmatched nodes of query graph; k_1 and k_2 – weights.

One feature of the domain is that for each stored case its description contains the result state after action application. Thus, the difference of assessments of the initial and final states of the case can be used as an effectiveness criterion E. It allows evaluating the utility of the case solution for the CBR-query in two ways: (a) in terms of similarity of initial states of stored case and query; (b) in terms of efficiency of proposed actions taking into account the decision maker's preferences:

$$E = \frac{\sum_{i=1}^{N} diff(ASSI_i, ASSR_i) \cdot W_{ASSI_i}}{\sum_{i=1}^{N} W_{ASSI_i}}, \tag{23}$$

where E – effectiveness metric, $ASSI_i$ – assessment of case initial state by i-th aspect, $ASSR_i$ – assessment of case result state by i-th aspect, $diff$ – difference between assessments, W_{ASSI_i} – weight factor of i-th aspect. The following formula was proposed to calculate $diff$:

$$diff\,(ASSI_i, ASSR_i) = CBS\,(ASSR_i, A_b) - CBS\,(ASSI_i, A_b) \qquad (24)$$

Thus metric E represents the level of relevance of the case C solution for the CBR-query Q. Metrics Sim shows how much the case C solution needs to be adapted in order to satisfy the query. Since adaptation result depends heavily on domain knowledge, metric E is more preferable than metric Sim if their values do not differ much.

The main steps of the developed retrieve algorithm are as follows:

1. Define preferences of decision maker $PREF_i$ and weighting factors W_{A_i};
2. Compute Sim and E for each case C_j from case base C_B;
3. Form empty result vector SC: $SC_j = (C_j, v_j)$, where v_j - confidence factor for C_j;
4. Form set of cases C_p for which $\forall C_j \in C_P : Sim\,(C_j, Q) > Sim_{MIN} \cap E\,(C_j, Q) > 0$, where $Sim_{MIN} = \min\limits_{C_j \in C_B} Sim\,(C_j, Q)$;
5. Add to list SC not more then M pairs (C_j, v_j), for which $C_j : C_j \in C_P \cap E\,(C_j) = E_{MAX}$, state $v_j = E\,(C_j)$;
6. Add to list SC not more then M pairs (C_j, v_j), for which $C_j : C_j \in C_P \cap Sim\,(C_j, Q) = Sim_{MAX}$, state $v_j = SIM\,(C_j, Q)$.

Vector SC is the output of retrieve algorithm.

6.2   Case Adaptation Algorithm

The knowledge-intensive adaptation methods can be broadly classified into the following three categories [25], [26]: substitution methods, transformation methods and ranking retrieved cases. We used the multistage transformational adaptation on the basis of general domain knowledge about dependencies between individual control actions, this approach allows combining the control actions to elaborate the most effective complex of measures.

Developed case adaptation algorithm uses a table of action interference and a path of case similarity computation in addition to the expert adaptation rules. Use of the similarity path allows defining the usability of each of individual actions for problem situation stated in query and selecting the most effective actions. The table of action interference allows to eliminate negative mutual influences between actions and to select actions which combination produces maximal cumulative effect.

The following actions can be used during adaptation procedure: the components of solutions of retrieved similar cases; the components of solution obtained by means of inferring on the ontology in accordance with adaptation rules. The table of action interference MI has dimensionality $K \times K$ (where $K = |\overline{Ac}|$), element MI_{ij} possesses the value 1, if actions Ac_i and Ac_j when used together give a positive cumulative effect, and value (-1) — in case of negative cumulative effect. Thus, the value of the function $E(Ac_i)$ can be considered as a lower bound of the effectiveness metric of acceptable solutions, and the value of the function $E(Ac_i \cup Ac_j : MI_{ij} > 0)$ — an upper bound.

The main steps of the developed adaptation algorithm are as follows:

1. Form empty list $AcSC$ of pairs $\{Ac, va\}$ where Ac - action, va - confidence factor;
2. For each pair $\{C_j, v_j\}$ from SC do:
   (a) For each action Ac_i from C_j add pair $\{Ac_i, v_j\}$ to $AcSC$ list (i.e. add actions from retrieved cases with confidence factor v);
3. Perform reasoning on ontology;
4. For each action AcR inferred in accordance with adaptation rules, add pair $\{AcR, 1\}$ to $AcSC$ list;
5. If list $AcSC$ is empty, when case base and ontology is not applicable to current DSS-query, adaptation is unsuccessful; otherwise
6. Sort list $AcSC$ by descendant of confidence factor va;
7. Remove incongruous actions from $AcSC$ list:
   (a) Set $i = 0$;
   (b) For each $|AcSC| > j > i$ remove pair $\{Ac_j, va\}$ from $AcSC$ if $MI_{ij} = -1$;
   (c) Set $i = i + 1$;
   (d) If $|AcSC| > i$ then go to step (b)
8. Form case solution list AcS that consists of actions Ac_i from list $AcSC$.

The case solution list AcS is the output of adaptation algorithm.

6.3 Case Revising Algorithm

If a case solution generated by the adaptation stage is not correct, it should be revised, this stage consists of two tasks: evaluation of the case solution generated by adaptation, if successful, retain new case; otherwise repair the case solution using domain-specific knowledge [17]. For evaluation of adapted solution we propose to use the consistency rules, for solution repair - case qualitative model and qualitative simulation. The revision procedure uses effectiveness $E(C)$ as a criterion of success. The case revision algorithm implementing such approach consists in general of the following steps:

1. Generate new case C as an individual of "Case" class which has index Ind coincident with CBR-query Q and solution Acs;
2. Perform the procedure "classify taxonomy" on ontology;
3. If case C was classified as individual of "inconsistency" class (in accordance with consistency rules), then revision is unsuccessful, remove case C;
4. Simulate the qualitative model for case C and define assessment A_i^- for obtained result state;
5. Compute $E(C)$ using (23);

6. If $E(C) < 0$, then revision is unsuccessful, remove case C;
7. If $0 \leqslant E(C) < E^-$, where E^- is average E-value for stored cases, then revision is quasi-successful, use solution Acs for current problem, but don't retain case C in case base;
8. If $E(C) \geqslant E^-$, then revision is successful, retain case C in case base.

Developed algorithms for case retrieve, adaptation and revision were implemented within the framework of intelligent decision support system jRAMWASS.

7   Intelligent Decision Support System jRAMWASS

The CBR-based IDSS jRAMWASS for floodplain management of Elbe Riverland was designed using object-oriented analysis and design technologies and UML modeling language. The Java2 technology was selected for implementation of the system, because it facilitates both fast and convenient prototyping the cross-platform system. Three-level architecture Data-Logic-Interface was used for system implementation. The general architecture of intelligent decision support system jRAMWASS is presented in Fig. 5.

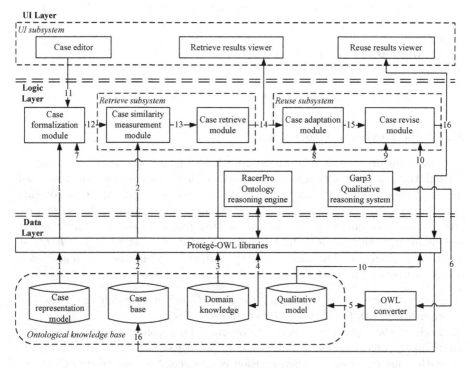

Fig. 5. System architecture

In Fig. 5 the following notation is used: 1 - case structure, 2 - stored cases, 3 - domain knowledge in form of DL-rules, 4 - asserted and inferred knowledge, 5 - case qualitative model in OWL-format, 6 - case qualitative model in GARP3-format, 7 - redefinition rules, 8 - adaptation rules, 9 - consistency rules, 10 - qualitative simulation results, 11 - problem description, 12 - CBR-query (case index), 13 - values of similarity measures, 14 - set of similar cases, 15 - adapted solution, 16 - new case.

The data layer contains classes for ontology access and provides facilities for such operations on classes and individuals of ontology as creation, deletion, modifying, linking, creation of complex classes hierarchy and individuals tree. The logic layer contains classes implementing the algorithms of cases retrieval, adaptation and revising for CBR cycle. The interface layer contains classes for graphical user interface implementation.

The process of decision making using developed IDSS jRAMWASS consists of the following main steps:

1. Formalization of problem description – identifying the aim hierarchy, aim attributes and values, priorities of decision maker.
2. Formulation of CBR-query in framework of case representation model.
3. Redefinition of CBR-query using inference on expert rules and generation of case index (description of problem situation).
4. Retrieve of the similar cases in case base using retrieve algorithm based on CBS and SBS similarity metrics.
5. Selection of the relevant cases for reuse.
6. Adaptation of the selected cases' solutions to the new problem using adaptation algorithm based on inference on adaptation rules.
7. Revision of the new adapted solution using simulation on case qualitative model and inference on consistency rules.
8. Generation of a new case for the solved problem in framework of case representation model.
9. Retention of the new case in the case base for further use.

System testing was performed using the case base which contains the results of observations of the test area Elbe Riverland during the period of 2006-2008 years. To assess the validity of decision making we compared the obtained decisions with the expert decisions with the same input data.The test results showed that the system decisions coincided with expert decisions on average by 88 percents. This fact allows to draw a conclusion that developed system is an effective tool for intelligent support of decision making in floodplain water management.

8 Summary

The concept of intelligent support of decision making in river floodplain management was proposed on the base of CBR coupled with QR and ontology. The ontological model for knowledge representation was developed including case representation model, domain ontology and case qualitative model. In detail CBR reasoning algorithms, including case search and retrieval algorithms, case adaptation and revision algorithms were designed and implemented within the framework of proposed concept. The intelligent decision support system jRAMWASS in water management of Biosphere Reserve Elbe River Landscape in Lower Saxony was developed on the basis of proposed models and algorithms. The system was implemented using object-oriented analysis and Java2 technology.

Acknowledgments. The authors would like to thank Bärbel Koppe (LUG), Tobias Keienburg (ABRE) and Frank Krüger (LUG) for participation as experts in design and testing of jRAMWASS.

References

1. RAMWASS, http://www.cimne.com/ramwass/
2. Matthies, M., Guipponi, C., Ostendorf, B.: Environmental decision support systems: Current issues, methods and tools. Environmental Modeling and Software 22, 123–127 (2007)
3. McIntosh, B.S., et al.: Environmental decision support systems (EDSS) development Challenges and best practices. Environmental Modelling and Software 26(12), 1389–1402 (2011)
4. Pallottino, S., Sechi, G.M., Zuddas, P.: A DSS for water resources management under uncertainty by scenario analysis. Environmental Modelling and Software 20(8), 1031–1042 (2005)
5. Burlekamp, J., Lautenbach, S., Graf, N., Reimer, S.: Integration of MONERIS and GREAT-ER in the decision support system for the German Elbe river basin. Environmental Modeling and Software 22, 239–247
6. Karmperis, A.C., et al.: Decision support models for solid waste management:Review and game-theoretic approaches. Waste Management. Elsevier, Amsterdam (2013)
7. Ramflood Decision support system for risk assessment and management of floods. Project of the IST Programme of the EC. IST IST-2001-37581 (2005), http://www.cimne.com/ramflood
8. Cabanillas, D., Llorens, E., Comas, J., Poch, M.: Implementation of the STREAMES Environmental Decision-Support System. In: iEMSs 2004 Artificial Intelligence Techniques for Integrated Resource Management, Osnabruck, Germany, pp. 33–39 (2004)
9. Ceccaroni, L.: Integration of a rule-based expert system, a case-based reasoner and an ontological knowledge-base in the wastewater domain. BESAI 8, 1–10 (2000)
10. Cortes, U., Sánchez-Márre, M., Ceccaroni, L., R-Roda, I.: Artificial intelligence and environmental decision support systems. Applied Intelligence 13, 77–91 (2000)
11. Sánchez-Márre, M., et al.: Intelligent environmental decision support systems. Environmental modelling, software and decision support: state of the art and perspectives, pp. 119–144. Elsevier, Amsterdam (2008)
12. Marling, C., Rissland, E., Aamodt, A.: Integrations with case-based reasoning. The Knowledge Engineering Review 13, 21–26 (2005)
13. Aarts, R.J., Rousu, J.: Qualitative knowledge to support reasoning about cases. In: Leake, D.B., Plaza, E. (eds.) ICCBR 1997. LNCS, vol. 1266, pp. 489–498. Springer, Heidelberg (1997)

14. An, A., Cercone, N., Chan, C.: Integrating rule induction and case-based reasoning to enhance problem solving. In: Leake, D.B., Plaza, E. (eds.) ICCBR 1997. LNCS, vol. 1266, pp. 499–508. Springer, Heidelberg (1997)
15. Prentzas, J., Hatzilygeroudis, I.: Categorizing approaches combining rule-based and case-based reasoning. Expert Systems 24(2), 97–122 (2007)
16. Sánchez, M., Bladé, E., Avci, B., Koppe, B.: Report on available EO and on-site environmental data for the three testing sites chosen (D2.1).RamWass Consortium (2007)
17. Aamodt, A., Plaza, E.: Case-Based Reasoning: Foundational Issues, Methodological Variations, and System Approaches. AI Communications 7(1), 39–59 (1994)
18. Prentzas, J., Hatzilygeroudis, I.: Combinations of Case-Based Reasoning with Other Intelligent Methods. International Journal of Hybrid Intelligent Systems - CIMA 6(4), 189–209 (2009)
19. Wriggers, P., Siplivaya, M., Zhukova, I., Kapysh, A., Kultsov, A.: Integration of a case-based reasoning and an ontological knowledge base in the system of intelligent support of finite element analysis. CAMES 14, 753–765 (2007)
20. Wriggers, P., Siplivaya, M., Joukova, I., Slivin, R.: Intelligent support of engineering analysis using ontology and case-based reasoning. Eng. Appl. of AI 20(5), 709–720 (2007)
21. Wriggers, P., Siplivaya, M., Joukova, I., Slivin, R.: Intelligent support of the preprocessing stage of engineering analysis using case-based reasoning. Eng. Comput (Lond.) 24(4), 383–404 (2008)
22. Bredeweg, B., Linnebank, F., Bouwer, A., Liem, J.: Garp3 - Workbench for Qualitative Modelling and Simulation. Ecological Informatics 4(5-6), 263–281 (2009)
23. Gonzales-Calero, P., Diaz-Agudo, B., Gomez-Albarran, M.: Applying DLs for retrieval in case-based reasoning. Applied Intelligence 22, 125–134 (2004)
24. Bergmann, R., Wilke, W., Vollrath, I.: Integrating general knowledge with object-oriented case representation and reasoning. In: 4th German Workshop: Case-Based Reasoning - System Development and Evaluation, Universitat Berlin, Germany, pp. 120–127 (1996)
25. Wilke, W., Begmann, R.: Techniques and knowledge used for adaptation during case based problem solving. In: Mira, J., Moonis, A., de Pobil, A.P. (eds.) IEA/AIE 1998. LNCS, vol. 1416, pp. 497–506. Springer, Heidelberg (1998)
26. Mitra, R., Basak, J.: Methods of Case Adaptation: A Survey. International Journal of Intelligent System 20(6), 627–645 (2005)

Semantic Collaborative Task Management Tool with Social Media Integration

Maria-Iuliana Dascalu[1], George Dragoi[1], Nicoleta-Cristina Stroescu[1], and Alin Moldoveanu[2]

[1] Faculty of Engineering in Foreign Languages,
University Politehnica of Bucharest, Romania
maria.dascalu@upb.ro, george.dragoi@ing.pub.ro,
nicoleta.stroescu@live.com
[2] Faculty of Automatic Control and Computers,
University Politehnica of Bucharest, Romania
alin.moldoveanu@cs.pub.ro

Abstract. The paper proposes a model for improving task scheduling in light project management. The model is implemented in a collaborative task management tool, which provides automatic task allocation based on ontological representations of project tasks and team members' profiles, social media integration, customization of notification, task plan templates, task progress awareness and reminders. The paper presents the methodology used to gather the requirements for the tool, the principles applied to obtain a successful product, the technical and functional description of the application, as well as the way in which it can improve the workflow of project management activities in a cross-functional virtual team. The novelties brought by the tool are the fact that it exploits the social profiles of the users: when a project is started, it provides a recommendation of the project team members based on their workload (extracted from their declared events) and on their expertise.

Keywords: task management, cross-functional virtual team, social integration, task allocation ontology.

1   Introduction

Task management plays an important role in knowledge work [1] and, in turn, knowledge work is the main lever to ensure the success of today's businesses [2]. According to some studies, the e-mail is still the most used instrument in task management [1], but there are obvious drawbacks of this approach: e-mail clients don't make task tracking, don't associate attachments to specific tasks, and don't allow task planning or automatic extraction of useful information. There are a lot of task management applications, developed to optimize the coordination and organization of project activities: some of them are stand alone, some are modules of complex project management environments [3]. Assigning knowledge workers to suitable tasks [4], supporting the collaboration between them and extracting the meaningful information

A. Kravets et al. (Eds.): JCKBSE 2014, CCIS 466, pp. 214–227, 2014.

from the working environment [1] are some of the problems which have to be taken into account when developing task management software. Collaborative task management software comes even with a greater challenge: it has to optimize the organization of those tasks which are characterized by non-routineness and highly interdependence [5]. A task is considered a non-routine when substantial information-processing is required [6] and it is prone to a high degree of misunderstandings [7]. A task is highly interdependent when several team members interact and "depend on each other for information, materials, and reciprocal units" [8]. If knowledge workers are organized in virtual teams [9] or in virtual enterprise networks [10], a complex software platform for collaborative task management becomes imperative.

The paper proposes a model for a collaborative task management application, the research methodology applied to develop the model, the technological choices made to implement the model, its distinctive features and the way in which it improves the project management activities within a virtual team in which the members have different profiles. In order to enhance collaboration between team members, useful information extracted from social media is automatically integrated in the knowledge workflow of the application. The application is presented in the context of other task management applications, which were critically analyzed taking into account multiple criteria.

2   Task Management Applications

There are many task management applications available on the market. After analyzing the features of several such applications, we chose to test five of them: Todo, GetItDone, Task Manager Professional, Producteev and Toodledo. Each of these products was studied from the following points of view: functionality, price, platform and usability.

Todo[11] is a Windows 8 and Windows Phone native application that manages personal tasks, which are organized into lists, the default ones being Home Tasks and Work Tasks. It also provides a series of filters that offer easy access to different tasks according to date, completion or due date. The tasks are simple and intuitive. A task can be repetitive and subtasks can also be created. The tool is oriented to personal projects: it serves as an organizer that sends notifications to the user. It is touch-screen optimized. The "Todo" application is only available for Windows 8, Windows Phone and the 8.1 upgrade. As strong points, it is simple to use, intuitive, the tasks have the basic properties and the notifications are handled well and it is synchronized with the Microsoft account. As weak points, the software is not team-focused, it doesn't have automatic features for allocating tasks and it does not provide a calendar. The notifications cannot be customized, are not sent via email and cannot be prioritized. The application is limited in the free version.

GetItDone [12] is an application designed to be used both in web browsers and smart phones and it serves as a task manager and team-project organizer. The software is structured into areas of responsibility, such as "Work", "Home", "Hobby", that need to be created by the user. The graphic user interface of the application is intuitive and easy to use. GetItDone is available for iOS, Android and has also the Windows 8, Windows Phone and the 8.1 adaptation. As strong points, it is a versatile application, with multiple platform versions and several functionalities. It can be easily used for allocating manual task to colleagues and to set tasks and to-dos of your own. It synchronizes between devices. As weak points, the full version of the application requires a rather expensive subscription if one plans to use it for a small project or for personal and occasional task delegation. The Windows 8 version of the software does not fit the Window8 UI model, as it is not designed specifically for it. The automatic task allocation is not implemented.

Task Manager Professional [13] is a native Windows 8 application, designed using Metro UI style and it is touch screen optimized for tablets with this operating system. The functionalities of the application are the classical ones of project and time management: creating workspaces, projects, tasks, subtasks. All these are structured in a hierarchy in the following way: workspaces are a collection of one or more projects, projects have tasks which may be composed by one or more sub-tasks. It does not require internet connection. This type of application uses toast notification, which is a "transient message to the user that contains relevant, time-sensitive information and provides quick access to related content in an app. It can appear whether you are in another app, the Start screen, the lock screen, or on the desktop" [14]. The application provides "Quick-Tasks", in order to manage simple to-dos and organize them in lists. As strong points, it is a native application, with basic functionalities; it is suitable for touch screen devices and provides basic task management functionalities. As weak points, it is not very intuitive, takes a long time to get used to the concepts and the organization of data. It is not collaborative and has no automatic features.

Producteev [15] is a project management software tool, with multiple platform versions (Windows, iPhone, Android, OS X). It is based on teamwork collaboration and implements features such as interactive timers and time tracking. The software is a SaaS (Software as a Service), which is a model of delivering software that is centered in cloud environment and is accessed by users through internet. Many applications use SaaS as a common model for delivery, as it helps at reducing costs and simplifying the implementation [16]. Firstly, the application is structured into networks, which allows the user to divide his/her projects according to the people he/she works with or to different environments. Secondly, it is divided into projects, which can be accessed by the others according to the permissions which are set for them. The automatic allocation of tasks is not available. Producteev, unlike other task management products that have been included in the study, is a more complex software that uses a team-centered, network communication approach. It integrates team management functionalities such as delegating permissions and tasks, sending messages, notification and grouping users into networks. With its filters and categories on the left side and content on the right side, Producteev's interface may seem, at the first sight, more or less similar to a user interface of a mailing application. Taking in consideration the functionalities that it offers, the display is not crowded and does not need a long time to adjust to it. As a drawback, there is no way to personalize the interface appearance. It does not provide a calendar or the possibility of seeing other people calendars. The application is free. As strong points, the software offer strong functionalities in an easy and natural way. It eases collaboration and communication. As weak points, it doesn't have automatic features for allocating tasks and the calendar feature is missing. The notifications cannot be customized.

Toodledo [17] is a web task and note manager application with corresponding versions for IOS. The software enables users to apply the GTD methodology in order to organize their to-do lists, ideas and notes. The GDT methodology implies that projects and tasks should be broken into actionable work items so that a person can concentrate on taking action on specific tasks [18]. It is destined to personal use rather than for business or team-work projects as it does not provide multiple user collaboration, allocation of task, permission delegation or share of calendars. The software can track the priority, start date, due date, status, time and duration of each task. Tasks can also be assigned to a context or a folder and also to a location on the IOS version. The users can create notes, time-track their task plan. There exists also the possibility of adding multiple tasks in one. The software does not provide an automatic way of task allocation. As mentioned before, "Toodledo" is not team-focused: it is strictly for personal organization and time management. The application is free for web use and cost for iOS. The two versions, web and iOS, can be synchronized. As strong points, the software offers time tracking, location finding, recursive tasks, and notifications. As weak points, it does not have a calendar and it does not synchronize with calendar application such as Outlook. The logic behind it is not intuitive enough to know how the user should organize its data from the beginning.

From the collaborative perspective, only Producteev includes team management functionalities, delegation of tasks, messaging and communication between people from a network. The others are personal task oriented. Automatic allocation of task or social media integration is not taken into consideration by any of these applications. The team management, cost friendliness and usability are analyzed and graded for all the five applications in Fig. 1.

In order to achieve collaborative features, the analyzed application could have exploited semantic technologies. A very good example in that direction is the Social Semantic Desktop (SSD) [1]: information objects on the desktop (documents, multimedia resources, e-mails) are represented as semantic web resources; the Personal Information Model Ontology (PIMO) is used to allow the user to structure one's individual information objects according to individual needs; a task management mechanism is included in the SSD, by the aid of a Task Model Ontology (TMO). Other task management applications make use of the connection to social networks, in order to achieve collaboration between team members [19]: SocialBase, HootSuite or CoTweet are some examples. But none of them combines social networks with semantic technologies and does note exploit the social profile of the team members to improve the distribution of workforce to tasks.

All the analyzed applications did not provide automatically allocation of tasks: this could have been solved with an algorithm for the famous resource-constrained project scheduling problem (RCPSP), which is a strongly NP-hard problem [20]. RCPSP means finding a schedule (project plan) that meets all resources and precedence constraints of tasks, while minimizing the makespan. Several algorithms are available, among them: a heuristic deterministic greedy one [21], a genetic one [22] or another based on empirical hardness models [23]. Other researchers didn't focus just on the makespan, but on multiple objectives, such as: obtaining shortest development time; satisfying budget constraint or achieving high workforce utilization [4]. For that, they developed different fitness functions for a Particle Swarm Optimization algorithm.

Fig. 1. Comparative analysis for task management applications

3   Research Methodology

In order to build the requirements for our product, we conducted a survey on potential users. Thus, we aimed to diminish the risk of obtaining yet another task management tool. The survey consisted in five questions that the respondents had to complete online. The questions were: (1) "Did you ever use a task management application?"; (2) "Did you use it/them for personal or professional purposes?"; (3) "Why did you use it?"; (4) "Can you name a feature that you used and find very important for the software?"; (5) "What feature would you like to add? Did you feel the need of a certain functionality?".

The sociometric analysis shows that from the 30 respondents, 83.3% have a technical education, 23% and have already graduated from college and the rest are students in the third or fourth year of faculty. The question "Did you ever use a task management application?" was a filter that reduced the number of respondents: 16.6% answered with "no". 50% of the remaining respondents used the applications for professional purposes, 37% for personal purposes, the rest for both. Twenty-five respondents answered the question "Why did you use the application?". The answers were centered on the idea of time management, helping them to better organize themselves, easing the job that they had to perform. Fifty percent brought in discussion the team work and keeping track of team progress. A very interesting answer was related to the "feeling" of keeping an organized work which helped the team progress. The same persons answered the question "Can you name a feature that you used and find very important in this software?". The responses were given taking into consideration various perspectives such as: usability, team collaboration, permanent connectivity and synchronization. Respondents appreciated the synchronization, being all the time aware of the progress that is made, customization of alarms and being able to use it on a mobile phone. Thirty-tree percent of the students emphasized the importance of well-done design and having a nice interaction with the interface. The responses of the last question, "What feature would you like to add? Did you feel the need of a certain functionality?", offer an overview of what the low points of most of the applications are. 26.6% of the respondents considered the intuitiveness of the application extremely important, as they would not like to spend a large amount of time to figure out the necessary steps. 16.6% of the respondents are pleased with the applications that they have used and the same number would appreciate automated task changing and notifications, especially on different devices.

4 "Assign-Me" – The Collaborative Task Management Tool

Based on the survey described in the previous section, and on the analysis of similar applications, we can say that the features that bring value to our application are the features that exceed clients' minimum expectations, which in our case are: automatic task allocation, social media integration, customization of notification, project templates, integration with maps, task progress awareness and reminders. As the IT market is continuously fast-moving and emerging, it is crucial that an application is designed in a way that allows future enhancements, integrations with new technologies and updates so that it can be coordinated with the user's new expectation. This is the fact on which we based our technological choices.

Our task management software "Assign.me" is a native Windows 8 application, which exploits Azure Mobile Services and has social media integration and enhanced collaborative features. The overall objective of the application is to provide an efficient project collaboration and effective task management within a project and between projects within the same portfolio, as well as self-organization functionalities (automatic allocation of tasks and workforces).

4.1   General Functionalities

The application is designed in a Windows 8 metro style, using Modern UI, which gives a nice feeling and an increased usability: see Fig. 2. It is optimized for touch screen devices.

The application gives the possibility to the users to:

- Create an account in order to use the application
- Create list of friends (workforce), by adding other users that also have accounts in our application and by interrogation the social profile of the current user
- Create projects, which can be personal projects or team projects
- Create portfolios of projects
- For each project/portfolio create a team and add people to the team
- Allocate permissions to people that work in that project/portfolio
- Add tasks to projects, tasks that should have the following properties: task type (private, public) , if the user wants to allocate it to another member manually or automatically, name, description, urgency, star date, due date, estimated allocated time, notification type (e-mail, phone message, notification within the application)
- Add projects to portfolios
- Add notes to a project/portfolio
- Have access to a calendar and also see the team calendar
- Add personal tasks in calendar.
- Communicate with the others by sending messages to other users or teams

Fig. 2. The Interface of "Assign.me" Collaborative Task Management Application

4.2   Semantic and Social Functionalities

As previously stated, the application has Facebook integration: at each login, there is a timer job which extracts the Facebook friends and the events at which those friends participate. This information is stored in the cloud. The extraction can be stopped, if, for some reason, the user decides so. The friends with matching profiles to our project/portfolio needs are added in the friends' list: each member of the list has a graphical note attached (highly matching, moderate matching, low matching, no matching). Their profiles can also be consulted: the profile contains their calendar (filled with the event information data taken from Facebook), as well as their education and work information. The last two attributes allows us to create the professional background (skills) of each friend. The Facebook Graph API provides the information needed to build the profiles, which can be further improved by manual annotations. The workload (the calendar) is taken into account only when the automatic allocation of resources to tasks is performed. When manual allocation is performed, it is displayed just to help the project manager to decide on one's team components. Also, the application lets us add other members from the database with suitable profile for the project/portfolio in use: one can make a search on matching profiles in the database.

The automatic allocation of resources can be made at project level or at portfolio level. We applied a genetic algorithm [25] in which we wanted to determine what friends (workforce) are as close as possible to the competences needed by each project task/portfolio project: this was done by calculating an ontological distance between the available competences and the desired one. For that, the creation of the task allocation ontology was required: our ontology is based on the Task Model Ontology TMO model [26], but we have concepts describing the workforce and concepts describing the tasks; the one describing the workforce represents friends' competences and availability; the one describing the tasks represent the requested competences to implement the project.

5 Technological Aspects in Developing the Collaborative Task Management Tool

The application is developed using Visual Studio and it is a native application for Windows 8. This is why, after the whole application is deployed, it will be accessible from the Windows Store. All the data for the application is stored in the cloud, more precisely on the Azure database servers. All the tables are stored and accessed by the application using some particular queries of Insert/Read/Delete actions. The scripts are uploaded to Azure and they are applied when the corresponding actions are being performed. For uploading the application to the cloud, it was necessary to create a developer account and after that upload the app package in order to be accessed through the Store. The application architecture is available in Fig 3.

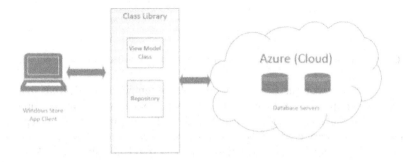

Fig. 3. Architecture of "Assign.me" Collaborative Task Management Application

Windows Azure is the Microsoft solution for cloud computing. It provides PaaS (Platform as a Service) as well as IaaS (Infrastructure as a Service), and it serves for building applications and services. Using Azure Mobile Services, our application was connected to a mobile service in Windows Azure [23]. The data of the application is stored using Windows Azure table storage. All the users are authenticated using the OAuth protocol provided App ID and Secret for Facebook. Users are enabled to use their Facebook account in order to sign into the application and we are able to access its data which is stored in the SQL Database in Windows Azure. If we take in consideration the client-server authentication model, we can identify how the client uses its credentials to access its resources hosted by the server. OAuth introduces a third role to this model: the resource owner. In the OAuth model, the client which is acting on the behalf of the resource owner, requests access to resources hosted by the server [24]. In our case, the client is our client application, the resource owner is the user and the server is the Facebook server. The data of the Facebook account are the protected resources that we want to access throughout our application. Our flow is what is called a 3-legged flow. Our user must use OAuth to gain access to the Facebook data. When support for Facebook login was added to our Windows 8 application, we obtained a set of client credentials (client identifier and secret) from Facebook to be used with our application OAuth-enabled API, as one can see in Fig. 4.

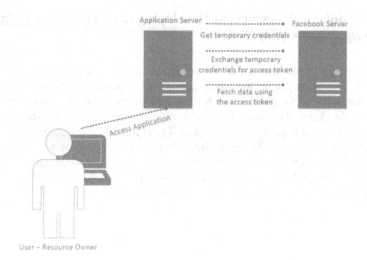

Fig. 4. Authentication mechanism in "Assign.me" Collaborative Task Management Application

Our application requests from Facebook a set of temporary credentials that are not resource-owner-specific, and can be used by our application to gain resource owner approval from the user to access Facebook data. The moment when our application receives the temporary credentials, it redirects the user to the OAuth User Authorization URL with the temporary credentials. The next step is to ask Facebook to redirect the user back once approval has been granted to our application. He/she has been redirected to Facebook and is requested to sign into the site. OAuth requires that Facebook servers first authenticate the resource owner (the user), and then ask them to grant access to the client (our application). For security reasons, OAuth allows the user to keep his/her username and password private and not share them with other application. The user does not introduce at any time the credentials into our application. After successfully logging into Facebook, the user is asked to grant access the client. Facebook informs the user of the request and the type of access being granted so that the user can approve or deny access. Facebook marks the temporary credentials as resource-owner-authorized which allows our application to know it has access to the data from the user's Facebook account. Our application uses the authorized Request Token and exchanges it for an Access Token. The difference between those two is that while Request Tokens have the capability of obtaining user approval, the Access Tokens are used to also access Protected Resources. Firstly, our application exchanges the Request Token for an Access Token and secondly it actually requests the data of the Facebook account.

In certain scenarios, an explicit "trust" cannot be established between the two applications so in this case OAuth will have to utilize an identity broker. Even though the two apps that need to exchange data do not trust each other, both apps will trust the identity broker that will be generating access tokens. Consider the same scenario, with the difference that an explicit trust does not exist between the two applications and for OAuth to work, the two applications trust a common "Identity Broker". Here is the sequence of events (available in Fig. 5):

1. User selects our application
2. Facebook requests a "context token" from the identity broker
3. Facebook sends the context token to the user (browser)
4. User sends the context token to our application
5. Our application sends the context token to Azure
6. Trusted identity broker generates an access token and sends back to our apllication based on the context token
7. Our application uses the access token to retrieve user's photos from Facebook

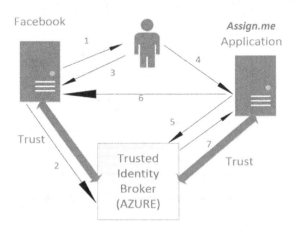

Fig. 5. Application authentication architecture with Trusted Azure Mechanism

The technical choices we made bring a set of additional constraints: in order to run the application, Windows 8 or 8.1 is required. Other hardware requirements include a Processor of 1 gigahertz (GHz) or faster, 1 gigabyte (GB) (32-bit) or 2 GB (64-bit) of RAM; 16 GB (32-bit) or 20 GB (64-bit) hard disk space and a Microsoft DirectX 9 graphics device with WDDM driver graphics card. In order to use the touch features, a tablet or a monitor that supports multi-touch is needed. In order to access the application, it should be downloaded from the app store so an Internet connection is mandatory and also a screen resolution of at least 1024 x 768. A Microsoft account is also required. We consider that these constraints are worth taking into account the gains they brought: data stored in cloud, flexibility, quick social media integration.

6   Using "Assign.Me" to Improve the Workflow of Project Management Activities in a Cross-Functional Virtual Team

In order to explain the utility of our application, we described in Fig. 6 a process taken place within any project management activities: the workforce allocation. After building their workforce list, the users of our application have to define the tasks for the current project, and then choose if they want to allocate the workforce manually or automatically. If they want to apply the automatic functionality, they have the possibility to refuse or not our recommended allocation.

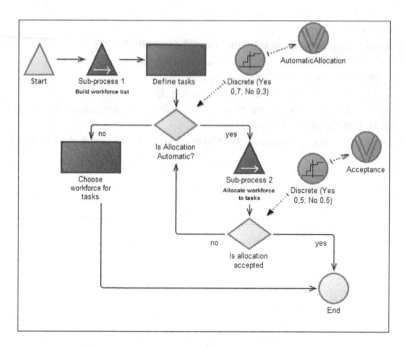

Fig. 6. Workflow of project management activities

Two important sub-processes of the process represented in Fig. 6 are detailed in Fig. 7: the first sub-process represents the way in which the workforce can be gathered and the second sub-process highlights in which way we use the Task Allocation Ontology to allocate automatically the workforce to tasks. The workforce one can use in a project is taken by executing FQL (Facebook Query Language) queries to his/her list of Facebook friends, which don't have an "Assign-me" account. The friends with education and work place suitable for the project needs are selected. In parallel, the database is interrogated also for friends with interesting profile for the project: the Facebook friends with application accounts are already in the database. Synchronization between friends' profiles stored in the application and their FB profiles is always recommended. In order to match the education and workplace with workforce competences needed by the project, we use the classification mechanism of our Task Allocation Ontology: if Allan has Informatics_Faculty and if Allan has JavaDeveloper_Job, then Allan is classified to have Java_programming_skills. By using the ontology automated classification, the user who builds the project team doesn't have to know much about the qualification obtained after graduating a certain faculty, thus cross-functional teams are easily built. Still, an expert is needed to create all the necessary concepts in the Task Allocation Ontology.

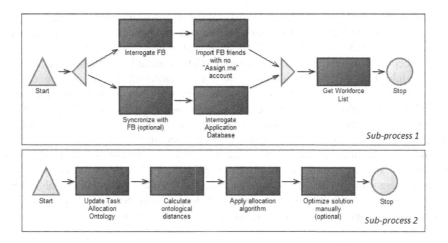

Fig. 7. Required sub-processes for workforce allocation in project management activities

In order to make the distribution of friends from the workforce list to project tasks, we adapted the genetic algorithm proposed by Nammuni, Levine and Kingston [25]: instead of allocation tutors to tutorial groups, we allocated individuals to tasks. An individual can be allocated to several tasks, but a task can't be allocated to several individuals: this is the main drawback of the algorithm. The main change was done to the fitness function: we took into consideration only the skills and the time availability of each worker. In order to calculate the ontological distance between the competences of the individuals from the workforce list and the competences required by the project, we made the following steps: attached a weight to each pair of leaves from the ontological tree (two siblings have a lower weight than two cousins), classify all the competences (of workforce and those required by project) using the ontology concepts and choose the weight taking into account the types of our classified competences.

In order to test if the automatic allocation of workforce to tasks brings added value to project management activities, we simulated the allocation process with ADONIS software, by using two random generators, as seen in Fig. 6. We noticed that the duration of resources allocation decreases if automatic allocation is chosen, thus the project management activities are optimized.

7   Conclusions and Future Work

Our task management tool was designed for light project management: the available workforce is seen as a list of friends, social network are highly queried and the automatic allocation module does not take into consideration any budget constraints. The strength of our application comes from the technological choices we made (the data are stored in cloud, thus facilitating the collaboration of virtual teams) and from combining the ontological expressivity with social power. Although ontologies were previously used by other task management applications [1] [25] [27] to solve automatically the allocation of tasks and resources within projects, none combines this method with social information. By exploiting the social profile of each user's friends, the collaboration in "Assign.me" is taken at an upper level. The competences of the workforce are a priori known by the project manager who can quickly decide upon acceptance or rejection of the recommendation made by our automatic allocation module. Our collaboration tool permits the sharing of resources in a certain project, but also between the projects in a certain portfolio: in this way, the collaboration between knowledge workers goes one step further. Also, by classifying the available workers to the Task Allocation Ontology, a common vocabulary is used to represent their skills, even if they have different educational and professional backgrounds. For the moment, we use the same ontology to represent the competences of the workers and the needed competences in the projects, but in the future we could separate them into two different ontologies and use an ontology alignment algorithm to make the queries [28]. Also, the project ontologies could be created automatically by querying semantic repositories [29] for specific domain ontologies.

Acknowledgement. The work has been funded by the Sectoral Operational Programme Human Resources Development 2007-2013 of the Ministry of European Funds through the Financial Agreement POSDRU/159/1.5/S/132397.

References

1. Riss, U.V., Grebner, O., Taylor, P.S., Du, Y.: Knowledge work support by semantic task management. Computers in Industry 61, 798–805 (2010)
2. Drucker, P.F.: The Age of Discontinuity: Guidelines to Our Changing Society. Heinemann, London (1969)
3. Obradovic, V., Jovanovic, P., Petrovic, D., Mihic, M., Bjelica, D.: Web-based project management influence on project portfolio managers' technical competencies. Procedia - Social and Behavioral Sciences 119, 387–396 (2014)
4. Shao, B.B.M., Yin, P.-Y., Chen, A.N.K.: Organizing knowledge workforce for specified iterative software development tasks. Decision Support Systems 59, 15–27 (2014)
5. Nikas, A., Argyropoulou, M.: Assessing the impact of collaborative tasks on individuals' perceived performance in ICT enabled Project Teams. Procedia - Social and Behavioral Sciences 119, 786–795 (2014)
6. Tushman, M.L.: Work Characteristics and Subunit Communication Structure: A contingency analysis. Administrative Science Quarterly 24, 92–98 (1979)
7. Te'eni, D.: Review: A cognitive-affective model of organisational communication for designing IT. MIS Quarterly 25, 251–312 (2001)
8. Campion, M.A., Medsker, G.J., Higgs, A.C.: Relations between work group characteristics and effectiveness: Implications for designing effective work groups. Personnel Psychology 46, 823–850 (1993)
9. Aldea, C., Draghici, A., Dragoi, G.: New Perspectives of Virtual Teams' Collaboration. In: Putnik, G.D., Cruz-Cunha, M.M. (eds.) ViNOrg 2011. CCIS, vol. 248, pp. 176–185. Springer, Heidelberg (2012)
10. Dragoi, G., Rosu, S.M., Pavaloiu, I.-B., Draghici, A.: Knowledge Applications Development at the SMEs Level in a Virtual Business Environment. Procedia Technology 9, 431–441 (2013)
11. Todo Task Management Application, http://www.appigo.com/

12. GetItDone Task Management Application, https://getitdoneapp.com/
13. Task Manager Professional, http://windows.appstorm.net/reviews/productivity-reviews/task-manager-professional-project-management-in-windows-8/
14. Toast Notification, http://msdn.microsoft.com/en-us/library/windows/apps/hh779727.aspx
15. Producteev Task Management Software, http://www.producteev.com/
16. Rezaei, R., Chiew, T.K., Lee, S.P., Aliee, Z.S.: A semantic interoperability framework for software as a service systems, Expert Systems with Applications 41, 5751–5770 (2014) in cloud computing environments
17. Toodledo Task Management Application, http://www.toodledo.com
18. David, A.: Getting Things Done, http://gettingthingsdone.com/
19. Social Media Task Management, https://gigaom.com/2011/06/20/socialbase-social-media-task-management/
20. Blazewicz, J., Lenstra, J.K., Rinnooy Kan, A.H.G.: Scheduling subject to resource constraints: Classification and complexity. Discrete Applied Mathematics 5, 11–24 (1983)
21. Goncharov, E.: A greedy heuristic approach for the Resource-Constrained Project Scheduling Problem. Studia Informatica Universalis 9(3), 79–90 (2011)
22. Valls, V., Ballestín, F., Quintanilla, S.: A hybrid genetic algorithm for the resource-constrained project scheduling problem. European Journal of Operational Research 185(2), 495–508 (2008)
23. Microsoft, Azure, http://www.windowsazure.com/en-us/services/mobile-services/
24. OAuth Protocol, http://hueniverse.com/oauth/guide/intro/
25. Nammuni, K., Levine, J., Kingston, J.: Skill-based Resource Allocation using Genetic Algorithms and Ontologies. Informatic Research Report EDI-INF-RR-0174, School of Informatics, University of Edinburgh (2002)
26. Task Model Ontology (TMO), http://www.semanticdesktop.org/ontologies/2008/05/20/tmo/
27. Marques, A.B., Carvalho, J.R., Rodrigues, R., Conte, T.: An Ontology for Task Allocation to Teams in Distributed Software Development. In: Proceedings of the 2013 IEEE 8th International Conference on Global Software Engineering (ICGSE), pp. 21–30. IEEE (2013)
28. Bodea, C., Dascalu, M., Serbanati, L.D.: An Ontology-Alignment Based Recommendation Mechanism for Improving the Acquisition and Implementation of Managerial Training Services in Project Oriented Organizations. In: Proceedings of the 9th International Conference and Workshops on Engineering of Computer Based Systems (ECBS), pp. 257–266. IEEE (2012)
29. Vasilateanu, A., Goga, N., Moldoveanu, F., Moldoveanu, A., Taslitchi, C.: Questor: Medical Report Search Engine. In: 2013 IEEE International Conference on Healthcare Informatics (ICHI), pp. 478–479. IEEE (2014)

Evaluation of Hardware Implementations
of CORDIC-Like Algorithms
in FPGA Using OpenCL Kernels

Andrey Andreev[1], Evgueni Doukhnitch[2], Vitaly Egunov[1], Dmitriy Zharikov[1],
Oleg Shapovalov[1], and Sergey Artuh[1]

[1] Volgograd State Technical University, Volgograd, Russia
{andan2005,sergeynexx}@yandex.ru,
{vegunov,dimitrol}@mail.ru,
oshapovalov@mail.com
[2] Novorossiysk State Maritime University, Novorossiysk, Russia
evgenydukhnich@gmail.com

Abstract. The FPGA implementation of CORDIC-like hardware-oriented algorithms, including multidimensional version, with OpenCL kernels are considered. This class of algorithms is also named as discrete linear transformation (DLT). Altera OpenCL SDK is used as a high-level synthesis tool to generate a project for Altera Stratix FPGA family from OpenCL kernels. For the obtained projects clock speed and space requirements are estimated. With this approach, first, the characteristics of the FPGA implementations of multidimensional DLT reflection algorithms are evaluated, in particular, unitary version of Householder-CORDIC reflection. The paper also discusses the possibility of automating the OpenCL kernels generation for the DLT of different dimensions.

Keywords: CORDIC, CORDIC-like algorithms, discrete linear transformation (DLT), multidimensional DLT, Householder-CORDIC, unitary transformations, OpenCL kernels, FPGA, Altera OpenCL SDK, HLS tools.

1   Introduction

One approach to improve computing performance is specialization of computing device according to the implemented algorithm. Besides extracting high performance from algorithm through parallelization and pipelining such approach reduces overhead on unnecessary infrastructure in the device and its power consumption. Problems of this approach are the high cost of custom VLSI design and manufacturing, as well as the complexity of designing special-purpose schemes. The solution of the first problem consists partly in the use of such elemental base, as FPGA, it allows to change the circuit configuration, which is placed in internal memory of the device. The second problem is perhaps more complicated and can partly be overcome with the help of modern high level synthesis (HLS) tools.

Development of specialized devices often requires the use of special versions of algorithms oriented to hardware implementation. One class of such algorithms are CORDIC-like, which is the development of Jack Volder's CORDIC algorithm [1].

A. Kravets et al. (Eds.): JCKBSE 2014, CCIS 466, pp. 228–242, 2014.

Despite the large number of publications devoted to CORDIC-like algorithms, most of them belong to the CORDIC algorithm itself, its variants and applications. Description of these algorithms implementation with custom VLSI-s and FPGA are also largely related to CORDIC [2]. Hardware implementation of other algorithms from this class (including multidimensional and unitary transformations) is considered by the authors either in general, or does not apply to the FPGA. As for the description of the implementation of these algorithms with the help of HLS - such publications are not known for authors. At the same time it should be noted that this issue is of interest because many of the characteristics of possible implementation of these algorithms are only estimated and often very approximate. On the other hand, many of these algorithms are still not fully investigated. In these conditions it would be useful to estimate more realistic parameters of the hardware implementation of CORDIC-like multidimentional algorithms based on available FPGA devices, which is the main research point of this paper.

2   CORDIC-Like DLT Algorithms

The most famous representatives of the hardware-oriented algorithms are iterative algorithms, known as CORDIC-like, which use simple arithmetic operations. The generalization of these methods on the implementation of linear algebra procedures leads to the class of so-called algorithms of discrete linear transformations (DLT) [3-6]. In the DTL algorithms matrix of a given linear transformation is represented in the form of convergent infinite product of simple matrices A_i:

$$A = \prod_{i=0}^{\infty} A_i \; . \tag{1}$$

In this case, instead of a linear transformation of the vector x with the matrix A, the iterative process takes place, that can be easily implemented on the pipeline:

$$y_{i+1} = A_i \cdot y_i$$

$$\text{where } i = 0, \ 1, \ \dots , \ \text{n-1} , y_0 = x. \tag{2}$$

As a result, when $n \rightarrow \infty$, $y_n \rightarrow y = Ax$. The transformation parameters for each iteration are known beforehand (with accuracy up to signs) and chosen so, that the elements of the matrices A_i will be only zero and algebraic sum of integer powers of radix (for most computing systems - the power of two). Therefore they only need to define the signs that depend on the values of the components of the transformed vector obtained at the previous iteration. As a rule, the iterative process is built in such a manner that a linear convergence is provided, and therefore the number of steps n is comparable to the operands word length. After each iteration the next digit of the result is clarified. The calculations at each iteration are reduced to the simple ("short") operations of addition and shift, which decreases the time of transformation and permits to organize the effective pipelines with a minimum tick time.

Thus, iterative DLT methods allow building special-purpose devices with high performance and reasonable hardware costs and provide the required accuracy.

The most known DLT algorithm is the Jack Volder's algorithm for implementing orthogonal transformation of plane rotation

$$A = \begin{bmatrix} \cos\alpha & -\sin\alpha \\ \sin\alpha & \cos\alpha \end{bmatrix} \tag{3}$$

in the two-dimensional case [1]. The device on its basis is called CORDIC - COordinate Rotation DIgital Computer. In this algorithm the rotation is performed by the iterative procedure in view of (1) without calculating the matrix (3):

$$\mathbf{y}_{i+1} = \mathbf{R}_i \cdot \mathbf{y}_i \;;$$

$$\mathbf{R}_i = \begin{bmatrix} 1 & -\xi_i \cdot 2^{-i} \\ \xi_i \cdot 2^{-i} & 1 \end{bmatrix} ; \tag{4}$$

$$\alpha_{i+1} = \alpha_i - \xi_i \Delta\alpha_i \;; \quad \Delta\alpha_i = arctg2^{-i} \;;$$

$$i = \overline{0, n-1} \;; \; \mathbf{y}_0 = \mathbf{x},$$

where $\xi_i = \pm 1$ is the rotation direction on the i-th iteration. At each iteration rotation is carried out at a fixed angle $\Delta\alpha_i$. The choice of ξ_i and α_0 depends on the mode of the algorithm. When rotating the vector x at a given angle (the rotate mode of CORDIC or "rotation") they use:

$$\xi_i = sgn\,\alpha_i \;; \; \alpha_0 = \alpha. \tag{5}$$

If they want to rotate the vector x to align the x-axis (vectorization, module computing or "vector") they use:

$$\xi_i = -sgn\,y_{2i} \;; \quad \alpha_0 = 0. \tag{6}$$

The calculation of the angle in the explicit form (4) may not be carried out, then the algorithm is called as implicit one.

A time of hardware implementation of a single iteration of the algorithm (4) is coming to a runtime of one addition.

The vectorization mode (5) in DLT algorithms in general is also called the mode of calculation of the transformation parameter, and the rotation mode (6) - mode of parameter application. In the CORDIC algorithm, in particular, the transformation parameter is the rotation angle α. An important feature of the DLT algorithms is the possibility to run the iterations with calculation of the transformation parameter for one set of input data, and the iterations applying these parameters for other sets of data in parallel. It is useful in execution of various matrix operations. To date, there are known a large number of basic DLT algorithms and their modifications to perform common orthogonal and some of unitary transformations [1-12].

3   Algorithms of Multidimensional and Unitary DLT

Among the DLT algorithms there are many multidimensional transformations [2-12]. Most of the DLT algorithms (besides the CORDIC algorithm and its modifications) are those. Algorithms of complex rotation, based on the Kronecker product of rotation matrices [12], or quaternion conversion [8], can be considered as multidimensional as well.

Algorithms of multidimensional DLT often exploit one common approach - consolidation of transformation performed at each iteration of DLT, as an alternative to conventional iteration with two-dimensional CORDIC in varying combinations. It should be noted here that although in many processing matrix tasks (for example, QR decomposition) orthogonal rotation transformation can replace other orthogonal transformations (for example, reflection). In other cases these transformations (reflection, quaternion, octonion and others) cannot be replaced and their implementation is of independent interest. In this paper, we, however, will compare the parameters of the obtained implementations of multidimensional algorithms with implementation based on CORDIC-processors. First, multidimensional orthogonal transformation is often an alternative to plane rotations, indeed. Secondly, it is interesting to estimate the overall cost of this approach, whether it gives some real advantages, particularly when implemented on an FPGA. This question is often ignored in the literature, or described in the context of the implementation in ASIC. There are also known some estimations, that multidimensional DLT is not efficient when implemented on an FPGA or ASIC.

Illustrative case for which you can compare two approaches (the use of a plane rotations or multidimensional transformation), is the task of vectorization (module calculation / orientation along one of the axes) of N-dimensional vector. If we solve the problem using the pyramid of CORDIC blocks, we need $\log_2 N$ stages, each of them takes m iterations (Fig. 1 for N=3,4,5,9, colored boxes indicate CORDIC conversions to preserve scaling factor). Using one device for DLT-reflection (for example, Householder-CORDIC) allows obtaining the result in one stage (taking the same m or $m + k$ steps, where k is the number of repeated iterations).

In this work we consider the implementation of the multidimensional DLT reflection of Householder (Householder-CORDIC [7]) for real and complex cases. For implementing DLT of Householder reflection there are two possible forms of algorithm: vector one and matrix one [13].

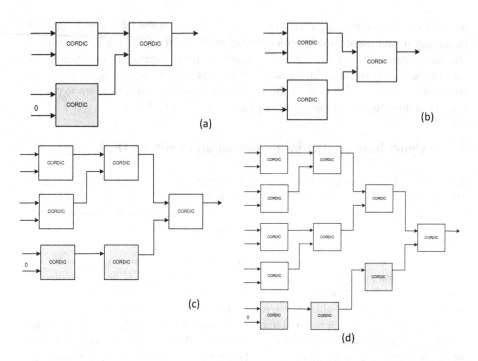

Fig. 1. Structural scheme to compute module of 3 (a), 4 (b), 5 (c), 9 (d) - dimensional vectors on the basis of CORDIC

Basic iterative expressions of the vector form of the algorithm is as follows :

$$
\left.
\begin{aligned}
y_1' &= \left(1 + 2^{-2i+l}\right) y_1 \;-\; 2\left(\sum_{k=1}^{m} f(k)\,\xi_k\, y_k\right) \\
y_j' &= \left(1 + 2^{-2i+l}\right) y_j \;-\; 2\left(\sum_{k=1}^{m} f(k)\,\xi_k\, y_k\right) 2^{-i}\,\xi_j
\end{aligned}
\right\}
\tag{7}
$$

where

$$
f(k) = \begin{cases} 1, & k = 1 \\ 2^{-i}, & k > 1 \end{cases}, \qquad
\xi_k = \begin{cases} 1, & k = 1 \\ \operatorname{sgn}(y_1)\operatorname{sgn}(y_k), & k > 1 \end{cases},
\tag{8}
$$

m - the dimension of the vector, $m = 2^l + 1$,

i - the number of the iteration, $i = \overline{0,\ n}$,

j - the number of components of a vector, $j = \overline{2,\ m}$,

y_p - components of the initial,

a$y_p{'}$ - and transformed vector.

In the vector form scalar product in brackets to the right in the equations (7) is calculated once explicitly and then used in all of m equations.

For matrix Householder-CORDIC DLT basic iterative expressions are as follows:

$$
\begin{aligned}
y_1' &= \left(2^{-2i+l} - 1\right) y_1 - \left(\sum_{k=2}^{m} 2^{-i+1} \xi_k \, y_k\right) \\
y_j' &= \left(1 + 2^{-2i+l}\right) y_j - 2^{-2i+1} y_j - 2^{-i+1} \xi_k \, y_1 - \\
&\quad - \left(\sum_{k=2}^{j-1} 2^{-2i+1} \xi_{jk} \, y_k\right) - \left(\sum_{k=j+1}^{m} 2^{-2i+1} \xi_{jk} \, y_k\right)
\end{aligned} \right\} , \qquad (9)
$$

where

$$
\xi_{jk} = \operatorname{sgn}\!\left(y_j\right)\operatorname{sgn}\!\left(y_k\right) \,, \quad \xi_k = \operatorname{sgn}\!\left(y_1\right)\operatorname{sgn}\!\left(y_k\right) \qquad (10)
$$

In (7) and (9) it is assumed that the dimension m is

$$
m = 2^l + 1, \qquad (11)
$$

in common case 2^{-2i+l} in (7 - 9) is transformed into $2^{-2i}\,(m-1)$.

From a practical point of view the most useful variants are the implementations of Householder-CORDIC algorithm for vectors of dimensions from 2 to 10 (with increasing of vector dimension the number of additional iterations in algorithm to ensure convergence also grows [6]). For dimension m, satisfying the condition (11) hardware costs will be lower. In the range $m = 2\ldots 10$ this condition corresponds to $m = 3, 5, 9$, therefore, we will address these cases, and $m = 4$ for comparison.

Also in this paper we consider the implementation of the complex (unitary) DLT reflection on the basis of the Householder-CORDIC algorithm described in [14-16].

Iterative formulas for vector form of algorithm [15, 16]:

$$
\begin{aligned}
y_{1Re}' &= \left(2^{-2i+l} - 1\right) y_{1Re} - 2^{-i+1} \sum_{k=2}^{m} S_1\!\left(\xi_{kRe}, \xi_{kIm}, y_{kRe}, y_{kIm}\right) \\
y_{1Im}' &= \left(2^{-2i+l} - 1\right) y_{1Im} - 2^{-i+1} \sum_{k=2}^{m} S_2\!\left(\xi_{kRe}, \xi_{kIm}, y_{kRe}, y_{kIm}\right) \\
y_{jRe}' &= \left(1 + 2^{-2i+l}\right) y_{jRe} - 2^{-i+1} S_3\!\left(\xi_{jRe}, \xi_{jIm}, y_{1Re}, y_{1Im}\right) - \\
&\quad - 2^{-2i+1} S_4\!\left(\xi_{jRe}, \xi_{jIm}, a_{Re}', a_{Im}'\right) \\
y_{jIm}' &= \left(1 + 2^{-2i+l}\right) y_{jIm} - 2^{-i+1} S_5\!\left(\xi_{jRe}, \xi_{jIm}, y_{1Re}, y_{1Im}\right) - \\
&\quad - 2^{-2i+1} S_6\!\left(\xi_{jRe}, \xi_{jIm}, a_{Re}', a_{Im}'\right)
\end{aligned} \right\} \qquad (12)
$$

where

S_t, $t = \overline{1,6}$ - selection function defined as follows.

$$S_1\left(\xi_{kRe}, \xi_{kIm}, y_{kRe}, y_{kIm}\right) = \begin{cases} \xi_{kRe} y_{kRe}, & \xi_{kRe}\xi_{kIm} > 0 \\ \xi_{kIm} y_{kIm}, & \xi_{kRe}\xi_{kIm} < 0 \end{cases},$$

$$S_2\left(\xi_{kRe}, \xi_{kIm}, y_{kRe}, y_{kIm}\right) = \begin{cases} \xi_{kRe} y_{kRe}, & \xi_{kRe}\xi_{kIm} < 0 \\ \xi_{kIm} y_{kIm}, & \xi_{kRe}\xi_{kIm} > 0 \end{cases}, (13)$$

$$S_3\left(\xi_{jRe}, \xi_{jIm}, y_{1Re}, y_{1Im}\right) = \begin{cases} \xi_{jRe} y_{1Re}, & \xi_{jRe}\xi_{jIm} > 0 \\ \xi_{jRe} y_{1Im}, & \xi_{jRe}\xi_{jIm} < 0 \end{cases},$$

$$S_4\left(\xi_{jRe}, \xi_{jIm}, a'_{Re}, a'_{Im}\right) = \begin{cases} \xi_{jRe}\left(a'_{Re} - a'_{Im}\right), & \xi_{jRe}\xi_{jIm} > 0 \\ \xi_{jRe}\left(a'_{Re} + a'_{Im}\right), & \xi_{jRe}\xi_{jIm} < 0 \end{cases},$$

$$S_5\left(\xi_{jRe}, \xi_{jIm}, y_{1Re}, y_{1Im}\right) = \begin{cases} \xi_{jIm} y_{1Im}, & \xi_{jRe}\xi_{jIm} > 0 \\ \xi_{jIm} y_{1Re}, & \xi_{jRe}\xi_{jIm} < 0 \end{cases},$$

$$S_6\left(\xi_{jRe}, \xi_{jIm}, a'_{Re}, a'_{Im}\right) = \begin{cases} \xi_{jRe}\left(a'_{Re} + a'_{Im}\right), & \xi_{jRe}\xi_{jIm} > 0 \\ \xi_{jRe}\left(a'_{Re} - a'_{Im}\right), & \xi_{jRe}\xi_{jIm} < 0 \end{cases},$$

and a' are defined through S_1 and S_2

$$a'_{Re} + a'_{Im} = \sum_{k=2}^{m} S_1\left(\xi_{kRe}, \xi_{kIm}, y_{kRe}, y_{kIm}\right) \tag{14}$$

$$a'_{Re} - a'_{Im} = \sum_{k=2}^{m} S_2\left(\xi_{kRe}, \xi_{kIm}, y_{kRe}, y_{kIm}\right).$$

4   Altera OpenCL SDK

Design of devices on FPGA can be conducted by directly entering schemes in FPGA CAD using the graphical editor, using the hardware description languages (HDL), or using any high-level synthesis tool (HLS), which implies the use of a programming high-level language (HLL), most often C. In the first two cases, we can get the most effective implementation, but they require more time-consuming efforts compared to HLS. In addition, HLS tools often offer not just HLL support, but also the infrastructure for work with memory and co-processor bus interface to the host machine. Among many HLS tools, the authors have chosen Altera OpenCL SDK, that is connected with availability for authors of the coprocessor Terasic DE5-Net (based on Stratix V FPGA) supporting this tool. The basis of this HLS is the use of OpenCL standard.

Development of the standard for parallel cross-platform programming language OpenCL has been carried out from the summer of 2008. The purpose of development is to transfer parallel algorithms from platform to platform with minimum costs. The OpenCL is based on the C language with specific to parallel programs extensions. In fact, OpenCL is focused on co-processors.

OpenCL involves building the application of two blocks. The host part is performed on the microprocessor (CPU or embedded in FPGA) – it is a standard C/C++ program. It is suggested to place computationally intensive parts of the application in the second block of the so-called kernels - which will run on the accelerator (standard implies the possibility of GPU use as well as FPGA and other types). For coding kernels we use the same C, but with special extensions to use parallelism of the accelerator. To connect two parts of the application OpenCL API is used that is a set of functions for the host part, allowing to communicate with the accelerator, and to run the kernel for execution. One of the leading world manufacturers of the FPGA - Altera company in November of 2012 published the first results of the development of OpenCL compiler for using kernels in their FPGA families Stratix IV/V [17].

5   Implementation of DLT with OpenCL

First of all, it is necessary to note some of peculiarities of implementation:

1) Traditionally DLT algorithms are built using the representation of numbers with the fixed comma, so this implementation was chosen. This allows to avoid difficulties with support for floating point across HLS tools and the need to assess the quality and special features of this support. The word length of all numbers is 32 bits.

2) Because HLS tool chosen for implementation uses C (with OpenCL extensions) as the input language, the original versions of algorithms are also implemented in C. To assess the implementation with the fixed comma integer type was used as the base type (32 bit).

3) To exclude automatic generation of divide and multiply blocks using HLS, all shift operations were realized through the «<<» and «>>» operations explicitly.

4) As a base the CORDIC algorithm without calculating angles (the "implicit CORDIC") in vectorization mode only was considered. Both pipelined (each iteration is performed on its stage after cycle unroll) and non-pipelined variants were investigated.

5) As the output information to evaluate the implementation the data from FPGA CAD system Quartus II 13.1 was used: number of occupied logical elements/blocks (LE), other resources of FPGA employed (FF, DSP), clock frequency and the number of possibly executed OpenCL kernels per second.

6) To evaluate the implementation of the algorithm using Altera OpenCL SDK, they must prepare the OpenCL kernel, which is actually a normal C program with some restrictions. In particular, it is necessary to refuse from calling functions that do not return void, to use special pointers, do not use nested loops, and so on.

The Altera OpenCL Compiler (AOC) generates pipelines by unrolling cycles using pragma

```
#pragma unroll<N>,
```

where N is the maximum number of steps that is needed to be unrolled (without <N> the maximum number of steps is used by default).

Also it should be noted that in this case Altera OpenCL was not used for generating the actual firmware for FPGA, because this process takes several hours, even on a very powerful machine. Instead the quick generation was used with a preliminary estimate of the parameters of the resulting schema:

```
aoc  -c  CORDIC.cl  --report --estimate-throughput
```

Code of OpenCL kernel for the CORDIC algorithm (4) looks like this:

```
__kernel void CORDIC( __global const int *x,
    __global const int *y, __global int *restrict xo,
    __global int *restrict yo)
{
    int X, X2;
    int Y, Y2;
    int sign;

    X2 = *x;    Y2 = *y;

    #pragma unroll 32
    for (int i = 0; i < 32; i++)    {
        X = X2;
        Y = Y2;
        sign = Y >= 0 ? 0 : 1;
        X2 = X + (sign ? -Y : Y) >> i;
        Y2 = Y - (sign ? -X : X) >> i;
    }
    *xo = X2;
    *yo = Y2;
}
```

The implementation of the vector form of the Householder-CORDIC algorithm (dimension of vectors is equal to 3) as an OpenCL kernel on Altera OpenCL SDK was developed in the same way and can be illustrated with the activity diagram on Fig. 2.

For effective implementation, it was required to remove all the internal loops, unrolling them explicitly. In addition, to reduce the complexity of the generated schema it was necessary to get rid of the operations of the form $x_k * sign(x_i) * sign(x_j)$ where the $sign()$ takes a value of ± 1. Despite the fact that according to the Altera documentation on code optimization, multiplication by ± 1 is implemented as simply as the multiplication by the power of 2, or changing sign, actually using the multiplication $sign(x_i) * sign(x_j)$ led to the increasing complexity of schemes in the implementation of the pipeline by an order (apparently, the compiler generates multiplier for this operation). In the result this multiplication was changed to the analysis of logical variables using the XOR operation and preliminary formation of the operands $X[i]$, $Y[i]$ with the correct signs :

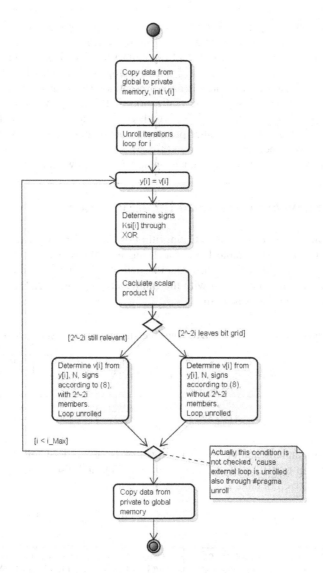

Fig. 2. Activity diagram for vector form of Hausholder-CORDIC algorithm implemented as an OpenCL kernel

```
ksil[0] = y[0] >= 0 ? 0 : 1;
ksil[1] = y[1] >= 0 ? 0 : 1;
ksil[2] = y[2] >= 0 ? 0 : 1;

ksi12 = (ksil[0]&&(!ksil[1])) || ((!ksil[0])&&ksil[1]);
ksi13 = (ksil[0]&&(!ksil[2])) || ((!ksil[0])&&ksil[2]);
// ...
Y[0][1] = ksi12 ? -y[1] : y[1];
Y[0][2] = ksi13 ? -y[2] : y[2];
```

Implementation of OpenCL kerenels for other dimensions of vectors looks the same, but becomes more cumbersome at increase of dimension.

The implementation of OpenCL kernel for unitary DLT of Householder-CORDIC reflection algorithm in vector form (12) was developed also. It looks analogical to above for a real transformation, but also not presented here because of the amount of code. Let us pay attention only to the realization of Boolean functions to select the signs of the operands according to (13), which is also made with the help of XOR function and "?" operator in a manner presented above, and the need to repeat some iterations for convergence, as described in [14,15].

Interested reader can found source codes in appendixes to work [16].

6   Evaluation of the Received Implementations

Features of realization of the CORDIC algorithm on Altera OpenCL SDK (version of Quartus II 13.1) are given in table 1 (the following are only indicators of kernel itself, without regard to the additional environment schemes). Parameter of total use percent of FPGA is shown for comparison with the implementation of other DLT algorithms on Altera OpenCL for the same chip.

Table 1. Characteristics of the CORDIC algorithm implementation using Altera OpenCL

Implementation	Complexity of devices (logical blocks,LE / registers, FF)	Using of FPGA, %	Clock frequency, MHz	Bandwidth, (M tasks /s)
Pipelined	5790 / 5073	1.63	250	250
Without pipeline	2413 / 6747	1.23	250	7,81

Indicators of implementation of vector form of Householder-CORDIC algorithm for dimensions up to 10, satisfying the condition (11), and also to dimension 4 (for comparison) are given in table 2.

Table 2. The pipelined implementation of vector algorithm Householder-CORDIC on Altera OpenCL SDK

Algorithm option (the dimension of the processed vector)	Complexity of devices (logical blocks,LE / registers, FF)	Using of FPGA, %	In relation to the pyramid of CORDIC, %	Bandwidth, (M tasks/s)
3-dimensional	12681 / 9743	3,42	-30 (+5)	250
4-dimensional	23195 / 18132	6.29	+70.46	250
5-dimensional	19152 / 15031	5.2	-46,8 (-20)	250
9-dimensional	39819 / 29639	10.62	-40,77(-18.6)	250 (222)

For all dimensions satisfying the condition (11) hardware expenses economy is observed in comparison with the decision on the basis of CORDIC from 18% to 47%.

For dimension 4, not satisfying the condition (11), the performance is even worse than for 5. Interestingly, that this is achieved at the same clock speed and performance that is not always possible in the general case with the hardware implementation. It should be noted that implementation of the Householder-CORDIC algorithm was conducted without the required number of extra iterations to ensure convergence, which for the dimensions < 10 is about 3 [7] (while whole number of iterations, according to [7] is less than for the CORDIC algorithm).

Features of the vector algorithm of complex reflection DLT implementation (for dimension 3) are given in table. 3

Table 3. Features of the vector algorithm of complex DLT reflection implementations (for dimension 3)

Implementation	Complexity of device (logical blocks,LE / registers, FF)	Using of FPGA, %	In relation to CORDIC use, %	In relation to House-holder CORDIC use,%	Bandwidth, (M tasks/s)
Pipelined	41346 / 33277	11.32	-42	-3.5	250
Without pipeline	4725 / 13346	2.43	-83.5	-64	15,63

In this implementation repeated iterations are considered, as described in [14,15] - about 8 iterations of the first half (totally we have 40 iterations for 32 - bit numbers). The table shows a comparison of complexity (by percentage of the use of FPGA) with alternative implementations of complex reflection considered in [8, 9]:

- processing of the vector with 3 blocks of complex rotations (CR), composed of 4 CORDIC blocks (Fig. 3 shows the CR block built on 4 CORDICs, and pyramid of CR blocks corresponds to Fig. 1a with replacement CORDIC into blocks of CR);
- processing of the vector with the help of two blocks of real-area Householder-CORDIC and m blocks of CORDIC (in this case m=3) (Fig. 4) [9].

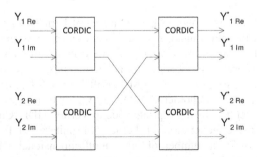

Fig. 3. The block of the complex rotation built on CORDIC

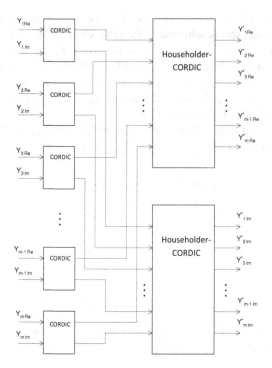

Fig. 4. Processing of the complex vector with the help of two blocks of real Householder-CORDIC and m blocks of CORDIC

7   Automating the Generation of Kernels

As noted above, for the effective implementation of the DLT algorithm in the OpenCL kernel for Altera OpenCL SDK you will need to unroll explicitly all cycles, except the external, and also to implement rather cumbersome expressions to select signs of the operands.

At increase of dimension of a multidimensional DLT, especially unitary, the complexity of the kernel's code dramatically increases, so it makes sense to automate the process of their creation.

On the one hand, this will help to get the codes of kernels for higher dimensions (more than 10). On the other hand, automatic code generation engines for OpenCL implementation of DLT algorithms can then be used in a more general system of automation of creating parallel applications for heterogeneous computer systems.

Currently, a small test application in Microsoft Visual C# is created to generate kernels for real DLT of Householder-CORDIC in vector form. Besides OpenCL kernels, the program generates the appropriate code in Verilog HDL. Currently a revision of the program for the generation of kernels of unitary DLT of Householder-CORDIC, as well as for a number of other multidimensional DLT algorithms is carried out. Also it is scheduled to compare the implementation of DLT based on Altera OpenCL SDK and on the basis of the HDL.

8   Conclusions

Assessment of the characteristics of Altera FPGA hardware implementation for some DLT algorithms using high-level design tool Altera OpenCL SDK is considered. Using Altera OpenCL SDK authors for the first time got the estimation of the features of multidimensional reflection DLT algorithms implementation using OpenCL kernels written in high level language C. The analysis of performance and complexity of circuits that implement the DLT algorithms of Householder-CORDIC reflections was made. For the first time estimations of hardware implementation on FPGA where obtained for the algorithm of unitary DLT reflection, developed earlier by authors. Only approximate analytical evaluation of complexity and performance where made for it before. The obtained results allow assert that the considered algorithms can be effectively implemented in FPGA according to the descriptions in OpenCL. Also it was shown that a multidimensional DLT of Householder-CORDIC implemented in a vector form, including unitary, for the dimensions 3, 5, 9 reduce hardware costs when the pipeline handles vectors of corresponding dimensions in comparison with traditional CORDIC algorithm from 4 to 80% (by 30-40% average). A prototype of the software module for automated generation of OpenCL kerenels for algorithms of multidimensional DLT was developed.

Acknowledgements. The authors are grateful to Altera Corporation for granting Altera OpenCL development tools within University program and Gamma company (Vyborg, Russia) for their help in expanding cooperation with Altera.

References

1. Volder, J.E.: The CORDIC Trigonometric Computing Technique. IRE Trans. on Electronic Computers EC-8(3), 330–334 (1959)
2. Andraka, R.: A Survey of CORDIC Algorithms for FPGAs // FPGA 1998. In: Proceedings of the 1998 ACM/SIGDA Sixth International Symposium on Field Programmable Gate Arrays, Monterey, CA, February 22-24, pp. 191–200 (1998)
3. Doukhnitch, E.: About one approach to execute digital linear transform. Cybernetics and Systems Analysis (5), 96–98 (1982) ISSN 1060-0396
4. Doukhnitch, E.: On one class of algorithms for coordinates discrete transforms. Processor Arrays 7, 102–108 (1976)
5. Doukhnitch, E.: Set of Hardware-implemented Algorithms for Design of Problem-oriented Processors with New Architecture. In: Proc. of Intern. Conf. Computers 1989, Bratislava, Czechoslovakia, pp. 42–47 (1989)
6. Doukhnitch, E., Kaliaev, A.: Algorithms for hardware realization of discrete coor-dinate transforms. Automatic Control and Computer Science (2), 79–82 (1977) ISSN 0146-4116
7. Hsiao, S.-F., Delosme, J.-M.: Householder CORDIC Algorithms. IEEE Transac-tions on Computers 44(8), 990–1001 (1995)
8. Cavallaro, J.R., Elster, A.C.: A CORDIC Processor Array for the SVD of a Complex Matrix. In: Vaccaro, R. (ed.) SVD and Signal Processing II, pp. 227–239. Elsevier Science, Amsterdam (1991)

9. Hsiao, S.-F., Delosme, J.-M.: Parallel Singular Value Decomposition of Complex Matrices Using Multidimensional CORDIC Algorithms. IEEE Trans. On Signal Processing (3), 256–272 (1996)
10. Doukhnitch, E.: Highly parallel multidimensional CORDIC-like algorithms. Artificial Intelligence (3), 284–293 (2001) ISSN 1561-5359
11. Doukhnitch, E.: Multidimensional CORDIC-like algorithms for DSP. In: Proc. of the Sixteenth Intern. Symp. on Computer and Information Sciences, Antalya, Turkey, pp. 368–375 (November 2001)
12. Doukhnitch, E., Salamah, M., Andreev, A.: Effective Processor Architecture for Matrix Decomposition. Arabian Journal for Science and Engineering 39(3), 1797–1804 (2014)
13. Doukhnitch, E., Egunov, V.: Algorithms of multidimensional reflections, suitable for systolic implementation (Algorithmy mnogomernyh otrazheniy, orientirovany na sistolicheskuju realizatsiju (in Russian)). Projectirovanie EVM:Megvuzovskiy sbornik nauchnykh trydov.- Ryazan: RSRA, pp. 57–63 (1994)
14. Doukhnitch, E.: Hardware implementation of unitary transformations with the help of DLT (Apparatnaya realizatsiya unitarnyh preobrazovany s pomoschju preobra-zovany DLP (in Russian)); Doukhnitch, E.I., Andreev A.E.: Conceptualnoye projec-tirovanie v obrazovanii, technike I technologii: Sb. nauch. tr. / VSTU - Volgograd, pp.68–70 (1999)
15. Andreev A.E. Hardware-oriented algorithms of basic unitary transformations in linear algebra. PHD thesis. Apparaturno-orientirovannye algorithmy tipovyh uni-tarnyh preobrazovany lineinoy algebry. Dissert. na soiskanie uch. stepeny k.t.n. Volgograd, p. 203 (1998) (in Russian)
16. Andreev, A.E., Egunov, V.A., Zharikov, D.N., Maloletkov, V.A.: Implementation of computational-intensive algorithms on a hybrid systems with reconfigurable coprocessors (Realizatsiya vychislitelno-intensivnyh algorithmov na hybridnykh systemah s reconfigurirujemymi soprocessorami: monograph), p. 180. VSTU. – Volgograd (2013) (in Russian)
17. Achieve Power-Efficient Acceleration with OpenCL on Altera FPGAs (Elec-tronic Resource), Mode of access: `http://www.altera.com/products/software/opencl/opencl-index.html`

The Beta Version of Implementation Tool
for SURE Model

Uranchimeg Tudevdagva[1,2,*], Tumurchudur Lkham[1], and Wolfram Hardt[2]

[1] Mongolian University of Science and Technology, Ulaanbaatar, Mongolia
[2] Technische Universitaet Chemnitz, Chemnitz, Germany
{uranchimeg,chuugii}@must.edu.mn,
{uranchimeg.tudevdagva,
wolfram.hardt}@informatik.tu-chemnitz.de

Abstract. This paper describes beta version of implementation tool which we developed to test structure oriented evaluation model for e-learning. The structure oriented evaluation (SURE) model consists of eight steps where included all essential parts of evaluation processes. The Mongolian University of Science and Technology and Technische Universitaet Chemnitz first time used this evaluation model for inner evaluation processes. To test advantages of SURE model we developed web based application - tool for SURE model. The beta version of tool was used in evaluation processes of above mentioned two universities. This application includes main functions of evaluation process: to create online survey based in the evaluation goal structures, to collect data online, to process data using calculation rules of SURE model, to produce graphical and statistical diagrams by evaluation scores.

Keywords: structure of goals, evaluation model, evaluation goal, online evaluation, tool for evaluation.

1 Introduction

An evaluation process is high political and complex task. Main reason is in this complex process involving many subjects and meet expectations of each involved groups as usual challenge for evaluation team. To solve this problem evaluation team have to use as it is possible objective evaluation model with clear data processing part. Second possibility to meet expectations of involved groups is data collection part have to run automatically without influence of subjects. Structure oriented evaluation model use logical structure to describe evaluation goals. In detailed example we refer to [37]. It helps to involved groups to accept criteria of evaluation and further checklist. Especially logical structure of main goals is useful to make clear expectations of stakeholders.

Many researchers and scientists developed different approaches and models for educational evaluation. R.Tyler [39], [40], D.Kirkpatrick [15] - [17], M.Scriven [31] - [33], M.Alkin [1] - [3], J.Messick [19], [20], D.Stufflebeam [28], [29] and J.Phillips

---

* Corresponding author.

A. Kravets et al. (Eds.): JCKBSE 2014, CCIS 466, pp. 243–251, 2014.
© Springer International Publishing Switzerland 2014

[23] - [25] are pioneers in educational evaluation theory. Other researchers such us M.Patton [21], [22], U.D.Ehlers [8] - [10], B.Khan [12] - [14], F.Colace [6], [7], P.Lam [18], V.Ruhe [27], E.Taylor-Powell and E.Henert [36] extended and continued this research.

However, no approach for evaluation of e-learning could reach a general acceptance until now. For a corresponding overview we refer to the report of Swedish National Agency for Higher Education [5]. This report contains an excellent survey on the European view on e-learning and quality assessment. Concise further overviews on quality research in e-learning are given by D.Ehlers [8], V.Ruhe and D.Zumbo [27]. For some additional or special aspects we refer to B.Khan [12], D.Kirkpatrick [17], D.Stufflebeam [28], P.Zaharias and A.Poulymenakou [43], E.Taylor-Powell and E. Henert [36].

Educators can use different evaluation models or methods. The main condition is that the evaluation process should be transparent and traceable for involved groups of the e-learning process. The quantitative models for evaluation of e-learning usually used are additive evaluation models. That means, depending on the considered evaluation goals, which are measured based on a defined scale, a linear function containing corresponding weight factors is used.

According to our observations there is a gap here. The existing evaluation models usually have no clear data processing part. The planning of evaluation, to create survey or checklist, to report evaluation result, all these parts of evaluation process are extensively discussed in literature. But it is not easy to find materials which explain in detail how the collected data should be processed.

By our view collected data have to be processed transparent and as objective as possible without any subjective influence. This was the starting point for development of our evaluation model which has clear calculation rules to process collected data.

The challenge of our research was to create and develop an evaluation model which fits to rapidly changing learning environment of e-learning. Aims of our research are:

- to develop an evaluation model that supports scientific evidence;
- to develop adapted calculation rules for the model;
- to test the model with simulated and authentic data.

Hence in this study, we develop an evaluation model which can be used by all groups which are involved in an e-learning project. Result of this research is a basic evaluation framework that can be collaboratively used by all groups of evaluation process.

The SURE model consists of eight steps [38]. Each step plays equal important role in evaluation process. Output of one step is become input of next step. By means, all steps related and connected one to other strongly. In the web based application - tool for SURE model automated several steps of SURE model: creation of online survey (Step 4), data collection (Step 6), data processing (Step 7) and preparation of evaluation report (Step 8).

Step 4: In our days exists various versions of online survey software. For example, Monkey [59], fluidsurveys [49], iPerceptions [51], free online survey [50], kwik survey [52], easy polls [45], survey planet [60], Sogo survey [57], eSurveypro [48], esurvey creator [47], Stellarsurvey [58], Questionpro [55], esurv [46], questionform

[53], panel place [54], survey crest [61] and addpoll [44. This procedure is integrated in our beta tool. Step 6: Data collection procedure programmed based on the online checklist (Step 4). Data collects by online and will send to sub data base of tool. Step 7: SURE model has own calculation rules based on the general measure theory. These calculation rules are programmed in this procedure. Step 8: beta tool included user graphical interface for evaluation reports by evaluation scores.

Let us explain advantage of logical structure of evaluation goals by example. Suppose we have to evaluate process = A. The evaluation team has to define key goal of evaluation in first step of SURE model. Number of key goals will depend of evaluation object and interest of involved groups in this process. In our example we will accept that was defined three key goals. Key goals designed by series logical structure (Fig. 1).

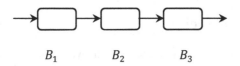

B_1 B_2 B_3

Fig. 1. Logical structure of key goals

The key goals linked between them by logical 'AND' relation. By means, if just one of these key goals cannot achieve own aim general evaluation of process will be failed.

In second step of SURE model evaluation team if it necessary can define detailed evaluation goals. We called it sub goal. Sub goal designed by parallel logical structure. In our example it can be look by Fig. 2.

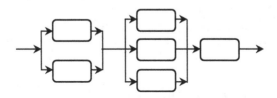

Fig. 2. Logical structure of sub goals

Sub goals are different solutions which can be used to reach defined key goal. These goals linked between them logical 'OR relation. From here we can see that of just one of defined sub goal is achieved own aim this key goal will evaluate successful.

Second main advantage of SURE model is calculation rules for data processing step. We developed adapted calculation rules to process collected data based on the general measure theory (for detail see [38]).

$$Q_q^*(C) = \frac{1}{n} \sum_{k=1}^{n} \sqrt[r]{\prod_{i=1}^{r} \left(1 - \sqrt[s_i]{\prod_{j=1}^{s_i} \left(1 - q_{ij}^{*(k)} \right)} \right)}$$

Here, q – is normalized evaluation score of single participants of online survey. s_i– is set of the participants' answer. r – is number of sub goals and k – is number of key goals. $Q_q^*(C)$ – is calibrated score of evaluation process.

Advantage of this model is data processing part can be program by defined calculation rules which are adapted to logical structure of evaluation goal. By means, the SURE model has calculation formulas for collected data with measure theory background. This is new effort to process data relating to defined evaluation goal. As usual after collection of data, collected data processed by standard tools like SPSS software. The SPSS software is statistical software for general case. If we will use calculation formulas which are directly related to defined evaluation goal than evaluation score by collected data will be more nearly to the true evaluation value.

Limitation of this model is not enough tested with real evaluation processes.

2   The Design of Tool

The structure oriented evaluation model use in two authentic evaluation processes. The Mongolian University of Science and Technology use model to evaluate success of faculty, the TU Chemnitz use to measure success of distance learning course.

In Fig. 3 shows data flow diagram of SURE tool.

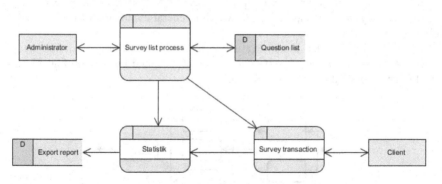

Fig. 3. Data flow diagram of SURE tool

Admin creates online survey based on the goal structures of evaluation. The tool storages several surveys parallel. The admin manages created surveys by wish or need of evaluation processes. Online survey can be "active" and visible or "passive" and invisible. Question list has different access. Admin has all right here and user works only with own created surveys. Applicants will receive unique account which generate by random function and will have access only survey questions. Collected data will be processed by defined calculation rules of SURE model. The tool can produce different type graphics and tables with evaluation results.

Fig. 4 shows relation of objects and In Fig. 5 shows activity diagram of tool for SURE model.

Main target of tool design was to establish basic architecture, which can be improved by other developers and coders in next improvement of tool. The screen design has to change depending on the browser and digital devices which use end users and admin.

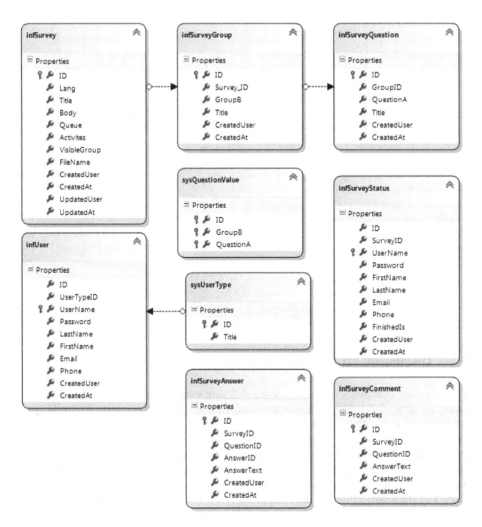

Fig. 4. Object relation diagram

In beta version we include next basic functions:

- Create online survey based on the defined logical goal structures of evaluation. Online survey or adapted checklist of evaluation can be edited after creation.
- Manage surveys in survey data base. Owner of survey can do next procedures: active or deactivate, make visible or invisible, delete or reorder surveys.
- Process collected data by SURE formulas. Calculation rules or formula of SURE model programmed in this beta version.
- Prepare reports by evaluation scores. It can be visual graphical or in table statistical types.

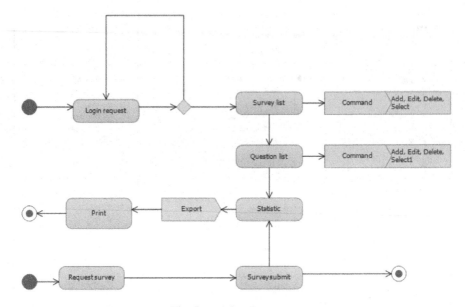

Fig. 5. Activity diagram

3   Discussion on the Beta Version

The structure oriented evaluation model defining evaluation goals by logical structures. These goal structures are start point of whole evaluation process. To create goal structures of evaluation is not integrated in beta version of tool. This step has to do manually yet. When logical structure of main and sub goals defined and confirmed by evaluation team admin can create adapted online survey based on accepted evaluation goal structure. Main target of beta tool was to automate data processing step using SURE model rules. Evaluation team will create online survey by defined goal structures and data will collected from applicants by online. Collected data have to be processed by beta tool. Evaluation team can produce different statistical information and graphics and tables by evaluation scores.

New aspect of this beta tool that it is designed only for SURE model. Without logical structure of evaluation goal this application has no meaning. Because, data processing step will use SURE model calculation rules and these rules are adapted to logical structures of evaluation goal.

The tool has selection possibility of languages. Actually version we has only two versions: English and Mongolian. Further plan is extend language options by other languages. We expect to use this beta version for evaluation processes in different activities. Based on the feedback of further users we plan to develop tool functionality for SURE model. Especially we are looking to possibility to use this tool with parallel of other free and open tools. It helps to us to compare and find gaps in our beta version.

If compare this beta version with existing online software which we listed above this software was designed for SURE model. Architecture of this application was adapted to structure oriented evaluation model. Internet based online survey software as usual has no any logical structure for evaluation goal. Not transparent how processing collected data in such us software. In our application data processing part is traceable and transparent by clear defined calculation rules. In detail we refer to [37], [38].

4   Conclusion

An evaluation is one the most important task of educational institutions. Each evaluation process has to be objectively and open as it is possibly to applicants. A software or application which we calling tools will be helpful to evaluators to do objective, open evaluation processes.

To create and develop tool which supports performance of evaluation process is important issue of software engineering field. Each complex application need a lot of time to verify and improve that tool. We are in ongoing progress of such us project. To distribute idea of SURE model and to establish tool for this model is our challenge. The theoretical background of data processing part is helpful to evaluators to create more objective evaluation. Calculation rules of SURE model are easy to implement by programming and traceable to control for evaluators. The beta version of tool was tested successful. In next step we improve visualization of data processing and support tools for evaluation report.

References

1. Alkin, M.C.: Evaluation Theory Development. Evaluation Comment 2, 2–7 (1969)
2. Alkin, M.C., Fitz-Gibbon, C.T.: Methods and Theories of Evaluating Programs. Journal of Research and Development in Education 8(3), 2–15 (1975)
3. Alkin, M.C., Christie, C.A.: An Evaluation Theory Tree, pp. 12–65. SAGE Press (2004)
4. Community Tool Box. A Framework for Program Evaluation: A Gateway to Tools, ch. 36. Work Group for Community Health and Development at the University of Kansas (2014)
5. E-learning quality, Aspects and criteria for evaluation of e-learning in higher education. Hoegskoleverket, Swedish National Agency for Higher Education, Report 2008:11 R (2008)
6. Colace, F., De Santo, M., Vento, M.: E-learning platform: Developing an Evaluation, Strategy in a Real Case. In: Frontiers in Education 35th Annual Conference, pp. 20–25
7. Colace, F., De Santo, M., Pietrosanto, A.: Evaluation Models for E-Learning Platform: an AHP approach. In: 36th ASEE/IEEE Frontiers in Education Conference, pp. 1–6 (2006)
8. Ehlers, U.D.: Quality in e-learning: use and dissemination of quality approaches in European e-learning: a study by the European Quality Observatory. Office for Official Publications of the European Communities (2005)
9. Ehlers, U.D., Pawlowski, J.M. (eds.): Handbook of Quality and Standardisation in E-Learning. Springer, Heidelberg (2006)
10. Ehlers, U.D.: Low Cost, Community Based Certification for E-learning in Capacity Building, Bonn (2010)
11. Joint Committee on Educational Evaluation, Sanders, J.R. (Chair): The program evaluation standards: how to assess evaluations of educational programs. Sage Publications, Thousand Oaks (1994)
12. Khan, B.H.: The People, process and product continuum in e-learning: The e-learning P3 model. Educational Technology 44(5), 33–40 (2004)
    http://asianvu.com/bookstoread/etp/elearning-p3model.pdf

13. Khan, B.H.: Managing e-learning: Design, delivery, implementation and evaluation. Information Science Publishing, Hershey (2005)
14. Khan, B.H.: Flexible Learning in an Information Society. IGI Global, Hershey (2006)
15. Kirkpatrick, D.L.: Techniques for evaluating training programs. Journal of American Society of Training Directors 13(3), 21–26 (1959)
16. Kirkpatrick, D.L.: Evaluating Training Programs. San Francisco: Berrett-Koehler Publishers, Inc. (1994)
17. Kirkpatrick, D.L., Kirkpatrick, J.D.: Evaluating Training Programs, The Four Levels, 3rd edn., San Francisco (2006)
18. Lam, P., McNaught, C.: A Three-Layered Cyclic Model of ELearning Development and Evaluation. Journal of Interactive Learning Research 19(2), 313–329 (2008)
19. Messick, S.J.: The Once and Future Issues of Validity: Assessing the Meaning and Consequences of Measurement, ETS Research Report. RR-86-30 (1986)
20. Messick, S.J.: The Interplay of Evidence and Consequences in the Validation of Performance Assessments. Educational Researcher 23(2), 13–23 (1994), http://edr.sagepub.com/content/23/2/13.full.pdf
21. Patton, M.Q.: Qualitative Evaluation Methods. Sage Publication, Beverly Hills (1980)
22. Patton, M.Q.: Utilization-focused evaluation. Sage Publications, Inc. Ruhe,V and Zumbo, B. D, Evaluation in distance education and learning: the unfolding model. The Guilford Press, New York (2008)
23. Phillips, J.J.: Handbook of Evaluation and Measurement Methods. Gulf Press, London (1991)
24. Phillips, J.J.: Return on Investment in Training and Performance Improvement Programs. Gulf Publishing Co., Houston (1997)
25. Phillips, P.P., Phillips, J.J.: ROI Fundamentals: Why and When to Measure Return on Investment (Measurement and Evaluation Series). Pfeiffer, San Francisco (2008)
26. Phillips, P.P., et al.: ASTD Handbook of Measuring and evaluating training. ASDT, Alexandria (2010)
27. Ruhe, V., Zumbo, B.D.: Evaluation in distance education and elearning: the unfolding model. The Guilford Press, New York (2009)
28. Stufflebeam, D.L.: The CIPP model for Program Evaluation. Evaluation in Education and Human Services 6, 117–141 (1983)
29. Stufflebeam, D.L.: The CIPP Model for Evaluation. Evaluation in Education and Human Services 49, 279–317 (2000)
30. Shadish, W.: Evaluation theory is who we are. American Journal of Evaluation 19(1), 1–19 (1998)
31. Scriven, M.S., et al.: The methodology of evaluation. In: Perspectives of Curriculum Evaluation, AERA Monograph Series on Curriculum Evaluation, vol. (1), pp. 39–81. Rand McNally, Chicago (1967)
32. Scriven, M.S.: Pros and cons about goal-free evaluation. American Journal of Evaluation 12(1), 55–76 (1991)
33. Scriven, M.S.: The nature of evaluation part II: Training. Practical Assessment, Research and Evaluation 6(12), 1–5 (1999)
34. Stufflebeam, D.L.: The CIPP model for Program Evaluation. Evaluation in Education and Human Services 6, 117–141 (1983)
35. Stufflebeam, D.L.: The CIPP Model for Evaluation. Evaluation in Education and Human Services 49, 279–317 (2000)

36. Taylor-Powell, E., Henert, E.: Developing a logic model: Teaching and training guide. Board of Regents of the University of Wisconsin System. Program Development and Evaluation, Madison (2008), http://www.uwex.edu/ces/pdande/evaluation/pdf/lmguidecomplete.pdf
37. Tudevdagva, U., Hardt, W.: A new evaluation model for eLearning programs. Technical Report CSR-11-03, Chemnitz University of Technology, Chemnitz, Germany (2011)
38. Tudevdagva, U., Hardt, W.: A measure theoretical evaluation model for e-learning programs. In: Proceedings of the IADIS on e-Society 2012, Berlin, Germany, March 10-13, pp. 44–52 (2012)
39. Tyler, R.W.: Basic principles of curriculum and instruction. The University of Chicago Press, Chicago (1949)
40. Tyler, R.W.: General statement of evaluation. The Journal of Educational Research 35(4), 492–501 (1972)
41. Weiss, C.: Have we learned anything new about the use of evaluation? American Journal of Evaluation 19(1), 21–33 (1998)
42. Yarbrough, D.B., Shulha, L.M., Hopson, R.K., Caruthers, F.A.: The Program Evaluation Standards: A Guide for Evaluators and Evaluation Users, 3rd edn. Sage Publications (2011)
43. Zaharias, P., Poulymenakou, A.: Developing a usability evaluation method for e-learning applications: beyond functional usability. International Journal of Human-Computer Interaction 25(1), 75–98 (2009)

Web Resources

44. Addpoll, http://www.addpoll.com/
45. Easy polls, http://www.easypolls.net/
46. Esurv, http://esurv.org/
47. Esurvey creator, https://www.esurveycreator.com
48. Esurveyspro, http://www.esurveyspro.com/free-onlinesurvey.aspx
49. Fluid Surveys, http://uidsurveys.com/
50. Free online survyes, http://freeonlinesurveys.com/
51. Iperceptions, http://signup.iperceptions.com/
52. Kwik Survey, http://kwiksurveys.com/
53. OnlQuestionform, http://questionform.com/
54. Panelplace, http://www.panelplace.com/
55. Questionpro, http://www.questionpro.com/
56. Quick Surveys, https://www.quicksurveys.com/
57. Sogo survey, http://www.sogosurvey.com/
58. Stellar survey, http://stellarsurvey.com/
59. Survey Monkey, https://de.surveymonkey.com
60. Survey planet, https://www.surveyplanet.com/
61. Surveycrest, http://www.surveycrest.com/

Evaluation of Flexibility to Changes Focusing on the Variable Structures in Legacy Software

Takanori Sasaki[1,*], Nobukazu Yoshioka[2], Yasuyuki Tahara[3], and Akihiko Ohsuga[3]

[1] University of Electro-Communications & Canon Incorporation, Tokyo, Japan
tsasaki@nii.ac.jp
[2] National Institute of Informatics, Tokyo, Japan
nobukazu@nii.ac.jp
[3] University of Electro-Communications, Tokyo, Japan
{tahara,ohsuga}@uec.ac.jp

Abstract. Light weight development processes like Agile have emerged in response to rapidly changing market requirements. However such processes are inadequate for software in embedded systems. As embedded software undergoes frequent refactoring, targeting only immediate requirements. As a result maintainability decreases because the system is not designed to respond to changes in the associated hardware. In this paper, we propose a method for detection of variation points and variability mechanisms. We also propose a technique for evaluation of flexibility to changes. Our approach is based on analyses of the call graph and the inheritance structure of source code to identify a layer structure that is specific to embedded software. These techniques provide us with objective and quantitative information about costs of adding functionality. We applied the proposal method to an actual product's code before and after the refactoring and could verify an improvement in system's variability.

Keywords: legacy code, variability, flexibility, evaluation.

1   Introduction

Recently, in software technology innovation is accelerating and new product concepts are appearing such as mobile, cloud, augmented reality and so on. As a result software system is getting more and more complex, while market needs are also changing in parallel. Therefore, if the market needs changes during development or immediately after production, it becomes difficult to create profit using the conventional processes like Waterfall Model in which making a lot of products after developing process such as accuracy forecasting future market, making specification, making design, implementing code, testing as in the conventional. In response to such challenges Light Weight development processes like Agile [1] are becoming popular. These process aims to finish developing only simple feature and mechanism, striving for shorter time-to-market without forecasting future accurately and designing

---

[*] Corresponding author.

A. Kravets et al. (Eds.): JCKBSE 2014, CCIS 466, pp. 252–269, 2014.
© Springer International Publishing Switzerland 2014

mechanism in advance. Once feedback from the market is received, additional features are developed. Thereby it mineralizes the gap between market needs and product feature. However, in case of such a development process, it is difficult to apply the Software Product Line (SPL) that is to do feature analysis [2] at first, is to identify variation points in product and to construct software system along the roadmap to compliant various requirements.

In Agile process development, legacy code is frequently refactored to develop new features which are only targeting immediate requirements [1]. Such process is especially inadequate for software in embedded systems. As the system is not designed to respond to changes in the associated hardware(s), its maintainability gradually decreases. Reason for such behavior can be attributed to the fact that usually embedded software numerous patches in order to accommodate hardware changes without inflating costs (full scale refactoring is very costly). For example, some hardware needs to initialize in a fixed order or needs to access with specialized format/protocol etc.

There are many papers about the method of refactoring to improve the maintainability in terms of implementation [7]. Also there are many papers about the method of variability design and feature analysis [2, 15] before implementation of product. However there are very few papers about the method of refactoring in terms of variability or the method of feature analysis for legacy code. Therefore conventional papers cannot say how to identify which feature is the most easy to maintain.

In this paper, we aim to provide with objective and quantitative information about costs of adding functionality and costs of maintenance in the future. Our contributions are to propose a method for detection of variation points and variability mechanisms in legacy code for embedded systems and to propose technique for evaluation of the flexibility to changes. Our approach consists of the following three steps: (1) to analyze the call graph and the inheritance structure of source code, (2) to identify a layer structure from them that is specific to embedded software in order to identify variation points and variability mechanisms, and (3) to compute the variability scores according to the types of the identified elements. We applied the proposal method to an actual product's code before and after the refactoring and computed the result of improvement in variability.

This paper is organized as follows: Section 2 explains the problem in embedded system software targeted in our scope. Section 3 proposes the method of flexibility to changes in each feature. Section 4 describes the experiment using actual code. Section 5 discusses the results in this study. Section 6 provides the related works. Finally Section 7 conclusions and directions for future work.

2   Problems in Embedded System

2.1   Scope

Lately, embedded systems are being developed and used widely. This paper targets fresh embedded system; products for which hardware specification has not matured, a new area which has unknown market needs and have customizable characteristics which should be adapted by variation and improvement.

These embedded systems are increasingly involved with high-speed network, miniaturization of sensor, high-performance computer chip immediately. For example, wearable computer, humanoid robot, networking home electronic facility which is connected to internet always, cooperation systems in home or office, automotive which is added new safety function and so on. These are new embedded system that does not complete the specification of the conventional software systems.

2.2   Problem

In our targeted embedded system, because of the swiftly changing market needs, it is difficult to use sequential development process like Waterfall, which ensures the detailed specification and allows development without rework.   Therefore it is easy to apply light weight development process like Agile without implementing for additional mechanism. These processes achieve to sell product to be shorter time-to-market with adapting changing market needs. And then it needs to consider variability design of making SPL which should be designed at the first in case of other process after product is a success. However in case of having legacy code, it becomes difficult to determine the location for introducing changes, additionally to appraise the costs of such changes is also laborious. As legacy code is often abstruse it's difficult to analyze the impact of these changes on the maintainability of software.

In case of refactoring, it is not avoidable to depend on the programmer for modification of place or method. In case of software maintainability, it is easy to increase costs by large spaghetti software regardless of unified concept.   Therefore using only legacy code, it is important to provide with objective and quantitative information to maintain with minimum costs compliant changing specification or improvement of hardware.

However it needs variability design point of view such as feature analysis based on requirement in general. Therefore it is difficult to find variability of product using only legacy code. Furthermore in case of making class diagram or call graph by software reverse engineering, it gets difficult to grab its structure. The reason why that it is getting to increase class relationship and number of callings involved increasing number of classes.

3   A Method for Evaluation of Flexibility to Change

3.1   Overview

As shown in Fig. 1, we propose a method that can evaluate the flexibility to changes quantitatively by computing variability score for each feature.

This method consists of 3 steps. First, we analyze source code from two points of views (call graph and inheritance which is important mechanism for object-oriented language) [12, 13] to prevent explosion of number of classes. Next, we find layer structure, inheritance structure, variation points and variability mechanisms in legacy code to remove dependence on programmer to decipher means or location for modification. In this paper, we define the variation point as a location of changing functionality in legacy code, which is realized by replacing class to other similar ones. We also define a variability mechanism as an implementation way which replaces class.

A feature usually has many functionality which is replaced at variation point. Finally, we map variability mechanism on layer structure and compute variability score to conduct an objective and quantitative evaluation for each feature.

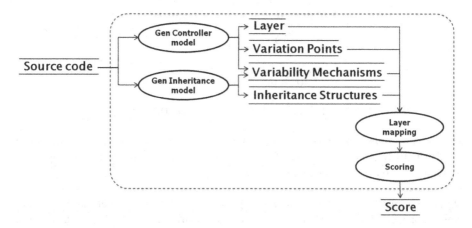

Fig. 1. Proposal Overview

3.2   Finding Variation Points and Variability Mechanism

Variability Design. We can identify the candidate of variation point as a class which has dependency on other classes and provides some functionality. Fig. 2 illustrates variation point [14] and controller class. We can find its candidate in Controller model diagram which is generated in terms of call relationship between classes. We define controller class to control internal instructions of system. A candidate of variation point can be identified by counting relationship with other classes. This class should be called by only one class and should call some other classes. These criteria are necessary to allow variation point class to change functionality (a). Furthermore if it also generates these classes exclusively, we can confirm that it is a variation point. Similarly, we can infer a class as controller class if it is called by some classes and calls some other classes due to intersection of many controls of feature (b).

This Controller model diagram has less number of classes than a class diagram generated by reverse engineering because classes which do not corresponded with aforementioned condition for example abstract class, calls which are only called by others etc. are removed.   Therefore we can observe variability design.

Inheritance Structure. Inheritance structure is important for object-oriented language [3, 11]. Also it is important to map variation points to variability mechanism for this paper. From inheritance model diagram (generated in terms of inheritance and instantiation of classes) we can classify two types of inheritance structure corresponding to variability mechanism.

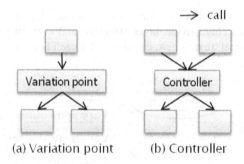

Fig. 2. Structures in Controller Model Diagram

Simple Inheritance Structure. Fig. 3 (a) illustrates a simplest inheritance structure. It is inherited from same base class. It is used by a variability mechanism to replace a derived class to another using base class as interface.

Different Layer Inheritance Structure. Fig. 3 (b) illustrates an inheritance structure which connects different inheritance trees to an abstract class at a higher layer. It is inherited from different base class. It is used by a variability mechanism to replace a derived class to another using same abstraction class as interface for improving cohesion.

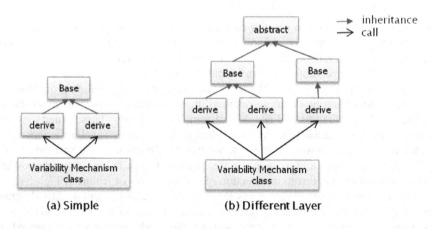

Fig. 3. Inheritance Structure

Variability Mechanism. Variability mechanism is a class created to allow changes in the software functionality. We can spot a variability mechanism using Controller model and Inheritance model diagram. It is a class which accesses some of leaf node of inheritance model and also accesses its parent class. It is classified in five design patterns [5, 6] in terms of using and creation.

Mixed Creation and Use. In this pattern logic to create and use part classes is defined within the class. This kind gets affected by changing parts or change in creation condition. This pattern decreases system understandability as class logic is usually complex. Fig. 4 (a) illustrates a sample of this pattern in Controller model diagram.

Factory. In this pattern, a class specifies a control logic accesses, via an abstract class, another class encapsulating the logics to create parts used in the control logic from the part classes. The former class does not create parts for itself. Part creation responsibility is delegated to factory class. Parts classes are created by specialized creation class. Simply put, it separates between use and creation of class. Though, in case of increase in number of part classes, specialized creation class gets larger and more complex. Fig. 4 (b) illustrates a sample of this pattern in Controller model diagram.

Factory Method. This pattern is similar to *Factory* pattern. Here we separate logic into two portions. 'Common part' which should reside in base class and 'part specific logic' which should be placed in derived class, therefore avoiding complex creation logic. However the system understandability decreases as number of parts increases because number of classes is also increased. This pattern is similar to Abstract *Factory* pattern in Controller model diagram.

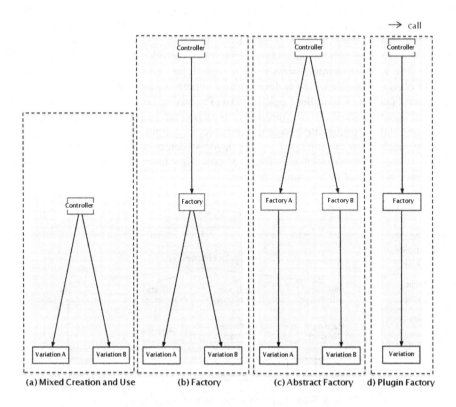

Fig. 4. Example of Variability Mechanism in Controller model diagram

Abstract Factory. This pattern hides composite structures of parts from user class by creating Factory Class for each variation. If there are some different composite structures for creating parts, it is easy to add the pattern of the structures. However if new parts is added to the structure, all classes involved in the structure gets affected. Therefore in case of frequently changing part classes the flexibility to changes decreases. Fig. 4 (c) illustrates a sample of this pattern in Controller model diagram.

Plugin Factory. Here parts can be generated dynamically without any creation of logic. Generating parts are expressed in inheritance model. However access to abstraction class from part class is not expressed in controller model because of absence of creation logic in code. It has very small impact as a change because of the aforementioned reason. However this pattern is difficult to use in cases where performance overhead involved in changing functionality cannot be ignored, as this pattern involves dynamic loading. Fig. 4 (d) illustrates a sample of this pattern in Controller model diagram.

3.3   Specified Layer Structure and Mapping Variability Mechanism

Software structure can be dissected into multiple layers having similar abstraction level. It is important to determine in which layer the variability mechanism is implemented. Fig. 5 illustrates the basic 3 layered structure for embedded system on which one can map variability mechanism. Each class called by controller class represents a feature tree. Whole feature trees connect at control layer. The controller calls logic class for each feature. The logic class implements logic at logic layer. The logic class calls hardware abstract class or algorithm class at detail layer. Furthermore Logic Layer is separated into two layers Hardware Controller Logic and Data Processing Logic.

Data is transmitted from hardware to algorithm class via controller, after processing data is transmitted back to hardware for output. Variation points and variability mechanism are mapped to this layer structure after separating controller model. If the variation point was found at controller layer, the logic related to this inheritance is deemed to be a single feature.

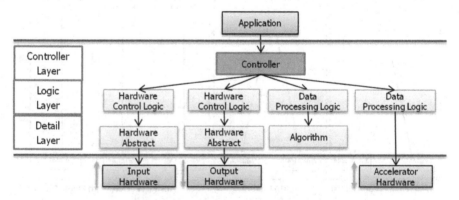

Fig. 5. Basic Layer Structure in Embedded System

3.4   Scoring of the Flexibility to Change of Software

The scoring of the flexibility to changes is computed for individual feature because requirements of changing each feature are different. For example, hardware device is depends on a product planning of each sensor. An algorithm is also depends on requirements of changing form market. In particular, an algorithm where valuable to product, it might increase. Therefore it is important to have the flexibility against the change. On the other hand a feature can exist for which changes has not been forecasted and might not have flexibility, but is designed for performance (often case in embedded). Therefore it needs to grasp the flexibility to changes quantitatively for each feature. We can compute score it by equation (1).

$$\text{Score} = \sum_{i=0}^{n} Score_L(i) + \sum_{j=0}^{n} Score_I(j) + \sum_{k=0}^{n} Score_P(k) \tag{1}$$

$Score_L$: the Score of each Layer
$Score_I$: the Score of each Inheritance structure
$Score_P$: the Score of each variability mechanism
i:Layer, j : Type, k : pattern

The score for each feature is merged with score of implementing of variability mechanism layer ($Score_L$), the score of Inheritance structure ($Score_I$), the score of variability mechanism pattern ($Score_P$). Value of following each score is a sample.

Table 1 illustrates the score of implementing of variability mechanism layer. As this evaluation aims to identify the location for implementation of variability mechanism (Controller layer or Logic layer) we evaluate about the three layers such as Controller Layer, Logic Layer and Detail Layer. Each layer has a different score and score is defined in such a way, so as, further if it away from controller, better is the score. It is necessary to implement variability mechanism away from controller layer because controller tended to be complex by adding feature.

Table 1. The Score of Layer

Layer	Score
Controller	0
Logic Layer	1
Detail Layer	2

Table 2 illustrates the score of inheritance structure. Each type of it has a different score. Further the score is defined that *Different Layer Inheritance structure* type is better. Because *Different Layer Inheritance structure* type can be minimized affection against changing in each inheritance tree. As compared with the case where no inheritance structure in class, class user side can access to necessary functionality via abstraction class. Also the flexibility to changes is strengthened by using it at variation points due to add functionality easily.

Table 2. The Score of Inheritance Structure

Type	Score
Simple Inheritance structure	1
Different Layer Inheritance structure	2

Table 3 illustrates the score of variability mechanism. This score is based on two criteria:

- Effect of change on legacy code. Low effect leads to high score.
- Separation of class generation and use mechanism. If the two mechanisms have low cohesion, changes can be introduced with least impact, hence low cohesion between generation and use leads to higher variability score.

Among the five patterns only *Mixed Creation and Use* pattern has no separation between class generation and use. Other pattern has varying impact on introduction of change. For example, in case of adding to replace parts of some permutation as specification, *Mixed Creation and Use* pattern needs to modify a code where use is written and add new parts. Similarly *Factory* pattern needs to modify a code where the factory is written and add new parts. While *Factory method* needs to add some factory class for each part, new parts and call of the each factory. Similarly *Abstract Factory* pattern needs to add a factory class for additional variation, new parts and call of the factory. *Plugin Factory* needs to add new parts.

Table 3. Sample Score of Variability Mechanism

Pattern	Score
Mixed Creation and Use	1
Factory	2
Factory Method	3
Abstract Factory	4
Plugin Factory	5

Therefore we can compare the flexibility to changes of legacy code quantitatively by score. Therefore we can predict which changing of hardware makes us big impact or which feature should be refactored in advance. Also the feature which gets high score is smaller costs of implementation than the feature of low score in case of changing specification. Incidentally a Data Processing Logic related Hardware Logic directly is sometimes affected by changing of hardware. Therefore it is better that both features hold same score.

4 Experiment and Result

We conducted an experiment with one of the products from Canon Incorporation The product was written in C++ language and was developed toward new market area. A part of this code was evaluated by proposal method for flexibility to change.

4.1   Finding Variation Points and Inheritance Structures

Fig. 6 illustrates the Controller model diagram which is generated in terms of call relationship between classes only. Table 4 illustrates the elements of Controller model. At first glance we can see that this software system is single layer system because number of detected Controller class is only one. Fig. 6 illustrates this system has nine features in Logic Layer. Also number of variation points was detected is 8.

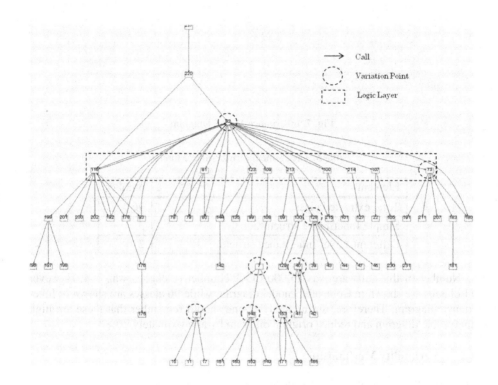

Fig. 6. Controller Model Diagram

Table 4. The Element of Controller Model

Element	Number
Total extracted class	71
Controller class	1
Variation point	8
Feature	9

Fig. 7 illustrates the Inheritance model Diagram in terms of inheritance. Table 5 illustrates the elements of Inheritance model. Number of the *simple inheritance structure* was detected is 3 and number of the difference layer inheritance structure was detected is 2. Both types of structures are used by variability mechanism.

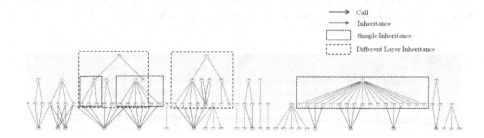

Fig. 7. Inheritance Model Diagram

Table 5. The element of Inheritance model

Element	number
Total extracted class	96
Simple Inheritance structure	3
Different Layer Inheritance structure	2

Number of this software was 23,000 LOC. Number of classes was 254. However 71 classes are shown in Controller model diagram while 96 classes are shown in Inheritance diagram. Therefore, during analysis one should remember that these are high analyzable diagram and reduce original diagram by approximately 70%.

4.2   Variability Mechanism

Fig. 8 illustrates where variability mechanism is implemented and of what type. Table 6 illustrates number of variability mechanisms for each layer. Table 7 illustrates number of variability mechanisms. We already found 9 features in Controller model. However two features which were detected are merged because a variation point of one variability mechanism was detected in Controller layer. Therefore number of features was reduced to 8. Following Variability mechanism pattern was detected among 8 features.

- *Abstract Factory* and *Factory Method*
- *Abstract Factory*
- *Factory Method*
- *Factory*

Further 3 variability mechanisms were detected in terms of implementation in Controller model.

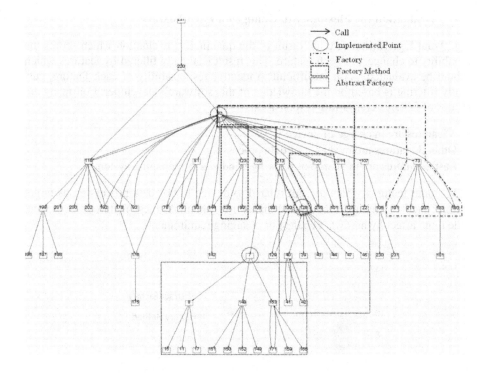

Fig. 8. The Place of Variability Mechanism and Type

Table 6. Number of Variability Mechanism at Each Layer

Layer	number
Controller	3
Logic Layer	0
Detail Layer	2

Table 7. Number of Variability Mechanism Pattern

Pattern	number
Mixed Creation and Use	0
Factory	1
Factory Method	2
Abstract Factory	2
Plugin Factory	0

4.3   Evaluation the Flexibility to Change on Each Feature

Fig. 9 and Fig. 10 illustrate the result of the quantitative evaluation which scores the flexibility to changes for each feature. This result is already filtered by features which should be evaluated. As it is difficult to identify responsibility of each feature, currently filtering is based on the knowledge of this software's developer. Following are groups of features concerning responsibility.

- 3 features are in charge of device I/O.
- Other 3 features are in charge of data processing.
- Last 2 features are in charge of painting windows or managing system.

We omit features which are not related to device I/O or data processing as target feature: such as painting window and managing system. As these features would have little to no affect by hardware change or changing requirements.

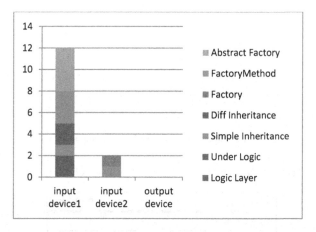

Fig. 9. The Evaluation of Hardware Logic

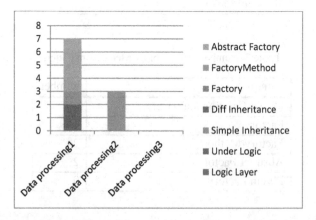

Fig. 10. The Evaluation of Data Processing Logic

Fig. 9 and Fig. 10 also illustrate the score of flexibility to change for each feature. This score is sum of all the scores related to the feature. This graph separates Hardware Logic group and Data Processing group.

We can see that input device1 (Fig. 9) implements *Factory Method* pattern as variability mechanism to change functionality at logic level. Furthermore it also implements *Difference Layer Inheritance* structure and *Abstract Factory* pattern to change functionality at algorithm level.

Score of the flexibility to changes for output device is zero. This is because it (output device) aims to improve performance and simplify structure than flexibility because of no changing plan.

In case of Data processing logic, one feature (Data processing1) implements Abstract *Factory* pattern in some places far from controller layer. Another feature (Data Processing2) is implemented through *Factory Method* pattern. However this feature has no variation point currently.

Thus we can compare the flexibility to changes for each feature quantitatively. Also we can know the reason of the score for each feature. Furthermore we can predict the impact on legacy code for each feature by changing a specification.

5   Evaluation

5.1   Comparison of the Refactoring Method in Convention

By convention, programmer needs to search related code after getting requirements of changing. However the code size is increased, it becomes difficult to understand perfectly. Therefore this work depends on programmer's knowledge and experiments and the quality of maintainability is difference in each changes. Also it is difficult to evaluate validation of changing code objectively. Therefore sometimes changes exceed or fall behind the requirements, as review is done by other developers who cannot understand source code deeply. Another disadvantage of convention method is the inability to evaluate efficiency of refactoring besides lines of code or number of classes and so on. The proposal method can provide other useful metrics for refactoring.

5.2   The Efficiency of Improvement Using Proposal Method

Against same project code, project has done refactoring. It aims to be more flexible against the changing of the data processing and then be able to customize freely. Therefore one of data processing logic was modified to plugin mechanism. In the before and after refactoring, the number of classes has increased to 254-291 and statement lines of code has increased about 3000 lines.

Fig. 11 and Fig. 12 illustrate the result of the evaluation of the flexibility to changes. Fig. 11 illustrates the controller model diagram after refactoring and additional variability mechanisms. One inheritance tree and related call tree are added. Then new two variability mechanisms are implemented. *Factory Method* pattern in the previous diagram (Fig. 9) is modified to contain a variation point because of addition of new functionality. While one variability mechanism is *Plugin Factory*, this pattern does not contain code to change functionality. Therefore this is advantageous as costs to modify are low and flexibility is high.

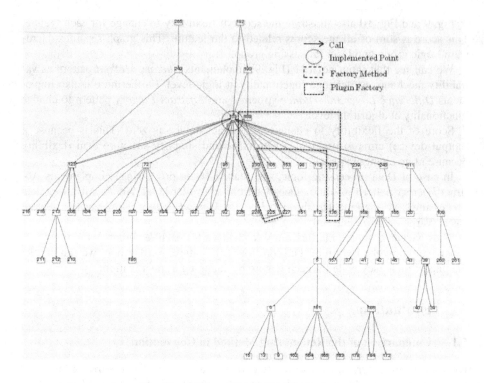

Fig. 11. Additional Variability Mechanism

Fig. 12 illustrates the evaluation of the flexibility to changes regarding Data processing Logic. As compare to Fig. 10, the score of Data processing2 is improved from 3 to 9.

This result is validated by an interview with the project developer. Also the project plan to modify the data processing logic3 which is still 0 and the input device2 which is still low score.

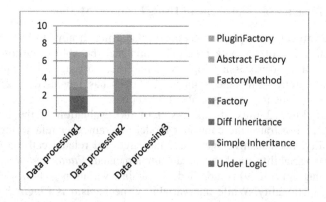

Fig. 12. The Evaluation of Data Processing Logic

5.3   Restriction of Proposal Method and Expand Area to Apply

In this paper, we deal with object-oriented language [12, 13] which has features like class inheritance, delegation and others to capture designer's intent. However there are many projects which use non object-oriented code in embedded system. Therefore we need to study how this proposal method can be dealt with non-object-oriented code.

In this paper, this proposal method is limited to the embedded system in a specific condition. We need to study whether it can be apply any other area's products if the product has already code.

6   Related Work

Walkinshaw et al [4] proposed an approach to object-oriented feature extraction using landmarks method and barrier methods. This approach extracts feature or use case by slicing the call graph. They removed unnecessary call graph to avoid explosion. In this paper, features are extracted using call graph and inheritance graph and not by slice-based approach. Also unnecessary classes are reduced in terms of variability mechanisms.

Keepence et al [6] defined three patterns of class structure design. These patterns are closely similar to the mandatory, alternative, and optional feature property in the feature oriented domain analysis. In this paper, five patterns are identified in terms of implementation in variation point. These patterns correspond to the degree of flexibility.

Yinxing [8] proposed an approach to integrate the domain analysis and clone detection to recover the variability. Duszynski et al [16] evaluated reusability by extracting variability mechanisms and common features. These are the extraction method of variation points or variability mechanisms by comparison of some similar products family. In this paper, variation points and variability mechanisms are extracted from single product using inheritance structure and call graph.

Ribeiro et al [9] said there are many type of variability mechanisms such as Inheritance, Configuration Files, Aspect-Oriented Programming (AOP). Further it is difficult to select appropriate mechanism. Therefore they develop a tool which suggests the appropriate variability mechanism depending on the criteria like modularity, LOC, scalability, binding time, place, type. They have also made for comparison using different mechanism such as Mixin and AOP. However it is difficult to use these mechanisms in our targeted embedded system generally due to language specification. In this paper, variability mechanism which is based on inheritance structure is detected in legacy code in terms of specialized pattern using inheritance.

Makkar et al [10] said there is a relationship between depth of the inheritance tree and reusability. As depth of inheritance tree increases, reusability decreases. They also said the threshold is within 3 layers. Therefore they created an equation relating the two quantities. In this paper, we compute the inheritance tree involved variability mechanism, which is placed under 3 layers.

Bansiya et al [12] mapped object-oriented design components to design metrics and design quality attributes. Hudli et al [13] validated various object-oriented metrics. For object-oriented language, various evaluation methods are proposed in terms of design or metrics. This paper is described about the method of evaluation of design in legacy code in terms of variation.

Claudia et al [15] proposed the method of evaluation variability mechanisms. They said there is variability implementation mechanism, selection of option and binding time as an evaluation point of view. In this paper, variability implementation mechanisms are detected in legacy code automatically.

Babar [17], Bengtsson et al [18], Castaldi et al [19] said the method of evaluation of software product line architecture. As they said, the method based on scenario such as SAAM and ATAM have been established. In this paper, we propose the method of evaluation by analyzing legacy code.

Hattori et al [20] evaluated the method for analysis of change impact. This analysis analyzes the affection against actual change. In this paper, we can evaluate affection each feature against change before actual changing.

7   Conclusion and Future Work

This paper has proposed a method to evaluate software's flexibility to changes in embedded system. This method is focused on variable structure such as Variability mechanism and Variation point in legacy software, consequently the evaluation is done for each feature. We applied the proposal method to an actual product's code before and after the refactoring and could compute the result indicating improvement in variability. Furthermore it could reduce classes by 60% to 70% in comparison to regular reverse modeling. This proposal method makes us to select location of variation point and implement variability mechanism appropriately depending on project's available capacity especially Agile development process.

In future, we intended to compare of the flexibility to change between different embedded systems.

References

1. Ghanam, Y., Andreychuk, D., Maurer, F.: Reactive Variability Management Using Agile Software Development. In: The International Conference on Agile Methods in Software Development, Orlando, pp. 27–34 (2010)
2. Kang, K., Lee, J., Donohoe, P.: Feature-Oriented Product Line Engineering. IEEE Software 19(4), 58–65 (2002)
3. Sheldon, F.T., Jerath, K., Chung, H.: Metrics for maintainability of class inheritance hierarchies. Journal of Software Maintanance:Research and Practice 14(3), 147–160 (2002)
4. Walkinshaw, N., Roper, M., Wood, M.: Feature Location and Extraction using Landmarks and Barriers. In: Proceedings of International Conference on Software Maintenance, Paris, pp. 54–63 (2007)
5. Niere, J., Schafer, W., Wadsack, J.P., Wendehals, L., Welsh, J.: Towards pattern-based design recovery. In: Proceedings of the 24rd International Conference on Software Engineering, Orlando, FL, pp. 338–348 (2002)
6. Keepence, B., Mannion, M.: Using Patterns to Model Variability in Product Families. IEEE Software 16(4), 102–108 (1999)

7. Du Bois, B., Demeyer, S., Verelst, J.: Refactoring - Improving Coupling and Cohesion of Existing Code. In: Proceedings of 11th Working Conference on Reverse Engineering, pp. 144–151 (2004)
8. Xue, Y.: Reengineering legacy software products into software product line based on automatic variability analysis. In: 33rd International Conference on Software Engineering, Honolulu, pp. 1114–1117 (2011)
9. Ribeiro, M., Borba, P.: Improving Guidance when Restructuring Variabilities in Software Product Lines. In: 13th European Conference on Software Maintenance and Reengineering, Kaiserslautern, pp. 79–88 (2009)
10. Makkar, G., Chhabra, J.K., Challa, R.K.: Object oriented inheritance metric-reusability perspective. In: International Conference on Computing, Electronics and Electrical Technologies, Kumaracoil, pp. 852–859 (2012)
11. Breesam, K.M.: Metrics for Object-Oriented Design Focusing on Class Inheritance Metrics. In: 2nd International Conference on Dependability of Computer Systems, Szklarska, pp. 231–237 (2007)
12. Bansiya, J., Davis, C.G.: A hierarchical model for object-oriented design quality assessment. IEEE Transactions on Software Engineering 28(1), 4–7 (2002)
13. Hudli, R.V., Hoskins, C.L., Hudli, A.V.: Software Metrics for Object-oriented Designs. In: Proceedings of IEEE International Conference on Computer Design: VLSI in Computers and Processors, Cambridge, MA, pp. 492–495 (1994)
14. Rajasree, M.S., Janaki, R.D., Jithendra, K.R.: Pattern Oriented Approach for the Design of Frameworks for Software Productlines. In: Proceedings of International Workshop on Product Line Engineering: The Early Steps: Planning, Modeling, and Managing, pp. 65–70 (2002)
15. Claudia, F., Andreas, L., Thomas, S.: Evaluating Variability Implementation Mechanisms. In: Proceedings of International Workshop on Product Line Engineering: The Early Steps: Planning, Modeling, and Managing, pp. 59–64 (2002)
16. Duszynski, S., Knodel, J., Becker, M.: Analyzing the Source Code of Multiple Software Variants for Reuse Potential. In: 18th Working Conference on Reverse Engineering, Limerick, pp. 303–307 (2011)
17. Babar, M.A.: Evaluating Product Line Architectures- Methods and Techniques. In: 14th Asia-Pacific Software Engineering Conference, Aichi, p. 13 (2007)
18. Bengtsson, P., Lassing, N., Bosch, J., van Vliet, H.: Analyzing software architecture for modifiability. HK/R Research Report (2000)
19. Castaldi, M., Inverardi, P., Afsharian, S.: A Case Study in Performance, Modifiability and Extensibility Analysis of a Telecommunication System Software Architecture. In: Proceedings of the 10th IEEE Int'l Symp. on Modeling, Analysis, & Simulation of Computer & Telecommunications Systems, pp. 281–290 (2002)
20. Hattori, L., Guerrero, D., Figueiredo, J., Brunet, J., Damasio, J.: On the precision and accuracy of impact analysis techniques. In: Proceedings of the Seventh International Conference on Computer and Information Science, Portland, Oregon, pp. 513–518 (2008)

The Adoption of Machine Learning Techniques for Software Defect Prediction: An Initial Industrial Validation

Rakesh Rana[1], Miroslaw Staron[1], Christian Berger[1], Jörgen Hansson[1],
Martin Nilsson[2], and Wilhelm Meding[3]

[1] Computer Science & Engineering, Chalmers, University of Gothenburg, Sweden
[2] Volvo Car Group, Gothenburg, Sweden
[3] Ericsson, Gothenburg, Sweden
rakesh.rana@gu.se

Abstract. Existing methods for predicting reliability of software are static and need manual maintenance to adjust to the evolving data sets in software organizations. Machine learning has a potential to address the problem of manual maintenance but can also require changes in how companies works with defect prediction. In this paper we address the problem of identifying what the benefits of machine learning are compared to existing methods and which barriers exist for adopting them in practice.

Our methods consist of literature studies and a case study at two companies – Ericsson and Volvo Car Group. By studying literature we develop a framework for adopting machine learning and using case studies we evaluate this framework through a series of four interviews with experts working with predictions at both companies - line manager, quality manager and measurement team leader.

The findings of our research show that the most important perceived benefits of adopting machine learning algorithms for defect prediction are accuracy of predictions and ability to generate new insights from data. The two most important perceived barriers in this context are inability to recognize new patterns and low generalizability of the machine learning algorithms.

We conclude that in order to support companies in making an informed decision to adopt machine learning techniques for software defect predictions we need to go beyond accuracy and also evaluate factors such as costs, generalizability and competence.

Keywords: Machine Learning, software defect prediction, technology acceptance, adoption, software quality.

1 Introduction

Modelling software reliability and predicting defect prone files/modules have been a practical challenge for software project and quality managers [1]. A number of methods are available to address the challenge of Software Defect Predictions (SDP) – ranging from mathematical reliability growth modelling [2], regression based models

A. Kravets et al. (Eds.): JCKBSE 2014, CCIS 466, pp. 270–285, 2014.

[3], analogy based predictions [4] and expert opinions [5]. The main limitation of these methods is the fact that they are based on existing patterns (or trends) in defect inflows or software metrics and thus are not robust to changes in these patterns. Recently data mining and Machine Learning (ML) techniques have been applied in this domain with acclaimed success [6], which can address the robustness limitations. Given easy access to growing amount of data and nature of software engineering problems, the use of ML in this area is expected to grow too [7].

While a number of companies have tested or started using these methods/tools [8], the methods are still used in a limited manner - which indicates that there are number of barriers preventing companies from adopting them in practice. A number of studies have evaluated different machine learning techniques for the purpose of software defect predictions [6] [9] [10], but they focus mainly on predictive accuracy of these methods while disregarding the ease of introduction or ability to evolve together with the data sets. On the other hand, when companies consider adopting new methods/techniques, they are also concerned with a range of other factors that are currently not adequately addressed. In this paper we investigate which of these factors are important for companies when they consider using machine learning for software defect predications. The research question we address is:

What are the factors that are important for companies to make informed decision to adopt (or not adopt) ML algorithms for the purpose of software defect predictions (SDP)?

Based on review of technology adoption/acceptance and machine learning literature, we developed a framework and outlined factors that potentially affect the adoption of ML in industry in our earlier work [11]. In this paper we present the initial validation of same from the perspective of its users i.e. the industry. The main objective is to provide insights of which factors companies regard as being important to them when they consider adoption of ML techniques in this context and what their main concerns are. These insights are useful for multitude of players in this domain from researchers to tool venders and the companies themselves who can use this explicit knowledge to make better decisions using a structured framework/approach.

The remainder of this paper is organized as follows. In following section (2) we summarize the traditional and machine learning approach to software defect prediction. Section 3 introduces the model for adoption of ML techniques in industry, which is explained with the example of software defect prediction. An initial industrial validation of introduced model is done using a case study; section 4 gives the case study design while section 5 provides the results from the case study. The paper ends with conclusions and ideas for future work in this area.

2   Related Work

ML has already been applied for predicting defects or defect proneness using code and change metrics and achieved good accuracy. Using code metrics data of projects from NASA IV&V facility Metrics Data Program (MDP), Menzies et al. [10] model based on naïve Bayes predicted with accuracy of 71% (pd, probability of detection) and probability of false alarm (pf) of 25%. Iker Gondra [9] also using NASA project data set (JM1) and obtained correct classifications of 72.6% with ANNs and 87.4% with SVMs. Using data from 31 projects form industry and using BNNs Fenton et al. [6] obtained an R^2 of 0.93 between predicted and actual number of defects. In [12] Menzies et al. tested different feature subset selection and report that software defect detection using machine learning approach is not too difficult in practice. As it can be observed from above cited studies - most compare and report performance with respect to predictive accuracy of different ML based algorithms, but performance evaluation on other dimensions either is limited or simply do not exist.

On the other hand studies within the area of technology adoption/acceptance have shown that adoption of complex technologies depend on multitude of factors [13] [14]. Building on the Theory of Reasoned Action (TRA) [15], Davis [16] developed the Technology Acceptance Model (TAM) to explain user acceptance of computer-based information systems. TAM has been applied and extended in number of previous studies for example to explain the adoption/acceptance of computer based technologies such as object oriented development processes by individual software developers [17], to explain the gender differences in perception of email usage [18] and predicting use of web-based information systems [19]. Wallace and Sheetz [14] used TAM in their attempt to provide a theoretical foundation for explaining and predicting the adoption of software measures. Chau and Tam [13] applied Tornatzky et al. [20] adoption framework, to explain factors affecting adoption of open systems in organizational computing, they found that organizations tend to focus more on their ability of adoption than on the benefits from adoption. Further the authors show that organizations take a reactive approach towards adoption of opens systems rather than a proactive attitude which have strong managerial implications.

We adapt and customize the TAM and Tornatzky et al. adoption framework [20] to explain which factors are relevant for explaining the adoption (or non-adoption) of machine learning techniques for software defect predictions [11]. In this paper we provide the perception of industry to these factors – which factors and their sub-dimensions (or attributes) are deemed important by the industry. The perception of industrial practitioners in this context is important as it provides useful insights on what is desired from these techniques. The framework and understanding of level of importance of attributes also help to set the direction for future research where different ML techniques can be compared on these attributes, which accelerates the technology transfer and its adoption.

3   Study Design

The overview of the research process employed in this study to capture the factors important for acceptance/adoption of machine learning in industry is presented in Fig. 1.

ML & technology acceptance
literature + Interviews

Attributes mapping to
framework of ML in Industry

Framework validation
with industrial partners

Fig. 1. Research process overview

The main steps in the process were:

- Existing research literature on machine learning and technology acceptance/adoption was explored for list of important benefits and challenges in applying ML in industry.
- The information was used to drive discussions with the industrial practitioners and a framework for ML adoption in industry (for software defect prediction) was developed [11].
- Attributes are mapped for each factor within this framework.
- Industrial practitioners validate the framework and mark the level of importance of each attribute in relation to making adoption decisions.

3.1 Case Study Context

Following the taxonomy and guidelines for conducting and reporting case studies in software engineering by Runeson and Höst [21], we conducted an exploratory case study using flexible design principle. We studied two large companies from widely different industrial domains (Automotive and Telecom) with significant focus on development of embedded software. Given the differences in domain, the study is designed as an embedded case study with two units of analysis (each company); Fig. 2 and Table 1 present an overview of the case study design and summary of case units.

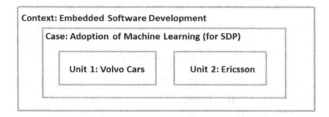

Fig. 2. Case study design overview

Two companies were selected that come from two different domains:

- Volvo Car Group (VCG), A company from the automotive domain
- Ericsson, A company from the telecom domain

The divisions we interacted with have one thing in common, they have not yet adopted machine learning as their main method/technique for predicting software defects, but they are considering evaluating it as a possible technique to compliment the current measurement/prediction systems in place. Since the objective of this paper is to present the factors affecting the adoption of machine learning in industry for software defect prediction, the subjects selected are considered appropriate for the purpose.

Table 1. Overview of case units

Unit of analysis (Domain)	Software development process	Current methods for SDP	Current state of adoption of ML for SDP
VCG (Automotive)	V-shaped software development	Focus on status visualization and analogy based prediction	Considering evaluation
Ericsson (Telecom)	Lean and Agile development	Various modes of presenting current status and predictions methods	Considering evaluation

3.2   Data Collection and Analysis Methods

The main source of data for the case study is obtained through semi-structured interviews, which is a more open method compared to structured interviews – this allows for adaptation of questions to given context and exploration of new ideas during the interview. Data collected through interviews is a form of first degree methods [21], that are although expensive to collect but offer larger control. Since the objective for this research is to explore, identify and validate factors affecting adoption of ML in industry, direct methods in form of interviews was assessed as appropriate.

Stronger conclusions can be drawn by using triangulation i.e. using data from several sources [21], therefore we complement the information obtained through interviews with document analysis from these companies. The archival documents analysed related to the information needs within the organization with respect to software defects and information demanded by various stakeholders within the organization.

Semi-structured interviews were conducted with managers responsible for providing software defects related information to different stakeholders within the organizations, these interviews were also complemented by interviews with managers responsible for quality. This setting provides us with both - the perspectives of practitioners responsible for delivering the information (roles responsible for applying/implementing ML techniques for software defect predictions) and the end users of this information who use it at various levels for decision support. The interviewees included:

- Manager at Volvo Cars Group within the department responsible for integrating software sourced from different teams and suppliers, the manager has more than 20 years of experience working with software development and testing. As ensuring safety and quality is a major responsibility in this role we refer to this manager by (VCG, QM).
- Team leader responsible for collection, analysis and reporting of project status with regard to software defects and their predictions (VCG, MetricsTL), the team leader has more than three decades of experience in various roles at the company.

- A senior quality manger whose experience with software (mainly within quality assurance) spans more than three decades (Ericsson, QM), and
- Team leader of metrics team at Ericsson; metrics team is the unit at Ericsson that provide the measurement systems within the organization (Ericsson, MetricsTL).

4   Factors Affecting Adoption of ML Techniques in Industry

The framework for adoption of ML in industry with how each factor is likely to affect the probability of this adoption is represented in Fig. 3. In the figure (+/-) indicates the possibility (hypothesis) of existence of positive/negative relationship with medium strength between a given factor and probability of adoption of ML in industry; a double (++/--) indicate a strong relationship.

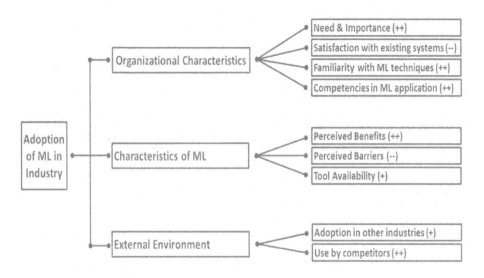

Fig. 3. A framework for ML adoption in Industry

4.1   Organizational and ML Characteristics

The factors of ML adoption framework are further broken down to sub-dimensions (or attributes) which represents the tangible measures the industrial practitioners can use to comment on their level of importance. The attributes for ML and organizational characteristics are shown in Fig. 4.

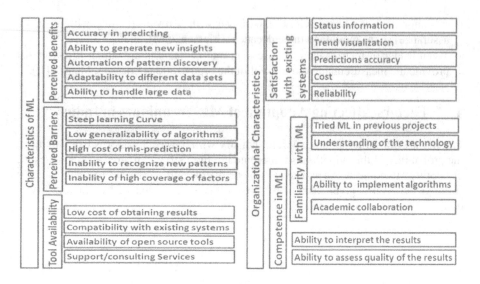

Fig. 4. Overview of attributes which relate to acceptance of ML for defect prediction

4.2   Operationalization of Factors

Factors were operationalized by asking interviewees to give the level of importance to each attributes on a five-point Likert-type scale. The levels that could be selected were:

(a) Very Low (VL)
(b) Low (L)
(c) Medium (M)
(d) High (H)
(e) Very High (VH)

The levels of scale reflect the degree of importance that an attribute has for adoption/acceptance of ML techniques for software defect predictions. The levels are used in different contexts; Table 2 summarizes the definitions used for each level.

Table 2. Defining the levels for different contexts

Level	Need and importance (Table 2)	Level of Satisfaction (Table 3)	Level of importance (Table 4)
Very Low (VL)	The information is not needed.	Not satisfactory, improvement is needed.	The attribute is not needed for analysis.
Low (L)	The information is desired, but not considered important.	Not satisfactory, improvement is desired.	The attribute can be considered but not required.
Medium (M)	The information is desired and is considered of value (if available).	Satisfactory, but could be improved.	The attribute is useful for making the analysis.

Table 2. (*continued*)

High (H)	The information is deemed as needed and is considered important.	Satisfaction is high.	The information on given attribute is needed for making the analysis.
Very High (VH)	The information is a must and should be provided with high accuracy.	Satisfaction is very high, with low scope for further improvement.	Cannot make a decision without information about this attribute.

5   Findings

5.1   Information Need and Its Importance for SDP

When it comes to defect management in software development, mature organizations collect and monitor wide range of defect related metrics. There is also need for various types of predictions to manage defects (and software quality) effectively and efficiently. The interviewees from two case units were asked to indicate the importance of different information needs.

Table 3. Examples of information need and its importance in industry

Prediction Needs w.r.t software defects	VCG (QM)	VCG MetricsTL	Ericsson (QM)	Ericsson MetricsTL
Classification of defect prone files/modules	L	H	VH	VH
Expected number of defects in SW components	H	H	L	VH
Expected defect inflow for a project/release	H	H	L	VH
Release readiness/expected latent defects	H	VH	H	VH
Severity classification of defects	VH	M	H	H

Table 3 shows that different organizations information needs can be different – among others this is dependent on factors such as how the software is developed, tested and verified within an organization. At VCG similar to most OEMs (Original Equipment Manufacturers) in automotive domain, Model Based Development (MBD) is prevalent. Much of the software in this company is developed using Simulink[1] models where code is generally auto-generated from models or sub-contracted to suppliers. In such environments classification of files/modules prone to defects is not the top priority. While for Ericsson which has more code-centric approach predicting defect prone files/modules holds very high importance.

Assessing release readiness is important (High) for both case units as is the case with severity classification of defects. It is interesting to note differences in their information need due to differences in their software testing and quality assessment approach. While at Ericsson finding smaller set of files/modules more prone to defects helps testing and quality teams to focus the limited resources to achieve high quality, at VCG knowing number of expected defects in a software component or expected defect inflow at a given point in time is more useful to mobilize their testing efforts to meet high quality demands.

---

[1] Simulink® is a block diagram environment for multidomain simulation and Model-Based Design. Matlab and Simulink are products and registered trademark of The MathWorks, Inc.

5.2   Current Status of Each Case unit

The same scale (five-point Likert-type) was used to indicate the level of satisfaction with current defect management/prediction systems, familiarity and in-house competence of ML techniques. The results are summarised in Table 4.

Table 4. Current status of each case unit

Factors	VCG (QM)	VCG MetricsTL	Ericsson (QM)	Ericsson MetricsTL
Satisfaction with existing systems				
Status information	H	H	H	H
Trend visualization	H	M	M	H
Predictions accuracy	M	M	L	H
Cost (current costs are low)	VH	VH	-	VH
Reliability	VH	H	VH	M
Familiarity and competence with ML techniques				
ML tried in previous project	L	L	-	M
Understanding of the technology	L	L	-	M
Ability to implement algorithms in-house	VL	M	-	M
Academic collaboration	M	H	-	M
Ability to interpret the results	H	H	-	M
Ability to assess quality of results	H	M	-	M

*In the fields marked (-), The Quality Manager interviewed at Ericsson was unable to provide assessment with high confidence, thus they are left out from analysis.

It is observed (from Table 4) that for companies currently not using ML for software defect prediction, satisfaction with existing defect monitoring and prediction systems is high, while the need to enhance the in-house competence in ML techniques is recognised.

Satisfaction with Existing Systems

- Stakeholders such as quality managers within these companies are satisfied to a high degree with how the defect related information is presented and trend visualized using existing systems.

- The accuracy of predictions is realized to be satisfactory, while it is considered improvements can be made.

- Cost is an important factor when choosing the prediction method - *"Cost of obtaining results is very important factor and the current systems we use are very cheap to run and maintain"*   *– QM at VCG.*

Since the existing systems have been in place for at least two years in each case, the running costs are very low and operational reliability very high.

Familiarity and Competence with ML Techniques

- It is recognised that there is a need for training before ML techniques can be used for software defect prediction. The improvement potential has also been realised with respect to in-house competence of implementing such algorithms.

- Participating companies in the study show medium to high confidence with their ability to interpret the results from such analysis which is related to the need for training (see point c) above). This is due to fact that experts in these organizations have deep understanding of their process, products and impact of different factors on these gained through experience of multiple projects over long periods of time.

5.3   Level of Importance of Factors

Table 5 presents the level of the importance of different attributes that affect the adoption/acceptance of machine learning algorithms in industry.

Table 5. Level of importance of attributes for the case units

Factors	Level of importance			
Attributes	VCG (QM)	VCG MetricsTL	Ericsson (QM)	Ericsson MetricsTL
Perceived Benefits				
Accuracy in predicting	H	H	VH	VH
Automation of pattern discovery	M	H	VH	VH
Adaptability to different data sets	M	H	VH	VH
Ability to handle large data	H	H	M	VH
Ability to generate new insights	H	M	H	H
Perceived Barriers				
Steep learning curve	L	VH	VH	VH
Inability to recognize new patterns	VH	M	VH	VH
High cost of mis-predicitons	M	M	VL	L
Low generalizability of algorithms	H	H	H	VH
Need for high coverage of relevant attributes	M	M	L	VH
Tool availability				
Compatibility with existing systems	M	L	H	VH
Availability of open source tools	L	H	M	VH
Low cost of obtaining results	VH	H	H	M
Support/consulting services	H	M	L	VL
External factors				
Adoption by other industries	L	L	L	M
Use by competitors	H	M	L	M

It is observed that while there are some variations depending on the case units, attributes related to perceived benefits and barriers are considered highly important for making adoption decisions. Attributes related to tool availability are deemed important but not critical, while external factors had little influence on adoption decisions of ML techniques in industry for SDP. Specifically,

Perceived Benefits

- Accuracy of predictions, automation, adaptability and ability to handle large are generally regarded as high or very high importance. Some interesting comments highlight these, *"When it comes to the benefits, accuracy and automation are the top priorities for us"* – *MetricsTL at Ericsson.*

- Using causal models such as Bayesian Networks that can provide range of decision-support and risk assessment capabilities for project mangers [6] is perceived as an important benefit of ML techniques application to SDP.

Perceived Barriers

On the other hand uncertainty over if the ML based techniques can be effective for detecting new patterns in the data and concerns over their generalizability are barriers that are considered highly important for making adoption decisions.

- Technology/innovations that need high upfront investment in terms of new knowledge acquisition can slow the adoption process. The respondents in our study also considered this attribute as highly important, except for the QM at VCG, according to him *"Steep learning curve is not a major problem if only few people (experts) need to know it to generate the results as long as they are easy to interpret by rest of the stakeholders" – QM at VCG.*

- Mispredictions can be costly for an organization and usually considered a barrier for prediction systems, but managers at both case units emphasized that this is not a show stopper. *"Since all predictions generally go through number of experts if the predictions are not close to reality they would not be accepted by these experts." – MetricsTL at VCG.*

Tool Availability

It was revealed that availability of tools is important for organizations, while if the tools are open source or proprietary does not have same impact on the adoption of new techniques.

- Information that is relevant to companies with respect to tools is the cost of running it (in terms of resources) should be low; i.e. it should be fairly easy to feed in the data and generate the results.

- Availability of support/consulting service for given tool is another factor that depends on given company preferences, companies like VCG in our case study, prefer to use a sub-supplier to provide services which are new to the company and generally incorporate them within in-house systems when confidence in their usability and effectiveness is well established. *"Even if open source tools are available, we typically need a vendor in between to do tool integration, manage upgrades and do maintenance work – we do not have resources for that" – QM at VCG.*

While at Ericsson, the departments which are supported by a specialized in-house team to cater the need of measurement systems, for these departments in order to achieve high transparency and provide greater flexibility prefer to develop in-house measurement systems than relying on external vendors where possible.

External Factors

- When it comes to external factors, adoption of a new method/techniques by industries outside of given industrial domain have low impact, while the knowledge that similar techniques are being used within the domain can highly motivate their evaluation within a given company. *"We are not afraid of trying new things and be-*

ing the first one, but if it is used in automotive sector and we have not tried it surely helps the case"   – QM at VCG.

The perspective on some attributes within the company is also dependent on the role. This is mainly due to the fact that some roles (as quality manger) are consumers of the information/measurement system, while in others (as a team leader of metrics team) the responsibility is to supply this information (responsible for building and maintaining the measurement/prediction systems).

The difference can be large for some attributes, while QM is not concerned with maintenance aspects, MetricsTL said with respect to ML techniques for software defect predictions: *"I am not confident that maintenance cost is low with respect to competence and technology we have today"*   *– MetricsTL at Ericsson.*

Explaining it further MetricsTL highlighted *"first developing a prediction system is time consuming task and further if I have to update it often then costs will be too high. Other thing is that we change our technology (for e.g. tools) from time to time – so what does that mean as a developer of ML based prediction system?"*

5.4   Specific Challenges in Adopting ML Techniques in Industry for SDP

Apart from common factors identified in previous section, in this section we present the specific challenges that were raised during the interviews towards accepting the ML techniques for software defect prediction.

Lack of Information to Make a Strong Business Case: Does ML techniques save company time or will they reduce risk? If so how much? These are some of the important questions mangers need - to make a strong business case for motivating the use of new techniques within their team and within the company.

"Time is a critical factor, especially in automotive domain where a new functionality is promised to the market long before it is completely ready, then the clock is ticking and the product development divisions are expected to deliver on time with superior quality" – QM at VCG.

If expected time savings or reduction in risk could be quantified for a given company, their decision on adoption becomes much easier.

Uncertainty on Applicability of ML When Access to Source Code Is Not Available: In cases where software is purchased from suppliers, the access to code and change metrics may not be available. It is unclear if ML based algorithms can still be useful and effective for SDP.

How to Adapt ML Techniques for Model Driven Development: Model driven development is predominant in many industries such as aerospace and automotive domain model. The question that is yet unanswered for these organizations is if ML based prediction systems can be effectively applied for their specific context.

Some of the important questions are - can we adapt ML based techniques to analyse models (e.g. UML, Simulink etc.) for the purpose of defects or quality predictions? Or can the metrics obtained from code (which is usually auto-generated from these models) be appropriate for SDP using current ML based approaches?

How to Effectively Use Text Base Artefacts for SDP: While most ML based techniques for SDP use quantitative data, some of the major software artefacts such as requirements and defect reports are largely text based. The ability of ML based methods to reliably handle textual data will boost confidence of industry in these methods, Menzies and Marcus [23] work is a good example of type of work these companies want to see more.

Uncertainty over Where ML Fits in Context of Compliance to Standards: Industrial domains with safety critical software usually follow stringent safety standards. For example in automotive domain, ISO 26262 is the new functional safety standard which recommends using formal methods for software verification and validation for high safety critical applications. How does ML based software prediction techniques fit in this framework and how can they contribute towards ensuring compliance to such standards is another area currently not well understood but important for organizations in such domain.

5.5   Validity

Threats to validity in this study are addressed in manner as described by Wohlin et al. [22]. There exists threat to internal validity to this study with respect to the selection of case units – both case units have not adopted ML widely for software defect predictions. For example it can be expected that there may be a difference between the perceived benefits among companies that have adopted such techniques and those that have not. In this study we only report how important these units feel these attributes are for taking an adoption decision thus minimizing the mentioned threat. This also aligns well with the objective of this study where our aim is to explore and list the important factors and not what the case units in this study's assessment is about ML techniques and tools.

Threat to construct validity exists with respect to if or not all factors that are important for making adoption decisions of ML in industry are taken into account. We explored the factors and attributes closely with the companies involved in this study. The attributes and model were again validated with the companies involved which limit the possibility of miss-interpretation which minimizes the threat to construct validity.

Incorrect conclusions about relationships can pose threat of conclusion validity. The presented study is designed as an exploratory case study. We present the perception of industry of which factors they deem as important with indications of possible relationship to the adoption framework. The future study planned that quantitatively assesses these relationships will have to seriously evaluate this threat to validity, but for present study it does not pose a major threat.

Threat to external validity is a major threat to this study, since only two units within two large software development organizations are used for validation, but numbers of steps are taken to minimize this threat. Firstly the adoption framework is based on wider technology adoption/acceptance literature, secondly the model is claimed to be only initially validated with these case units, comprehensive validation and quantitative assessment is planned as future work. Further using case units from widely different industrial domain and using different job roles within the units and two stage interviews help minimize the threat to external validity.

6   Conclusions and Future Work

In large software development organizations, a software defect prediction is important for project and quality mangers to realise the goal of zero known defects by the release date. Machine learning techniques offer an alternative to methods based on statistical regression or expert opinions. ML based methods have been compared to traditional methods for aspect such as predictive accuracy, but for companies considering adoption of ML based techniques, a number of other factors are also important.

In this paper we set out to investigate, *What are the factors that are important for companies to make informed decision to adopt (or not adopt) ML algorithms for the purpose of software defect predictions (SDP)?* We identified a total of nine important factors and 27 related attributes that affect the adoption of ML based techniques for software defect predictions. The framework for adoption of ML for SDP is validated using a series of interviews with experts on quality and team leaders responsible for providing software defects related information at two large software development organizations.

The results suggest that information needs can be different for different companies based on their software development and testing process. The existing systems in place for presenting and visualizing information related to software defects are deemed satisfactory, they offer low running costs and high reliability. The need for training to increase competence in ML techniques is also recognised in these companies. The study further show that for adopting ML techniques, predictive accuracy and ability to generate new insights from large data are most important perceived benefits. At the same time low generalizability and steep learning curve are perceived barriers that need to be overcome to gain higher adoption of ML in industry. Availability of tools and support services can also accelerate the adoption process in this respect.

Impact of understanding such factors is at multiple levels: for companies themselves it explicitly lists the factors that are implicitly deemed important by them when they make adoption decisions on ML based techniques/tools. Listing and visualizing important attributes for such decisions also makes it easier for mangers to see the big picture and objectively evaluate new ML based techniques and tools for their usefulness and applicability for a given problem at a given point in time. The adoption framework is also useful for companies that provide tools and services to larger organizations developing software. With knowledge of important factors they can customize their products (e.g. tools) and services offerings to closely fit the need of these organizations.

In future work we plan to quantitatively evaluate the effect size of important attributes towards ML adoption decision using large scale survey of companies that have already adopted ML techniques and ones that are yet to embrace it. Research with regard to which factors are important for industry and evaluative studies of ML based techniques/tools on these factors can complement the existing and on-going work on establishing the characteristics of ML techniques and thus contribute toward their adoption in industry and society.

Acknowledgements. The research presented here is done under the VISEE project which is funded by Vinnova and Volvo Cars jointly under the FFI programme (VISEE, Project No: DIARIENR: 2011-04438). We are thankful to companies involved in this study, namely Volvo Car Group, and Ericsson for providing the data and interview participants for sharing their knowledge and time. We also acknowledge the support of Software Center at Chalmers/University of Gothenburg.

References

1. Fenton, N.E., Neil, M.: A critique of software defect prediction models. IEEE Trans. Softw. Eng. 25, 675–689 (1999)
2. Lyu, M.R.: Handbook of software reliability engineering. IEEE Computer Society Press, CA (1996)
3. Nagappan, N., Ball, T., Zeller, A.: Mining metrics to predict component failures. In: Proceedings of the 28th International Conference on Software Engineering, pp. 452–461 (2006)
4. Staron, M., Meding, W., Söderqvist, B.: A method for forecasting defect backlog in large streamline software development projects and its industrial evaluation. Inf. Softw. Technol. 52, 1069–1079 (2010)
5. Li, M., Smidts, C.S.: A ranking of software engineering measures based on expert opinion. IEEE Trans. Softw. Eng. 29, 811–824 (2003)
6. Fenton, N., Neil, M., Marsh, W., Hearty, P., Radliński, Ł., Krause, P.: On the effective-ness of early life cycle defect prediction with Bayesian Nets. Empir. Softw. Eng. 13, 499–537 (2008)
7. Zhang, D., Tsai, J.J.: Machine learning and software engineering. Softw. Qual. J. 11, 87–119 (2003)
8. Fenton, N., Neil, M., Marsh, W., Hearty, P., Marquez, D., Krause, P., Mishra, R.: Predicting software defects in varying development lifecycles using Bayesian nets. Inf. Softw. Technol. 49, 32–43 (2007)
9. Gondra, I.: Applying machine learning to software fault-proneness prediction. J. Syst. Softw. 81, 186–195 (2008)
10. Menzies, T., Greenwald, J., Frank, A.: Data mining static code attributes to learn defect predictors. IEEE Trans. on Softw. Eng. 33, 2–13 (2007)
11. Rana, R., Staron, M., Nilsson, M.: A framework for adoption of machine learning in industry for software defect prediction. Presented at the Submitted to ICSOFT-EA, 2014 , Vienna, Austria (2014)
12. Menzies, T., Ammar, K., Nikora, A., DiStefano, J.: How simple is software defect detection. Submitt. Empirical Softw. Eng. J. (2003)
13. Chau, P.Y., Tam, K.Y.: Factors Affecting the Adoption of Open Systems: An Explora-tory Study. Mis Q. 21 (1997)
14. Wallace, L.G., Sheetz, S.D.: The adoption of software measures: A technology accep-tance model (TAM) perspective. Inf. Manage. 51, 249–259 (2014)
15. Ajzen, I., Fishbein, M.: Understanding attitudes and predicting social behaviour (1980)
16. Davis Jr., F.D.: A technology acceptance model for empirically testing new end-user information systems: Theory and results (1986), http://www.researchgate.net/publication/35465050_A_technology_acceptance_model_for_empirically_testing_new_end-user_information_systems__theory_and_results_/file/9c960519fbaddf3ba7.pdf

17. Hardgrave, B.C., Johnson, R.A.: Toward an information systems development acceptance model: the case of object-oriented systems development. IEEE Trans. on Eng. Manag. 50, 322–336 (2003)
18. Gefen, D., Straub, D.W.: Gender Differences in the Perception and Use of E-Mail: An Extension to the Technology Acceptance Model. MIS Q. 21 (1997)
19. Yi, M.Y., Hwang, Y.: Predicting the use of web-based information systems: self-efficacy, enjoyment, learning goal orientation, and the technology acceptance model. Int. J. Hum.-Comput. Stud. 59, 431–449 (2003)
20. Tornatzky, L.G., Fleischer, M., Chakrabarti, A.K.: Processes of technological innovation (1990)
21. Runeson, P., Höst, M.: Guidelines for conducting and reporting case study research in software engineering. Empir. Softw. Eng. 14, 131–164 (2009)
22. Wohlin, C., Runeson, P., Höst, M., Ohlsson, M.C., Regnell, B., Wesslén, A.: Experimentation in Software Engineering. Springer, New York (2012)

Mixed Diagnostic Testing:
Tasks with Formula Type Answer[*]

Yury Kostyuk, Alex Fux, Irina Fux, Vladimir Razin, and Anna Yankovskaya[**]

National Research Tomsk State University, Tomsk, Russia
ayyankov@gmail.com

Abstract. The paper deals with using formal languages in intelligent teaching-testing systems based on mixed diagnostic tests that allow to apply the test tasks with responses in the form of formulas. A simple intuitive language for writing formulas is described. A technology is proposed to verify an answer-formula compliance with a formula given by the test developer. A checking algorithm uses the LL(1)-parser, Postfix Polish Notation string generator and an interpreter to calculate the answer-formula value for the prearranged set of input data.

Keywords: teaching-testing system, mixed diagnostic tests, context-free language, LL(1)-parser, Postfix Polish Notation.

1 Introduction

To increase the efficiency of using the mixed diagnostic tests [1-3] at the different stages of testing, it is necessary to apply test tasks requiring answers in the various forms [4]. In the traditional tests, tasks are divided into the following types [5]:

— closed-form answer tasks that require choosing a single correct or incorrect answer;
— multiple choice tasks that require choosing several right or several wrong answers from the list;
— tasks with establishing correspondence between two sequences;
— tasks with establishing the correct sequence;
— tasks with an open answer that are supposed to have a number, a word or a text in the arbitrary form as its answer.

It is easy to implement answer verification programmatically for all types of tasks given above except for the tasks with an open answer when multiple variations of an answer can be correct. In most cases, the answer to the tasks of that type must be written in a strict form (e.g. numerical value in a fixed format), which significantly limits tests applicability. Some of the new computer systems for testing learners' knowledge allow open answer tasks described by a regular expression [6]. In this case, the answer is considered to be correct if it corresponds to some regular expression (pattern)

---

[*] Supported by Russian Foundation for Basic Research, projects no. 13-07-98037-r_sibir_a, 13-07-00373 a, 14-07-00673 a and partially by Russian Humanitarian Foundation project no. 13-06-00709.
[**] Corresponding author.

A. Kravets et al. (Eds.): JCKBSE 2014, CCIS 466, pp. 286–293, 2014.

predefined by the test developer. However, this way is rather specific and does not cover all the variants of tasks with an open answer.

A written work in the form of essay can also be an answer to the task of that type. Technologies to check these types of an open answer – Automated Essay Scoring and Calibrated Peer Review – are described in [7].

In testing students' knowledge in the different subjects the tasks with the algebraic formula type answer are among the most effective. Usually, these formulae include variables given in the task itself as well as common constants and operations. In this case, the main problem of using computer testing is establishing the equivalence of the two formulae: the formula given by the test developers and the formula written as an answer. Generally, there is no universal decision for this problem. In this paper, a particular solution that could be convenient in use and effective in practice, is suggested.

2   General Principles of Formula Type Answer Check Up

The algebraic formulae involving the calculation of one or several variables are to be considered. In general, a programming language can be used for formulae notation, however, the learner is supposed not just to know the language as it is, but also to be able to program in it. If the knowledge of the subject other than Computer Science is tested, it is a tall order. That is why we introduce an intuitively understandable simplified language for the formulae notation, in which only the variables that are defined in the task itself are allowed. The formulae given in this language should be written in one or several lines, and all the operations should be clearly signified. The notation of variables and constants is restricted to one or several Latin letters and/or Arabic numbers.

The algorithm of answer checkup is executed as follows:

1. Formula-answer (or a set of formulae) written by the learner is sent to the testing system and then analyzed, following which it is translated into a Postfix Polish Notation (PPN). If some formal (syntactic) errors in the notation are found, the testing system must immediately inform the student that he has to correct the errors and give the right answer. This is of great importance since the testing is aimed at the knowledge check up in the particular field rather than the language of formulae notation.
2. If there are no errors in the formula notation, PPN received by the testing system is transferred to the interpreter that makes the appropriate computation, giving the input data prepared beforehand as its input. Matching of the results obtained is made using values prepared by the test developers. If they are in full agreement, the formula is considered to be right. If approximate numbers are involved, matching should be made in terms of the computational error.

Therefore, in developing the test of this kind it is necessary not only to state the task distinctly but also to provide several sets of input data and the relevant results which the learner must get when applying the appropriate formula.

3   Formula Notation Language

The simple language of formulae is proposed. In a formula, variables predefined in the task, variables defined by the formula and numerical constants, are used. The variables are written according to the rules worked out in programming languages, i.e. they can consist in several Latin (lower- and upper-case) letters and numbers and they are to begin with the letter. The constants are written in numerical values, they can be integers and real numbers, fixed-point numbers and/or decimal exponent, either signed or unsigned. In the latter case, the letter e goes before the exponent. For some mathematical constants various alphabetical characters, e.g. pi, can be reserved. If one must use specific constants (for example, the physical ones), their notation should be given in the task.

Each formula notation is restricted by one line, if there is more than one formula, a semicolon and/or a new line should be used. The notation starts with the variable that must be computed, after that goes the equal mark, then – the expression with variables, constants and round brackets. Operations are grouped by their priorities. Of highest priority is raising to the power operation (sign ^). Next are unary operations requiring only one operand. Among them are unary plus and minus, as well as operations which define the standard mathematical functions: square root (sqrt), sinus (sin), cosinus (cos), and so on. After that go multiplication (sign *) and division (sign /) operations. Of lowest priority are addition and subtraction operations (with two operands). Any part of the expression can be restricted with round brackets either on the right or on the left so as to change the order of the execution of operations.

The syntax of the language like this one can be written as the set of productions of context-free grammar [8]. For brevity sake, nonterminals (syntactic notions) are to be written with upper case Latin letters. Right and left parts of the production will be divided by the arrow, and terminals (by groups) written in the following way: raising to the power operation - sign ^, unary operations (apart from plus and minus) – letter s, multiplication and division operations - sign *, plus and minus - sign +, variables – letter a, constants – letter k, brackets – round brackets, formula separator (semicolon or new line) – sign ;.

Strictly speaking, the notation of variables and constants as well as operation designations requiring more than one character, are not grammar terminals. However, at the preliminary processing of the formula being analyzed the lexer [8] can be of use. It recognizes such grammar structures (lexical units) and translates them into terminals at the output. Lexer makes it possible to facilitate and speed up the further analysis.

Given below are productions of the formulae language, with vertical line dividing different right parts for the group of rules, whose left parts are the same.

$$P \to P\,;\,A \mid A \mid A\,;$$

$$A \to a = S$$

$$S \to S + T \mid T$$

$$T \to T * F \mid F$$

$$F \to W \mid + F \mid s\,F \tag{1}$$

$$W \to W \wedge G \mid G$$

$$G \to (S) \mid a \mid k$$

In these productions the initial terminal – P.

4   LL(1)-Parsing of Formulae

One of the most effective methods of the analysis of character strings produced by context-free grammar is LL(1)-parsing [9]. In order to apply this method of parsing it is necessary to transform it to Greibach normal form when the right parts can be either empty or start with terminal character in all the productions. The grammar of this kind admits determinative LL(1)- parsing if for each group of productions with the same nonterminal in the left part, the right parts will be distinguishable by the first terminal.

Let entry string of characters be always completed with the boundary character $\perp$. In order the LL(1)-analyzer to work, it is necessary to draw a table whose columns are designated with terminals, the boundary character $\perp$ included, and strings – with nonterminals of the transformed grammar. For all productions of grammar given as

$$A \to a\gamma,$$

where A – a nonterminal, a – a terminal, γ – a string of both terminals and nonterminals, the right part of the rule $a\gamma$ is placed on the intersection of the line marked with nonterminal A with the column designated as terminal a. If the production is in the form of

$$A \to \lambda,$$

where λ is the empty string, all the cells designated with nonterminal A and free of the other rules are written as λ.

Before the work starts, first the boundary character $\perp$ is put into the stack of the parser, then goes the initial nonterminal. At each stage the parser gets yet another terminal from the lexer and executes one of the two actions:

1. if there is a nonterminal on top of the stack, depending on what another entry terminal is, this nonterminal is changed in the stack by the right part characters of the corresponding production, with these characters written in the reverse order. If for another entry a terminal character written in the table is λ, a non-terminal is removed from the stack. If there is an empty cell in the table, the parser fixes the error in the input string;
2. if there is a terminal on top of the stack, it is compared with the another entry character. If there is a match, a terminal is removed from the stack and the transition to the following character in the input string is made. Lack of match gets the parser to register the error.

The work of the parser ends when the entry string of characters turns out to be looked over. If, in this case, the stack is empty, the entry string of characters is considered correct, if it isn't empty, the string is erroneous.

PPN generation is carried out while LL(1)-parser is at work. It is done in the following way. The second stack is necessary for PPN generator, its work being done simultaneously with that of the recognizer with its stack. Written in the second stack is the sequence of semantic characters that denote the actions generated by PPN elements. The actions on PPN generation will be done when the characters are removed from the second stack.

For the implementation of PPN generator together with the main table of LL(1)-parser it is necessary to give a semantic table. Its size fits with that of the main table. Moreover, for each non-empty cell of the main table, where there is a right part of any production, the sequence of operations is put into the semantic table. The number of these operations is equal to the length of the right part of this production.

Since terminal characters in the context free grammar are, indeed, lexical units, recognized by the lexer, such lexical units as variables names and constants contain additional semantic information – links to tables of variables or tables of constants, i.e. the same terminals can be different semantically in the context free grammar.

PPN generation also involves forming the two tables: the table of constants and the table of variables. Besides, the constants and the variables that are required for the computations to be made in accordance with the conditions must be written in the table prior to the action of the LL(1) parser. Those constants and variables should be given by the test developer.

Let's consider the semantic actions on PPN generation for the formula grammar. The actions indicated by the following characters are included in the sequence:

- a – writing in a PPN variable;
- k – writing in a PPN constant;
- $=$ – writing in a PPN assignment operation;
- $+$ – writing in a PPN binary addition operation;
- $-$ – writing in a PPN binary subtraction operation;
- $*$ – writing in a PPN multiplication operation;
- $/$ – writing in a PPN division operation;
- $[-]$ – writing in a PPN unary subtraction operation;
- s – writing in a PPN standard function operation, for example, **sqrt**;
- $\wedge$ – writing in a PPN raising to power operation;
- $\square$ – empty action.

While a variable is entered into PPN, search is made in the table of variables. If there is a variable with the same name in the table, the link to it is entered into PPN. Otherwise, a new variable is entered into the table of constants and the link to it is written in PPN.

The actions indicated by the characters given above will be executed simultaneously with the pop of corresponding characters from the second stack.

In Table 1 one can find the parser's table which overlaps with the semantic table of PPN generator where there is only one column marked with terminal s. In the actual table for each operation computing a standard function there must be a column like that. Productions put into the table are derived from grammar rules (1) by their transformation to Greybach normal form.

Table 1. Integrated table of Parser and PPN Generator

	+	−	*	/	^	s	(	)	a	k	=	;	⊥
P	λ	λ	λ	λ	λ	λ	λ	λ	*a=SB* *a□□=*	λ	λ	*;P* □□	λ
B	λ	λ	λ	λ	λ	λ	λ	λ	λ	λ	λ	*;P* □□	λ
S	*+FVU* □□□□	*−FVU* □□[−]□				*sFVU* □s□□	*(S)WVU* □□□□□□		*aWVU* a□□□	*kWVU* k□□□			
U	*+TU* □□+	λ	λ	λ	λ	λ	λ	λ	λ	λ	λ	λ	λ
T	*+FV* □□□	*−FV* □□[−]				*sFV* □s□	*(S)WV* □□□□□		*aWV* a□□	*kWV* k□□			
V	λ	λ	**FV* □□*	*/FV* □□/	λ	λ	λ	λ	λ	λ	λ	λ	λ
F	*+F* □□	*−F□* □□[−]				*sF□* □□s	*(S)W* □□□□		*aW* a□	*kW* k□			
W	λ	λ	λ	λ	*^GW* □□^	λ	λ	λ	λ	λ	λ	λ	λ
G							*(S)* □□□		*a* a	*k* k			

Consider the work of parser and RPN generator. Let the input formula with a, b, c variables and numerical constants be as follows:

$$a=-(b+c)*b^{3}/(b-2.5) \qquad (2)$$

Formed at the output are the table of (a, b, c), variables and the table of (3, 2.5) constants and PPN in which the links to the table of variables are in curly brackets while the links to the table of constants are in square brackets.

$$\{1\}\{2\}\{3\}+[-]\{b\}[1]^{\wedge}*\{2\}[2]-/ \qquad (3)$$

5   Formula Computation Using Postfix Polish Notation

Computation with predefined PPN can be made by the interpreter that uses an additional stack [8]. For the formulae language under consideration the structure of the stack is as follows. The stack consists in cells, each cell having two parts: 1) content type, 2) content that can serve either as a link to the variable in the table or a numerical value. Besides, for each variable in the table there must be space to store the current value as well as the tolerated error of computation since in the general case numerical values can be approximated.

For each input variable the test developers should predefine numerical values and put them into additional table where input data are presented as sets. Moreover, for each input variable, which must be defined by formulae, the tolerated error must be given.

Algorithm for computation is usually executed recursively in the following way. The number of loop iterations is the same as the number of sets of input data. Loop execution starts with writing the input values of the current set of data into the table and the tolerated error for the output variables. From here on, sequential scanning of generated PPN and actions with the stack are made according to the following rules:

— if the current element of PPN is a variable, the link to it is copied from PPN to the stack, the type of cell in the stack being defined in " link":
— if the current element of PPN is a constant, by the link the value of that constant is copied from the table of constants to the stack, the type of cell being defined in "value";
— if the current element of PPN is a unary operation, the top element is removed from the stack, if it is of "link" type, the value by that link is read in the table of variables and if it is of "value" type, it is used, after that the unary operation is executed and its result is put into the stack, the type of cell being defined in "value";
— if the current element of PPN is a binary operation (apart from operation =), then , like in the case of unary operation, only one value is removed either from the stack or the table of variables and (unlike the unary operation) the other value is removed either from the stack or the table of variables whereupon the unary operation is executed and its result is put into the stack again;
— if the current element of PPN is operation =, like in the case of the unary operation, the value is removed from the stack or from the table of variables, then the link is removed from the stack, after that the retrieved value is put into the table of variables by the link.

After the computation has ended for the current set of input data matching of the values of input data put into the table is made using prepared by the developers' true values in terms of the computational error. If for each set of data matching is successful, the formula type answer is considered correct.

6   Conclusion

The use of the tasks with the algebraic formula type answer improves the quality of testing in the different subjects, especially, when the mixed diagnostic tests are implemented. The proposed method makes it possible to computerize the checkup of such answers, and the knowledge of complicated programming languages is not required.

References

1. Yankovskaya, A.E., Semenov, M.E.: Foundation of the Construction of Mixed Diagnostic Tests in Systems for Quality Control of Education. In: Proc. 13th IASTED International Conference Computers and Advanced Technology in Education (CATE 2010), Maui, Hawaii, USA, August 23-25, pp. 142–145 (2010)

2. Yankovskaya, A.E., Semenov, M.E.: Intelligent System for Knowledge Estimation on the Base of Mixed Diagnostic Tests and Elements of Fuzzy Logic. In: Proc. IASTED International Conference on Technology for Education (TE 2011), Dallas, USA, December 14-16, pp. 108–113 (2011)
3. Yankovskaya, A.E., Semenov, M.E.: Application 34. Mixed Diagnostic Tests in Blended Education and Training. In: Proceedings of the IASTED International Conference Web-based Education (WBE 2013), Innsbruck, Austria, February 13-15, pp. 935–939 (2013)
4. Yankovskaya, A.E., Fuks, I.L., Dementyev, Y.N.: Mixed Diagnoctic Tests in Construction Technology of the Training and Testing Systems. IJEIT 3, 169–174 (2013)
5. Avanesov, B.S.: Composition of test tasks: Textbook. – 3 edd., add. – M.: Testing centre, – 240 c (2002)
6. Naprasnik, S.V., Tsimbaluk, E.S., Shkill, A.S.: Computer System for Testing Learners' Knowledge. In: OpenTEST 2.0 Materials of 10 International Conference UADO Education and Virtuality, Kharkov, Yalta, pp. 454–461. KhNURE, Kharkov (2006)
7. Balfour, S.P.: Assessing Writing in MOOCs: Automated Essay Scoring and Calibrated Peer Review[TM]. Research & Practice in Assessment. Special Issue: MOOCs & Technology. Virginia Assessment Group 8, 40–48 (2013)
8. Aho, A.V., Ullman, J.D.: The Theory of Parsing, Translation and Compiling. Parsing, vol. 1. Parsing. Printice-Hall, Inc., Englewood Cliffs (1972)
9. Aho, A.V., Ullman, J.D.: The Theory of Parsing, Translation and Compiling. vol. 2. Printice-Hall, Inc., Englewood Cliffs (1973)

Thematic Clustering Methods Applied
to News Texts Analysis

Anastasia N. Soloshenko, Yulia A. Orlova,
Vladimir L. Rozaliev, and Alla V. Zaboleeva-Zotova

Volgograd State Technical University, Volgograd, Russia
{nastyasolan,yulia.orlova,
vladimir.rozaliev,zabzot}@gmail.com

Abstract. This paper is devoted to a problem of partition documents from the news flow into groups, where each group contains documents that are similar to each other. We use thematic clustering to solve this problem. The existing clustering algorithms such as k-means, minimum spanning tree and etc. are considered and analyzed. It is shown which of these algorithms give the best results working with news texts. Clustering is a powerful tool for text processing, but it can't give a complete picture of news article semantics. This paper also presents a methodic of comprehensive news texts analysis based on a combination of statistical algorithms for keywords extracting and algorithms forming the semantic coherence of text blocks. Particular attention is paid to the structural features of the news texts.

Keywords: thematic clustering, clustering algorithms, news articles, document representation.

1 Introduction

Internet resources development has exacerbated the problem of information overload. American research service Cyveillance reported in the early XXI century that the number of pages in the Internet exceeded 4 billion, and every day increases by 7 million. Particularly, online news resources audience growth exceeds almost twice the growth of the total number Internet users. This audience is 43.2% of Russian Internet users nowadays (according to the Nielsen//NetRatings research) [13]. The number of daily posts in Twitter closes to the mark of 400 million records per day, whereas in April 2012 this index was 340 million per day.

Raw unstructured data constitute a large part of the information with which users deal every day. So many organizations (automated library information systems, broadcasting channels, news feeds and etc.) and individual users feel needs in means of automatic technologies analyzing natural language. Automatic clustering, i.e. partition documents from the news flow into groups (possibly hierarchical) marked by some semantic descriptors, is one of the priority tasks solved by information systems.

A. Kravets et al. (Eds.): JCKBSE 2014, CCIS 466, pp. 294–310, 2014.

2   Overview of Existing Text Analysis Systems Enabling Document Clustering

A large number of software products that provide function of text documents clustering are known nowadays.

It is TextAnalyst, Galaktika-ZOOM among Russian and a powerful tool for texts analyzing IBM Text Miner among foreign. TextAnalyst includes opportunities of semantic network creation, annotation, text search, automatic classification and texts clustering. IBM Text Miner contains classification, clustering keywords search and texts annotation utilities. However, the most of the leading systems don't focus on news texts processing.

Russian system Yandex News automatically classifies data in news stories and makes abstracts based on news documents cluster. Service InfoStream provides access to timely information from the search mode considering semantic similarity of documents. Mobile news aggregator Summly bought in March 2013 by the Yahoo! company also performs news articles grouping by their topics. However, the application is unsuitable for the processing of Russian texts.

Thereby the existing software systems don't solve posed problem in whole. It is necessary to develop a product for news texts analysis combining clustering of news articles with complex text analysis.

3   News Texts Structure Features Applied to Clustering Problem

Having reviewed a number of articles submitted at the well-known news sites such as Lenta.ru, NewsRu.com, Kommersant.ru, Expert (and others related to the top 30 news portals of Ru.net), we can build a common structure of the news text (figure 1).

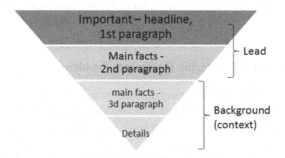

Fig. 1. Structure of the news text

This structure is based on the principle of "inverted pyramid", which requires placement of basic information at the beginning of the material and its subsequent detailed disclosure.

- Headline of the news reflects its topic and contains no more than 10 words (80 characters). So, for example, not more than 15 words in the title displayed in Yandex, Google displays up to 70 words.
- Basic facts about the events reflected in paragraphs 1-2, and constitute the so-called lead of text (covers the main theme).
- 3rd and subsequent paragraphs make a background of news (context). As a rule, details of happening are disclosed there, the information directly related to the news is given.

So we have a formula: (Who? + What? + Where? + Why? + When? + How?) for the content of the news. This so-called law of «five W and one H», attributed to R. Kipling [9]. If all news reports construct according to a single structure, the solution of clustering problem could be significantly simplified.

4   Thematic Clustering of News Streams

Clustering is the task of grouping a set of objects in such a way that objects in the same group (called a cluster) are more similar to each other than to those in other groups. The number of clusters can be fixed or not fixed. Main groups of clustering algorithms are hierarchical and non-hierarchical, crisp (hard) and fuzzy algorithms.

A hierarchical clustering method produces a classification in which small clusters of very similar documents are nested within larger clusters of less closely-related documents. A non-hierarchical method generates a classification by partitioning a dataset, giving a set of (generally) non-overlapping groups having no hierarchical relationships between them.

Hard clustering methods are based on classical set theory, and require that an object either does or does not belong to a cluster. Hard clustering means partitioning the data into a specified number of mutually exclusive subsets. Fuzzy clustering methods, however, allow the objects to belong to several clusters simultaneously, with different degrees of membership. In many situations, fuzzy clustering is more natural than hard clustering.

4.1   Formalization of Clustering Documents Problem

Let's consider the problem of clustering documents more formally.

Let X – set of objects, Y – set of numbers of clusters. Function of the distance between objects defined as $\rho(x, x')$. There is a finite training sample objects $X^m = \{x_1, ..., x_m\} \subset X$. It is necessary to split the sample into disjoint subsets, called clusters, so each cluster consists of objects that are close to metric ρ, and objects of different clusters significantly differed. In this case cluster's number y_i is attributed to each object $x_i \in X^m$.

Clustering algorithm is the function $a : X \rightarrow Y$ that assigns to any object $x \in X$ cluster's number $y \in Y$ [6].

4.2   Clustering Algorithms

Let's consider only few algorithms optimal for news stream processing from our point of view.

Agglomerative Clustering. This is a «bottom up» approach: each observation starts in its own cluster, and pairs of clusters are merged as one moves up the hierarchy.

This method builds the hierarchy from the individual elements by progressively merging clusters. In our example, we have six elements {a} {b} {c} {d} {e} and {f}. The first step is to determine which elements to merge in a cluster. Usually, we want to take the two closest elements, according to the chosen distance.

Optionally, one can also construct a distance matrix at this stage, where the number in the i-th row j-th column is the distance between the i-th and j-th elements. Then, as clustering progresses, rows and columns are merged as the clusters are merged and the distances updated. This is a common way to implement this type of clustering, and has the benefit of caching distances between clusters. A simple agglomerative clustering algorithm is described in the single-linkage clustering page; it can easily be adapted to different types of linkage (see below).

Suppose we have merged the two closest elements b and c, we now have the following clusters {a}, {b, c}, {d}, {e} and {f}, and want to merge them further. To do that, we need to take the distance between {a} and {b c}, and therefore define the distance between two clusters. Usually the distance between two clusters A and B is one of the following:

- The maximum distance between elements of each cluster (also called complete-linkage clustering):

$$\max\{d(x.y): x \in A, y \in B\}$$

- The minimum distance between elements of each cluster (also called single-linkage clustering):

$$\min\{d(x.y): x \in A, y \in B\}$$

- The mean distance between elements of each cluster (also called average linkage clustering):

$$\frac{1}{|A| \cdot |B|}\sum_{x \in A}\sum_{y \in B}d(x, y).$$

- The sum of all intra-cluster variance.
- The increase in variance for the cluster being merged (Ward's method)
- The probability that candidate clusters spawn from the same distribution function (V-linkage).

Each agglomeration occurs at a greater distance between clusters than the previous agglomeration, and one can decide to stop clustering either when the clusters are too far apart to be merged (distance criterion) or when there is a sufficiently small number of clusters (number criterion) [6].

Advantages: does not require the number of clusters to be known in advance, no input parameters, computes a complete hierarchy of clusters, good result visualizations integrated into the methods. Disadvantages: may not scale well: runtime for the standard methods – O (n^2 log n), no explicit clusters: a «flat» partition can be derived afterwards, no automatic discovering of «optimal clusters».

K-means Algorithm and Its Modifications. The K-means algorithm is an iterative clustering technique that evolves K crisp, compact, and hyperspherical clusters in a data set such that the measure

$$J = \sum_{j=1}^{n} \sum_{k=1}^{K} u_{kj} \cdot \| \bar{x}_j - \bar{z}_k \|^2 \tag{1}$$

is minimized. Here, u_{kj} is equal to 1 if the j-th point belongs to cluster k, and 0 otherwise; $\bar{z}_k$ denotes center of the cluster k, and $\bar{x}_j$ denotes the j-th point of the data. In K-means, cluster centers are first initialized to K randomly chosen points from the data set. The initial partitioning is formed using the minimum distance criterion. The cluster centers are subsequently updated to the means of the respective clusters.

The process of partitioning followed by updating centers is repeated until one of the following becomes true: (a) the cluster centers do not change in subsequent iterations, (b) the J value becomes smaller than a threshold, or (c) the maximum number of iterations has been exhausted. The different steps of the K-means algorithm are enumerated further [3].

Step 1: Choose K cluster centers $z_1, z_2, ..., z_k$ randomly from the n points $x_1, x_2, ..., x_n$.

Step 2: Assign point x_i, $i = 1,2,...,n$ to cluster C_j, $j \in 1,2,...,k$ k

If $\| x_i - z_j \| < \| x_i - z_p \|$, $p = 1,2,...,k$ *and* $j \neq p$, ties are resolved arbitrarily.

Step 3: Compute new cluster centers $z_1^*, z_2^*, ..., z_k^*$ as follows:

$$z_i^* = \frac{\sum x_j \in C_i^{x_j}}{n_i}, i = 1,2....,K$$

where n_i is the number of elements belonging to cluster C_i.

Step 4: If $z_i^* = z_i$, $i = 1,2,...,K$ then terminate.

Otherwise, $z_i = z_i^*$, $i = 1,2,...,K$ and continue from step 2.

Fig. 2. The K-means algorithm

The K-means algorithm has several limitations. K-means algorithm may converge to values that are not optimal, depending on the choice of the initial cluster centers. Also, global solutions of large problems cannot be found with a reasonable amount of computation effort. Moreover, this technique assumes that clusters are of hyperspherical shape and more or less equal in size. Finally, K-means is not robust to outliers. It is because of these factors that several other methods for clustering have been developed (such as K-means++, K-medoids algorithms).

Fuzzy Clustering Algorithms – FCM. Fuzzy C-means is a widely used technique that uses the principles of fuzzy sets to evolve a fuzzy partition matrix for a given data set. The set of all c×n, where c is the number of clusters, non-degenerate constrained fuzzy partition matrices, denoted by M fcn, is defined as

$$M_{fcn} = \left\{ U \in R^{c \times n} \mid \sum_{i=1}^{c} u_{ik} = 1, \sum_{k=1}^{n} u_{ik} > 0, \forall i \text{ and } u_{ik} \in [0,1]; 1 \le i \le c; 1 \le k \le n \right\}. \quad (2)$$

The minimizing criterion used to define good clusters for fuzzy C-means partitions is the FCM function, defined as

$$J_{\mu}(U,Z) = \sum_{i=1}^{c} \sum_{k=1}^{n} (u_{ik})^{\mu} D^{2}(\bar{z}_{i}, \bar{x}_{k}). \quad (3)$$

Here, $U \in M_{fcn}$ is a fuzzy partition matrix; $\mu \in [1, \infty]$ is the weighting exponent on each fuzzy membership; $Z = [\bar{z}_{1}, .., \bar{z}_{c}]$ represents c cluster centers; $\bar{z}_{i} \in R^{N}$; and $D(\bar{z}_{i}, \bar{z}_{k})$ is the distance of $\bar{x}_{k}$ from the i-th cluster center [3]. The fuzzy C-means theorem states that, if $D(\bar{z}_{i}, \bar{z}_{k}) > 0$, for all i and k, then (U,Z) may minimize J_{μ}, only if $\mu > 1$ and

$$u_{ik} = \frac{1}{\sum_{j=1}^{c} (\frac{D(\bar{z}_{i}, \bar{x}_{k})}{D(\bar{z}_{j}, \bar{x}_{k})})^{\frac{2}{\mu-1}}}, \quad for \ 1 \le i \le c, 1 \le k \le n \quad (4)$$

and

$$\bar{z}_{i} = \frac{\sum_{k=1}^{n} (u_{ik})^{\mu} \bar{x}_{k}}{\sum_{k=1}^{n} (u_{ik})^{\mu}}, 1 \le i \le c. \quad (5)$$

A common strategy for generating the approximate solutions of the minimization problem in Eq. 3 is by iterating through Eqs. 4 and 5. A detailed description of the FCM algorithm can be found in [4].

Although in fuzzy clustering the final output is a crisp partitioning, the user can utilize the information contained in the partition matrix. The FCM algorithm shares the problems of the K-means algorithm in that it also gets stuck at local optima depending on the choice of the initial clusters, and requires the number of clusters to be specified apriori.

So, the advantages of this algorithm are: 1) it gives best result for overlapped data set and comparatively better then k-means algorithm; 2) unlike k-means where data point must exclusively belong to one cluster center here data point is assigned membership to each cluster center as a result of which data point may belong to more than one cluster center.

Disadvantages are: 1) apriori specification of the number of clusters; 2) with lower value of u_{ik} we get the better result but at the expense of more number of iteration; 3) Euclidean distance measures can unequally weight underlying factors.

Minimum Spanning Tree Algorithm. Minimum Spanning Tree (MST) is a subgraph that spans over all the vertices of a given graph without any cycle and has minimum sum of weights over all the included edges. In MST-based clustering, the weight for each edge is considered as the Euclidean distance between the end points forming that edge. As a result, any edge that connects two sub-trees in the MST must be the shortest. In such clustering methods, inconsistent edges which are unusually longer are removed from the MST. The connected components of the MST obtained by removing these edges are treated as the clusters. Elimination of the longest edge results into two-group clustering. Removal of the next longest edge results into three-group clustering and so on.

Coefficient of variation (Coeff_Var) is defined as the ratio between standard deviation (σ) and the arithmetic mean (μ). In the proposed method, we use the coefficient of variation to measure the consistency. By consistency, we mean how the distance between the points is uniform from one another. The more uniform the points are, the more consistent they are said to be and the lower the coefficient of variation, the greater is the consistency. Given a set of data points $x_1, x_2, ..., x_n$, we express the coefficient of variation mathematically as follows [14, 15]:

$$Coeff\_Var = \frac{\sigma}{\mu} , \qquad (6)$$

where

$$\sigma = (\frac{1}{n}\sum_{i=1}^{n}(x_i - \mu)^2)^{\frac{1}{2}} = (\frac{1}{n}\sum_{i=1}^{n}(x_i^2 - (\frac{1}{n}\sum_{i=1}^{n}x_i)^2)^{\frac{1}{2}} \text{ and } \mu = \frac{1}{n}\sum_{i=1}^{n}x_i$$

We use a threshold value on the coefficient of variation (Coeff_Var) to determine the inconsistent edges for their removal from the minimum spanning tree of the given data set in order to produce the clusters.

A detailed description of the MST based clustering algorithm can be found in [15].

Advantage of this algorithm is comparatively better performance than k-means algorithm, disadvantage is threshold value and step size needs to be defined apriori.

Neural Networks. It is possible to use the neural network with so called unsupervised learning for cluster analysis that is based on evaluation of the difference (distance) of the weighted vector w of the neural network from the vector of input pattern x and search of neuron, whose weighted coefficient have the minimum distance of w from x. This neuron, which won among the neurons of the network, has the right to adjust its weights and the weights of neurons in its surroundings and thus the response on submitted learning pattern to better value. After submitting of a further learning pattern it can win another neuron of the net that can adjust its weights and the weights of neurons in its surroundings and thus to increase better answer etc. The clusters are thus created in the net that in certain places of the network optimally respond to certain symptoms of submitted patterns, as well as unknown patterns. The "map" of patterns is created. This network was presented by Kohonen in 1982 and it is called Kohonen self-organizing map. The schema of this network is presented at the figure 3 [1].

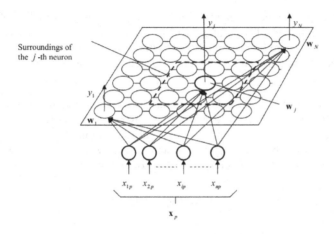

Fig. 3. Sample schema of the Kohonen network

The network contains n distributing nodes that are fed by single components of the vector of input pattern $x_p = (x_{1p}, x_{2p},..., x_{ip},..., x_{np})^T$ and N efficient neurons distributed on imaginary surface (one-layer network), for example on the surface of specific configuration such as rectangular structure, where the efficient neurons are found in individual crossing lines of the rectangular structure (there are used other structures, such as with glory in efficient neuron using other structure, such as hexagon). The neurons have among themselves the bindings, so that it is possible to define the surroundings of each neuron. Further, it is possible to think over lateral activity of neuron on the neighbouring neurons according to the rule: the nearest surroundings are represented by exciting bindings and further surroundings by inhibitive bindings. The action of the i-th component xi on the j-th neuron is done by weight coefficient w_{ji} (real value). The weight vector of the j-th neuron is $w_j = (w_{j1}, w_{j2},..., w_{jn})^T$.

The input vector (for the p-th input pattern) has the form $x_p = (x_{1p}, x_{2p}, ..., x_{np})^T$.

It is calculated for each neuron its distance D_j (of the vector w_j from the vector x_p) as an Euclidean distance $D_j(w_j, x_p) = |w_j - x_p|$. For the evaluation of D_j is used the formula

$$D_j = \sum_{i=1}^{n} (x_{ip} - w_{ji})^2, \; where \; j = 1, ..., N. \tag{7}$$

The competition of neuron consists in the fact that the neuron is found, that has the weighted coefficients with the smallest distance from values of relevant components of the vector x_p. This neuron is considered to be a winner.

The algorithm of learning of the neural network is as follows [10]:

1) Set up of the number of input variables n according to the structure of input pattern and determination of a number N of efficient neurons according to condition: $L \le N / (4 \log N)$ where L is the number of patterns to be recognized by net.

2) Set up of initial values that are selected as random values in the range $\langle -0.5; 0.5 \rangle$.

3) Set up of the shape and radius of initial environs of winning neuron NE(t0), at first it is greater, major, then it is decreased step by step to be Rc(t) = 1.

4) The use of the first learning pattern x_1 and foundation of the winning neuron is done in such a way, that the Euclidean distance of its weighted vector w_j from x_1 is the smallest. The calculation is done according to the formula

$$D_j = \sum_{i=1}^{n} (x_i(t) - w_{ji}(t))^2 \to \min \; for \; j = 1, ..., N.$$

The ideal case is the situation $\min_{j} D_j \to 0$.

5) The adaptation of weighted coefficients is done according to the formula

$$w_{ji}(t+1) = w_{ji}(t) + \alpha(t)(x_i(t) - w_{ji}(t)), \; for \; j \in NE_c(t)$$

and

$$w_{ji}(t+1) = w_{ji}(t), \; for \; j \notin NE_c(t)$$

The teaching is done so long, until the weighted coefficients do not change if random pattern from the collection of learning patterns is used.

4.3   Comparison of Clustering Methods According to the News Texts Processing

We should consider following features of news streams choosing the optimal news clustering algorithm:

— Ever-growing collection of documents;
— The same article may reflect several stories;
— News has a certain structure of the text;
— Different parts of the document should have a different weight during similarity detection;
— Stories and documents can be cross-referenced to each other.

According to this features we present a table review of the existing news streams clustering algorithms.

Table 1. Clustering algorithms

	Agglomerative	EM-algorithm	K-means	FCM	BIRCH	MST
Non-hierarchical			+	+		+
Hierarchical	+	+			+	
Hard	+	+	+		+	+
Fuzzy				+		
Incremental					+	
Number of clusters should be set			+	+		

We consider that news clustering algorithm should be non-hierarchical, fuzzy and incremental. Therefore, the most optimal methods for this application are FCM algorithm or neural networks.

Further we consider aspects of the news text semantic analysis.

5   News Texts Proceedings after News Streams Clusterization

So, news aggregators are complex hardware and software systems that solve a wide range of tasks: the actual clustering, ranking documents within the cluster, overview annotation, identifying key subjects, thematic classification, news search and etc. [5], [8]. Semantic analysis is one of major functions of news aggregators besides clustering. It can be divided into several stages (figure 4).

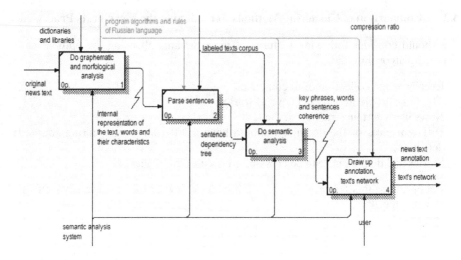

Fig. 4. The procedure of news text semantic analysis

5.1   Initial Stage of News Text Analysis

The information necessary for further processing by morphological and syntactic analyzers produce at the initial stage of text processing – graphematic analysis [6]. This stage includes internal representation of the news text structure as a triplet $T = <P, S, W>$, where P - paragraphs, S - sentences, W - words. Correct identification of the title and of the first sentence in the paragraph that contains the basic facts of the article is also necessary at this stage

The next step is the morphological analysis. It has a purpose to construct the morphological interpretations of words from input text. All methods can be divided into two groups - the vocabulary and probability-statistics (without using a dictionary). The disadvantages of the first are the large amount of lexicons, poor performance on a small sample, the lack of precise linguistic methods. The second method (vocabulary) is based on the connection of dictionary or thesaurus and it gives the most comprehensive analysis of the word's form [2].

Some morphological library should be used for this step, for example, Lemmatizer, FreeLing, NLTK, MCR, tokenizer. A lot of morphological interpretations such as the morphological part of speech, lemma (for example, the nominative singular noun or infinitive verb), a plurality of grammemes sets - elementary descriptors that identify word form to any morphological class (gender, number, case) is given for each word from the input text. Porter's stemmer can be used in order to work with unfamiliar words (its implementation is available for many languages).

5.2   Parsing

Syntactic analysis (parsing) is considered as a problem of constructing a sentence dependency tree. It includes syntax highlighting, definition of subordination fragments.

We give an overview of the main parsing tools [17], which may be used in your project.

Table 2. Parsers

Title	Method	Languages	Platform
AOT	grammar HPSG	Russian, English, German	GNU/Linux, Microsoft Windows
MaltParser	machine learning	Russian, English	Java
Link Grammar Parser	grammar links	Russian, English	GNU/Linux, Microsoft Windows
NLTK	machine learning	English	Python
Solarix	rules	Russian, English	GNU/Linux, Microsoft Windows

5.3   Keywords Extraction, Drawing Up Annotation

There are a big number of keywords extraction methods now. The most famous of them are TF-IDF and C-Value.

TF-IDF, term frequency–inverse document frequency, is a numerical statistic which reflects how important a word is to a document in a collection or corpus. TF is the number of times that term t occurs in document d, IDF is a measure of whether the term is common or rare across all documents. It is obtained by dividing the total number of documents by the number of documents containing the term, and then taking the logarithm of that quotient.

$$IDF = \log \frac{|D|}{|(d_i \supset t_i)|} \qquad (8)$$

where $|D|$ - the total number of documents in the corpus; $|(d_i \supset t_i)|$ - number of documents where the term ti appears (when $n_i \neq 0$).

TF-IDF is the product of two statistics, term frequency and inverse document frequency.

The C-value is given as follows:

$$C-Value(a) - \begin{cases} \log_2 |a| \cdot freq(a), & a \text{ is not nested} \\ \log_2 |a| \cdot freq(a) - \frac{1}{P(T_a)} \cdot \sum_{b \in T_a} freq(b) & \text{otherwise} \end{cases} \qquad (9)$$

where a – is the candidate string, |a| - is the number of words in string a, freq(a) – is the frequency of occurrence of a in the corpus, Ta – is the set of extracted candidate terms that contain a, P(Ta) – is the number of these longer candidate terms [12].

However, software modules for keywords and entities extraction have already existed. These modules include PullEnti, written entirely in C #. NET.

We have developed the keywords extraction algorithm for our program.

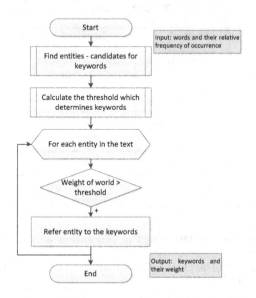

Fig. 5. Key phrases extraction algorithm

It's combining the extraction of named entities from news text (based on the results of morphological analysis and the plug-PullEnti work results) and counting the weight of words considering the frequency of its occurrence.

The relative frequency of a word-candidate for keywords with the index equal (0,2 × number of entities) is a threshold for the recognition word as a keyword. This experimental value is calculated on a sample of 500 texts.

As a result the body of knowledge structure S of the news text can be defined as follows: S = {M, F}, where M - set of all concepts of knowledge body, F - ratio «semantic connection». It can be used a semantic network as a formal model of the structure of knowledge, defined as a directed graph G = (E, V), where E - the set of vertices delivered in a one- to-one correspondence with the set of concepts; V - set of oriented arcs; arc leaves from the top, corresponding to the basic concept A, and is included in the node corresponding to the concept which combines by the meaning with notion A [7], [11], [16]. Thus, content of news can be represented graphically in the form of key concepts and relationships between them, either in the form of so-called mind map (figure 6).

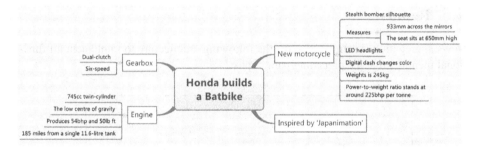

Fig. 6. Mind map of news text

It is also necessary to perform the following processing of sentences before drawing up the news text annotation (figure 7).

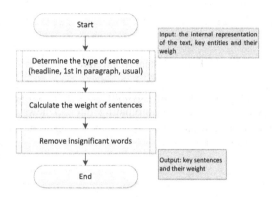

Fig. 7. Sentences analysis algorithm

Calculation of sentences weight is based on its location in text. It is calculated as follows:

$$W_s = N_{kw} \cdot Rf_{kw} \cdot ParagraphWeight \cdot k \qquad (10)$$

where W_s – sentence weight; N_{kw} - the number of keyword occurrences in the sentence; Rf_{kw} - the relative frequency of the keyword, paragraph weight - the relative weight of the paragraph in the text, it is 0.35 for the first paragraph (lead), 0.2 for the second, 0.1 for others (context); k - coefficient of sentence significant within a paragraph. It is equal 1 for the first sentence of the paragraph, for others - 0.8.

The annotation includes the sentences with the greatest weight, and it's based on adjusted compression ratio.

6   Results

News aggregation system must have the following architecture to implement all functional mentioned at the preceding paragraphs:

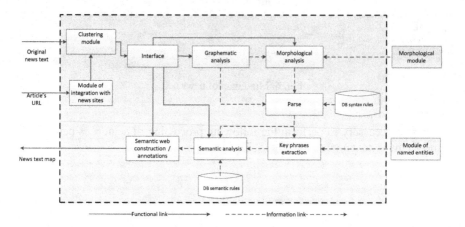

Fig. 8. System architecture

There was carried out an experiment which proves that the efficiency of processing online news articles has increased by automating internet news streams processing (i.e. processing time has decreased and the quality of the result has improved). We obtained following results:

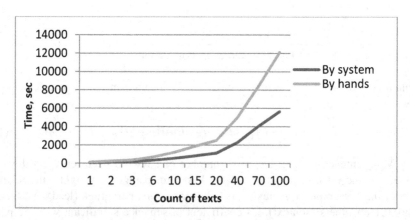

Fig. 9. Dependence of processing time on the number of texts

Time by system includes not only time for directly preparation of text's annotation but also the time required for adjusting a final text.

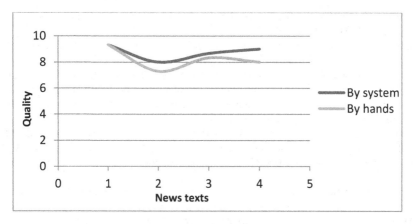

Fig. 10. Quality of annotations

The quality of result annotation can be evaluated by means of the following measures: preservation of key facts, semantic coherence of news article and preservation of text's syntactic structure after the removal of non-significant parts. Each of these measures was assessed by experts on a scale of 0 to 10 and then to assess the quality of the annotation we took the arithmetic mean of these three indicators for each text.

So the quality of the news is treated at the same level as in human text analysis and processing time is reduced at least several times.

7   Conclusions

So, news texts analysis includes tasks of clustering documents and subsequent complex processing of articles. News stream and its features, clustering algorithms for news articles were analyzed. We offer the most appropriate solution for our problem - FCM algorithm or neural networks applied to internet news texts processing. However, it should be noted that it is not only true, as it is necessary not only to experiment with a selection of measures distances, but sometimes even change the algorithm to achieve a better results. We have also implemented part of online news aggregation system and have investigated the effectiveness of its work.

References

1. Ali, M., Dapoigny, R.: Advances in Applied Artificial Intelligence. Springer, Heidelberg (2006)
2. Artem'ev, K.: Probabilistic method of the morphological analysis for full-text indexed search tasks. In: Proceedings of the Russian Conference of Young Scientists in Information Retrieval, RuSSIR, pp. 6–12 (2008)
3. Bandyopadhyay, S., Saha, S.: Unsupervised Classification. Springer, Heidelberg (2013)
4. Bezdek, J.C.: Pattern Recognition with Fuzzy Objective Function Algorithms. Plenum, New York (1981)

5. Bol'shakova, E.I.: Automated processing of natural language texts and computational linguistics. MIEM, Moscow (2011)
6. Manning, C.D., Raghavan, P.: Information Retrieval. Cambridge University Press (2008)
7. Dmitriev, A.S., Zaboleeva-Zotova, A.V., Orlova, Y.A., Rozaliev, V.L.: Automatic identification of time and space categories in the natural language text. In: Applied Computing 2013 Proceedings of the IADIS International Conference, Fort Worth, Texas, USA, October 23-25, pp. 187–190. IADIS (International Association for Development of the Information Society), UNT (University of North Texas) (2013)
8. Dmitriev, A.S., Zaboleeva-Zotova, A.V., Orlova, Y.A., Rozaliev, V.L.: Processing of Spatial and Temporal Information in the Text. In: World Applied Sciences Journal (WASJ), vol. 24(spec.issue24), pp. 133–137. Information Technologies in Modern Industry, Education & Society (2013)
9. Dobrov, B.V.: Basic line for news clusterization methods evaluation. In: Proceedings of the 12th Scientific Conference on Digital Libraries: Advanced Methods and Technologies, Digital Collections, RCDL 2010, Kazan, pp. 287–295 (2010)
10. Dostal, P., Pokorny, P.: Cluster analysis and neural network. Brno University of Technology (2007)
11. Grune, D.: Tokens to Syntax Tree – Syntax Analysis. Springer, New York (2012)
12. Kiryakov, A.: Semantic annotation, indexing, and retrieval. Web Semantics: Science, Services and Agents on the World Wide Web 2, 49–79 (2004)
13. Lande, D.V.: Knowledge Search in INTERNET. Professional work. Dialectics, Moscow (2005)
14. Pera, M.S., Ng, Y.-K.D.: Using maximal spanning trees and word similarity to generate hierarchical clusters of non-redundant RSS news articles. J. Intell. Inf. Syst. 39, 513–534 (2012)
15. Petrica, C.: Pop: The Generalized Minimum Spanning Tree Problem. University of Twente (2002)
16. Rozaliev, V.L., Bobkov, A.S., Orlova, Y.A., Zaboleeva-Zotova, A.V., Dmitriev, A.S.: Detailed Analysis of Postures and Gestures for the Identification of Human Emotional Reactions. In: World Applied Sciences Journal (WASJ), vol. 24(spec. issue 24), pp. 151–158. Information Technologies in Modern Industry, Education & Society (2013)
17. Zaboleeva-Zotova, A.V., Orlova, Y.A., Rozaliev, V.L., Fomenkov, S.A., Petrovskij, A.B.: Formalization of initial stage of designing multi-component software. In: Multi Conference on Computer Science and Information Systems 2013: Proceedings of the IADIS International Conference Intelligent Systems and Agents, Prague, Czech Republic, July 23-26. IADIS (International Association for Development of the Information Society), Prague, pp. 107–111 (2013)

Extracting the Translation of Anime Titles from Web Corpora Using CRF

Maiko Yamazaki[1], Hajime Morita[2], Kanako Komiya[3], and Yoshiyuki Kotani[4]

[1] Tokyo Institute of Technology
yamazaki@lr.pi.titech.ac.jp
[2] Kyoto University
morita@nlp.ist.i.kyoto-u.ac.jp
[3] Ibaraki University
kkomiya@mx.ibaraki.ac.jp
[4] Tokyo University of Agriculture and Technology
kotani@cc.tuat.ac.jp

Abstract. Unknown words whose translation is not listed in general dictionaries, have been a problem in cross-language information retrieval and machine translation. Since the new terms are created one after the other, it is difficult to cover all such terms using general bilingual dictionaries. Therefore, researches on automatic extraction of translations for unknown words have been performed for the purpose of building a bilingual dictionary at low cost using Web corpora. In this paper, we focus on anime titles; they are commercially important, and propose a method to extract Japanese candidate translations corresponding to the English anime titles using Conditional Random Fields (CRF). We used transliteration features as well as features of bag of words, part of speech, and so on because we focused on the fact that when the Japanese anime titles were translated into English, they were transliterated in many cases. The experiments were performed using one hundred Web pages at most collected from the search engine, whose queries were Japanese-English anime title pairs extracted from Wikipedia. The results showed that the number of acquired titles significantly increased when the transliteration features were used.

1 Introduction

E-commerce has become widely used throughout the world and had enabled people to purchase products from abroad. However, there are some cases where non-Japanese buyers are unable to find products they want through Japanese shopping Web sites because they require Japanese queries. If English product names could be translated into Japanese automatically, they would be useful for the product search. We focused on products related to Japanese anime because they were commercially important; Japanese pop culture such as that exemplified by manga, anime, and gaming has gained popularity with young generations in recent years. However it is particularly difficult to translate product names such as titles of anime or movies using machine translation. That made it possible to use part of speaches as features. Moreover, since the new anime are

A. Kravets et al. (Eds.): JCKBSE 2014, CCIS 466, pp. 311–320, 2014.

broadcasted one after the other, it is difficult to translate the title of them using existing dictionaries. In this paper, we propose a method to extract candidate translations of Japanese corresponding to the English anime title by Conditional Random Fields (CRF). We designed the features focusing on the fact that when a Japanese anime title was translated into English, it was often transliterated.

2   Related Work

Parallel corpora are necessary for automatic extraction of the translation of Out of Vocabulary(OOV) terms, however, they are limited. Thus, translation extraction using the text on the Web has attracted attention. Many works on automatic extraction of the translation of OOV terms in Web corpora are accomplished[5][2].

Chang et al. (2013) described automatic extraction of the translations[1]. They extracted the translations of terms in various field from mixed-code snippets of a search engine using CRF. Translation, transliteration and distance are used as features, and candidate translations are ranked by frequency of appearance.

Our work targets Japanese-English translation pair, whereas most previous works targeted Chinese-English translation pair. Therefore, morphological analysis was conducted and CRF tagged each morpheme in our work, while it tagged every Chinese characters in previous works.That made it possible to use part of speeches as features. Moreover there are many translation pairs whose original title was not only English but also Japanese because we targeted anime titles. Since Japanese anime titles were often transliterated, we focused on transliteration when we designed the feature, considering romanization Japanese and English loan words.

On the other hand, Japanese subculture has attracted worldwide attention and extraction of anime-related words are commercially useful. For example, Takase et al. (2013) presented named entity extraction that has focused on anime-related words using CRF[3]. In this paper, we automatically extracted the Japanese translations of English Anime titles.

3   System Summary

Our system carried out automatic extraction of the candidate translations of Japanese anime titles as follows:

1. Input an English anime title into search engine as query and obtain the top 100 Web pages that search engine output.
2. Perform morphological analysis on each Web page acquired in step 1 and create eleven types of feature for each morpheme.
3. Label morphemes using a model learned in advance. Candidate translations are extracted based on the labels.

System flow is shown in Figure 1.

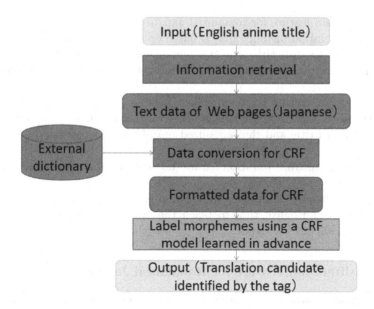

Fig. 1. System summary

4   Feature Design

The following eleven types of feature were used as features of CRF for each morphemes in this system. Transliteration features in Japanese and English are described in section 4.1 and 4.2.

1. Bag of words
2. Part of speech(POS)
3. Subcategory of POS
4. Type of character(Hiragana, Katakana, Alphabet, Kanji, and Others)
   Hiragana is character type mostly used for words of Japanese origin and Katakana is mostly used for western loan words. Kanji is character of Chinese origin and mostly used for words of Chinese origin. Others include marks.
5. The number of morphemes between the English title and the morpheme in question. Here, the numbers is negative if the morpheme was before the title.
6. Whether or not the morpheme in question is listed in the translation dictionary. After calculating the translation probabilities using the GIZA ++[1] based on Japanese-English Bilingual Corpus of Wikipedia's Kyoto Articles[2], translation pairs whose probability is 0.1 or more are stored in the translation dictionary.

---

[1] http://www.statmt.org/moses/giza/GIZA++.html
[2] http://alaginrc.nict.go.jp/WikiCorpus/

7. Transliteration feature for romanized Japanese
   It is transliteration distance that is based on the edit distance between each word in the English title and the romanized morpheme. The value is 0-10. Transliteration distance is the closeness of the sound between the morphemes.
8. Transliteration feature for English loan words
   It is transliteration distance that is based on the edit distance for each word in the English title and the romanized morpheme in question. The value is 0-10.
9. Smaller value of transliteration feature for romanized Japanese and English loan words
10. Whether or not the morpheme in question is in the parenthese.
11. BIOES tags of English title to teach the system the original title whose translation should be output.

4.1   Transliteration Feature for Romanized Japanese

There are many anime titles whose English translation is transliterated from Japanese such as "Kimi to Boku"(literaly means "You and Me"). We introduced transliteration feature for romanized Japanese that measures the degree of matching between each word in English title and each romanized Japanese word, in order to extract such translations. Simple romanization rules that depends on pronunciation are used to romanize Japanese words and we focused on them for this feature.

Transliteration feature value is calculated as follows. First, the candidate transliteration distances are calculated between English candidate strings and Japanese candidate strings. Here, English candidate strings include all words in the English title and conpound words of all successive two words in the English title. Japanese candidate strings are the morpheme in question and the strings that consist of the morpheme and one morpheme before or after the morpheme itself. These candidates were made in the case morphological analyser mistakes. Some of them are artificial words because these candidate strings were made automatically. Next, the minimum value is selected and divided by the length of the Japanese candidate string for the feature value. After that it is multiplied by ten and rounded.

Transliteration feature for romanized Japanese value, TJ, is calculated as follows.

$$TJ = \min_{e_i \in E, n_j \in N} \left(\frac{d(e_i, n_j)}{length(e_i)} \right) \times 10 \tag{1}$$

E denotes the set of all words and conpound words of all successive two words in the English title. N denotes the morpheme in question and the strings that consist of the morpheme and one morpheme before or after the morpheme itself. $d(e_i, n_j)$ denotes edit distance between e_j and n_j.

How to calculate the feature value "ダーティペア (Da-teipea)", which is in "キディグレイド/と/ダーティペア/の/比較 (Kideigureido to da-teipea no hikaku)"(Slash means morpheme delimiter.) that was acquired from English title "Dirty Pair"is described for example. First, the "ダーティペア (Da-teipea)" is romanized and we get "da-teipea". After that, levenshtein distances between "da-teipea" and each word in the English title and compound word of two adjacent words included in the English title, namely, levenshtein distances between "da-teipea" and "Dirty", "Pair", and "DirtyPair" are calculated respectively like Figure 2.

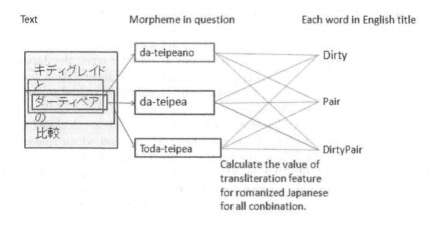

Fig. 2. Calculate transliteration feature for romanized Japanese value

Then, five which is the smallest value of edit distance from "da-teipea" and "Dirtypair", is divided by 9, the length of the character string "da-teipea". Finally, the value 0.56 is obtained.

Next, "とダーティペア (to da-teipea)" was made from the morpheme in question and the previous morpheme of it and it was romanized as "toda-teipea". The edit distances between "toda-teipea" and each word in the English title and conpound word that consists of two adjacent words in English titles are calculated. Then six, the smallest value of the edit distance was selected. It was divided by eleven, i.e., the length of "toda-teipea" and the value 0.55 was obtained. The smallest distance between "ダーティペアの (Da-teipea no)" and English words was calculated in the same way.

Finally, the smallest value, 0.55, was selected. It is multiplied by ten and rounded; We got six for the value.

As shown in this example, this system could deal with a case that one morpheme in Japanese corresponded to two words in English by using not only the English words in title but also compound words of two adjacent words in the title. In addition, it could also deal with the case that two morphemes in Japanese corresponded to one word in English, such as "月/姫 (Tsukihime, literaly means "moon princess")" by using conpound words of two adjacent Japanese morphemes.

When the Japanese morpheme was written in alphabet, the edit distance between English candidate strings and the morpheme was calculated so that the system could deal with Japanese titles that include both alphabet and Japanese character such as "ビッグ X（Big X）".

4.2 Transliteration Feature for English Loan Words

If the value of the transliteration feature for romanized Japanese of the "Felix" and "フィリックス (firikkusu)" is calculated, edit distance is large though they should be zero. As shown in this example, they are sometimes not similar based on simple transliteration rules but their sounds are similar when the Japanese title was English loan words. Therefore, we introduced transliteration feature for English loan words in order to extract the translations that described in Japanese as they sound in English.

The value of transliteration feature for English loan words is calculated using dynamic programming that maps the morpheme in question which romanized to each word that is included in the English title. This method related to the method of Tsuji et al. (2012) that maps phonemes to katakana by dynamic programming [4]. It should be noted that the transliteration feature for English loan words is calculated only if the character type of morpheme in question was Japanese.

Here after, we call a word in English title "English pronounciation string" and a morpheme in question "Japanese pronounciation string". Cost is zero when two strings are exactly the same or when they become the same using the conversion rules for English loan words, which were simple rules for transliteration from English into romanized Japanese (c.f. "igh" is read as "ai") which have been created in advance. Otherwise the cost is one .

Simple rules for transliteration from English into romanized Japanese have been created as the conversion rules for English loan words.

The alignment of "ドロップ (doroppu)" and "drop" is shown in Figure 3 for example. The Japanese pronunciation string "do" could be converted into the English pronunciation string "d" and the Japanese pronunciation string "pu" could be converted the English pronunciation string "p" using the rules.

First, "ドロップ" is converted to Roman alphabet "doroppu". "Drop" is set to English pronunciation string and "doroppu" is set to Japanese pronounciation string. Alignment is started from the zero point in the most lower left. From the zero point, the path to the following four points is given. Coordinates are expressed as (English pronunciation string, Japanese pronunciation string).

- No English pronunciation string is aligned with the Japanese pronunciation string. (1,0)
- No Japanese pronunciation string is aligned with the English pronunciation string. (0,1)
- "D" in Japanese pronunciation string is aligned with "d" in English pronunciation string. (1,1)

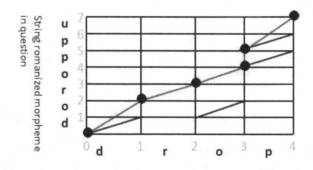

Each word in the English title

Fig. 3. Association of string

- "Do" in Japanese pronunciation string is aligned with "d" in English pronunciation string. (1,2)

Transitions from the zero point to the point of (0,1) or (1,0) cost one, and transitions from the zero point to the point of (1,1) or (1,2) cost zero. In this step, all costs of transition are stored. Next, the path from the four points obtained above are derived. All the path from each point are obtained and their costs are stored recursively in this way and the route with the lowest cost is finally chosen as the alignment. In the case of Figure 1, the path $0 \rightarrow (1,2) \rightarrow (2,3) \rightarrow (3,4) \rightarrow (3,5) \rightarrow (4,7)$ is finally selected, and its cost is one from (3,4)-(3,5). The costs are calculated by the following equation 2. Here, TE denotes the transliteration feature value for English loan words.

$$TE = \frac{Cost}{length\ of\ morpheme\ in\ question} \times 10 \qquad (2)$$

5   Experiments and Evaluation

5.1   Experimental Data

English-Japanese anime title pairs were extracted from English Wikipedia dump data of 2012[3]. Thus, 2134 pairs of English-Japanese translations of anime titles were obtained. These title pairs were used as queries for a search engine whose target language was set to Japanese. Here, the Japanese translation as well as original English title was input into the system for the experiment. For each title, the top 100 Web pages at most were obtained. Google[4] has been utilized as a search engine. Five-fold cross validation was used for the experiment : one fifth of titles were used for the test and rest of them were used for the training for one validation.

---

[3] http://dumps.wikimedia.org/enwiki/
[4] http://www.google.com/

5.2 Experimental Set-Up

First, each Web page must include one English title as well as at least one Japanese translation. The Web pages that does not match this condition were removed. Web pages were also removed when the Japanese title was the same as the English title. As a result, 1282 titles whose Web pages were in this experiment.

If two or more English titles were in one Web page, the English tags of titles except the one that comes out the first were removed so that every Web page could have only one English title in one Web page. Further, only candidate translations within 25 morphemes from English title were extracted based on the idea that the translations of the English title tend to appear nearby the title.

In the experiments, MeCab[5] was used as a morphological analyzer and CRF++[6] was used as a CRF tool.

5.3 Evaluation Method

We regarded the Japanese translation that the system output was correct only when it was exactly the same as the Japanese title extracted from Wikipedia. The system output more than one candidate translation for one title. The coverage, the ratio of the titles whose correct translation could be extracted at least once was evaluated. In addition, recall, precision, and F-measure of BIOES tags were evaluated as reference. In this experiment, a model based on all the eleven kinds of features and a model based on eight features i.e. excluding the features related to transliteration, transliteration feature for romanized Japanese, transliteration feature for English loan words, and smaller value of transliteration feature for romanized Japanese and English loan words, were compared.

6 Experimental Result

Coverages of the system with and without transliteration features are shown in Table 1. Micro and macro average of recall, precision, and F measure based on the tags are shown in Table 2.

Table 1. Coverage

Feature	The titles that the system output	Coverage
All	922	0.719
-Transliteration	806	0.629

Table 1 shows the coverage fell more than nine points when the transliteration features were not used. It shows transliteration features are effective to extract

---

[5] http://mecab.googlecode.com/svn/trunk/mecab/doc/index.html
[6] http://crfpp.googlecode.com/svn/trunk/doc/index.html

Table 2. Micro and Macro average of recall, precision, and F-measure

	Feature	Recall	Precision	F-measure
Micro average	All	0.514	0.739	0.606
	- Transliteration	0.352	0.741	0.477
Macro average	All	0.488	0.588	0.533
	- Transliteration	0.335	0.531	0.411

translations of anime titles. Further, Table 2 shows the recall and F-measure fell but the precision did not be changed when the transliteration features were not used.

7 Discussion

Titles such as "星銃士ビスマルク"(Seijyushi bisumaruku, Bismark) and "戦場の ヴァルキュリア"(Senjyou no varukyuria, Valkyria Chronicles) could be extracted by addition of transliteration feature.

We think that this is because the transliteration feature worked effectively because the sounds of the titles of Japanese and English were similar. On the contrary, titles such as "とんでぶーりん"(Tonde bu-rin, Super Pig) and "紅の 豚"(Kurenai no buta, Porco Rosso) were not extracted by addition of transliteration features. These must be extracted using features of part of speech or distance, since the sounds are not similar, but they could not be extracted because the weight of transliteration became large as a result of learning.

Further, "ヤマトよ永遠にやまと"(Yamato yo towa ni yamato) is obtained erroneously for the translation for "BE FOREVER YAMATO" from the text "… (アニメ) ヤマトよ永遠にやまとよとわに … "((Anime) Yamato yo towa ni yamato yo towa ni), although the correct title was "ヤマトよ永遠に (Yamato yo towa ni)".

We think that the system extracted two words "ヤマト (Yamato)" and "や まと (Yamato)" whose value of transliteration feature is small and that is why the system extracted the translation including them.

Moreover, we regarded the parts of titles such as "アリエッティ"(Ariettei, Arriety) in "借りぐらしのアリエッティ"(Karigurashi no ariettei, The Borrower Arriety) as incorrect in this experiments, but they may be sufficiently useful for the real use of product search.

8 Conclusion

In this paper, we extracted the Japanese translations of English anime titles, with a focus on the transliteration features. The experiments showed that the coverage was improved more than nine points when the system used three transliteration features, "transliteration feature for romanized Japanese", "transliteration feature for English loan words", and "the smaller value of transliteration feature".

References

1. Chang, J.Z., Chang, J.S., Jang, J.-S.R.: Learning to find translations and transliterations on the web based on conditional random fields. IJCLCLP 18(1), 19–45 (2013)
2. Huang, F., Zhang, Y., Vogel, S.: Mining key phrase translations from web corpora. In: Proceedings of Human Language Technology Conference and Conference on Empirical Methods in Natural Language Processing, pp. 483–490 (2005)
3. Takase, M., Komiya, K., Kotani, Y.: Named entity recognition for animation-related words using CRF. In: Proceedings of the 3rd Corpus Japanese Workshop, pp. 179–182 (2013)
4. Tsuji, R., Nemoto, Y., Luangpiensamut, W., Abe, Y., Kimura, T., Komiya, K., Fujimoto, K., Kotani, Y.: The transliteration from alphabet queries to japanese product names. In: Proceedings of the 26th PACLIC, pp. 456–462 (2012)
5. Zhang, Y., Wang, Y., Xue, X.: English-chinese bi-directional oov translation based on web mining and supervised learning. In: Proceedings of the ACL-IJCNLP 2009 Conference Short Papers, pp. 129–132 (2009)

Method of Ontology-Based Extraction
of Physical Effect Description from Russian Text[*]

Sergey Fomenkov, Dmitriy Korobkin, and Sergey Kolesnikov

Volgograd State Technical University, Volgograd, Russian Federation
cad@vstu.ru

Abstract. The paper presents the method of information extraction of physical effect description from Russian text. Physical Effect is an objective relation between two or more physical phenomenon, each of which is described appropriate physical quantity. The representation model of knowledge about physical effects based on an ontologic approach is developed. Logical and physical representation of domain ontologic model is designed. The method of physical effects extraction on the basis of semantic analysis system by AOT and creating queries to ontologic model is developed. The developed system efficiency was tested on a special documents array. Efficiency increase in comparison with existing program "IOFFE" developed by employees of CAD department of Volgograd State Technical University is demonstrated.

Keywords: Domain ontology, fact extraction, text mining, physical effect.

1   Introduction

Nowadays one of the most important tasks is automation of early stages of designing (requirements specification and technical proposal stages) of new technical systems and technologies on the base of which are made fundamental decisions about principles of operation and structure of design object. One of the most promising approaches to realize early stages of requirements specification is concerned with use of structured physical knowledge in the form of Physical Effects (PE) for automatic synthesis and choice of physical operating principle of developed technical system.

Physical Effect [1] is an objective relation between two or more physical phenomenon, each of which is described appropriate physical quantity. As any physical phenomenon realize in material medium so a representation diagram of PE in the form of "black box" is visual and useful:ABC where A - input, B - object, C - output.

Now the problem of process support of PE database update (which the basic procedures are an automated search and extract descriptions of new PE) has not received in any decision, except an approach described in works of A.I. Polovinkin and developed by employees of CAD department of Volgograd State Technical University [2].

---

[*] This work was partly supported by the RFBR (grants 13-07-97032 and 13-01-00302).

A. Kravets et al. (Eds.): JCKBSE 2014, CCIS 466, pp. 321–330, 2014.

However the method of modifying the physical effects database created by this approach and implemented to software "IOFFE" [3] has serious drawbacks:

- use of insufficiently effective algorithm of the semantic analysis (low precision and recall),
- as the knowledge base is used the thesaurus,
- as a extraction method is search for patterns which does not provide due precision of natural language texts processing.

The ontology representation in this approach is not standardized which complicates system integration and use of the results in other systems. Thus, increase of efficiency of search and extraction of FE descriptions at the expense of new, more productive approaches is actual.

2   Method of Ontology-Based Extraction of Physical Effect Description

Domain ontology was chosen as representation model of knowledge about physical effects. Unlike production model, a semantic network, frames and formal logic models, the ontology is the most formal model. Ontology is the most widespread form of the knowledge description of any subject domain, has sufficient expressiveness and easy integration with information systems.

Currently, there are many tools for creating and supporting ontology. These tools are in addition to standard viewing and editing functions also perform import and export of various formats and languages, documenting ontologies, support visualization and graphical editing, provide support for documenting ontologies, etc. Consider the most known tools of engineering of the ontologies which main characteristics are presented in Table 1.

For development of the domain ontology the Protégé tool was chosen. This choice is reasonable by criteria of ergonomics, and also possibilities of visualization of concepts taxonomy, presence of the editor of formal axioms, also possibility of saving of the ontology in various formats, ensuring compatibility with development tools.

3   Domain Ontology "Physical Effect"

The domain ontology based on knowledge from physical effects database was developed for the organization of extraction process of physical effects descriptions developed by employees of CAD department of Volgograd State Technical University and also based on model of the physical effect description [1].

The main requirements to the developed domain ontology:

- possibility to extract physical effect description;
- possibility to support and add new concepts;
- possibility to integrate into information systems.

Table 1. Review of design tools of ontologies

Software / Comparing factor		Onto-lingua [4]	OntoEdit [5]	Protégé [6]	OilEd [7]	Onto-Saurus [8]
Availability		Free license	Free license	Open source	Open source	Open source
Software architecture	Architecture	Client - server	three-component structure	three-component structure	Three-component structure	Client - server
	Expansibility	-	Plug-ins	Plug-ins	-	-
	Storage of anthologies	Files	Files	Files, DBMS	Files	Files
Model of knowledge	Formalization	Frames + FOL	Frames + FOL	Frames + FOL, DL	DL	DL
	Main language of knowledge representation	Onto-lingua	OXML	OKBC	DAML + OIL	LOOM
	Formal language of axioms	Onto-lingua	F-logic	PAL	-	LOOM

The physical effect in the developed ontology is presented according to the physical effect model: {Input, Output, Object}.

Relations connecting the model elements were introduced in the ontology for extraction of physical effect description:

- "To have influence on" ("Иметь воздействие на" in Russian). The relation connecting concept "Physical Effect" and concept "Physical Effect Output".
- "To have object of influence" ("Иметь объект воздействия" in Russian). The relation connecting concept "Physical effect" and concept "Physical Effect Input".
- "Located in" ("Находиться в" in Russian). The relation connecting concept «Physical Effect» and concept "Physical Effect Object".

Also the relations characterizing fundamental concepts of the domain ontology - a matter and properties of elements of a matter were entered:

- "To have properties of a field" ("Иметь свойства поля" in Russian). Connects concepts of a field and possible properties;
- "To have properties of substance" ("Иметь свойства вещества" in Russian). Respectively - for substance;

- "To have a unit of measure" ("Иметь единицу измерения" in Russian). Allows to characterize physical quantity.

Other relations reflect the class hierarchy of the domain ontology and have "SuperclassOf" designation.

Ontology was designed using Protégé tool and is presented on Figure 1.

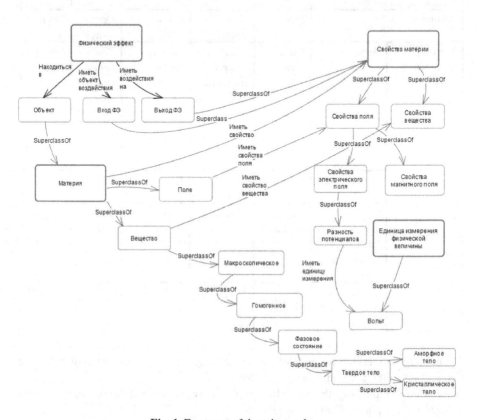

Fig. 1. Fragment of domain ontology

The language used for description ontology - OWL [9]. As a dialect was chosen OWL DL, which provides the maximum expressiveness without loss of completeness and resolvability of calculations.

Figure 2 shows scheme in the form of a network which reflects the most significant relationships between classes.

Ontology physical schema is shown in Figure 3. In ontology added physical effect description: "The influence of potential difference to the magnetic field in the solid" ("Воздействие разности потенциалов на магнитное поле в твёрдом теле" in Russian)

When developing the domain ontology the existing model of representation was modified by introduction of new relations and new structure. It allowed to get the following advantages:

- decision of synonymy problem by use objects classes. Synonyms are added in the ontology as objects of classes;
- possibility of knowledge extraction from the domain ontology. The presence of tools for automatic analysis and visualization;
- flexibility to ontology update and support.

Fig. 2. Taxonomy of domain ontology classes

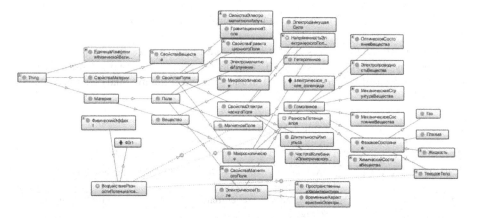

Fig. 3. Fragment of ontology physical schema

4   Extraction of Physical Effects Descriptions from Natural Language Text

At the initial stage of extraction of physical effects descriptions (Figure 4), it is necessary to localize the text area containing PE descriptions. This process is implemented with search of keywords defining possibility of presence of physical effect in the text, such as: "Dependence", "Cause", "Influence", "Reduction", "Increase" ("Зависимость", "Воздействие", "Влияние", "Уменьшение", "Увеличение" in Russian) etc.

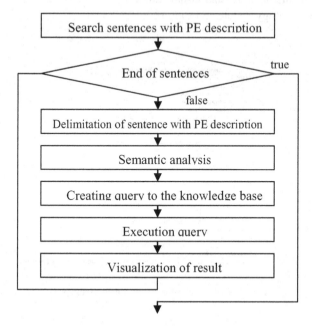

Fig. 4. The algoritm of physical effects extraction

For semantic analysis was used tool for automated processing of Russian texts developed by AOT.ru [10] group. Its output is a semantic network with a defined relationship. List of relationships used in the selected semantic analyzer is presented in Table 2.

Table 2. List of the semantic relations

Name	Symbol	Examples	Structure
ЗНАЧ	VALUE	"Action in the environment"	VALUE (Action, environment)
ОБ	OBJ	"Influence on the current strength"	OBJ (Influence, current strength)
ПАРАМ	PARAM	"Potential difference"	PARAM (Difference, Potential)
ПРИЗН	PROPERT	"Magnetic field"	PROPERT (Field, Magnetic)
СУБ	SUB	"Influence of the difference"	SUB (Difference, Influence)
ЛОК	LOC	"Flow in the conductor"	LOC (Conductor, Flow)
ЗАВИС	F-ACT	"Dependence of viscosity"	F-ACT (Dependence, Viscosity)
ЗАВИС ОТ	S-ACT	"Dependence on temperature"	S-ACT (Dependence, Temperature)

Developed ontology structure allow the use of queries to the knowledge base the purpose of which in this case will be to extract of physical effects descriptions.

One of the most common formal and supported by automated tools approaches to create queries to ontology is a method based on language SPARQL[11].

Let's define a physical effect description in accordance with the selected language and model:

```
SELECT DISTINCT? result WHERE {
? resultSuperClass ns:иметьВоздействиеНа ns:ВыходФЭ
("ns:toHaveInfluenceOn ns: PhysicalEffectOutput" in Eng-
lish)
? resultSuperClass ns:иметьОбъектВоздействия ns:ВходФЭ.
("ns:toHaveObjectOfInfluence ns: PhysicalEffectInput" in
English)
? resultSuperClass ns:находитьсяВ ns:ОбъектФЭ.
("ns:locateIn ns: PhysicalEffectObject" in English)
? result rdfs:subClassOf? resultSuperClass. }
```

Differently, for extraction of physical effect description it is necessary to reveal three components according to model: What object is influenced by physical effect? What influence contains in physical effect? Where the physical effect is localised?.

Since the above description is common to all physical effects specific physical effect will be a subclass of this description.

Example:

```
Class ({ (Influence of a potential difference on a mag-
netic field in a solid) })
partial { restriction (toHaveInfluenceOn allValuesFrom
(Magnetic field)),
restriction (toHaveObjectOfInfluence allValuesFrom (Po-
tential difference)),
restriction (locateIn allValuesFrom (Solid)) })
```

Query is generated from the results of the semantic analysis of sentence with the expected physical effect description. It is necessary to unite the semantic relations in groups and the query to the knowledge base of physical effects is comparable each of groups.

To convert a semantic graph we will make its bypass in a direct order with fixing relationships and nodes. We introduce the following rules that associate semantic relations and their respective present representation in the knowledge base (Table 3).

Table 3. Semantic relations and corresponding query

AOT relations	Transformed relations	Query SELECT DISTINCT? result WHERE
SUB (Influence, Difference) + PARAM (Difference, Potential)	Input (Influence, Potential difference)	? resultSuperClass ns:toHaveObjectOfInfluence ns: Potential difference
VALUE (Difference, Solid) + PROPERT Solid, Crystal)	Object (Crystal solid)	? resultSuperClass ns:locateIn ns: Crystal Solid
OBJ (Influence, Field) + PROPERT (Field, Magnetic)	Output (Influence, Magnetic field)	? resultSuperClass ns:toHaveInfluenceOn ns: Magnetic field

Thus, the presence of correspondences between semantic relations and queries to the knowledge base allows to unequivocally interpret fragment structure with the expected physical effect description.

Example of the physical effect description:

Input data:	Temperature infuences on volume of gaseous bodies ("Воздействие температуры на объем газообразных тел" in Russian)
Semantic analysis:	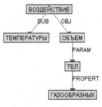
Query to the ontology:	SELECT DISTINCT? result WHERE {? resultSuperClass ns: toHaveObjectOfInfluence ns: Temperature ? resultSuperClass ns: locateIn ns: Gaseous body ? resultSuperClass ns: toHaveInfluenceOn ns: Volume }
Result:	Physical Effect «Thermal expansion of liquid and gaseous bodies».

5   System of Extraction of Descriptions of Physical Effects

Developed system will search for domain ontology's concepts and execute the query to the knowledge base of physical effects. Description of the extracted physical effect appears at the bottom of the window, the extraction result is shown on Figure 5.

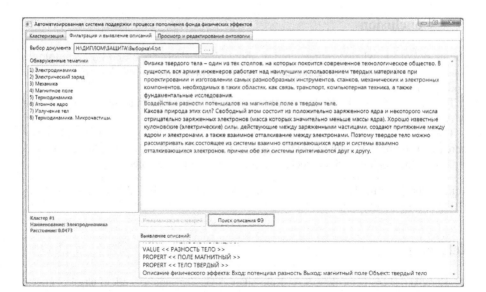

Fig. 5. The description of the extracted physical effect

The system efficiency was tested on a special documents array which consists of 50 documents with 80 physical effects description ($D^{rel} = 80$ PE).

D^{rel}_{retr} – a number of relevant primary PE descriptions,

D^{nrel}_{retr} – a number of irrelevant primary PE descriptions,

D_{retr} – a number of constructed PE descriptions.

Average results of the test program shown in Table 4.

Table 4. Results of system efficiency verification

Efficiency index	Value
D^{rel}_{retr}	50
D^{nrel}_{retr}	64
D_{retr}	114
Precision	0,412
Recall	0,625

Comparison of efficiency indexes of the developed system and IOFFE system [2] are presented in Table 5.

Table 5. Comparison of efficiency indexes

Efficiency index	IOFFE	Our system
Precision	0,306	0,412
Recall	0,518	0,625

6   Conclusion

The model of knowledge representation about physical effects based on an ontologic approach is developed. Logical and physical representation of domain ontologic model is designed.

The method of physical effects extraction on the basis of semantic analysis system by AOT and creating queries to ontologic model is developed.

The developed system efficiency was tested on a special documents array. Efficiency increase in comparison with existing program "IOFFE" developed by employees of CAD department of Volgograd State Technical University is demonstrated.

Acknowledgement. This work was partly supported by the RFBR (grants 13-07-97032 and 13-01-00301).

References

1. Korobkin, D.M., Fomenkov, S.A., Kolesnikov, S.G.: Semantic network of physical effects descriptions in natural language context. In: WWW/Internet 2013: Proceedings of the IADIS International Conference, Fort Worth, Texas, USA, October 22-25. IADIS (International Association for Development of the Information Society) (2013)
2. Korobkin, D.M., Fomenkov, S.A., Kolesnikov, S.G., Orlova, Y.A.: A multi-stage algorithm for text documents filtering based on physical knowledge. World Applied Sciences Journal 24(24), 91–97 (2013)
3. Korobkin, D.M., Fomenkov, S.A., Kolesnikov, S.G., Voronin, Y.F.: System of physical effects extraction from natural language text in the internet. World Applied Sciences Journal 24(24), 55–61 (2013)
4. Fikes, R., Farquhar, A., Rice, J.: Tools for Assembling Modular Ontologies in Ontolingua. Knowledge Systems, AI Laboratory (1997)
5. Sure, Y., Staab, S., Angele, J.: OntoEdit: Guiding Ontology Development by Methodology and Inferencing. In: Meersman, R., Tari, Z. (eds.) CoopIS 2002, DOA 2002, and ODBASE 2002. LNCS, vol. 2519, pp. 1205–1222. Springer, Heidelberg (2002)
6. Musen, M.: Domain Ontologies in Software Engineering: Use of Protege with the EON Architecture//Methods of Inform. Medicine, 540–550 (2010)
7. Bechhofer, S., Horrocks, I., Goble, C.A., Stevens, R.: OilEd: a Reason-able Ontology Editor for the Semantic Web. In: Description Logics. CEUR Workshop Proceedings, vol. 49. CEUR-WS.org (2001)
8. Swartout, B., Patil, R., Knight, K., Russ, T.: Ontosaurus: A tool for browsing and editing ontologies. In: 9th Banff Knowledge Aquisition for KNowledge-based Systems Workshop, Banff, Canada (1996)
9. McGuinness, D.L., van Harmelen, F. (eds.): OWL Web Ontology Language. Overview:W3C Recommendation, February 10 (2004), Access mode: http://www.w3.org/TR/owl-features/
10. Sokirko, A.: Morphological modules on the website. In: Proc. "Dialogue-2004", Protvino, Russia, pp. 559–564 (2004) (in Rus.), http://www.aot.ru
11. Arenas, M., Gutierrez, C., Hurtado, C., Pérez, J.: Semantics and complexity of SPARQL. ACM Transactions on Database Systems (TODS) TODS Homepage Archive 34(3) (August 2009)

Two-Stage Segmentation Method
for Context-Sensitive Image Analysis

Aleksey V. Alekseev, Yulia A. Orlova, Vladimir L. Rozaliev,
and Alla V. Zaboleeva-Zotova

Volgograd State Technical University, Volgograd, Russia
{alekseev.yeskela,yulia.orlova,
vladimir.rozaliev,zabzot}@gmail.com

Abstract. This article considers two-stage segmentation method for context-sensitive image analysis. We represent a combination of two methods: pyramidal segmentation and Grabcut. The results of the pyramidal segmentation are used for the Grabcut as input data. The resulting regions should be used for further detailed recognition. In conclusion shows the comparative results of pyramidal segmentation, Grabcut segmentation and two-stage segmentation.

Keywords: image segmentation, pattern recognition, image analysis.

1   Introduction

Image often prepended to the observer as a set of homogeneous regions, differing from each other by certain characteristics. A number of different types or classes usually small portions, the whole picture is divided into non-overlapping areas, each of which is filled with one type of image. In the analysis of such images observer or automatic goal is to determine geometric areas and designation for each room type (class). Sometimes a set of information about the source image called her card. Image processing, allowing getting a card, called segmentation.

Segmentation is an important task in image processing that plays a leading role in understanding images. It can be defined as the process of decomposing an image into regions which are homogeneous according to some criteria. The goal of segmentation is to simplify and/or change the representation of an image into something that is more meaningful and easier to analyze. Image segmentation is typically used to locate objects and boundaries (lines, curves, etc.) in images. More precisely, image segmentation is the process of assigning a label to every pixel in an image such that pixels with the same label share certain visual characteristics. Investigation of the question of image segmentation subject of numerous papers, however, the process of segmentation is one of the fundamental problems of image analysis. All methods of image segmentation divide to two types: automatic or interactive. The Automatic segmentation methods are fast can be used for batch image processing or in computer vision, but, generally, they show the worst results as compared with interactive methods. The Interactive methods better, but they need user intervention, which is to enter some

A. Kravets et al. (Eds.): JCKBSE 2014, CCIS 466, pp. 331–340, 2014.

initial data depending on the method of segmentation (like the subject area or vice versa – an area not belonging to an object).

Methods used in the segmentation, more varied than the features that distinguish individual classes. It should be noted that a single universally accepted, effective approach that would lay the basis for all or at least most of the methods do not exist.

In this work we combine two methods of segmentation: the first is automatic - pyramidal segmentation and the second is interactive – Grabcut. Pyramids are hierarchical structures which have been widely used in segmentation tasks [1]. The result regions of the pyramidal segmentation are used for the Grabcut as input data. For designing software than demonstrate a result of segmentation used [2].

2   Pyramidal Segmentation

The problem is formulated as textural and color image segmentation. Initial data are multiple; so the approach to the construction of a segmentation algorithm was selected from a plurality of the last two classes of methods: splitting images into homogeneous region by analyzing the similarities in the feature space. The main criterion in this case is the distance between the projections of the elements in the feature space, which is performed on the basis of association of adjacent elements, or a boundary between them. Although the algorithm used and significant segmentation feature space, but in contrast to the classical solution of the problem of clustering is not analyzed the distribution density, and estimate the proximity of points in this space. Thus one of the most important issues is the choice of the metric in it.

Considered algorithm contains two levels (stages). On the first image is divided into many small clusters by using a pyramidal algorithm and the second is their final fusion. Schematic structure of the algorithm is as follows. Originally constructed combined N- dimensional feature space that contains the converted color and texture characteristics of isolated and a transition to a so-called a vector image, which is a two-dimensional array of N-dimensional vectors in this space. The resulting vector is processed pyramidal algorithm, converts it to the primary graph clusters in which each pixel is correlated to a particular cluster - the corresponding node of the graph. Thus, each node of the graph displays the corresponding cluster, and edges - possible connections between neighboring clusters. Required characteristics of the clusters and their relationships with neighboring clusters are combined into a list of clusters used in the second stage. Obtained at this stage of the graph of clusters is only a preliminary segmentation result , because the size of the primary clusters are much smaller than the size of the image , and the number , respectively , significantly more than the number of objects .

In the second stage of pairwise analyzes neighboring clusters having common borders merges those clusters whose parameters are close enough, and there is simplification of the constructed graph. Since the merger of clusters leads to a change in their average parameters, then the process continues with the iterative scheme. Closure criterion is the absence of a merger of pairs of clusters with distance less than a predetermined threshold. The result of this operation is a segmented image.

One of the most important aspects in solving the problem of image segmentation as a selection of homogeneous areas is the question of "similarity" of elements and / or clusters of images, i.e. proximity of their symptoms. Since both the elements and clusters can be displayed in the same feature space, the question measuring proximity can be reformulated as the introduction of the metric in the feature space. It is important to note that there is no universal metric; it is not even for the color subspace. [3][4]

3   Grabcut Segmentation Algorithm

As applied in the auditorium of computer vision, Grabcut can be employed to efficiently solve a broad variety of low-level computer vision problems (abet on vision), such as image smoothing, the stereo correspondence infuriate, and many addendum computer vision problems that can be formulated in terms of computer graphics minimization. Such vibrancy minimization problems can be edited to instances of the maximum flow difficulty in a graph (and for that excuse, by the max-flow min-graze theorem, define a minimal scrape of the graph). Under most formulations of such problems in computer vision, the minimum vibrancy unchangeable corresponds to the maximum a posteriori estimate of a good. Although many computer vision algorithms liven up up opinion acid a graph (e.g., normalized cuts), the term "graph cuts" is applied specifically to those models which employ a max-flow/min-scratch optimization (tally graph acid algorithms may be considered as graph partitioning algorithms).

"Binary" problems (such as denoising a binary image) can be solved exactly using this access; problems where pixels can be labeled considering subsequent to more two another labels (such as stereo correspondence, or denoising of a grayscale image) cannot be solved exactly, but solutions produced are usually oppressive the global optimum.

The theory of Grabcut was first applied in computer vision in the paper by Greig, Porteous and Seheult of Durham University. In the Bayesian statistical context of smoothing frightful (or corrupted) images, they showed how the maximum a posteriori estimate of a binary image can be obtained exactly by maximizing the flow through an similar image network, involving the inauguration of a source and sink. The difficulty was hence shown to be efficiently solvable. Prior to this outcome, approximate techniques such as simulated annealing (as proposed by the Geman brothers), or iterated conditional modes (a type of selfish algorithm as suggested by Julian Besag) were used to solve such image smoothing problems.

Although the general k-colour problem remains unsolved for k > 2, the showing off in of Greig, Porteous and Seheult has turned out to have broad applicability in general computer vision problems. Greig, Porteous and Seheult approaches are often applied iteratively to a sequence of binary problems, usually submissive muggy optimal solutions; see the article by Funka-Lea et al. for a recent application.

Grabcut methods have become popular alternatives to the level set-based approaches for optimizing the location of a contour (see for an extensive comparison).

However, graph graze approaches have been criticized in the literature for several issues:

Metrication Artifacts: When an image is represented by a 4-linked lattice, Grabcut methods can exhibit unwanted "blockiness" artifacts. Various methods have been proposed for addressing this issue, such as using added edges or by formulating the max-flow shackle in continuous look.

Shrinking Bias: Since Grabcut finds a minimum clip, the algorithm can be biased toward producing a little contour. For example, the algorithm is not moreover than ease-suited for segmentation of skinny objects with than blood vessels (see for a proposed affix).

Multiple Labels: Grabcut is unaccompanied light to locate a global optimum for binary labeling (i.e., two labels) problems, such as foreground/background image segmentation. Extensions have been proposed that can locate approximate solutions for multilabel Grabcut problems.

Memory: the memory usage Grabcut adding speedily as the image size amassing. As an illustration, the Boykov-Kolmogorov max-flow algorithm v2.2 allocates $24n+14m$ bytes (n and m are respectively the number of nodes and edges in the graph). Nevertheless, some amount of operate has been recently curtains in this management for reducing the graphs previously the maximum-flow computation. [5][6]

The results of the algorithm are shown in Fig. 1.

Fig. 1. GrabCut segmentation

4   Two-Stage Segmentation Algorithm

We present a two-stage image segmentation, which is to use two algorithms: pyramidal segmentation and Grabcut. First run pyramidal segmentation, in order to mark the initial regions, the output obtained regions received automatic segmentation; they are not good enough to use them as reliable information about the existing regions in the image. To improve the result, each region is presented as submitted by the user, and it has already caused Grabcut segmentation, which use energy minimization shows the best result. The results of the algorithm are shown in Fig. 2.

Segmentation algorithm should clearly define where one ends and the other begins segment. As a rule, the boundaries are characteristic changes in brightness or shades of color occurring in areas subject background. And if the drop is more of a threshold, then it must follow that they are different segments. But there is a small problem: differences can vary greatly for different objects, and segments difficult to separate is uniquely specified threshold. For a table surface on wall background: swings neighboring pixels along the table surface would be relatively small, but on the table - border wall will jump, which divide segments.

Fig. 2. Two-stage segmentation

5   Applications

Our method can be applied in various application areas such as:

- Content-based image retrieval (architectural and engineering design, art collections, crime prevention, geographical information and remote sensing systems, intellectual property etc.)
- Machine vision
- Medical imaging (locate tumors and other pathologies, measure tissue volumes, diagnosis, study of anatomical structure, surgery planning, virtual surgery simulation, intra-surgery navigation)
- Object detection (pedestrian detection, face detection, brake light detection, locate objects in satellite images (roads, forests, crops, etc.))
- Recognition Tasks (face recognition, fingerprint recognition, iris recognition)
- Traffic control systems
- Video surveillance

For some problems, our method is better suited for some of the worst in the first place it is associated with specific topics, for example, in the case of medical imaging, it is more logical to use the segmentation, which will identify the different levels (bone, tissue, etc.). Our method is good for object recognition, as will allow to separate from the background.

6   Appointment

This algorithm is planned to apply for a modification of the algorithm coloring grayscale images. Coloring grayscale images in a way that seems realistic to most human observers is a problem that has recently attracted renewed interest within the computer graphics community. The coloring problem amounts to replacing a scalar value stored at each pixel of a grayscale image by a vector in a multi-dimensional color space. This problem doesn't have a unique solution, because in the transition to grayscale image unsalvageable lost color information.

Today, there is some of software that allows coloring grayscale images. But in these systems humans must meticulously hand-color each of the individual image regions.

We propose to change comparing images stage. Original coloring process is as follows Fig.4. Technique to color grayscale image use information from database of color images and database of objects (Fig. 3.). The technique consist of two steps: colorize overall part of image and colorize objects, if they are found. User can add and delete images of base of color images, but can't add or delete objects of base of objects, because to objects are put forward more stringent requirements.

Two-stage segmentation allows changing search algorithm color image source. Now it works by comparing signatures of images. Signature – 128 float values, obtained from normalized histogram of 1 channel lab color space. In [7] has been shown that 128 – optimum number of elements signature. Fig. 5 demonstrates a process for preparing signature. In the case of a two-stage segmentation can be obtained separately to compare regions on the basis of a wide variety of metrics. One of the options - not to compare the signatures of all the images [8], but separate regions, with similar image regions are more likely to belong to the images with the same colors. Another option - we can take the regions separately, using different images to color one, it will increase the resulting quality [9] of the individual parts, but can harm the overall combination, so it need post processing [10].

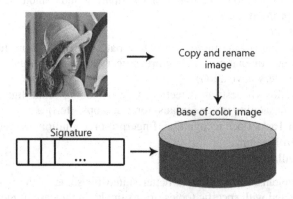

Fig. 3. Base of color image

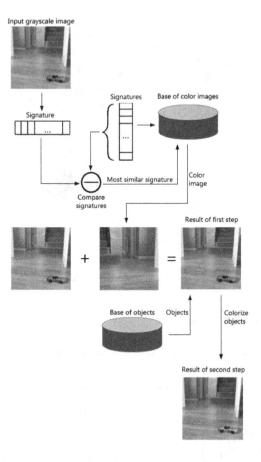

Fig. 4. Colorize technique

Images are computed signature image and signatures are compared on the basic of correlation (1) between them:

$$d_{correl}(H_1, H_2) = \frac{\sum_i^N H_1'(i) * H_2'(i)}{\sqrt{\sum_i^N H_1'^2(i) * H_2'^2(i)}},$$

(1)

where H_1 and H_2 – signatures, N equals number of elements signature (N = 128) and $H_k'(i)$ equals (2):

$$H_k'(i) = H_k(i) - \left(\frac{1}{N}\right)\left(\sum_j^N H_k(j)\right)$$

(2)

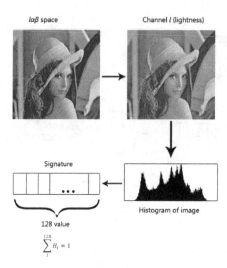

Fig. 5. Signature of image

7   Parallel Computing

To speed up segmentation we used parallelization results are shown in Table 1.

Table 1. Parallelization

Image size	Serial code, s		OpenMP, s		Acceleration, times
360x270	2,61	2,45	1,03	1,03	2,36
	2,41		1,04		
	2,40		1,02		
	2,39		1,02		
480x360	4,22	4,12	1,68	1,65	2,50
	4,10		1,64		
	4,09		1,66		
	4,08		1,63		
720x540	9,06	9,01	3,45	3,53	2,55
	8,99		3,51		
	8,99		3,67		
	9,00		3,49		
960x720	15,16	15,18	5,66	5,70	2,66
	15,15		5,75		
	15,15		5,69		
	15,26		5,70		
1024x768	17,66	17,61	6,57	6,55	2,69
	17,53		6,53		
	17,78		6,52		
	17,46		6,58		

Using the OpenMP library, we were able to achieve acceleration in 2.69 times for an image size of 1024x768 pixels. Time specified in the table - the time spent on the whole problem, not only segmentation.

8   Related Work

In the future we plan to work on the following issues:

- Change the first stage of segmentation pyramid for effective segmentation graphs. Perhaps it will get acceleration without significant loss of quality.
- Plan to add database objects and looking for known objects to segmentation based on descriptors of the key points (SURF [11]). The data obtained can be used as input data for the segmentation. It will improve the quality of segmentation.
- Using deep learning for pre-known locations (such as a city or forest). This allows sophisticated features to recognize, as compared with traditional neural networks, and effectively used for the segmentation images problem.
- Using the GPU to accelerate computation (parallel computing architecture NVIDIA CUDA), scheduled to receive a significant acceleration and achieve real-time video processing (30 FPS).

9   Conclusion

In this paper, the algorithm was considered a landmark two-stage segmentation method based on automatic segmentation pyramid and interactive method Grabcut. The results obtained by the automatic method does not greatly inferior method Grabcut, and the introduction of automation allows you to handle collections of images automatically, which can also be used for video, were presented a description of two algorithms separately and their combined result. On test images were shown practical results obtained combination algorithms. We provide the basic features two-stage segmentation and describe its role in the developed world supersystem. We show experimental results on parallel computing and the resulting acceleration, and identify the main areas of improvement work.

References

1. Alekseev, A., Rozaliev, V., Orlova, Y.: Automatization colorize grayscale images based intelligent scene analysis. In: 11th International Conference of Pattern Recogni-tion and Image Analysis: New Information Technologies (PRIA-11-2013), September 23-28, vol. I, pp. 151–154. Image Processing Systems Institute of the RAS [et al.], Samara (2013)
2. Zaboleeva-Zotova, A.V., Orlova, Y.A., Rozaliev, V.L., Fomenkov, S.A., Petrovsky, A.B.: Formalization of inital stage of designing multi-component software. In: Multi Conference on Computer Science and Information Systems 2013, Proceedings of the IADIS International Conference Intelligent Systems and Agents 2013, Prague, Czech Republic, July 23-26, pp. 107–111 (International Association for Development of the Information Society), Prague (2013)

3. Antonisse, H.: Image Segmentation in Pyramids. Computer Graphics & Image Processing 19, 367–383 (1982); [AGBB] Alpert, S., Galun, M., Basri, R., Brandt, A.: Image segmentation by probabilistic bottom-up aggregation and cue integration. In: IEEE Conf. on Computer Vision and Pattern Recognition (CVPR 2007) (2007)
4. Marfil, R., Molina-TancoL, B.A., Rodríguez, J.A., Sandoval, F.: Pyramid segmenta-tion algorithms revisited. Pattern Recognition 39(8), 1430–1451 (2006)
5. Boykov, Y., Jolly, M.-P.: Interactive graph cuts for optimal boundary and region segmentation of objects in N-D images. In: Proc. IEEE Int. Conf. on Computer Vision (2001)
6. Boykov, Y., Kolmogorov, V.: Computing Geodesics and Minimal Surfaces via Graph Cuts. In: Int. Conf. on Computer Vision, ICCV (2003)
7. Vieira, L.F.M., et al.: Fully automatic coloring of grayscale images. Image and Vision Computing 25(1), 50–60 (2007)
8. Rozaliev, V.L., Orlova, Y.A.: Model of emotional expressions in movements. In: Cognition and Exploratory Learning in the Digital Age (CELDA 2013): Proceedings of the IADIS International Conference, Fort Worth, Texas, USA, October 22-24, pp. 77–84. Inter-national Association for Development of the Information Society, University of North Texas (2013)
9. Zaboleeva-Zotova, A.V., Bobkov, A.S., Orlova, Y.A., Rozaliev, V.L., Polovinkin, A.I.: Automated identification of human emotions based on analysis of body movements. In: Multi Conference on Computer Science and Information Systems 2013: Proceedings of the IADIS International Con-ferences Interfaces and Human Computer Interaction and Game and Entertainment Technologies 2013, Prague, Czech Republic, July 23-26, pp. 299–304. IADIS (International Association for Development of the Information Society), Prague (2013)
10. Rozaliev, V.L., Bobkov, A.S., Orlova, Y.A.: Detailed Analysis of Postures and Gestures for the Identification of Human Emotional Reactions. In: World Applied Sciences Journal (WASJ), vol. 24(spec. Issue 24), pp. C.151–C.158. Information Technologies in Modern Industry, Education & Society (2013)
11. Bay, H., et al.: Speeded-up robust features (SURF). Computer Vision and Image Understanding (CVIU) 110(3), 346–359 (2008)

Super-Resolution Approach to Increasing the Resolution of Image

Vladislav Agafonov

Volgograd State Technical University, 28 Lenin Avenue, Volgograd, 400005, Russia
Agafonov.Vladislav@gmail.com

Abstract. Super-resolution (SR) is a class of techniques that enhance the resolution of an imaging system by combining complimentary information from several images to produce high resolution images of a subject. Fast non-iterative and iterative algorithms are described in this article. The metrics to compare the images are investigated also. In conclusion shows the comparative results of these methods. Test results showed good practical applicability of the developed algorithms.

Keywords: Super-Resolution, increasing image resolution, multi-frame image processing.

1 The Problem of Increasing Image Resolution

Increasing the image resolution in the usual form is a very simple task. The problem arises when it is necessary to save good quality in the process of increasing resolution of the image. For this it is necessary to introduce the concept of image quality.

1.1 The Concept of Image Quality

Image quality is a characteristic that evaluates human-readable image degradation.

There are several methods using that we can objectively measure image quality. They can be classified into two types: full-reference and no-reference. In the first case, the quality of the test image is evaluated by comparing it with the reference image, which has an excellent quality. In the second case, the methods are trying to estimate the quality of the image without any reference to the original.

In this paper, the resulting images will be defined as a deviation from the original.

1.2 Causes of Quality Digital Photos Loss

During the registration process digital images, there are natural loss of spatial resolution caused of optical distortion, blurring during fast moving caused of limited speed of shutter, or noise which is generated inside the sensor [1].

As can be seen from Figure 1 the obtained at the output recording device image quality is very different from the original scene.

A. Kravets et al. (Eds.): JCKBSE 2014, CCIS 466, pp. 341–355, 2014.

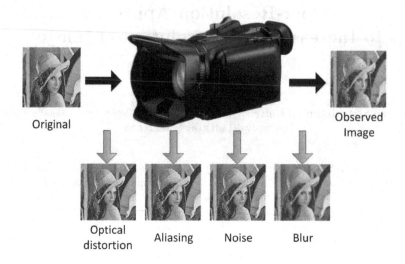

Fig. 1. The process of image registration

1.3 Methods of Increasing Image Resolution

Presently there are many algorithmic methods for increasing image resolution. Most of them are based on the one image processing. But due to the fact that the information amount of the image is constant, using these methods we can not achieve a high quality.

In this paper it is consider another approach to improve the resolution of images based on technology of Super-Resolution (SR). Its main idea is to use information from several images. In this case information sources are multiple images of the same object taken with a slight offset relative to each other.

1.4 Mathematical Model of Image Degradation

Consider a high resolution image size ($N_1 \cdot L_1 \times N_2 \cdot L_2$), and designate it as x. Parameters L_1 and L_2 are the coefficients in the image sampling model of observation in the horizontal and vertical directions, respectively. So we can find that each low resolution image has a size of $N_1 \times N_2$. We write the original high-resolution image as $x = [x_1, x_2, \ldots, x_N]^T$, where $N = (N_1 \cdot L_1 \times N_2 \cdot L_2)$, and k-th low-resolution image $y_i = [y_{i1}, y_{i2}, \ldots, y_{iM}]^T$, where $M = N_1 \times N_2$. Considering all the distortion that can occur when the image recording images, the observation model can be represented as:

$$y_i = DH_iF_ix + N_i, \tag{1}$$

where F_i – The geometric deformation matrix with size ($N_1 \cdot L_1 \cdot N_2 \cdot L_2) \times (N_1 \cdot L_1 \cdot N_2 \cdot L_2)$; H_i – The warp matrix with size ($N_1 \cdot L_1 \cdot N_2 \cdot L_2) \times (N_1 \cdot L_1 \cdot N_2 \cdot L_2)$; D – matrix of discretization size($N_1 \cdot N_2) \times (L_1 \cdot N_1 \cdot L_2 \cdot N_2)$; N_i – noise [2].

Used in this model deformation matrix F_i characterizes geometric transformations (shift, rotation) that occur during the registration process i-th image, the matrix H characterizes the degree of image blur.

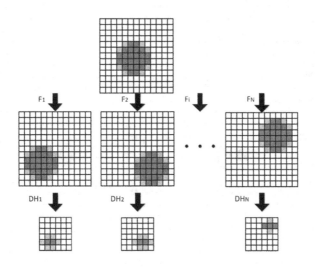

Fig. 2. The process of image registration

Thus, the problem of constructing low-resolution frames at a known high-resolution image is reduced to the generation of several geometric deformation matrices, the value of which will set the movement of object, and the consistent application of the filter H and the operator D. Schematically it is illustrated in Fig. 2

The problem of increasing the resolution is the problem of minimizing the error:

$$x_r = \arg\min_x \sum_i \|DH_iF_ix - y_i\|, \tag{2}$$

where DH_iF_i – is the operator of decreasing the resolution. That is the problem of finding such high resolution image, which will give the minimum deviation from the low-resolution images, if it is reduced [3].

2   Methods of Super-Resolution

Process of obtaining a high-resolution image is divided into three phases: registration, interpolation and restoration. Image Registration is the parameter estimation of scene motion from frame to frame. The process of estimating the parameters of the motion is to determine the parameters of the geometric transformation between the observed low resolution images and some basic coordinate system. An important factor for the successful resolution enhancement is accurate estimation of the parameters of scene motion on frames, so the registration methods should provide sub-pixel accuracy.

In phase interpolation occurs union low-resolution images and overlay them on the grid of high-resolution image. After that the methods are used to eliminate noise and frequency distortions. Super-Resolution Methods differ from each other by different approaches in implementing these steps.

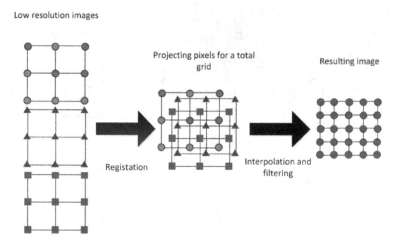

Fig. 3. General scheme of Super-Resolution

General scheme of Super-Resolution shown in Figure. 3. There is a sequence of images of a scene with a low resolution. They all have a slight offset relative to one another. First, determined the motion between frames. Using these estimates nonuniformly distributed pixels arranged in a grid of high-resolution image. Then, with the aid of one of the interpolation methods are calculated uniformly distributed pixels in an image with high resolution. Then computed frequency distortion. After that, occurs the traditional solution to the problem of image reconstruction.

2.1   Iterative Back Projection Method

There is a sequence consisting of K low-resolution images $y_{1,...,K}$ size of $N_1 \times N_2$. Need to build an image x size $(L_1 \cdot N_1) \times (L_2 \cdot N_2)$, which minimized the error function

$$E(x) = \sum_{i=1}^{K} ||P_i(x) - y_i||, \qquad (3)$$

where $|| \bullet ||$ is any norm; $P_i(x)$ is the projection of the image x on the grid image y_i.

Construction of high-resolution images based on iterative approach [2]. Selected an arbitrary initial approximation images with high resolution $x^{(0)}$, then simulated the process of obtaining a set of low-resolution images $y_k^{(0)}$. Difference $\{y_k - y_k^{(0)}\}$ used to refine the initial approximation, and iterative process continues until minimizing the error function. If it turns out that j iteration $x^{(j)}$ is "right" solution, then the simulated image $\{y_k^{(j)}\}$ must be absolutely identical images y_k. Mathematically, we can describe method IBP the following iterative scheme:

$$x^{(n+1)} = x^{(n)} + \frac{1}{K} \sum_{k=1}^{K} F_k^{-1}(((y_k - y_k^{(n)})) \uparrow s) * h), \qquad (4)$$

where $x^{(n)}$ $x^{(n+1)}$ is high-resolution image on n and $n+1$ iterations; K - number of low-resolution images; y_k - the k-th low resolution image; $y_k^{(n)}$ - he k-th low resolution image, obtained on the n-th iteration of the image $x^{(n)}$; F_k- operator geometric transformation linking images x and y_k; h – kernel of dispersion function. $\uparrow s$ – operator increase the image size.

2.2   Fast Super Resolution

Solving of (2) can take a lot of time, and very often it is important to get a quick approximation of the SR problem [4]. Fast SR algorithm quickly solves this problem and consists of the following steps:

1. Fix the first image y_1 and calculate the offset between y_1 and $y_k, k = 2, 3, \ldots, n$, n – is the number of different images. The offset between y_1 and y_1 is zero.
2. Upsample every image given their offset from the first image:

$$Y_k = F_k U y_k, \qquad (5)$$

where U – is Gauss upsampling operator. The basis of this algorithm is fast computation $F_k U$.
3. Calculate an average image

$$X = \frac{1}{N} \sum_{k=1}^{N} Y_k. \qquad (6)$$

4. Deblur the resulting image.

To upsample the image for fast SR, we use Gauss resampling to calculate [5][6]. Gauss method for change the image scale with scaling factor p looks as follows:

$$W_k(px, py) = \frac{\sum\limits_{(x_i, y_j) \in \Omega} e^{\frac{-(x-x_i)^2 - (y-y_i)^2}{2\sigma^2}} w_k(x_i, y_i)}{\sum\limits_{(x_i, y_j) \in \Omega} e^{\frac{-(x-x_i)^2 - (y-y_i)^2}{2\sigma^2}}}, \qquad (7)$$

where w_k – low resolution image, W_k – high resolution image, σ – radius of the Gauss filter, (x_i, y_i) is pixel value w_k.

Application warping operator F_k to (7) is a shift of values (x_i, y_j) by motion vectors:

$$W_k(px, py) = \frac{\sum\limits_{\Omega} e^{\frac{-(x-x_i+u_{i,j})^2-(y-y_i+v_{i,j})^2}{2\sigma^2}} w_k(x_i, y_i)}{\sum\limits_{\Omega} e^{\frac{-(x-x_i+u_{i,j})^2-(y-y_i+v_{i,j})^2}{2\sigma^2}}}. \tag{8}$$

To perform fast computation of (8), numerator and denominator of this fraction is represented as a convolution of the delta function with a Gaussian filter. In discrete form, we form two images (W_k^* and W_k^{**}), initially zero-filled. Next, for each point (x_i, y_j) of w_k computed its coordinates in the high resolution image W_k:

$$(x_i, y_j) \to (p(x_i - u_{i,j}), p(y_i - v_{i,j})) = (x_{i,j}^*, y_{i_j}^*). \tag{9}$$

After that, the values of $w_k(x_i, y_j)$ are added to $W_k^*(x_{i,j}^*, y_{i,j}^*)$ and ones to $W_k^{**}(x_{i,j}^*, y_{i,j}^*)$. . If coordinates $(x_{i,j}^*, y_{i,j}^*)$ are not integer, then we approximate the convolution with a single delta function as a convolution with a sum of delta functions defined at integer coordinates using bilinear interpolation [7].

After the images W_k^* and W_k^{**} formed, we apply Gauss filter to both, then divide W_k^* on W_k^{**} elementwise:

$$W_k = W_k^*/W_k^{**}. \tag{10}$$

2.3   Super Resolution with Bilateral Total Variation

Among the many algorithms that estimate a high resolution image from a set of low resolution images, the most important are those, that can work with distorted and noisy low resolution images. Reconstruction quality of many algorithms decreases when they arrive at the input low resolution image containing noise. Furthermore, existence of outliers, which are dened as data points with different distributional characteristics than the assumed model, will produce erroneous estimates. A method which promises optimality for a limited class of data and noise models may not be the most effective overall approach. Algorithms that are not so sensitive to errors in the input data, will provide a much better and stable result.

Super resolution problem is an ill-posed [8]. There is an infinite set of solutions that satisfy (1). A solution obtained unstable algorithms with a small amount of noise will produce incorrect results. Therefore, considering regularization in super-resolution algorithm as a means for picking a stable solution is very useful, if not necessary. Also, regularization can help the algorithm to remove artifacts from thefinal answer and improve the rate of convergence.

Regularization compensates unknown or incorrect information on the LR images, it is usually implemented as a penalty factor in the generalized minimization cost function:

$$\widehat{x} = \arg\min_{x} \left[\sum_{k=1}^{N} p(y_k, D_k H_k F_k x) + \lambda \Upsilon(x) \right],$$ (11)

where λ – the regularization parameter, Υ – is the regularization cost function.

One of the most successful regularization methods for denoising and deblurring is the total variation (TV) method. The regularizing function looks like:

$$\Upsilon_{BTV}(x) = \sum_{\substack{l=-P \\ l+m\geq 0}}^{P} \sum_{m=0}^{P} \alpha^{|m|+|l|} \|x - S_x^l S_y^m x\|_1,$$ (12)

where operators S_x^l and S_y^k shift x by l and y by k pixels in horizontal and vertical directions respectively, α – weight coefficient $0 < \alpha < 1$, applied to the spatial distribution of regularization.

As a result, the problem of super resolution is reduced to the problem of minimizing the following function:

$$\widehat{x} = \arg\min_{x} \left[\sum_{k=1}^{N} \|D_k H_k F_k x - y\|_1 + \lambda \sum_{\substack{l=-P \\ l+m\geq 0}}^{P} \sum_{m=0}^{P} \alpha^{|m|+|l|} \|x - S_x^l S_y^m x\|_1 \right],$$ (13)

To find the minimum of this function uses the steepest descent method:

$$\widehat{x}_{n+1} = \widehat{x}_n - \beta\{ \sum_{k=1}^{N} F_k^T H_k^T D_k^T sign(D_k H_k F_k \widehat{x}_n - y_k)$$

$$+\lambda \sum_{\substack{l=-P \\ l+m\geq 0}}^{P} \sum_{m=0}^{P} \alpha^{|m|+|l|} [I - S_y^{-m} S_x^{-l}] sign(\widehat{x}_n - S_x^l S_y^m \widehat{x}_n) \},$$ (14)

where β – is a scalar defining the step size in the direction of the gradient. S_x^{-l} and S_y^{-m} is shift corresponding S_x^l S_y^m, but in the opposite direction. Function $sign$ defined as:

1. 0, if the corresponding pixels x and y are equal
2. +1.0, if a pixel x greater than the corresponding pixel y
3. −1.0, if a pixel x is less than the corresponding pixel y

The matrices F, H, D, S and their transposes can be exactly interpreted as direct image operators such as shift, blur, and decimation. Noting and implementing the effects of these matrices as a sequence of operators spares us from explicitly constructing them as matrices. This property helps this method to be implemented in an extremely fast and memory efficient way. [8].

3   Comparison of the Quality of Algorithms

This section will demonstrate the results of the algorithms super-resolution. The test suite will consist of highly detailed images, pictures with a blurred background, pictures with different levels of Gaussian noise and spike noise and images with distorted text. In this section, all the examples are synthetic obtained using a low resolution image generator. For the existence of sub-pixel shift small areas were cut from the original image with an arbitrary shift. After that, all obtained test images were compressed into a few times, so some of the information was lost. To compare two images using metrics PSNR and MSSIM [9] [10].

3.1   Processing of Images without Defects

Result of the algorithms on the first test image shown in Figure 4. Images obtained by the methods BTV SR, IBP SR visually look much better than the images obtained by the methods of the bilinear interpolation and Fast SR.Fast SR method worse than iterative methods, but better than bilinear interpolation method.

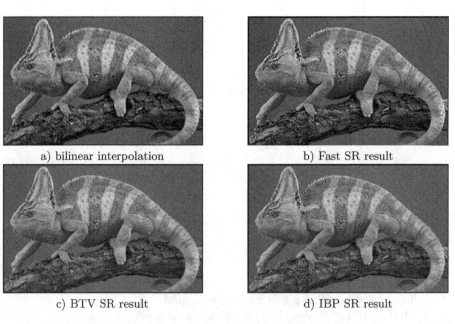

a) bilinear interpolation   b) Fast SR result

c) BTV SR result   d) IBP SR result

Fig. 4. The results of the algorithms on the first test

In Figures 5 – 7 are enlarged images of some areas of the original image. In Figure 5, the image obtained using the bilinear interpolation very blurred and has a low detail. Image obtained by Fast SR is not blurred, but there are aliasing on the borders that probably is the result of the last step of the algorithm.

The last two images obtained by BTV SR and IBP SR, have a higher visual quality. They do not have aliasing, there is a high detail.

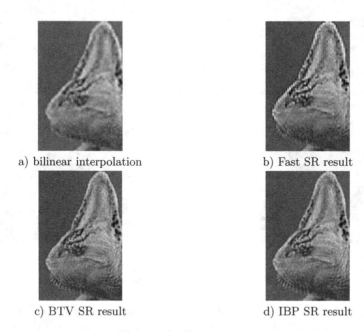

a) bilinear interpolation   b) Fast SR result

c) BTV SR result   d) IBP SR result

Fig. 5. The first test, area 1

In Figure 6 spikes on his back are practically invisible when using linear interpolation method. Spikes on the image obtained by the algorithm Fast SR looks more separable, however, as before, left the field with a high level of blur. Results BTV SR algorithms and IBP SR as before give very good results.

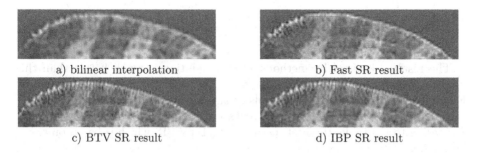

a) bilinear interpolation   b) Fast SR result

c) BTV SR result   d) IBP SR result

Fig. 6. The first test, area 2

In Figure 7 bilinear interpolation method is completely blurred image.

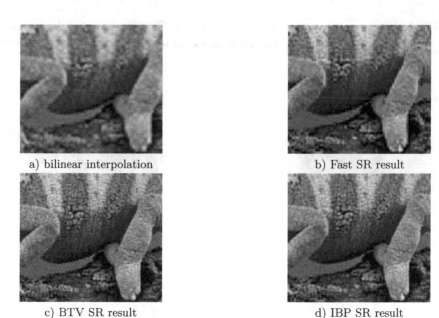

a) bilinear interpolation   b) Fast SR result

c) BTV SR result   d) IBP SR result

Fig. 7. The first test, area 3

Comparisons of quality of the original image and the image obtained using bilinear interpolation, Fast SR, BTV SR, IBP SR are presented in Table 1. Time of iterative methods have been measured at 70 iterations.

Table 1. Results of quality assessment methods

	PSNR(db)	MSSIMR	MSSIMG	MSSIMB	Time(sec)
Bilinear interpolation	21, 647	0, 661	0, 640	0, 658	0, 118
Fast SR	22, 078	0, 697	0, 679	0, 693	0, 713
BTV SR	23, 303	0, 789	0, 776	0, 786	31, 795
IBP SR	23, 208	0, 780	0, 766	0, 777	25, 148

The results obtained by methods super resolution is much better than the image enlarged using bilinear interpolation. The table shows that the method of Fast SR inferior to the other methods of super resolution, but this is compensated by the fact that this method works much faster then iterative methods. According to the table, the best method is to BTV SR, which is based on regularization.

The same results are presented in the form of graphs(Fig. 8).

Result of the algorithms on the first test image shown in Figure 9.

On this test, we consider the possibility of algorithms to recover the text information. In Figures 10 and 11 presented specific areas.

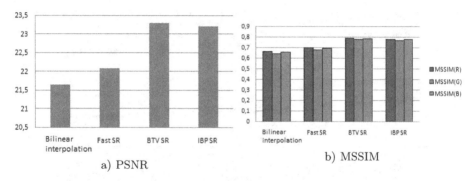

a) PSNR

b) MSSIM

Fig. 8. Graphic metrics to first test

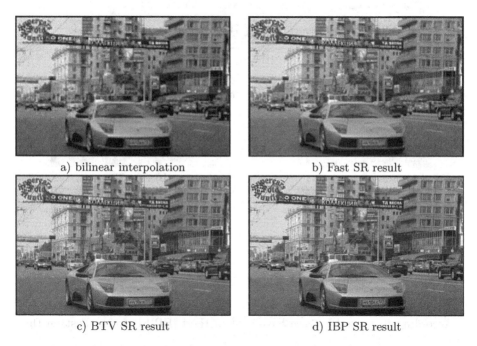

a) bilinear interpolation

b) Fast SR result

c) BTV SR result

d) IBP SR result

Fig. 9. The results of the algorithms on the second test

In Figure 10, the image obtained by bilinear intrepolyatsii is not readable because of strong blur. Fast SR method eliminated the blur a little, but most of the test is still not readable. BTV SR iterative method shows good results, the text is perceived much better. Algorithm IBP SR got most readable image.

In Figure 11 images obtained by bilinear interpolation and Fast SR are not readable.

On images, obtained by BTV SR can see the numbers, but letters as before blurred. Visually algorithm IBP SR got the best image quality.

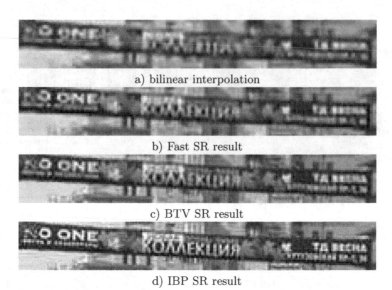

a) bilinear interpolation

b) Fast SR result

c) BTV SR result

d) IBP SR result

Fig. 10. The second test, area 1

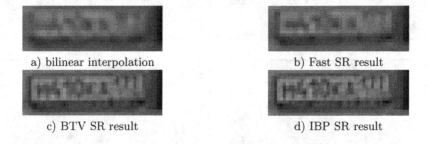

a) bilinear interpolation   b) Fast SR result

c) BTV SR result   d) IBP SR result

Fig. 11. The second test, area 2

According to the table 2 we have that method IBP SR works best on this test.

Table 2. Results of quality assessment methods

	PSNR (db)	MSSIMR	MSSIMG	MSSIMB	Time(sec)
Bilinear interpolation	21, 697	0, 680	0, 681	0, 676	0, 132
FastSR	22, 115	0, 715	0, 716	0, 713	0, 812
BTV	23, 566	0, 786	0, 786	0, 783	33, 135
IBP	24, 004	0, 791	0, 790	0, 789	27, 643

The same results are presented in the form of graphs(Fig. 12).

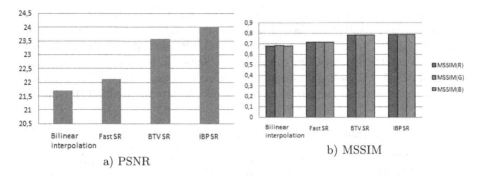

a) PSNR   b) MSSIM

Fig. 12. Graphic metrics to second test

3.2   Processing of Noisy Images

Ability to remove noise from the image is important for improving the quality of the algorithms. Among the methods of super resolution method only BTV SR was created specifically to eliminate defects.

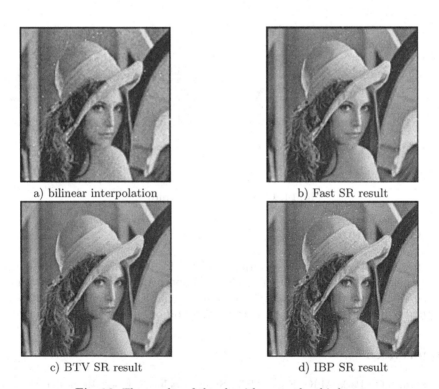

a) bilinear interpolation   b) Fast SR result

c) BTV SR result   d) IBP SR result

Fig. 13. The results of the algorithms on the third test

For the experiment was chosen an image that has a Gaussian and spike noise. Bilinear interpolation method did not remove any noise. As a result of the method Fast SR, spike noise has become more, although it became less noticeable. BTV method completely removed the noise and get a good image. As expected, this is the best method in accordance with the table 3. IBP method is not removed noise. On the contrary, he has accumulated it with all the images.

Table 3. Results of quality assessment methods

	PSNR(db)	MSSIMR	MSSIMG	MSSIMB	Time(sec)
bilinear interpolation	24, 165	0, 564	0, 596	0, 596	0, 105
FastSR	25, 049	0, 665	0, 695	0, 707	0, 643
BTV	27, 049	0, 695	0, 712	0, 726	25, 476
IBP	24, 767	0, 582	0, 602	0, 612	21, 216

The same results are presented in the form of graphs(Fig. 14).

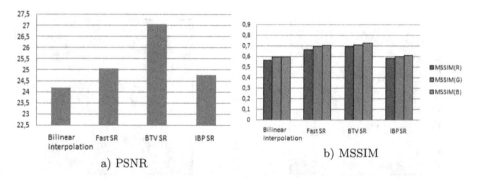

a) PSNR   b) MSSIM

Fig. 14. Graphic metrics to third test

4   Conclusion

The paper deals with super-resolution methods for increasing the resolution of digital images. Application of these methods opens the possibility of obtaining higher resolution images using existing hardware base. Comparative analysis of methods showed their advantage over the method of bilinear interpolation.

References

1. Park, S.C., Park, M.K., Kang, M.G.: Super-Resolution Image Reconstruction: A Technical Overview. IEEE Signal Processing Magazine, 21–36 (2003)
2. Rashupkin, A.V.: Methods of remote sensing data processing to improve the quality of output images. Bulletin of the Samara State Aerospace University 2, 124–132 (2010)

3. Lukin, A., Krylov, A., Nasonov, A.: Image Interpolation by Super-Resolution. In: 16th International Conference Graphicon 2006, pp. 239–242. Novosibirsk Akademgorodok (2006)
4. Krylov, A., Nasonov, A., Ushmaev, O.: Image Super-Resolution using Fast Deconvolution. In: 9th International Conference on Pattern Recognition and Image Analysis: New Information Technologies: Conference Proceedings, Nizhni Novgorod, vol. 1(2), pp. 362–364 (2008)
5. Krylov, A., Nasonov, A., Sorokin, D.: Face image super-resolution from video data with non-uniform illumination. In: Proceedings of 18th International Conference on Computer Graphics, GraphiCon 2008, pp. 150–155 (2008)
6. Krylov, A.S., Nasonov, A.V., Ushmaev, O.S.: Video super-resolution with fast deconvolution. Pattern Recognition and Image Analysis 19(3), 497–500 (2009)
7. Nasonov, A.V., Krylov, A.S.: Fast super-resolution using weighted median filtering. In: Proceedings of International Conference on Pattern Recognition, Istanbul, pp. 2230–2233 (2010)
8. Farsiu, S., et al.: Fast and Robust Multi-Frame Super-Resolution. IEEE Transactio
9. Bovik, A.C., et al.: Structural and Information Theoretic Approaches to Image Quality Assessment. In: Multi-Sensor Image Fusion and Its Applications, pp. 473–497. CRC Press, United Kingdom (2005)
10. Hor, A., Ziou, D.: Image Quality Metrics: PSNR vs. SSIM. In: 20th International Conference on Pattern Recognition, Istanbul, August 23-26, pp. 2366–2369 (2010)

Design and Implementation
of a Context-Based Security Model

Tadashi Iijima and Satoshi Kido

Faculty of Science and Technology, Keio Univ., Japan
{iijima,s_kido}@ae.keio.ac.jp
http://www.iijima.ae.keio.ac.jp/project/sec

Abstract. This paper proposes a context-based security model and describes one of the design and implementation of enforcement mechanism of it. In this access control model, a kind of object-oriented petri-net with nets-within-nets semantics is adopted as a context representation.

This approach is, particularly, expected to be suitable for dynamic access control within inter-organizational business processes. The overall architecture of the access control model is designed by extending XACML standard architecture. And a Scala-based internal Domain Specific Language is designed to specify security policies.

Keywords: Access Control Model, Context Sensibility, XACML, Domain Specific Language.

1 Introduction

This paper proposes a concept of context-aware access control. The access control model adopts an object-oriented Petri-net concept to represent context sensibility of access control. So far, if we access only single data source, DBMS for the data source is utilized for access control as a facade of several information-flow with the data source, so it's unnecessary to embed an access control model into individual software applications. In recent years, however, this premise is not always satisfiable. The recent application softwares have to access information among multiple data management organizations, so a brand-new mechanism is needed to manage consistency among inter-organizational information. Therefore, we try to construct a common facade framework by externalizing the mechanism for access control of distributed multiple data resources. Needless to say, we need to construct an access control mechanism which observes the status of resources and application software and enforces access control policies to them.

The so-called object-oriented Petri-net is an extension of original Petri-net to introduce modularity based on the concept of object-orientation, and each the modules behave cooperatively. This type of Petri-net has abilities to represent contexts of access information from multiple views, such as inter-organizational workflow, workflows in individual organizations, state transitions of actors that access managed information, and state transitions of data resources. This point corresponds with the above-mentioned purpose of context representation.

A. Kravets et al. (Eds.): JCKBSE 2014, CCIS 466, pp. 356–370, 2014.

In the next section the necessity of Context-Aware Access Control (CxAC) is described through case studies. The section 3 introduces the object-oriented Petri-net based on net-within-net semantics[1]. The section 4 proposes CxRBAC, which is added context to Role-Based Access Control (RBAC)[2]. It is one of subclasses of CxAC. And in section 5 the design of the policy enforcement system is proposed as an extension of the XACML model.

2   Case Studies and Problems to Be Solved

We adopted the case studies from the field of medical information. The first case study is situation-sensitive dynamic access authorization change. In recent years, the necessity to get required information of patients for emergency life-saving has been recognized. The first clue to get the required information for emergency life-saving is identification of the patient. And then, anamnesis (history of past illness), allergic or not, medical contraindications, and information about taking medicine and so on are important. These pieces of information are effective for not only decisions of rescue workers(emergency life-saving technicians), but also for appropriate supervising from doctors and for the provision in the hospital to which the patient has been carried.

However, rescue workers should not be permitted to access the information except for under emergency. Moreover, in spite of emergency, the process to get the information is complicated because of the possibility to distribute some information among hospitals, clinical examination place, and pharmacy. There are the following three requirements:

(1) quick accessibility of a wide range of medical information of a patient who has a serious condition,
(2) ability to extend access authorizations dynamically as necessary, and
(3) spontaneous accessibility of integrated information at emergency, according to prepared workflow of the complicated process of getting information.

To satisfy the requirement (3), rather than evaluating the rights to access a single operation as in the conventional access control models, it's necessary to focus on the tracking of multiple operations dispersed in the workflow. So we have adopted the Petri-net to express workflows, treated transitions of the Petri-net as landmark events to specify accessor's characteristic operations and their order, and have developed access-right evaluation mechanism as an extension of XACML architecture.

The other case study is medical information sharing. In recent years, spread of electronic medical records has progressed, but, on the one hand, information sharing does not wholly advance. It has been increasing for patients to take a medical diagnosis not at a single medical institution but multiple medical institutions as a second opinion in order to select a better remedy, and then some medical institutions have a specialized outpatient department for a second opinion. However, the outpatient department for a second opinion needs to be provided with medical information required for diagnosis, such that records of examination and treatment from the doctor-in-charge, because in such the department it's general not to treat and examine the patient, but just to give an opinion as a reference. In order to provide such information, it is major to use paper medium except for a part of image information because the preparation for electronic medical information sharing infrastructure has not been enough even if a patient permits to share it.

There are obstacles of mutual compatibility on the electronic medical system, difference of information management policy among each medical institution and so on. However, in case of just reading and/or brawsing, it's possible to distribute information through the network under an appropriate access control. We need to consider the right of both patients and medical institutions creating medical records.

Moreover, repeating the same examination may increase the burden of medical expenses when a patient transfers to another hospital, because the medical collaboration system among medical institutions has not yet been established. Such a transfer tends to take place, whenever a cerebral infarction patient shifts to a convalescence and also rehabilitation phase from an acute phase. It is always not bad to distribute the examination data that belongs to not only medical institutions, but also clinical examination companies under the patients' permissions. This is related to the view that examination data and medical records should originally belong to examinees, just patients. In addition, there is a possibility of cooperation with so-called Personal Health Records (PHRs) that accumulate daily health records of weight, blood pressure and so on. In this way, the existing access control model is deficient because it only has the access control model to the database management system as a facade accessing centralized managed database in only a single organization. We have to implement Context-Aware Access Control (CxAC) to share information under different local access control policies of different data management organizations. So we have adopted the Object-oriented Petri-net instead of conventional Petri-net.

3   Object Oriented Petri-Net: OPeN

3.1   What Is the Object Oriented Petri-Net

In our project, we adopt an Object-oriented Petri-net as a context representation. An Object-oriented Petri-net is an extended model of original Petri-net by adding modularity based on the object orientation concept, but there are many varieties. This project adopts the Reference-Net, which is one of the Object-oriented Petri-Net varieties, based on nets-within-nets semantics[1].

In this reference net, there are two types of tokens typically. One is a simple token (Black Token) on usual P/T nets (Place/Transition nets). Simple tokens on a place are used to express the number of ordinary tokens. The other is a Reference Token, which is equivalent to a reference (namely a pointer) to subnet expressing another subsystem.

Places can be classified into the simple place for a simple token and the reference place for a reference token.

- Simple Token (Black Token)[1]
- Reference Token

The subnet referring the reference token is called Object Net and has an identity as one object. The reference token can be transferred in a network like a simple token, but a reference token can be copied according to fire of transitions with branching outgoing arcs. Please note that there are copying references, not copying objects (i.e. sub-nets). Like that we mention later(the left hand side of Fig.1), an instance method, which has the same name with a transition, is executed when the transition in the Petri-net referred by a reference token.

3.2   A Concrete Model of Reference-Net: OPeN

We have been developing the concrete Object-oriented Petri-Net model, OPeN, as one of the realizations of abstract Reference-Net model with nets-within-nets semantics. Several prototypes of tools have been developed. For example, an integrated editor/simulator, a static analyzing tool with model checkers, a server-type workflow engine, and so on. Sare under improvement continuously. We have improved such tools continuously, with repeating actual application.

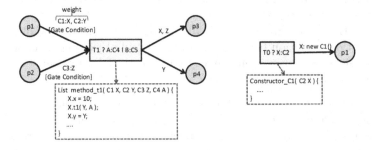

Fig. 1. An Example of Annotations of Arcs and Transion in OPeN

In the OPeN model, individual object-net is equivalent to an instance created by class description. The class description is divided into two files: one file is a class definition in an inscription language, such as Java, defines an object, and the other file defines a Petri-Net as an XML, named with file extension to provide compatibility with previous versions) . The object net defined by classes is a Petri-net describing behavior (life cycle) of the object, a property (instance variable) group of the object and a method group used when the object transitions on the life cycle.

In the OPeN model, individual object-net is equivalent to an instance created by class description. The class description is divided into two files: one file is a class definition in an inscription language, such as Java, defines an object, and

---

[1] Conventionally, this is called Black Token, but we called it a simple token because of easy to understand.

the other file defines a Petri-Net as an XML, named with file extension ".opn" (or "pnmlx" to provide compatibility with previous versions) . The object net defined by a class, which is constructed by a Petri-net describing behavior (life cycle) of the object, set of properties (instance variables) of the corresponding object, and set of methods used when the object transitions on the life cycle. The method is mainly used to describe gate conditions used in incoming arcs of transitions or to update property values when a transition fires. Fig. 1 shows the annotation of arcs and transitions in the OPeN model.

Fire of transition $t1$ makes method $t1$ with the same name execute[2]. On the current prototype specification, language specification for defining a type of property and a method is not defined strictly, but conforming to Fig.1, it is associated mutually because it is externalized to the class definition (class definition with the same name as a net) of the object oriented language (for example, Java or Scala) equipping the basic reflection function.

The system constituted by multiple object nets hierarchically, so we use a unit of "project" corresponding to a project file. However, this section conceptually expounds the semantics restricting hierarchies to not many but two in order to understand easily. The two hierarchies consist of an object (Petri-net) controlling overall behavior and a sub-object (Petri-net) group to behave under controlled. In this section we call one controlling overall behavior "system net" following EOS (Elementary Object System)) convention and call the others (i.e. controlled sub-objects "object nets")[3].

A part of transitions fire interactionally between a system net and object nets. The interactional relation between a system net and object nets is expressed as a set of a pair of both transitions. In a system net, the following three conditions are needed due to fire of a transition T[4].

(a) In the system net, the simple token B_i fulfills fire conditions.
(b) In the system net, the reference token B_i fulfills fire conditions.
(c) In the object nets referred by the reference token R_j related to fire of T, the transitions having interactional relation to T can fire.

From these fire mechanisms, we can recognize three fire rules of (a) interaction, (b) transport and (c) autonomous in the object-oriented Petri-net based on nets-within-nets semantics (or reference semantics) and the extension. First, there is a type that a system net and object nets interact and transition. This is called

---

[2] If $ts1$ interacting with $t1$ exists in a subnet of this net, the $ts1$ is necessary to be fiarable so that $t1$ becomes able to fire. Then, the $t1$ and $ts1$ fires simultaneously according to the firing rule (Interaction) of an objec t-oriented Petri-net, mentioned later. If $ts1$ is not firable, $t1$ cannot fire also. An incoming arc of transitions corresponds to input parameters of the corresponding method.

[3] In case of a hierarchical system, this object net is also equivalent to a system net relatively to lower sub-Petri-nets. The OPeN extends the notion of EOS, but as long as you do not be confused, we call a pair of a net and its direct successors "system net" and its "object nets".

[4] However, in case of OPeN, condition (c) is adapted recursively into lower object nets because of admitting not only two levels but multiple levels of hierarchy.

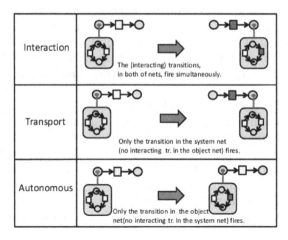

Fig. 2. Rules of Firing Transitions (modifyed from the Fig. in [1])

"interaction." Second, there is a type that a system net does not have object nets interacting and firing. This is called "transport." This name derives from that the situation that reference tokens on a system net transfer is related to transfer of mobile agents remaining not to transition state in object nets. Lastly, there is a type that transitions in object nets fire independently from a system net. This is called "autonomous." This name derives from that token transition is brought about in object nets not regulated by a system net (Fig. 2).

4 Context-Aware Role-Based Access Control

The Context-Aware Access Control (CxAC) that we proposed in this paper can be thought as a subclass of RBAC (Role-Based Access Control) model. We adopt a context-oriented role model to RBAC.

Generally speaking, access authorizations can be expressed by a set of permitting ones in possible tuples of subject–operation–resource. A role-based access control model defines access authorizations not each subject individuals, but each role that subjects are classified based on, and it can be standard substantially now. Classifying to roles makes the number of access authorizations reduces drastically. In the case of electric medical records, it defines access authorizations to not each medical staff, but each role for example doctors, nurses, pharmacists, clinical technologists, office workers and so on.

Structuring inheritance hierarchies of roles makes it systematize, amount of description reduce and maintainability of the policy improve. For instance, grouping doctors or nurses each hospital department and managers or section chiefs each position is possible. At these viewpoints of classifying, crossing classes can be considered, so having more complicated structure according to mixing-in multiple roles is possible if the structure is based on a simple inheritance hierarchy. For instance, classifying each hospital department based on whether he has the qualification of a board certified specialist or not or based on whether he is a doctor in charge for a specific patient or not is possible, but in case of subdividing a lot like that, that should be considered as a property-based access control model.

Generally speaking, assignments like this are not changed ad hoc. In short, a role like doctors or nurses is not changed easily, and it can be true that the position changes (be promoted or demoted) but saying it changes ad hoc is difficult. Therefore, dynamic alteration structure depending on conditions such as extension of access authorizations at only emergency is usually treated differently from long span assignments of roles.

However, at this section, we express ad hoc dynamic alteration as composition of policies each role, and then give each various particle role a set of

$$operation - target - permission - condition - obligation$$

as a policy. Dynamic composition (has the order) by multiple mixing-in policies each role establishes the authorizations. Permission is divided into three parts of permit/deny/indeterminate. In the case of policies according each other about operations, targets and permission, conditions are composed by logical product and obligations are composed by logical sum. We can use context as part of conditions. This context can be at both a subject side and a target side.

This policy description can use the internal DSL (Domain Specific Language) within programming language Scala and can be translated to XML expression used at XACML(Fig. 3). Fig. 4 and 5 is a screen image of the OPeN editor to specify synchronous firing of behaviors and policy context. Policies, including obligations, can be associated with Petri-nets also by using the OPeN editor.

Each behavior of subjects and resources (or servers) is expressed by the object-oriented Petri-net, coordinated actions are expressed by the interaction among transitions. Moreover, Policy Enforcement Point (PEP) enforces behavior that satisfy policies (such as execute an obligation) on subjects according to object-oriented Petri-nets and their interactional relationships.

The following shows a simple example. This example gives the policy when emergency medical technicians access the patient's medical information (high emergency stuff like allergy information) archived on an electronic medical record server in a medical center from an ambulance according to using their IC card. At the present system, if there are not concrete instructions (online medical control) from a doctor, the medical activity by emergency medical technicians is prohibited except for specified acts. However, when patient's life is in a dangerous condition on account of anaphylactic shock, emergency medical technicians can inject on behalf of doctors as long as patients are prescribed Epinephrine auto-injectors (adrenalin self-administration) in order to relieve symptoms and prevent from shock until undergoing medical treatment [5].

```
12⊖ case class DoctorPolicyEng() extends Policy {
13
14    policy(0) {
15      ID is "DoctorPolicy"
16      name is "Doctor's Policy"
17      ruleCombiningAlgID is Permit_Overrides
18      target is {
19        subject is doctor
20        resource is any_resource
21        action is any_action
22      }
23
24      rule(0) {
25        ID is "Rule0"
26        effect is Permit
27        target is {
28          subject is doctor
29          resource is consultation or allergiesInfo
30          action is edit
31        }
32        timelimit is_from "09:00:00" to "17:00:00"
33      }
```

(a) a piece of policy representation in DSL

```
obligations {
  in_case_of Permit idCardReader must scan(RFID)
  in_case_of Deny PEP must send(errorMessage) from (PEP) to (hospitalA)
}
```

(b) obligation representations in DSL

```
<?xml version="1.0" encoding="UTF-8"?>
<Policy xmlns="urn:oasis:names:tc:xacml:2.0:policy:schema:os"
xmlns:xsi="http://www.w3.org/2001/XMLSchema-instance"
RuleCombiningAlgId="urn:oasis:names:tc:xacml:1.0:rule-combining-algorithm:permit-overrides"
PolicyId="DoctorPolicy" xsi:schemaLocation="urn:oasis:names:tc:xacml:2.0:policy:schema:os
http://docs.oasis-open.org/xacml/access_control-xacml-2.0-policy-schema-os.xsd">
    <Description>Doctor's Policy</Description>
 - <Target>
   - <Subjects>
     - <Subject>
       - <SubjectMatch MatchId="urn:oasis:names:tc:xacml:1.0:function:string-equal">
           <AttributeValue
               DataType="http://www.w3.org/2001/XMLSchema#string">doctor</AttributeValue>
           <SubjectAttributeDesignator DataType="http://www.w3.org/2001/XMLSchema#string"/>
         </SubjectMatch>
       </Subject>
     </Subjects>
   - <Resources>
       <AnyResource/>
     </Resources>
   - <Actions>
       <AnyAction/>
     </Actions>
   </Target>
 - <Rule Effect="Permit" RuleId="Rule0">
   - <Target>
     - <Subjects>
       + <Subject>
         - <SubjectMatch MatchId="urn:oasis:names:tc:xacml:1.0:function:string-equal">
             <AttributeValue
                 DataType="http://www.w3.org/2001/XMLSchema#string">doctor</AttributeValue>
             <SubjectAttributeDesignator
                 DataType="http://www.w3.org/2001/XMLSchema#string"/>
           </SubjectMatch>
         </Subject>
       </Subjects>
     - <Resources MatchId="urn:oasis:names:tc:xacml:1.0:function:or">
       - <Resource>
         - <ResourceMatch MatchId="urn:oasis:names:tc:xacml:1.0:function:anyURI-equal">
```

(c) a piece of translated XML representation of policy (a)

Fig. 3. An example of DSL representation of Security Policy and its translation to XACML-based XML

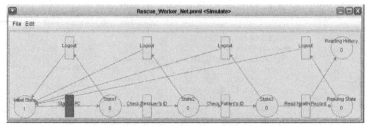

(a) a behavior of an emergency life-saving technician

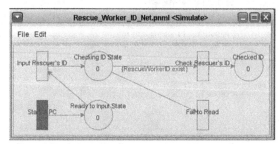

(b) a behavior of a rescue worker ID server

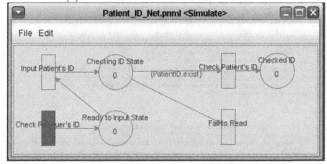

(c) a behavior of a medical record server

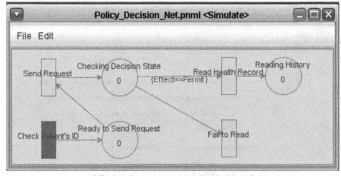

(d) a policy context to be enforced

Fig. 4. Policy descriptions of an actor and resources, and policy context

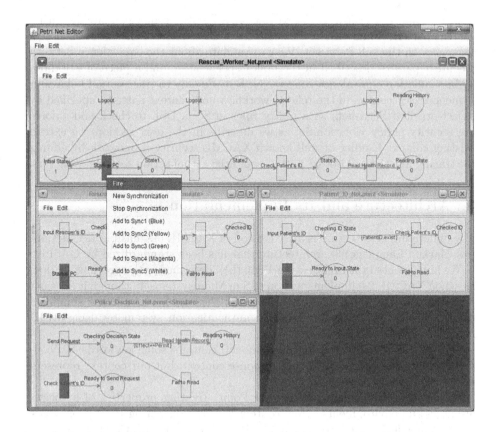

Fig. 5. Editing screen image of synchronous firing of behaviors and policy context

In this example, the context pattern implies "before the medical technician to access the patient's medical record, they finished the authentication using the ID card of both of them as obligations."

In the object-oriented Petri-nets, object-nets can express the behavior of individuals and a system-net can express their cooperation. According to having more than two hierarchies, it can express a workflow among related actors(subjects to access information), resources (targets to be accessed) and their individual behaviors (transitions). A situation can be treated as a marking at Petri-nets. Therefore, time series of situation, namely the conditions can be expressed by a Petri-net (subnet of a workflow) creating time series of a marking trying to designate. Then, in this report, a context is expressed by firing sequence of transitions.

A subject can access an information resource, if and only if the transitions of both object-nets that mean the subject and the resource fire as interaction. A context is expressed by a set of practicable fire series on a sub-Petri-net of a workflow, and it is called a context pattern[5]. A firing sequence matches with a context pattern if and only if the sequence is an element of the set of all firable sequences on the sub-Petri-net. We can validate about the equivalence between a context pattern described in the policy specification and a piece of workflow, by bi-simulation equivalence concept [6]. But it's only to trace actual behaviour sequences of accessors in the related workflow and context patterns specified by object-oriented Petri-nets with policy rules in Scala DSL to check and enforce the security policy violation.So, as we describe in the next section, we extend existing context handler of well-known XACML security framework by adding the tracing function of context patterns and the actual action sequence of actors.

5   Architecture and Its Implementation

The underlying architecture is an extension of XACML (eXtensible Access Control Markup Language)[3] architecture that has been standardized by OASIS.

We implemented the architecture(Fig.6 (b)), described in the previous section, based on XACML 2.0 implementation of Sun Microsystems[4], though it does not correspond to the newest XACML 3.0. And then we have built the simplified medical health record service with an authentication system by using REID readers of Phidgets[6] (Fig.7).

The XACML architecture(dataflow model) contains some keywords of a context handler, resource-context and response context, but our context representation is treated at their points.

We extend PIP (Policy Information Point) treating properties of subjects, resources and environments before context handler connecting PDP (Policy Decision Point) deciding permission and PEP (Policy Enforcement Point) executing access control (We name it Contextual Information Point = CIP). The module drew by dotted line on figure. 5 is the extended point. We have extended the following four modules in the existing Sun's implementation to integrate with our OPeN system and simplified medical record system:

- /com/sun/xacml/support/SimplePDP.java
- /com/sun/xacml/ctx/ResponseCtx.java
- /com/sun/xacml/ctx/Rusult.java
- /com/sun/xacml/AbstractPolicy.java

It's necessary to justify context information in order to avoid "spoofing context information." However, our proposed model premises spread resources under different managers, so on account of justifying context information of subjects and resources under other management structures, we decide to need approval of an external reliable third party.

---

[5] A sub-Petri-net "$sub(n)$" of a Petri-net "n" is a Petri-net consisting of a subset of a set of transitions, Petri-nets and arcs.

[6] http://www.phidgets.com/

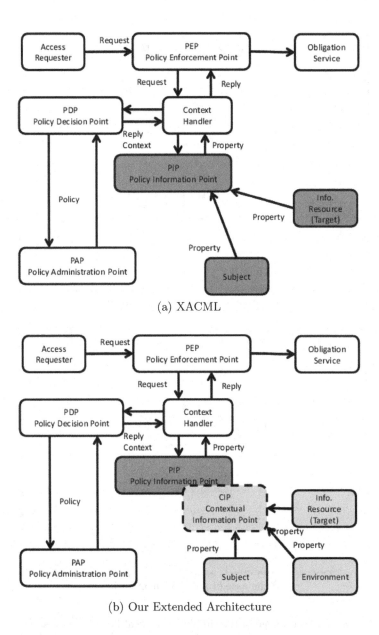

(a) XACML

(b) Our Extended Architecture

Fig. 6. The architecture of XACML and its extention

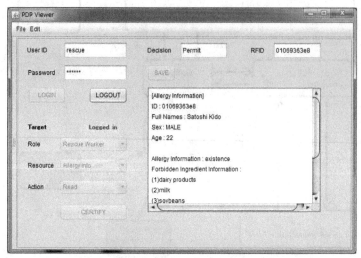

(a) the case of successful authentication

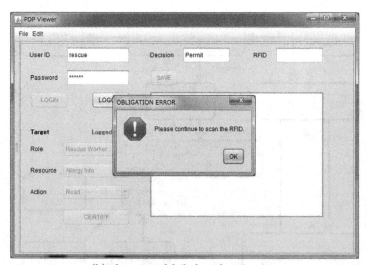

(b) the case of failed authentication

Fig. 7. A screen image of the simplified medical health record service

6   Evaluation

We compare the CxAC with simple RBAC, TMAC(Team based Access Control) [7] and SA(Security Automata)[8], which treats simple context conceptually. The comparison table is described in table. 1.

Table 1. Comparison with existing Security Models

Criteria	CxAC	RBAC	TMAC	SA
Complexity	Medium	Low	Low	High
Understandability	Simple	Simple	Simple	Simple
Easy of use	Medium	High	High	Medium
Applicability	High	High	Medium	Medium
Groups of Users	Yes	Yes	Yes	Yes
Policy Specifications	Yes	Yes	Yes	Yes
Policy Enforcement	Yes	Yes	Yes	Yes
Fine-Grained Control	High	Low	Medium	High
Active / Passive	Active	Passive	Active	Active

7   Conclusions

This paper describes the following five items:

(1) the proposal of a context-aware access control concept,
(2) an access control model according to the concept by using the object oriented Petri-net as a context representation,
(3) a design of policy enforcement mechanism as an extension of XACML architecture,
(4) a design of security policy notation as internal DSL of Scala, and
(5) an implementation based on the Sun's XACML implementaion.

In order to realize access control according to fine-grained situations, a representation of patterns of context to represent the status is required. Rather than evaluating the rights to access a single operation as in the conventional access control models, it's necessary to focus on the tracking of multiple operations dispersed in the workflow. The representation of context pattern is bound with corresponding security policy includes obligations. By using the object-oriented Petri-net in common with the workflow representation to represent the context pattern for situations and tracing each other, our method can select the appropriate policy to apply and enforce obligations. So we have adopted the Petri-net to express workflows, treated transitions of the Petri-net as landmark events to specify accessor's characteristic operations and their order, and have developped access-right evaluation mechanism as an extension of XACML architecture. Object-orientation of the OPeN is effective to express mutual compatibility of a group of accessors and target resources, and inter-organizational collaboration.

A part of the effectiveness of this method was confirmed through an example on how to check the authority of an emergency medical technician in order to access electronic medical record, from the inside of an ambulance car. In this example the proposed system enforces to comply with context pattern that implies "Before the medical technician accesses the patient's medical record, they finished the authentication using the ID card of both of them as obligations." But in this simple example we cannot make use of ability to describe parallelism of the Petri-net effectively. Effective use of concurrency is an issue in the future. And refinement of policy representation also remains a challenge for the future work. Accumulating more complex case studies is necessary to improve the DSL Policy expression. We think that the foundation to achieve this purpose was built.

References

1. Valk, R.: Object Petri Nets. In: Desel, J., Reisig, W., Rozenberg, G. (eds.) Lectures on Concurrency and Petri Nets. LNCS, vol. 3098, pp. 819–848. Springer, Heidelberg (2004)
2. Sandhu, M.S., Coyne, E.J., et al.: Role-based access control models. IEEE Computer 29(2), 38–47 (1996)
3. OASIS Standard: eXtensible Access Control Markup Language(XACML) 3.0 (January 22, 2013), http://docs.oasis-open.org/xacml/3.0/xacml-3.0-core-spec-os-en.pdf
4. Sun Microsystems, Inc.: Sun's XACML Implementation (July 16, 2004), http://sunxacml.sourceforge.net/
5. Health Policy Bureau of Ministry of Health, Labor and Welfare, Japan: For partial revision of the scope of the emergency life-saving treatment (in Japanese), Health Policy NotificationN o.0302001 (March 2, 2009), http://www.mhlw.go.jp/topics/2009/03/dl/tp0306-3a.pdf
6. Nielsen, M., Winskel, G.: Petri nets and bisimulation. Theoretical Computer Science 153(1-2), 211–244 (1986)
7. Thomas, R.K.: Team-based access control (TMAC): a primitive for applying role-based access controls in collaborative environments. In: RBAC 1997 Proceedings of the Second ACM Workshop on Role-based Access Control, pp. 13–19 (1997)
8. Deng, J., Brooks, R., Taiber, J.: Security Automata Integrated XACML and Security Validation. In: Proc IEEE SOUTHEASTCON 2010, pp. 338-343 (March 2010)

Mobile Security Solution for Enterprise Network

Alla G. Kravets, Ngoc Duong Bui, and Mohammed Al-Ashval

Volgograd State Technical University,
28 Lenin Avenue, 400005, Volgograd, Russia
agk@gde.ru, ramsetii@gmail.com

Abstract. This paper discusses an approach to Mobile security solution for enterprise network. It describes a secure solution for protect user devices and corporate information with end-to-end mobile security extending to data, users, devices, applications outside or inside of enterprise network. This solution improves the security of enterprise network by resolve the mobile security problems, increase work process efficiency. As a result, it will deliver data, services in a secure scalable, reliable way across multiple networks with multiple devices and guarantees high usability of system.

Keywords: mobile security, bring your own device, mobile device management, enterprise network.

Introduction

Mobile devices today become so inexpensive that they are standard equipment at many enterprises. Everyone with the own portable device (e.g. laptops, tablets, mobile phones, PDA) has IP-based wireless network (cellular network, Wi-Fi, WiMAX...) can access the enterprise's sensitive data (emails, plans, corporation's events, documents, private data etc.) at every location in the world as well as the ability in some models to work on spreadsheets. Although this increases the work efficiency, promote the performance of the employees working in the company but there is the issue of data privacy and information security of the company also increased [1, 2, 3, 4].

However, the phenomenal growth in mobile and wireless communications entails the serious problem of security. The causes, mainly due to the frangibility of wireless and mobile features and the variety of applications and services, fall into the following categories:

- Physical disabilities and limitations of mobile and wireless communications (for example, high rate of errors and unpredictable behavior error due to external interference and mobility, to impose influence on the characteristics of not only performance, but also safety).
- Fully to the environment air radio and wireless field devices provides many more features being exposed to malicious attacks and/or be subject to occasional interference.
- Applications are becoming more and more important than ever, including mobile applications and services in the field of military, health care, business, finance,

A. Kravets et al. (Eds.): JCKBSE 2014, CCIS 466, pp. 371–382, 2014.

etc. other services can bring users to easily in touch with possible threats of invading privacy, for example, location awareness of services and applications based on the context.

-     The content of services, most of which are media-type, are valuable not only to subscribers, but also composers and suppliers, and thus secure the protective measures.

So on, access and even, theft company owner's data has never been easier. Critical enterprise information is leaking onto mobile devices whose risk of loss or theft is much higher than it is for PCs at the office with more easy way. Therefore, companies need to have the owner policies and measures to manage the mobile devices of employees in the company access to sensitive resources of the company. The number of cases of leaking confidential business information via mobile devices continues to increase. Many enterprises have been aware for resolve these problems and apply management systems as well as mobile devices management (MDM) and/or bring your own device (BYOD) with matching policies to monitor status and control functions of smart phones and tablet computers to solve problems of enterprise data security secrets leaked whenever a device is lost or stolen [5, 6]. However, no standard has been set as yet assess whether such management systems mobile devices correctly provide basic security functions required of an enterprise and has functions such be developed safely.

By introducing the solution to resolve mobile security problems in the enterprise network environment while ensuring efficient working of the employees to access corporate data remotely on mobile devices inside or outside enterprise network. Our goal, propose a security solution to managed mobile devices when accessing corporation's resources using secure characteristic of HIP protocol [7] with end-to-end framework of Mobile Device Management [13] and Bring your own device [14].

By the defines, HIP protocol add a new layer, called Host Identity (HI) Layer, in the original TCP/IP stack between the network layer and transport layers. HIP also is an end-end security protocol for naming of endpoints and creates, performs authentication IPSec security associations between host-host. The IP address in current TCP/IP stack is using for location and identifier of host. However, in HIP protocol, the IP address of only is used for location, also host identity tag (HIT) – a 128-bit hash of the HI, is using for identifier parameter of host. In the HIP protocol, firstly, the endpoints establish session keys with the HIP Base Exchange [9], after which all packets are protected using IPSec ESP [10]. Finally, there is a re-addressing mechanism to support IP address changes with mobility and multihoming [11].

[12, 13, 14] gives some definitions of mobile security, mobile device management, bring your own device, it as follows:

-     Mobile security is the protection of smartphones, tablets, laptops and other portable computing devices, and the networks they connect to, from threats and vulnerabilities associated with wireless computing. Mobile security is also known as wireless security. Securing mobile devices has become increasingly important in recent years as the numbers of the devices in operation and the uses to which they are put have expanded dramatically. The problem is compounded within the enterprise as the ongoing trend toward IT consumerization is resulting in more and more employee-owned devices connecting to the corporate network.

-     Mobile device management (MDM) is the administrative area dealing with deploying, securing, monitoring, integrating and managing mobile devices, such as smartphones, tablets and laptops, in the workplace. The intent of MDM is to optimize the functionality and security of mobile devices within the enterprise, while simultaneously protecting the corporate network. Mobile device management software allows distribution of applications, data and configuration settings and patches for such devices. Ideally, MDM software allows administrators to oversee mobile devices as easily as desktop computers and provides optimal performance for users. MDM tools should include application management, file synchronization and sharing, data security tools, and support for either a corporate-owned or a personally owned device.

- Enrollment and Configuration Mobile Devices.
- Centrally Manage Mobile Devices.
- Proactively Secure Mobile Devices.
- Distribution Enterprise Resource on to Mobile Devices.☐ Monitor and Report on Mobile Devices.

-    Bring your own device (BYOD) refers to the policy of permitting employees to bring personally owned mobile devices (e.g. laptops, tablets, and smart phones) to their workplace, and to use those devices to access privileged company information and applications. There are four basic options, which allow:

- Unlimited access for personal devices.
- Access only to non-sensitive systems and data.
- Access, but with IT control over personal devices, apps and stored data. ☐
- Access, but prevent local storage of data on personal devices.

The widespread proliferation of consumerization of IT means more personal consumer computing devices are brought to the workplace by employees for use and connectivity on the enterprise network. The phrase BYOD (bring your own device) has become widely adopted to refer to these employees. Mobile device management is one way that an enterprise can deliver secure mobile solutions to its BYOD workforce.

The paper is structured as follows. First, we describe the mobile security issues in enterprise network, in Sect. 1. Next, in Sect. 2, we present the concept of HIPbased mobile device management system. Afterward, we give our solution's system descriptions in Sect. 3. Then, we present some related works in Sect. 4. Finally, we conclude the paper in Sect. 5.

1   Mobile Security Issues in Enterprise Network

From the definition above, there are some important mobile security issues of a mobile device management system in the enterprise network [5, 6, 15, 16]:

-    Man-in-the-middle at-tack, Denial of service attack, Replay attack, Session hijack, unauthorized access.
-    Loss of sensitive data, Intercepted or corrupted data, Impersonation, - Data packet sniffing / modification or recovery.
-    Devices rooting, jail breaking or losing, rootkit, application removal / stop or decompile, malware.

2   HIP-Based Mobile Device Management System

2.1   System Model and Working Environment

A HIP-based mobile device management system comprehensively manages mobile devices by monitoring their status and controlling their functions remotely using untrusted wireless Internet connection (Over-the-Air (OTA)/Wi-Fi) to manage the required business resources.

Companies are alarmed at the rate of employee adoption of mobile devices to access corporate data. MDM is now touted as a solution for managing corporateowned as well as personal devices in the workplace. The primary challenge is the ability to manage the risks associated with mobile access to data while securing company issued and Bring Your Own Device for mobile devices.

Typically HIP-based MDM solution is client – server type application and includes two components: client-side application and server-side components of solution.

a) Client-Side Application

Client-side application roles as mobile agent and is installed in the employment's owner mobile devices. Its main functions is collection all client's status and reporting to MDM server. It applies enterprise's policies to the mobile device and transmits the result back to the MDM server. Client-side application also deploys policies received from the MDM server to the mobile device and transmits the result back to the MDM server.

b) Server-Side Components of MDM Solutions

Server-side components of MDM solutions is maintains components of MDM system. It controls, monitors mobile device that connects to enterprise network. It also protects enterprise network against network secure problems. It includes 6 following components:

- MDM server: MDM server manages the data received from user's client and distributes the mobile device management policies to the client.
- HIP-based gateway: This is the gateway between the internal network and external network. The mobile devices from outside of enterprise network connect to the system through its.
- Certificate server [19]: This is the most important component in the PKI system [8]. It provides user's certificate information when MDM server request.
- Directory server: Directory server is a shared server for control information infrastructure for locating, managing, administering, and organizing common items and resources in the enterprise network (e.g. folders, files, users, groups, devices etc.).

- Application server [20]: Application server provides an environment where applications can run, no matter what the applications are or what they do
- Database server [21]: Database server provides database services to serve other services in the enterprise network. In MDM solution, it provides trusted information of user for PKI certificate when is requested.

MDM server sends out the management commands to the mobile devices, and a client component, which installed on the mobile device, receives and implements the management commands. One of the next steps was to allow a client initiates to update, similar to when a user requests a client update. Central remote management, using commands sent over the air, is the next step. A system administrator at the mobile operator, an enterprise IT data center can use an administrative console to update or configure any one or groups of mobile devices.

Figure 1 shows the MDM solution model and working environment [13, 17, 18].

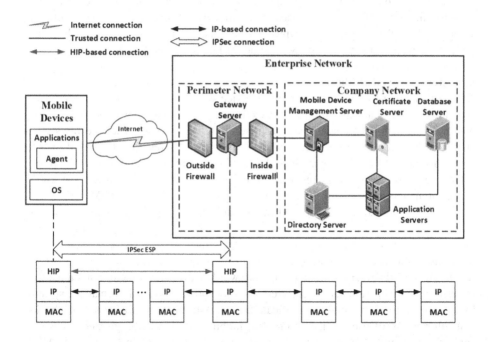

Fig. 1. The working environment of a MDM system in Enterprise Network

2.2   Secure Mobile Connection Process

There are three phases in the process when a mobile device connects to the enterprise network through Mobile device management (MDM) system, as follows: application access phase, HIP-based exchange phase, system associated phase.

a) Application Access Phase

When the employments access sensitive data from outside enterprise network by their mobile devices, they will access to enterprise network through MDM system. Application's client side in mobile device uses PIN code to restrict unwanted access to the system. User need type the PIN code every time necessary to access application.

b) HIP-Based Exchange Phase

When user completed access client-side application, start HIP-based four-way handshake for the establishment of HIP connections between mobile device and Gateway of MDM system. This phase is described same as in [7, 9]. After this fourway handshake, the mobile devices secure connected to the gateway of system. Most legacy applications can run unmodified over HIP [32]. HIP-based exchange process is transparent to normal users. By using HIP protocol, the transfer data time will be increased with short delay time but it is very short. Users do not recognize its participation in the process of exchange data between mobile devices and enterprise network though HIP-based gateway. The information exchange between mobile device and MDM system is encrypted (IPSec data exchange), no data is lost and system can resist some type of network attack (Man in the middle, DoS etc.).

c) System Associated Phase

After establishing a connection of mobile device with the MDM system by HIPbased type through the gateway, initiate data exchanges and mobile device start associate with the system applications in the enterprise's internal networks. The gateway serves all traffic between mobile devices and MDM system. It converts HIP-based packet from outside network to normal IP packet for internal network and otherwise. When MDM server receives access requests from client-side application, it ask the user's login parameters same as in the database of system. In addition, MDM server will send onetime password or the second factor authentication parameters to the user by other way [29, 30, 31]. The user enters the owner identification information, system login password and onetime password or the other second factor authentication parameters into the client-side application in the mobile device for sends to MDM server. At the MDM server, the onetime password or the second factor authentication is verified. If this parameter is corrected, the user's identification information, system login password will be send to certificate server. After that, certificate server checks that information of user. If it is corrected, mobile device will be granted access to enterprise's resource corresponding with their policy and right in the system. After this process, the licensed mobile devices can start working with the system.

The whole of connecting process of the mobile device with MDM solution in the enterprise network as described in Figure 2.

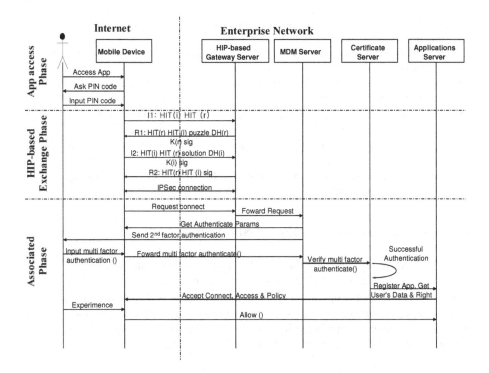

Fig. 2. Sequence diagram of connection process

2.3   Interactions of Solution

When mobile device completes connection process with MDM system, there are some interactions between the main components:

- Safely enroll new or existing devices over-the-air (OTA) initiating the installation of a configuration profile on their own mobile device. By apply the policy of MDM for each individual device; data on device (personal, enterprise etc.) are registered with MDM server.
- Configure one or multiple devices to enforce company policies and procedures.
- Collect and analyze relevant hardware and software data, such as device type, model, serial number, memory and installed apps.
- Collect hardware data, including processor, memory, hard drive space and battery life. Also, view and manage inventory of installed applications.
- Capture carrier network, phone number and data roaming settings.
- Secure authenticate, report to MDM server the information of mobile device to verify whether match registered data, which stored in the database server.
- Secure customers' networks through safety policies and restrictions.
- Enforce restrictions, such as access to the app stores, camera and browser security.

- Define password complexity for unlocking the phone and number of login attempts before the device locks.
- Centrally manage all mobile devices across all customer sites from a single interface.
- Takes control mobile device with the functions according to the mobile device control policy / command.
- Implemented some of the secure control commands of MDM server on the mobile device. Remotely reset passcodes, lock devices or wipe devices.
- Client application with built-in agent reports the status, parameter to the MDM server.
- Safely apply enterprise settings for individual mobile device, including special policy, configure and applications such as ERP, CRM, CMS etc.

3   Architecture Description of Solution

In this section, we will describe the main key components of our built-in clientserver MDM solution architecture. Reliable parts of the client placed inside protected mobile agent, responsible for the operation of the assets applications that need protection. We also will describe the main components of solution's architecture and how they work in order to ensure the level of security required for using in the enterprise network.

Figure 3 shows the components of MDM solution architecture.

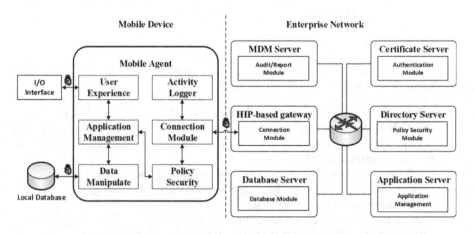

Fig. 3. The components of MDM solution architecture

The authentication module in certificate server authenticates the client platform and user to its counterpart in the enterprise network, which the first is the MDM server. This module generates a verifiable report of the client's identity that is bound to the MDM server. The report also includes information about the user manipulating the enterprise's data at mobile device. The MDM server verifies the report to ensure that it is communicating with corresponding user-right by using policy security module in the directory server. This determines that the user is part of an organizational domain in the enterprise that is authorized to access the authorized data in the database server.

The client and server engage in a one-time provisioning protocol that results in application secrets being securely sealed to the mobile device using HIP protocol. These secreted data, which was sealed before transmission and can only, be unsealed at other side by corresponding key, protocol, authorized user. In addition, because HIP protocol secure communication with each separate session, so very difficult for eavesdrop to intercept communications between mobile devices and enterprise network (e.g. man in the middle attack, DoS attack etc.).

Table 1, 2 describe the client-side components and server-side components of MDM solution architecture.

Table 1. Client-side components of MDM solution architecture

User Experience	Provides human-machine interface for access device and enterprise data, service.
Application Management	Manages applications in the mobile device (install, uninstall, update, execute etc.
Data Manipulate	- Encrypts temporary data to store at the local database. - Decrypts stored data from local database to process.
Activity Logger	Records all events, parameters in the mobile device.
Connection Module	Provides secure communication with enterprise network by using virtual HIP-based network driver.
Policy Security	Manages configurations, policies, instructions and verifies the policy to prevent all unauthorized actions.

Table 2. Server-side components of MDM solution architecture

Audit/Report	Manages all audit, report data that stored at database.
Connection Module	Provides HIP-based secure connections to the agents in the mobile devices. Convert between HIP-based protocol packet and IP packet.
Database Module	Stores all information for MDM solution.
Authentication Module	Enrolls, authenticates and identifies all user with their mobile devices.
Policy Security Module	Provides policy security configuration related to other modules.
Application Management	Management the list of allow and deny applications.

In our solution architecture, data use policy and encryption keys are stored at database server inside the enterprise network. The data owner specifies use policy and access control using the policy security engine that runs inside agent at mobile device.

The policy is then uploaded to the database server through the secure communication channel between the mobile device and enterprise network.

The protected data is encrypted within the agent with a randomly generated key, which is stored on the database server, and later distributed to authorize for processing with original mobile application. The encrypted data themselves need not be stored at database server and can be disseminated to intended recipients by various means (document repositories, email etc.).

An authorized device, upon receipt of an encrypted trusted data corresponding directory policy, can manipulate it using the secure data sandbox (user experience module) component of the client application, running inside agent in the mobile device. The policy engine, after validating that the use policy (downloaded securely from the server into the mobile agent) of the data is compatible with the user operation (e.g., editing or viewing), also gets the data decryption key and transfers control to the user experience module. This module decrypts the data inside the agent, parses the content and generates corresponding data for processing on the client application in the mobile device. Since the path between application memory and the user experience module that holds the decrypted before processing is insecure, we use technology to deny processing caching memory to protect that data. The encrypted data are transferred to the human-machine interface for processing via I/O bus.

Finally, the secure activity logger, also running inside the agent on mobile device, records every user activity related to data manipulates, transmits, reports it to the server where it is stored. This capability enables features such as auditing of employment's data access and nonrepudiation of user actions.

The untrusted part of the solution, consisting of the outside of agent on the mobile device and libraries used to avail of kernel services (e.g., file I/O, thread management etc.), untrusted network between devices and enterprise network. The interface was designed to ensure that no secrets from the trusted part are allowed to leak out to the untrusted part, and the independent platform mobile agent ensure that the secrecy and integrity of the data and code inside the agent-resident trusted part is maintained at all times. The security and safety of information within enterprise networks by traditional security solutions perform charge (IDS, NAC, AAA, XMS, Policy Directory, Firewall etc.).

The MDM server and other servers work in the secure trusted environment of enterprise network and connected with the mobile devices though the secure HIP-based gateway. Inside enterprise network consists of the application server, authentication and identification management module in certificate server, a directory server for maintaining user and platform information, and the database that stores information about device informations, status; whitelisted client platforms; client-server session state; application data policies and keys; and user activity logs. All communication between the MDM server and mobile device is secured, encrypted and offers integrity and replay protection to provide end-to-end security for various use cases by HIPbased gateway.

4   Related Works

There are some researches about mobile device management system and enterprise mobility such as [22, 23, 24, 25, 34]. In these researches, the authors use the ISO/IEC 15408 - The Common Criteria for Information Technology Security Evaluation [26] to resolve the mobile device management problem. L. Liu et al. [33] present their design for a portal to provide remote management access to virtualized device management servers hosted in a service cloud. Their design is targeted to hide the details of the device management behind a standard-based, uniform control interface that can be viewed from a cross-platform agent that can run on multiple mobile platforms. However, these works of these authors have not fully resolved the network problems, such as Man in the Middle [27] or DoS [28].

5   Conclusions

In this paper, we proposed a mobile security solution to resolve mobile issues in the enterprise networks for protect sensitive data of corporation, stability of network operation and employment's owner device etc. Our method retrieves the combinatorial effect from the security of Host Identity Protocol, Bring your own device and Mobile device management to protect data transfer over untrusted, anonymous network. Also with using these secures characteristics, our solution can protect enterprise network and employment's device avoid mobile devices' threat, risk (data loss, devices lost/theft, unauthorized / incorrect access, DoS attack, man in the middle etc.) but ensure high usability of system.

In the future, we intend to implement and experiment this solution in the cloud environment with virtual host, and experimental results show that it has good usability and supported to resolve mobile securities in the enterprise network as well.

References

1. Kietzmann, J., Plangger, K., Eaton., B., Heilgenberg, K., Pitt, L., Berthon, P.: Mobility at work: A typology of mobile communities of practice and contextual ambidexterity. Journal of Strategic Information Systems 3 (4), 16 pages (retrieved November 9, 2013)
2. Borg, A.: Enterprise Mobility Management Goes Global: Mobility Becomes Core IT. Aberdeen Group, Inc. (retrieved August 24, 2011)
3. Drake, S.: Embracing Next Generation Mobile Platforms to Solve Business Problems. Computerworld Inc. IDC, 8 pages (retrieved August 24, 2011)
4. Alms, D.: Understanding Mobility Management: Trends, Priorities and Imperatives. Visage Mobile, 6 pages (retrieved August 24, 2011)
5. Huawei Technologies Co., Ltd.: Huawei AnyOffice Mobile Security Solution, 12 pages (2013)
6. IBM.: Mobile device management solutions secure & manage mobile assets, across your enterprise, http://www.sdsems.co.kr/WebContent/product/vpn.jsp
7. Moskowitz, R., Nikander, P.: Host Identity Protocol (HIP) Architecture. RFC 4423. IETF (May 2006)
8. Carlisle, A., Steve, L.: Understanding PKI: concepts, standards, and deployment considerations, pp. 11–15. Addison-Wesley Professional (2003)
9. Moskowitz, R., Nikander, P.: Host Identity Protocol. RFC 5201. IETF (April 2008)
10. Kent, S.: IP Encapsulating Security Payload (ESP). RFC 4303. IETF (December 2005)

11. Nikander, P., Henderson, T., Vogt, C., Arkko, J.: End-Host Mobility and Multihoming with the Host Identity Protocol. TFC 5206. IETF (April 2008)
12. Definition: mobile security, http://whatis.techtarget.com/definition/mobile-security
13. Definition: mobile device management, http://searchmobilecomputing.techtarget.com/definition/mobile-device-management
14. Definition: Bring your own device, http://en.wikipedia.org/wiki/Bring_your_own_device (accessed March 28, 2014)
15. Citrix.: 10 "must-haves" for secure enterprise mobility, 12 pages (2013)
16. International Organization for Standardization (2004), ISO/IEC TR 13335-1: Information technology – Security techniques – Management of information and communications technology security – Part 1: Concepts and models for information and communications technology security management., http://www.iso.org/iso/iso_catalogue_tc/catalogue_detail.htm?csnumber=39066 (accessed March 29, 2014)
17. Liyanage, M., Gurtov, A.: Secured VPN Models for LTE Backhaul Networks. In: 2012 IEEE Vehicular Technology Conference (VTC Fall), September 3-6, pp. 1–5 (2012)
18. Nikander, P., Komu, M.: Host Identity Protocol. RFC 5338. IETF (September 2008)
19. Definition: Certificate server, http://en.wikipedia.org/wiki/Certificate_server (accessed March 29, 2014)
20. Definition: Application server, http://en.wikipedia.org/wiki/Application_server (accessed March 29, 2014)
21. DB-Engines Ranking, http://DB-Engines.com (retrieved December 28, 2013)
22. Rhee, K., Won, D., Jang, S., Chae, S., Park, S.: Threat modeling of a mobile device management system for secure smart work. Electronic Commerce Research, 1–14 (2013)
23. Rhee, K., Eun, S., Joo, M., Jeong, J., Won, D.: High-Level Design for a Secure Mobile Device Management System. In: Marinos, L., Askoxylakis, I. (eds.) HAS 2013. LNCS, vol. 8030, pp. 348–356. Springer, Heidelberg (2013)
24. Rhee, K., Jeon, W., Won, D.: Security Requirements of a Mobile Device Management System. International Journal of Security and Its Applications 6, 353–358 (2012)
25. Rhee, K.: A Study on the Security Evaluation of a Mobile Device Management System. Ph. D. Dissertation, Sungkyunkwan University, Suwon (2012)
26. CCMB: Common Criteria for Information Technology Security Evaluation Part 1: Introduction and general model Version 3.1 Revision 4 (2012)
27. Definition: Man in the middle attack, http://en.wikipedia.org/wiki/Man-in-themiddle_attack (accessed March 29, 2014)
28. Definition: Denial of service attack, http://en.wikipedia.org/wiki/Denial-of-service_attack (accessed March 29, 2014)
29. Machani, S., Pei, M., Rydell, J.: TOTP: Time-Based One-Time Password Algorithm. RFC 6238. IETF (May 2011)
30. Bellare, M., Hoornaert, F., Naccache, D., Ranen, O.: HOTP: An HMAC-Based One-Time Password Algorithm. RFC 4226. IETF (December 2005)
31. Rydell, J., Bajaj, S., Machani, S., Naccache, D.: OCRA: OATH Challenge-Response Algorithm. RFC 6287. IETF (June 2011)
32. Henderson, T., Nikander, P., Komu, M.: Using the Host Identity Protocol with Legacy Applications. RFC 5338. IETF (September 2008)
33. Liu, L., Moulic, R., Shea, D.: Cloud Service Portal for Mobile Device Management. In: Proceedings of IEEE 7th International Conference on e-Business Engineering (ICEBE), p. 474 (January 2011)
34. Kravets, A.G., Gurtjakov, A.S., Darmanian, A.P.: Enterprise intellectual capital management by social learning environment implementation. World Applied Sciences Journal 23(7), 956–964 (2013)

The Control System of the Eight-Legged Mobile Walking Robot

Andrey Andreev[1], Victor Zhoga[1], Valeriy Serov[2], and Vladimir Skakunov[1]

[1] Volgograd State Technical University, Russia
andan2005@yandex.ru,
{zhoga,svn}@vstu.ru
[2] JSC "CCB "Titan", Russia
va-serov@mail.ru

Abstract. The paper considers the control system of the autonomous mobile robot CS-7 with eight supporting legs, installed on four hard frames in pairs. Advantages of the chosen design: energy absence to support machine weight and simpler algorithms of trajectory and reference points motion management.

Onboard control is designed as a scalable, modular distributed low-level microprocessor system, which comprises two major subsystems: information measurement for processing sensors data and robot actuators control.

Supervisory control mode is supported by the vision system based on time-of-flight cameras and a set of ultrasonic and infrared sensors, geosteering module for local and global robot positioning. Measuring information is transmitted to the control computer via Wi-Fi module.

Software for the upper-level computer and library of functions for low-level units are developed for the implementation of various robot motion algorithms. Functions define the basic parameters of orthogonal movers depending on the given route and environment map.

Keywords: eight-legged mobile walking robot, mobile robot, the distributed control system, controllers, sensors, supervisory management.

1   Introduction

Currently, robotics is becoming an important part of many spheres of human activity. The range of applications of robotics is extremely wide. Among the many types of robots one can distinguish autonomous mobile robotic system, the hallmark of which is the ability to move in space. The primary function of mobile robots is their using in the course of intelligence operations in a non-deterministic environments, inaccessible or dangerous to humans: in places of technogenic catastrophes, during the demolition debris, in places with increased radiation background, during the mine clearance [1, 2]. One of directions of robotics development is a use of robots in technological processes of agricultural production. The interaction of technical objects with a nature is the most complex. For technological operations robot requires orientation on the land taking in consideration relief, soil dampness, locations of the plants [3].

A. Kravets et al. (Eds.): JCKBSE 2014, CCIS 466, pp. 383–392, 2014.

For ensuring of mobility wheeled, tracked, walking or combined propulsion devices are mainly used, and each of that has own merits and demerits [4]. It is impossible to create a universal mover capable of effectively and confidently move in any conditions. For robots, which movement is expected to occur on the roads with hard coating, wheel drivers are usually applied, as they provide a maximum movement speed. For driving on deformable surfaces crawler movers are applied. Using of the walking way of movement leads to qualitative growth of various basic operating indicators of mobile robots compared to wheeled and tracked. Among these features there are, in particular, a higher possibility of adaptation to the roughness of the support surface, essentially higher profile cross-country ability and maneuverability, allowing the machine movement in any direction and turns on the spot, the ability to work on soils with low bearing capacity, the ability to manage a support reactions and stabilization of the body position during movement. The use of walking propulsion allows the robot to move indoors, in narrow hallways and doorways, on stairs, gives an opportunity to make maneuvering in confined spaces. Prospects for the application of such robots are determined, in particular, by their energy efficiency. The movement of walking robots on a deformable surface is accompanied by energy consumption to maintain their weight, to perform work against gravity, to overcome friction in kinematic pairs of mechanisms of striding and transmission, on lifting, lowering and transfer of legs, deformation of the soil, acceleration, braking and turning of machine, as well as on the functioning of the control system.

Problems of robots with walking mechanisms are associated with a creation of control systems which adapt to the roughness of the support surface and have the best (from the point of view of operating speed and (or) energy consumption) law of relative movements of the parts of the propeller and body. Thus, the choice of the propulsion type is associated with operating conditions. Often for greater versatility a combination of several types of propulsion are applied.

The complexity of the control algorithms, ensuring coordination of separate links of each swalking mechanism as well as mutual motion of different mechanisms among themselves, largely depends on the kinematic scheme of the used striding walking mechanisms and schemes of the robot. Orthogonal kinematic scheme of the walking propulsion has minimum requirements for control system. In addition, orthogonal mover has significant advantages of energy consumption because the robot during the motion on a horizontal surface doesn't expend the job to keeping its weight. Application of orthogonal schemes of mobile robot propulsion allows us to use building block design based on the functional modules that have all the necessary elements: actuators, feedback sensors, a control unit with microprocessor. There are constructions of robots used for mine detection [6]. In these robots walking mechanisms with three managed degrees of freedom are applied and a multilevel control system is developed for the implementation of programmable motions. In our opinion, the complexity of the control system is not due to the complexity of the robot tasks, but the complexity of its mechanical structure. Its number of degrees of freedom exceeds the minimum necessary to perform asked movements. Complex mechanical design of such robots together with a complex control system leads to their high cost and reduces the ability to resist extreme external influences [7, 8].

2   The Design of the Robot

For the purpose to create a mobile robot platform for the placement of technological equipment for various destinations robot with orthogonal-rotary walking propulsion (Fig.1) is designed and manufactured in the Volgograd State Technical University. The present paper describes the design of the robot, the dynamics of controlled motion and algorithms of a control system functioning for the robot with orthogonal walking propulsion [9].

The robot consists of a top frame 1, connected by the rotation mechanism with the bottom body 2.

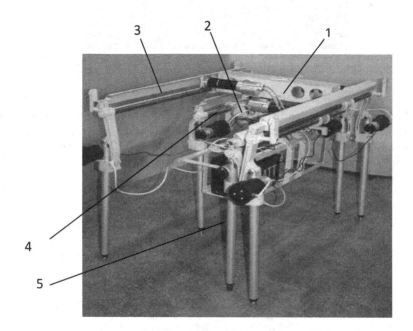

Fig. 1. An eight-legged mobile walking robot

Each of the body parts are connected with pair of guide blocks 3,4 made in the form of a splined shaft with a ball screw LBST30 DD CL, with a stroke of 942 mm and 1,042 mm, with the horizontal displacement drives. The drives of the company «Maxon motors» are used as horizontal displacement drives and rotation drive. Each drive includes a servo motor RTG060, planetary gear, brake, position sensor (encoder HEDL9140, 500 imp/rev). Twisting moment on the drive shaft of horizontal movement is 4 Nm; angular velocity is 425 rev/min. Maximum twisting moment on the rotating drive shaft is 34 Nm; the angular velocity of the output shaft is 17 rev/min (Fig. 2).

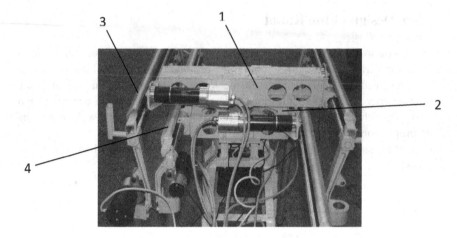

Fig. 2. The drive of the horizontal movement of robot frames

Robot vertical adaptation drives 5 to the supporting surface are mounted at the ends of the rods. The linear actuators CAT33Hh400h4AG1F, «SKF group» are used as drives. Bearing rod dynamic load is 500 N; the speed is 0.174 m/s; the stroke is 400 mm. (Fig. 3). The robot is powered by the battery with the voltage of 24 V.

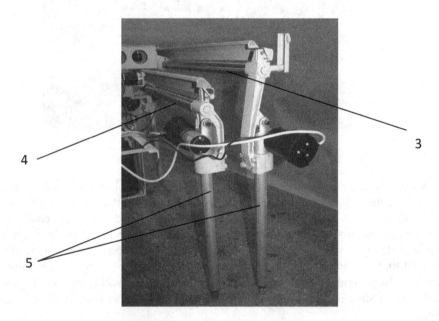

Fig. 3. The drive of vertical adaptation

3   Programmable Movement

Depending on the operating conditions and the nature of tasks performed by a robot, there are various algorithms to move it. Robot movement speed during the execution of these algorithms depends in many respects on parameters of a roughness of the support surface.

Any movement of the robot with orthogonal walking propulsion can be decomposed into a number of elementary movements, the sequence of their execution depends on the operator's choice of one of the possible motion algorithms. These walks are characterized by the presence of motion intervals, during which there are no relative horizontal movement of robot frames (start-stop mode). The necessity of these phases is conditioned by the requirement of unstressed contact of the vertical posts at the robot adaption to the supporting surface. Kinematic scheme of the robot allows us to implement a walk, in which the robot body moves continuously, and unstressed adaptation of the robot to the roughness of the support surface is provided by the programmatic laws of the relative movement of its parts [10].

The robot maneuvering is carried out in several ways: discrete turn, at which the center of mass of the robot will not move; discrete turn at which the center of mass moves in a broken curve; the progressive movement of one of the frame relative to the other at rectilinear movement of the body.

The sensors of the information support system should monitor the results of the relative movements of the parts of the robot and to determine its position relative to signposts in the external environment, which allows to solve the problem of choosing points of foot setting on the support surface and the choice of the motion law The described structure of a mobile robot, designed for autonomous functioning in the unstructured work space adapts well to programmable movements.

4   Settlement Scheme

The considered robot consists (Fig.4) of mechanical part, electric motors with gearboxes, control system block, sensor system and power unit.

The mechanical part is represented as six massive rigid bodies. The lower part of the robot body (1) with mass m_1 hosts the block of the control system and power unit. The top part (2) with mass m_2, is associated with the bottom part of a body with the cylindrical hinge of fifth grade. On each part of the body to guide are fixed, in which installed bars 3, 4 with the possibility of horizontal travel each weighing m_3, m_4, associated with horizontal movement drives.

Retractable legs 5 interact with the bearing surface at the point, and the response surface is determined by the forces $\vec{N_i}(i = 1 \div 8)$ .The robot motion is relative to the fixed coordinate system $O\xi\eta\varsigma$ without taking into account the rotation of the upper part of the robot relative to lower. The coordinate axes C_1XYZ connected with the center of mass of the lower part of the body and move onward relative to the fixed coordinate system. The position of the center of mass is determined by the radius - vector $\vec{r_1}$, the velocity vector $\vec{V}$ and the vector of angular velocity $\vec{\omega}$. With each of solid bodies, comprising the mechanical part of the robot, moving coordinate systems $C_kX_kY_kZ_k$ $(k = 1 \div 6)$ are connected, which axes are the principal Central axes of inertia. Directions in the space of the principal Central axes of inertia of all parts of the robot are the same. Their positions relative to the axes C_1XYZ, are specified by the Euler ship angles φ, ψ, θ. The body movement is possible when all eight legs are on the support. Thus, the analyzed robot is a mechanical system with variable structure.

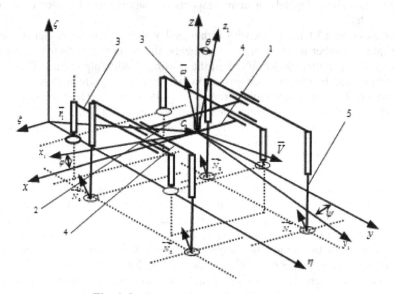

Fig. 4. Settlement scheme of mobile robot

5   Mathematical Model

The equations of robot motion under the gravity forces, forces of reactions of supporting surface at the points of base plates contact were made in the form of a Lagrangian equations of the 2nd kind. The kinetic energy of the robot, as a systems of rigid bodies is determined by the expression

$$T = \sum_{i,k=1}^{i=3,k=6} (\tfrac{1}{2}m_k \dot{r}_k^2 + \tfrac{1}{2}I_{ik}\omega_{ik}^2), \tag{1}$$

where $\dot{r}_k$ - is the speed of the center of mass of the robot in an absolute coordinate system; I_{ik}, ω_{ik} - the principal Central moments of inertia and the projection of the angular velocity vector of each part of the robot on the axis of mobile coupled system of coordinates.

Differential equations of the robot motion in a matrix form

$$A\ddot{q} = B(q,\dot{q}) + F(t) + N(q,\dot{q}), \tag{2}$$

where A - 10x10 symmetric matrix of the coefficients of inertia; $B(q,\dot{q})$ - the column matrix of components that depend on the generalized coordinates and velocities; $F(t)$ - column matrix of control forces; $N(q,\dot{q})$ - column matrix of reactions forces of support surface.

6   The Structure of the Motion Control System

The control system is a problem-oriented complex of specialized typical devices. System components are joined by the internal interface and provide a sufficiently complete amount of measurement data and computing resources.

Onboard control system is divided into two levels: the upper level makes decisions on forming the main control actions for executive devices depending on the operation modes of the robot, and the lower level implements functions of assessment of environment condition, control functions and governs the propulsion. In the supervisor mode the external interface is used to select the algorithm of programmable movement, formation of the route and management objectives. Through this interface an information from sensors and vision systems is transferred to the remote computer for analysis and solution of navigation problems.

The structure of the movers control system of walking robot is shown in Fig. 5. On the upper level the main control functions are executed by the Host controller SK-iMX53-MB+OEM. Structurally the controller is made on the motherboard SK-iMX53-MB, on which a processor module SK-iMX53-OEM is installed. The basis of the module is a high-performance processor FreeScale iMX536 with ARM Cortex-A8 architecture and frequency up to 800MHz, complemented by a wide number of peripherals and high-speed interfaces (USB, Ethernet, LVDS USB, Audio, CAN, UART, SPI, I2C, and many others).

On the lower level there are two main subsystems: subsystem for electric drives control, made taking into account features of control circuits for different linear motors types, and sensor subsystem that supports the supervisory mode of the robot operation.

In the horizontal movement drives and in the turn actuator the control functions are performed by special position controllers EPOS2 70/10. Controllers can manage the engines with Hall sensors and the encoder at an inclusion (plugging) in the network as a slave device connected to the Host controller via USB.

To control the vertical support actuators a typical data preprocessing and linear motors autonomous control modules are designed. The modules perform a functions of signal generator for engine control via direct commands received from Host controller. As well they perform a software implementation of algorithms of digital filtration (filters Kalman-Bucy) for data from ultrasound and infrared distance sensors separately for each vertical support and processing of servo feedback signals for supports linear drives control by the position. The speed and direction of movement of vertical sliding bearings is managed through bridge amplifiers schemes built on dual-link drivers - integrated circuits VNH3SP30.

Data preprocessing module is built on a development board STM32F3DISCOVERY. In the base of the board there is 32-bit ARM microcontroller STM32F303VCT6 from the ARM Cortex-M4 family with built-in interfaces: USB, SPI, I2C, converters ADC, DAC and other peripherals. In addition, a digital accelerometer and a gyroscope are integrated (installed) on the board, the data from them is used in the algorithms of the spatial orientation.

The vision system is built on the sensor controller ASUS Xtion PRO Live - camera of structured light, allowing to obtain a three-dimensional picture of the environment.

In the module of local and global navigation a GPS satellite navigation systems sensor as well as ultrasonic and infrared distance sensors, antenna arrays, digital gyroscope and an accelerometer to determine the longitudinal and cross tilt of mobile robot platform are applied.

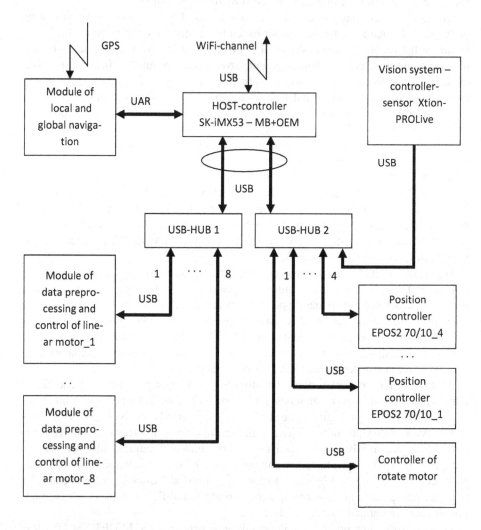

Fig. 5. The structure of the walking robot control system

7   The Software Structure

Information exchange between software of the lower and upper levels is carried out by a protocol based on the developed system of control commands. Software of walking robot consists of three main components.

1. Module of robot control that implements a graphical user interface. It allows us to set the mode of the robot motion and the parameters for the specified mode. The module operates as a Windows application on a personal computer of a supervisor that communicates via a wireless network connection (Wi-Fi) with the module of programmable   movement assignment, and also allows us to view the image from the camera of the robot in the real-time mode.
2. Module of the robot programmable movement assignment   that implements the control algorithm for the selected mode of the robot motion: rectilinear motion on a flat surface, driving on uneven surfaces (with auto-leveling), crossing the barrier, turn. The module is functioning as a server process on board Host controller running Linux. The module provides the ability to connect a client application of a supervisor to perform basic motion algorithms, distributes commands to peripheral controllers according to the motion algorithm and monitoring the state of each of the movers to get the required trajectory of motion of the robot as a whole.
3. Module of interaction with peripheral controllers in modules of data preprocessing and linear motor control ensures the delegation of drivers management functions and   obtaining the work status of each controller, performs distribution of requests to peripheral controllers connected to the central controller via USB by a their unique addresses in the onboard system of the robot, receives and processes measurement information flow from the sensory system.

Interaction with peripheral controllers is provided by software library written in C for Linux OS. Each of peripheral controllers provide a management of one linear motor (raise/lower of vertical sliding supports, horizontal movement or rotation of the platform), and the collection and processing of information from the associated with this propulsion sensors (linear position sensor, sensors of longitudinal or transverse roll, distance sensors to the surface).

8   Conclusion

The kinematic scheme of the considered robot allows to perform comfortable movement on an undetermined support surface. Algorithms of programmable motion of robot body are implemented   by independent movements of walking propeller links. Two-layered control system lets implement random movements of robot in supervisor mode. The structure of the control system assumes its development with an increase of   amount and quality of information about the operating environment [11].

Acknowledgement. The work was supported by the Russian Foundation for Basic Research (project 13-08-00387 - a), (project 12-08-00301 - a).

References

1. Livshitz, A., Petrenko, E., Rachkov, M.: Humanitarian Demining Technologies in Russia. In: Pros 2003 ICAR, Coimbra, Portugal, vol. 1, pp. 544–549 (2003)
2. Zhoga, V.V.: Computation of Walking Robots Movement Energy Expenditure. In: Proc. 1998 IEEE Internationai Conference on Robotics and Automation, Leuven, Belgium, vol. 1, pp. 163–164 (1998)

3. Gerasun, V.M.: The particular qualities of an agricultural robots and their requirements(Osobennostisel'skokhozyaystvennykhrobotovitrebovaniya k nim(in Russian)); Gerasun, V.M., Nesmiyanov, I.A., Zhoga, V.V.:Robototekhnikaiiskusstvennyyintellekt: mater. V vseros. nauch. - tekhn. konf. smezhdunar. uchastiyem, g. Zheleznogorsk, 15 noyab, g. / Pod nauch. red. V.A. Ugleva; Sibirskiyfederal'nyyun - t, Zheleznogorskiy filial SFU. - Zheleznogorsk, pp. 26–28 (2013)
4. Zhoga, V.V.: The quality metrics system for walking transport machines(Sistema pokazateleykachestvashagayushchikhtransportnykhmashin(in Russian)). Inzhenernyzhurn (5), 21–28 (1997)
5. Hirose, S., Kato, K.: Development of Quadruped Walking Robot with the Mission of Mine Detection and Removal-Proposal of Shape-Feedback Master-Slave Arm. In: Proc. 1998 IEEE International Conference on Robotics & Automation Leuven, Belgium, vol. 3, pp. 1913–1718 (1998)
6. Nonami, K., Huang, Q.J.: Humanitarian Mine Detection Six-Leggad Walking Robot COMET-II with two Manipulators. In: Prog. of the 4rd Int. Conf. on Climbing and Walking Robots, pp. 989–996 (2001)
7. Briskin, Y.S., Zhoga, V.V., Pokrovskiy, D.N., et al.:Mobile robotics complex for humanitarian demining(Mobil'nyyrobototekhnicheskiykompleksdlyagumanitarnogorazminirovaniya(in Russian)). Mekhatronika, Avtomatizatsiya, Upravleniye (3), 28–37 (2007)
8. Tambouratzis, T., Chalikias, M.S., Souliou, D., Gregoriades, A.: Dimensionality Reduction of Accident Databases for Minimal Tradeoff in Prediction Accuracy. In: IKE, pp. 64–71 (2010)
9. Zhoga, V.V., Skakunov, V.A., Eremenko, A.V., Fedchenkov, P.V., Gerasun, V.M., Nesmiyanov, I.A., Dyashkin-Titov, V.V.: Patent 2476372 RF, MПКC1. Accident Rescue Vehicle. Volgograd state technical university (2013)
10. Gavrilov, A.E., Zhoga, V.V., Fedchenkov, P.V.: Synthesis of optimal program law for movement of a robot with orthogonal walking drives. Journal of Computer and Systems Sciences International 50(5), 847–857 (2011)
11. Tambouratzis, T., Souliou, D., Chalikias, M., Gregoriades, A.: Combining probabilistic neural networks and decision trees for maximally accurate and efficient accident prediction. In: The 2010 International Joint Conference on Neural Networks (IJCNN), pp. 1–8. IEEE (July 2010)

Development of a Protocol to Ensure
the Safety of User Data in Social Networks,
Based on the Backes Method

Lê Xuân Quyến and Alla G. Kravets

Volgograd State Technical University, Volgograd, Russia
agk@gde.ru

Abstract. This article discusses the security issues of user data in social networks, such approaches to security. Analyses existing approaches based on their own protocol is being developed that uses the social network representation as a queuing network. Arguments in favour of the proposed approach effectiveness are considered, it is implemented based on the method of Backes, as well as numerical simulation results of its work.

Keywords: social net, cryptography, protocol, authentication, digital signature.

1 Introduction

One of the central problems in the development of distributed systems is the design of cryptographic protocols that meet the desired functional requirements and meet the implementation of the security properties.

Over the past few years online social networks (OSN) have become a tool to communicate with people and take part in many social activities such as exchange of information, exchange of opinions, events, publications and advertisements. Based on this, we concluded that the lack of access control mechanisms (for example, to restrict access to pictures, videos and messages on the wall) can lead to unpleasant consequences, for example, employers have the possibility of monitoring the personal lives of their employees. In such conditions, the privacy of public relations is a fundamental property, in fact, as the anonymity of users.

We introduce a cryptographic framework to achieve access control, privacy of social relations, secrecy of resources, and anonymity of users in social networks.

Combining the concepts of anonymity forms of access control is crucial to ensure that certain documents could be read-only or available only certain persons, as opposed to users who are not. Anonymity and confidentiality are also desirable in a variety of applications that can work with social networks such as content sharing and feedback reports.

2 Theoretical Basis

Proof-Carrying Authorization has been successfully deployed in the context of web applications [1], mobile devices [2]. Maffei and Pecina [3] extended the concept of

A. Kravets et al. (Eds.): JCKBSE 2014, CCIS 466, pp. 393–399, 2014.

Authorization with confirmation (TSA) (Proof-Carrying Authorization). Expanding TSA is based on a powerful combination of digital signatures and confirmation of non-disclosure of signatures. The first step is used to justify the witness logical formulas, the last-to selectively hide confidential data. The extension supports various properties of privacy, such as data privacy and user anonymity.

$$\frac{\text{SIGNED}}{\Gamma \vdash \text{digital\_signature}(s, A, F)} \qquad \frac{\text{NAME-I}}{\Gamma \vdash A \text{ says } F} \qquad \frac{F}{A \text{ says } F}$$

$$\frac{\text{NAME-IMP-E}}{A \text{ says } F \qquad A \text{ says } F \to G}$$
$$\frac{}{A \text{ says } G}$$

Fig. 1. Say method

$$S \quad := \quad \text{ver}(u_s, u_A, F) \mid S_1 \wedge S_2 \mid \exists x.\, S$$

$$[S] \quad = \quad \begin{cases} u_A \text{ says } F & \text{if } S := \text{ver}(u_s, u_A, F) \\ [S_1] \wedge [S_2] & \text{if } S := S_1 \wedge S_2 \\ \exists x.\, [S'] & \text{if } S := \exists x.\, S' \end{cases}$$

$$\frac{\text{ZERO-KNOWLEDGE}}{\Gamma \vdash \text{ZKProof}(S)}$$
$$\frac{}{\Gamma \vdash [S]}$$

Fig. 2. Deduction rule

Distinctive features of the method say are shown in Fig 1. Interference rules are parametrized to the environment Γ which can contain formulae, creating security policies, also formulae like $digital\_signature(s; A; F)$. $SIGNED$ maintaining connections between signatures and logical formulae, if the environment Γ contains statement $digital\_signature(s; A; F)$ then Γ issay F. Backes [4] suggests that this rule $COMM - J, COMM - A$ describes the cryptographic communication messages exchange. Figure $3 COMM - A$ shows an embodiment $COMM - J$ which is introduced to simulate anonymous communication: In this embodiment, the sender's identity is replaced with the special character "?" and it is unknown to receiver.

$$\frac{\text{ENSUE}}{A \text{ knows } \Gamma} \qquad \frac{\text{P-A}}{A : F} \qquad \frac{\text{P-S}}{A : vk_A \text{ says } F} \qquad \frac{\text{P-ZK}}{A \text{ knows } \Gamma \quad \Gamma \vdash_{\text{ZK}} S \quad \text{ver}_{\text{zk}}(M, S)}$$
$$\frac{\Gamma \vdash F}{A \text{ knows } F} \qquad \frac{}{A \text{ knows } F} \qquad \frac{\text{ver}_{\text{sig}}(M, vk_A, F)}{A \text{ knows } M} \qquad \frac{}{A \text{ knows } M}$$

$$\frac{\text{COMM-J}}{\begin{array}{c} \text{if } F_B \text{ then } B \text{ sends } F \text{ to } p \\ \text{if } F_A \text{ then } A \text{ receives } F' \text{ from } q \\ B \text{ knows } F_B \, \eta \quad B \text{ knows } M \quad A \text{ knows } F_A \, \theta \\ p\eta = A \quad q\theta = B \quad [M] = F \quad F'\theta = F \end{array}}{A \text{ knows } M}$$

$$\frac{\text{COMM-A}}{\begin{array}{c} \text{if } F_B \text{ then } ? \text{ sends } F \text{ to } p \\ \text{if } F_A \text{ then } A \text{ receives } F' \text{ from } ? \\ B \text{ knows } F_B \, \eta \quad B \text{ knows } M \quad A \text{ knows } F_A \, \theta \\ p\eta = A \quad [M] = F \quad F'\theta = F \end{array}}{A \text{ knows } M}$$

Fig. 3. Communication rule

3 Protocols for Social Nets

Backes [2] introduced a number of protocols for social nets register, getResource. Here we use a combination shown on fig. 1,2,3; inherit approach but add statement: $AsaysOperations(op)$, op := R|W|RW, R- read data,W- write data,RW- read and write data. With the addition of $AsaysOperations(op)$ increased security of user data in the network, increased choice for users. Fig. 4 is a friendly request from kA (social relations unidirectional) Statement $B\ says\ FriendReq(A)$.

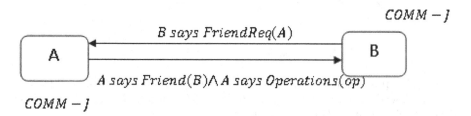

Fig. 4. Register protocol

Statement $AsaysFriend(B)\wedge AsaysOperations(op)$ represents a corresponding confirmation of friendship. B can use this information to be engaged in certain activities.

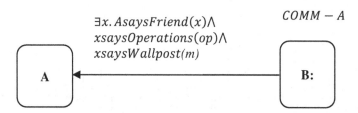

Fig. 5. B posts message on the A's wall

Assume for example that the access to the wall A is limited only to friends: B can anonymously post messages on the A wall using the existential quantification of his personality, as shown below (Figure 5).

Let B interested in photography, available for viewing only by friends of A, B can prove that he is a friend, without revealing his identity in Figure 6.

Cryptographic Implementation. Let us describe all cryptographic primitives needed to build the aforementioned zero-knowledge proof, the use of bilinear mappings makes these primitives particularly effective.

Bilinear Mapping: Bilinear mapping [1] of electronic card elements $G_1 \times G_2$ in the target group G_T is bilinear. More precisely, the equality holds for all values G, H, x, и y
$.e(x \cdot G, y \cdot H) = e(G, y \cdot H)^x = e(x \cdot G, H)^y = e(G, H)^{xy}$

Digital Signature Scheme. We use a digital signature scheme recently proposed in the papers of Abe [3].

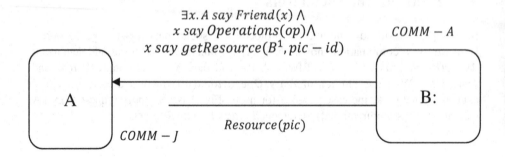

$$\exists x. A\ say\ Friend(x)\ \wedge$$
$$x\ say\ Operations(op)\wedge$$
$$x\ say\ getResource(B^1, pic - id)$$

COMM − A

A

B:

COMM − J

Resource(pic)

Fig. 6. Operation overview. Data B transferred to A.

Groth-Sahai proof system without disclosure is very flexible and the overall system. It is multiplication of equations G_1 and G_2 and equation pair products. We will use SXDH proof systems by Groth-Sahai [4,5,6].

3.1   Simulation Modeling of Authentication Systems in Social Networks

We use the Lukjanov [7] approach: modeling assessment services lectures in Figure 7.

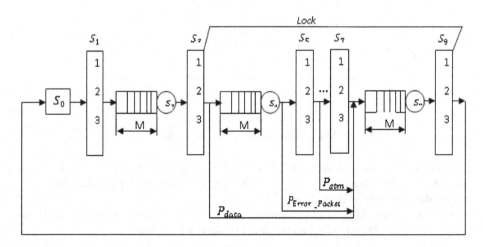

Fig. 7. Shema Authentication Protocol getResource a queuing network

S_0: - duration of service in the center S_0 is exponentially distributed with parameter λ. S_1: centre formalizing the module of TCP-operating system when establishing a connection. M-number of service channels, no queue. The center formalizes the work of the TCP module of operating system. It handled customer orders when establishing a connection with the implementation of the so-called three-step handshake. Service discipline in the center of IS. S_2- the main thread of the application server, the application retrieves from a queue on the establishment. Maximum queue length L L is set to the center of the server application. Service discipline in the center of FCFS-M/M/1. S_3, S_{11}- Centers S_3, S_{11} have M service channels (server threads) and when beginning of the application service $i - M$ in the center S_3 it is considered busy until the completion of service $i - M$ in the channel S_{11}. Thus, the center $S_3 и S_{11}$ channel is blocked. S_3, S_{10} IS discipline service nodes (serviced without delay). S_4 - center, which extracts the evidence. Figure 4 and 5 show the proofs. S_4 with servicing discipline PS (processor sharing), and a queue length M . S_5 - Centre formalizing authentication assertions job: $ProfsayRegistered(id, course)S_5$IS discipline service nodes S_6 - Centre formalizing authentication assertions job: $idsayEvaluation(course, grade)S_6$IS discipline service nodes S_7 - Centre formalizing authentication assertions job: $SSP(id, s, psd)S_7$IS discipline service nodes S_8 - centre formalizing authentication assertions job: $SSP(id, s', psd')$, S_8 IS discipline service nodes S_9 - Centre formalizing authentication assertions job: $(psd', \_) \notin x_l$, S_9 IS discipline service nodes S_{10} - centre formalizing the module server responses generation module S_{10} with servicing discipline PS (processor division) and queue length M.

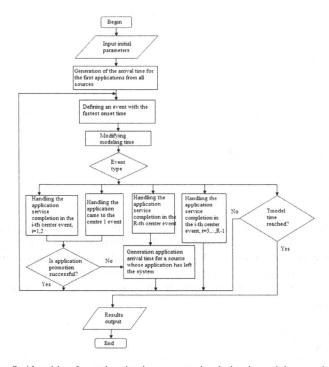

Fig. 8. Algorithm for authentication system simulation in social networks

4 Numerical Simulation Results of Authentication Systems in Social Networks

Authentication systems modeling in social networks have been carried out with a program developed in C # on the basis of the above simulation model algorithms. On the fig. 9. In the simulation, the following parameters of the system have been used:

The maximum number of simultaneously open network connections 50. Allowed time the TCP connection-20.0s. Allowable time waiting for service after the TCP connection-20s. The extraction of the application queue for service and create a child-stream server application 0.12s. Simulation time 10s, queue size 80 applications. The maximum number of server threads$M = 200$. Duration is $RTT - 0.05s$. Duration of authentication $S_5 - 1.2s$. Duration in $S_6 - 0.4s$. Duration in $S_7 - 0.3s$. Duration in $S_8 - 0.2s$.

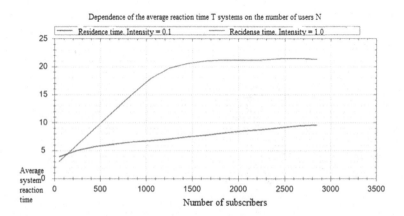

Fig. 9. Dependence of the application average service time on the number of system users

5 Conclusion

In this paper we developed the idea based on the method Backes [2] to increase the security of user data in social networks, authentication systems functioning in social networks as a queuing network. Algorithm for authentication system simulation in social networks [10] in the experimental part is shown in Figure 9. Based development, explores language for confidentiality help users have more options for confidential information.

References

1. Abe, M., Fuchsbauer, G., Groth, J., Haralambiev, K., Ohkubo, M.: Structure-preserving signatures and commitments to group elements. In: Rabin, T. (ed.) CRYPTO 2010. LNCS, vol. 6223, pp. 209–236. Springer, Heidelberg (2010)

2. Backes, M., Maffei, M., Pecina, K.: Automated Synthesis of Privacy Preserving Distributed Applications. In: Proc. Network and Distributed System Security Symposium (NDSS 2012). Internet Society (2012)
3. Blazy, O., Fuchsbauer, G., Izabachène, M., Jambert, A., Sibert, H., Vergnaud, D.: Batch groth–sahai. In: Zhou, J., Yung, M. (eds.) ACNS 2010. LNCS, vol. 6123, pp. 218–235. Springer, Heidelberg (2010)
4. Camenisch, J., Dubovitskaya, M., Lehmann, A., Neven, G., Paquin, C., Preiss, F.-S.: Concepts and Languages for Privacy-Preserving Attribute-Based Authentication. In: Fischer Hübner, S., de Leeuw, E., Mitchell, C. (eds.) IDMAN 2013. IFIP AICT, vol. 396, pp. 34–52. Springer, Heidelberg (2013)
5. Ghadafi, E., Smart, N.P., Warinschi, B.: Groth–Sahai proofs revisited. Springer (2010)
6. Groth, J., Sahai, A.: Efficient Non-interactive Proof Systems for Bilinear Groups. In: Smart, N.P. (ed.) EUROCRYPT 2008. LNCS, vol. 4965, pp. 415–432. Springer, Heidelberg (2008)
7. Lukjanov, V.S., Cherkovasky, I.V., Skakunov, A.V., Bykov, D.V.: Model of computer networks with certification centres: monograph, p. 242. VSTU, Volgograd (2009)
8. Maffei, M., Pecina, K.: Position Paper: Privacy-Aware Proof-Carrying Authorization. In: Proc. ACM SIGPLAN Workshop on Programming Languages and Analysis for Security (PLAS 2011) (2011)
9. Maffei, M., Reinert, M.: Security and Privacy by Declarative Design. In: 2013 IEEE 26th Computer Security Foundations Symposium (CSF) (2013)
10. Chumak, A.A., Ukustov, S.S., Kravets, A.G., Voronin, J.F.: Social Networks Message Posting Support Module. World Applied Sciences Journal 24, 191–195 (2013)

Algorithms of Ranking and Classification
of Software Systems Elements

Irina Kosmacheva[1], Irina Kvyatkovskaya[2], Irina Sibikina[1], and Yuliya Lezhnina[2]

[1] Astrakhan State Technical University, Department of Information Security, Russia
ikosmacheva@mail.ru, isibikina@bk.ru
[2] Astrakhan State Technical University, Department of Information Technology, Russia
I.Kvyatkovskaya@astu.org, lejninau@mail.ru

Abstract. Algorithms of ranking of software systems elements are considered. Usually, there is a large number of indicators on the base of which the software systems elements are ranked; and these indicators are measured in different scales. Experts with subjective perception to some extent often estimate the indicators. Ranking algorithms using meta parameters in conditions of lack of information, as well as algorithm of fuzzy ranking of element enable to formalize the decision support processes for software engineering. The developed algorithm of fuzzy ranking data types within a single scale using standard fuzzy classifier for categorizing competencies of objects.

Keywords: Ranking algorithms, competence, expert estimates, factor set.

1 Introduction

One of the major problems of information development of Russia at the present stage is the estimating and selection of technology of software engineering. In order to choose the techniques with best performance characteristics software developers are forced to deal with choice of the means and technology of the process improve; identifying a set of performance values, which should be achieved for successful certification; gathering the necessary data and using of trails criteria for evaluation functionality and quality, etc. When we analyze the results of the evaluation and the selection criteria are applied, it may be recommended to acquire technology. If there is no suitable technology, in this case, it is recommended to develop a new technology, to modify an existing one or to refuse from the implementation.

In this way, there are tasks of selecting and ranking criteria, definition of technology candidates, collecting the necessary data, and the use of criteria for evaluation to identify the tools with the best indicators. For example, the combination of economic and environmental factors can be expressed by taking into account such factors as: minimal labour intensity for software development; maximal productivity; best quality of the software to be developed; investments compensation; minimal expenses for the software support; minimal time of introduction of software and hardware; minimal expenses for introduction of software and hardware; minimal period of compensation for introduction of software and hardware.

A. Kravets et al. (Eds.): JCKBSE 2014, CCIS 466, pp. 400–409, 2014.

The issues of classification, ranking and selection of technology of the software development require science-based approach. There is a large number of indicators on the base of which the software systems elements are ranked; and these indicators are measured in different scales. However, the ranking algorithms and classification of objects, based on the methods of multi-choice and decision theory, are used in most management tasks. Problems of this type are related to the objectives of decision making under risk and uncertainty. The usefulness of the decision depends on various external random factors: for example, information about integration with existing means, including both integration with each other and their integration with the software development and exploitation in an organization. Many of the criteria relating to future periods often can only be evaluated subjectively (e.g., expected needs in teaching; resources used during and after transition to the new software, possible risks related to implementation of the plan etc.) and often depend largely on expert evaluations. Utility matrix describ the situation of choice under uncertainty or risk (while setting probabilistic characteristics of environmental conditions). Special role in decision-making belongs to the relation between a decision-making person (DMP) and the level of his/ her awareness for decision-making.

2   Materials and Methods

Let us consider the cases of changes in knowledge of DMP in the evaluation of objects when moving from DMB's total uncertainty in the choice to partial one, and then - to the change in the class of problems. Let us use the definitions of DMP with varying degrees of awareness, imposed by Yu. V. Kandyrin [1-3]. *Poorly informed* DMP has the opportunity to highlight the quality indicators for the evaluation of alternatives, but finds it difficult to choose priorities among them. *Mid-informed* DMP is able to allocate a set of quality indicators and to set priorities among them in the adopted super-system meta-indicators of quality. *Well informed* DMP is able to single out quality indicators and to set priorities among them. In the first case for poorly informed DMP Pareto or Slater criterion is used, allowing to separate linearly ordered layers of non-dominated alternatives.

Let us introduce the concept of competence of a participiant, which is a formal description of a system that is suitable for the measurement of the two states of objects in retrospective and future periods: the party is potential to perform a given basic project (BP); the result of this BP. In the first case, Pareto or Slater criterion is used for mid-informed DMB, allowing to separate linearly ordered layers of non-dominated alternatives. The use of the notion of competence can decompose many farmers into groups with similar characteristics, solving one of the problems of decision theory - the task of classification.

For such a solution, it is possible to perform the so-called line bundle of alternative classes. If object competences are evaluated by means of quantitative or qualitative data to determine the quasi-linear order of the objects, using Pareto layers. This is determined by the selection function $C^P(OBJ)$ on the principle of Pareto. For this purpose the first layer is defined $OBJ^1 = CP(OBJ)$, the second one: $OBJ^2 = OBJ \backslash CP(OBJ \backslash OBJ^1)$, the third one $OBJ^3 = OBJ \backslash CP(OBJ \backslash OBJ^1 \backslash OBJ^2)$, P-layer: $OBJ^P = OBJ \backslash CP(OBJ \backslash OBJ^1 \backslash ... OBJ^P-1)$, until $|OBJ^P| \neq 0$. In order to separate a subset of non-dominated elements, any of option functions can be used that separates alternatives, obviously belonging to Pareto multiplicity [4]: n-circular tournament selection function or option function taking into account the dominant criteria.

To solve the problem of object ranking under the conditions of low awareness, two algorithms are available: an algorithm that uses algebraic methods for expert information processing, based on the introduction of the distance between the estimates; the algorithm of fuzzy rating, bringing the entire ranking system to a single metric scale with the use of fuzzy multiplicities. Both algorithms utilize a preference table (Table 1), that joins estimates n of criteria $Komp_i$, $i=\overline{1,n}$ with objects Obj_j, $j=\overline{1,m}$. Each i-row of the table contains estimates of i-criterion for n objects: $Komp_i(Obj_j)= K_i(Obj_j) = (K_{i,1}, K_{i,2}, \ldots K_{i,m})$, $i=\overline{1,n}$.

Table 1. Table of expert estimates

	Obj_1	Obj_2	...	Obj_m
$Komp_1$	$K_{1,1}$	$K_{1,2}$	...	$K_{1,m}$
...	...	...	...	...
$Komp_n$	$K_{n,1}$	$K_{n,2}$	...	$K_{n,m}$

Examination of object criteria involves employees of higher levels of the hierarchy of management: representatives of industry, economists, computer programmers and managers. Each of them performs the expertise in his/ her own scale, which makes post-processing and analysis of results difficult, so the proposed algorithm makes use of transition to a uniform ordinal scale [5].

2.1   Algorithm of Object Ranking with Unordered Competencies

Let us describe the necessary elements for this algorithm:

$A_1=\{Metr1, Ind1, Alg1, Int1\}$, where $Metr1 = \{$any ordinal scales$\}$; $Ind1^{Inp} = \|Komp_i(Obj_j)\|$, $i=\overline{1,n}$, $j=\overline{1,m}$; $Alg1 = \{$algorithms for solving problems of allocation: Hungarian algorithm, Mack method; calculation of weights according to Fishburn rule$\}$; $Int1^{Out} = \{i_1, i_2, \ldots, i_m\}$ – object ranking in terms of preference decrease, where i_j – number of j-object in the ranking.

Algorithm Description

1. Let's evaluate all the assessments of object competences in an ordinal scale and determine whether preference may be evaluated with ranks.
2. For each i-row of the table let's set preference vector $\lambda^i=(\lambda_{i,1}, \lambda_{i,2}, \ldots, \lambda_{i,m})$, whose each element $\lambda_{i,j}$ shows, in terms of what number of estimates j-element of vector K_i is more preferable than all the m estimates of this vector.
3. Let's join all the acquired n of rankings $\Lambda=\{\lambda^1, \lambda^2, \ldots, \lambda^n\}$, into the matrix Λ, whose columns correspond with expert assessments of each object $\Pi=\{\pi^1, \pi^2, \ldots, \pi^m\}$ and are evaluated with ranks.

4. Let's develop a matrix $R = \{ r_{kl} \}$, where $r_{kl} = d(\pi^k, \pi\varepsilon^l)$, $k = \overline{1,m}, l = \overline{1,m}$, The value r_{kl}, characterizes "disagreement" of experts with the set of i alternative on j-position in the resulting ranking. any vector preferences, in which k -alternative consistently takes place from the first to the last, it is distance between the rankings, defined with the formula of Kemeny-Snell median.

5. Let's find out the final ranking $\lambda_0 = Arg \min\limits_{\lambda \in \Lambda} \sum\limits_{i=1}^{n} d(\lambda, \lambda^i)$.

6. Let's solve the problem of allocation, reduced to the minimization of a functional:

$$\sum_{k=1}^{m}\sum_{l=1}^{m} r_{k,l} \cdot x_{k,l} \to \min, \ \sum_{k=1}^{m} x_{k,l} = 1, \sum_{l=1}^{m} x_{k,l} = 1, x_{k,l} \geq 0, \tag{1}$$

where X – binary matrix of allocations:

$$x_{k,l} = \begin{cases} 1, & \text{if } k - \text{object takes the } l - \text{place,} \\ 0, & \text{otherwise.} \end{cases} \tag{2}$$

7. Analyzing X, we'll acquire ranking $\{i_1, i_2, \ldots, i_m\}$, where i_j shows the rank of j-object.

8. Using Fishburn weighting scheme, we will define coefficients of preference for each object, comparing decreasing sequence of priorities of objects i_j and the system of decreasing, according to the rule of arithmetic progression, weights w_j. If a mixed system of preferences is available, object weights are defined in the form of a rational function:

$$w_j = \frac{u_j}{V}, j = \overline{1,m}, \tag{3}$$

where numerator u_j is defined according to recursion scheme:

$$u_{j-1} = \begin{cases} u_j, & \text{if } i_{j-1} = i_j \\ u_j + 1, & \text{if } i_{j-1} > i_j \end{cases}, \quad u_m = 1, j = \overline{m,2}; \tag{4}$$

Common denominator of all Fishburn functions is determined according to the formula:

$$V = \sum_{j=1}^{m} u_j. \tag{5}$$

2.2   Algorithm of Fuzzy Object Ranking

Let's describe the necessary elements for this algorithm:

$A_2 = \{Metr2, Ind2, Alg2, Int2\}$, where $Metr2 = \{$any ordinal scales$\}$; $Ind2^{Inp} = \|Komp_i(Obj_j)\|$, $i = \overline{1,n}$, $j = \overline{1,m}$; $Alg2 = \{$transform algorithm $\|Komp_i(Obj_j)\|$ to linguistic scale with function F_{np}}; $Ind2^{Out}$= {i_1, i_2,..., i_m} – object ranking in terms of decreasing preference, where i_j – the number of j-object in the ranking; $Int2$ = {RK} – non-vector integral indicator. The algorithm is applied when transition from heterogeneous ordinal scales to a single evaluation system of qualitative and quantitative ratings, based on fuzzy evaluation system, is necessary [6].

Algorithm Description

1. Transform data from different ordinal scales to a single scale of ratios using a transform function F_{np}, whose form is defined by an expert. F_{np} characterizes the degree of quality manifested, using linguistic gradations, for example, using a five-factor classifier {«Very High», «High», «Middle», «Low», «Very Low»}, which sets multiplicity {"VH", "H", "M", "L", "VL"}.
2. Define linguistic variable as a sequence ⟨β, T, D⟩, where β– the title of linguistic variable «Value of object competence»; T– multiplicity {"VH", "H", "M", "L", "VL"}; D_β– universal fuzzy variables, included in the linguistic variable β To determine the linguistic variable, trapezoidal or triangular membership functions should be applied.
3. Define competence value with onto function F_{np} : $K_i \rightarrow [0,1]=\mu_\beta(K_i)$, where K_i– indicator in the ranking; β– described linguistic gradation of the degree of competence expressiveness and estimates from the rank [0, 1], corresponding to it. Set finite fuzzy relation $Q_H=\{K,\mu_{Qh}(K)\}$ as a matrix form.
4. Define β in the premise that the quality of all indicators increases linearly with the increase in the indicator value (Table 2).

Table 2. Linguistic gradation of quality

N	B_n	$D_\beta=[a;b]$	$\mu_\beta(d)$
1	Very high	[0,65;0,8]	$f(x;a,b)=\begin{cases}0, x \le a \\ (x-a)/(b-a), a \le x \le b \\ 1, x \ge b\end{cases}$
2	High	[0,5;0,8]	$f_\Delta(x;a,b,c)=\begin{cases}0, x \le a \\ (x-a)/(b-a), a \le x \le b \\ (c-z)/(c-b), b \le x \le c \\ 0, x \ge c\end{cases}, b=(a+c)/2$
3	Middle	[0,35;0,65]	$f_\Delta(x;a,b,c)=\begin{cases}0, x \le a \\ (x-a)/(b-a), a \le x \le b \\ (c-z)/(c-b), b \le x \le c \\ 0, x \ge c\end{cases}, b=(a+c)/2$
4	Low	[0,2;0,5]	$f_\Delta(x;a,b,c)=\begin{cases}0, x \le a \\ (x-a)/(b-a), a \le x \le b \\ (c-z)/(c-b), b \le x \le c \\ 0, x \ge c\end{cases}, b=(a+c)/2$

Table 2. (*continued*)

5	Very low	[0,2;0,35]	$f(x;a,b) = \begin{cases} 0, x \le a \\ (b-x)/(b-a), a \le x \le b \\ 1, x \ge b \end{cases}$

Rank the objects Obj_1, Obj_2, ..., Obj_m using the acquired assessment matrix M. For example, to aggregate obtained values of competencies of i-object into a non-vector indicator using the integral function and weights, assigned by experts. The base values K for each term of a linguistic variable are proposed: Very high – 0,8; High – 0,65; Middle – 0,5; Low – 0,35; Very low – 0,2. The weight values correspond to the points where the membership function for each term of a linguistic variable takes the value of one. The aggregate value of the index is determined by the formula:

$$RK_{i,j} = \sum_{l=1}^{kt} \kappa_l \cdot \mu_l(K_{i,j}),$$ (6)

where kt– number of terms of a linguistic variable; K_l – parameter of weight of l-term; μ_l– value of membership function for l-term.
5. Calculate complex value of the ranking:

$$RK_j = \sum_{i=1}^{n} c_i \cdot RK_{i,j}$$ (7)

where c_i – weight of i-competence, which is equal to 1 only in case if all of them are equally significant.
6. Order the objects in terms of descending ranking RK.

2.3 Algorithms of Ranking of Software Development Technology Using Meta-indicators under Conditions of Partial Knowledge

Let us consider the case of partial awareness of DMB, who only has an idea of the priorities of competencies in terms of the super-system, or the priorities assigned to the higher level of the hierarchy of elements. The proposed algorithm establishes a partial order of objects by recursive procedures for ordering.

$A_3 = \{Metr3, Ind3, Alg3, Int3\}$, where $Metr3 = \{n$ of ordinal scales$\}$; $Ind3^{Inp}$ = relation data model $\|Komp_i(Obj_j)\|$, $i = \overline{1,n}$, $j = \overline{1,m}$; set of meta-indicators $\{ K_1, K_2\}$; $Alg3 = \{\pi$-rule, L-rule$\}$, $Ind3^{Out} = \{\{i_1, i_2,..., i_m\}$, where i_j – number of j-object in the ranking $\}$.

Algorithm Description

1. Define a set of competencies $Komp_1$, ..., $Komp_n$, which are used to compare the objects from the set $OBJ=\{Obj_1, ..., Obj_m\}$.
2. Select composite indexes (K_1, K_2) and find coordinates of each competence on the subspace OK_1K_2.

3. Build n linear orders $L(OBJ/Komp_i)$.
4. Determine by an expert the coordinates of competencies in the space of super-system indexes (K_1, K_2).
5. Develop associative matrixes of factor sets AM_i, $i = \overline{1, n}$ for each linear order in the form of (Table 3):

Table 3. Associative matrix AM for factor set F_{OBJ}/K_i of linear order $L(OBJ/K_i)$

Objects/Nhoods	$O_1(Obj_1)$	$O_2(Obj_2)$	...	$O_m(Obj_m)$
Obj_1	0			
Obj_2		0		
...	...	...	...	
Obj_m				0

Each column sets the nhood $O_j(Obj_j)$ of j-object, $j = \overline{1, m}$, and includes a set of all dominant and equivalent objects for this object Obj_j.

$$am_{i,j} = \begin{cases} 1, & \text{if } i - \text{var} iant \text{ is included in the nhood of } j - object , \\ 0, & otherwise \end{cases} \tag{8}$$

6. Develop a quasi-linear order of competences, using Pareto layers. Divide the initial set of n competencies into p layers: $KOMP_1$, ..., $KOMPp$. For all the competences of one Pareto layer find the intersection of associative matrixes by **π-rule**[2]: Assume that a set of numbers of competencies within the p-layer of the Pareto $\{i_1,...,i_{/KOMPpl}\}$ is set
$F=F_{OBJ}/\{KOMP_{i1},...,KOMP_{i/KOMPpl}\}=F_{OBJ}/\{KOMP_{i1}\}\cap...\cap\Phi_{OBJ}/\{KOMP_{i/KOMPpl}\}$.
7. L-rule allows determining the indiscernibility of objects under the conditional L-criterion. In order to do this, compare the hood of indiscernible objects within the original associative matrixes AM_i: If $am^i_{j*,k*}=am^i_{k*,j*}=1$, $j^* \in \{1,...,m\}$, $k^* \in \{1,...,m\}$, then $am_{j*,k*}$ – indiscernible element. By L-rule all the elements of AM matrix are transferred in the resulting matrix, which correspond to factor set F, except for indiscernible elements on whose place the result of the conjunction of a given element $am^i_{j*,k*}$ is fitted into the resulting matrix and matrix element which corresponds to factor F.
8. The resulting matrix determines a strict ranking of objects.

Let's Consider the Application of This Algorithm on a Specific Case Study: An initial set of five software development technology is fixed, for each of which three competencies are selected: "Productivity", "Compatibility with other software technologies", "Costs of implementing of technology" (Table 4). It is necessary to order the objects by competencies ($Komp_1\uparrow, Komp_2\uparrow, Komp_3\uparrow$).

Table 4. Initial data

Objects	$Komp_1\uparrow$	$Komp_2\uparrow$	$Komp_3(mln.\ roubles)\downarrow$
Obj_1	70	90	3,24
Obj_2	85	140	2,45
Obj_3	90	130	1,68
Obj_4	80	60	2,45
Obj_5	60	100	2,6

Solution

1. Select summary meta-indicators of quality: $K_1 = \{\text{Significance}\}$, $K_2 = \{\text{Cost}\}$.
2. Set priorities for competences in the set a space of meta-indicators (Table 5).

Table 5. Initial data

Competences	Coordinates of competences in meta-space $\mathbf{R}^2$	
	$K_1\downarrow$	$K_2\downarrow$
$Komp_1$	1	3
$Komp_2$	2	2
$Komp_3$	1	1

3. Develop linear orders for $Komp_1, Komp_2, Komp_3$: $L(OBJ/Komp_1)=\{Obj_3, Obj_2, Obj_4, Obj_1, Obj_5\}$; $L(OBJ/Komp_2)=\{Obj_2, Obj_3, Obj_5, Obj_1, Obj_4\}$; $L(OBJ/Komp_3)=\{Obj_3, \{Obj_2, Obj_4\}, Obj_5, Obj_1\}$.
4. Build three associative matrixes for each linear order (Table 6, 7, 8).

Table 6. Associative matrix AM1 for factor set F_{OBJ}/K_1

Objects/Nhoods	$O(Obj_1)$	$O(Obj_2)$	$O(Obj_3)$	$O(Obj_4)$	$O(Obj_5)$
Obj_1	0	0	0	0	1
Obj_2	1	0	0	1	1
Obj_3	1	1	0	1	1
Obj_4	1	0	0	0	1
Obj_5	0	0	0	0	0

Table 7. Associative matrix $AM2$ for factor set F_{OBJ}/K_2

Objects/Nhoods	$O(Obj_1)$	$O(Obj_2)$	$O(Obj_3)$	$O(Obj_4)$	$O(Obj_5)$
$Obj1$	0	0	0	1	0
$Obj2$	1	0	1	1	1
$Obj3$	1	0	0	1	1
$Obj4$	0	0	0	0	0
$Obj5$	1	0	0	1	0

Table 8. Associative matrix $AM3$ for factor set F_{OBJ}/K_3

Objects/Nhoods	$O(Obj_1)$	$O(Obj_2)$	$O(Obj_3)$	$O(Obj_4)$	$O(Obj_5)$
Obj1	0	0	0	0	0
Obj2	1	0	0	1	1
Obj3	1	1	0	1	1
Obj4	1	1	0	0	1
Obj5	1	0	0	0	0

5. We will construct a line bundle of competence classes according to Pareto principle of distribution of competences in a given space of meta-indicators: $KOMP=\{Komp_1,Komp_2,Komp_3\}$; $KOMP1=KOMP^P=\{Komp_3\}$; $KOMP2=KOMP\backslash KOMP^P=\{Komp_1,Komp_2\}$. Thus $\pi(KOMP)=\{Komp_3,\{Komp_1,Komp_2\}\}$. The solution begins with $Komp_3$, associative matrix for it has already been built (Table 8), then $Komp_1$ and $Komp_2$ participate, incomparable with each other.

6. Let's build associative matrix $AM12$ (table 9) for factor set $F_{OBJ}/\{K_1, K_2\}$,whose elements are acquired by means of Boolean conjunction over the elements of matrixes $AM1$ and $AM2$: $F_{OBJ}/\{K_1, K_2\} = F_{OBJ}/K_1 \cap F_{OBJ}/K_2$.

Table 9. Associative matrix $AM12$ for factor set $F_{OBJ}/\{K_1, K_2\}$

Objects/Nhoods	$O(Obj_1)$	$O(Obj_2)$	$O(Obj_3)$	$O(Obj_4)$	$O(Obj_5)$
Obj1	0	0	0	0	0
Obj2	1	0	0	1	1
Obj3	1	0	0	1	1
Obj4	1	0	0	0	0
Obj5	0	0	0	0	0

7. We will develop the end set, which establishes the order on OBJ, be means of intersection of matrixes $AM12$ and $AM1$ by L-rule: we will select from matrix $AM3$ indiscernible elements. This is $am3_{24}=am3_{42}=1$. We will figure out the conjunction of elements (2,4) (row 2, column 4) и (4,2), taking the same positing in matrix $AM12$ and $A3$ and enter them into the new matrix $AM123$:

$am123_{24}=am12_{24}\&am3_{24}=1\&1=1$; $am123_{42}=am12_{42}\&am3_{42}=0\&1=0$.

The rest of the elements are indiscernible and are transferred from matrix $A3$ into the end matrix $A123$ (Table 10).

Table 10. End associative matrix

Objects/Nhoods	$O(Obj_1)$	$O(Obj_2)$	$O(Obj_3)$	$O(Obj_4)$	$O(Obj_5)$
Obj1	0	0	0	0	0
Obj2	1	0	0	1	1
Obj3	1	1	0	1	1
Obj4	1	0	0	0	1
Obj5	1	0	0	0	0

8. We will find out with the end matrix the relation of the order: $L(OBJ/\{Komp_1,Komp_2, Komp_3\})=\{ Obj_3, Obj_2, Obj_4, Obj_5, Obj_1\}$. The solution is acquire.

3   Discussion

Studies have shown that in Russia in the management of quality of the software development process there are no practical methods, allowing to carry out the process of decision-making in the tasks: the choice of software development technology for support in the form of grants and investments; to determine the volume of investment for individual companies; to assess the impact of support received; to choose software development technology, which are most typical for a given company. For DMP, who are acting with sufficient awareness, the ability to set priorities among the competencies, algorithms are developed based on the procedures of P-ordering (according to Podinovskiy V.V.) and t-ordering (according to Chernorutskiy I.G.) [10].

4   Conclusion

The above-mentioned approaches and algorithms can be used when creating an information system to support management decision-making in the implementation of technologies for creating software. The objectives of such a system include ranking of technologies for different purposes: the inclusion of the technologies specific for a given organization, the selection for investment support, etc. To solve these problems, characterized by multiple evaluations of objects in different scales of measurement, the results of this work are present.

References

1. Kandyrin, Y.V., Moskovskiy, A.E., Shkurina, G.L.: Methodology of the optimal queuing repairs on the technical characteristics of objects. News of Volgograd State Technical University 2, 110–114 (2007)
2. Kandyrin, Y.V., Kurbatova, E.N.: Conceptual design of data structures for automated selection. News of Volgograd State Technical University 5, 44–46 (2004)
3. Kandyrin, Y.V., Koshelev, A.M.: Automation of multi-structuring alternatives based on their serial ordering. News of Volgograd State Technical University 8(5), 31–36 (2008)
4. Taymaskhanov, K.E.: State support as a mechanism to ensure sustainable development of agriculture in a depressed region (theory, methodology, practice), author's doctoral thesis, Moscow (2011)
5. Barkalov, S.A., Bakunets, O.N., Gureeva, I.V., Kolpachev, V.N., Russman, I.B.: Optimization models of the distribution of investment in the company by type of activity. Institute of Management Problems of the Russian Academy of Sciences 68 (2002)
6. Makarov, I.M., Vinogradskaya, T.M.: The theory of choice and decision-making, p. 328. Nauka, Home Edition Physical and Mathematical Literature, Moscow (1982)
7. Kvyatkovskaya, I.Y.: The theory of decision-making: Manual, Astrakhan State Technical University, p. 100 (2002)
8. Kvyatkovskaya, I.Y.: The line bundle of classes of alternatives to the use of the logical form of the selection function. Bulletin of Astrakhan State Technical University 1(36), 116–119 (2007)
9. Gayrabekova, T.I., Kvyatkovskaya, I.Y.: Formation of rational set of performers of business processes in agriculture. News of Volgograd State Technical University 4(91), 98–103 (2012)
10. Chernorutskiy, I.G.: Decision-making, p. 416. BHV-Petersburg (2005)

Fuzzy and Hierarchical Models for Decision Support in Software Systems Implementations

Vladimir Ivanovich Averchenkov, Vyacheslav Vasilievich Miroshnikov,
Alexander Georgievich Podvesovskiy, and Dmitriy Aleksandrovich Korostelyov

Bryansk State Technical University, Bryansk, Russia
apodv@tu-bryansk.ru

Abstract. The decision models and algorithms for choice of optimal software system configuration have been presented. The generalized choice algorithm includes three stages (and there are three models respectively): a class of system is chosen at the first stage, a type of system is chosen at the second stage, and a particular configuration is chosen at the third one. The Analytic Hierarchy Process (AHP) and the Resources Allocation methods including the AHP as one of their components, underlie the mentioned models. The model and algorithm for choice of class of system have been described for both crisp and fuzzy environments.

Keywords: software system configuration, the Analytic Hierarchy Process, the Resources Allocation Method, fuzzy interval.

1 Introduction

Informatization is the most effective way for industrial development today. That means application of progressive information technologies for automation of design and manufacturing (CAD/CAM/CAE systems), production management (ERP/MRP systems), documents circulation (Workflow systems), etc. Today the software market presents a number of such systems, which differ according to functional possibilities, scale of tasks being solved, requirements to the hardware environment, costs and expenses for maintenance. Therefore, entering the way of informatization, an industrial plant often faces a problem of choosing such a software system and its configuration, which would most satisfy the specific problems of this plant, taking into consideration its financial possibilities. The importance of such a choice being right is predetermined first of all by the fact, that any mistake at this stage may cancel the whole effect of the system introduction, and this may cause significant financial loses for the plant, because of high cost of such systems (in the order of hundreds thousand USD).

A computational methodology for choice of optimal configuration for a software system of any class and type is presented in the paper. Using of this methodology would increase the scientific and technical validity of decisions being made by an

A. Kravets et al. (Eds.): JCKBSE 2014, CCIS 466, pp. 410–421, 2014.

industrial plant while applying of new information technologies, and also would make investments for these purposes less risky. The methodology is based on application of the AHP (Saaty and Vargas, 2001) in combination with elements of fuzzy sets theory (Zimmermann, 2001).

2   The Generalized Algorithm for Choice of Optimal Software System Configuration

The choosing process is carried out in the framework of such taxonomic hierarchical structure of software systems as "family – class – type – configuration". At the same time it is subject to the framework of a certain family of systems. In other words, configurations can be chosen among the family of either CAD/CAM/CAE or ERP/MRP or Workflow systems, etc. Next, for example the classes of systems from the CAD/CAM/CAE family are "heavy", "medium" and "light". The "heavy" CAD/CAM/CAE systems class contains such types of systems as CATIA, Pro/ENGINEER, UNIGRAPHICS, EUCLID, etc. The methodology being described implies the three-stages approach for the choosing process. A class of system is chosen at the first stage, a type of system is chosen at the second stage, and a particular configuration is chosen at the third one. This approach is shown in fig. 1 as a generalized choice algorithm scheme.

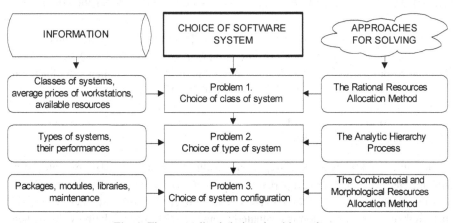

Fig. 1. The generalized choice algorithm scheme

The kind of informational environment (crisp or fuzzy) for the problem is taken into consideration in the frameworks of this algorithm. Therefore the descriptions of the particular stages are given separately for crisp and fuzzy cases.

3   The Choice of Optimal Decision in Crisp Environment

3.1   The Choice of Class of System

The developed by the authors mathematical model for this stage is based on the method of Rational Resources Allocation (Andreychikov and Andreychikova, 2013). According to this model, the problem for choice of class of system can be formalized as follows. Let A j (j = 1, ..., k) be the names for the classes of software systems belonging to a certain family. Let Z be the minimal total number of workplaces necessary for the plant, P be the available financial resources, dj be the average price of one workplace for the system of the class A j. It is required to find the i-th combination of the classes {A j} and the numbers of workplaces m_{ji} in that combination, so that the following objective function would be maximized:

$$Q_i = \left(E(C_{ni}^k) \big/ D(C_{ni}^k) \right) \to \max ,$$ (1)

where Qi is the efficiency degree for the software system per price unit, C_{ni}^k is the i-th combination of classes containing n classes of the system among k possible classes (i.e. it is a certain set containing n classes, and being a subset for the given set containing k classes, n ≤ k), $E(C_{ni}^k)$ is the functionality degree for the combination

C_{ni}^k, and $D(C_{ni}^k)$ is price of this combination. The following requirements have to be satisfied as well: 1) The price of any combination must not exceed the available financial resources; 2) No combination may contain identical elements; 3) Each pair of combinations must differ in at least one element; 4) The whole set of combinations must contain all the unary, binary, ternary, etc. combinations of classes; 5) The total number of workplaces for all the classes forming any combination must not be less than minimally possible value Z.

The functionality degrees $E(C_{ni}^k)$ are evaluated using the AHP by calculating with the help of pairwise comparison matrix (PCM) the vector of priorities for all possible combinations of existing classes. The number m_{ji} of workplaces of the j-th class in their i-th combination is evaluated using the AHP by calculating with the help of PCMs the vectors of priorities for various percentage ratios of workplaces numbers in each possible combination of classes.

The optimal solution for the above-formalized problem is found among all the combinations of classes by means of exhaustive search. Additionally, various percentage ratios of workplaces numbers (with respect to their priorities) are looked through while examining each binary, ternary, etc. combinations of classes. The search algorithm has the following steps:

1. The initial set of alternatives is formed. It must include all possible combinations of classes for the given family of systems. The total number of these combinations is:

$$A = k! / (n!(k-n)!)$$
$$(2)$$

For instance if the number of existing classes k = 3 then there are the following combinations:

$$C_{11}^3 = A_1, \quad C_{12}^3 = A_2, \quad C_{13}^3 = A_3, \quad C_{24}^3 = A_1 A_2, \quad C_{25}^3 = A_1 A_3, \quad C_{26}^3 = A_2 A_3,$$
$$C_{37}^3 = A_1 A_2 A_3$$
$$(3)$$

2. The PCM for the obtained set of alternatives is formed, and the vector of priorities is evaluated:

$$W_n^k = (w_1, ..., w_A),$$
$$(4)$$

where A is defined by (2). The elements wi of this vector are just the functionality degrees $E(C_{ni}^k)$ for the corresponding combinations of classes. For instance if k=3 then we will have:

$$E(C_{11}^3) = w_1, \quad E(C_{12}^3) = w_2, \quad E(C_{13}^3) = w_3,$$

$$E(C_{24}^3) = w_4, \quad E(C_{25}^3) = w_5, \quad E(C_{26}^3) = w_6, \quad E(C_{27}^3) = w_7.$$
$$(5)$$

3. The numbers m_{ji} of workplaces is determined for each class in every combination, subject to the requirement 5, i.e.

$$\sum_{j=1}^{k} m_{ji} \geq Z; \ i = 1, ..., A$$
$$(6)$$

For each unary combination we can set $m_{ji}=Z$ if the i-th combination is represented by the class A j, and $m_{ji}=0$ otherwise. In case of binary, ternary and other combinations we can evaluate m_{ji} by AHP in the following way: The subset containing all the combinations except unary ones is separated out of the initial set of alternatives. The number of elements in that subset is A–k. Let α_{ji} be the relative number (percentage) of the workplaces for the class A j in the i-th combination. It is obvious that:

$$\sum_{j=1}^{k} \alpha_{ji} = 100 \tag{7}$$

A PCM is formed for every combination belonging to that subset. The object for comparison is the acceptability (for the plant) of various percentage ratios of workplaces numbers for different classes. For instance if k=3 then we have four matrices (i=4; 5; 6; 7), and each of them is aimed at comparing acceptability of various values for the following kinds of ratios (respectively):

$$(\alpha_{14}/\alpha_{24})_{A_1 A_2}, \quad (\alpha_{15}/\alpha_{35})_{A_1 A_3},$$

$$(\alpha_{26}/\alpha_{36})_{A_2 A_3}, \quad (\alpha_{17}/\alpha_{27}/\alpha_{37})_{A_1 A_2 A_3}. \tag{8}$$

For example the expression $(\alpha_{14}/\alpha_{24})_{A_1 A_2} = 10/90$ means that the combination $C_{24}^3 = A_1 A_2$ contains 10 % workplaces of the class A1 and 90 % workplaces of the class A 2. Another example, the expression $(\alpha_{17}/\alpha_{27}/\alpha_{37})_{A_1 A_2 A_3} = 5/10/85$ means that the combination $C_{37}^3 = A_1 A_2 A_3$ contains 5 % workplaces of the class A 1, 10 % workplaces of the class A 2, and 85 % workplaces of the class A 3.

The priority vectors corresponding to each of the described matrices are evaluated. The values of components for a certain vector determine preferences of different percentage ratios for numbers of workplaces of different classes in their particular combination. As a result, we can find the most preferable percentage ratio for every combination. The corresponding absolute values m_{ji} can be calculated using the formula:

$$m_{ji} = r\left(Z \cdot \alpha_{ji}/100\right), \tag{9}$$

where r(x) means rounding of x to the nearest greater integer (this keeps the condition (6) satisfied).

4. At this step the obtained values m_{ji} are checked for satisfying the requirement 5 connected with the total price of the system. In other words, the following condition is checked:

$$D(C_{ni}^k) = \sum_{j=1}^{k} d_j m_{ji} \leq P; \quad i=1,...,A \tag{10}$$

The set of feasible alternatives is formed as the result of that check. An alternative, represented by only one class, is considered to be feasible if it satisfies the condition (10); in this case the sum in (10) has only one non-zero component. An alternative, represented by binary, ternary, etc. combination of classes must be also checked for satisfying the condition (10), and if the alternative does not, the next percentage ratio (respect to decreasing of the priorities) is taken: the new values m_{ji} are obtained using (9), and the corrected in this manner alternative is checked for satisfying (10) again, etc. It can be shown that the set of feasible alternatives is not empty if and only if the following condition holds:

$$d_* \cdot Z \leq P, \tag{11}$$

where d_* is the minimal element in the set $\{d_j \mid j=1, ..., k\}$ (i.e. it is the price of the cheapest workplace).

5. Now we can find the optimal solution for the problem connected with choice of class of system. The optimal solution is found among the feasible solutions using the formula (1). The obtained solution should be drawn up as a specification containing the classes having been chosen and numbers of workplaces determined for each class.

3.2   The Choice of Type of System

We solve this problem by direct using of the AHP. The solving algorithm has the following steps:

1. The initial set of alternatives $\{A_1, A_2, ..., A_n\}$ is formed. Each alternative represents a certain type of software systems for the class having been chosen at the previous stage.
2. The hierarchy having several levels is constructed. The highest (nearest to the root) level contains a set of group criteria $\{Q_1, ..., Q_K\}$, the next one contains a set of criteria $\{Q_{11}, ..., Q_{1m}; ...; Q_{K1}, ..., Q_{Kl}\}$ detailing the corresponding group criteria, etc. For instance, the following two-level hierarchy can be used for CAD/CAM/CAE systems of the "heavy" class: the higher level of this hierarchy contains nine generalzied criteria ($K = 9$): $Q_1 = $ "User Interface", $Q_2 = $ "User Support", $Q_3 = $ "Geometric Data Exchange", $Q_4 = $ "Geometric Modelling", $Q_5 = $ "Design Documentation", $Q_6 = $ "Applied Tasks", $Q_7 = $ "Programming for Numerical Control Machines", $Q_8 = $ "Database Management System", $Q_9 = $ "Reverse Engineering". A certain set of the particular criteria from the lower level corresponds to each of the above-mentioned criteria from the higher level. For example, the criteria corresponding to Q_4 ("Geometric Modelling") are: $Q_{41} = $ "Skeleton Modelling", $Q_{42} = $ "Surface Modelling", $Q_{43} = $ "Solid-state Modelling", $Q_{44} = $ "Parametric Modelling", $Q_{45} = $ "Preliminary Designing", $Q_{46} = $ "Assembly Designing", $Q_{47} = $ "Associative Connections between Details".
3. The vectors of priorities for alternatives respect to the last but one hierarchy level are calculated by forming and processing the corresponding PCMs. The PCMs for remaining hierarchy levels are processed analogously, and the priorities for the elements of a certain hierarchy level respect to the higher level elements being

connected with them are calculated. Thus, we get the set of all priority vectors generated by the existing hierarchy.

4. The synthesis is executed, that means successive calculation of priorities for alternatives respect to the elements belonging to all the hierarchy levels. This process has the direction from the lower hierarchy levels to the higher ones, subject to the particular connection mode between elements of adjacent levels. The ultimate aim is evaluating the priorities of alternatives respect to the root element of the hierarchy.

3.3   The Choice of Configuration for a Workplace

The developed by the authors mathematical model for this stage is based on the Combinatorial and Morphological Resources Allocation method (Andreichicov and Andreichicova, 2000). The model is underlain by the idea of using a morphological table, the structure of which is shown in Fig. 2. This table describes a set of possible configurations for a software system of a certain type in compact and clear form.

Component parts for configurations		ALTERNATIVES (A_{ij})			
Names	Specifications				
Part 1	Alternatives (A_{ij})	A_{11}	A_{12}	...	$A_{1\,kl}$
	Efficiency (E_{ij})	E_{11}	E_{12}	...	$E_{1\,kl}$
	Price (d_{ij})	d_{11}	d_{12}	...	$d_{1\,kl}$
	Quantity (z_{ij})	z_{11}	z_{12}	...	$z_{1\,kl}$
Part 2	Alternatives (A_{ij})	A_{21}	A_{22}	...	$A_{2\,k2}$
	Efficiency (E_{ij})	E_{21}	E_{22}	...	$E_{2\,k2}$
	Price (d_{ij})	d_{21}	d_{22}	...	$d_{2\,k2}$
	Quantity (z_{ij})	z_{21}	z_{22}	...	$z_{2\,k2}$
...					
Part n	Alternatives (A_{ij})	A_{n1}	A_{n2}	...	$A_{n\,km}$
	Efficiency (E_{ij})	E_{n1}	E_{n2}	...	$E_{n\,km}$
	Price (d_{ij})	d_{n1}	d_{n2}	...	$d_{n\,km}$
	Quantity (z_{ij})	z_{n1}	z_{n2}	...	$z_{n\,km}$

Fig. 2. The structure for morphological table of configurations

According to fig.2, a workplace configuration has the following structure:

1. There is a set of component parts (subsystems, units, details, modules, packages, etc.), determined by their names. Let n be the total number of the available component parts.
2. Each component part is determined by three sets of specifications: efficiency (E_{ij}), price (d_{ij}) and quantity (z_{ij}). The efficiency is evaluated by the AHP similarly to the efficiency evaluating for the types of system (see 2.3). The sources of information

about the prices are vendors' price-lists. The quantity is determined by the functional characteristics of the systems.

3. Each component part is realized by a finite set of alternatives A_{ij}. The maximum value $(k_1, k_2, \ldots, k_m)$ of the column index j here is different for each row i.

Thus, the configuration choice problem for the software system of a certain type can be formalized in the following way. Assume the morphological table of configurations has been set (with the similar structure to the one shown in Fig. 2). Let R be the highest allowed price for configurations. It is required to find a combination {Aij} of alternatives, so that the following objective function would be maximized:

$$Q = \left(\sum_{i=1}^{n} E_{i\,j(i)} \middle/ \sum_{i=1}^{n} d_{i\,j(i)} \cdot z_{i\,j(i)} \right) \to \max \tag{12}$$

The following requirements have to be satisfied here:

1. The price of any combination must not exceed the specified upper limit, i.e.

$$\sum_{i=1}^{n} d_{i\,j(i)} \cdot z_{i\,j(i)} \leq R \tag{13}$$

2. Each combination must include an alternative A_{ij} from every row of the morphological table respect to the specified quantity z_{ij}. This requirement is rather strong and in some situations it may be weakened. For example, in case of limited financial resources it may be sometimes impossible to allocate the latter among all the rows of the morphological table. In such cases the following requirement should be used instead of the current one: 2a) Each combination should include an alternative from a certain subset of the morphological table rows respect to the specified quantity z_{ij}.

The algorithm for the specified configuration choice problem has the following steps: 1) Form the morphological table; 2) Specify the highest allowed price for configurations; 3) Form the set of all possible combinations of alternatives, using exhaustive search, respect to the condition 2 or 2a; 4) Calculate the total price for each obtained combination, and check if the condition (13) is satisfied. Thus, the set of feasible solutions is formed; 5) Find the optimal solution among the feasible ones using the formula (12). The obtained structure of optimal configuration should be drawn up as a specification to a contract for the sale of software system of the chosen type.

4 The Choice of Optimal Decision in Fuzzy Environment

The above-described models and algorithms for optimal decision choice correspond to the case when all the initial data for the choice problem are well-defined and exactly known. But this usually does not occur. First, limits for price of software system and for number of workplaces are usually not strict enough – the sets of allowed values for those parameters have usually vague bounds; the last fact may have interpretation of different preference levels for different values. Second, values of many parameters characterizing a software system are often uncertain (the average price of workplace is good example here). The information about those values is usually available in the form of expert judgements, which are often expressed in linguistic form. Thus, the initial mathematical model for the choice problem has to be adapted for taking into account uncertainty and ambiguity of initial information. The mathematical conception of fuzzy sets, fuzzy numbers and linguistic variables (Zimmermann, 2001) seems to be the most effective here.

We will view here the way for fuzzification of the model for choice of class of system, described in 3.1. For the sake of simplicity we will assume that only the desired price of a software system P and the average price of workplace dj (see 3.1) are fuzzy. Additionally, let the values of the parameter dj be estimated by experts in linguistic form using expressions like these: "high", "medium", "low", "not very high", "more or less low", etc. We will use fuzzy numbers or fuzzy intervals generalizing them (Dubois and Prade, 1979) for formalization of fuzzy values. According to its definition, fuzzy interval is fuzzy subset of the real line with membership function having the following structure:

$$\mu_C(x) = \begin{cases} L_C(x), a_0 \leq x \leq a_1, \\ 1, a_1 < x < b_1 \\ R_C(x), b_1 \leq x \leq b_0, \\ 0, \text{ otherwise} \end{cases} \qquad (14)$$

where L_C, R_C are piecewise-continuos functions such that L_C increases in the segment [a0, a1] from $L_C(a0)=0$ to $L_C(a1)=1$, and R_C decreases in the segment [b1, b0] from $R_C(b1)=1$ to $R_C(b0)=0$. If a1=b1 then C is fuzzy number. The functions L_C and R_C are called left and right branches of the membership function of fuzzy interval C respectively. In some cases one branch may be missing (i.e. may be a0=a1 or b1=b0).

Assume the following notation. Let R+ be the set of $(0, \infty)$, $U = [u_*, u^*] \subset R^+$, where u_*, u^* are respectively left and right bounds for the set of all possible prices of the workplaces for a software system of a certain type. We will formalize the values of dj using linguistic variable, and we will define the latter using the conventional structure (Zimmermann, 2001):

$$< L, T(L), U, G, M >, \qquad (15)$$

where L is the name of variable, T(L) is the set of names of its primary linguistic values (terms) with each value being a fuzzy interval defined on the universal set U, G is a syntactic rule for generating the complex terms, and M is a semantic rule for formalizing the latter. In our case L = "Price of Workplace";

T(L) = {"low", "medium", "high"}; the terms are represented in the form of fuzzy intervals on the above-defined set U ⊂ R+. The model for membership functions of the primary terms is shown in fig. 3.

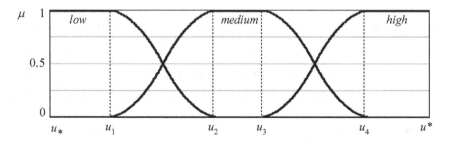

Fig. 3. The primary terms of the linguistic variable *"Price of Workplace"*

The values for u1, u2, u3, u4, and particular form for the branches of the membership functions should be set by experts on the basis of existing information on prices of workplaces for the software system being chosen, taking into account some known from literature recommendations on membership functions constructing. The syntactic rule G allows to generate complex terms subject to the syntactic diagram shown in Fig. 4. The semantic rule M associates concentrating (squaring) with the "very" modifier, dilatation (square rooting) with the "more or less" modifier, and complement with the "not" modifier. It can be shown that under these conditions any complex term will keep the property of being fuzzy interval. So, $dj \in G[T(L)]$, where $G[T(L)]$ is the extended set of terms for the linguistic variable L, containing all possible values of it, and each value is represented by a fuzzy interval on the set U.

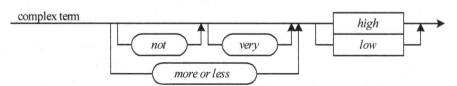

Fig. 4. Syntactic diagram for generating the complex terms

A fuzzy interval on the set R+ is used for representation of the desired price P. The membership function has the structure similar to (14). The degree of membership for a certain value to that interval may be interpreted as degree of acceptability of the corresponding price for the plant. Thus, the prices within the limits of [a1, b1] are fully acceptable, and the prices out of the limits of [a0, b0] are fully inadmissible.

Because of fuzziness of some initial parameters of the problem, the algorithm for its solving (searching for optimal combinations of the classes of system) described in 3.1 is modified as well. Particularly, the 4-th and 5-th steps are modified, and instead of them we have the following steps:

4a) The price for an i-th combination of classes is calculated by the following formula:

$$D(C_{ni}^k) = \sum_{j=1}^{k} d_j m_{ji}$$

$$\text{(16)}$$

Since the values of dj are fuzzy, the using of fuzzy arithmetic (Dubois and Prade, 1979) is necessary in (16). Thus, the value of the price $D(C^{k^{ni}})$ becomes a fuzzy interval as well. The obtained price $D(C_{ni}^k)$ is compared with the desired price P in order to evaluate the acceptability degree for the combination C_{ni}^k with respect to price. The concept for inclusion indices of fuzzy sets (Fuzzy Sets, 1982) can be used here. Assume A and B are arbitrary fuzzy sets on a set X. We take the following index, which evaluates the inclusion degree of A into B.

$$I(A,B) = |A \cap B| / |A|$$

$$\text{(17)}$$

where $|A| = \int_X \mu_A(x)\,dx$, and the used definition for fuzzy intersection is product-oriented (Zimmermann, 2001). We should note the following properties of the above-defined index (Fuzzy Sets, 1982): a) $0 \le I(A, B) \le 1$; b) $I(A, B)=0$ if and only if supp A $\cap$ supp B = $\varnothing$; c) $I(A, B)=1$ if and only if $A \subseteq B1$, where B1 is the core of the set B (i.e. the set of elements which membership degrees are 1); d) if $C \subseteq A$ then $I(C, B) \le I(A, B)$. Due to these properties we can make the following definition for the acceptability degree for an alternative with respect to price:

$$F(C_{ni}^k) = I(D(C_{ni}^k), P)$$

$$\text{(18)}$$

The alternative is considered to be feasible if $F(C_{ni}^k) > 0$. Otherwise, as it was in crisp case, the next percentage ratio (respect to decreasing of the priorities) is taken, and the operations are repeated. It can be shown that the set of feasible alternatives is not empty if and only if the following is true:

$$[Z \cdot u_*, \ Z \cdot u^*] \cap supp\, P \neq \varnothing$$

$$\text{(19)}$$

5a) Unlike in crisp case, we have the acceptability degree for combination of classes with respect to price instead of its price. Therefore, we cannot use directly the objective function (1) for evaluating the efficiency of the feasible alternatives. But if we treat efficiency as a generalized criterion being detailed by the criteria of functionality and acceptability with respect to price, we can use the AHP for efficiency evaluation. In other words, we can construct the hierarchy with these two criteria. We do not need to calculate the priorities of alternatives respect to these criteria, because we already have them: the values of $E(C_{ni}^k)$ have been calculated on the step 2, and the values of $F(C_{ni}^k)$ have been calculated on the step 4a.

5   Conclusion

Using of the AHP in combination with elements of fuzzy sets theory enables to formalize and effectively solve the complicated, multi-objective and ill-defined problem of optimal software system configuration choice and therefore decrease the mistaken decisions and the sequent significant financial loses risk level. The developed decision models and algorithms were tested on different tasks connected with optimal software systems configuration choice (Averchenkov, Podvesovskiy and Brundasov, 2004). In addition, as it was shown in (Averchenkov, Lagerev and Podvesovskiy, 2012), these model are invariant and can be applied for decision support in other problem domains.

References

1. Andreychikov, A.V., Andreychikova, O.N.: System Analysis and Synthesis of Policy Decision in Innovatics. Librokom, Moscow (2013) (in Russian)
2. Averchenkov, V.I., Lagerev, A.V., Podvesovskiy, A.G.: Presentation and Proceedings of Fuzzy Information in Multi-criteria Decision Models for the Problems of Socioeconomic Systems Management. Herald of Bryansk State Technical University 2(34), 97–104 (2012)
3. Averchenkov, V.I., Podvesovskiy, A.G., Brundasov, S.M.: Automation of Multi-criteria Program-technical Decision Choice Based on Semantical Extension Hierarchical and Network Decision Models. Herald of Bryansk State Technical University 1(1), 183–193 (2004)
4. Dubois, D., Prade, H.: Fuzzy Real Algebra: Some Results. Fuzzy Sets and Systems 2, 327–348 (1979)
5. Yager, R.R. (ed.): Fuzzy Sets and Possibility Theory: Recent Developments. Pergamon Press, New York (1982)
6. Saaty, T.L., Vargas, L.G.: Models, Methods, Concepts & Applications of the Analytic Hierarchy Process. Kluwer Academic Publishers, Boston (2001)
7. Zimmermann, H.: Fuzzy set theory and its applications. Kluwer Academic Publishers, Boston (2001)

In Process Homogeneous Object-Binding Structure for Preference Zone Based Decision Making

Daniel Reißner and Wolfram Hardt

Technische Universität Chemnitz, Chemnitz, Germany
{daniel.reissner,wolfram.hardt}@informatik.tu-chemnitz.de

Abstract. This paper leads on research of decision support methods for software engineering. Regulation of temperature for Ensuring of cooling chain, triggering of grouped maintenance tasks, sensor based filling and sorting out of bottles, cutting, positioning, assembling and sorting in in high rack warehouse are typical examples for control decisions in factories. By the favorable technological innovation rate immense numbers of sensors and actors are available in highly complex machine factories. Modern production and quality optimization incorporates complex cooperative not context-aware control commands. To improve energy-efficiency of existing control and logistics systems and to provide context for new complex software engineering solutions, structure, objects and wide and compressed parameter evaluation is required. To improve robustness and quality of logistics solutions we developed idea of a homogeneous object-binding structure for an object-zone-based preference. Preference integrates real-time decision zones, energy zones and a zone-compressed application gradient for self-organization of sensor-actor-tasks.

Keywords: zone-based preference, object-binding, decision making, key-value, energy-efficient, adaptive learning, quality.

1 Introduction

In order to automatically produce goods of high quality in an energy-efficient way, control tasks have to be transferred to production machines to right point in time by maintenance and logistics solutions using context knowledge of factory structure.

Main idea is to create objects by object-binding to provide object-context bound data for maintenance and logistics entities. Thereby binding is applicable to many machines by a generic homogeneous key-value attribute format.

One main focus of factory planning researchers is energy-efficient load distribution and self-organized carrier distribution to on demand usable specialized machines. Homogeneous format allows for generic controlling of such machines while preference integrates homogeneous structure and other parameter to self-organized routing and control decisions.

A Preference of an object is a weighted sum of quality criteria used as comparison criteria between objects in simple case by greedy monotony criteria. Furthermore target formulation, machine learning optimality by preference exchange mechanism,

A. Kravets et al. (Eds.): JCKBSE 2014, CCIS 466, pp. 422–432, 2014.

weighting and update rules have to be considered. Preference allows self-organisation by an application gradient. Furthermore it allows routing under extreme conditions with fluctuation energy levels, signal disturbances and technology breakdowns by exploitation of factory structures. A gateway level takes the load from autarkic sensor network and on highest hierarchy level a centralized server with database is used Fig. 1 [1].

In order to bind sensor data a probabilistic approach is presented which uses a tolerance value [2].

Content management Systems like Joomla [3], Django [4] or bootstrap [5] allow the higher level creation of web applications using predefined objects and template systems.

Social services like Twitter and Facebook enhance simple unstructured common sense message transfers by user preference relevant parameters like likes, number of followers, favourites, retweets-dependencies, hashtag keys and general data about persons.

Mechanical Engineering tool Labview allows for mapping of extern data from wifi or plc to fixed addresses for fixed evaluation.

Object oriented databases allow storing of objects and access via object oriented programming function calls [6].

In sensor network routing target is to reduce overhead of transferring messages to not requiring nodes to save energy for unneeded transmission. Approaches are e. g. formulation of network as dominating set problem or introduction of reliability parameters to reduce sending to all nodes called broadcasts with the problem of possibly not shortest paths any more [7].

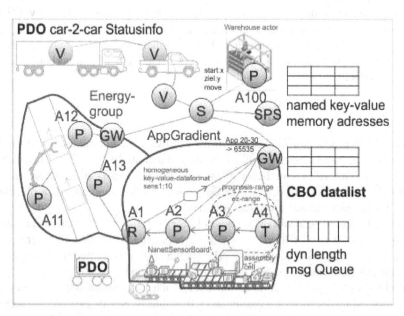

Fig. 1. Hierarchical network (Process node, Technical node, GW Gateway, Server, Vehicle) with carrier belt objects and portal device objects for zone based self-organized preference decisions for data and carrier

2   Homogeneous Object-Binding Structure

An abstract *Object* is defined, which represents data of real world depending on grouping conditions as "key-value" pairs. This way homogeneous object binding structure abstracts classical key-value format to general group-value format allowing for application required individual grouping in objects, by objects (most required groups) and in between of objects. The preference leads the object-data to a decision (forwarding, suggestion generation) on basis of object-progress-bound real word parameters. The groups are described as zones too and may realize hierarchical layers.

The key-value attribute format is as variant of group-value format without group assignment. The group-value format is generic while human readable. Redundancy occurs on useful data for better error correction while saving in special case not required general header overhead. Parameters of current machine stack could be selected fine granular. Parameters of various machines could be easily exchanged without limitations of fixed ordered addresses. Equipment of one machine may miss a sensor which will influence the receiving order. This could be considered and resolved by using such key identifiers across systems.

Decision finding problem is formulated based on preference-based decision making. Decision finding problem is to produce under given parameters p_i of unknown influence strength, a qualitative decision variable called preference P by weighting w_i of parameters: $P = w_1 p_1 + w_2 p_2 + \ldots + w_n p_n$. Thereby required target dependencies e. g. in form of monotony criteria can be as well integrated as generic model-rate-tracking approaches of application area by weight adapting mechanism. In order to lead the parameter to decision variable in a simple, homogeneous and energy-efficient way, parameters are represented in requirement-variable key, variable value count homogeneous object-binding structure. Key information can also only represent a preference and fixed parameters to realize keyless fixed data format without overhead of type variable.

2.1   Factory Object-Binding Preference

In case of big production facilities with many PLCs, for process control over PLC zones arises the requirement to collect the data in a central maintenance instance for coordination. This allows for better maintenance times, carrier distribution and also additional information of security relevant processes for team member outside of factory for fast alerting and resolving of issues.

In order to provide carrier bound data to factory solution an abstract object, *carrier belt object* (CBO) is introduced. The CBO groups data based on node hierarchy of gateway-layer of autarkic sensor network. The data are represented as homogeneous key-value pairs of sensor type and value.

On GW-Layer a preference is introduced, which realizes the object-binding und makes forwarding decisions for carrier and CBO-objects. Sensor data are on reception assigned to a carrier belt object in gateway. The assignment takes place by the preference according to the logic progress of sensor data detection. Furthermore, the preference integrates the timely progress of carrier to estimate the logic progress in case of lost sensor data. This way carrier movement progress dimensions are not missed and estimations for carrier position for data binding are not required.

The logic progress is refined by the detection of PLC (e.g. RFID) aside from the reception of sensor data of nodes. The timely progress is refined by timestamps of sensor nodes, reception times and PLC known belt movement speed. The next target is provided from QR-code part list scans of sensor nodes or from warehouse system. Based on progress model and the next target the GW-level preference determines the next forwarding target for carrier. Furthermore parameters like node disturbances and energy are integrated in preference. Additionally the routing decision of preference leads to forwarding of data to next following gateway.

For energy-efficient data acquisition by the autarkic sensor network, the dimensions of the gateway network are defined by sending power requirements. The resulting energy zones assign far away nodes to the next gateway-level energy-zone by discover timeout request of the far away node.

For reliable transfer, nodes may define real-time zones. These zones are characterised by stable connection paths to current point in time. In case of typical disturbance in wireless networks, the real-time zone may exist furthermore. Therefore in past the now required data had to be sent and a timely buffer for sending of new data is adhered. Additionally, in case of breakdown of areas, preference can evaluate status using real-time zone parameter. This way in dense networks preference may decide to switch to alternative zone or activate a real-time backup technology. On top of the real-time zones fault-tolerant and stable real time paths are constructible and token based guaranteed distribution mechanism is implementable.

The in [1] introduced application gradient can be realized with low memory requirements by mapping to the energy zones Fig. 1. This is deciding, because this way without explicit target address a self-organized routing is realizable by one time distribution of compressed structure.

2.2   Person and University Topics Data Object-Binding Preference

Existing workflow tools like workflow server [9] do not allow view restrictions in explicit order of workflow by possibilities, indirections and spreading of an partial order graph. They organize the workflow itself so one can select a task and required time after finishing the task externally. They do not realize the tasks as web processable GUI to integrate solving the task. Furthermore they only provide generic view and are not able to generate state required dynamic GUI elements as needed, limiting overview possibilities. An integrated solution which allows for object data organisation of topics, students, and supervisors as well as task/workflow organisation by dynamic by property extendable flexible objects was required.

In order to show the simple transferability of homogeneous object binding preference it was applied to person and university topics management system advising next steps in processing student object related group-value data. A preference makes suggestions for next to process keys by user defined preference of editing person and current study progress of student.

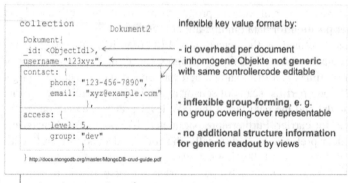

```
collection          Dokument2        infexible key value format by:
  Dokument{
    _id: <ObjectId1>,  ←——————————— - id overhead per document
    username "123xyz",  ←——————————— - inhomogene Objekte not generic
    contact: {                          with same controllercode editable
        phone: "123-456-7890",
        email:  "xyz@example.com"      - inflexible group-forming, e. g.
                        },             no group covering-over representable
    access: {
        level: 5,                      - no additional structure information
        group: "dev"                   for generic readout by views
                }
  }  http://docs.mongodb.org/master/MongoDB-crud-guide.pdf
```

structure extension
+ more flexible more general format redesign

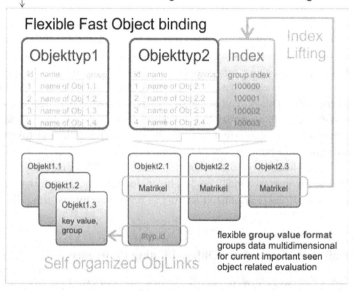

Flexible Fast Object binding

Objekttyp1   Objekttyp2   Index   Index Lifting

flexible group value format
groups data multidimensional
for current important seen
object related evaluation

Self organized ObjLinks

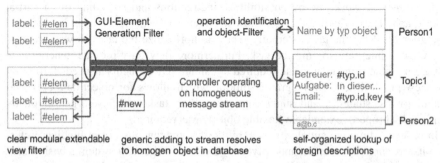

| clear modular extendable view filter | generic adding to stream resolves to homogen object in database | self-organized lookup of foreign descriptions |

Fig. 2. Overview of table realization near concept of homogeneous object binding structure; top: type object allows redundancy reduction for id and indexes by index lifting, bottom: group value format allows very flexible mighty e. g. filtering, self-organized database-update, view-generation from gradient partial order graph operations on homogeneous message stream

Unstructured text like from twitter could be represented as key-value attributes for key words and hash tags stored in person or problem object to organize person data or get problem relevant common sense solutions from preference. Integration of such user preference bases data are under consideration on basis of smartphone bases planning tool.

Homogeneous Object binding structure allows easy changes on level of full access to all functionality. This is often wished by programmers to overcome limitations of architectures for individual realizations. On the other hand by usage of parameterized GUI Objects a higher application specific abstraction and lower editing effort could be provided compared to originalities of predefined encapsulated access methods.

The group value format allowed for flexible dynamic generated web-views integrating self-organized followed object links in a generic controller processing on the homogeneous message stream. This way it could be seen as a structure extension and more flexible format redesign compared to Mongo DB [8] Fig. 2 [9].

Instead of direct filtering on message stream and form generation, frameworks like ckan [10] have a higher integration overhead in their architecture by function overhead, to implement plugins and requirement for many interfaces. Homogeneous object binding structure avoids this overhead by direct working on data, while representing further mechanisms as readable structure e.g. security and access groups. Thereby structure not disturbs in case not required, e.g. resolving value if available but automatic resolving object link if present. Additional groups can be used but must not be considered in simple scenarios. GUIs are fast individual generatable enhanced by attributes for generation but not required attributes or interfaces.

This way programmer do not have to encapsulate functionality, but simply select what he/she want on preference requirements, allowing for low maintainable code and individual requirement GUIs. This is especial useful for faster extending and external framework related update break outs. Thereby programmer can get faster overview of what he has written to extract environmental framework interaction causes for faster and in many cases because of full accessibility of base functionality only so possible resolving. During changes of server and API by TU-Chemnitz Corporate Design Conversion, this way basic loading order requirements of web site content could be adapted to changing server behavior and framework update related CSS displaying issues could be fast identified to the frameworks and by redefinitions resolved.

3   Current Results

A homogeneous key-value object structure for fusion of sensor data was realized using nanett boards (msp430 microcontroller, cc2420 radio chip) Fig 3. Thereby the preference progress decision was supported by detections of barcode and qr-code updates from android-smarthones transfered via bluetooth. The homogeneous key-value format was also used to control a high-bay warehouse Fig. 3. Therefore a node application tranforms the homogeneous key-value requests to value changes at named memory adress keys. The connection to the warehouse was done using TCP. Preference-based robot arm move decisions where tested with simple sorting algorithms (bubble sort, selection sort, Schiebefix, ...). The CBO Structure was realized in Laptops as Gatewaylevel and the database was realized by a WLan accessable service of TU-Chemnitz. From the provided CBO, machine and carrier entities where generated. These Entities were transfered to a GUI-Server Laptop which displayed the high-bay warehouse movements detected by smartphone qr-codes and allowed for generation of homogeneous key-value tasks for Festo warehouse.

In order to access data of Experimentier- und Digitalfabrik an opc client was realized, which bridges the data over local network to a database controller. The database controller sends the opc named adresses as homogeneous message stream to our database for creation of PLC object. Despite the distribution of research laboratories in Straße der Nationen of TU Chemnitz and Factory in Erfenschlager Straße, homogeneous architecture allows real time integrated representation of distributed data in single mysql server integrating wlan and lan technologies.

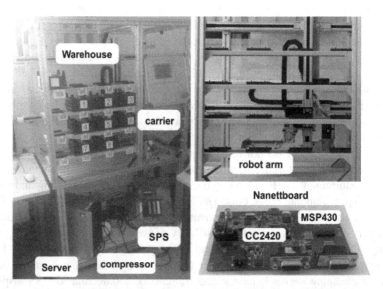

Fig. 3. Demonstrator components read and controlled using homogeneous object binding structure

Choosen PLC known in and out ports of machines for rfid detection and manual and automatic processing and lift across unit was mapped by plc-program to adresses of a generic data block. This data blocks are extracted by our opc interface, transferred over local network to database controller and send to database as homogeneous stream. This way all PLC available parameters of experimental factory are controlable via homogeneous object binding structure to support better preference decisions. The database alows for more secure access than additional indirection over web service. Control over homogeneous key identifier is easier than get to know the meaning of in plc blocks distributed program. By generic reading out keys, installation of new machine and normal setup in plc could in futur realizations result in automatic extraction of inputs and outputs to database. For security and control of by extraction provided data, currently a one time manual enabling of machine data level for later on demand extraction is required.

Because of the wide acceptance and easy usage, realisation of objects was done using relational database model mysql. In case of student management there is a table for each student and common object like inventar. Each object holds a key, value and grouping collumn. Because indexing is done using key a search for an request simply is a traversation of all relevent objects m and a indexed key selection per object. This way joins (mxn) are avoided. Redundancy could be eliminated by creation of objects for common features. A general object table holds all objects. By avoiding inheritance with related consistency checks and method dependencies of object oriented databases [6] and usage of acid capabilities of relational databases the real time applicability of the homogeneous object binding approach is strengthen. In case of factory szenario it holds the cbos and pdos. For evaluation of current progess and next steps metainformation of target number (e. g. "t1" label) is used by this name for the

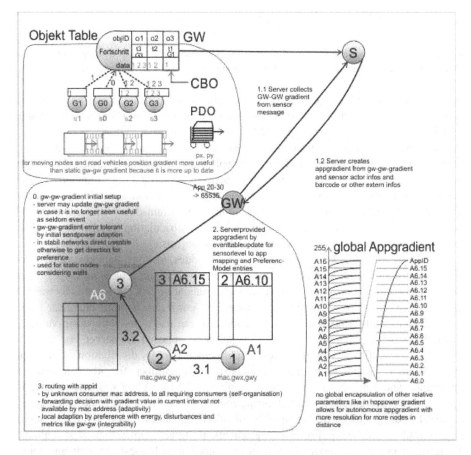

Fig. 4. Sensor object-binding in gateway; and application gradient routing details

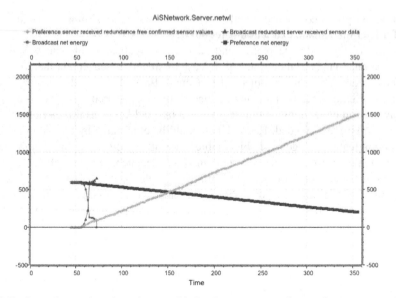

Fig. 5. Basic preference based routing considering hop-power-gradient and energy outperforms redundant broadcast approach in network lifetime and number of delivered packets

key. Furthermore old measure state from sensor data and qr-code and new state by GUI movement tasks should be realized as corresponding keys. Progress time model, division of measure state and next control state and database transaction consistency should ensure consistency with real world events. Furthermore for application layer a central controller in server should manage application order dependencies. Controller is basicaly enhanced by index lifting mechanism by which data are transferred from objects to typ object collumn for generic fast lookup without redundancy of index data. This way a generich controller first lookup in collum data with fast relational database index access speed eg for often required matriculation number is possible, while also can lookup flexible seldom used data in objects.

In order to allow this key value pairs in sensor nodes, received data key-value pairs are currently stored in a character queue to allow dynamic length messages. This queue can be enhanced by own key-value measurement or task pairs and is forwarded as a message of resulting length to next node. For sensor data a single character value was sufficient while control tasks for warehouse where also tested with string-values.

In this paper application gradient propagation is proposed via server Fig. 4 (1.2). Further energy-efficiency improvement could be achieved by distribution of gradient by each node. Application gradient consists of a number for identification of application and a number to describe strength of gradient. A big strength variable is more promising to get data to target during routing decision. Without knowing mac-id of target node, by using higher level applicationtarget information, (single or multi target) routing following promising gradients to target application was realized. Thereby, in preference model of a node, neighbor with biggest gradient and other homogen integrated and weighted high-valued properties is selected.

First simulation results showed that preference based routing using homogeneous object binding structure outperforms simple broadcast mechanism in exponential way Fig. 5. Current integration of other parameters showed linear in parameter energy savings over time considering signal quality, timing, and shortest path. The diagram in Fig. 5 was created with a simulation scenario in Omnet++ like in Fig. 1 with server, gateways, process and technical nodes using preference bases routing approach. Same scenario was realized then with simple broadcast routing for comparison. In Oment++ realized Homogeneous message format is variable to support both routing strategies in a generic way. Homogeneous message format was realized in hash map representation for clearer direct array style code and decoding operations minimizing interface overhead, while by generic representation stays connectable to other modules.

4   Outlook

The planned Maintenance and Logistics solutions should be implemented. The homogeneous object binding structure and preference zone based decision making was sucessfully applied to student data management system for TU Chemnitz. There preference makes group-, user-wish- and progess- of student based decissions for next tasks in editing the student data. The easy applying of the structure allows also for inventar management, termin management and line lock level file version management in one database connected system. The number of applications should be increased to extract further common features.

5   Conclusion

In this paper a flexible unifying object binding structure was presented and its simple application was demonstrated on factory sample. Based on this structure, zone parameters where combined to a preference forwarding decision for data and carrier. Thereby knowledge about the weighting of parameters can be directly realized and extended by generic rate approaches. In order to demonstrate the high group-value grouping flexibility, application of homogeneous object binding structure to thesis management system was illustrated. In both samples homogeneous object binding structure allows as far as we know for gradient based decision structures not possible before. In case of factory scenario, decision structure is realized by application gradient fine granular routing decision mechanism and in case of thesis management by preference generated user GUIs and process logic generated from partial-order progress-gradient-graph. Thereby in factory scenario results preference controlled self-organized routing from sensor to actor and in thesis management case preference controlled flexible self-organized retrieval, update and insertion of data.

References

1. Reißner, D., Strakosch, F.: Energy Efficient Communication by Preference-based Routing and Forwarding. In: 11th International Multi-Conference on Systems, Signals & Devices, SSD 2014 (2014)
2. Cheng, W., Jin, X., Sun, J.-T.: Probabilistic Similarity Query on Dimension Incomplete Data. In: Ninth IEEE International Conference on Data Mining, ICDM 2009, December 6-9, pp.81–90 (2009), doi: 10.1109/ICDM.2009.72
3. Joomla CMS (April 2014), http://www.joomla.org/
4. Django CMS (April 2014), https://www.django-cms.org
5. Bootstrap Framework (April 2014), http://getbootstrap.com/
6. Lee, J., Son, S.H., Lee, M.-J.: Issues in developing object-oriented data-base systems for real-time applications. In: Proceedings of the IEEE Workshop on Real-Time Applications, July 21-22, pp. 136–140 (1994), doi:10.1109/RTA.1994.316160
7. Pongthawornkamol, T., Nahrstedt, K., Wang, G.: HybridCast: A Hybrid Probabilistic/Deterministic Approach for Adjustable Broadcast Reliability in Mobile Wireless Ad Hoc Networks. In: IEEE International Conference on Communications, ICC 2009, June 14-18, pp. 1–6 (2009)
8. MongeDB, http://www.mongodb.org
9. Reißner, D., Hardt, W.: Management System for University Topics Based on Homogeneous Object Binding Structure. In: CSR-14-01, ChemnitzerInformatik-Berichte, International Summerschool Computer Science 2014, Proceedings of Summerschool, July 7-13, Juni 2011, Chemnitz (2014)
10. Workflow Server (April 2014), http://www.mycontrol.de/workflow/
11. CKan Tutorials (April 2014),
    http://docs.ckan.org/en/latest/extensions/tutorial.html,
    http://docs.ckan.org/en/ckan-1.7/forms.html

Hybrid Expert System Development
Using Computer-Aided Software Engineering Tools

Natalia A. Polkovnikova and Victor M. Kureichik

Federal State-Owned Autonomy Educational Establishment of Higher Vocational Education,
Southern Federal University, Russia
natalia-polkovnikova@mail.ru, kur@tgn.sfedu.ru

Abstract. The purpose of this article is to demonstrate a way of intellectualization of automated information and diagnostic systems using knowledge bases, databases and algorithms for the formalization of procedures in terms of the development of an expert system for marine diesel engines.

The aim of this work is to develop an expert system's architecture with data mining tools for solving the problem of technical exploitation of marine diesel engines based on fragmented, unreliable and possibly inaccurate information. The architecture of such expert system allows moving from normal monitoring to «information monitoring» in the specialized intelligent human-machine systems. Application of data mining technology allows optimizing database processing queries that retrieve the required information from the actual data in order to detect important patterns. An approach based on data mining and fuzzy logic in the expert system is shown on an example of solving technical exploitation of marine diesel engines problem.

Keywords: decision support system, expert system, data mining, database, knowledge bases, computer-aided software engineering, diesel-engines, fuzzy logic, linguistic variable, membership function.

1 Introduction

Due to the constant increase in the overall volume of automation controlled parameters, stringent requirements to ensure safe and efficient operation, the ship's mechanic is experiencing great difficulties in the analysis of received information. In these conditions, an important way to increase the reliability and efficiency of technical exploitation (TE) of main marine diesel engines is the use of modern information technologies to accommodate better the actual use of technical modes, maintenance and repair, as well as information support for operator (mechanic) in decision making.

For this purpose, an integrated approach to the TE tasks of marine engines solution based on system organization of information and modern information technologies in the development of data processing algorithms, search and detection of failure causes, technical condition forecasting, the automation of decision making support procedures was proposed. This approach was implemented with the following basic tasks

A. Kravets et al. (Eds.): JCKBSE 2014, CCIS 466, pp. 433–445, 2014.

of main engine TE: evaluation of technical conditions and identification of failures; assignment of allowed mode taking due to the technical and external navigation conditions; preventing sudden and forecasting gradual failures; determination of the amount and priority of maintenance, overhaul and between docking periods.

At the core of these problems solving it is necessary to use various information from hardware means of technical diagnostics, onboard systems of centralized control, as well as requirements of various regulatory documents. For formalizing procedures of data evolution in information system of marine diesel engine, a technique has been developed using statistical models of different types and levels: standard and current (adaptive), local and integral, which requires a database of measured parameters, software and database models.

The application of expert systems (ES) increases significantly the efficiency of main marine diesel engine diagnosis since ES can quickly analyze a variety of information about current situation features, make the necessary recommendations on the possibility of eliminating one or another failure to take into account nonlinearity and uncertain nature of its processes and make optimal decisions to operate engine.

The expert system developed called "Diesel expert" - represents an intelligent program that can give practical recommendations for mechanic about technical condition of the engine on basis of inferences and knowledge about possible workflow and fuel supply parameters values. Domain knowledge required to operate expert system in a certain way is formalized and presented in the form of a knowledge base in main module of the program and failures database, which may be amended and supplemented during system development [1-3].

The distinctive feature of this expert system is presence of knowledge bases with different structures and various types of logical inference that is why expert system is called "hybrid".

2   Expert System Development

In developing of expert system "Diesel expert" computer aided software engineering (CASE) tool for automation software design – Rational Rose has been used. Rational Rose allows creating model of the future system, easy for understanding algorithms, relationships between objects by which subsequently a software (expert system) framework is created. Using completed model design, flaws are easy to spot on the stage when their fix does not require significant cost yet. All classes and diagrams have been designed using Rational Rose code generator – Ensemble Rose Delphi link.

At the first stage in Rational Rose use-case diagram was developed, with which were determined functional requirements to expert system. The first action of the user is entering data on the results of engine indicating. Then expert system makes calculations and plotting; outputs failures with recommendations to address and solve them, creates a report and adds new failures in database.

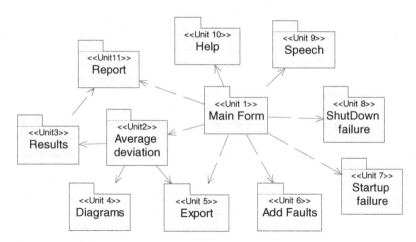

Fig. 1. The interaction scheme of expert system modules (Main Logical View)

The following step in Rational Rose designing environment was the creation of interaction diagrams for application modules (Main Logical View). Fig. 1 shows the interaction of expert system modules, which minimal element is package (🗀).

Package includes one functional module and group of form elements of the program and is used to determine the behavior of larger objects scenarios with further details.

Each package corresponds to a software module of the expert system. In this step it was determined that from the main window of expert system – Unit 1 (Main Form) the whole functional capabilities of each module will be available.

The Interaction scheme of expert system modules includes the following packages (Fig. 1):

Unit 1 (Main Form) – main window of the expert system;
Unit 2 (Average Deviation) – calculation of parameters deviations;
Unit 3 (Results) – output failures and their solutions;
Unit 4 (Diagrams) – charting the results of calculations;
Unit 5 (Export) – exporting tables to MS Office;
Unit 6 (Add Faults) – adding new failures to the database;
Unit 7 (Startup Failure) – failure diagnosis at the engine start up;
Unit 8 (Shut Down Failure) – failure diagnosis at the engine shut down;
Unit 9 (Speech) – voice menu for program control;
Unit 10 (Help) – help about the program;
Unit 11 (Report) – report on found failures and recommendations.

Further in Rational Rose prototyping expert system modules have been made. For example, let us consider the class diagram for Form 3, containing output of detected failures (Fig. 2).

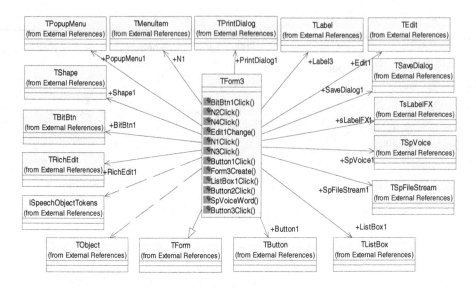

Fig. 2. The class diagram for Form 3 of expert system

In the center of diagram there is class TForm3, which is characterized by events. Events are actions that are associated with visual or non visual objects on the form. It was determined that the Form 3 will contain two RichEdits to display detected failures and their solutions, drop-down and main menus with options to print, export and change the font, text and voice control engine.

This form contains three types of relationships between classes:

- Generalization (normal arrows) – relationship type, showing that TForm3 is a child of the main form of the program TForm, because all raw data to calculate and detect failures will be entered in the main form.
- Dependency (dashed arrows) – relationship type, showing on this form that classes: ISpeechObjectTokens – reading troubleshooting solutions by Russian and English engine voices and TObject – for creating report to MS Word, are exported from the main form–server, i.e. class TForm3 uses classes ISpeechObjectTokens and TObject as parameters in different methods.
- Unidirectional association (empty pointer arrow) – relationship type (one-way communication) is common and the weakest form of communications between class with class or class with interface.

As a result of sharing Rational Rose with the programming language Delphi user interface prototype of expert system has been obtained, the detailed model of interface classes, basic architectural features of the system and full lifecycle support have been developed. The basic idea of this approach is the use of reverse engineering (round-trip engineering): all programming code changes in Delphi are displayed in the object model, built in Rational Rose and, conversely, changes in classes, methods, and other elements in the object model respectively correct the programming code in Delphi. Then to the obtained prototype of expert system functionality in RAD Studio 2010 has been added.

Expert system "Diesel expert" includes: the database of failures and database of troubleshooting solutions; the knowledge base, containing rules for identifying failures. In the formalization of procedures for assessment of technical condition "the concept of deviations" has been used. Identification of failures on individual cylinders is made by developed diagnostic matrix. The operator gets on the monitor screen graphical display of numerical values of parameters deviations in the cylinders, and text message about probable failure.

Fig. 3 shows the main window of the expert system, which contains the main menu, the table of current workflow settings and fuel supply in the cylinders with calculation of mean values, reference parameters of the engine, interactive form of failure diagnosis at the start up and shut down of the engine.

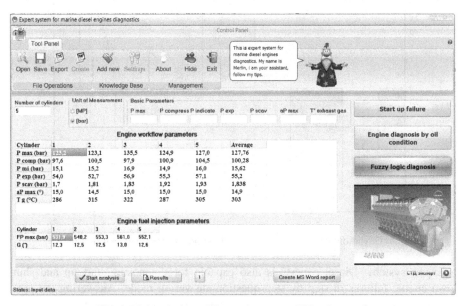

Fig. 3. Main window of the expert system "Diesel expert"

As the result of diagnostic and predictive procedures, operator has the ability to output tables and graphs trends of diagnostic parameters to the screen that provides necessary information support for recognition of sudden and forecasting gradual failures. For the timely recognition of sudden failure it is important to identify the most informative one (for this type of failure) option and provide its continuous monitoring. For parameters that are not dependent on engine operating mode, recognition and switching of sudden alarm failure is provided when the controlled parameter is in excess within confidence intervals of actual and limit values, and when a parameter has critical rate of rise.

For fault identification of the main engine individual cylinders diagnostic algorithms and matrix have been developed, in accordance with it, values of controlled parameters are compared with their average values. Failure sign of single cylinder will be in case if at least one parameter exceeds the allowable deviation limits. Failure identification has been produced by corresponding set of features. Fig. 4 shows the expert system chart window with maximum pressure (p_{max}) deviations from average in cylinders.

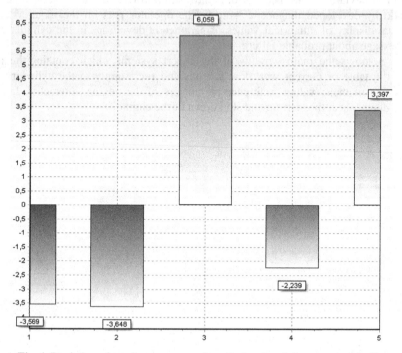

Fig. 4. Deviation of maximum pressure in cylinders (p_{max}) from average in %

Expert system "Diesel expert" is also capable for diagnosing start up and shut down engine failures in step by step question-answering mode. Answering the proposed questions, mechanic builds a logical chain, reducing time for finding trouble-shooting nodes. Such a question-answering mode is a classic for expert systems, since the first expert systems worked in this way. The advantage of this method is in as close as possible approach to the real expert's logic in finding troubleshooting. The disadvantage of this method lies in case of situations with large number of questions for diagnosis that leads to great time loss. According to the results of research that was conducted by George Miller [4], human short-term memory can hold from 7 to 9 entities at the same time. That is why this question-answering mode is ideal for the amount of questions 7 ± 2, which was implemented in "Diesel expert" system. The architecture features of developed expert system were considered in the context of three main characteristics of performance: speed, flexibility, and understandability.

"Diesel expert" fully meets the requirements of flexibility: the database of faults can be changed and supplemented during development process; system meets the requirements for clarity: expert system has Microsoft Office Assistant technology, which helps user to make right steps and actions, also it has speech recognition technology by Microsoft Speech API for voice menu and Russian voice engines – Digalo and Elan; and at last, expert system has necessary speed for solving problems in open sea conditions.

Integration of data mining tools in expert system is an innovative approach to the problem of database analysis according to indicating results in marine diesel engines failure diagnosing. Figure 5 shows the architecture of expert system designed for deployment in vessel operating conditions.

The main feature of proposed expert system architecture is logical separation in three parts: a client, application server and data server, each of which can run on its own computer. Marked parts of the application interact with each other by exchanging messages in a pre-agreed format (API, SQL, filtering).

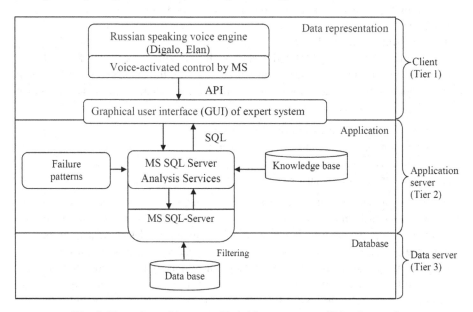

Fig. 5. Three-tier architecture of hybrid expert system "Diesel expert"

3   Advantages of the Proposed Architecture

Three-tier architecture in comparison with two-tier (client-server or file server architecture) has the following advantages:

- high reliability and security;
- configurability – isolation of levels from each other allows quick and simple means to reconfigure the system within one level when failure or scheduled maintenance;
- low performance requirements and technical characteristics of terminals.

The distinctive feature of developed expert system is the presence of voice interface that provides the following advantages:

- efficiency and natural control;
- minimum of special user training;
- possibility of using both manual (keyboard, computer mouse) and voice information input;
- operator mobility in controlling process.

Structure of implemented voice interface includes two main components:

- voice recognition in managing expert system using Microsoft Speech API 5.1 library;
- speech synthesis for reading aloud found troubleshooting using Russian Digalo and Elan voice engines.

All knowledge in the knowledge base is divided into algorithmic and non-algorithmic:

• **Algorithmic (procedural)** – those algorithms that compute functions and transformations on exactly defined tasks. In formalizing procedures for technical conditions assessment used "the concept of deviations"; the parameters' deviations of each cylinder from average values in accordance with technical maintenance rules of marine diesel engines should not exceed the following limits:

1) mean indicated pressure Δp_{mi} $\pm 2,5$ %;
2) maximum pressure in cylinder $\Delta p_{max} \pm 3,5$ %;
3) pressure in the end of compression $\Delta p_c \pm 2,5$ %;
4) temperature of exhaust gases $\Delta t_r \pm 5$ %.

Increasing actual value deviation of the controlled parameter from its average value should be considered as development of deteriorating condition and can be detected long before the controlled parameter limit which provides alarm activation.

• **Non-algorithmic** – consist of mental objects called concepts or rules. For fault identification established rules and their interconnections to malfunctions were used.

Microsoft SQL Server provides an integrated environment for creating data mining models and working with them. MS SQL Server Analysis Services includes the following algorithms:

- Microsoft Decision Trees;
- Microsoft Clustering;
- Microsoft Naive Bayes;
- Microsoft Time Series;
- Microsoft Association;
- Microsoft Neural Network;
- Microsoft Linear Regression;
- Microsoft Logistic Regression.

By using these algorithms combination it is possible to create solutions for the problems to detect hidden regularities in large and multidimensional databases.

4   Development of a Fuzzy Expert System Model

The model of expert system based on fuzzy logic is a set of production rules written in natural language by specialists for hard forming complex diagnostic process. Fuzzy expert systems allow not only taking into account the uncertainty, but also providing an opportunity to simulate the reasoning, based on professional experiences of experts. Fuzzy logic module call is carried out by pressing the "fuzzy logic diagnosis" button through the main window of expert system (fig. 3).

Fig. 6 shows the block diagram of expert system based on fuzzy logic. Dynamical system is diagnosed object (engine) in the use conditions with defined set of parameters at any given time. Monitoring system reads the data from engine and provides this data to the operator. Then, the operator inputs the received data to the expert system and executes processing mechanism.

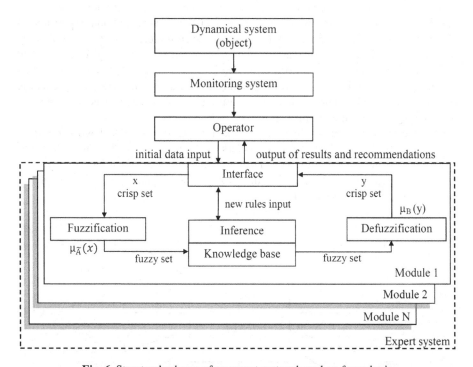

Fig. 6. Structural scheme of an expert system based on fuzzy logic

Fuzzification is conversion of input data that is crisp set, into a fuzzy set, defined by membership functions. The purpose of fuzzification step is establishment of correspondence between numerical values of the individual input and corresponding value of membership function with its linguistic variable. Input data is vector $\{x_1, x_2 \dots x_i\} \in X$, where i – is number of diagnosed parameters, obtained by monitoring system. Then takes place linguistic evaluation of each parameter in accordance with predetermined membership functions in the system. After this, a crisp set of input parameters is transformed into a fuzzy set Ã and used as linguistic variables in logical rules of knowledge base. After this, a crisp set of input parameters is transformed into a fuzzy set Ã and used as linguistic variables in logical rules of knowledge base. Defuzzification is the inverse transformation of a fuzzy set in a crisp set B. Thus, the system values are the probabilities of each failure $\{y_1, y_2 \dots y_j\} \in Y$, where j – the number of failures (or states).

Fuzzy set is the dependency $\mu(x) = \mu_{\tilde{A} \to B}(y)$ as function from output variable y. Thus, failure identification is performed with the assessment of probabilities. Such a system called the Mamdani-Zadeh logical inference system. Choice type of Mamdani fuzzy model caused by the fact that the rules of the knowledge base are clear and intuitive, whereas for Takagi-Sugeno-type models is not always clear what kind of linear dependence "input - output" is necessary to use and how to get them.

The proposed structural scheme of expert system based on fuzzy logic can be applied to any system for technical condition determination and decision support systems for complex processes, when there is no mathematical model and expert knowledge about the object or process can be formulated in linguistic form. The operating process of main marine diesel engines is characterized by instability: different load modes, changing external conditions of navigation, switching to different sorts of fuel and human factor influence. Therefore, taking into account the objectively existing uncertainty, incomplete and unclear information about the object, it is reasonable to use fuzzy logic for failure identification.

Fig. 7 shows a functional scheme for cylinder diagnostics in MATLAB fuzzy inference system editor. The inputs are parameters of cylinder, obtained from engine indicating. Outputs are probable cylinder failures, typical for the input data. Fuzzy logic module call is carried out by pressing the "fuzzy logic diagnosis" button through the main window of expert system (fig. 3).

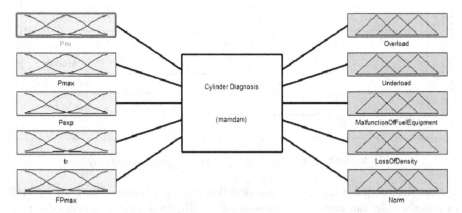

Fig. 7. Functional scheme for fuzzy failure identification

Cylinder can have the following states: overloaded, underloaded, malfunction of fuel equipment, loss of density and normal state. Each parameter has its own range of change. The linguistic evaluation value of each variable is performed using three terms: low, normal, high. Membership function has a trapezoidal shape: y = trapmf (x, [a, b, c, d]), where the argument a – is a minimum allowable value with zero probability of normal state, interval between the arguments [b, c] shows the parameter belonging to the normal state with probability 1. And, correspondingly, the argument d – is a maximum allowable value with zero probability of normal state. Choice of trapezoidal membership functions caused by the fact that normal state probability is determined not by a single variable value, but some range of acceptable values.

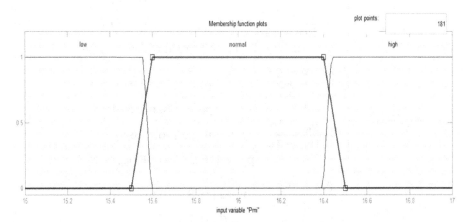

Fig. 8. Membership functions of mean indicated pressure (p_{mi})

Low value of mean indicated pressure p_{mi} is in range [15...15,6], normal – [15,6...16,4] and high is [16,4...17] (fig. 8). The parameter values for linguistic variable range have been calculated in accordance with acceptable deviations in technical regulations from average values. For mean indicated pressure possible values are the following set:

$$p_{mi} = (15; 15,3; 15,6; 16; 16,4; 16,6; 17) \tag{1}$$

Each element in set has its own degree of membership: the higher the degree of membership, the greater the probability that parameter value in norm [5-7]. Membership functions or information for their construction are given by experts on the basis of subjective preferences and are not random. The resulting fuzzy set has the following form:

$$\tilde{A}_{p_{mi}} = \left(\frac{0}{15}, \frac{0,3}{15,3}, \frac{1}{15,6}, \frac{1}{16}, \frac{1}{16,4}, \frac{0,5}{16,6}, \frac{0}{17} \right) \tag{2}$$

Since the p_{mi} set is finite and contains 7 elements, the fuzzy set $\tilde{A}_{p_{mi}}$ can be written as:

$$\tilde{A}_{p_{mi}} = \sum_{i=1}^{7} \frac{\mu_A(Pmi_i)}{Pmi_i}, \tag{3}$$

where $\mu_A(Pmi_i)$ – is membership degree of $Pmi_i \in$ Pmi to fuzzy set $\tilde{A}$. The membership degree - is a number from range [0...1]. The higher the degree of membership, the more the element of the set corresponds to the properties of fuzzy set. For the parameter p_{mi} (fig. 8) membership functions have three qualitative representations, which fuzzy inference mechanisms mathematically formalized in the following way:

$$\mu_{low}(p_{mi}) = \begin{cases} 1 & p_{mi} \in [15 \ldots 15,6] \\ 1 - \dfrac{p_{mi} - 15,5}{15,6 - 15,5} & p_{mi} \in [15,5 \ldots 15,6] \\ 0 & p_{mi} \in [10\ 15]\ OR\ p_{mi} > 15,6 \end{cases} \tag{4}$$

$$\mu_{normal}(p_{mi}) = \begin{cases} \dfrac{p_{mi} - 15,5}{16 - 15,5} & p_{mi} \in [15,5 \ldots 16] \\ 1 & p_{mi} \in [15,6 \ldots 16,4] \\ 1 - \dfrac{p_{mi} - 16}{16,5 - 16} & p_{mi} \in [16 \ldots 16,5] \\ 0 & p_{mi} \in [10 \ldots 15,4]\ OR\ p_{mi} > 16,5 \end{cases} \tag{5}$$

$$\mu_{high}(p_{mi}) = \begin{cases} \dfrac{p_{mi} - 16,3}{16,5 - 16,3} & p_{mi} \in [16,3 \ldots 16,5] \\ 1 & p_{mi} \in [16,5 \ldots 17] \\ 0 & p_{mi} < 16,3 \end{cases} \tag{6}$$

After completing fuzzification, all input variables have identified specific values of membership functions for each of the linguistic terms, which are used in terms of "**IF** parameter N **IS** (**low / normal / high**)" in the rule base of fuzzy inference system [8, 9].

Thus, the application of fuzzy logic in conjunction with other diagnostic algorithms, allows approximating to the experts' logic and "Diesel expert" can be attributed to the class of hybrid expert systems.

5   Conclusion

This article describes and discusses the intellectualization method of information and diagnostic automated systems using knowledge bases, databases and algorithms regarding formalization procedures in order to develop an expert system aimed at marine diesel engines. Steps of expert system development using computer-aided software and design engineering tools have been shown. Effective ways of heterogeneous knowledge interaction in hybrid expert system for solving marine diesel engines technical maintenance problems have been suggested.

Expert System "Diesel expert" designed to operate with VLCC tankers and provides with mathematical analysis of measurements, retrospective information analysis. Designed voice interface provides interactive mode with the computer. Operator (mechanic) gets an information support and guidance in solving technical operation problems that allows making correct decisions.

Represented architecture of the developed expert system provides diagnostics of main marine diesel engines on the basis of objective information obtained by hardware as well as by subjective knowledge of experts that refers this system to the class of hybrid expert systems.

References

1. Kureichik, V.M.: Features of decision making support system design. Izvestiya SFedU. Engineering Sciences (7), 92–98 (2012)
2. Kureichik, V.M., Polkovnikova, N.A.: Development of hybrid expert system for main marine diesel engines. In: XVI International Conference on Soft Computing and Measurements (SCM 2013), May 23-25, pp. 27–30 (2013)
3. Polkovnikova, N.A., Kureichik, V.M.: Development of an expert system model based on fuzzy logic. Izvestiya SFedU. Engineering Sciences 1(150), 83–92 (2014)
4. Miller, G.A. The magic number seven plus or minus two: some limits on our capacity for processing information. Psychological Review (63), 81 – 97 (1956)
5. Li, D., Du, Y.: Artificial intelligence with uncertainty, p. 347. Tsinghua University, Beijing, Chapman & Hall/CRC (2008)
6. Zadeh, L.A.: Is there a need for fuzzy logic? Information Sciences 178, 2751–2779 (2008)
7. Pegat, A.: Fuzzy modeling and control M.: BINOM. Laboratory of Knowledge, p. 798 (2009)
8. Sivanandam, S.N., Sumathi, S., Deepa, S.N.: Introduction to fuzzy logic using MATLAB, p. 441. Springer (2007)
9. Buckley, J.J., Jowers, L.J.: Simulating continuous fuzzy systems, p. 202. Springer (2006)

Forecasting Model of Small City Depopulation Processes and Possibilities of Their Prevention

Elena Georgievna Krushel, Ilya Victorovich Stepanchenko,
Alexander Eduardovich Panfilov, Ivan Mikhailovich Haritonov,
and Elena Dmitrievna Berisheva

Kamyshin Technological Institute of the Volgograd State Technical University,
Kamyshin, Russia
stilvi@mail.ru

Abstract. A simple simulation model of depopulation dynamics is presented. It is based on the agent-based simulation and stochastic finite automata theory results. The computation experiments on the long-term prediction of the number of population and proportions among the different age groups prove the danger of 50% reduction in the number of population, degradation of the capable and reproductive age group population and undesirable increase of the number of pensioners. The simulation (agent) technique was applied to detect the possibilities of the depopulation process termination and favorable age structure restoration.

The model of long-term dynamic planning of the small business development is formulated in the terms of non-linear mathematic programming theory. It can be applied to detect the small business rational specialization and estimate the resources required for the small business successful development which can prevent the depopulation process.

Keywords: Agent technique, decision methods, life quality, simulation model, depopulation process, non-linear mathematic programming.

1 Introduction

The demographic evolution models overview [1,2], [4,5,6], [11] shows that the purpose of major known mathematical models consists of the global demographic tendencies prediction and so such models are incompletely suitable to examine the factors of the folk relocation due to the people outflow from small towns and villages to megalopolises.

The social and economic reasons of small cities depopulation (described at [3] in the terms of regression models) are applicable to extrapolate the current depopulation effects on the future time periods. But such models have lack of facilities to search for ways to prevent depopulation process as a result of implementation of several strategic initiatives.

Thereby the development of a small city depopulation special model is reasonable. The purpose of such model is to illustrate the small city dangerous demographic

A. Kravets et al. (Eds.): JCKBSE 2014, CCIS 466, pp. 446–456, 2014.

situation decay as a result of an inadmissible disproportion between the salaries of small city and megalopolis workers and the lack of workplaces.

The model described below allows estimating the undesirable changes of both the small city inhabitant number and different age group ratios. It is also suitable to determine long term after-effects of the current negative social and economic factors and to examine the effectiveness of different strategies to terminate the depopulation process.

2   A Brief Description of the Approach

The small city demographic situation is roughly characterized by the number of citizens and their distribution between different age groups. The problem of the demographic situation forecasting is considered for each t-th year of the given T- years prediction period.

The agent-based model (ABM) is chosen as the tool of demographic situation forecasting. For each t-th year of T- years prediction period the folk outcome / income flow simulation is considered for a virtual city settled by artificial inhabitants (agents). For each agent the stochastic prediction of its state change within t-th year is carried out (i.e. either income in the virtual city with corresponding age value, either outcome, or remain in the city with corresponding age increase). Although the state change determination of each agent is senseless the average indicators for each age group can be obtained and justified by the results of the numerous computation experiments with small city ABM-model.

The process of model parameter identification was supported by the life quality SWOT-analysis implementation of a typical Russian small city (i.e. the estimation of the existing strength and weakness aspects as well as future favorable opportunities and threats). The SWOT-analysis was based on the independent statistical data of megalopolis and small city life quality indicator comparison as well as on the results of the different age citizen questionnaires treatment.

Although the proposed model cannot pretend to possess high accuracy because of the essential uncertainty of future the simulation results may be useful as the quantitative addition to the conceptual qualitative verbal proofs. The model may also be applied by the municipal governance in order to choose ways to terminate the depopulation process.

3   An Overview of the Model Main Features

The description of the demography situation dynamics is carried out in the terms of the stochastic finite automata theory [9], [12]. The computations are executed cyclically starting at $t = 1$.

1. The demographic state $S(\tau[t])$ at a certain moment $\tau[t]$ within t-th year of the prediction period is presented as a set of virtual city inhabitants (agents). Each

element $s_j(\tau[t]) \in S(\tau[t])$ corresponds to the age of j-th agent as an inhabitant of the virtual city at the moment $\tau[t]$. The age of such an agent has to be determined during the simulation process as the integer number $V_j(t)$, $j \in M_{live}(\tau[t])$; $M_{live}(\tau[t])$ is the agents index marks set. The initial age value $V_j(0)$ is supposed to be known from the citizen census data or (in case such data lack) $V_j(0)$ is nominated randomly corresponding to the virtual city age distribution law.

2. Each agent's state changes are considered at the following distinct time moments within t-th year of prediction period:

$\tau[t_b]$ – the date at the year start preceding the virtual yearly agent census;

$\tau[t_n]$ – the date at the year start after yearly agent census completion;

$\tau[t_f]$ – the date at the end of the year after the re-counting of the agents remaining in the virtual city.

3. Each agent's state change is emulated for every moment $\tau[t]$, $\tau[t] \in (\tau[t_b]; \tau[t_n]; \tau[t_f])$, $t = 1,.., T$. The junction to the state $S(\tau[t_b])$ emulates the replay of the state $S(\tau[t_f - 1])$ (i.e. the set of agents living in the virtual city at the moment of the yearly agent census simulation start at t-th year). The junction from the state $S(\tau[t_b])$ to the state $S(\tau[t_n])$ emulates the growth of agent number due to the set of birthday and immigration action simulation. The sum $N_{new}[t]$ of new-born and immigrant agents' number is considered as the parameter the change of which is possible for different simulation session. The junction from the state $S(\tau[t_n])$ to the state $S(\tau[t_f])$ emulates the change of the agents' number for the period between the agent census simulation at $\tau[t_n]$ and the end of t-th year $\tau[t_f]$. After the junction from state $S(\tau[t_f])$ to the state $S(\tau[t_b + 1])$ the age of each agent is increased by 1 and agents with the ages more than the bound V_{max} value are eliminated.

4. The process of agent retention / elimination within the time interval $\tau[t_n] \le \tau[t] \le \tau[t_f]$ is emulated by the stochastic algorithm which generates the binary token $w_j[t] \in \{0;1\}$ for each j-th agent. The probabilities of the retention $P(w_j[t] = 1)$ or the elimination $Q(w_j[t] = 0) = 1 - P(w_j[t] = 1)$ are supposed to depend both on the agent's age $V_j(t)$ and the yearly migration parameter values.

5. The demography parameter prediction problem dimension was simplified (with essential dimension reduce) by means of the agent state aggregation at the few age groups. Such simplification is justified by the statistically detected existence of the ages with raised out-migration tendencies (i.e. school leaver, college and institute graduate ages, the able-bodied citizens at ages less than 30 years etc.). The agent age bounds $[\underline{V}_g; \overline{V}_g)$; $\underline{V}_g < \overline{V}_g$ for each g-th age group, $g = 1,.., G$, correspond to the age intervals with weak influence of agent ages on the migration probabilities

and so these probabilities are assumed equal for each j-th agent of corresponding age: $\forall j: V_j \in [\underline{V}_g; \overline{V}_g)$ $P(w_j[t]=1) = P_j[t]$, $g = 1,.., G$.

6. The simulation session results represent both the estimation of the virtual city total agent number and their age distribution between G groups for each t-th year of T-years prediction period.

The model described above is purposely simplified by reason of objectively lacking reliable statistical data and the demographic processes dependence on non-predictable future circumstances. Therefore we knowingly refused to take into account several demography factors (i.e. marriage statistics, decrease of megalopolis attraction because of the ecology quality worsening as well as serious transport problems etc.) Nevertheless the presented model allows obtaining and forecasting small cities alarming depopulation effects.

4   Examples of Computer Experiments Results

Fig. 1 illustrates several simulation sessions results illustrating expected changes of the citizen number throughout the next 50-year prediction period. The initial conditions and the model parameters correspond to one of the Volga region small cities with evident depopulation effect appearance. Although the model has stochastic elements the trajectories obtained in various simulation sessions (Fig. 1) are similar.

If the existing depopulation rate was kept up at the present level the citizen number should be shortened year by year achieving the stable value almost twice less than initial state.

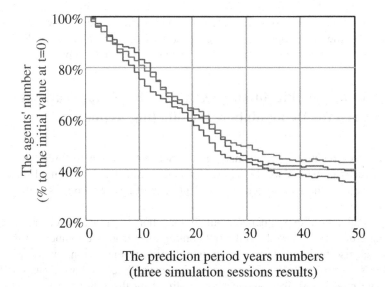

The predicion period years numbers
(three simulation sessions results)

Fig. 1. The prediction of small city inhabitant number

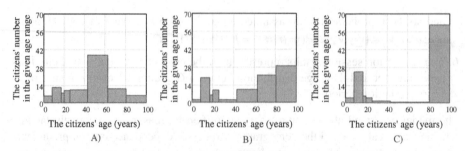

Fig. 2. Age structure change estimation: A) 1st year of the prediction period; B) 20th year of the prediction period; C) 50th year of the prediction period

The results of age distribution forecasting seem to be much more disappointing (Fig.2).

Due to the variety of the retention / elimination probabilities of different age groups of citizens the undesired able-bodied worker group number reduction is predictable. In addition to the whole citizen number reduction the abrupt raise of pensioner number part and the retention of pre-school and school age part are expected (i.e. the grandchild generation would be entrusted to the grandparents due both to the small city high-quality ecology state and to the lack of time which parents are able to dedicate to children in the existing life conditions).

The city with such undesirable citizen age structure without any doubt would be in need of subventions and so the level of people profit would be even less than now. Therefore the market net would be cut down and the consumption of high-quality long-time usage goods would be reduced.

Because of the capable personnel lack the city enterprises would feel the heightened demand for highly qualified workers. The influence of this factor on the depopulation process is ambiguous. The interest of owners in business growth would result in preventing the depopulation. Vice versa the lack of such interest would force the enterprises to close correspondingly accelerating the depopulation process.

5   A Demographic Situation Change Model Application to Search for Depopulation Terminating Actions

The set of computation experiments were carried out in order to forecast the demographic processes which would follow the actions causing the essential raise of income flow due to the appearance of a great number of new workplaces with attractive salaries.

The computation experiments emulate the short-term yearly elevation of the incoming citizens comparable to the out-coming ones from the moment of the hypothetic enterprise building start up to its introduction in the nominal working regime. Afterwards the probabilities of the citizens' income and outcome were supposed to be equal. The model described above was amplified by the following parameters: the year's numbers of the hypothetic enterprise start and completion of building as well as the coefficient (more than 1) of the ratio between the income / outcome flow mean values.

Fig.3 illustrates the expected influence of the large-scale enterprises cluster development with high salary values and stable successful marketing on the citizens' number changes. The effectiveness of this action depends on the term of the enterprise startup. The early startup (Fig.3-A) is much more preferable than later ones (Fig.3-B, C) and the procrastinating results in depopulation effects (Fig.2-C). The cluster specialization can be chosen by the SWOT-analysis detection of the promising small city local resource availability.

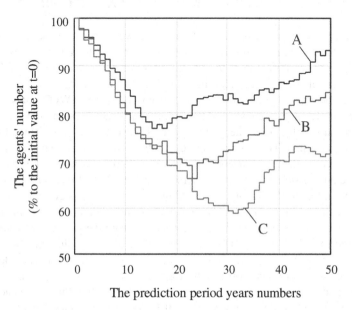

Fig. 3. Modeling the process to overcome the depopulation on various schedules of building start. A – in 5 years, B – in 10 years, C – in 20 years since the start of modeling.

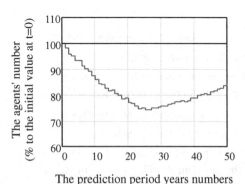

Fig. 4. Restoring the pre-crisis population as a result of the implementation of small and medium businesses

The depopulation effects may be softening also due to the growth of the purposeful small and medium business oriented on the local resource treatment (Fig. 4).

The simulation results show that the demographic after-effects of the small business step-by-step growth are preferable to once-only powerful enterprise making but only while the small business growth should be intensive enough (the necessary intensity can be estimated via the simulation sessions). Therefore both of depopulation terminating variants are hopeful.

6   The Model of Small Business Specialization Choice

The model of small business specialization choice was carried out in the terms of the optimal dynamic planning approach [10]. The purpose of planning consists of the expected efficiency estimation of the small business enterprise development by means both of owner self-support and loan investments. The list of the probable production assortment is supposed to be known (being prompted by the SWOT-analysis results) and so the subject of plan consists of the investment strategy estimation (i.e. the decisions on the sum of the investments and its yearly distribution between the prescribed investment addresses). The planning strategy determination was treated as the optimization problem with the criterion (objective) suited to achieve the concordance between the enterprise owners and workers interests taking into account the depopulation terminating goal. Particularly the maximizing criterion was chosen as the worker motivation fund value being summarized across the planning period interval. The dependences of the necessary resources restrictions from the yearly investment values are supposed to be known as well as the dependence of the production demands on its price values. Also the demand of investment self-accounting was included in the set of optimization problem constraints. Currently with the decision making on the investment addresses the inner parameters are determined (i.e. the yearly each assortment position volumes, the sum of yearly self-supported investments values, the yearly requested and returning loans etc.).

1. The problem statement is presented below in the following **designations**:

- N_{asr} – the prescribed assortment positions number;
- N_{res} – the prescribed resources number;
- T – the prescribed planning period (number of years);
- N_{inv} – the prescribed number of investment addresses;
- $i = 1,.., N_{asr}$ - assortment position index mark set;
- $m = 1,.., N_{res}$ - resource kind index mark set;
- $k = 1,.., T$ – planning period year index mark set;
- $n = 1,.., N_{inv}$ - the investment address index mark set;
- T_n^* – the prescribed term of n-th enterprise making (years);

- $\overline{T}_n^* = T - T_n^*$ – the number of year after which the making of the n-th enterprise could not raise the criterion value;
- $t^*(n) = 1,..,\overline{T}_n^*$ – the period of the n-th enterprise effective making;
- $\overline{T}' = T - \min_n T_n^*$ – the period of the justified loan demands;
- I_n^* – the prescribed value of the investments necessary for n-th enterprise making;
- E_{imk} – the m-th resource kind charge necessary for the unit production of i-th assortment position the k-th year of planning period (the value E_{im1} for the 1st year supposed to be known) ;
- $\%E_{imn}$ – the m-th resource kind charge decreasing due to the n-th enterprise making for the unit of i-th production assortment position (in % of initial value achieved to the planning interval beginning);
- E_k^{cc} – the prescribed conditionally constant expenses the k-th year;
- $\%E_n^{cc}$ – the decrease of the conditionally constant expenses due to the n-th enterprise making (in % of initial value achieved to the planning interval beginning);
- E_k^{other} – the prescribed other expenses the k-th year;
- $\%E_n^{other}$ – the decrease of the other expenses due to the n-th enterprise making (in % of initial value achieved to the planning interval beginning);
- $\overline{E}_m$ – the prescribed yearly expenses restriction for the m-th resource kind purchasing;
- K_0 – the prescribed start investment value;
- $\%L$ – the prescribed rate of loan payment, %;
- $\%R^{mun}$ – the prescribed utmost exceeding value of the price upon the manufactory costs (being fixed by the municipal governance, %);
- $\%D_k$ – the annual discounting coefficient of the k-th year.

2. The variables values which have to be **determined** are as follows:

- R_{ik} – the expected price value of the i-th assortment position the k-th year;
- V_{ik} – the production volume of the i-th assortment position k-th year;
- $M^*_{n,t^*(n)}$ – the binary index marks eliminating the decision making of n-th enterprise startup $t^*(n)$-th year;
- L_k – the loan requested at the k-th year, $\forall t > \overline{T}' \; L_t = 0$;
- $E^{loan}_{t',\tilde{t}(t')}$ – the loan returning at the year $\tilde{t}(t')$ being received the t'-th year, $\tilde{t}(t') = t',..,T$;

- P_k – the part of the profit directed for the worker motivation fund the k–th year.

3. The **auxiliary** variables are as follows:

- MD_{ik} – the market demands on the i-th assortment position at k-th year (its dependence on the production price was considered as linear with known parameters a_i, b_i: $MD_{ik} = a_i - b_i \cdot R_{ik}$);
- MC_{ik} – the manufactory cost of the i-th assortment position unit k-th year:

$$MC_{ik} = \sum_{m=1}^{N_{res}} E_{imk} ;$$

- PP_k – the enterprise pure profit value the k-th year:

$$PP_k = \sum_{i=1}^{N_{asr}} \left[V_{ik} \cdot (R_{ik} - MC_{ik}) \right] - E_k^{cc} + (\overline{I}_k^{inv} - I_k^{inv}) - \sum_{t=1}^{k} E_{t,k}^{loan} ;$$

- I_k^{inv} – the expenses on the enterprises making the k-th year: $I_k^{inv} = \sum_{n=1}^{N_{inv}} I_n^* \cdot M_{n,k}^* ;$

- $\overline{I}_k^{inv}$ – the utmost investment volume which may be used the k-th year: $\overline{I}_k^{inv} = L_k + PP_{k-1} \cdot (1 - P_{k-1});$

- E_{imk} – the expenses for the m-th resources kind for the production unit of i-th assortment position the k-th year: $k = 2,.., T$ (for $k = 1$ the value is prescribed):

$$E_{imk} = E_{im1} \cdot \left(1 - \sum_{n=1}^{N_{inv}} \frac{\% E_{imn}}{100} \cdot \sum_{q=1}^{k-T_n^*} M_{n,k-q}^* \right) .$$

4. The set of **restrictions** includes following:

- The production volume should be nonnegative and should not exceed the market demands:

$$V_{ik} \le MD_{ik}; V_{ik} \ge 0; \tag{1}$$

- The production price should not exceed the manufactory costs more than the value assigned by the municipal governance the year preceding the planning period start:

$$R_{ik} \le \left(1 + \frac{\% R^{mun}}{100} \right) \cdot MC_{i1} \tag{2}$$

- The restrictions for the resources expenses are following:

$$\sum_{i=1}^{N_{asr}} E_{imk} \cdot V_{ik} \le \overline{E}_m, \quad \forall k = 1,..,T \tag{3}$$

- The restrictions on the part of the yearly profit directed for the worker motivation fund k-th year:

$$P_k \leq 1, \quad P_k \geq 0 \tag{4}$$

- The demand of the only-once each enterprise making during the planning period:

$$\sum_{t=1}^{\bar{T}_n^*} M_{n,t} \leq 1 \tag{5}$$

- The restrictions of the investment volume the k-th year:

$$I_k^{inv} \leq \bar{I}_k^{inv}, \tag{6}$$

$$I_t^{inv} = 0, \ \forall t > \bar{T}' \tag{7}$$

(7) corresponds to the enterprises for which the startup after $\bar{T}'$-th year cannot lead to criterion raise;

- The initial investment is considered as the profit of the year preceding the start of the planning period:

$$PP_0 = K_0 \tag{8}$$

- The worker motivation fund value the year preceding the start of the planning period is accepted at zero level:

$$P_0 = 0 \tag{9}$$

- The restrictions on the requests and returns of loans are as follows:

$$L_{t'} = \sum_{t=t'}^{T} \left[E_{t',t}^{;oan} \middle/ \left(1 + (t - t' + 1) \cdot \frac{\%L}{100}\right) \right]; \ L_{t'} \geq 0; \ E_{t',\bar{T}(t')}^{loan} \geq 0 \tag{10}$$

5. **Optimization Problem Formulating:** with the respect of restrictions (1)-(10) find the variables enumerated in the sections 2, 3 maximizing the T-years summary of the workers motivation fund value:

$$J = \sum_{k=1}^{T} \left[\sum_{i=1}^{N_{asr}} V_{ik} \cdot \left(R_{ik} - \sum_{m=1}^{N_{res}} E_{im1} \cdot \left(1 - \sum_{n=1}^{N_{inv}} \frac{\%E_{imn}}{100} \cdot \sum_{q=1}^{k-T_n^*} M_{n,k-q}^* \right) \right) - \right.$$

$$\left. - E_k^{cc} + \left(L_k + PP_{k-1} \cdot (1 - P_{k-1}) - \sum_{n=1}^{N_{inv}} I_n^* \cdot M_{n,k}^* \right) - \sum_{t=1}^{k} E_{t,k}^{loan} \cdot P_k \cdot \%D_k \right] \to \max; \tag{11}$$

The problem is related to the class of the partially digit non-linear mathematical programming problems.

7   Conclusion

The simulation results show that the small cities depopulation processes offer a real danger of the province decay. The authors hope that the proposed models would be useful for decision makers worried to terminate the small cities depopulation.

Acknowledgements. The article was based on work supported by grants of Russian Foundation for Basic Research Povolzhie No. 13-07-97033, No. 14-07-97011.

References

1. Bramezza, I.: The Competitiveness of the European City and the Role of Urban Management in Improving the City's Performance, p. 160. Purdue University Press, Rotterdam (1990)
2. Hall, P.: Planning Strategies for Cities and Region. Town and City Planning, 139–142 (1995)
3. Zadesenec, E.E., Zarakovskij, G.M., Penova, I.V.: Metodologija izmerenija i ocenki kachestva zhizni naselenija Rossii. Mir izmerenij (in Russia),
   http://ria-stk.ru/mi/adetail.php?ID=37667
4. Kapitza, S.P.: The phenomenological theory of world population growth. Physics-Uspekhi 39(1), 57–71 (1996)
5. Korotaev, A.V., Malkov, A.S., Khalturina, D.A.: Mathematical model of population growth, economics, technology and education. Preprint Inst. Appl. Math., the Russian Academy of Science, Moscow (2005)
6. Podlazov, A.V.: Master Equation of the Theoretical Demography and a Model of the Global Demographic Transition. Preprint Inst. Appl. Math., the Russian Academy of Science, Moscow (2001)
7. Bonabeau, E.: Agent-based modeling: methods and techniques for simulating human systems. Proc. National Academy of Sciences 99(3), 7280–7287 (2002)
8. Sallach, D., Macal, C.: The simulation of social agents: an introduction. Special Issue of Social Science Computer Review 19(3), 245–248 (2001)
9. Hopcroft, J.E., Motwani, R., Ullman, J.D.: Introduction to Automata Theory, Languages, and Computation, 2nd edn., p. 521. Addison-Wesley (2001)
10. Gavrilets, E.Z., Krushel, E.G., Lifshits, A.L., Polyak, E.G.: Business games with dynamic planning models. Automation and Remote Control 42(2 pt.1), 173–181 (1981)
11. Grübler, A., O'Neill, B., Riahi, K., Chirkov, V., Goujon, A., Kolp, P., Prommer, I., Scherbov, S.: Regional, national, and spatially explicit scenarios of demographic and economic change based on SRES Original Research Article. Technological Forecasting and Social Change 74(7), 980–1029 (2007)
12. Krushel, E.G., Stepanchenko, I.V., Stepanchenko, O.V., Panfilov, A.E.: Landscaping State Modeling in a Small Town. World Applied Sciences Journal 25(12), 1669–1675 (2013)

Developing a Model of Multi-Agent System of a Process of a Tech Inspection and Equipment Repair

Vladislav Panteleev, Aleksey Kizim, Valery Kamaev, and Olga Shabalina

Volgograd State Technical University, Volgograd, Russian Federation
{panteleev.vlad,o.a.shabalina}@gmail.com, kizim@mail.ru,
kamaev@cad.vstu.ru

Abstract. This paper examines the issues of efficiency upgrading of using existing tools and possibilities to maintain and repair equipment, and to reduce the workload of the staff. The MRO process of the facility is analyzed in this report. The basic models and the functions they perform are defined in this report. The agent-based approach is used to model a simulation of MRO process. Conceptual and logical models of MRO process are developed here.

Keywords: equipment, maintenance, repair, maintenance and repair, maintenance and repair organization, methodical and software and information support of maintenance and repair, maintenance and repair methodologies, agent-based modeling, multi-agent systems, intelligent methods, automation.

1   Introduction

The main objective of improving the quality of operation of the equipment is to ensure a long and trouble-free processing of the parts with specified performance, accuracy as well as with minimal time, labor and money on maintenance and repair (MRO), which are necessary to restore the technical qualities of machines which, lost during the process of operation. To solve this problem facility organizes system of maintenance and repair (M&R) process of tech equipment (TO).

M&R Management MOT carried with impact on MRO regime characterized by periodic maintenance and maximum admissible (critical) determines the deviation parameter (criterion of limiting state) equipment from the normative values. Consequence of the effective implementation of this intervention is to improve the content of the existing equipment and a clear realization of all kinds of its systematic maintenance and planned repairs. It increases the adaptability of operating period of the life cycle of machines, in other words maintainability, which should be used as a criterion of effectiveness of MRO process [1].

Choice of the methodology takes a major role in increasing the efficiency of MRO, in this report we will consider the methodology MRO according to actual technical condition.

Methodology MRO based on the actual technical condition is aimed to prevent equipment failures and it involves constant monitoring of its technical condition, identification of existing or developing defects and also to determine the optimal time

A. Kravets et al. (Eds.): JCKBSE 2014, CCIS 466, pp. 457–465, 2014.

to start the repair process. This methodology is based on the fact that there is a relationship between the possible malfunctions of equipment and structural elements by the respective technical indicators. It means that conducting monitoring of various parameters, which characterize the operation of the equipment, can detect the change of its condition in time and it allows conducting technical service only when there is a real threat, in other words, when the parameters show unacceptable performances[2].

Practical usage of this methodology involves fulfilment of the following conditions:

1.   Deep understanding of structure of the equipment: for each piece of equipment the following characteristics must be defined:

— a set of indicators, each of which defines the technical condition of the component instance equipment, and the entire set of fully reflects the state of the instance. Moreover, for each of Index defined a certain critical level, the achievement of which means high probability of breakage;
— a list of faults (failures). Fault type is determined by the values of a set of technical indicators for this instance of equipment. The necessary work and supplies to eliminate malfunctions are known.

2.   Each piece of tech equipment must be monitored in real time to check its technical indicators (usually solved by using PCS).

3.   Keep the statistic data of the values of technical indicators, and the history of each instance of MRO equipment. This information serves as a basis for revising critical values of indicators and standards of technical maintenance and repair [3].

In this case, simulation modelling is used, in some sources it called dynamic modelling. Simulation model can be viewed as a set of rules (differential equations, maps of states, machines, networks, etc.), which define the transformation of the current state to the other state. In this case imitation is the process of "making" model, the conducting it through the (discrete or continuous) state changes in time. Generally for complex problems, which involve time and dynamic issues this simulation, is a more powerful tool for analysis.

Advances in the development of approaches and media development of simulation models make them virtually uncontested by support decision-making for complex systems. Recent advances in the field of computer simulation is an agent-based modelling. There exists many definitions of agent and agent-based approach to simulation. Common to all these definitions is that the agent is an entity that has an activity, autonomous behavior, it can make decisions according to a certain set of rules and it can interact with the environment and other agents. Agent-based models are used to study the de-centralized systems, dynamics functioning of which is determined not by the global rules and laws, but on the contrary, these global rules and laws are integral results of individual activity of multiple agents[4,5].

Agent-based approach to simulation modelling has been successfully used in many fields of knowledge - for example, in engineering, sociology, economy and ecology. Reflecting the impact of this approach recently is the selection the independent directions in the various social science disciplines such as "computational economics", "computational sociology", etc. [6].

It is obvious that the application of this modelling approach is most convenient when we are interested in the behavioral characteristics of the whole system, which are defined as the integral characteristics by the set of these agents. One and the same system can be built under different paradigms depending on the goal modelling[7].

Thus, now is the actual task of optimizing the system control maintenance and repair of process equipment engineering facilities by maintainability impact on MRO regime based on the implementation of the principles of the process approach[8].

Current scientific developments in this field were reviewed such as the development of a simulation model predicting the dynamic changes of the status of technical systems for effective planning of a cost for maintenance and repair [9]. Creating simulation models based on the MRO intelligent agents [10]. Development of support MRO decision-making process described in [11, 12]. Approach study process of repair and maintenance of the equipment of the facilities integrated in [13]. Modelling of process MRO in aviation and astronautics described in [14, 15].

2   Goals and Objectives

The goal of this work is to improve the efficiency of the use of available funding for the maintenance and repair of equipment, reducing the load on the experts, as well as development of software that would allow simulating the MRO process of a facility.

To achieve this goal we have defined following tasks:

1. Study domain - Maintenance and repair of equipment;
2. Research a MRO facility;
3. Development of conceptual and logical models of MAS of the MRO process.
4. Development of software tools to implement the prototype of MAS, which models the MRO process.

3   Researching of the Subject's Field

The object of the research is the process of inspection and repair. In order to research and to model this process we have selected a repair and service company, which performs maintenance and repair of various equipment for various customers in many geographically dispersed locations.

The subject of our research is the process of repair and maintenance of the repair-service facility, to be more exact it is the way a repair team, which is specialized in one type of the equipment, performs this process. For example, dynamic equipment: pumps. A repair team works by the repair technology according to a factual condition of equipment.

Repair team performs the following tasks:

— periodic inspection of the equipment;
— apply for a parts from store;
— repair of equipment;
— start \ stop equipment;

During MRO, repair team can identify the following periods:

— inspections of equipment;
— deciding if a repair is necessary;
— stop equipment;
— filling and submitting an application for the necessary parts at the store;
— sending a request for missing parts in stock to the supplier;
— obtaining details from the supplier;
— storing parts and giving it to a master;
— obtaining of a set of parts and repairing equipment;
— launch equipment..

The main essence of the MRO process was highlighted:

1. Equipment is technological equipment, which is loaded with materials or blank means, and technological snap to perform a specific part of the process. These include, for example, casting machines, presses, machine tools, test equipment, etc.
2. Master is a skilled worker engaged in inspection, technical maintenance and repair of equipmentt;
3. Warehouse is a space (or a complex of it) for storing the material values and the provision of storage services. In logistics warehouse performs the function of accumulation of reserves of material resources, needed for vibration in the supply and demand, as well as for syncing speed of the flow of goods in the transportation systems from the manufacturers to consumers or material flows in industrial production systems.
4. Supplier is any legal entity (organization, company, institution) or a human who is supplying goods to customers. Supplier carries out business activities in accordance with the terms of a contract, which is a type of a sale contract. In the supply contract, the Contractor shall transmit goods produced or purchased by him to the due date or dates to the buyer for use in entrepreneurial activities or other purposes not related to personal, family, household, or other similar use.

4   Results

The work was investigated and analyzed the process MRO repair - service enterprise, clearly shown in Fig. 1.

During a detailed analysis of the MRO process of the servicing company, the main model objects and sets of functions that they perform were highlighted.

Based on a detailed analysis the model of the multisystem was developed. Another "Mai Engineer" was added who supervises work of all "Engineer" objects. Takes repair requests and distributes their employment depending on the workload remaining.

Agents «Agent» in the model are: the identifier ID (name of agent), O – multitude of agents that are associated with this agent, the action repetition frequency of the owner's agent with other agents Freq, and a plurality of basic organizational structures - ORG^A, relevant to specific functions (roles) agents:

$$Agent = \{ID, O, Freq, ORG^A\} \tag{1}$$

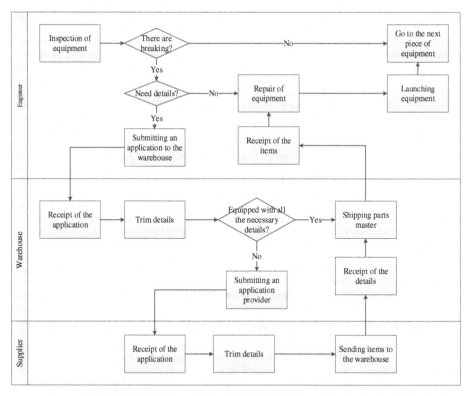

Fig. 1. MRO process of repair and maintenance company

Table 1. Basic model objects and functions

Object	Functions
Equipment	Change in efficiency status.
Engineer	Equipment inspection; Equipment stoppage Parts Ordering; Details acquisition; Equipment launch.
Warehouse	Receiving the order; Order fulfillment; Details acquisition; Parts Ordering; Items reception.
Supplier	Receiving the order; Order fulfillment; Details acquisition;

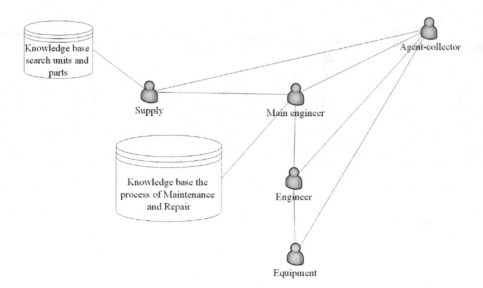

Fig. 2. Model of the MAS

The organizational structure of the agent is formally described as:

$$ORG^A = <S^A, R^A, CP^A, ACT^A, Rem^A, STR^A, L, ST, SL, T> \qquad (2)$$

where S^A - Agent's goals set that it has to perform to complete for its task ;

R^A- agent roles set which he must act to achieve the relevant objectives;

CP^A - the agent skills and abilities set, which he must possess to give to fulfill the respective roles;

ACT^A- set of the agent's actions;

Rem^A – Agent's memory that stores the actions performed by the agent;

STR^A- agent's behavior strategies set which leads towards achieving the relevant objectives;

ST - set of states of the agent;

SL – agent's operation limitations set.

T - generalized transition function

$T: ST \times ACT \times SL \rightarrow 2ST$, satisfies the following conditions:

a) for any st, act, ACT, sl, SL, if the state st satisfies restriction of φ, st $\models \varphi$, and a pair of <act, φ>,sl, то T<st, act, sl> -> φ;

b) for any st, act,ACT, sl1, sl2 , SL, if sl1 > sl2 , then T<st, act, sl1>˝T<st, act, sl2>.

Agent memory - preserving processes executed by the agent is represented as:

$$Rem^A = Save\ (st_0 - (act^{0/}/sl_0)\text{fi } st_1 - (^{act_1}/sl_1)\text{ fi } ...st_n - (^{act_n}/sl_n/)\text{fi } ...) \qquad (3)$$

The repetition rate of the owner's agent actions with other agents is presented as a function depending on the interacting Ce, certificate, the relationship between them and the history of the agent Rem^A:

$$Freq=f(Agent, O, Rem^A) \qquad (4)$$

Where the function f – the processing of interacting actions frequency repetition and a descending sorting of agents' familiar O-sets.

Agent "Equipment" has the following states:

— work;
— idle;
— breakdown.

He also includes a list of parts and relationships that make up the equipment. Several key parameters for each element by which the values of the state of the equipment are determined.

Agent "Engineer" has the following states:

— diagnostic an equipment;
— launching an equipment;
— repair of an equipment;
— stoppage of an equipment;
— sending an equipment state data to " Chief Engineer " agent;
— receiving instructions from agent "Chief Engineer";
— obtaining materials for the repair of the agent " Chief Engineer".

Agent " Main Engineer " has the following states:

— receiving a report on the state of the equipment from the agent "Engineer";
— analysis of the resulting report;
— deciding on a repair necessity;
— ordering the necessary parts for repair;
— obtaining the necessary parts for repair;
— transfer advice and parts needed for repair to agent "Engineer";
— load distribution between the agents "Engineer".

For a decision on the need to repair agent «Main engineer " uses the knowledge base. Now there is still no generally accepted methodology and universal MRO. Therefore, different methodologies for modeling process MRO must use the knowledge base, designed specifically for the chosen methodology. What complicates the process a little modeling.

Agent «Supply» has the following states:

— receive a list of items from the agent " Main Engineer ";
— order parts from the supplier;
— receipt of the items from the supplier;
— transmission parts agent " Main Engineer ";
— search and order these parts.

In the absence of the necessary parts, agent "supply" can prolime search similar items with the use of a knowledge base on the coincidence of structural parameters and function.

To search for similar items developed knowledge base based on AND / OR graph. Which consists of the following elements:

- Repair Facility - equipment. Contains functions.
- Functions - actions that can be performed to repair or nodes. Contains links and details.
- Node - elements of equipment that can perform a set of functions separately from the hardware. Contains functions.
- Detail - the item is not carrying in itself or any functional singularities.

The developed model is used to determine the amount of labor management technicians servicing company, by building models MRO process with different variations of congestion specialists. Data modeling of these processes are analyzed and compared with each other to determine the most optimal process MRO with an approximately equal load on specialists. Just the proposed improvements on the supply stage can significantly speed up the search process and get the details now.

5   Conclusion

In this paper, we have reviewed and analyzed the modern scientific developments in the field of modeling the process of maintenance and repair of equipment. Reviewed and analyzed the process of MRO repair - service enterprise. The basic model objects and sets of functions that they perform. Developed conceptual and logical models MAC MRO process.

We are planning to use software tools in order to embody the MAS prototype, which models the MRO process and after we are planning to use the developed model.

In the future we plan to implement the software tool for the implementation of the prototype MAC modeling process MRO and validation of the developed model.

This work was supported by RFBR grant № 13 -01- 00798_a.

References

1. Sergushicheva, M.A.: Proyektirovaniye application-oriented the multiagentnykh of systems with usage of a packet of DISIT (An electronic resource) (2009), Access mode: http://www.sai.vstu.edu.ru/load/multiagent_shvec_serg.doc
2. Kizim, A.V., Chi-kov, E.V., Melnik, V.Y., Kamaev, V.A.: Programmno-informacionnaya podderjka tehnicheskogo obslujivaniya i remonta oborudovaniya s uchetom interesov subektov processa. Informatizaciya i svyaz (3), S.57–S.59 (2011)
3. Century Romanenko, H.: Simulation modeling of process of aging of difficult systems (Electronic resource) (2012), access mode: http://www.nbuv.gov.ua/PORTAL/natural/Ptekh/2012_3/118-123.pdf

4. Denisov, M.V., Kizim, A.V., Matokhina, A.V., Sadovnikova, N.P.: Repair and mainten-ance organization with the use of ontologies and multi-agent systems on the road sector example. World Applied Sciences Journal 24(24), 31–36 (2013)
5. Kizim, A.V., Kravets, A.D., Kravets, A.G.: Generation of intelligent agents to support tasks of maintenance and repair (Generacija intellektual'nyh agentov dlja zadach pod-derzhki tehnicheskogo obsluzhivanija i remonta). In: IzvestiaTPU, pp. 131–134 (2012)
6. Denisov, M.V., Kamaev, V.A., Kizim, A.V.: Organization of the Repair and Maintenance in Road Sector with Ontologies and Multi-agent Systems. Original Research Article Pro-cedia Technology 9, 819–825 (2013)
7. Shurygin, A.N.: Simulation modeling of maintenance service (Electronic resource) (2009), Access mode: `http://dspace.susu.ac.ru/xmlui/bitstream/handle/0001.74/776/14.pdf?sequence=1`
8. Kizim, A.V.: Establishing the Maintenance and Repair Body of Knowledge: Comprehen-sive Approach to Ensuring Equipment Maintenance and Repair Organization Efficiency. Original Research Article Procedia Technology 9, 812–818 (2013)
9. Reshetnikov, I.: Agent management model MRO integrated production structure. RISK: Resources, information, supply, competition (4), 169–171 (2010)
10. Kizim A.V., Kamayev V.A., Denisov of M. of Century: An information system of a deci-sion support (ИСППР) for scheduling of TOIR of road technique. Innovations on the basis of information and communication technologies T. 1., 402–404 (2013)
11. Nechval, N., Purgailis, M., Cikste, K., Berzins, G., Rozevskis, U., Nechval, K.: Prediction Model Selection and Spare Parts Ordering Policy for Efficient Support of Maintenance and Repair of Equipment. Analytical and Stochastic Modeling Techniques and Applications, 321–338 (2010)
12. Zhuravlev, A.V., Portnyagin, A.L.: Implementation of a comprehensive approach to the study of the processes of maintenance of equipment of oil and gas industry. Journal of Cy-bernetics (11), 17–23 (2012)
13. Thomas, A.J., Francis, M., Rowlands, H.: Defining an Asset Management strategy for aero-space MRO functions using Monte Carlo methods. In: IET and IAM Asset Manage-ment Conference, pp. 12–18 (2011)
14. Li, H., Ji, Y.-J., Qi, G.-N., Gu, X.-J., Zhang, D., Chen, J.-X.: Integration model of complex equipment MRO based on lifecycle management. Computer Integrated Manufacturing Systems (2010)
15. Liu, Y.-B., Xu, Y.-L., Zhang, L.: MRO system modeling based on multi-layer model. Computer Integrated Manufacturing Systems (2010)

Performance Analysis of Alternative Open Source Parallel Computing Approach to OpenMP on Multicore Processors

Satyadhyan Chickerur[1], Dadi Mohan Krishna Rayudu[2],
Srinidhi Hiriyannaiah[2], and Olga Shabalina[3]

[1] Centre for High Performance Computing,
B.V. Bhoomaraddi College of Engineering and Technology, Hubli, India
[2] IBM-ISL, Bangalore, India
[3] Computer-Aided Design Department, Volgograd State Technical University,
Lenin av., 28, Volgograd, Russia
{Chickerursr,rayudu.mohan,srinidhi.hiriyannaiah,
o.a.shabalina}@gmail.com

Abstract. In this era of evolving computing field, parallel computing is one of the fastest changing fields. There have been numerous researches made and still the research is going on in the areas of data decomposition, parallel algorithms to get more performance through parallelism. In this paper we have achieved parallelism by using an open source made available with the name libdispatch (implementation of Grand Central Dispatch Services). This package has been ported to the FreeBSD, however this can also be used under open source environment. In this paper we have experimented with matrix multiplication in sequential and parallel programs. The categories of experimentation done are: Sequential Programming with GCC and Clang; Parallel programming with OpenMP and clang with dispatcher. Better performance has been observed in Clang for both sequential and parallel computations

Keywords: Parallel programming, Clang, OpenMP, Grand Central Dispatch.

1   Introduction

The life cycle of processors has evolved from single processors to multi-core processors with the advent of data and computation to process large sets of data. Some but not all programs are being shifted from serial to parallel programming to handle large data sets. In present scenario all hardware configuration are reached to its limits so in this present situation we have to improve our way of executing parallel programming. In order to utilize efficiently multi-core processors the program in execution must be written to achieve parallelism. Most of the programs or software fails because of under utilization of multi-core processors. However, the process of achieving parallelism is a tedious task as it involves data decomposition, analyzing task dependency graphs, mapping of tasks to processors.

A. Kravets et al. (Eds.): JCKBSE 2014, CCIS 466, pp. 466–476, 2014.

Matrix multiplication has been used as a primary block in many of the subject areas [1]. Graph theory uses matrix multiplication to obtain the distance between a pair of nodes. In computer graphics it plays a prominent role in rendering. Hence, with the advent of multicore architectures it is important to explore mechanisms for enhancing the performance of matrix multiplication by parallelization [6]. In this paper we present the evaluation of sequential programming of matrix multiplication using GCC and clang, then parallel programming of matrix multiplication using lib-dispatch.

2   State of the Art

Computer Programs are written using programming languages that specify the classes for computation. Computer processes a particular sequence of instructions and not program texts. Therefore, the program text must be translated to a suitable one before the computer processes it. This process of translation can be automated with the help of a compiler.

2.1   GCC

GCC is one of renowned compilers used for execution of both serial and parallel programs since few decades. Majority of the research community has immensely benefitted by the compiler, which once was treated as one of the Best. In the recent days some new compilers have arrived which show better performance than the compiler of the previous generation the GCC. The details of GCC are given at the free software foundations GNU Project website [2].

2.2   Clang

Clang is written using C++ and a cross compiler. Since LLVM is also written using C++ clang can effectively optimize the algorithms to produce an efficient code and easily adapt to new architectures. But, the main focus of clang team was to present errors in a user-friendly manner even though it is a command line based compiler [3][4][5]. This is taken care by the diagnostics engine of clang that diagnoses the error and presents it in a user-friendly manner. It prints the source code and points out the location where the parser went wrong. But, since it is a young project, efforts are being made to execute parallel programs using clang with Polly.

2.3   Generic Parallel Programming Using OpenMP

In the area of high performance computing parallel programming is an important area of research [6]. OpenMP provides a parallel programming model that reply to utilize parallel platforms with portable across different architectures. A combination of libraries, directories and environment variables is used by open MP to exploit the platform in C/C++ and Fortran programs.

Compiler directories are the main technique used in OpenMP to exploit or derive parallelism in programs [7][8]. These directives are added to the locations where parallelism is needed and provides an indicator to the compiler the region which has to be parallelized along with some instructions that specify how the region is to be parallelized [10].

```
Ex: #pragma omp parallel
      {
            printf("Hello World");
      }
```

The execution of a program with OpenMP is based on fork-join model [14]. When a program with OpenMP constructs is executed, execution table place on simple thread, master thread until OpenMP construct #pragma omp parallel is encountered then fork () call executes to create a team of threads. The team of threads created executes the statements that are enclosed in parallel regions. When the execution of these threads is over, then join () call is executed for synchronization, some of threads have to wait until all the threads are finished and finally terminated learning behind masters thread.

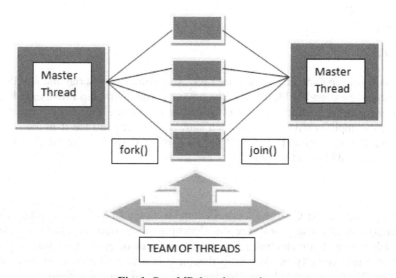

Fig. 1. OpenMP thread execution

3   Proposed Alternative Approach

Multi core processors have changed the field of advanced computing requiring the developer to adapt to the changing threads of development and write applications according to it [12][13].

GCD is a new approach that helps the developers to adopt their applications to the varying trend of multi core processors by allowing the thread management to operating system and thus reduce the overheads of threading issues. GCD provides a new way of multi-core programming with optimal thread management, simplified event handling and synchronization based on queues.

It uses queues which can be either system defined or user-defined which consists of blocks. Whenever a block has been dispatched, t is assigned the available thread from the pool of threads and thus overcome the disadvantages of pool of threads and thus overcome the disadvantage of creating and managing threads, thus reduce the latency of executions[14].

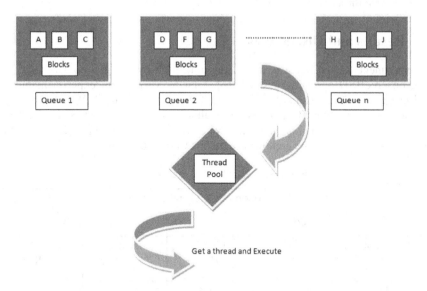

Fig. 2. GCD block execution

The number of threads created in the thread pool depends on the cores available in the system. Once the thread pool is available, GCD allocates the block to available thread and proceeds with execution. Since the system is responsible for management and execution of threads, the program or code runs efficiently on single processors, multiprocessor system and everything in between.

The two main components of GCD are

- Blocks
- Queues

Blocks help to define self-contained units of work .It is denoted by a caret at beginning of a function.

```
Ex:  ^{printf ("hello world")};
```

Queues: Blocks that needs to be executed are scheduled to queues. These are lightweight data structures that are more efficient than normally managing threads and code. Queues are able to monitor resource demand across the entire OS. The system used wide enable to balance supply& demands of threads across multiple applications [14]. Various types of queues in GCD are:

Global Queue: There is a global queue associated with concurrent processors in GCD. Whenever a block is en queued on one of the global queues, he available threads are searched and one of thread is assigned to the clock.

Private Queues: These are serial queues created by a developer that has access to shared data structure. They are scheduled using global queues. Each serial queue has its own target queue when a block is added to the queue; the queue itself is added to the target queue. When it turns comes queue gets executed with blocks one after the other.

Main Queue: Every process has main queue which is a unique serial queue associated with main thread of program.

4   Results and Discussions

The experiment carried out was matrix multiplication by using compilers GCC and Clang on FreeBSD operating system [16]. First we carried out experimentation on serial programs. These results are shown in Table 1 and Figure 3. We observed that execution time of both GCC and clang was almost the same till matrix size 700x700. But, as the matrix size increased further we observed that clang takes less execution time compared to GCC. The architecture used is Core2Duo system.

Table 1. GCC and CLANG execution times

Comparison of GCC and CLANG				
	2 cores		4 cores	
Matrix Size	GCC (Sec.)	CLANG (Sec.)	GCC (Sec.)	CLANG (Sec.)
100x100	0.0468	0.0468		
200x200	0.258	0.289	0.039	0.054
300x300	0.656	0.570	0.179	0.171
400x400	0.859	0.617	0.382	0.375
500x500	1.578	1.281	0.859	0.843
600x600	2.508	2.188	1.820	1.742
700x700	3.883	3.305	3.507	3.500
800x800	5.734	4.867	5.460	5.437
900x900	8.922	7.719	8.328	8.125
1000x1000	13.336	11.930	11.781	11.320
1200x1200	23.023	20.602	20.601	19.523
1400x1400	36.547	32.586	32.851	31.031
1500x1500	44.672	39.711	40.632	38.085
1600x1600	54.344	48.461	50.406	46.328
1800x1800	77.195	68.922	70.414	65.820
2000x2000	91.508	81.59	61.890	53.140
2300x2300	138.398	123.00	93.250	80.398

Table 1. (*Continued*)

2500x2500	181.711	161.719	121.375	104.203
2600x2600	199.289	177.492	131.976	115.945
2900x2900	283.508	252.383	187.867	163.718
3000x3000	305.445	271.578	202.453	177.937

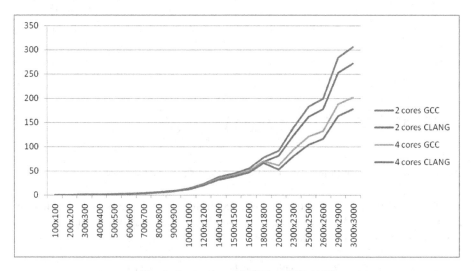

Fig. 3. Comparison of GCC and CLANG

Table 2. OPENMP ON 2 CORES AND 4 CORES

OPENMP		
MATRIX SIZE	2 CORES(Sec.)	4 CORES(Sec.)
200X200	0.05	0.04
300x300	0.17	0.14
400x400	0.45	0.45
500x500	0.93	0.81
700x700	2.59	3.57
1000x1000	8.71	7.84
1200x1200	15.22	25.31
1500x1500	30.06	51.65
1700x1700	45.65	60.91
2000x2000	83.78	128.51
2500x2500	186.7	241.77
3000x3000	339.58	431.25

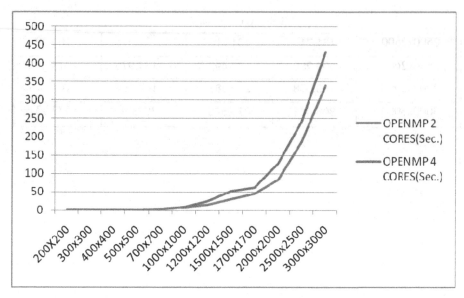

Fig. 4. Comparison Of OpenMP On 2 Cores And 4 Cores

Table 3 and Figure 5 lists the values of execution time of Clang with Dispatcher on 2 cores and 4 cores. We observe that with the increase in matrix size the execution time is less on 4 cores compared to 2 cores.

Table 3. Clang with Dispatcher on 2 Cores and 4 Cores

CLANG with Dispatcher		
MATRIX SIZE	2 CORES(Sec.)	4 CORES(Sec.)
200X200	0.04	0.03
300x300	0.11	0.05
400x400	0.35	0.07
500x500	0.42	0.22
700x700	0.86	0.44
1000x1000	1.24	0.93
1200x1200	1.88	1.34
1500x1500	2.93	2.14
1700x1700	3.71	2.72
2000x2000	5.41	3.83
2500x2500	7.9	5.9
3000x3000	12.81	11.03

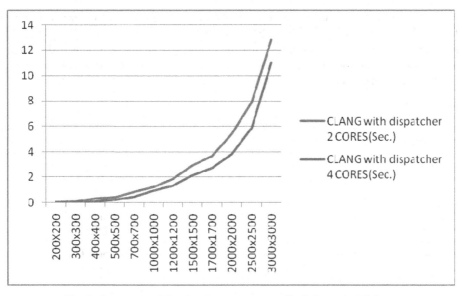

Fig. 5. Comparison Of Clang With Dispatcher On 2 Cores And 4 Cores

Table 4. Comparision Of Openmp And Clang With Dispatcher

Comparison of OPENMP and CLANG with Dispatcher				
	2 cores		4 cores	
Matrix Size	GCC with OPENMP	CLANG with Dispatcher	GCC with OPENMP	CLANG with Dispatcher
200X200	0.05	0.04	0.04	0.03
300X300	0.17	0.11	0.14	0.05
400X400	0.45	0.35	0.45	0.07
500X500	0.93	0.42	0.81	0.22
700X700	2.59	0.86	3.57	0.44
1000X1000	8.71	1.24	7.84	0.93
1200X1200	15.22	1.88	25.31	1.34
1500X1500	30.06	2.93	51.65	2.14
1700X1700	45.65	3.71	60.91	2.72
2000X2000	83.78	5.41	128.51	3.83
2500X2500	186.7	7.9	241.77	5.9
3000X3000	339.58	12.81	431.25	11.03

Next, we carried out our further experiment on parallel program of matrix multiplication with OpenMP and Clang with dispatcher on 2 cores and 4 cores. These results are shown in table 4. From the results we observe that until matrix size 400x400 there is a minor difference in execution time in 2 cores. But, as the matrix size increases from 500x500 we can observe that relative time of execution with OpenMP is dramatically greater than Clang with dispatcher. So, a speedup of 26.5x is achieved with a matrix size of 3000x3000. Hence, as the matrix size increases the speedup with dispatcher is also increased.

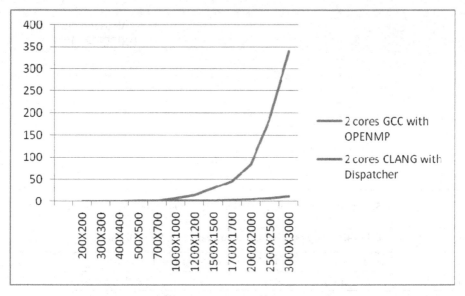

Fig. 6. Comparison Of OpenMP and Clang With Dispatcher On 2 Cores

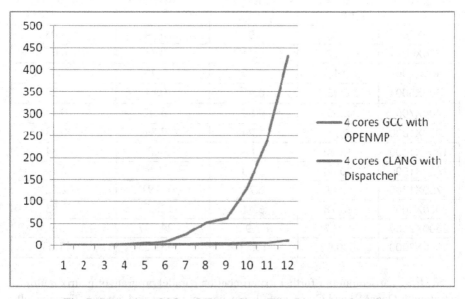

Fig. 7. Comparison Of OpenMP and Clang With Dispatcher On 4 Cores

It also shows the results of same program executed on a 4 core system. We can observe that it takes much less time than on a 2 core system. From the graph we can observe that there is a much difference between OpenMP and dispatcher. These results are shown in table 4 and Figure 6 and Figure 7.

5   Conclusion

GCC is one of the most widely used compilers for execution of all programs. But Clang is another compiler that can be used that produces results in less time compared to GCC. OpenMP is a widely used technique to exploit parallelism among programs with GCC as the compiler. Libdispatch is one of the alternative techniques that can be used to exploit parallelism using Clang compiler. This approach provides a better way to achieve parallelism by abstracting the details of shared and private variables thread management from the developer and thus concentrate on the decomposition of the problem into parallel pieces. It not only provides the ease of development but also produces more scalable programs.

References

1. Ismail, M.A., Mirza, S.H., Altaf, T.: Concurrent Matrix Multiplication on Multi-Core Processors. Altaf Concurrent Matrix Multiplication on Multi-Core Processors. IJCSS 5(2), 208–220 (2011)
2. https://gcc.gnu.org
3. Fandrey, D., Fuchß, T.: Clang/LLVM Maturity Evaluation Report Karlsruhe University of Applied Sciences Computer Science department (June 6, 2010)
4. Guntli, C.: Architecture of clang, Analyze an open source compiler based on LLVM; HSR - University of Applied Science in Rapperswil (June 3, 2011)
5. http://clang.llvm.org/
6. Grama, A., Karypis, G., Kumar, V., Gupta, A.: Introduction to Parallel Computing, 2nd edn. Pearson Publishers (2003)
7. Jin, H., Jespersen, D., Mehrotra, P., Biswas, R., Huang, L., Chapman, B.: High Performance Computing Using MPI and OpenMP on Multi-core Parallel Systems. Journal Parallel Computing 37(9), 562–575 (2011)
8. Allen, E., Chase, D., Flood, C., Luchangco, V., Maessen, J.W., Ryu, S., Steele, G.L.: A Multicore Language for Multicore Processors. Project Fortress: Linux Magazine (September 2007)
9. Bircsak, J., Craig, P., Crowell, R., Cvetanovic, Z., Harris, J., Nelson, C.A., Offner, C.D.: Extending OpenMP for NUMA Machines. In: Proceedings of the 2000 ACM/IEEE Conference on Supercomputing, Dallas, TX (November 2000)
10. Chamberlain, B.L., Callahan, D., Zima, H.P.: Parallel Programmability and the Chapel Language. International Journal of High Performance Computing Applications 21(3), 291–312 (2007)
11. Novillo, D.: Openmp and automatic parallelization in gcc. In: The Proceedings of the GCC Developers' Summit (June 2006)

12. Weinberger, A., Mentor, T.: Dr. David Hastings, Shippensburg University Multicore programming using Apple's Grand Central Dispatch
13. Grand Central Dispatch: A better way to do multicore. Apple Inc. Technical Brief (2009)
14. Concurrency Programming Guide. Apple Inc. Developer Connection (2011)
15. http://www.OpenMP.org
16. http://wiki.freebsd.org/GCD/

Iteration Multilevel Method
for the Travelling Salesman Problem

Nikolay V. Starostin and Ilya V. Klyuev

Lobachevsky State University, Department of Computational Mathematics and Cybernetics,
Chair of Informatics and Scientific Research Automation, Nizhny Novgorod, Russia
nvstar@iani.unn.ru, kluev.ilya@gmail.com

Abstract. This document presents iteration multilevel method of solving the travelling salesman problem. The multilevel method reduces graph dimension (reduction phase), searches for a solution with a coarse graph and consistently restores the obtained solution on the source graph (restoration phase). The suggested iteration approach allows to improve the originally obtained cycle through multiple reduction and restoring the problem. The results obtained during testing testify of perspective of this approach.

Keywords: Travelling salesman problem, Iteration method, Multilevel optimization.

1 Introduction

The classic travelling salesman problem is considered in symmetrical setting with a sparse graph. Displayed NP hard problem makes solution of very high dimension tasks by precision methods practically impossible.

In the original problem a marked graph $G = (V, E, w)$ is set, where V – vertex set $|V| = n$; $E \subseteq V^{(2)}$ – edge set; $w_{ij} \in R^+$ – real number showing weight of edge $\{v_i, v_j\} \in E$. It is required to find such $\rho = (\rho_1, \rho_2, ..., \rho_n) \in \Pi$ repositioning that complies with Hamiltonian cycle $(v_{\rho_1}, v_{\rho_2}, ..., v_{\rho_n}, v_{\rho_1})$, $v_{\rho_i} \in V, \{v_{\rho_i}, v_{\rho_{i+1}}\} \in E$, $\{v_{\rho_n}, v_{\rho_1}\} \in E$, $i = 1, n-1$ of minimal weight

$$\min_{p \in \Pi} \left(w_{p_n p_1} + \sum_{i=1}^{n-1} w_{p_i p_{i+1}} \right) \to \min \qquad (1)$$

2 Transition to a Task with Entire Graph

The problem of searching a permitted Hamiltonian cycle with a any non-oriented graph belongs to the class of NP-full problems [1]. To overcome difficulties related to

A. Kravets et al. (Eds.): JCKBSE 2014, CCIS 466, pp. 477–482, 2014.
© Springer International Publishing Switzerland 2014

enumeration of feasible solutions a technology of reducing the task to an entire non-oriented weighted graph is suggested, which allows to efficiently operate a nonempty set of feasible solutions even for very sparse graphs. The technology provides for adding the source graph to a full one $\tilde{G} = (V, V^{(2)}, a)$: weights of existing edges $\{v_i, v_j\} \in E$ remain unchanged $a_{ij} = w_{ij}$; for any pair $v_i, v_j \in V$ of nonadjacent vertexes $\{v_i, v_j\} \notin E$ a edge weighing $a_{ij} = d_{ij} + m_{ij} \cdot \sum_{i=1}^{n} w_{ij}$ is created, where d_{ij} and m_{ij} are total edge weight and the number of transitional vertexes of the shortest way between vertexes v_i and v_j correspondingly. It is easy to show that the optimal cycle at such entire graph is a solution of the task with a sparse graph.

Exact algorithms [2,3] are not applicable for solving applied problems, which stipulated development of approximate [4] and heuristic approaches [5,6,7,8] for the travelling salesman problem. The so called meta-algorithms [9,10] are particularly interesting, in particular their demonstrative representative – the class of multilevel algorithms, which was successfully used for the first time for the problem of partitioning the graph [11],[13].

3   Multilevel Algorithm

For soling the considered problem the multilevel approach is suggested based on the technology of reducing the dimension by graph reduction method, search of the cycle in the reduced graph with its subsequent restoration to the original graph.

```
1   cycle ML_TSP(graph g)
2   {
3       int level = 0;
4       while (level < LEVELS)
5       {                               Cycle of sequential
6           g = coarse(g);              graph reductions.
7           level++;
8       }
9       cycle x = find(g);              Searching a cycle.
10      while (level > 0)
11      {                               Cycle of consistently
12          x = unproject(g, x);        restores the obtained
13          g = uncoarse(g);            solution on the source graph
14          x = refine(g, x);           with local search.
15          level--;
16      }
17      return x;
18  }
```

Listing 1. Multilevel algorithm

The primary objective of reduction is obtaining the reduced graph "version" by edges identification method. The reduction algorithm is based on heuristics (function **coarse**): the priority is given to edges with the lowest weight. The algorithm selects a system of nonadjacent edges, identifies them, thus building a coarse version of the source graph.

The same algorithm may be applied to a coarse graph version and obtain a new, more coarse graph. A series of sequential reductions end, when a coarse graph of acceptable order is obtained.

The coarsest graph is used for searching a cycle with a heuristic algorithm based on "greed" (function **find**) – the next cycle element is chosen as an edge with the lowest weight. Algorithm cycle generation is started from a randomly chosen vertex and is finished upon inclusion of all graph vertexes into the cycle.

Then a restoration procedure is done for the obtained solution (function **unproject**) –it is a process of sequential transfer of the found solution from the coarse graph to the source graph (function **uncoarse**). At this stage the algorithms based on the local search play the key role, which are used after each transfer of solution from a coarser graph to a less coarse one. It allows refining the solution using new information missing in the coarser graph versions. As local optimization algorithms two special cases of r-optimization are used, suggested by Kernighan and Lin [8]: 2-optimization and 3-optimization (function **refine**).

4   Iteration Multilevel Algorithm

Traditional multilevel schemes are intrinsically practical and provide no way for improvement of the obtained solution. A concept of multilevel iteration algorithm is suggested (see listing 2), which through repeated reduction and restoration of the problem and its solution allows improving the originally obtained cycle.

```
1   cycle ML_TSP(graph g, cycle x)
2   {
3       for (int iter = 0; iter < ITERS; iter++)      Cycle of iteration mul-
4       {                                             tilevel algorithm.
5           int level = 0;
6           while (level < LEVELS)
7           {                                         Reduction phase.
8               g = coarse(g, x);                     Graph reduction and
9               x = project(g, x);                    solution reduction.
10              level++;
11          }
12          x = refine(g, x);                         optimize the existing
13          cycle y = find(g);                        solution or find new
14          if (record(y, x)) y.copyTo(x);            solution.
15          while (level > 0)
16          {                                         Restoration phase.
17              x = unproject(g, x);                  Solution restore.
18              g = uncoarse(g);                      Graph restore.
19              x = refine(g, x);                     Local search.
20              level--;
21          }
22      }
23      return x;
24  }
```

Listing 2. Iteration multilevel algorithm

Major change is in the reduction procedure. The objective of the new reduction is identification of the edges having a high chance of falling into the optimal cycle. Such reduction allows providing favorable conditions for designing the remaining fragments of the optimal cycle (function project). As experiments showed that edges falling into the originally found cycle have high chances, therefore the "lightest" of them are reduced first of all.

The same changes refer to the stage of searching a chain in the coarse graph – in the iteration multilevel scheme 2 strategies are used: the first one tries to locally optimize the existing solution, and the second one is aimed at the search of principally new solution based on the above greedy heuristics.

5   Experiment

In computational experiments the well-known public collection [14] of graphs (column "graphs") and the record shortest cycles (column "record") was used, for which various algorithms were evaluated for years and repeatable record results have been obtained. The suggested algorithm was tested on 75 test problems from the above collection (see Table 1).

Table 1. Experiment results

graph	$|V|$	$|E|$	record	MATRUZ record	%	graph	$|V|$	$|E|$	record	MATRUZ record	%
a280	280	78120	2579	2675	3.7	kroE100	100	9900	22068	22244	0.8
ali535	535	285690	202339	209347	3.5	kroA150	150	22350	26524	26732	0.8
att48	48	2256	10628	10653	0.2	kroB150	150	22350	26130	26297	0.6
att532	532	282492	27686	28467	2.8	kroA200	200	39800	29368	29776	1.4
bayg29	29	812	1610	1610	0.0	kroB200	200	39800	29437	30284	2.9
bays29	29	812	2020	2020	0.0	lin105	105	10920	14379	14382	0.0
berlin52	52	2652	7542	7544	0.0	lin318	318	100806	42029	43090	2.5
bier127	127	16002	118282	118838	0.5	p654	654	427062	34643	34927	0.8
brazil58	58	3306	25395	25395	0.0	pa561	561	314160	2763	2916	5.5
brg180	180	32220	1950	1990	2.1	pcb442	442	194922	50778	52799	4.0
burma14	14	182	3323	3323	0.0	pr76	76	5700	108159	109471	1.2
ch130	130	16770	6110	6149	0.6	pr107	107	11342	44303	44301	-0.0
ch150	150	22350	6528	6654	1.9	pr124	124	15252	59030	59412	0.6
d198	198	39006	15780	15954	1.1	pr136	136	18360	96772	97578	0.8
d493	493	242556	35002	36097	3.1	pr144	144	20592	58537	58587	0.1
dantzig42	42	1722	699	699	0.0	pr152	152	22952	73682	73843	0.2
eil51	51	2550	426	433	1.6	pr226	226	50850	80369	80551	0.2
eil76	76	5700	538	559	3.9	pr264	264	69432	49135	49993	1.7
eil101	101	10100	629	652	3.7	pr299	299	89102	48191	48894	1.5
fl417	417	173472	11861	12114	2.1	pr439	439	192282	107217	108941	1.6
fri26	26	650	937	937	0.0	rat99	99	9702	1211	1219	0.7
gil262	262	68382	2378	2426	2.0	rat195	195	37830	2323	2426	4.4
gr17	17	272	2085	2085	0.0	rat575	575	330050	6773	7044	4.0
gr21	21	420	2707	2707	0.0	rat783	783	612306	8806	9175	4.2
gr24	24	552	1272	1272	0.0	rd100	100	9900	7910	7981	0.9
gr48	48	2256	5046	5055	0.2	rd400	400	159600	15281	15659	2.5
gr96	96	9120	55209	55995	1.4	si175	175	30450	21407	21408	0.0
gr120	120	14280	6942	7065	1.8	si535	535	285690	48450	48646	0.4
gr137	137	18632	69853	70159	0.4	st70	70	4830	675	682	1.0
gr202	202	40602	40160	40840	1.7	swiss42	42	1722	1273	1273	0.0
gr229	229	52212	134602	136890	1.7	ts225	225	50400	126643	130078	2.7
gr431	431	185330	171414	176037	2.7	tsp225	225	50400	3916	3988	1.8
gr666	666	442890	294358	304707	3.5	u159	159	25122	42080	42392	0.7
hk48	48	2256	11461	11556	0.8	u574	574	328902	36905	38097	3.2
kroA100	100	9900	21282	21344	0.3	u724	724	523452	41910	43407	3.6
kroB100	100	9900	22141	22558	1.9	ulysses16	16	240	6859	6859	0.0
kroC100	100	9900	20749	20750	0.0	ulysses22	22	462	7013	7013	0.0
kroD100	100	9900	21294	21384	0.4						

The results of the iteration multilevel algorithm are the following (column MATRUZ): in 12 graphs we managed to repeat a record result (7% instances); in 28 graphs deviation from the record result does not exceed 0.5% (37% instances); maximum deviation from the record result does not exceed 3.7%; in graph pr107 the obtained result was 44301, which exceeded the record one of 44303 by 2 units (see Table 1).

Below (see Table 2) presented new record cycle for graph pr107, which was obtained by the iteration multilevel algorithm.

Table 2. Cycle with weight 44301 in graph pr107 [14]

№	vertex	№	vertex	№	vertex	№	vertex	№	vertex	№	vertex
1	88	19	105	37	39	55	22	73	0	91	74
2	90	20	54	38	36	56	19	74	1	92	77
3	57	21	49	39	33	57	16	75	62	93	79
4	93	22	52	40	32	58	13	76	65	94	82
5	56	23	53	41	30	59	17	77	63	95	81
6	95	24	50	42	35	60	14	78	66	96	78
7	96	25	51	43	34	61	15	79	64	97	80
8	94	26	48	44	31	62	12	80	67	98	59
9	97	27	45	45	28	63	11	81	68	99	83
10	99	28	44	46	25	64	10	82	71	100	58
11	102	29	42	47	29	65	7	83	70	101	85
12	101	30	47	48	26	66	9	84	69	102	86
13	98	31	46	49	27	67	8	85	72	103	84
14	100	32	43	50	24	68	6	86	61	104	87
15	55	33	40	51	21	69	4	87	73	105	89
16	103	34	37	52	20	70	5	88	60	106	92
17	104	35	41	53	18	71	2	89	75	107	91
18	106	36	38	54	23	72	3	90	76	108	88

During experiments an iteration multilevel algorithm was launched in the following mode: the number of reduction levels equaled 10, each reduction iteration reduced graph dimension by 10%, number of multilevel iterations equaled 10. It should be noted that during solving any of the tasks presented in Table 1 on PC (configuration i7 2 GHz / 16 Gb, OS MS Windows 7x64) did not exceed 5 seconds.

6   Conclusion

The suggested original iteration multilevel approach demonstrated clearly the potential for solving the considered class of travelling salesman problems. The method of multilevel reduction allows to efficiently reduce complexity of high dimensional problems, and multilevel local search allows successful repeated optimization of the found solution. The developed academic version of algorithm software realization demonstrates relatively low computational costs in search of "good" solutions for the known travelling salesman problems.

References

1. Karp, R.M.: Reducibility Among Combinatorial Problems. In: Miller, R.E., Thatcher, J.W. (eds.) Complexity of Computer Computations, pp. 85–103. Plenum, New York (1972)
2. Carpaneto, G., Fischetti, M., Toth, P.: New lower bounds for the symmetric travelling salesman problem. Mathematical Programming 45, 233–254 (1989)
3. Carpaneto, G., Toth, P.: Some new branching and bounding criteria for the asymmetric travelling salesman problem. Management Science 26, 736–743 (1980)
4. Christofides, N.: Worst-case analysis of a new heuristic for the travelling salesman problem, Report 388, Graduate School of Industrial Admin (1976)
5. Norback, J., Love, R.: Heuristic for the Hamiltonian path problem in Euclidean two space. Journal of the Operational Research Society 30, 363–368 (1979)
6. Karp, R.M.: A patching algorithm for the nonsymmetric traveling-salesman problem. SIAM Journal on Computing 8, 561–573 (1979)
7. Lin, S.: Computer solutions of the traveling salesman problem. Bell Syst. Tech. J. 44, 2245–2269 (1965)
8. Lin, S., Kernighan, B.W.: An Effective Heuristic Algorithm for the TravelingSalesman Problem. Operations Res. 21, 498–516 (1973)
9. Grefenstette, J., et al.: Genetic algorithms for the traveling salesman problem. In: Proc. Intern. Conf. of Genetic Algorithms and their Applications, pp. 160–165 (1985)
10. Dorigo, M., Stutzle, T.: Ant Colony Optimization. Massachusetts Institute of Technology (2004)
11. Karypis, G., Kumar, V.: A Fast and High Quality Multilevel Scheme for Partitioning Irregular Graphs. SIAM J. Sci. Comput. 20(1), 359–392 (1998a)
12. Kernighan, B.W., Lin, S.: An efficient heuristic procedure for partitioning graphs. Bell System Tech. (1970)
13. Walshaw, C.: A Multilevel Approach to the Graph Colouring Problem. Technical Report01/IM/69, Comp. Math. Sci., University Greenwich, London, UK (May 2001b)
14. Traveling salesman problem library (TSPLIB) at the University of Heidelberg, http://comopt.ifi.uni-heidelberg.de/software/TSPLIB95/

Component-Based Approach to Multi-Agent System Generation

Alla G. Kravets, Sergey A. Fomenkov, and Andrey D. Kravets

Volgograd State Technical University, Volgograd, Russia

Abstract. The paper contains general information on development process of multi-agent system generator. Generator in question uses component-based approach as a general methodology in construction of multi-agent systems and modules. Component-based module of the generator consists of a set previously created agent templates and typical connections between them. Authors propose visual programming paradigm in order to supply a user with an opportunity to create multi-agent modules without special education as a software developer. Visual programming module of the generator allows a user to construct a scheme of inter-agent collaboration with agents of component-based module set.

Keywords: component-based approach, multi-agent system, code generation, visual programming.

1 Introduction

Model of multi-agent systems initially developed for representation of system of a number of collaborating objects sharing the same or familiar structure nowadays is proven worthy of use in a great number of scientific areas. Multi-agent systems modeling have shown great results in physics, medicine, chemistry, agriculture and etc. Being used in data mining and software engineering for robotics the concept of agent as an object vested by a set of user's rights in order to accomplish its objectives was established. That concept of agent allowed determining agent as a complex system that can be based on intellectual methods within a multi-agent collaboration model. Due to implementation of multi-agent model into a vast number of informational systems authors stated a goal of creating a source generating platform which would allow creating multi-agent systems and modules by experts of subject area without involvement of developers[1].

2 Literature Review

2.1 Multi-Agent Systems

The key idea of every multi-agent system is a delegation to an agent of a certain task and associated rights similar to user's ones which are required for automated decision

A. Kravets et al. (Eds.): JCKBSE 2014, CCIS 466, pp. 483–490, 2014.

making[8]. Agent is an active object that exceed traditionally stated limitations of object in object-oriented programming and moreover using these objects in order to fulfill its goals be means of management changing their states and statuses. According to this definition of agent the minimal basis characteristics set of common agent[7]:

• Activity as a ability to product and realize goals;
• Self-containment as an absolute or comparative independence from environment which among externals contains other agents and presence of "freedom of the will" which provides a behavior required for continuity of agent's resource provision;
• Sociability that manages an opportunity to complete tasks using abilities of other agents and provided by highly developed communication protocols;
• Purposefulness assuming existence of self-motivation sources and moreover special intentional characteristics.

Delegation of complex tasks to program systems (agents) allows representing and solving of non-formalizable problems using more natural approach[6].

2.2   Multi-Agent Generation Systems

In order to create a model of the multi-agent system generator authors have analyzed several environments used by developers of multi-agent systems[2]. According to authors the most important of those systems are:

• Multi-agent programmable environment NetLogo;
• JADE multi-agent development library for Java;
• MASON multi-agent library core.

The analysis of existing development tools revealed several common weaknesses[9]:

• Each analyzed system requires involvement of personnel high-qualified as a software developer. This requirement restricts access of an subject area expert to vital steps of project in development;
• Those systems can be used in order to create a multi-agent system with any structure of agents and their collaboration, but applying of new collaboration structure to the system or slightly changing it in order to comply with changing of environmental situation makes an organization interested in that multi-agent system to attract significant resources to the process of development which must be started from the outset.
• An implementation of intellectual methods in agent's structure allowing easier connection between environment and an agent provides new obstacles to the developer due to possible requirement to use other development system for that purpose.

3   Development of Multi-Agent System Generator

Nowadays process of development of MAS project requires of almost non-stop collaboration of developer and an expert of subject area yet some of the major steps are
performed in the absence of expert. For example, the step of choosing development
tools is viral for the entire project, since these tools put their requirements and probable weaknesses to all of the following development processes. Also a great number of
developed multi-agent systems don't use a complex agent structure based on intellectual methods and behavioral algorithms since the choice of their usage mostly rests
with the developer while expert only specifies goals of agent on the step of agent
structure development[3, 4, 5].

As a result of multi-agent systems development analysis authors descried that
every multi-agent system uses several types of agents only. Agents of the same type
used under different options and settings. Authors propose using a component-based
approach in order to generate agents of several types.

Also authors stated a goal of creating an interface which allows users to create
multi-agent systems and modules without special developer qualification in order to
bring experts closer to the development process. Authors supposed to achieve that
goal by using methods of visual programming paradigm.

Thus multi-agent systems generator includes two major modules which guarantee
fulfillment of statements lying behind its creation:

— Bank of components
— Visual programming module

To-be diagram of generation system functioning process is represented by figure 1.

3.1   Bank of Components

Component-based software is a desirable concept in constructing expandable software
applications[10]. By reusing previously designed parts to construct application software, the productivity of development process can be improved dramatically. In their
operations users of multi-agent systems continually face a need to expand its functionality in order to achieve tasks and improve convergence between desired result of
system functioning and actual system output. Authors propose development of bank
of components as an implementation of component-based approach into the generator.
Bank includes two types of components:

— Agents
— Possible connections between agents

Agents
Agent is and autonomous entity which observes environment through sensors and interact with it using actuators and directs its activity towards achieving rational goals.
Agent in the bank is not a fully prepared multi-agent system part yet a template of a
real functioning agent. Bank of these templates is continually expands including new

types of agents so that multi-agent systems created through using of the generator can obtain wider functionality. Each agent in the bank must meet several requirements:

— Each agent has a fully documented interface which includes possible input and output parameters
— Each agent has a list of settings which allow users to create different agents according to subject area and environment of multi-agent system functioning
— Each agent has an intellectual algorithm implemented in it for agent to achieve maximum adequacy in interaction with environment[14]

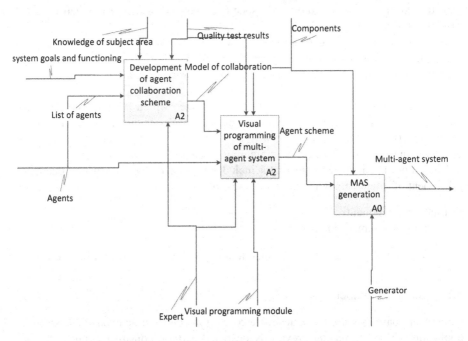

Fig. 1. Generator functioning. To-be diagram.

Connections

List of connections in the bank includes all possible types of connections between agents. Connections are used to create an inter-agent collaboration structure by connecting interfaces of each agent. It is desirable to have at least on type of connection for each pair of agents.

3.2   Visual Programming Module

The question of creating an interface to be used by a non-developer users have been discovered by the authors at the beginning of development of the generator since the concept of the generator included that the main role in functional structure development was granted to a subject area expert. Authors propose development of a visual programming module as the solution to this question[15]. Current solution is based on "boxes and arrows" idea which includes agents as boxes and connections between them as arrows. Figure 2 represents a screen of a visual programming module user interface.

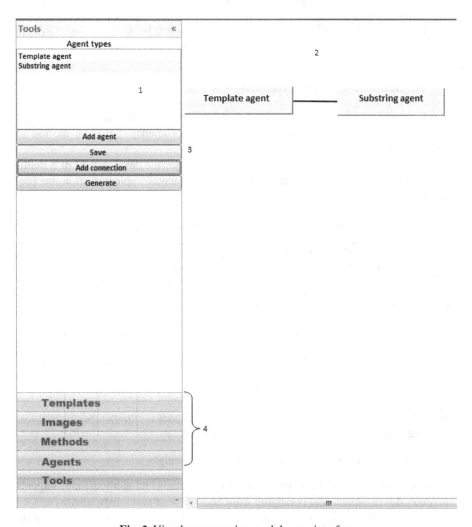

Fig. 2. Visual programming module user interface

At figure 2 numerals indicate:

1. List of agents from bank of components
2. Work area. This area is used to construct an inter-agent collaboration scheme using agents and connections
3. Functional buttons. These buttons are used to interact with the work area of the module. That group includes "Add agent", "Save", "Add connection", "Generate" buttons.
4. System mode buttons. These buttons are used to switch between modes of system functioning, such as agent testing, agent settings or visual programming module.

4   Implementation and Results

The main result of this study is multi-agent systems tools development, which helps to improve the multi-agents systems design process efficiency, based on the use of intelligent agents.

Systems have passed the experimental introduction for the development of 3 multi-agent systems[11, 12, 13, 16]. The results of experimental implementation are presented in Table 1.

Table 1. The results of experimental implementation

System name	Multi-agent module development time (hours)			Client-user losses (users number)			Management costs (development costs, thousand rubles RUR)		
	before	*after*	*decrease on*	*before*	*after*	*increase on*	*before*	*after*	*decrease on*
Collection and intelligent analysis of data about nanotechnologies MAS	16	10	38%	18	21	17%	24.0	15.6	35%
Maintenance and equipment repair support MAS	23	10	57%	56	62	11%	115.0	98.0	15%
Multi-agent CRM-system of tourist enterprise	7	4.5	36%	34	43	26%	76.0	56.2	26%

We achieve effectiveness criteria, described above, namely:

• through the use of intelligent agents predefined patterns and methods, multi-agents modules development time is ranging from 36 to 57% of previously spent;
• the use of intelligent techniques has allowed to obtain agents, the most adequate and easily accomplishing their goals in a changing environment, which results in the elimination of 11 to 26% loss of user clients generated multi-agent modules;
• by expanding the expert role in the development and rapid prototyping methodology application, allowing to make changes to the generated functional modules from the early stages, reducing management costs for businesses ranged from 15 to 35%.

5   Conclusion

Authors performed a task of development of multi-agent systems generator. During the task two new modules of the generator were developed. These are bank of components and visual programming module. Bank of components is being expanded including new types of agents to form multi-agent systems and new types of connections between these agents. Visual programming module allows non-developer users and experts to construct schemes of multi-agent systems functioning and generate multi-agent systems based on that scheme.

References

1. Antonets, A.S., Kravets, A.G.: Multi-agent module for vacancy information gathering from recruitment agencies portals in the scopes of intellectual environment 'Staff Reserve' (in Russian). Messenger of Computer and Informational Technologies 2, 38–42 (2007)
2. Ding, L., Finin, T.W.: Characterizing the semantic web on the web. In: Cruz, I., Decker, S., Allemang, D., Preist, C., Schwabe, D., Mika, P., Uschold, M., Aroyo, L.M. (eds.) ISWC 2006. LNCS, vol. 4273, pp. 242–257. Springer, Heidelberg (2006)
3. Kravets, A.D., Fomenkov, S.A.: Development of intellectual agents generation model (in Russian). SWORLD Scientific Digest 5(3), 59–61 (2012)
4. Kravets, A.D., Fomenkov, S.A.: Intellectual multi-agent systems generator design (in Russian). SWORLD Scientific Digest 1(4), 42–46 (2012)
5. Kravets, A.G., Shevchenko, S.V.: Agent generator for multi-agent system of perspective technologies data mining (in Russian). News of KPI 29, 92–97 (2012)
6. Krizhanovsky, A.I., Pihtin, P.S.: Usage of cooperative learning and data retrieval in multi-agent systems (in Russian). News of Volgograd State Technical University 6(8), 106–110 (2010)
7. Iarovenko, V.A., Fomenkov, S.A.: Features of multi-agent model implementation in development of structured physical data mining system (in Russian). News of Volgograd State Technical University 4(13), 164–166 (2010)
8. Iarovenko, V.A., Fomenkov, S.A.: Freeagent platform for multi-agent systems development (in Russian). News of Volgograd State Technical University 4(13), 164–166 (2012)
9. Nguen, D.H., Kamaev, V.A.: Multi-agent based system of documents flow organization (in Russian). Security in Informational Technologies 1, 130–132 (2012)
10. Lampka, K., Perathoner, S., Thiele, L.: Component-based system design: analytic real-time interfaces for state-based component implementations. International Journal on Software Tools for Technology Transfer, 1–16 (2012)
11. Kravets, A.G., Gurtjakov, A., Kravets, A.: Corporate intellectual capital management: learning environment method. In: Proceedings of the IADIS International Conference ICT, Society and Human Beings, pp. 3–10 (2013)
12. Kizim, A.V., Kravets, A.D., Kravets, A.G.: Generation of intellectual agents for tasks of maintenance and repair support. Izvestia Tomskogo Politechnicheskogo Universiteta 321(5), 131–134 (2012)
13. Bosenko, V.N., Kravets, A.G., Kamaev, V.A.: Development of an Automated System to Improve the Efficiency of the Oil Pipeline Construction Management. World Applied Sciences Journal. Information Technologies in Modern Industry, Education & Society 24, 24–30 (2013)

14. Kravets, A.G., Kravets, A.D., Korotkov, A.A.: Intelligent Multi-Agent Systems Generation. World Applied Sciences Journal. Information Technologies in Modern Industry, Education & Society 24, 98–104 (2013)
15. Romanenko, E.V., Kravets, A.G.: Development and Implementation of Multi-Agent Approach to Support the Process of Requests Execution in a Distributed Information System "Toureast: CRM AI". World Applied Sciences Journal 24, 145–150 (2013)
16. Ukustov, S.S., Makarov, I., Kravets, A.G., Romanenko, E.V.: On Math Approach to Tourist Project Team Formation Problem Concerning Performance and Cooperative Effects. World Applied Sciences Journal. Information Technologies in Modern Industry, Education & Society 24, 238–242 (2013)

Using an Automatic Collection Method
to Identify Patterns during Design Activity

Jonatan Hernandez, Hironori Washizaki, and Yoshiaki Fukazawa

Waseda University, Tokyo, Japan
jhernandez@asagi.waseda.jp, {washizaki,fukazawa}@waseda.jp

Abstract. Although design is an extremely important activity in software development, it is subjective because it depends on the designers' knowledge and skills. Every designer has her or his own strategies to solve design problems. Herein we model the design process as an ordered sequence of logical actions of "Create", "Delete", and "Modify" applied to the elements of a UML class diagram, and propose an automatic approach to collect information about the design process to elucidate design strategies. The strategies considered are top-down, bottom-up, breadthfirst, depth-first, and opportunistic. By mining the ordered sequences of actions for frequent patterns and analyzing the position and distribution of the actions in the sequence, we obtained two types of relationships in the design process: micro-patterns and macro-patterns. Then we evaluated our approach with two case studies. The first one, which occurred over a short time frame with seven subjects, identified the strategies used, while the second, which involved three subjects over a long period, revealed that there is not a universal strategy, but a combination of strategies.

1 Introduction

"All software is designed" [1]. Design is a fundamental step in the software development process, but it is subjective because the abilities of the designers greatly influence the final product. Hence, explicitly identifying successful strategies and patterns will not only increase the understanding of the design process, but will also help improve the skills of software designers.

1.1 Design Strategies

Here the term *strategic knowledge* [2] represents the strategies or approaches applied by the designers, such as top-down or bottom-up. These strategies can be identified using the order in which the elements are created, deleted, and modified. The main elements of a UML class diagram are entities and their relationships. These elements are classified at a different levels of abstraction; classes and relationships are in the higher level of abstraction because they are general, while methods and attributes are in the lower level of abstraction because they are more specific. The elements and their abstraction levels in this paper are listed below:

A. Kravets et al. (Eds.): JCKBSE 2014, CCIS 466, pp. 491–504, 2014.
© Springer International Publishing Switzerland 2014

– High level of abstraction

  1. Classes and Interfaces Entities

  2. Relationships Relationships among the entities such as dependency, generalization, and aggregation

– Low level of abstraction

  3. Attributes and Operations Entity details

UML specifications contain several types of diagrams (e.g., Activity Diagrams, Sequence Diagrams, Collaboration Diagrams, etc.). Every diagram has its own specific elements (e.g., Actors, Activities, etc.) [3]. Initially we chose the UML class diagram and its main elements as the starting point. The strategies considered are [4], [5]:

Bottom-up Operations and attributes are defined before classes.

Top-down Classes are defined before methods.

Breadth-first Operations are defined before being refined.

Depth-first Operations are defined in the class and immediately refined before creating the next method.

Opportunistic Frequent changes between different levels of abstraction.

It is important to note that there are some constraints when using a UML tool. For example, a bottom-up approach is more difficult because methods or attributes cannot be created without first creating a class.

1.2   Challenges

There are challenges when analyzing design activities. One is data collection. Previous research used verbal protocols to collect data about the design process in which the participants were asked to verbalize their thinking processes [4] [6] [7]. These protocols require an extensive analysis of the recorded sessions, which makes data collection time-consuming. Moreover, most of the elements created during an activity very short lived, and evidence is non-existent or quickly discarded (e.g., notes or talks with colleagues and co-workers) [1]. A method for fast, automated data collection should help establish an explicit record of the creative process.

Another is how to evaluate design. Design is difficult to evaluate in terms of correct or incorrect. As stated in [4], "design problem solutions are more or less 'acceptable' or 'satisfying', they are not either 'correct' or 'incorrect'". Thus, each design problem has multiple solutions. A method that provides details about the process step-by-step should help realize a better evaluation design evaluation.

2   Proposal: Our Approach

We model the design process as an ordered sequence of actions. Each action is an operation over an element of the UML diagram. The operations are "Create", "Delete", and "Modify", and are applied on entities such as classes and interfaces as well as relationships like generalizations and associations. Figure 1 shows an example of our model of this process.

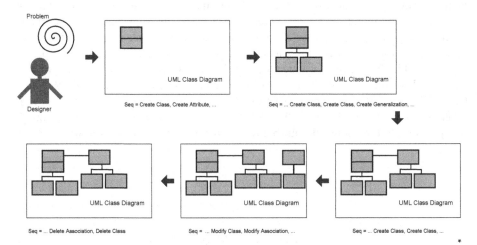

Fig. 1. Representation of the design process as a sequence of actions

Every diagram creation process is represented as an ordered sequence S of actions a and elements e such as $\{a_1,e_1,a_2,e_2,...,a_n,e_n\}$, where $a \in \{Create,Delete,Modify\}$ and $e \in \{class,attribute,operation,...\}$. Using this step-by-step process representation of how the design elements are created, we can analyze the importance of elements, the order of creation, and the number of changes to the elements. Two tools were used to collect the sequences of these actions: a collection tool that we developed for ArgoUML [8] by using JAspect [9], and a collection tool provided by Sparx Systems Japan for Enterprise Architect [10]. Two patterns emerged: macro- and micro-patterns. Macro-patterns indicate the relationships between actions and sequences, including the position, distribution, and the total number of actions in a sequence. Examples of macro-patterns include the location of the Create operation, and the ratio between the total numbers of Create actions and Delete actions.

In contrast, micro-patterns represent the relationships between sequence actions, such as the frequent subsequences of actions. To find these relationships, we used the apriori algorithm to search for frequent subsequences and performed a typical term and pattern-counting search [11]. An example micro-pattern is a frequent subsequence like an action of Create Class followed by Modify Class. Using the apriori algorithm we obtain rules, which are implications of the form $X \Rightarrow Y$ where $X,Y \subseteq a,e$ and $X \cap Y = \emptyset$ [12]. In other words a rule represents how likely an element X will be followed by an element Y in one subsequence. To create the subsequences we divided the main sequence into smaller subsequences of size 2, 3, 4, ..., up to *max.lenght*. These subsequences are repeated at least two times in the main sequence. Thus the *max.length* is the length in which no more subsequences that repeated at least two times are found.

Two metrics are used to evaluate the rules: support [13] and confidence [14]. Only rules that meet a minimum value for both metrics are considered. Support is defined as the number of sequences in which the subsequence is present. For example, if a subsequence is found in six of seven transactions, its support is 6/7 or 0.86. Confidence is defined as *support($X \cup Y$)/support(X)*, and indicates the percentage that a rule is true for all transactions containing both elements X and Y . For example, a support of 0.50 for the rule {Create Class}⇒{Rename Class} indicates that the rule is true in half of the cases when a transaction contains both Create Class and Rename Class. Finally we show one example a diagram evolution. Figures 2, 3, and 4 show a diagram for minute 9, 30, and 50, respectively. The sequence began with defining many classes, but relationships, attributes, and methods, were added over time.

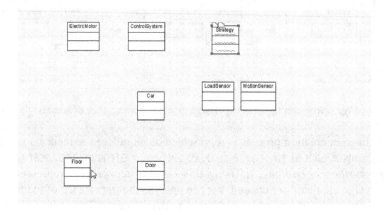

Fig. 2. Minute 9 of E2

3   Case Study 1: Short Time-Frame Exercise

This case study involved a small design exercise, which lasted approximately one hour. The subjects (seven total) were asked to use the open source UML tool ArgoUML [8] to analyze the parts and control elements necessary for an elevator to work properly. The objective was to create a UML class diagram with elements and relationships appropriate to model an elevator and its control system. The subjects were volunteers from the Department of Computer Science and Engineering of Waseda University. All the diagrams can be reviewed online at [15].

The elements considered were *class*, *interface*, *attribute*, *operation*, *generalization*, and *association* from the UML standard (Table 1). In this ArgoUML case study, the "Modify" action was renaming of the elements.

The experiments and subjects are referenced as E1...E7 and S1...S7, respectively. Table 2 indicates the academic year of the subjects.

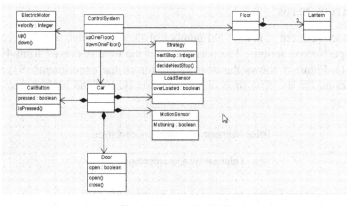

Fig. 3. Minute 30 of E2

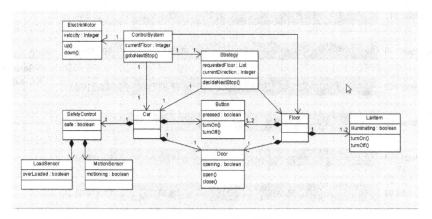

Fig. 4. Minute 50 of E2

Table 1. Abbreviations for the actions collected from the users by our tool in the short time-frame exercise

	Create	Delete	Modify
Class	CC	DC	MC
Interface	CI	DI	MI
Attribute	CA	DA	MA
Operation	CO	DO	MO
Generalization	CG	DG	MG
Association	CS	DS	MS

Table 2. Subjects listed by academic year

Experiment	Subject	Year
E1,E3,E4,E5, E6	S1,S3,S4,S5,S6	Undergraduate students
E2,E7	S2,S7	Graduate students

3.1   Macro-patterns

The first macro-pattern was the total number of Delete actions, which were the least frequently performed actions. The percentage of the total is ranged from 4% (E5) to 23% in (E1). Figure 5 shows the distribution for all the experiments. S1, who used UML diagrams for the first time in this case study, had the highest percentage of Delete actions.

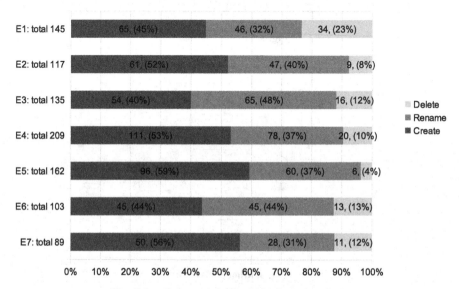

Total Number of Actions Combined

Total per type, (percentage)

Fig. 5. Percentage of the Total Number of Actions

Table 3. Ration of Create to Modify actions for class, attribute, and operation by subject

	Ratios	
(Create/Modify) Class	(Create/Modify) Attribute	(Create/Modify) Operation
E1 0.62	0.7	0.57
E2 0.93	0.88	1
E3 0.44	0.82	0.94
E4 1.12	0.87	0.96
E5 1.46	1.06	1
E6 0.8	0.78	0.83
E7 0.75	1	2

The second macro-pattern was the ratio between Create and Modify actions. Action targets were classes, attributes, and operations, which were the most used elements in all the diagrams. Table 3 shows their relationships where a value closer to one denotes fewer changes, while a value less than one indicates that the final name of the classes were altered several times (i.e., the number of modifications is higher than the number of created classes).

Closely related to the previous macro-pattern was the ratio between the total number of classes and the Create Class action (Table 4). Similar values indicated fewer changes in the classes during the exercise, and are associated with fewer errors.

Table 4. Ratio of the total number of classes to Create actions by subject

Ratio	E1	E2	E3	E4	E5	E6	E7
Total Classes/CC	0.72	0.85	0.64	0.28	0.4	0.75	0.92

The third macro-pattern was related to the distribution of actions (Fig. 6). Figure 7 shows the sequences used in E1, E2, E3, and E7. In E2, 9 of the 11 final classes of the diagram were created in the first 10 minutes of the experiment. In E3, all 7 of the final classes were created in the first 10 minutes. In E7, 9 out of the 11 classes were created at the beginning. In contrast, classes in E1 were created and removed throughout the experiment.

In E2 and E7 not only were classes created at the beginning, but they were created sequentially. Classes were created one after another in a long sequence of creation of classes. In E2 nine classes were created in a row, while in E7 seven classes were created in a row. Thus, this design used the same level of abstraction and the same type of elements.

3.2   Micro-patterns

The highest transition rates occurred when executing an action on an element and when continuing with more actions on the same type of element (Table 5). The highest rates were for class, attribute and operation, which are the basic elements of a UML class diagram. This micro-pattern of executing actions on elements with the same level of abstraction was related to a breadth-first approach. Two more interesting transitions also resulted from a relationship, such an association or a generalization to a class. Consequently, design occurred at a high level of abstraction.

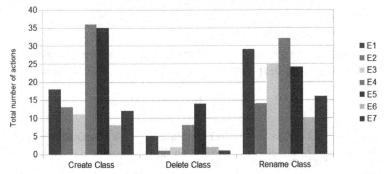

Fig. 6. Number of Create actions

After a Delete or Modify action, the action with the next highest probability was Create (Table 6), indicating that a modification action created a new element, especially after a Modify action.

Table 5. Transition rates of elements

Transition		Probability	Transition		Probability
Class	→ Class	0.70	Generalization	→ Class	0.22
Attribute	→ Attribute	0.71	Association	→ Class	0.31
Operation	→ Operation	0.74			
Interface	→ Interface	0.45			
Association	→ Association	0.50			
Generalization	→ Generalization	0.48			

There was the second micro-pattern in the transition rates of the actions (Table 6). After the Delete action, there was a 0.39 probability of continuing with a similar action. Similarly, after a Create action, there was about 0.33 probability of repeating the same operation. The most interesting rates were from Create to Modify and vice versa. After creating an element, it seemed natural to modify it, whereas after an element was modified, creating a new element seems logical.

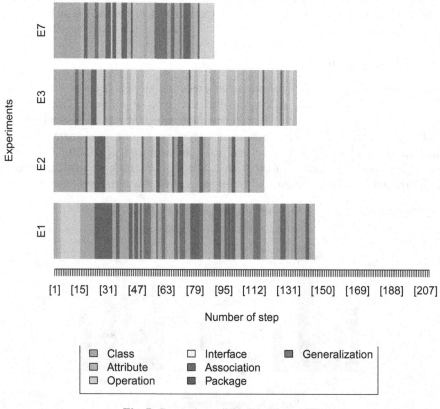

Fig. 7. Comparison of E1, E2, E3, and E7

The rules for Create and Modify actions had a high confidence (Table 7). These rules were related to designing elements at a same, high level of abstraction (i.e., design at the level of classes, which is a high level of abstraction) or designing at the same, more detailed level of attributes and operations.

3.3   Relationship between Strategies and Patterns

In this first case study, several students used a top-down, breadth-first approach. In particular, in the sequences of E2 and E7 (Fig. 7) the subjects were graduate students with more experience in design methods and tools, and began their class diagrams by defining the majority of the classes, and then they refined their design by adding more detail using methods and relationships. This topdown approach, which is demonstrated in Figs. 2 and 3, was commonly used by designers, especially those who had experience in Object Oriented Programming [5]. The top-down approach depended on both designer's experience and difficulty of the problem. The top-down is the most common approach when the problem is known or the designer is experienced [16]. A common micro-pattern was creating and modifying elements on the same level of abstraction (Table 5), which is a breadth-first approach.

Table 6. Transition rates of actions

	→ Create	→ Delete	→ Modify
Create →	0.33	0.07	0.60
Delete →	0.48	0.39	0.13
Modify →	0.72	0.09	0.19

Table 7. Rules for the actions and elements

Rule		Support	Confidence
Modify Operation	→ Create Operation	0.18	0.77
Create Operation	→ Modify Operation	0.18	0.75
Modify Attribute	→ Create Attribute	0.18	0.73
Create Attribute	→ Modify Attribute	0.18	0.74
Modify Class	→ Create Class	0.30	0.79
Create Class	→ Modify Class	0.30	0.80

A second strategy used the opportunistic approach, where elements and relationships of the diagram were created on different levels of abstraction. E1 in Figure 7 had the highest variation in the abstraction levels.

4   Case Study 2: Long Time-Frame Exercise

In this second case study, we collected the logs of students in a Software Engineering class. The students used the UML tool Enterprise Architect [10] for their designs. Data was collected for three months. The objective of the class was for the students to learn the basic principles of Software Engineering by acquiring basic design techniques. Although several domains were presented in the class, herein the domain is a hotel reservation system. Table 8 lists the elements considered in this case study. For Enterprise Architect, the "Modify" action was to rename and to change the properties of an element.

This exercise involved three undergraduate students enrolled in a Software Engineering course and were using UML for the first time. The experiments and subjects are referenced as E8, E9, and E10 and S8, S9, and S10, respectively.

4.1   Macro-patterns

The first macro-pattern was the total number of actions (Create, Delete, Modify) (Fig. 8). The most common action was Modify, which occurred 71.86 % of the time.

Table 8. Abbreviations for the Actions collected from the users in the long time-frame exercise

	Create	Delete	Modify
Association	CCn	DCn	MCn
Attribute	CA	DA	MA
Method	CM	DM	MM
Class	CC	DC	MO
Object	CO	DO	MO

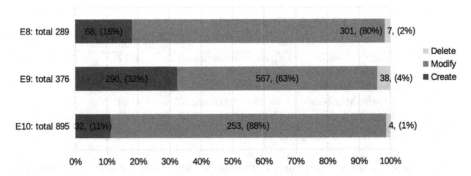

Fig. 8. Total Number of Create, Delete, and Modify Actions

Modifying existing elements was the most common operation, and the element most used was association. A second macro-pattern found was long sequences of Modify actions on the association elements. The longest sequence was 104 modifications of existing associations. Figure 9 shows some very long chains of actions on association elements.

4.2   Micro-patterns

Tables 9 and 10 show the transition rates of the elements and actions. The action with the highest probability was Modify, which was usually executed after any other action. Because examples were given during the class, the students used these examples as the basis for their own designs, which involved more modifications than creation of new elements. The diagrams [15] showed that of all of the students created similar designs.

Table 11 shows the rules for the elements of Enterprise Architect.

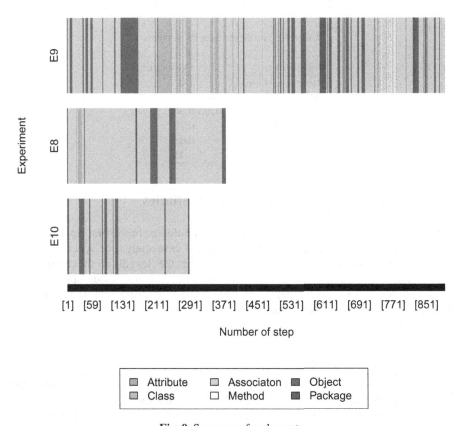

[1] [59] [131] [211] [291] [371] [451] [531] [611] [691] [771] [851]

Number of step

| ▨ Attribute | ▨ Associaton | ▨ Object |
| ▨ Class | ☐ Method | ▨ Package |

Fig. 9. Sequences for elements

4.3   Relationship between Strategies and Patterns

Although we expected for a top-down, breadth-first approach similar to the first case study, the subjects in the second case study used a combination of strategies. The most common pattern was the modification of the association elements, such as generalization, aggregation, and dependency. 72.88% of all actions in a sequence targeted and association element, and 71.86% of the steps the action was Modify. We believe this result was due to the numerous in-class examples, which were the basis of each subjects' design. The relationships of the elements are high-level abstraction elements. Consequently, the subjects designed at a high level of abstraction instead of using operations or attributes to realize a detailed design.

Table 9. Transition rates of actions

	→ Create	→ Delete	→ Modify
Create →	0.01	0.02	0.97
Delete →	0.27	0.24	0.49
Modify →	0.33	0.03	0.64

Table 10. Transition rates of elements

Transition	Probability
Attribute→Class	1.0
Method→Class	1.0
Association→Association	0.90
Object→Object	0.75
Class→Class	0.48
Package→Package	0.41

5   Comparing Results from the Case Studies

In the first (short time-frame) case study, the top-down, bread-first approach was clearly used, whereas the second (long time-frame) case study, one specific strategy was not employed. The difference seemed to be the length of the experiment. Moreover, the second case study involved students learning about objectoriented design for the first time, which explained why the level of abstraction were frequently changed in a more opportunistic approach.

6   Related Work

In [2], three teams' abilities to solve a design problem were compared by watching videos of the developers, and classifying the statements made during the design to identify the strategies that each team used. Herein our classification is based on the sequence of actions that each developer employed to create a class diagram.

In [7] the design activities of three designers were compared through the verbalization of different tasks. The strategy level of the design activity was analyzed while creating a program at two levels: global-control strategy and very particular strategies, (i.e. "reuse, consideration of the user of the system and simulation"). These strategies are at a different level of abstraction that those used in our study.

In [17] designer's experience is important because it affects his behavior. For example, simulation and note taking only occur when a designer has sufficient domain knowledge. If the designer already has a plan based on his experience, he will use that plan. In our case study, we also observed different strategies in each of the case studies, but we considered time to be the most important factor because the strategies differ in the short time-frame and long time-frame case studies.

In [18] is a study where two teams of two people each designed a traffic simulator, the strategies are divided by two factors: the approach to explore the possible designs: breadth-driven or deep-driven, and the problem solving strategy: problem-driven or solution-driven. The strategies in this study were obtained by observing the discussion of the teams using the recorded session in a video, and classifying the statements during the design session. The approach is different, at a higher level, and with the need of direct observation and analysis of the design process.

Table 11. Rules for actions and elements

Rule	Support	Confidence
Create Association→ Modify Association	0.56	0.97

In [19] forty professionals participated in a software design task and their strategies were analyzed with a verbal protocol. In this study the differences between high and moderate performers was evident only when analysing what it is called "task-irrelevant verbalizations", which shows the difficulties of analysing design activity with verbal protocols.

In [20] three design sessions, each consisting of a pair of designers working on a design problem were analyzed. The analysis in this paper was made by analysing the sessions, evaluating the discussion and ideas talk by the designers during the sessions. The analysis focused on dividing the sessions into cycles and describing the subjects in each session. This approach requires much analysis that can only be made by a researcher.

7   Conclusions and Future Work

We found macro- and micro-pattern relationships using a quick, non-intrusive method to collect the information about a design process. These patterns were used to identify the strategies employed by designers. The information collected using our process was very specific because it is composed of a set of basic actions that offer a simple but complete view of the design process. We identified two strategies. One was a top-down, breadth-first strategy where classes were initially defined and then the design details were considered. The other was an opportunistic approach where the elements of the diagram were created at different levels of abstraction.

We conducted our experiment on two different groups of students. All the subjects were students, therefore at this moment we cannot generalized our results to other groups of people. In the future we plan to experiment with different groups of subjects, such as professionals.

In the future, we plan to analyze the relationship between metrics and patterns. The strategies used might be related to the quality of the UML diagram, such as quality metrics of the design. We intend to use the elucidated patterns to help the designers inexperience designers to improve their designs.

References

1. Baker, A., van der Hoek, A., Ossher, H., Petre, M.: Guest editors' introduction: Studying professional software design. IEEE Software 29(1), 28–33 (2012)
2. Popovic, V., Kraal, B.: Expertise in software design: Novice and expert models. In: Proceedings of Studying Professional Software Design (2010)
3. Muller, P.-A.: Instant Uml. Wrox Press Ltd. (1997)
4. Visser, W., Hoc, J.: Expert software design strategies. In: Psychology of Programming, pp. 235–249. Academic Press (1990)
5. D´etienne, F.: Design strategies and knowledge in object-oriented programming: effects of experience. Human–Computer Interaction 10(2-3), 129–169 (1995)
6. Dorst, K., Dijkhuis, J.: Comparing paradigms for describing design activity. Design Studies 16(2), 261–274 (1995)
7. Visser, W.: Designers' activities examined at three levels: organization, strategies and problem-solving processes. Knowledge-Based Systems 5(1), 92–104 (1992)
8. Argouml, http://argouml.tigris.org/
9. Aspectj (December 2013), http://www.eclipse.org/aspectj/
10. Enterprise architect (December 2013), http://www.sparxsystems.com
11. Text analysis utilities (June 2013), http://cran.r-project.org/web/packages/tau/tau.pdf
12. Hahsler, M., Hornik, K.: Building on the arules infrastructure for analyzingtransaction data with r. In: Advances in Data Analysis, Proceedings of the 30th Annual Conference of the Gesellschaft fur Klassifikation e.V., Freie Universitat Berlin, March 8-10. Studies in Classification, Data Analysis, and Knowledge Organization, pp. 449–456. Springer (2006)
13. Agrawal, R., Srikant, R.: Mining sequential patterns. In: Proceedings of the Eleventh International Conference on Data Engineering, pp. 3–14. IEEE (1995)
14. Zaki, M.J.: Spade: An efficient algorithm for mining frequent sequences. Machine Learning 42(1-2), 31–60 (2001)
15. Diagrams (January 2014), http://www.fuka.info.waseda.ac.jp/~jonatan/ref/RD1.html
16. Rist, R.S.: Knowledge creation and retrieval in program design: A comparisonof novice and intermediate student programmers. Human-Computer Interaction 6(1), 1–46 (1991)
17. Adelson, B., Soloway, E.: The role of domain experience in software design. IEEE Transactions on Software Engineering (11), 1351–1360 (1985)
18. Tang, A., van Vliet, H.: Design strategy and software design effectiveness. IEEE Software 29(1), 51–55 (2012)
19. Sonnentag, S.: Expertise in professional software design: A process study. Journal of Applied Psychology 83(5), 703 (1998)
20. Baker, A., van der Hoek, A.: Ideas, subjects, and cycles as lenses for understanding the software design process. Design Studies 31(6), 590–613 (2010)

Knowledge Management for Business Processes: Employees' Recruitment and Human Resources' Selection: A Combined Literature Review and a Case Study

Miltiadis Chalikias[1], Grigorios Kyriakopoulos[2,*],
Michalis Skordoulis[3], and Michalis Koniordos[4]

[1] Laboratory of Applied Economic Statistics and Operations Research,
Department of Business Administration, School of Business and Economics,
Technological Institute of Piraeus, 250 Thivon & Petrou Ralli Av., 12244 Egaleo, Greece
mchalikias@hotmail.com

[2] School of Electrical and Computer Engineering, Electric Power Division,
Photometry Laboratory, National Technical University of Athens, 9 Heroon Polytechniou St.,
15780 Athens, Greece
gregkyr@chemeng.ntua.gr, gregkyr@gmail.com

[3] Laboratory of Management Information Systems and New Technologies,
Department of Business Administration, School of Business and Economics,
Technological Institute of Piraeus, 250 Thivon & Petrou Ralli Av., 12244 Egaleo, Greece
mskordoulis@gmail.com

[4] Department of Business Administration, School of Business and Economics,
Technological Institute of Piraeus, 250 Thivon & Petrou Ralli Av., 12244 Egaleo, Greece
laertis@teipir.gr

Abstract. Nowadays many businesses have been focused on the recruitment and selection of the appropriate employees, in order to deploy their entrepreneurial activities. Besides, on the employees' behalf, the increased competitiveness in a worldwide level of analysis necessitates that all employees to be facilitated with advanced capabilities throughout the organizational hierarchy. In effect, these businesses adopt and develop contemporary processes for their employees' recruitment and selection, in order to ensure increased productivity and effectiveness in a liquefied economic environment. The development of appropriate schemes of selection and recruitment, in line to the ongoing and in-field investment of education, skills and training, are determining factors to the prosperity of manufacturing industry. The ultimate goals of knowledge management in a strategic, innovative, and operational level of decision making is the achievement of greater awareness of the interactive role of science, engineering, and technology towards businesses' success, as well as the development of flexible organizational structures that encourage entrepreneurial creativity, structural flexibility, and managerial change. In the present study, the determining parameters of employees' recruitment and human resources' selection are presented in a literature

---

* Corresponding author.

A. Kravets et al. (Eds.): JCKBSE 2014, CCIS 466, pp. 505–520, 2014.

overview, while the inclusion of a Case Study –being based on an innovative-oriented pharmaceutical company– reveal this company's prominent role of in-dentifying new markets and opportunities that might emerge and then choosing to respond to these long-term visions by activating its competitive advantages in a Management-Technology-Strategy tripartite pattern, rather than being forced into action by competitors.

Keywords: Business processes, employment, human resources selection, knowledge management, recruitment, review.

1   Introduction

Employees' performance is an utmost importance factor that reflects the strategic pro-cedures' achievement, the development of competitive advantages over the competi-tors, as well as the overall prosperity of a company (Bowen and Ostroff, 2004; Wright et al., 2001). Employees' performance is associated with two parameters, the worker capabilities and his/her effort while working. Capabilities are related to selection and learning, either through already educated employees or as the accumulated result of ongoing work and lifelong education. In parallel, workers' effort is the combined result of businesses practice and incentives' provision towards the workforce (Wright et al., 1995). These practices are in accordance to wages, goals' determination, workplace specifications, as well as the communication paths between the employees and their employers. Nevertheless, the precondition of the above practices is that employees have obtained the relevant capabilities in order to implement them within their every-day working tasks (Gatewood et al., 2008).

Human Resource Management (HRM) refers to all necessary policies and proce-dures that a company adopts in order to manipulate its workforce in an optimum level. The main characteristics of an integrated Human Resources Management are the fol-lowing: acquaintance, belonging, motives, and human resources development (HRD) (DeCenzo and Robbins, 1988). Storey et.al. (1989) classified HRM into five characte-ristics, namely: selection, performance, evaluation, rewards, and human resources development, while Beer et.al. (1985) pointed out the critical role of employees within the HRM context.

Huselid (1995) stated that HRM practices contribute to the development of com-petitive advantages, which are aligned with the competitive strategies of a company. This study revealed the integrated approach of HRM with issues such as company turnover, company assets, as well as the Tobin Q index; the latter correlates the busi-ness worth with its assets. Finally, employees' selection is a prevalent factor to a company's prosperity, since it forms the substrate of effective motivation for its em-ployees and ensures that all employees are capable to complete their working tasks (Gatewood et al., 2008).

2   Features of Employees' Recruitment

Employees' recruitment is based on the HRM processes which predict current and future needs of workforce that should be satisfied with existing employees (internal recruitment) or as a new job position offered. The processes of employees' recruitment are the sources of recruitment, the employees who participate in the recruitment, the content of the recruitment (such as sources of information), as well as the development of the recruitment. Indicatively, according to Gatewood et al. (2008), sources of information affect the data collection and manipulation within a company. Indeed, it is commonly accepted the fact that advertisements and recruitment agencies are less contingent regarding the employees' qualification, while other more credible sources involve the internal processes of controlling the workforce, such as the recruitment of employees among University graduates or according to sources that are based on the reports of existing employees.

Employees are exposed to both positive and negative aspects of HRM/HRD (Breaugh and Starke, 2000). Rynes and Cable (2003) investigated the employees' involvement to HRM/HRD in line to demographic characteristics, the personality, the specialization and the specification of recruitment agencies, in order to reveal whether these features could affect the employees' behavior towards a job's description and offer package. Chapman et al. (2005) signified that businesses should proceed in employees' hiring on the ground of their positive interpersonal behavior.

The development of the recruitment is sparsely studied in the relevant literature. Particularly, Arvey et al. (1975) and Rynes et al. (1991) denoted that the development of recruitment is positively related to the accelerated pace of response to candidates during each recruiting step, whether they are eligible or not to the job offered. This prompt response of the business implies that either the business is credible, thus it is a worthy workplace for the candidate, or that the candidate has impressed the recruitment personnel thus s/he has good chance to be hired.

The content of the recruitment should be overly positive to a job applicant, implying wages' advantage, credible and supportive colleagues, cozy working environ-ment, hierarchy ranking opportunities, rewards, and working challenges. Contrarily, the above features should offer an illusive environment, while an employee could not meet these expectations. Wanous (1980) suggested a realistic job preview in order that candidates should balance out both the positive and the negative aspects of their job offered. This accrued information results in an auto-selection process, balancing out the confrontation of the negative aspects in a manageable manner. Therefore, candidates who remain active in the job offer consist the "human pool" which matches to the demands and specifications of the job offered (Wanous, 1973).

These realistic job previews should be incorporated within all steps of recruitment (Rynes and Cable, 2003), while it is also observed that job applicants are badly affected towards the negative aspects of a job company and its hosting company, preferring to work in a company that adopts traditional ways of recruitment (Bretz and Judge, 1998). Subsequently, the realistic job preview shows a weak positive association with job satisfaction and a weak negative association with the company turnover

(Buckley et al., 1997). Therefore, balanced information regarding the job offers and the company itself prerequisites the appropriate treatment of job applicants.

The potential decision of a job applicant to either keep his/her interest to a company or to express indifference, should be based on his anticipation and affection to this company (Gatewood et al., 1993). Even in the initial steps of the recruitment process, detailed information about the company are welcome and positively appreciated from the job applicants (Rynes and Cable, 2003), while other applicants value the quantity and the specification of information in line to the company notable brand name and status (Barber and Roehling, 1993).

2.1   Attractiveness and Goals in the Recruitment Procedure

Breaugh and Starke (2000) have described a model of employees' selection according to which a company should recruit its workforce by determining its goals. Subsequently, it is important for this company to draw his strategy in order to implement these goals, while the following steps of recruitment that should be accomplished are: sources, employees/job applicants, content of recruitment (incorporates known information), and development of recruitment. Conclusively, the results of the recruitment process are the number of job applicants, their cognitive and capabilities' level, the diversity of their expertise and the final number of successful applicants.

According to Chapman et al. (2005) the recruitment procedure incorporates the organizational activities, such as the selection of the collecting pool and the job advertisement, all of which affect the plethora of the specifically-qualified job applicants as well as their decision to accept of refuse a job offer. Rynes (1991) denoted the interlinking features between selection and recruitment, since selection specifications of a company play a dominant role to the sources of recruitment, regarding the legislative protection of equal opportunities and the collective bargaining. According to Gatewood et al. (2008), recruitment has three main goals:

- The accruing of an appropriate number of job applicants (at least ten candidates per job offer), while keeping the recruitment process in affordable cost.
- The need of the company to comply with its legislative and social responsibilities, regarding the demographic composition of its workforce.
- The increased possibilities of the appropriate applicant selection, eliminating the number of candidates with insufficient capabilities/qualifications throughout the steps of recruitment.

Koch and McGrath (1996) examined the association between the HRD design, recruitment, selection practices and the job productivity. These authors concluded that the productive workforce should be proven a valuable strategic advantage, since companies which developed effective processes to attract their workforce should obtain a competitive and incomparable "pool of trustworthy talents".

2.2   Sources of Employees' Recruitment

There is a distinct role of external and internal source of employees' recruitment that resides to the fact that the nature of data collection is distinct in both cases. In the external recruitment there are little previously known data, while the internal recruitment refers to existing employees who have already some level of affiliation with their company's function. Therefore, the audit of external to the company applicants prerequisites the practices of interviewing and examinations, whereas the relevant evaluation of the existing employees to a new job offer within the same company should be achieved through the discussion, re-evaluation, and matching of their qualifications to the upper ranking positions within the company's hierarchy (Gatewood et al., 2008).

Numerous studies have been devoted to the selection processes of appropriate job applicants. These studies have shown that in a long term basis, a combination of internal and external sources of recruitment enables to companies to survive and even developed in a continuously liquefied economic environment. The main internal sources of recruitment information are (Gatewood et al., 2008):

- Table of the company announcements, periodical issues, newspapers, intranet.
- Workforce databases.
- Employees' recommendations.
- Internal jobs' shift.
- Prior employees and walk-ins.

The main external sources of recruitment information are (Gatewood et al., 2008):

- Job agencies.
- Employees' databases.
- Internet facilities.
- Unions and professional bodies.
- Press advertisements.
- Colleges and educational centers from secondary education.

A wide range of studies have investigated the different traits of the aforementioned sources of recruitment information, leading to contradicting outcomes. Collins και Stevens (2002) postulated the interactive role of the recruitment sources, especially affecting the perceptions of job applicants regarding the decisive role of job specifications' and the company status.

Horwitz et al. (2003) studied the most and the least effective strategies that compound the administrative tool of companies in Singapore towards the recruitment, job package offer as well as the last longing employment of specialized employees. According to Horwitz et al. (2003), the most popular strategies of recruitment are:

- The targeted advertisement.
- The internal development of the employees' talents.
- The involvement of professionals to find and hire the appropriate employees ("headhunters").

- The attractiveness of Internet facilities.
- Career plans that are designed to workforce relocation.

Nevertheless, the aforementioned strategies do not guaranty their effectiveness. Contrarily, the following strategies, being positioned in a ranking hierarchy, are capable to attract job applicants to more viable manner (Horwitz et al., 2003):

- The competitive package offer.
- The internal development and promote of the talents among the existing employees.
- The notable status of the employer.
- The direct initiatives to attract competitive and ambitious job applicants.
- The targeted advertisement.

The least effective strategies to attract job applicants, are positioned in the following hierarchy ranking (Horwitz et al., 2003):

- The job attractiveness through Internet.
- Advertisements.
- Professional "headhunters".
- The recruitment reports.
- Interviews conducted from University students.

It is noteworthy that Internet facilities obtained a dominant role to employees' recruitment during the last years. The main web technique is the encouragement of a site visitor to submit his/her biographical data for future job offers through e-mailing (Cappeli, 2001). Therefore, this administrative tool to recruitment should express optimum benefits to both company and candidates, adopting the following suggestions (Foster, 2003):

- The recruitment of employees who are aware of the company features.
- The development of a web site that aims to attract employees.
- The pick up of energetic and dynamic employees.
- The determination, but no stigmatization, of the lazy job applicants.

The electronic application for job offers is a relatively new path of recruitment, thus there are limited studies devoted to investigate the effectiveness of this approach (Chapman and Webster, 2003). Dineen et al. (2001) introduced a web site for an imaginative company, offering information for open positions as well as its social assets and responsibilities. The hosting web site provided also feedback regarding applicants' suitability to their company. Dineen et al. (2003) concluded that this feedback affected the final decision of the job applicants to a final recruitment in this imaginary company.

Avery (2003) developed a web site of an imaginary company, attempting to manipulate the demographic diversity to its workforce and exposing a variety of gender and cultural features of people. The white visitors expressed indifference to this gender spectrum of exposing features, whereas the coloured visitors were attracted from this diversified job advertisement only in terms of the explicit reference to the company's executives.

Conclusively, the electronic approach should be proven especially effective for a company in case that the relevant advertisement has extensively structured towards the job description and the accompanying information to a straightforward manner to appropriate job applicants (Anderson, 2003). The role of the electronic advertisement is to affect the job applicants' decision, in a direct, trustworthy, and costless manner (Anderson, 2003).

3   The Fundamental Role of Human Resources' Selection in a Business

The organizational philosophy and its workforce features are determinant factors to employees' selection, since companies are developing the recruitment paths by focusing on their philosophy. Thus, a credible recruitment process involves the determination of non-suitable job candidates, the interactive role of tasks and human traits, and the organizational adjustment to the surrounding society context (Collins, 2007). The selection process incorporates the actions of data collection and evaluation for each applicant, prior to a final decision to be drawn regarding his hiring or not. The steps of a HRD are the following (McConnell, 2008): job description, determination of ways for measurable/quantified-qualified performance, determination of employees' capabilities, specializations, and cognitive capacities, and finally, the development of evaluation tools.

A process of employees' selection should incorporate detailed data from job applicants, not only regarding to their qualifications but also including the accomplishment of their aspirations, financial and ethical motives, as well as their personal goals in case of their hiring in a specific company. This detailed information are subjected to the evaluation of the overall recruitment effectiveness (Scroggins et al., 2008; Nye et.al.,2008; Gatewood et al., 2008). The necessary processes that accompany the appropriate data collection and employees' selection are (Mathis and Jackson, 1999):

- Curriculum Vitae.
- Preliminary interview or written exams.
- Application Form for the job offered.
- Psychological tests.
- Interview for selection.
- Confirmation of the information gathered.
- Medical tests.
- Final decision.
- Feedback.

A plethora of jobs are relevant to the mental health condition of applicants and their personality integrity, thus psychological tests enable the appropriateness of applicants' behavior as future employees (Scroggins et al., 2008; Nye et al., 2008). Breaugh (2009) and Wagenaar (2012) signified the meaningful contribution of medical data collection and the co-existence of ethical issues that are revealed due to these personal data registration. Finally, a new research direction upon the employees' selection addresses the issues of gender differences and the contradicting roles of maternity and work for women (Ellett et al., 2009; Chzhen and Mumford, 2011).

4   The Case Study

4.1   Introduction to the Case Study

The Case Study explores the main features and the entrepreneurial orientation of a pharmaceutical company that operates in Athens, Greece. This company has a lengthy experience, lasting over 40 years, and know-how in conventional and generic drugs accompanying by an extended collaboration net in the main European pharmaceutical companies. In parallel, the examined company offers a vertically integrated production and service that is client-oriented in a wider global context; supporting the whole Life Cycle Analysis of its products from the design up to the brand launch in the market. These products are distributed in the main Hellenic hospitals, thus actively covering all the main medical specifications and treatments.

In an entrepreneurial overview, the strategic design of the company is framed to the Research-Extrovert-Investment activities, while the future plans are focused on strengthening its business position in the globalized market by enhancing its exports, doubling its main entrepreneurial components and reinforcing its capital adequacy. Besides, continuous involvement in innovativeness and the accomplishment of 30 patents –that are approved from the main European and US Organizations, such as EPO and UPSTO– enable the company to co-fund projects of University-Research Center collaborations that are adapted in an industrial scale and make annual gross revenue of over 20 million Euros in Greece.

4.2   Methodology

The Case Study involves the construction and delivery of two different questionnaires. The first questionnaire, "Type 1", consists of 24 close-typed questions in a 5-level ranking scale; these are sub-divided in 3 groups of 8 question each. These groups are specifically based on Management (questions m.1 – m.8), Technology (questions t.1 – t.8) and Strategy (questions s.1 – s.8) issues. The second questionnaire, "Type 2", consists of 8 close-typed questions in a 5-level ranking scale; these are sub-divided in 3 groups that are also based on Management (questions m.1 – m.2), Technology (questions t.1 – t.3) and Strategy (questions s.1 – s.3) issues.

The first questionnaire was provided to the upper ranking administrative staff of the company and there were responses from one man and one woman. The second questionnaire was provided to the company's employees and there were responses from one man and nine women. Both questionnaires addressed the same objectives (questions) – per Type 1 or 2– within the following three periods: prior to 1990, 1990–1995, and 1995–2010. The questionnaires were delivered and collected during the December 2010. The outcomes of the Case Study are presented in the following Table 1.

Table 1. The outcomes of the Case Study, according to the delivered questionnaires

Period	Prior to 1990		1990-1995		1995-2010		Results
2 responses ("1", "2") for the Questionnaire-Type 1*	1	2	1	2	1	2	Total/Mean marks (out of 5.0)
Partial Sum of Management	15	15	18	16	22	19	105/2.19
Partial Sum of Technology	32	30	34	33	37	36	202/4.21
Partial Sum of Strategy	18	18	25	25	29	26	141/3.36
Total Sum: Man-Tech-Str	**65**	**63**	**77**	**74**	**88**	**81**	**448/3.25**
10 responses ("1-10") for the Questionnaire-Type 2	1-10						Total/Mean marks (out of 5.0)
Partial Sum of Management **	8-7-8-9-8-7-8-6-6-6						73/3.65
Partial Sum of Technology***	12-10-12-11-9-11-12-11-12-10						110/3.67
Partial Sum of Strategy***	13-12-13-12-13-11-11-12-11-12						120/4.00
Total Sum: Man-Tech-Str	**33-29-33-32-30-29-31-29-29-28**						**303/3.79**

*each response is summed up to maximum of 8 questions of 5 marks each= 40marks
** each response is summed up to maximum of 2 questions of 5 marks each= 10marks
*** each response is summed up to maximum of 3 questions of 5 marks each= 15marks

4.3   Discussion upon the Literature Review and the Case Study

4.3.1   Discussion upon the Employees' Recruitment and Human Resources' Selection Overview

Human resources' selection is a vital entrepreneurial process during the last 40 years. The earlier studies of human resources' exploitation had been focused on naval (Blanchard, 1975), trading, industrial and engineering systems (Askren and Lintz, 1975), while the methodological tools of experimental planning and raw sources' manipulation, such as interviewing and data storage, were similar to the main decisive techniques (Schwan, 1976; Heim, 1989).

A regional allocation of human resources' selection in published studies during the last 15 years is depicted in the following Table 2. These references are grouped in accordance to regional allocation and in reversed chronological order: from the newest to the earliest.

The findings of the above Table 2 revealed a wide spectrum of regional allocation and conceptual categorization upon the human resources' involvement in a business environment. Indeed, human resources' selection is subject to highly populated regions and megacities, such as in Western Europe and China, since human resources are associated with the patterns of goods' production and consumption as well as with the practices of a marketing mix that reinforces consumerism pattern for not merely satisfied but for delighted customers. Contrarily, less developed and sparsely populated countries –such as in Africa and in South America– are regulated from simpler forms of marketable brands and consumerism motives, possibly restricted to provision of only raw materials and outsourcing to developed countries, thus human resources' selection plays an inferior role within their context.

From an entrepreneurial overview, human resources' selection plays a vital role to businesses' profit and team working build up, while from the workforce overview, employees should attribute their business's growth and profitability as a personal accomplishment, feeling inseparable and vital stakeholders to their business prosperity. These regional distinct characteristics to human resources' selection were further

Table 2. Regional allocation of human resources' selection studies during the last 15 years

# Ref	Reference	Geographical area	Main notion	Number of references
1	Aguinis and Smith (2007)	North America, USA	The study introduced an innovative integrative framework by simultaneously co-evaluating the four concepts of test validity, test bias, selection errors, and adverse impact. Various selection systems are subjected to their degree of validity and bias, while a relevant computational program offered online calculations and performance.	
2	Snyder et al. (2006)	North America, USA	The study investigates the designing and validating selection procedures for information technology (IT) workers. Implications are discussed among the stakeholders, who are industrial/organizational psychologists, human resource managers, and managers of IT workers.	North America: 4
3	Bobko et al. (2005)	North America, USA	The study has addressed statistically based banding in order to manipulate test scores' outcomes that are developed to assess job applicants. The appropriateness of classical test theory and models that estimate standard and binomial errors are also discussed.	
4	Whyte and Sue-Chan (2002)	North America, Canada	Base rate data were collected and manipulated in line to a statistically-oriented scenario that describes the selection decision by individual and groups of human resources' managers.	
5	Raoudha et al. (2012)	Europe, France	Use of a the linguistic model TOPSIS as a decision making practical tool in relation to task requirements, management limitations and candidates competences from a University.	Europe: 3
6	Konig et al. (2011)	Europe, Germany	Cognitions of practitioners' thinking about selection procedures. The adopted methodological tools are established interviews and the repertory grid technique to the selection filed of application.	
7	Polychroniou and Giannikos (2009)	Europe, Greece	The study denotes the complexity, subjectivity and vagueness that interfere to human resources' selection. Therefore, a fuzzy multi-criteria decision-making methodology was based on the TOPSIS multi-criteria decision tool in order to select employees in a major Greek private bank. This methodology determines the limitations of imprecision and uncertainty, showing flexibility in a recruitment process.	
8	Sow and Oi (2011)	Asia, China	Creative human resource approaches to hire new employees, necessary skills, economic implications, and reasons of employees' turnover in the hospitality and tourism industry are addressed in the China context.	
9	Yang and Wang (2011)	Asia, China	A determining factor to human resource management is the outsourcing service provider. A well selected, developed, and evaluated outsourcing scheme reduces entrepreneurial risk, especially in the China context where outsourcing market is in the initial stage.	
10	Zhao and Jin (2010)	Asia, China	The study investigated the parameters of human resource management and the optimization of enterprise logistics systems towards the prosperity of businesses. Besides, the authors adopted an integrated optimization framework that is developed from the sub-systems of marketing, human performance and technical support	Asia: 4
11	Tsai et al. (2003)	Asia, Taiwan	In this study, an integrated computational method, the accompanying critical resource diagram and a design approach of Taguchi's parameter were implemented in order to explore the software resource human resources' selection problem. The outcomes are promising, since the methodological approach can achieve robust performance with apparently reduced project cost and duration.	
12	Zysberg (2009)	Middle East, Israel	The methodological tool of "process analytic" is adopted for human resources' selection. This tool was applied to large-scale studies, offering a theoretical and psychometric framework for vocational purposes, being based on symbolic processes and cognitive ability.	
13	Saidi Mehrabad and Fathian Brojeny (2007)	Middle East, Iran	The strategic role of human resources' selection was designed, modeled and implemented via an expert system for job preferences and organizational requirements, appointment of suitable applicants to a correct job rotation, and the matching of the salary schemes to the qualifications of applicants.	Middle East: 2
Total References				13

examined by Gerhart (2009) who adopted the diversification of locally-based "individuals/team-member cultures" as distinct and dominant motives that determine the "national culture constraints" and the "organization cultures". According to Gerhart (2009), the relationship among the above cultures is not always straightforward, since implications arise from the predominant influence of national culture differences in managing workforces as well as from the fact of balancing out the aforementioned inherit constraints and the ultimate importance of businesses' well being, solid development and economic profitability.

Carless (2009) pointed out that businesses' performance is linked to recruitment and selection, thus a sound psychological profile of employees is needed. Psychological tests that measure features of ability and personality have to be constructed in such a way in order to reveal applicants' traits and capabilities throughout the steps of employees' recruitment and selection.

Stevens and Campion (1994, 1999) developed a metric test that consists of 14 characteristics of team working, independently of each team responsibilities. These characteristics are grouped in the following categories: solution of conflicts, cooperative problems' solving, communication, targets' determination, performance management, and program and coordination of tasks. These characteristics pointed out necessary capabilities of team working, excluding personal or technical specializations.

McClough και Rogelberg (2003) revealed the relationship between team working capabilities and employees' performance in the light of team working interactions. Morgeson et al. (2005) denoted the dominant role of an appropriate socio-psychological environment of a company, focusing on the effectiveness of employees' selection and the successful implementation of teamwork members. Morgeson et al. (2005) introduced an interview pattern that measured a spectrum of social capabilities, a personality test, and a Stevens-Campion test, all concluding that adopted methodological tests of selection were related to personal and teamwork performance.

Bjorkman and Lu (1999) investigated the involvement of 65 Western countries on conglomerations to HRM in China. The study revealed that a wide range of Western-based practices were applied in China, while sporadic Western companies applied their policies to China, since they motivated in order to be benefited at applying policies and practices of Chinese culture and origins. Nevertheless, Child (1991) and Osland and Cavusgil (1996) denoted that HRM in China is a challenge to foreign countries that are operating within its context, since multinational companies have to either address issues of HRM and worldwide applicability to the China context, or they should be adapted to the Chinese cultural framework and its regional practices of HRM.

4.3.2 Discussion upon the Case Study

The critical questions that originate from the innovative orientation of the company are: Which are its innovative Departments?, In which way are its employees educated?, By which way are the company's Departments collaborate to each other?, Which methods monitor the innovativeness accomplishment?

In response to the above key-questions, the innovative products of the company were predominately based on the human workforce, the production line, and the financial management. These innovative-oriented features enabled the market control, the profitability, the competitive advancement, and the effective composition of the entrepreneurial scheme of Management-Technology-Strategy. According to the outcomes of the Table 1, the main enduring competitive advantage of the company was the constant technological superior position of all its technologically-based Departments, while the Strategy component, even though it was inspired from both the internal and external business environment, it had not proven such advantageous as the Technology was.

5   Conclusions and Future Orientations

The association of attraction and selection of employees is the subject of many published studies. Rynes and Barber (1990) denoted that the process of employees' attraction is positively associated with a complex spectrum of interrelated issues, including:

- Salary, benefits, children care, flexibility in working hours, job prosperities.
- Targeted pool of company applicants, level of education, working experience, demographic elements of age, gender, ethnicity.
- Market conditions and job specifications.

Numerous studies are focused on new patterns of employees' attraction and selection, in line to the businesses' organizational framework. Therefore, the traditional pattern of employment was devoted to a simple task, being compounded from a range of similar activities all of which were burdened one worker. On the other hand, while a product or service completion necessitates the remote task of a worker or a working team, current patterns of selection programs are focused on the integrated grid of activities and responsibilities to all members of the entrepreneurial hierarchy, involving both employers and employees within the same business (Gatewood et al., 2008).

It is also noteworthy that communication abilities and cooperation capabilities are recognized as utmost importance elements to selection and job offer. This finding is in accordance to new patterns of employees' attraction especially for team working specifications (Gatewood et al., 2008, Stevens και Campion 1994, Stevens and Campion, 1999, McClough and Rogelberg, 2003, Morgeson et al., 2005).

Finally, the Case Study revealed that each of the aforementioned 24 questions of the Questionnaire-Type 1 implied the necessity of different Life Cycle Analysis structure for each entrepreneurial activity, thus the plethora of responses to Questionnaire-Type 2, in comparison to only two responses of the Questionnaire-Type2, offered a more objective and credible evaluation of the outcoming results over the three chronological periods examined. Moreover, generalizing the main the main outcomes of the Case Study it should be stated that a contemporary business environment necessitates the adaptation of each national company to the external environment of the globalized market. This view of globalization enhances the interactive association between businesses and Organizations/Economies. The fulfillment of this adaptation should be achieved either with no changes in a business environment, thus no globalization occurs, or with a dynamic adaptation to the globalized market in line to the prominent role of the Management-Technology-Strategy entrepreneurial scheme.

References

1. Aguinis, H., Smith, M.A.: Understanding the impact of test validity and bias on selection errors and adverse impact in human resource selection. Personnel Psychology 60, 165–199 (2007)
2. Anderson, N.: Applicant and recruiter reactions to new technology in selection: A critical review and agenda for future research. International Journal of Selection and Assessment 11, 121–136 (2003)
3. Arvey, R.D., Gordon, M.E., Massengill, D.P., Mussio, S.J.: Differential dropout rates of minority and majority job candidates due to 'Time Lags' between selection procedures. Personnel Psychology 28, 175–180 (1975)
4. Askren, W.B., Lintz, L.M.: Human resources data in system design trade studies. Human Factors 17, 4–12 (1975)
5. Avery, D.R.: Reactions to diversity in recruitment advertising-Are differences black and white?". Journal of Applied Psychology 88, 672–679 (2003)
6. Barber, A.E., Roehling, M.V.: Job postings and the decision to interview: A verbal protocol analysis. Journal of Applied Psychology 78, 845–856 (1993)
7. Beck, J.W., Walmsley, P.T.: Selection Ratio and Employee Retention as Antecedents of Competitive Advantage. Industrial and Organizational Psychology 5, 92–95 (2012)
8. Beer, M., Lawrence, P.R., Mills, Q.N., Walton, R.E.: Human Resource Management. Free Press, New York (1985)
9. Bernerth, J.B., Feild, H.S., Giles, W.F., Cole, M.S.: Perceived fairness in employee selection: The role of applicant personality. Journal of Business and Psychology 20, 545–563 (2006)
10. Bjorkman, I., Lu, Y.: The management of human resources in Chinese-western joint ventures. Journal of World Business 34, 306–324 (1999)
11. Blanchard, R.E.: Human performance and personnel resource data store design guidelines. Human Factors 17, 25–34 (1975)
12. Bobko, P., Roth, P.L., Nicewander, A.: Banding selection scores in human resource management decisions: Current inaccuracies and the effect of conditional standard errors. Organizational Research Methods 8, 259–273 (2005)
13. Bowen, D.E., Ostroff, C.: Understanding HRM-Firm performance linkages: The role of the "strength" of the HRM system. Academy of Management Review 29, 203–221 (2004)
14. Breaugh, J.A., Starke, M.: Research on employee recruitment: So many studies, So many remaining questions. Journal of Management 26, 405–434 (2000)
15. Breaugh, J.A.: Employment contracts and health selection: Unhealthy employees out and healthy employees in? Human Resource Management Review 19, 219–231 (2009)
16. Bretz, R.D., Judge, T.A.: Realistic job previews: A test of the adverse self-selection hypothesis. Journal of Applied Psychology 83, 330–337 (1998)
17. Buckley, M.R., Fedor, D.B., Carraher, S.M., Frink, D.D., Dunnette, M.D.: The ethical imperative to provide recruits realistic job previews. Journal of Managerial Issues 9, 468–484 (1997)
18. Cappeli, P.: Making the most of on-line recruiting. Harvard Business Review, 139–147 (March 2001)
19. Carless, S.A.: Psychological testing for selection purposes: A guide to evidence-based practice for human resource professionals. International Journal of Human Resource Management 20, 2517–2532 (2009)

20. Chapman, D.S., Webster, J.: The Use of Technology in the Recruiting, Screening, and Selection Processes of Job Candidates. International Journal of Selection and Assessment 11, 113–120 (2003)

21. Chapman, D.S., Uggerslev, K.L., Caroll, S.A., Piasentin, K.A., Jones, D.A.: Applicant Attraction to Organizations and Job Choice: A Meta-Analytic Review of the Correlates of Recruiting Outcomes. Journal of Applied Psychology 90, 928–944 (2005)

22. Child, J.: A foreign perspective on the management of people in China. International Journal of Human Resource Management 2, 93–107 (1991)

23. Chzhen, Y., Mumford, K.: Gender gaps across the earnings distribution for full-time employees in Britain: Allowing for sample selection. Labour Economics 18, 837–844 (2011)

24. Collins, C.J., Stevens, C.K.: The Relationship between early recruitment-Related activities and the application decisions of new labor-market entrants: A brand equity approach to recruitment. Journal of Applied Psychology 87, 1121–1133 (2002)

25. Collins, S.K.: Employee recruitment: Using behavioral assessments as an employee selection tool. Health Care Manager 26, 213–217 (2007)

26. Dayan, K., Fox, S., Kasten, R.: The preliminary employment interview as a predictor of assessment center outcomes. International Journal of Selection and Assessment 16, 102–111 (2008)

27. DeCenzo, D.A., Robbins, S.P.: Personnel/Human Resource management, 3rd edn. Prentice-Hall, Englewood Cliffs (1988)

28. Dineen, B.R., Ash, S.R., Raymond, A.: A web of applicant attraction: Person-organization fit in the context of web-based recruitment. Journal of Applied Psychology 87, 723–734 (2002)

29. Ellett, A.J., Ellett, C.D., Ellis, J., Lerner, B.: A research-based child welfare employee selection protocol: Strengthening retention of the workforce. Child Welfare 88, 49–68 (2009)

30. Foster, M.: Recruiting on the web: Smart strategies for finding the perfect candidate. McGraw-Hill, New York (2003)

31. Gatewood, D.R., Field, H.S., Barrick, M.: Human Resource Selection, 6th edn. Thomson South-western (2008)

32. Gerhart, B.: Does national culture constrain organization culture and human resource strategy? The role of individual level mechanisms and implications for employee selection. Research in Personnel and Human Resources Management 28, 1–48 (2009)

33. Heim, K.M.: Organizational entry: Human resources selection and adaptation in response to a complex labor pool. Library Trends 38, 21–31 (1989)

34. Horwitz, M.F., Heng, T.C., Quazi, A.H.: Finders, keepers? Attracting, motivating and retaining knowledge workers. Human Resource Management Journal 13, 23–44 (2003)

35. Huselid, M.A.: The impact of human resource management practices on turnover, productivity, and corporate financial performance. Academy of Management Journal 38, 635–672 (1995)

36. Koch, M.J., McGrath, R.G.: Improving labor productivity: Human resource management policies do matter. Strategic Management Journal 17, 335–354 (1996)

37. Konig, C.J., Jori, E., Knusel, P.: The amazing diversity of thought: A qualitative study on how human resource practitioners perceive selection procedures. Journal of Business and Psychology 26, 437–452 (2011)

38. Mathis, L.R., Jackson, J.H.: Human Resource Management-Essential Perspectives, vol. 78. International Thomson Publishing (ITP), Canada (1999)

39. McClough, A.C., Rogelberg, S.G.: Selection in teams: An exploration of the teamwork knowledge, skills, and ability test. International Journal of Selection and Assessment 11, 56–66 (2003)

40. McConnell, C.R.: Conducting the employee selection interview: How to do it effectively while avoiding legal obstacles. JONA's Healthcare Law, Ethics, and Regulation 10, 48–56 (2008)

41. Morgeson, F.P., Reider, M.H., Campion, M.A.: Selecting individuals in team settings: The importance of social skills, personality characteristics, and teamwork knowledge. Personnel Psychology 58, 583–611 (2005)

42. Nye, C.D., Do, B.R., Drasgow, F., Fine, S.: Two-step testing in employee selection: Is score inflation a problem? International Journal of Selection and Assessment 16, 112–120 (2008)

43. Osland, G.E., Cavusgil, S.T.: Performance issues in U.S.-China joint ventures. California Management Review 38, 106–130 (1996)

44. Polychroniou, P.V., Giannikos, I.: A fuzzy multicriteria decision-making methodology for selection of human resources in a Greek private bank. Career Development International 14, 372–387 (2009)

45. Raoudha, H., Mouloudi, D.E., Selma, H., Abderrahman, E.M.: A new approach for an efficient human resource appraisal and selection. Journal of Industrial Engineering and Management 5, 323–343 (2012)

46. Rynes, S.L., Cable, D.M.: Recruitment research in the twenty-first century. Handbook of Psychology, 55–76 (2003)

47. Rynes, S.L.: Recruitment, job choice, and post-hire consequences: A call for new research directions. In: Dunnette, M.D., Hough, L.M. (eds.) Handbook of Industrial and Organizational Psychology, 2nd edn., vol. 2. Consulting Psychologists Press, Palo Alto (1991)

48. Rynes, S.L., Barber, A.E.: Applicant attraction strategies: An organizational perspective. Academy of Management Review 15, 286–310 (1990)

49. Rynes, S.L., Bretz Jr., R.D., Gerhart, B.: The Importance of Recruitment in Job Choice: A Different Way of Looking. Personnel Psychology 44, 487–521 (1991)

50. Saidi Mehrabad, M., Fathian Brojeny, M.: The development of an expert system for effective selection and appointment of the jobs applicants in human resource management. Computers and Industrial Engineering 53, 306–312 (2007)

51. Schwan, E.S.: The effects of human resource accounting data on financial decisions: An empirical test. Accounting, Organizations and Society 1, 219–237 (1976)

52. Scroggins, W.A., Thomas, S.L., Morris, J.A.: Psychological testing in personnel selection, part II: The refinement of methods and standards in employee selection. Public Personnel Management 37, 185–198 (2008)

53. Snyder, L.A., Rupp, D.E., Thornton, G.C.: Personnel selection of information technology workers: The people, the jobs, and issues for human resource management. Research in Personnel and Human Resources Management 25, 305–376 (2006)

54. Sow, H.C., Oi, M.K.: A study of human resources recruitment, selection, and retention issues in the hospitality and tourism industry in Macau. Journal of Human Resources in Hospitality and Tourism 10, 421–441 (2011)

55. Stevens, M.J., Campion, M.A.: The Knowledge, Skill, and Ability Requirements for Teamwork: Implications for Human Resource Management. Journal of Management 20, 503–530 (1994)

56. Stevens, M.J., Campion, M.A.: Staffing Work Teams: Development and Validation of a Selection Test for Teamwork Settings. Journal of Management 25, 207–228 (1999)

57. Storey, J.: New Perspectives on Human Resource Management. Routledge eds, London (1989)

58. Tsai, H.T., Moskowitz, H., Lee, L.H.: Human resource selection for software development projects using Taguchi's parameter design. European Journal of Operational Research 151, 167–180 (2003)

59. Wagenaar, A.F., Kompier, M.A.J., Houtman, I.L.D., van den Bossche, S.N.J., Taris, T.W.: Employment Contracts and Health Selection: Unhealthy Employees Out and Healthy Employees In? Journal of Occupational and Environmental Medicine 54, 1192–1200 (2012)

60. Wanous, J.P.: Organizational Entry: Recruitment, Selection, and Socialization of Newcomers, vol. 34. Addison-Wesley, Reading (1980)

61. Wanous, J.P.: Effects of a realistic job preview on job acceptance, job attitudes, and job survival. Journal of Applied Psychology 58, 327–332 (1973)

62. Whyte, G., Sue-Chan, C.: The neglect of base rate data by human resources managers in employee selection. Canadian Journal of Administrative Sciences 19, 1–11 (2002)

63. Wright, P.M., Dunford, B.B., Snell, S.A.: Human resources and the resource-based view of the firm. Journal of Management 27, 701–721 (2001)

64. Wright, P.M., Kacmar, K.M., McMahan, G.C., Deleeuw, K.: P=f(MxA): Cognitive ability as a moderator of the relationship between personality and job performance. Journal of Management 21, 1129–1139 (1995)

65. Yang, W., Wang, W.: Research of the evaluation and selection to human resource management outsourcing service provider. International Conference on Management and Service Science, MASS 2011, art. no. 5998726 (2011)

66. Zhao, L., Jin, J.: Study on enterprise logistics system optimization path selection based on human resources management. In: ICLEM 2010: Logistics for Sustained Economic Development - Infrastructure, Information, Integration - Proceedings of the 2010 International Conference of Logistics Engineering and Management, vol. 387, pp. 3055–3061 (2010)

67. Zysberg, L.: An emerging new component of cognitive abilities in human resources selection: Preliminary evidence to the existence of a 'process-analytic' factor in selection batteries. International Journal of Selection and Assessment 17, 69–75 (2009)

Knowledge-Based Support for Innovative Design on Basis of Energy-Information Method of Circuits

Viktoriya Zaripova and Irina Petrova

CAD department, Astrakhan State Institute of Civil Engineering, Astrakhan, Russia
{vtempus2,irapet1949}@gmail.com

Abstract. The article discusses a new scientific approach which was called "Automation of innovative processes» (Computer-Aided Innovation - CAI). CAI combines various interdisciplinary research in the sphere of innovation in order to increase the effectiveness of new product development (NPD). The analysis of international scientific experience and more than 150 software products in the field of automation of innovation processes gave us the classification of CAI tools. It is shown that complex CAI includes usually the subsystem for the management and generating ideas for new products development. The innovative design is a knowledge-intensive process which requires knowledge of diverse domains. However, it is unclear, how to model and represent this knowledge in a uniform and computable way. The article describes how knowledge-based techniques can be used to organize a computer support for innovative design based on energy-information method of modeling processes of different physical nature.

Keywords: CAI, innovations, creativity, university-enterprise cooperation.

1 Introduction

The innovation process is highly dynamic. Its effectiveness depends largely on the speed of response to changing market and economic situation. Hence enterprises need in complex software to operative and decision making support of the innovation process throughout the product lifecycle.

The Working Group WG 5.4. on Computer-Aided Innovation (CAI) was established in 2004 under umbrella of the Technical Committee "Applied Information Technologies" of the International Federation for Information Processing (IFIP) [1].

Computer-Aided Innovation (CAI) is a new scientific field that combines various interdisciplinary researches in the field of innovation in order to increase the effectiveness of New Product Development (NPD) [2]. Scientists and experts of the working group are studying the theoretical and practical aspects related to the development of automated systems to support innovation processes.

Innovation process is a complex iterative, interactive, multi-tasking process that depends on many factors. Here practitioners and academics in the field of management and economics, engineering, and information systems are working together to increase the likelihood of success and reducing time to market the new product.

A. Kravets et al. (Eds.): JCKBSE 2014, CCIS 466, pp. 521–532, 2014.

Therefore CAI should be integrated into existing models of business processes to manage the innovation process. The following sources of innovation could be listed: research (open new knowledge), market needs, existing knowledge (external to the company) and the knowledge gained in the process of learning by doing. Complex of the enterprise information systems must support innovations throughout the entire production cycle of a new product , including the generation and selection of the most promising ideas, systematic planning and management of intellectual property portfolio, project management, introduction of new products to market, etc.

There are a large number of different software to perform most of these functions. And this becomes an obstacle on the way of the creation of integrated automation system of innovation processes in the enterprise to increase the efficiency of creating new products (New Product Development - NPD).

The article describes the results of the analysis of scientific works devoted to Computer-Aided Innovations, the classification of computer-based CAI, and prospects for further development in this direction based on WEB 2.0 technologies. It is shown that one of the obligatory three CAI subsystems is a subsystem of control and generating ideas for new products (New Product Development).

Most products in the "management and the generation of ideas" group are various computerized methods of thinking activation for ideas generation (brainstorming, mindmapping, etc). Results (ideas) are collected in a database to be being analyzed by various methods further. However, these methods are ineffective in solving of complex engineering problems.

Therefore, this article discusses one of the methods of conceptual design, allowing to organize the Knowledge-Based Support For Innovative Design of Energy-based information models of circuits of various physical nature.

2   CAI Classification

Different approaches to the classification of computer CAI tools has been proposed by several authors in [3,4,5,6]. In [5,6], the authors S.Kohn, S.Hüsig (2007-2009 years) have analyzed about 150 software products that can be attributed to the CAI system and proposed to divide them into three groups (Figure 1):

- Idea Management,
- Strategy Management,
- Patent Management.

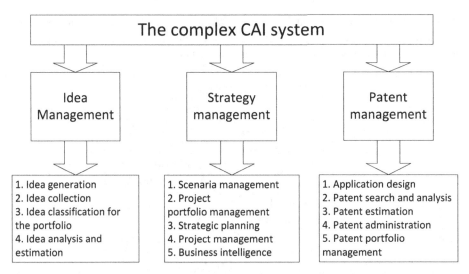

Fig. 1. Classification of Computer Aided Innovation (CAI) tools

The first group - "Idea management" includes software to control the initial stage of the innovation process from idea generation to collection, analyzing and classifying of ideas and their subsequent evaluation.

The second group - "Product development strategy management" includes software to support innovative managers who work with strategic issues, such as, scenario management, project portfolio management, project management and business analytics.

The third group is the "Patent management", ie company's intellectual property management. The intellectual property has a twofold role in the process of creating of a new product (NPD). Firstly, the patent - is the legal protection of innovations and secondly patent database can be used to generate new inventions and search of prototypes and analogues, detection and development of competing companies. Many software products from the first group of "Ideas management" use existing database inventions to find new areas of strategic development of the company.

In [7], we repeated the study on the up-to-date array of software products in order to identify new trends in the development of CAI systems. During the CAI market analysis we considered about 150 software products available on the market and intended for mass use on the enterprises in 2012. To determine the functionality of software products we studied materials on the manufacturers' websites, articles describing the product and the demo versions, if it was possible.

A summary table of the investigated software products is attached as the annex to the paper [7]. There are the product name, manufacturer, Internet address, and identification of the product with respect to a class and subclass of CAI- products classification.

As shown by further statistical analysis the largest part of CAI- tools (32%) are in the group of " ideas management," 25% are in CAI-products of the " strategies management " class , while 22 % belong to the group " patents management."

In addition, a separate group "complex solutions" (21 %) were recovered. It includes products that combine the functionality of the two or three groups. Figure 2 shows a diagram of distribution of software products in groups.

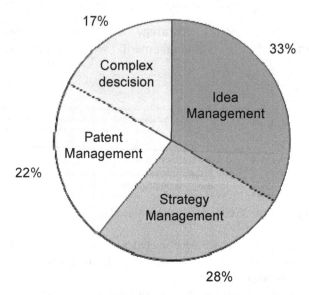

Fig. 2. Distribution of CAI tools in groups

Compared to researches in [4,5] the number of complex solutions significantly increased (from 4% in 2007 to 21% in 2013). This suggests that the CAI systems market has a clear trend towards the integration of functionality in the complex product. However, the market has lack of comprehensive solutions that integrate all functions of CAI in one product. But the tighter integration groups "idea management" and "management strategy" may be noted easily.

Most products in the group "ideas management" are analogs of computer-aided methods of psychological thinking activation (brainstorming and memory card) aimed to generate ideas. Results (ideas) are collected in a database, and then analyzed by various methods. However these methods are ineffective to solve complex engineering problems. They know a large number of more effective methods of systematic and targeted search for new technical solutions. For example morphological analysis, functional analysis, TRIZ, functional-physical method of R.Koller and others. But there are almost no software products that implement these methods. For example, - Goldfire Innovator ™, Innovation WorkBench ®, Pro / Innovator 5.0 use of TRIZ methodology, MA / CarmaTM use morphological analysis.

3   CAI Development Trends (Open and Closed Systems)

CAI-traditional tools are focused on intra-development of new products (NPD), i.e. the process of product lifecycle management from invention to innovation is provided by the staff of the company. External factors such as the opinion of suppliers and consumers were considered indirectly or were not considered at all. Therefore, these CAI systems are called a closed CAI (CAI 1.0).

Open innovations [7] are targeted usage of internal and external flows of knowledge and ideas to accelerate internal innovations, and expand both domestic and foreign markets to promote their own technologies.

In [8] the basic techniques used to implement open innovation are listed, such as the method of consumer innovation (E.Hippel), tools for client innovation (S. Tomka), innovation competitions aimed at ideas generation for all stages of the innovation process.

To implement these methods a special IT infrastructure is required. It is based on cloud technology to combine internal and external stakeholders in the process of creating innovation [3]. These developments are expanding the traditional concept of CAI-systems towards open innovation (Open CAI 2.0). Application of cloud technologies to create such systems as Open CAI 2.0 is reasoned by following features:

- cloud services can be quite easily accessible to the user through the network without the need to pre-install the software (SaaS system),
- cloud computing makes it easy to ensure scalability and dynamic generation of services.

Examples of implementation of such platforms are Virtual Innovation Agency of BMV Group (http://www.bmwgroup.com/via/), online community of brainstorming (https://www.atizo.com/), WEB-portal "Conveyor of Ideas" by FSUE "Russian Post" (http://www.konveer-idea.ru/about/), Ideas portal "Dom.ru" of Russian telecommunications holding by «ER-Telecom» (http://idea.domru.ru/). Some companies already specialize as intermediaries. They organize competitions or ideas exchange on their platform for other organizations, IdeaCrossing or IdeaConnection (http://www.ideaconnection.com/) are good examples (https://www.ideacrossing.org/).

Open CAI systems solve three major problems: the collection of ideas produced by a lot of people, and selection of the best of them, the creation of a technological platform that allows you to collect, document, and discuss ideas and concepts to improve them regardless of time and place, to facilitate the exchange between the community and the innovative companies, which are looking for new ideas outside.

Comparative analysis of open and closed CAI systems showed that for qualitative high-tech solutions it is necessary to use systematic methods and directed search of new technical solutions, involving representatives of professional associations, and experts of narrow specialization. Open innovation platforms using methods of brainstorming and mindmapping rather solve the problem of socialization of innovative ideas and identification of needs. But they rarely result in a high-tech solutions. Thus, a comprehensive platform that combines the methods of open innovation with effective work of R & D specialists and subject community experts will be the most appropriate.

Production of modern high-tech products requires a significant expansion of the spectrum of professional competencies of R & D specialists. At the beginning of the last century basic knowledge of electricity, elementary mechanics and signal processing was enough for the production of the first phones. But in the design of the latest generation of mobile phones you will need to use about 20 knowledge areas (optics , microelectronics , new materials , computers and information technology , signal processing, ecology , etc.). This leads to new requirements for design engineers, and R & D specialists. In the past their individual knowledge and skills were sufficient to meet the needs of the design process, but now there is a need to create interdisciplinary teams of specialists, the team with strong support by means of information technologies (bases of physical and technical knowledge, practices, as well as algorithms for synthesis of new technical solutions) .

Conceptual model of an open CAI system is based on WEB 2.0 technologies. It is considered in [9,16]. Core of the system is the CAI «Intellect-Pro» which supports the tasks of the first group «Ideas management" and, in part, a third group of "Managing patents" [10] . This software product implemented a systematic and efficient method for direct search for new technical solutions based on knowledge-based techniques. Later in the article it is described how knowledge-based techniques can be used to organize a computer support for innovative design based on energy-information method of modeling processes of different physical nature.

4   Computer Support for Innovative Design on Base of Energy-Information Method

As part of the science of engineering design scientists have developed a large number of design methods. Many methodologies have similar objectives, structure and inherit each other's design theory. Last complex extensive study which investigated 324 information source, is given in [11]. Important conclusions that have been made in this work identified trends in engineering design:

1. The creation of intelligent tools to support designers in the early stages of design is still relevant and useful task.
2. The creation of such tools need in establishment and use of vast storehouse of knowledge and ontological methods for fast and relevant search of these data to provide engineers with real and virtual space for co-working.

In [12] a classification of CAI-based models of innovative design is shown. According to the [12] the methods using a systematic approach and knowledge base of the physical effects of different nature are the most effective ones (Fig.3). The CAI system «Intellect-Pro» implements a systematic and efficient method for direct search of new technical solutions, based on the energy-information method.

The essence of engineering design process is the mapping between known physical knowledge given a required function into a description of a realizable design product. Every engineering domain contains a set of fundamental physical laws (physical effects and phenomena) thus providing a basis for designing new products through combining and instantiating these principles. The use of this knowledge governs tasks of routine design or redesign rather well. The problem arises when a designer experiences the lack of domain-dependent fundamental knowledge on the basis of which a new product can be designed. Essential there is that knowledge required for innovative design can be drawn from different domain and a new product can utilize physical principles from different domains. Transferring physical knowledge from one domain to another can significantly simplify a design. This suggests an independent field of innovative design, a new product based on a new physical principle, which was not used in this area before. Problem can be solved if synthesis of new technical solutions at the level of fundamental physical principles (physical phenomena or effects) will be organized.

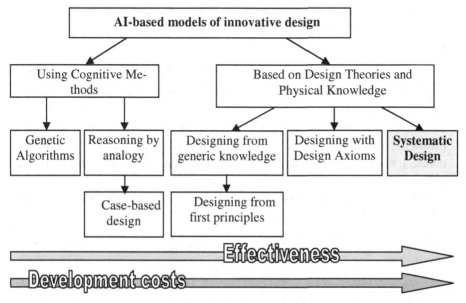

Fig. 3. Classification of AI-based models of innovative design [12]

Thus, the task of developing of a single system approach to knowledge organization for CAI system at the level of ideas generation (conceptual design) is topical. The system should be invariant to the physical nature of the phenomena or process. This approach should ensure that following will be provided:

- mathematical modeling of processes in the technical device, which is invariant to the physical nature of these processes,
- the possibility of processing of physical effects and phenomena that do not fit within a strict framework model,
- the possibility of a structural description of the physical principle of the device.

The basic ideas of energy-information method of modeling of processes of different physical nature (EIMC) are described in [13,14,15] . Distinctive features of this model are:

- presentation of a technical device (TU) as a set of circuits of different physical nature, interacting with each other,
- physical processes within each circuit are described by equations of the same type (EIMC criteria) via the generalized variables and parameters,
- circuits of different physical nature interact via interchain physical and technical effects (PTE).

The whole diversity of relationships between variables and the parameters could be presented in the form of a complex graph (Fig. 4) by using of energy-information model for describing circuits of different physical nature. The figure shows the graph of physical and technical effects and intrachain dependencies for n chains: mechanical, magnetic, electrical circuit and the i-th physical nature.

In this figure you can see:

- generalized values of different physical nature (U_e, U_μ, U_{ml}, U_i - action values; I_e, I_μ, I_{ml}, I_i - reaction values; Q_e, Q_μ, Q_{ml}, Q_i - charge values; P_e, P_μ, P_{ml}, P_i - momentum values);
- generalized parameters of different physical nature (R_e, R_μ, R_{ml}, R_i - resistance parameter; C_e, C_μ, C_{ml}, C_i - capacity parameter; L_e, L_μ, L_{ml}, L_i - inductance parameter), that reflect the relationship between the generalized quantities within the corresponding circuits of given physical nature;
- coefficients of physical and technical effects between circuits of different physical nature (K_{UmlQe}, $K_{Q\mu Ii}$, $K_{IeU\mu}$ and others).

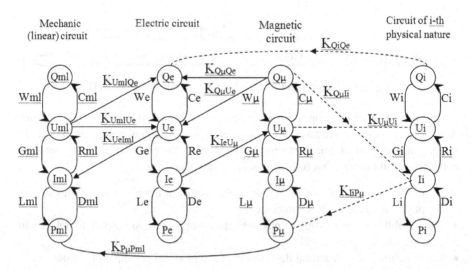

Fig. 4. Bond graph for n circuits of the various physical nature

CAI system knowledge base is a set of standardized descriptions of physical and technical effects (PTE) and intrachain dependencies that must meet the following requirements:

- Each PTE or intrachain dependence are formalized (in EIMC terms) description of the real phenomena occurring in the physical system and having a causal connection between two or more physical quantities. The system presents the physical effect as a ternary structure $B_{i\ in} \rightarrow KB_{i\ in} B_{j\ out} \rightarrow B_{i\ out}$, where $B_{i\ in}$ - input , $KB_{i\ in} B_{j\ out}$ - physical effect coefficient, and $B_{i\ out}$ - out. Physical effect coefficient reflects the relationship of input and output quantities. Analytical expressions for the physical and technical effects (PTE) coefficients and the numerical values of these coefficients, as well as a set of values of PTE technical characteristicsc, are determined from the results of theoretical and experimental research in the field of physics and technology, and available in various sources of scientific and technical information.
- Each PTE or intrachain dependency can have different technical implementation. The whole set of potential technical descisions could be described via morphological matrixes (a set of essential technical details – parameters, and a variety of their technical designs - attributes), the components of which are characterized by the same set of expert assessments of performance.
- Each PTE must have a standard formal description: PTE passport (name, EIMC formula, structural scheme element (PSS) showing the dependence between input and output, coefficient formula (also in details), average coefficient values, the values of performance, a list of references, the visual description of PTE technical implementation, short text description), a PTE describing map (the visual desception of PTE technical realization, PSS, PTE title, and the numerical values of its performance).

Examples of PTE passport and morphological matrix are given in [15].
New technical solutions search can be reduced to the following stages:

- I stage – search of all possible models describing the physical principle of (FP) sensor functionality. The search is made on base of structural parametric synthesis of information in data base of physical and technical effects and further selection of the best options on the aggregate performance estimation;
- II stage - selection of optimal design implementations of each element of the selected FP on basis of morphological synthesis;
- III stage - layout design and creation of conceptual design based on generalized techniques, which contains examples of the PTE performance in different conditions and exploitation manners collected from the patent information.

5   Composition of CAI - System Knowledge Bases and Its Architecture

To develop CAI system architecture (Fig. 5) the one should provide the establishment of the following knowledge bases:

- Knowledge base of the known physical effects and phenomena. Used for the synthesis of physical principle of technical systems. Knowledge is represented in the form of a formalized unified model based on the passport of physical and technical effect, which contains a brief review and full description of physical and technical effect, its input and output described in terms of EIMC, as well as the average values of standard performance and the formula for calculating the transmission coefficient based on the known physical laws.

- Base of morphological matrixes to describe all possible technical realizations of PTE. Morphological matrix should include attributes (list of the typical technical realization component parts) and their options, as well as result of expert comparative analysis of different option of the same attribute.
- Base of animated pictures, demonstrating the principle of action of physical laws and phenomena, as well as elementary morphological matrix' elements.
- Base of design techniques, used to improve the performance of technical solutions which contains information on the use of examples of a physical effect, collected from the patent bases.
- Database of patents used in the framework of expert analysis of information on PTE and decisions, received on the basis of the system.
- Base of new solutions, made by system users.

Database of experts who perform distributed data analysis and fill up the system knowledge base.

All these knowledge bases contain a variety of information, characterizes the same physical phenomenon from different perspectives. Therefore it is necessary to use methods of ontologies for the organization of fast and relevant search on these data set. Taxonomy and ontology for energy-information method of modeling the phenomena of different physical nature will allow engineers to work together in real or virtual space, reduces the complexity of the work of experts to formalize the knowledge about the physical and technical effects.

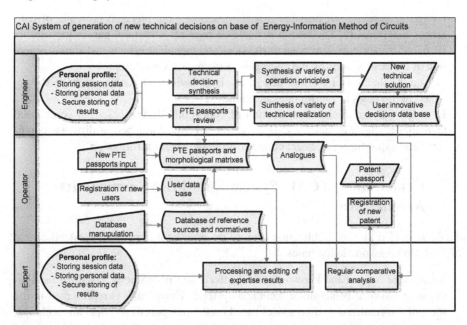

Fig. 5. Architecture EIMC CAI-system

6   Conclusion

1. Automation of innovative processes (Computer-Aided Innovation - CAI) is a new scientific field that combines various interdisciplinary research in the field of innovation in order to increase the effectiveness of new product development (New Product Development - NPD)

2. Based on the analysis of approximately 150 software products belonging to the class of CAI systems we showed that most of the examined CAI-tools (32%) falls into the group of " idea management," 25% - to the "strategy management", and 22% belong to the group " patent management" as well as 21% are separated into the group "integrated solutions", which implements the functions of two or three groups.

3. It is shown that there is a clear trend towards the integration of functionality in the one complex product on the market of CAI systems. However, the market is a lack of comprehensive solutions that integrate all CAI functions in one product, although tighter integration may be noted in groups " idea management " and " strategy management"

4. Most products in the group of "ideas management" are analogs of computerized methods of psychological thinking activation (brainstorming and mindmapping) aimed to generate ideas. However these methods are ineffective in solving of complex engineering problems,.

5. Software analysis identifies a new direction - so-called open-CAI system (CAI 2.0.). These systems using WEB 2.0 cloud technology. It allows to get ideas from a larger community of people (suppliers, customers , employees) and to identify the needs of society. Comparative analysis of open and closed CAI systems showed that for quality high-tech solutions it is necessary to use systematic methods and directed search for new technical solutions, involving representatives of professional associations and   subject experts.

6. When architecting CAI system you must provide the creation and useing of knowledge and extensive storages and system ontological methods for fast and relevant search of these data and to provide engineers with a special virtual space to work together in real-time.

7. It is proposed to use a single system approach to knowledge organization for CAI system on the level of ideas generation (conceptual design). This approach is invariant to the physical nature of the phenomena and processes (energy-information model circuits of different physical nature)

8. The article describes the CAI system architecture model at the level of ideas generation and structure of knowledge bases of such a system. To address issues of relatedness of these knowledge bases the development of taxonomy and ontology of energy-information modeling method of different physical phenomena of nature requires. It makes information search easier for experts and engineers interacting with the system.

References

1. IFIP Technical Committee 5: Information Technology Applications, http://ifiptc.org/?tc=tc5
2. Barczak, G., Sultan, F., Hultink, E.J.: Determinants of IT Usage and New Product Performance. Product Innovation Management (24), 600–613 (2007)
3. Kohn, S., Hüsig, S.: Open CAI 2.0 – Computer Aided Innovation in the era of open innovation and Web 2.0. Computers in Industry (62), 407–413 (2011)
4. Kohn, S., Hüsig, S.: Computer Aided Innovation – State of the Art from a New Product Development Perspective. Computers in Industry (60), 551–562 (2009)
5. Kohn, S., Hüsig, S.: Development of an empirical-based categorisation scheme for CAI software. Computer Applications in Technology (30, ½), 33-45 (2007)
6. Zaripova, V., Petrova, I.: Model of development of computer aided innovation tools (CAI). Prikaspiskii Journal: Management and High-Technologies 3(19), 111–129 (2012)
7. Chesbrough, H.W.: Open Innovation. The New Imperative for Creating and Profiting from Technology. Harvard Business School Press, Boston (2003)
8. Diener, K., Piller, F.: The market for Open Innovation: first study to compare the offerings, methods, and competences of intermediaries, consultancies, and brokers for open innovation. RWTH-TIM Group (2010), http://mass-customization.blogs.com/files/extract_the-market-of-open-innovation_2010-report.pdf
9. Zaripova, V.: Elaboration of automated system for supporting and training of creative thinking and designing for engineers. In (INTELLECT - PRO). 2-nd Advanced Research in Scientific Areas ARSA (2012), http://www.arsa-conf.com/archive/?vid=1&aid=2&kid=60101-45
10. Zaripova, V.: Automatization of engineering activity on the stage of concept design of sensors' elements, CAI "Intellect Pro". Software Registration Licence No 2006613930
11. Chandrasegaran, S.K., et al.: The evolution, challenges, and future of knowledge representation in product design systems. Computer-Aided Design 45, 204–228 (2013)
12. Sushkov, V., Alberts, L., Mars, N.: Innovative engineering design based on sharable physical knowledge. In: Artificial Intelligence in Design 1996: Proceeding of the International Conference Artificial Intelligence in Design, pp. 723–742 (1996)
13. Zaripov, M.F.: Energy-Informational Method of Scientific and Engineering Creativity. VNIIPI, Moscow (1988)
14. Zaripov, M., Petrova, I., Zaripova, V.: Project of creation of knowledge base on physical and technological effects. In: Joint IMEKO TC-1 & XXXIV MKM Conference Education in Measurements and Instrumentation, vol. I, pp.171–176 (2002)
15. Petrova, I., Zaripova, V.: Systems of teaching engineering work on base of internet technologies. International Journal Information Technologies and Knowledge 1, 89–95 (2007)
16. Zaripova, V.: Computer Aided Innovation model for university-enterprise cooperation. Proceedings ICTIC (Proceedings in Conference of Informatics and Management Sciences) 3(1), 377–382 (2014) ISBN: 978-80-554-0865-1, ISSN: 1339-231X

Solution on Decision Support in Determining of Repair Actions Using Fuzzy Logic and Agent System

Maxim Denisov, Alexey Kizim, Valery Kamaev, Svetlana Davydova,
and Anna Matohina

Volgograd State Technical University, Volgograd, Russia
{maxden33,matokhina.a.v}@gmail.com, kizim@mail.ru,
kamaev@cad.vstu.ru, s.davydova@bk.ru

Abstract. The paper describes the structure of a decision support for the industrial equipment maintenance and repair (MR) process based on multi-agent systems and fuzzy logic based on neural networks. The solutions of agent system`s basic subsystems and interaction mechanisms are described. The stages of the maintenance and repair organization continuous improvement process are described. The multi-agent system model was developed and examined on example of road equipment repair. Obtained results are allows to perform the equipment maintenance and repair much better.

Keywords: Program System, Industrial Equipment, Maintenance and Repair, Knowledge Model and Representation, Fuzzy Logic, Fuzzy Neural Network, Intelligent Agents, Multi-agent Systems.

1   Introduction

Today's market relations are showing the improving of production industries competitiveness, considerable attention has focused on reducing its cost. A significant part of the production costs are the costs of maintenance and operation of equipment, reaching the industry average of 8-12% (H&E, 2013). Volume of repairs of machinery and equipment absorb considerable resources. Implementation of technical and organizational innovations implemented in industrial plants primarily in the main production. This reinforces the disparity between the level of primary production and the level of maintenance of fixed assets in working condition. As a result, the efficiency of maintenance and repair (MR) is reduced (Kizim & Linev, 2008). This adversely affects the feasibility condition of the enterprise as a whole. First, the performance of industrial workers is largely dependent on the technical condition of the equipment and its duration downtime for repairs and secondly, without timely and quality repair and maintenance is impossible to provide good quality output, and thirdly, enterprises before the task to achieve the highest possible return on invested capital. All this necessitates a constant search for ways to improve the maintenance and repair of equipment such as enterprise-wide and individual industries and the national economy.

A. Kravets et al. (Eds.): JCKBSE 2014, CCIS 466, pp. 533–541, 2014.

There is the gap in knowledge about the equipment repairs feasibility, certain wear-out and operating time. Used equipment MR scheduling techniques are not always effective. Feed equipment failures increases with time, as its nodes condition worsens due to natural aging. Determination of the impact of the repair time is important. To take into account many parameters have to use the state of the equipment is not only quantitative but also qualitative characteristics and expert estimates. Such characteristics operate model based on fuzzy sets. To solve the problem of determining the types, volumes and time repair actions necessary to develop a decision support system using the fuzzy logic (Sugeno, 1994). It is assumed that the solution of the above problems can be used for industrial equipment in general, making no separation criteria equipment.

2   Knowledge Model of Maintenance and Repair

Since the quality information about the state of the equipment usually is incomplete and poor must have appropriate methods to solve the maintenance, repair and operation (MRO) problem. Problem of determining the timing and terms of the equipment failure repair actions against other support MRO tasks is particularly important. Analysis of existing solutions has shown that the inclusion of incomplete and qualitative knowledge can be performed using different approaches, widely known of which are the coefficients of confidence, fuzzy sets and fuzzy logic, probabilistic approach based on Bayes' theorem, the modified Bayesian approach, the theory of evidence (justification) Dempster - Shafer, and etc. (Dvoryankin, 2003).

Confidence coefficient (CS) – is an informal evaluation that adds to the expert conclusion. CS formula does not distinguish case contrary evidence from the case of insufficient information; it is sometimes useful (Forsyth, 1989). Fuzzy sets in the definition and description of the objects characteristics operate not only qualitative values. Interpretation of qualitative values is subjective in nature, i.e. they are interpreted differently by different people. Due to the vagueness (fuzziness) qualitative values, certain difficulties arise to transition from them to quantifying (Luger, 2009; Kamaev, 2010).

For the organization of inferences in intelligent systems with incomplete knowledge instead of the traditional deduction can be applies the abduction (as known, abduction is the process of forming an explanatory hypothesis based on the given theory and the available observations and facts) (Kamaev and Shcherbakov, 2011). The fuzzy neural network is a multi-layer neural network, in which the layers act as elements of the fuzzy inference system. Neurons of the neural network are characterized by a set of parameters that you can set as a result of the process of conventional neural networks learning. This method of knowledge representation is more perspective for solving. The prediction algorithm is developed for the numerical evaluation of an equipment node failure. It implemented on a computer. It provides performance calculations based on the equipment. The aim is to create a software algorithm that would allow calculating the expected time of failure of each part of the equipment.

As the initial information used data from the time of failure of machine parts throughout the year. Input parameters were specified interval, that is, for each of them to set the minimum and maximum values (confidence interval). When designing a fuzzy neural network for forecasting considered application of the following fuzzy inference algorithms: the algorithm Mamdani and Sugeno algorithm.

Mamdani algorithm implementation included the following stages: the formation of the rule base of fuzzy inference systems, fuzzification of input variables. And the aggregation of sub-conditions in fuzzy production rules (for finding the truth degree of the conditions of each of the fuzzy rules used productions paired fuzzy logic operations, we used the method min-activation

$$\mu'(y) = \min\{c_i, \mu(y)\}, \tag{1}$$

where μ (y) - a membership function of the term, which is the value of the output variable set on the universe of Y.

Accumulation conclusions of fuzzy production rules, defuzzification output variables. In this case, we used the method relative to the average of the center:

$$y_c = \frac{\sum_{i}^{M} \mu(y_{ci}) y_{ci}}{\sum_{i} \mu(y_{ci})} \tag{2}$$

y_{ci} where is the center of the i-th fuzzy rule; μ (y_{ci}) - the value of the membership function corresponding to this rule.

Sugeno algorithm included the following conditions: the formation of the rule base of fuzzy inference systems, in the rule base of fuzzy rules are used only as a product:

$$\text{RULE}: \text{ if } x_1 \text{ is } A_1 \text{ and } x_2 \text{ is } A_2, \text{ then } w = \varepsilon_1 a_1 + \varepsilon_2 a_2 \tag{3}$$

where ε_1 and ε_2 - some weights.

In Sugeno algorithm also includes:fuzzification of the input variables, the aggregation of sub-conditions in fuzzy production rules. In addition, activation in fuzzy production rules Mamdani algorithm performed similarly by the formula (2) then calculated at the fuzzy output values of each rule accumulation conclusions of fuzzy production rules, defuzzification output variables is performed using a modified method of the center of gravity for point sets.

$$y = \frac{\sum_{i=1}^{n} c_i w_i}{\sum_{i=1}^{n} c_i} \tag{4}$$

where n - the total number of active rules fuzzy productions.

Subsequently, based on testing network created with the use of these algorithms was chosen fuzzy neural network that implements the algorithm Sugeno. This is due to the fact that the fuzzy neural network algorithm has a lower error Sugeno learning and prediction error. To predict failure time items developed fuzzy neural network algorithm Sugeno. Fig. 1 shows an algorithm of the fuzzy neural network.

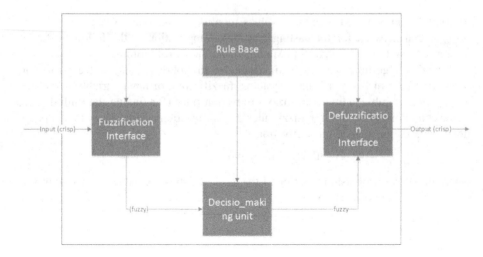

Fig. 1. Algorithm of fuzzy neural network

3   Maintenance and Repair Support Multiagent Systems Model

The approach, used in this paper, is that the solution of MR tasks can be distributed among intelligent agents which specialize in solving of particular problems. Parallel operations of such agents can significantly speed up the information processing and improve the reliability of the original problem. In solving this problem are found the special coordinator agent that can take collective decisions based on local decisions of other agents using the principles of the decision-making theory or different voting procedures. All local decisions are made in parallel mode, which speeds up the adoption of a collective decision.

For interaction monitoring and simplify the management structure of similar objects are used agents which grouped in the multi-agent systems (MAS). The MAS model, originally developed to represent the interaction processes of objects set with similar structure, has been used successfully in a variety of scientific fields (Weiss, 2013; Kizim et al, 2012). Using this model in the fields of robotics and data mining has led to the development of the concept of an agent as an object endowed with rights of the user and the ability to perform a similar range of applications. Thus, the developed agent is a complex system based on fuzzy sets.

Due to the heterogeneity and different geographic location of equipment is justified application of agent technology to address maintenance and repair (Kizim, 2009). Agents have characteristics that make them indispensable in MRO problems (Kizim & Chikov, 2012). Ability to respond appropriately to dynamically changing conditions makes MAS for flexible use in maintenance equipment is quite self-contained and the situation it changes dynamically. Agents have properties of flexibility, extensibility, and fault tolerance. In distributed task among the MAS agents, each of which is considered as a member of the group. The distribution of tasks involves assigning roles to each member of the group with the definition of measures of responsibility and experience requirements (Melnyk et al, 2011; Denisov, 2013b).

For all methods of predictions making equipment the MRO works within the automated system using agents can improve the speed and quality of drafting plans for work on equipment maintenance and repair. Accordingly, we propose the following model of the maintenance MAS (Denisov, et al, 2013a).

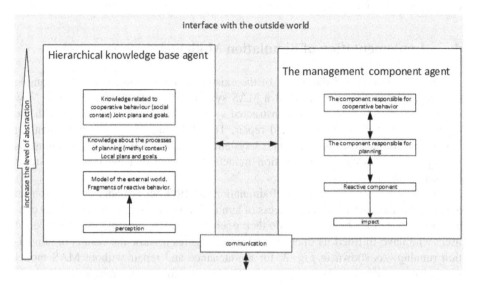

Fig. 2. Architecture MRO for road equipment based on multi-agent

Distributed problem solving by several agents in the multi-agent system is divided into these stages:

1. The machine agent manager analyzes failures of internal nodes, as well as prioritization of their repair

2. These tasks are distribute among the agents executing

3. Each executive agent decides its task, sometimes also dividing it into subtasks

4. To provide an overall result produced compositions are integrating of partial results corresponding to the selected task

5. The machine agent manager is used to determine the priority for repair of equipment importance grades, which were prepared according to the modified Reliability Centered Maintenance (RCM2) methodology (Denisov et al, 2013b; Kizim, 2013).

To implement the program of intelligent agents have been proposed and used a lot of different architectures. The InteRRaP-MAS architecture selected for this task. In this architecture, source control agent is multilevel. Every upper layer works with more abstracted (and aggregated) information (Glaser, 2002; Denisov et al, 2013a). InetRRaP was developed in order to meet the requirements of modeling dynamic agent societies such as interacting robots. Its main feature is that it combines patterns of behavior with explicit planning facilities. On the one hand, patterns of behavior allow an agent to react quickly and flexibly to changes its environment. On the other hand, the ability to devise plans is generally regarded necessary to solve more sophisticated tasks (Muller at al., 1995).

The software product has been developed. It is the basic of complex automated system. The first system is designed for the implementation of complex communication throughout the information space of MRO equipment. It is the cross-platform application, the client part of which can run on both operating systems of personal computers and mobile OS.

4   Implementation of Simulation Modeling

Therefore, we examined the model of the existing systems maintenance on example of road equipment repair, and built a MAS system of maintenance and repair. Now we test the effectiveness of the constructed system work and comparing it with the existing system of maintenance and repair. To fulfill this goal needs implementing simulation. In that work used Simplex3 system for the simulation implementation, as it supports the creation of simulation models of normal and agent-based systems (Schmidt, 2001).

The purpose of the execution of simulation is MRO performance comparison on MAS and without MAS. In the process of simulation implementation, have 1000 concurrent users that are beginning to do their operation. At the exit time is the number of users who have fulfilled its operation (output). Figures 3 show the results of simulation running. As shown in Fig. 3, for maintenance and repair without MAS model number of outputs increases over time. This means that some transactions are executed sequentially.

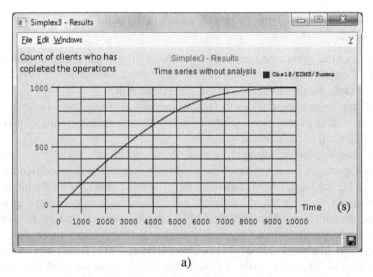

a)

Fig. 3. The result of simulation of MRO without MAS (a) and for MAS (b)

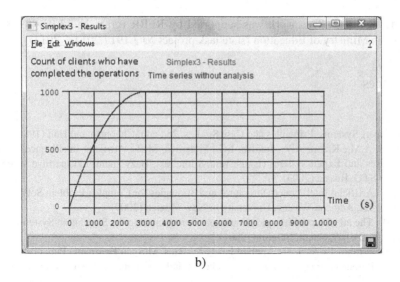

Fig. 3. (*Continued*)

In the process of simulation implementation modeling was used only MAS agents parallelism property, but was not involved in the possibility of storing agents. Thus, the speed of the MRO system on the MAS is higher than the existing maintenance and repair systems.

5   Conclusion

Was described the technique of determining the moment of industrial equipment repair action based on fuzzy sets. The algorithm of fuzzy sets was designed and implemented. The fuzzy neural network is a multi-layer neural network, in which the layers act as elements of the fuzzy inference system. The algorithm of the fuzzy neural network was developed. The repair and maintenance organization support used ontologies and multi-agent systems. The agents' composition and agent-based model planning system for maintenance and repair as multi-agent system was designed. The structure of intelligent agents corresponding to the model was developed. Maintenance and repair planning techniques used Case Based Reasoning method based on ontology. The stages of distributed problem solving by several agents in the multi-agent system were showed. The model of the existing systems maintenance was examined. The system approbation based on regional state enterprise for the construction and repair of roads and repair service contractor company which performing the repair of industrial equipment in several industrial areas. Development and implementation of complex software systems are manufactured in the organizational stages. Currently the automated system collects information on the operation, which is accounted for in the prototype of decision support system.

Acknowledgement. This work was supported by RFBR (grant № 13-01-00798_A) and Russian Ministry of Education (state task project № 2.1917.2014K_2014).

References

Book

Forsyth: Expert Systems: Principles and Case Studies, 2nd edn. Chapman and Hall (1989)
Dvoryankin, A.M., Kizim, A.V., Jukova, I.G., Siplivaya, M.B.: Artificial intelligence. Knowledge bases and Expert systems (Iskusstvennyi intellekt. Bazy znanii i ekspertnye sistemy), p. 140. VSTU, Russia (2003)
Luger, G.F.: Artificial Intelligence: Structures and Strategies for Complex Problem Solving, 6th edn. Pearson, Addison Wesley, University of New Mexico (2009)
Schmidt, B.: The art of modelling and simulation: introduction to the Simulation System Symplex3, SCS- BVBA, Ghent, Belgium (2001)
Sugeno, M., Terano, T., Asai, K.: Applied Fuzzy Systems. Morgan Kaufmann Pub. (1994)
Weiss, G.: Multiagent Systems. Intelligent Robotics and Autonomous Agents series. The MIT Press (2013)

Journal

Denisov, M.V., Kizim, A.V., Matokhina, A.V., Sadovnikova, N.P.: Repair and maintenance organization with the use of ontologies and multi-agent systems on the road sector example. World Applied Sciences Journal 24(24), 31–36 (2013a)
Kamaev, V.A., et al.: Application of fuzzy neural network models for the identification of the state of roads. Journal of Computer and Information Technology, Engineering (12), 36–41 (2010)
Kamaev, V.A., Shcherbakov, M.V.: Abduction in conceptual design, cognitive modeling and data mining [Abdukcia v konceptual'nom proektirovanii, kognitivnom modelirovanii i intellektual'nom analize dannyh]. Open Education (2, pt. 2), 62–67 (2011)
Kizim, A.V., Linev, N.A.: Research and development of methodic of automation of repairing work of enterprise (Issledovanie i razrabotka metodiki avtomatizacii remontnyh rabot predpriyatiya). Izvestia VolgGTU 4(2), 43–45 (2008)
Kizim, A.V.: Rationale for the automation of repair and maintenance of equipment. Izvestia-VolgGTU 6(6), 118–121 (2009)
Kizim, A.V., Melnyk, V.Y., Chikov, E.V.: Forecasting and planning for software and information support for the maintenance and repair of equipment. Open Education 2(85 pt. 2), 224–227 (2011)
Kizim, A.V., Kravets, A.D., Kravets, A.G.: Generation of intelligent agents to support tasks of maintenance and repair. Generacija intellektual'nyh agentov dlya zadach podderzhki tehnicheskogo obsluzhivanija i remonta 321(5), 131–134 (2012)
Melnik, V.Y., Kizim, A.V., Kamaev, V.A.: Decision support in the formation of the work queue using Automation planning of maintenance and repair of equipment 12(11), 107–110 (2011)
Muller, J.P., Pischel, M., Thiel, M.: Modeling Reactive Behavior in Vertically Layered Agent Architecture. In: Wooldridge, M.J., Jennings, N.R. (eds.) ECAI 1994 and ATAL 1994. LNCS, vol. 890, pp. 261–276. Springer, Heidelberg (1995)

Conference paper or contributed volume

Denisov, M.V., Kamaev, V.A., Kizim, A.V.: Organization of the Repair and Maintenance in Road Sector with Ontologies and Multi-agent Systems. In: Original Research Article Procedia Technology, vol. 9, pp. 819–825 (2013)

H&E Equipment Services, Inc., Reports for 2013-year results (2013), http://www.he-equipment.com

Kizim, A.V., Chikov, E.V.: Increasing efficiency of equipment maintenance and repair process using a systematic approach and a set of key perfomance indicators. In: Proceedings of the Congress on Intelligent Systems and Information Technologies, IS&IT 2012, Moscow, vol. 4 [an annotated report] / SFU [et al.], p. 32 (2012)

Kizim, A.V.: Establishing the Maintenance and Repair Body of Knowledge: Comprehensive Approach to Ensuring Equipment Maintenance and Repair Organization Efficiency. Original Research Article Procedia Technology 9, 812–818 (2013)

Vicente, E., Jiménes, A., Mateos, A.: A fuzzy extension of Margerit methodology for risk analysis in information systems. In: Proceedings of the International Conference Information Systems 2013, IADIS, Lisbon, Portugal, March 13-15, pp. 39–46 (2013)

Evaluation of Interaction Level between Potential Drug and Protein by Hydrogen Bond Energy Calculation

Ekaterina Tyulkina[1], Pavel Vassiliev[2], Timur Janovsky[1], and Maxim Shcherbakov[1]

[1] Volgograd State Technical University, Volgograd, Russia
{8marta_08,janovsky}@mail.ru, maxim.shcherbakov@gmail.com
[2] Volgograd State Medical University, Volgograd, Russia
pvassiliev@mail.ru

Abstract. Paper describes approach to evaluation of interaction level between potential drug molecule and protein molecule, what uses calculation of possible hydrogen bond energy. Information about atoms belonging to molecules and bonds between them can be extracted from text descriptions of molecule structures. Basing on experimental values of hydrogen bond energy between different atoms the total numeric value of bounding energy between the protein molecule and the potential drug molecule can be prepared. Thereby, the decision about strength of the interaction can be solved, and as a conclusion about drug's influence on illness, for the occurrence of what the protein is responsible. Barriers to recognition of applicability of the approach are described.

Keywords: hydrogen bond energy, protein molecule, potential drug, interaction level, program application, energy spectrum, graph of values, text analysis.

1 Introduction

There are many problems in the field of drug design nowadays. Before beginning of production of the new drug it must be subjected to numerous animal experimentations, and it is very expensive procedure. The computer methods of prediction of pharmacological activity of the compound prepared in chemical laboratories exist. For these methods it is necessary to specify the substances' chemical properties and parameters. Though this approach also has disadvantages: for example one of these methods – molecular docking – is a very time-consuming procedure (sometimes it can be conducted on multiprocessor cluster during a week), but the accuracy of results is not high. This paper describes process and results of the work to create the software that can operatively answer the question if the interaction between specific drug and specific protein should be studied in details. The more exact calculation of interaction energy (with using the special tools) and laboratory experiments are understood as more detailed studying of interaction. And ideal outcome of such work is the decision-making about the drug production.

The drug is any substance that can be used for diagnostic, prophylaxis, relief and treatment of human and animal diseases and birth control. When the drug comes in

A. Kravets et al. (Eds.): JCKBSE 2014, CCIS 466, pp. 542–555, 2014.

the human organism it influences on specific cell receptor. Cell receptor is a molecule of protein (rarely – lipid) situated on the surface of the cell or dissolved in cytoplasm of the cell. It reacts specifically on attaching of chemical substance molecule to it by changing of its dimensional configuration and transmits this signal into the cell. The substance which binds with receptor is called as ligand of this receptor. Changing of receptor conformation after binding with ligand leads to start of biochemical reactions cascade and as a result to changing of functional state of the cell.

Compound's biological activity modeling method by computer is called as virtual screening. It allows considering a great number of compounds though spends very small time in contrast with real experiments. Besides that virtual screening provides an opportunity to explore not yet synthesized compounds while reducing cost of experiments because it doesn't require the funds for purchasing and synthesis of chemicals. Usually virtual screening is used for preliminary selection of compounds which expensive methods of real screening would be applied to afterwards.

There are two groups among virtual screening methods. The first group includes algorithms that allow constructing of new molecules basing on famous active compounds structures (ligand-based design). The second group of methods comes from biological target structure (structure-based design).

The first category methods assess complementarity of ligands to receptor by determination of ligands similarity between each other. Traditionally they include various algorithms of compounds selection based on fundamental concept of two-dimensional structural similarity to the active drug molecules (2D-similarity) and three-dimensional similarity to the active molecules (3D-similarity).

For realization of methods of the second category knowledge about investigated biological target structure, features of its formation and form, composition of binding site is required. Features of interaction between famous ligand and specific target are also necessary to specify. Methods of 3D-molecular docking are based on this principle. Molecular docking procedure consists of design of protein 3D-model, determination of active site into it (place of the best interaction) and situation of ligand in protein active site. Herewith changings of protein and ligand conformations are considered and calculation of interaction energy is performed. There are many program systems that perform molecular docking: DOCK, FlexX, FRED, Glide, GOLD, Surflex and other. Ligand and protein models design is a very resource intensive task and has significance to implement only by using of multiprocessor clusters. But even having access to high performance computing, insufficient knowledge of many theoretic aspects of ligand-receptor interaction (such as consideration of their dynamics, all the possible conformations of ligand and protein, influence of solvent molecule and other substances, presented in solution) leads to the next situation. In many cases using of molecular docking doesn't cause improving quality of target-specific activity prediction in contrast with less resource intensive methods of two-dimensional structural similarity. Important factor is also that the vast majority of computer programs work in the conditional approximation nowadays. In accordance with it proteins are considered as stationary systems, and only area of direct binding is exposed to structural and energy variation. Obviously it can't reflect all the regularities of interaction in the system "ligand – biological target" to the full [1].

Despite the fact that virtual screening greatly facilitates and accelerates search of new drugs, any its method has disadvantages described above.

The next overall disadvantages inherent to molecular docking, 2D-similarity and molecular similarity methods can be generally noticed:

1. Licenses for software deciding tasks of new drug design are very expensive.
2. Calculation error may be so great that it sometimes raises the question about expediency of virtual screening method application.
3. In computer modeling an opportunity to specify all the properties of compound not always exists and rounding error makes result very far from truth (transmembrane proteins modeling).

Energy of interaction between ligand and protein can be calculated with great error and without specifying of absolutely all factors of such interaction. These circumstances may become the reason of that the calculated activity of well-binding substance is lower than activity of substance not binding with a protein. In this case the decision is the running of system for evaluation of interaction between protein and those ligands about which there is information that they bind with this protein, but specific data about level of this binding absent. It is necessary to have an instrument to receive such information. This instrument within an acceptable term must give an answer to question if one protein can interact with some ligand. It is not obligatory for instrument to characterize their interaction level, but it must be enough to determine if this interaction is possible. In this case acceptable term must be understood as a time, several times less (hundred times) than time of either molecular docking implementation (including calculation of all target protein conformations) or substructure search (big databases scanning). According to protein size (count of amino acids in its composition) process of interaction level evaluation can take time from few seconds (for amino acids amount less than 20) to few minutes (for proteins with complex structures), using developed program.

Thus results of virtual screening to be more plausible should be obtained for substances well-binding with protein. For receiving information about binding level the program for evaluation of interaction level between potential drug and protein was developed.

2   Methodology

The work was done towards the development of software that basing on structural formula could operatively determine whether to study interaction between one ligand and some protein more particularly. The presented method results in approximate numerical value of interaction level. The method takes as input data basic information about protein and ligand. This information does not change depending on the environmental conditions and this circumstance provides more reliable results. Because of protein primary structure (sequence of amino acid residues) is determined by protein genetic code, structures of higher exponents are determined by amino acid sequence. Thus input data was decided to be represented as ligand structural formula and peptide sequence. In order to generate multiple description of the protein, it was decided to perform the fragmentation of the input amino acid sequence.

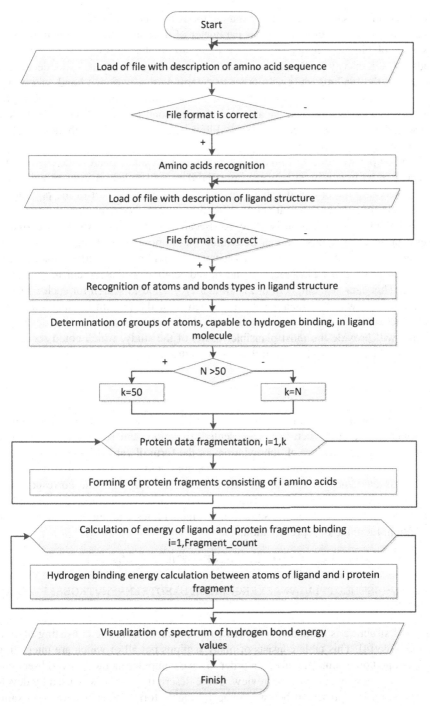

Fig. 1. Flowchart illustrating methodology

Because universal measure of any interaction is the energy, binding energy of protein and ligand was decided to use as parameter of their interaction evaluation. Whereas 80% of binding energy of «protein-ligand» complex is provided by hydrogen bonds [2], the energy of forming of hydrogen bond between atoms was decided to consider as the binding energy. In order to determine the hydrogen bond energy it is necessary to have the information about atoms or groups of atoms contained in protein and ligand structures and capable to hydrogen bond forming. Numeric values of hydrogen bond energy are necessary too. Flowchart of described methodology algorithm is represented in Fig.1.

At the output we get set of binding energy numeric values. Each value characterizes energy of hydrogen bond between potential drug molecule and some protein fragment. Analyzing the obtained values we can evaluate in what part of the protein the greatest binding strength is situated. With the protein fragmentation the variation of best binding place location is achieved. Because of this place will be occurred in several protein fragments we can determine the combination of amino acids what promotes the best binding and the exact location of binding site. Further this data can be used to more exact placement of the ligand relative to the protein in molecular docking. This data also can help in 2D-similarity method to search for such a ligand, the structure of which is identical to the structure of the protein binding site. As a result, the combination of a standard method of virtual screening and developed program will provide the most plausible results of the study, which could serve as a pretext for the laboratory testing of this potential drug.

2.1   Data-In

Data about protein and ligand molecule structures are necessary for program application running. Protein structure is represented as amino acid sequence. Amino acid sequence represents the set of abbreviations in the form of capital letters of the Latin alphabet. Each of these letters means some amino acid. Such protein structure description is contained in special file with extension *.faa. This file corresponds to FASTA-format of amino acid sequence representation [3]. It includes the single line with its contents description and some (one or more) lines with amino acid sequence description. Example of representation:

```
>gi|129295|sp|P01013|OVAX_CHICK GENE X PROTEIN
(OVALBUMIN-RELATED)
QIKDLLVSSSTDLDTTLVLVNAIYFKGMWKTAFNAEDTREMPFHVTKQESKPVQMMC
MNNSFNVAT
```

Ligand structure is redundantly described in chemical table file consisting of connection table [4]. This table consists of many sections not all of which are interesting for developed program. Therefore, in order to save computer memory several sections were intentionally excluded from review. Table description in the way used by developed program is represented below. Connection table format is considered on example of Alanine molecule.

Alanine

| 6 | 5 | 0 | 0 | 0 | 0 | 0 | 0 | 0 | 0999 | V2000 | | | | | | | | Counts line |

0.2062	0.3572	0.0000	C	0	0	0	0	0	0	0	0
0.2063	-1.0717	0.0000	N	0	0	0	0	0	0	0	0
-0.2062	-0.3572	0.0000	C	0	0	0	0	0	0	0	0
-1.0313	-0.3572	0.0000	C	0	0	0	0	0	0	0	0
-0.2062	1.0717	0.0000	O	0	0	0	0	0	0	0	0
1.0313	0.3572	0.0000	O	0	0	0	0	0	0	0	0

Atom block

3	2	1	1	0	0
1	3	1	0	0	0
3	4	1	0	0	0
1	5	2	0	0	0
1	6	1	0	0	0

Bond block

M END

Section «Counts line» contains information relating to the number of atoms, the number of bonds and the table version. To specify the number of atoms and the number of bonds 3 positions are reserved. There are 6 atoms and 5 bonds in Alanine molecule.

Atom block determines atom symbols and any atypical deviations from the mass, charge and stereochemical properties. Atom block consists of several lines the number of which is equal to the atom number in molecule. Each line describes atom coordinates (decimal fractions comprising 5 positions for storage of the integer part of the fraction and 4 positions for storage of the fractional part) and atom symbol for storage of which 3 positions are assigned. So, in Alanine molecule there are 3 Carbon atoms, 2 Oxygen atoms and 1 Nitrogen atom.

Bond block is made up of bond lines, one line per bond. Each line describes bond between two atoms, type of bond, bond topology (chain or ring). Each bond is represented by the number of the first bonding atom, the number of the second bonding atom and type of bond between these atoms (1 – single, 2 – double, 3 – triple, 4 – aromatic). The atom numbers are determined by the order of their consecution in the atom block. So, in Alanine molecule Oxygen atom (described the penultimate in the atom block, its number is 5) is double bonded with Carbon atom, described the first in atom block.

Information about Hydrogen atoms is not given in the connection table.

Line "M END" finishes description of the specific molecule structure.

Set of file formats containing some form of table of chemical elements connection is defined: molfiles (molecule files), RGfiles (Rgroup query files), rxnfiles (reaction files), SDfiles (structure-data files), RDfiles (reaction-data files). For this work molfiles and SDfiles are interesting.

Molecule file (*.mol) describes single molecule structure that can contain unconnected fragments. File of this format with ligand structure description is loaded in program. To store the data about ligand structure special class l_molecule, whose properties resemble the connection table was implemented in the program:

```
class l_molecule
{
public:
   l_molecule();
   ~l_molecule();
   void allocate();         //Allocation
   char l_name [50];
   unsigned int countAtom;  //Atom number
   unsigned int countConn;  //Bond number
   unsigned int ** conn;    //The atom bonds situation
   double ** coordinates;   // Two-dimensional array of
atom coordinates
   char ** atoms;           //Names of molecule atoms
   QMap <unsigned int,unsigned int> groups1;
   bool assign(FILE * F_L);
   void freealloc();
};
```

When mol-file describing the ligand structure is loading in the program, the method assign() is calling to read data from file. Then object of l_molecule class is created to store data about the ligand.

Structures of amino acids from protein content are also represented in the connection table format. When FASTA-file describing amino acid sequence is loading in the program, each letter meaning one amino acid gets in accordance object of the l_molecule class that describes structure of this amino acid. The structure of each amino acid may be conveniently described in molfile. However, in order to save CPU time spending on the reading N files describing amino acid structures (N is the input sequence length) it was decided to register data about 22 amino acids in the program code.

2.2   Atoms Capable of Hydrogen Bond Forming Recognition

In the paper [2] exploration results are published that confirm the next hypothesis: 80% of binding energy of protein-ligand complex is provided by hydrogen bonds. Two types of groups are necessary to form the hydrogen bond: proton-donor (COOH, OH, NH_2, S, C, F, Cl, Br, I, Se, P) and proton-acceptor (O, F, Ne, S, Cl, Ar, Cr, Mn) [5]. Hydrogen bond is formed between these groups. The opportunity of hydrogen bond formation can be determined by presence of these groups in ligand and protein molecule structures. The conclusion about molecular interaction strength can be made basing on their binding energy.

Analyzing the data from connection tables (atoms and bonds) of input structures the information about groups capable of hydrogen bond formation is received. The determination of groups is implemented by the next way. In the atom block the type of chemical element of each atom is analyzed, thus if this atom is one of atoms that can form hydrogen bond, its bonds are checked in bond block. Group is defined more exactly by type of its bonds.

In the program two-dimensional array hydro_energy of the double type is declared. It contains values of hydrogen bond energy between groups of atoms that can be met in amino acids and ligands. In the rows of this array groups that can be met in ligand structure are situated, in the columns – groups that can be noticed in amino acids. Experimental value of the hydrogen bond energy in kcal/mol is contained at the intersection of row and column. If bond can't be formed between some groups at the intersection of corresponding row and column null is situated. To store data about groups capable of hydrogen bond forming in molecules in the class l_molecule the next property is declared:

```
QMap <unsigned int,unsigned int> groups1;
```

groups1 is a two-dimensional container that stores data in a pair of "key-value". Identifier of hydrogen bond group plays a role of key, the number of these groups in the specific molecule plays a role of value. Group identifier determines number of row in hydro_energy array (for ligand) and number of column (for amino acid).

Groups that can form hydrogen bonds are previously known in each amino acid composition. The total number of existing amino acids is 22. These are groups containing either hydrogen or electronegative elements. For amino acid structure the container groups1 is initially filled. Ligand groups are identified in the moment of receiving its structure description represented in the input file. The energy of possible binding can be determined by knowing the group identifiers for protein and ligand structures.

2.3   The Protein Data Fragmentation

The amino acid chain defines a set of data that describes the protein. To obtain a meaningful representation of the protein structure it is necessary to deploy description submitted as a set of single amino acids structures into multidimensional space. It means to generate information that uniquely describes the specific protein. Fragmentation of protein data was selected as a method of multidimensional description obtaining.

Protein data fragmentation involves the allocation of several fragments out the basic amino acid chain. Each fragment consists of several amino acids. By default single fragments have already been received: every input letter of Latin alphabet gets in accordance structure of amino acid coded by this letter. Every amino acid contains NH_2 and COOH chemical groups. Both groups take part in the formation of a peptide bond between two amino acids. Carbon from COOH-group of the first amino acid is united with Nitrogen from NH_2-group of the second amino acid (Fig.2). As a result, water molecule and dipeptide are formed.

Dipeptide will also have NH2-group (remaining untapped from the first amino acid) and COOH-group (remaining untapped from the second amino acid) that can take part in further polypeptide chain increase (by 3, 4, 5 and more amino acids in one fragment). Polypeptide chain increase goes from left to right: from the left side fragment is situated consisting of k amino acids going in input sequence (k=1..N, if N≤50, and k=1..50, if N>50), from the right side – the single amino acid that is situated always the next in input series of the amino acids. After their linking fragment is formed consisting of amino acids whose number is k +1.

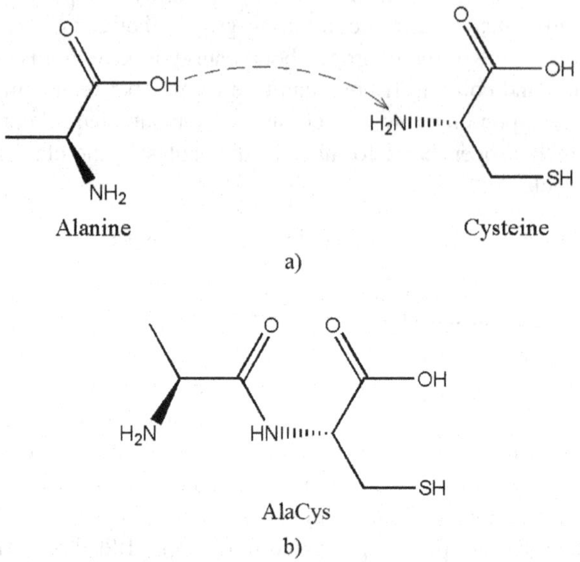

a)

AlaCys

b)

Fig. 2. Formation of peptide bond between Alanine and Cysteine: a) single acids; b) dipeptide

For example if input chain was ACGM then by fragmentation we can get 10 different protein fragments that are defined by input amino acid sequence. There are single A, C, G, M, double AC, CG, GM, triple ACG, CGM and quadruple ACGM (Fig.3).

To generate fragments by dint of peptide bond it is necessary to have information about atoms that take part in its formation. Location of Nitrogen atom from NH_2-group and Carbon atom from COOH-group is indicated in class acid that stores data about amino acids. Class acid inherits properties from class l_molecule described above and contains some new properties that are necessary to identify atoms forming peptide bond. These new properties are in the context of connection table of the substance:

```
    unsigned int Nnum;    //Number of Nitrogen atom from NH₂-
group
    unsigned int Cnum;    //Number of Carbon atom from COOH-
group
    unsigned int Ocon;    //Number of line where Oxygen atom
bond is described that must be deleted
    unsigned int Odecl;   //Number of line where Oxygen atom
is declared that must be deleted
```

Information about each atom used by this program includes only atom number in atom block and bonds in bond block. Then all initial information that is required to atom identification includes designation of its number in atom block.

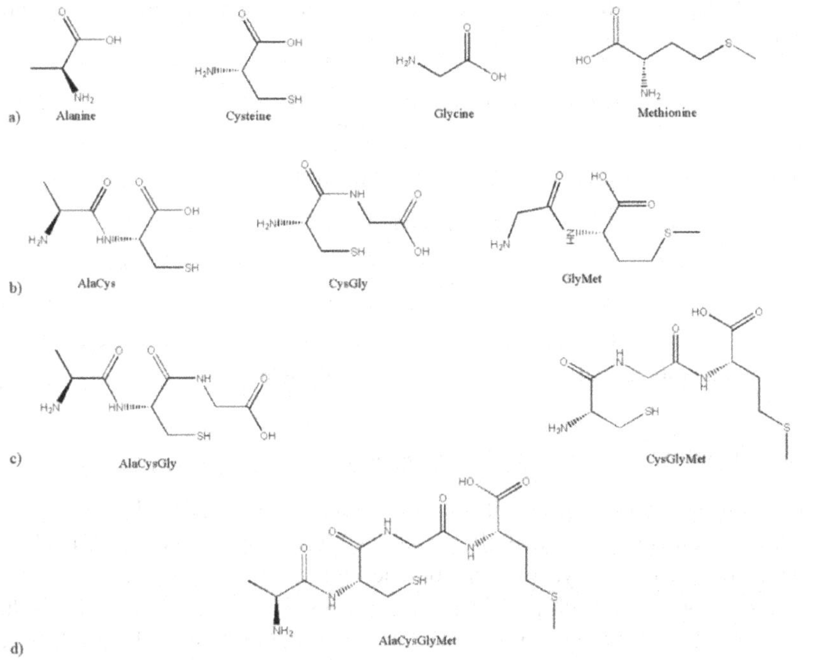

Fig. 3. Protein fragments: a) single; b) double; c) triple; d) quadruple

Therefore, for storing information about the Nitrogen and Carbon atoms data type unsigned int was used.

When fragment is formed the new connection table is generated. It is formed from connection tables of initial substances including the following changes:

- the number of atoms in formed table is equal to sum of the first operand atom number and the second operand atom number without 1;
- the number of bonds in formed table is equal to sum of bonds of the first and the second operand;
- serial numbers of atoms of the second operand are updated in consideration of serial numbers of atoms of the first operand;
- bond block is updated in consideration of updated serial numbers of atoms;
- from atom block of the first operand Oxygen atom that formed water molecule upon linking is deleted;
- bond of Carbon atom from the first operand with the second operand Oxygen atom that formed water molecule upon linking is deleted from bond block;
- values of properties showing the location of chemical binding groups are updated;
- bond of Carbon atom of the first operand with Nitrogen atom of the second operand is added to bond block;
- size of container groups1 containing list of groups capable of hydrogen bond forming is increased.

Number of protein fragments Fragment_count received from amino acid sequence which length is N, is defined by the formula (1).

$$Fragment\_count = \sum_{i=0}^{k} N - i \qquad (1)$$

Value of parameter k is defined by the next conditions:

$$k = \begin{cases} 50, if \ N \geq 50 \\ N, if \ N < 50 \end{cases} \qquad (2)$$

Thus, using of fragmentation can provide a unique representation of some polypeptide and avoid dispersal of information about protein structure.

2.4   Calculation and Visualization of Results

By determining groups capable of hydrogen binding in ligand and in every protein fragment we can calculate value of binding energy of both molecules. Calculation is performed by the next way: using hydro_energy array the opportunity of binding of each ligand group with each protein fragment group is checked. The value at the intersection of corresponding row-identifier of group (ligand) and column-identifier of group (protein fragment) is multiplied on the number of these groups in molecules. The number of groups is stored as value by key-identifier in container groups1 of molecule. Obtained for every pair of groups values of energy are summed. If bond is impossible (null value is situated at intersection) it doesn't influence on total sum. So one energy value can be obtained that will characterize the binding level of some protein fragment with ligand.

Calculating of value of hydrogen bond energy of every protein fragment with ligand we can get numeric spectrum of hydrogen potentials. The number of values in it is equal to number of formed protein fragments. This spectrum will characterize interaction of some ligand with protein.

Obtained spectrum of hydrogen potentials can be represented by 3 different ways:

1. Table of numbers. Floating-point numbers are contained in table, number of rows in which is equal to maximal number of amino acids in fragment, number of columns is equal to number of amino acids in protein content.
2. Graph of spectrum. Abscissa axis shows fragment numbers, ordinate axis shows numeric values of binding energy of fragments with ligand.
3. Text file. It contains energetic spectrum ligand-protein complex where numeric values are separated by tabs.

To increase the reliability of the results, the randomness criteria set should be applied [6], when a set of output data is formed.

3   Discussion and Results

Described methodology is largely suppositive because any computer prediction of interaction level of ligand-protein complex and pharmacological activity is suppositive. The main obstacle on the way of approbation of software that implements the represented methodology is the lack of reliable data basing on which the program operates and analyzes other data. The missing data are the values of the hydrogen bond energy between groups capable of its formation. Experimentally it is difficult to obtain the values of hydrogen bond energy (infrared spectroscopy method) because when chemical substances interact between each other, bonds of another nature can be formed and their energy also contributes to the total interaction energy. Furthermore, environmental parameters also influence on energy value. Directly calculation of hydrogen bond energy entails inverse errors: artificially created environmental conditions may not take into account a number of factors, but exclusion of them is wrongful.

At the moment array hydro_energy, that is the main data source in program, is almost empty. Only items, situated at the intersection of groups containing atoms F, O, N, have values. Because of these problems, today program can't provide user-pharmacologist with any reliable data.

Because of factors, described above, any real results of the developed software implementation are not achieved. Formally work of program can be demonstrated on the example of evaluation of interaction level of Divinatorin D [7] and kappa opioid receptor (identifier in universal protein knowledgebase is P41145) [8]. Structure of protein, which is under investigation, is represented as amino acid sequence in file KOR.faa:

```
>sp|P41145|OPRK_HUMAN Kappa-type opioid receptor OS=Homo
sapiens GN=OPRK1 PE=1 SV=2
MDSPIQIFRGEPGPTCAPSACLPPNSSAWFPGWAEPDSNGSAGSEDAQLEPAHISPA
IPVIITAVYSVVFVVGLVGNSLVMFVIIRYTKMKTATNIYIFNLALADALVTTTMPF
QSTVYLMNSWPFGDVLCKIVISIDYYNMFTSIFTLTMMSVDRYIAVCHPVKALDFRT
PLKAKIINICIWLLSSSVGISAIVLGGTKVREDVDVIECSLQFPDDDYSWWDLFMKI
CVFIFAFVIPVLIIIVCYTLMILRLKSVRLLSGSREKDRNLRRITRLVLVVVAVFVV
CWTPIHIFILVEALGSTSHSTAALSSYYFCIALGYTNSSLNPILYAFLDENFKRCFR
DFCFPLKMRMERQSTSRVRNTVQDPAYLRDIDGMNKPV
```

The structure of ligand is represented in molecule file Divinatorin D.mol.

Visualization of spectrum of hydrogen bond energy between these substances as a graph of dependence of energy value from protein fragment number is represented in Fig.4. By built graph we can understand that place of the best binding of the protein-ligand complex is presumably situated there where peak values are observed. Whereas same area of protein is repeated on the graph several times, the possible location of binding site is characterized by smooth transition between the values, because exactly there several protein fragments of amino acid chain take part in bond with ligand. This value is situated over the fragment with number of 1720.

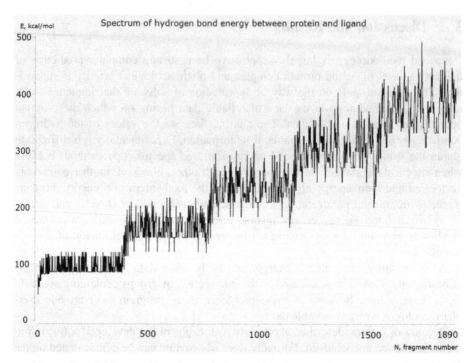

Fig. 4. Graph of values of hydrogen bond energy between protein fragments and ligand

4   Conclusion

Represented methodology describes way of evaluation of interaction level between potential drug and protein basing on structural formulas. Developed software differs from existing systems by that it doesn't implement time-consuming construction of 3D-models and large databases scanning. It provides less computational costs in comparison with existing systems and allows predicting interaction level between potential drug and protein with some degree of reliability.

In the future software can be improved and converted into learning system by creating of database. This database would store early received data about interaction of ligands with proteins. It will allow to execute analyze more rapidly and have an access to training sample instead of online-accumulation of information about ligand activities, that exists today.

Despite the disadvantages inherent to this approach, developed program executes analyze of interaction of protein and ligand. It allows performing forecast of potential drug activity in relation to predetermined protein. Moreover, the program calculates the possible interaction level much faster than existing systems (milliseconds and minutes versus hours and days).

References

1. Vassiliev, P.M.: New informational technologies in medicine. 3, 69-71 (2008) (in Russian)
2. Ferenczy, G.G., Keseru, G.M.: Thermodynamics of fragment binding. J. Chem. Inf. Model 52, 1039–1045 (2012)
3. Wageningen Bioinformatics Webportal, http://www.bioinformatics.nl/tools/crab_fasta.html
4. Dalby, A., Nourse, J.G., Hounshell, W.D., Gushurst, A.K.I., Grier, D.L., Leland, B.A., Laufer, J.: Description of several chemical structure file formats used by computer programs developed at Molecular Design Limited. J. Chem. Inf. Model. 32, 244–255 (1992)
5. Pimentel, G.C., McClellan, A.L.: The Hydrogen Bond. W. H. Freeman, San Francisco (1960)
6. Yanovskiy, T.A. Izvestiya VolgGTU. 54, 38–44 (2009) (in Russian)
7. Computational Systems Biology Laboratory, http://kanaya.naist.jp/knapsack_jsp/information.jsp?sname=C_ID&word=C00047216
8. Universal protein knowledgebase, http://www.uniprot.org/uniprot/P41145

Sleep Apnea Detection Based on Dynamic Neural Networks

Devjatykh Dmitry, Gerget Olga, and Olga G. Berestneva

National Research Tomsk Polytechnic University, Cybernetics Institute, Tomsk, Russia
ddv.edu@gmail.com, ogb6@yandex.ru, olgagerget@mail.ru

Abstract. One of widespread breath disruption that takes place during sleep is apnea, during this anomaly people are not able to get enough oxygen. The article describes method for breathing analyses that is based on neural network that allows recognition of breath patterns and predicting anomalies that may occur. Class of machine learning algorithms includes lots of models, widespread feed forward networks are able to solve task of classification, but are not quite suitable for processing time-series data. The paper describes results of teaching and testing several types of dynamic or recurrent networks: NARX, Elman, distributed and focused time delay.

Keywords: Sleep apnea, breath pattern, recurrent neural network.

1 Introduction

Breath disorders during sleep that patients with asthma suffer from may be described as a collective term – obstructive breathing disorders during sleep[1]. Such sleep disordersbeing combined with asthma are known as overlap syndrome. Degree of health damage that overlap syndrome does is much worse than each of its components does by its own[2,3]. The term health damage means reducing performance of body respiratory functions. Thus it is necessary to recognize and classify clinical data and provide better ways of detecting obstructive breathing disorders during sleep that asthma patients have.

From pathophysiological viewpoint breathing disorders during sleep are classified into 2 groups: apnea and hyperpnoea. They vary in degree of decreasing blood saturation with oxygen and breathing suspension. Both apnea and hyperpnoea may obstructive and central, such classification is based on mechanics of disorders.

Nowadays analyzing polysomnographyis common way of apnea diagnosing. It includes several synchronously recordedsignals. Such signals usually are: electrocardiography, oronasal airflow, blood oxygen saturation, such recordings are usually obtained in sleep laboratories. Another approach is based on evaluation of electrocardiography derived respiration.

There are numerous methods for sleep apnea diagnosing based on polysomnography and electrocardiography derived respiration. Most of them use analysis of the amplitude and frequency and precision of such approaches lies between 80% and

A. Kravets et al. (Eds.): JCKBSE 2014, CCIS 466, pp. 556–567, 2014.

90%. But despite of such satisfactory accuracy these methods don't provide information about exact start and end point of apnea episode and here's why. A very widely used standard for "scoring" (annotating) sleep studies is based on the now-obsolete technology of printing polysomnograms on fan-fold paper charts. By convention, these charts were printed at scales of 30 seconds per page (the pages were roughly A3 size -this was a lot of paper!), and the sleep physiologist would score them by marking the sleep stage (and notes about other events such as apneas, leg movements, etc) on either each page (once per 30 seconds) or each pair of facing pages (once per minute). This practice persists even though the polysomnograms are viewed and marked on-screen these days.

The majority of papers [4, 5, 6]describe methods that can count minutes with apnea episodes within an hour.Amount of minutes within an hour defines apnea–hypopnea index that indicates severity.

Our approach allows indicating apnea episodes not within minute or 30 seconds long records but within milliseconds range. Such results were obtained by using new type of data set and close cooperation with medical experts from Third Tomsk City Hospital. Mathematical models that we used to solve the task were recurrent neural networks, such architecture allows bypassing the restriction of classic perceptron (they can't work with time-series data).

2   Data and Methods

2.1   Data

For the purpose of research we used dataset that contained 39 recording. Records were obtained by pulmonology department of Third Tomsk City Hospital; on average recording were 8-10 hours long and included electrocardiography and oronasal airflow. Frequency of these signals was 11Hz. Most of the patients had asthma and represented different age brackets (25-60 years old). Each record was preliminarily analyzed by sleep physiologists who marked obstructive sleep episodes with high precision, unlike most data sets that could provide information about apnea–hypopnea index, our data was supported by annotations that revealed exact seconds when apnea began and when it did end. So each recording consists of two same dimensional time-series, the first includes oronasal airflow value with 11Hz frequency and the second included 0 and 1values, 0 values correspond to no apnea while several 1 values flagged current episode as time-series as apnea.

2.2   Neural Network Basics

Data processing mechanics of biological neural network may be transferred to mathematical model that is known as an artificial neural network. As its biological progenitor it includes neurons, basic blocks of network. The large number of different types of networks exists today. Despite constantly appearing various topologies they all have in common several features: neurons set, and connections (synaptic weights and biases) between them.

Artificial Neuron. The neuron is the basic unit of network it includes three basic elements. First off, the syntactical weights, they are represented as vectors. In terms of biology synapse of neuron cell is the one that provides a huge amount of operations brain is enabled to perform, same goes for mathematical model not the cell itself, but the connections between them defines computational power, each weight or synapse is presented as a number. Connection with negative value form creates an inhibitory influence, while positive value is considered as stimulative. Other elements of neuron are adder and activation function. These components of model imitate the actual performance of biological cells. Each component of the input vector is multiplied by corresponding weight values and summed. This linear combination is transferred to activation function, that controls the amplitude of the neuron's output value. Usually the range of output signal lies with 0 and 1, or -1 and 1. The process is described in figure 1.

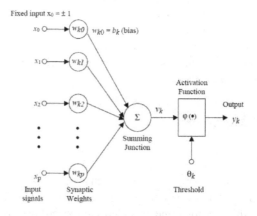

Fig. 1. Artificial neuron mathematical model

From this model the interval activity of the neuron can be shown to be:

$$v_k = \sum_{j=1}^{p} w_{kj} x_j \qquad (1)$$

Activation Function. The output value of neuron also known as the spike is computed as an outcome of some activation function which takes sum of products of input and weight vectors as an argument. It acts like a compressing function, so the current output of the neuron will not exceed restricting values that are defined by type of activation function. Common activation functions are logistic and hyperbolic tangent respectively:

$$\varphi(v) = \frac{1}{1 + e^{-v}} \qquad (2)$$

$$\varphi(v) = \frac{e^{2x} - 1}{e^{2x} + 1} \qquad (3)$$

These functions produce outputs between 0 and 1 or -1 and 1 respectively, also should be mentioned that their derivatives are easy to be calculated, what is vital for training process.

Neural Network Topology. Various types of neural network with unique architectures are made of neurons, that as was mentioned before are basic units. There are many ways of classifying neural network types. Because of practical medical solution that we are going to provide as experimental results diving into static and dynamic is fitting. Feedforward or static network has no delays, feedback elements and short-term memory. Such network generated output values directly from current input values, without taking into consideration previous internal states of network or outputs. Multilayer perceptron is a classic representative of feedforward network is shown in figure 1.

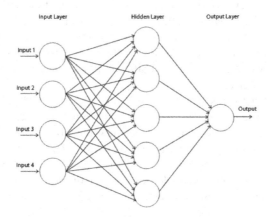

Fig. 2. Feed-forward neural network architecture known as perceptron

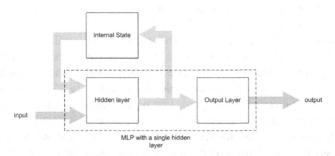

Fig. 3. Dynamic neural network architecture

In dynamic networks (shown at figure 3), the output depends not only on the current input to the network, but also on the current or previous inputs, outputs, or states of the network.

This type of network was invented to overcome fundamental limitation of perceptron that lies in its inaptitude for analyzing time-series data. Dynamic network possess more capabilities than static one, but usually it required more efforts for finding correct weight values (learning process). Short-term memory allows dynamic networks to be trained for recognizing time-varying patterns and predicting time-series data. In general static network are used as recognizing solution, while dynamic are fitted for time-series prediction, but there are papers [7,8] that proves that recognizing task may be presented as time-series prediction, and by combining these two approaches, dynamic network may extract additional knowledge from data set thus increasing accuracy.

2.3   Combining Pattern-Recognition and Time-Series Prediction

The dynamic neural network is a common instrument for time-series predicting. In this paper we used the dynamic feature of the network to recognize input sequences into different specified classes. Obviously these tasks do not much in common with. However, development of suitable inner structure for extracting additional features from input vector while performing classification tasks may be supported by time-series prediction approach.

Dynamic neural networks may solve both classification and predicting tasks by more efficient use of temporal information that lies in the input sequence. This means that during training or testing stages of network interconnections between current inputs, internal or even output values are processed to produce output and to put past information into short-term memory. While supervised training process these past targets and internal values compose additional source of information.

Whereas input signal presented to dynamic network is a time-series the target vector may be either a trivial sequence of constants or another time-series. For detecting apnea in polysomnograpy signals (i.e. labeling input sequence as "healthy" or "sick") the output is a constant label of class. For prediction tasks the output is presented as additional time-series.

These tasks are different from each other because target values present different type of information. However, there are papers that proves features of data extracted from data to perform time-series prediction may be strongly related to label (i.e. classify) a time-series. A significant example is presented in [5], [9], these papers performed learning of grammar by predicting next word in sentence, although grammatical inferencegrammar is more oftendescribed as a classification task. Network internal state analysis proved that resemblingtraits are presented in both tasks[10,11]. In the process of multitask learning it did turn out that increasing of information while training makes it easier for identifying relevant characteristics. The contemporaneous considering of somehow related tasks while performing learning can improve generalization results [12].

It is presented in [13] that pertinent characteristics that are to be presented in inner states of dynamic neural network for both classifying and predicting solutions are heavily related. Thus task of time-varying pattern recognition may be performed with more accuracy if within learning dynamic network is supplemented with additional units and target values, presented as sequences and not trivial constants. The apparentlyuntied tasks can be mutually combined during training.

2.4   Methodology

Topologies that we used in work are Focused-Time-Delay-Network, Distributed-Time-Delay-Network and Nonlinear-Autoregressive-Network.

Focused Time Delay. This topology of network is the most straightforward, it involves static feed-forward network with tapped-delay input. It is a general dynamic network, dynamics appears only on stage of presenting input signal which is supplemented by previous values. Despite being dynamic there is arguing whether this network is dynamic or static because it may be presented as multi-layer perceptron with additional input neurons.

Distributed Time Delay. This topology of network implies presence of tapped delay line memory not only for input signals, but also for hidden layer. That means that we present current input signal to corresponding layer of network, in additional though short-term memory lines we supplement network with additional past input signals. But the activations of hidden layer neurons are not instantly transferred to output neurons, but are circulating between input and hidden layer to generate internal states of network and only then the current output signal of network is computed.

Nonlinear Autoregressive Exogenous Inputs. NARX models have much in common with distributed networks. The distinction lies in additional signals that are given to network. While others dynamic network may extract additional information from input sequence by using past values of internal states, this topology allows supplementing of network with past values of output signals.

The defining equation for the NARX model is

$$y(t) = f(y(t-1), y(t-2), ..., y(t-n_y), u(t-1), u(t-1), u(t-n_u)) \quad (4)$$

Here, y defines output at t time step, u denotes input vector submitted to input layer at t time step. Themechanics of this architecture is thatthe next value of the output signal y(t) is dependent on pastoutput signalsand pastinput vectors.

As it was demonstrated in (5) current output of network depends of previous output and input signals. There are two ways to get previous output signals.

Open Loop. During supervised training of network the true output is known, and these true outputs are fed back to network for generating an output signal at t time step.

Close Loop. In real life situations it impossible to expect true output signals as previous values for NARX network. In close loop state network use its actual output signals at previous time-steps. Such state of network is usually turned on when training and validating processes are complete. The difference between two states is visualized at figure 11.

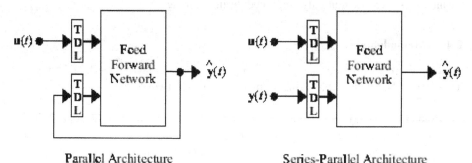

Parallel Architecture   **Series-Parallel Architecture**

Fig. 4. Parallel architecture(closed-loop) and series-parallel architecture(open-loop) scheme

Computations. Performing of classification with dynamic network, no matter what topology was chosen includes several steps. It starts with submitting "warm-up" input sequences, which length is defined by amount of time-delays applied to different layers of network. We used "1-of-N" encoding which means that amount of neurons in output layer is equal to number of classes we are recognizing. In every time step a winner-takes-all is performed i.e. the output neuron with highest values determines label of input sequence.

Process of network training is based on minimizing error. The classification error is given by rate misclassified input sequences in data set. However it is not the function that we use in supervised learning as performance measure. For adapting weights the mean-squared-error (4) is minimized.

$$E = \frac{1}{N \cdot T} \sum_{n=1}^{T} \sum_{t=1}^{T} \sum_{i=1}^{C} (o_{nti} - y_{nti})^2 \tag{5}$$

here, N denotes amount of time-series in date set; T the number of time steps in every time series; C amount of neurons in output layer. The variables o_{nti} and y_{nti} are defined as the output and target values of the ith output neuron at the tth time step of nth time series.

3   Experimental Results

This chapter reveals results of detecting sleep apnea using different architectures of dynamic neural networks.

3.1   Training and Testing Datasets

To recognize apnea we used several dynamic neural network types. As feature vectors we used two input signals from database, one of them took part in learning process another was picked for testing purposes. These signals are shown in figures 4-5.

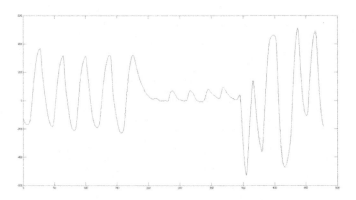

Fig. 5. Learning input signal

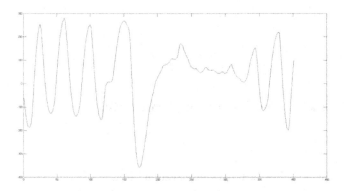

Fig. 6. Testing input signal

Input signals have different length, and that is significant advantage compared to static network, that are suitable for processing vectors of same dimensions. To each input signal we had corresponding target signals, shown at figures 6-7. They may look similar, but it should be considered that every target signal can be examined only in conjunction with corresponding input signal.

The more signals we present for learning the better network will work, however for purposes of this work we decided to take such small amount of signals because it reveals pros and cons of architectures much better. And each network was evaluated by comparing output signals, obtained from network.

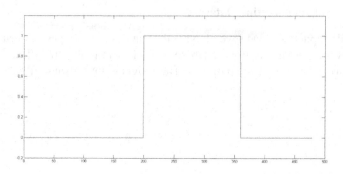

Fig. 7. Learning target signal

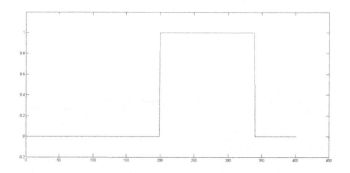

Fig. 8. Testing target signal

3.2   Network Training and Topology Characteristics

We researched three different architectures of network with several constants and variable parameters. Constants are:

- Training methods:Resilient back propagation
- Neurons in hidden layer:10
- Stop criterias
    - Successful validation checks(30% of learning input sequence)
    - Mean Square Error(MSE) value achieved(1e-4)
    - Maximum amount of iterations achieved(1000)
    - Minimum performance gradient achieved(1e-10)

Variable parameters are time-delays for layers of network. Each network was trained 4 times with one of stopping criterias being active. For every network we gained 4 training and testing results, depending on what stop criteria finished training. From these results we chose those, that provided lowest mean-square error. For creating, training and scoring network we used MatLab Neural Network Toolbox.

3.3   Apnea Detecting Results

Following tables represents network classification accuracy depending on amount of time-delays and topology type.

Table 1. Focused time delay network apnea detecting results

Topology											
FTDNN	Amount of time delays for input layer										
	1		5		10		20		40		100	
Lowest	Train	Test	Train	Test	Train	Test	Train	Test	Train	Test	Train	Test
MSE of 4												
attempts	0.022	0.106	0.012	0.110	0.002	0.157	1e-5	0.193	1e-8	0.263	1e-7	0.36

Focused delay showed that increasing time delays for input layer may increase performanceduring training, but it also reduces accuracy during testing process. Such tendencies took place for all 4 stopping criterias applied. None of networks achieved appropriate accuracy for testing sequence.

Table 2. Distributed time network apnea detecting results

Topology											
DTDNN	Amount of time delays for input : hidden layers										
	1:1		5:5		10:5		20:5		40:10		100:20	
Lowest	Train	Test	Train	Test	Train	Test	Train	Test	Train	Test	Train	Test
MSE of 4												
attempts	0.012	0.118	0.004	0.112	9e-4	0.094	3e-4	0.113	4e-5	0.17	1e-4	0.5

For this type of network it is not necessary to set same amount of time delays for input and hidden layers. Time delays for hidden layer significantly increased time of learning, not in terms of amount iterations, but in term of computational speed. Focused time delay also did not manage to achieve appropriate accuracy. For apnea detecting it is obvious that such types of dynamic networks like FTDNN and DTDNN require increasing of learning sequences. Even simple perceptron can provide good results with good learning data set. But creating such small learning sequence reveals abilities of networks.

NARX network showed best results; however it required finding precise number of input and output layer delays. Next table provides mean-square error values for training and testing in open-loop state of network and close-loop as well.NARX network was trained in open-loop state, in close-loop only testing operations were performed.

NARX network showed supremacy over distributed and focused delay networks in terms of MSE in both closed and open-loop states.Even with small amount of learning and testing sequences it showed appropriate results. It is interesting that asymmetrical delays (input delays amount was not equal to output) showed better accuracy than network with equally large amount of delays. In medical terms apnea episode is supposed to be approximately 10 seconds long, according to frequency of our input signal which was 11Hz we can make a conclusion that time delays should exceed or at least be equal to length of anomaly that we are going to detect in time-sequence, but this rule should determine amount of time-delays only for output layer, delays for input layer however may be significantly smaller, this improves accuracy a little bit, but more importantly it increases speed of learning because it exclude weights from network.

Table 3. Nonlinear autoregressive exogenousinputs network results

Topology										
	Amount of time delays for input:output layers									
NARX(open -loop)	1:1		5:5		10:10		20:20		40:40	
Lowest MSE of 4 attempts	Train	Test	Train	Test	Train	Test	Train	Test	Train	Test
	1e-3	5e-3	1e-6	0.921	8e-5	1.942	9e-4	0.429	9e-3	0.407
NARX(close -loop)	Train	Test	Train	Test	Train	Test	Train	Test	Train	Test
Lowest MSE of 4 attempts	0.337	0.312	0.98	2.32	1.152	2.316	2.561	3.017	1.125	1.141

	Amount of time delays for input : output layers									
NARX(open -loop)	60:60		100:100		150:150		170:170		25:170	
Lowest MSE of 4 attempts	Train	Test	Train	Test	Train	Test	Train	Test	Train	Test
	1e-5	0.338	1e-6	0.178	1e-7	0.082	1e-8	0.08	1e-8	0.064
NARX(close -loop)	Train	Test	Train	Test	Train	Test	Train	Test	Train	Test
Lowest MSE of 4 attempts	0.637	0.729	0.216	0.382	0.039	0.051	0.027	0.103	1e-4	0.048

4   Conclusions

In this paper we presented results of apnea detecting by analyzing polysomnography data using dynamic neural networks. The main issue that we faced was finding appropriate parameters of network, such as learning algorithm, amount of neurons in hidden layer, activation functions and foremost number of time-delays for dynamic networks. Not all dynamic networks are equally powerful, NARX network proved to be supreme in terms of accuracy. However this type of networks requires more complicated process of testing because of two states that we used: open-loop and closed-loop we had to calculate outputs twice. Assuming that in real-life medical operations there will be no opportunity to instantly get real output values we put in priority closed-loop state results, so if network would work accurate in open-loop, but would misclassify input sequences in closed-loop state we would consider such network as not appropriate. Although it was not a purpose of research to evaluate speed of learning methods, the more time-delays we assigned the more iterations it was required to find adequate solution in terms of weights.

As future work we are planning to start using physyonet.org data bases; increase learning and testing data sets for improving generalization ability of network and implement genetic algorithm for training dynamic neural networks.

References

1. Mangat, E., Orr, W.C., Smith, R.O.: Sleep apnea, hypersomnolence and upper airway obstructionsecondary to adenotonsillar enlargement. Arch. Otolaryngol. 103, 383–386 (1977)
2. Newman, A.B., Nieto, F.J., Guidry, U., Lind, B.K., Redline, S., ShaharE., P.T.G., Quan, S.F.: Relation of sleep-disordered breathing to cardiovascular disease risk factors: The Sleep Heart Health Study. Am. J. Epidemiol. 154, 50–59 (2001)
3. Cabrero-Canosa, M., Hernandez-Pereira, E., Mo-ret-Bonillo, V.: Intelligent Diagnosis of Sleep Apnea Syndrome. Engineering in Medicine and Biology Magazine 23(2), 72–81 (2004)
4. Avcı, C., Akbaş, A.: Comparison of the ANN Based Classification accuracy for Real Time Sleep Apnea Detection Methods. In: The 9th International Conference on Biomedical Engineering (BIOMED 2012), Innsbruck, February 15- 17 (2012)
5. Correa, L.S., Laciar, E., Mut, V., Torres, A., Jane, R.: Sleep Apnea Detection Based on Spectral Analysis of Three ECG—Derived Respiratory Signals. In: Annual International Conference of the IEEE Engineering in Medicine and Biology Society, September 3-6, pp. 4723–4726 (2009)
6. Tagluk, M.E., Sezgin, N.: Classification of Sleep Apnea through Sub-band Energy of Abdominal Effort Signal Using Wavelets and Neural Networks. Journal of Medical Systems 34(6) (2010)
7. Riedmiller, M.: Advanced supervised learning in multi-layer perceptrons – from backpropagation to adaptive learning algorithms. International Journal of Computer Standards and Interfaces 16(5), 265–278 (1994)
8. Elman, J.L.: Finding structure in time. Cognitive Science 14, 179–211 (1990)
9. Giles, C.L., Miller, C.B., Chen, D., Sun, G.Z., Chen, H.H., Lee, Y.C.: Extracting and learning an unknown grammar with recurrent neural networks. In: Moody, J.E., Hanson, S.J., Lippmann, R.P. (eds.) Advances in Neural Information Processing Systems, vol. 4, pp. 317–324. Morgan Kaufmann Publishers, San Mateo (1992)
10. Lawrence, S., Giles, C.L., Fong, S.: Natural language grammatical inference with recurrent neural networks. IEEE Transactions on Knowledge and DataEngineering 12(1), 126–140 (2000)
11. Ebrahimi, F., Mikaeili, M., Estrada, E., Nazeran, H.: Automatic Sleep Stage Classification Based on EEG Signals by Using Neural Networks and Wavelet Packet Coefficients. In: 30th Annual International IEEE Conference, Vancouver, pp. 1151–1154 (2008)
12. Jaeger, H.: Short term memory in echo state networks. GMD Report 152,GMD - German National Research Institute for Computer Science (2001a)
13. Box, G.E.P., Jenkins, G.M., Reinsel, G.C.: Time series analysis: Forecasting and control, vol. 734. Wiley (2011)

Multidimensional Data Visualization Methods
Based on Generalized Graphic Images

Irina A. Osadchaya, Olga G. Berestneva, Vitaly A. Volovodenko,
and Olga V. Marukhina

National Research Tomsk Polytechnic University, Cybernetics Institute, Tomsk, Russia
ogb6@yandex.ru

The main peculiarity of decision-making systems is their growing mathematization. The reason for applying mathematical principles is usability of simple procedures capable of being performed on a computer. In addition, most of the tasks solved on computer are of algorithmic nature; require solution existence and consistent computational methods. Classical solution is unique and reliable in a finite amount of time via search methods.

Studying decision-making methods in social and economic systems illustrates that these conditions are impossible to be met in many cases. Existence of a solution can be proved only in some instances. When turning from practical problem setting to its mathematical version, a great number of factors influencing the solution must be ignored. Practical problem setting analysis suggests the availability of several "solutions". In such cases a decision taker (DT) faces the situation when finding a solution grows into selecting a solution from a set of alternatives, usually based on contradictory conditions. It should be taken into account, that there are a lot of time-dependent factors in social and economic systems. Controlling the conditions of such systems is connected with the time series (TS) problem. These series have a high degree of uncertainty and require applying methods for their processing. Such methods do not guarantee high-quality accuracy. In this regard it's possible to indicate neural network and fuzzy models as well as artificial intelligence models.

Modelling the behaviour of social and economic systems is based on the models of fuzzy dynamic process named fuzzy time series (FTS). FTS multidimensionality is the property providing the complexity of data representation with the independency between the fixable indicators.

This paper considers the simplest case of presenting a multidimensional fuzzy time series (MFTS) by the indicators capable of being measured and presented in real numbers:

$$\mathbf{W} = \{V(t_1), V(t_2), ..., V(t_i), ..., V(t_k)\} \tag{1}$$

$\mathbf{W}$ is MFTS, the finite set of indicator vector; $t_1, t_2, ..., t_i, ..., t_k$ are points of time, when $V(t_i)$ is detectable and able of being registered:

$$V(t_i) = \{q_1(t_i), q_2(t_i), ..., q_n(t_i)\} \tag{2}$$

A. Kravets et al. (Eds.): JCKBSE 2014, CCIS 466, pp. 568–575, 2014.

Indicator vector is measured and registered at time point t_i.

Fuzziness is concealed in time pointers $q_j(t_i)$.

MFTS analyzing is impeded by inability of getting comprehensive quantitative data and its insufficiency.

Problem Setting. A given MTFS should be represented visually for a DT to make required manipulations and analysis.

As it follows from (1) and (2) the multidimentional fuzzy time series W is easier to represent as a spreadsheet or list of lists. In this case $V(t_i)$ is a row-vector which consists of various indicators measured and registered at time point t_i:

$$V(t_i) = \{q_1(t_i), q_2(t_i), ..., q_n(t_i)\} = \{q_{i_1}, q_{i_2}, ..., q_{i_n}\}, \qquad (3)$$

where $q_{i_n} \in R$; $V(t_i)$ can be considered to be a space point R_n for the time point t_i.

It follows from (1) that MTFS is the sequence of R_n points.

$$\mathbf{W} = \{V(t_1), V(t_2), ..., V(t_i), ..., V(t_k)\} = \{V_1, V_2, ..., V_i, ..., V_k\}.$$

This is the finite sequence and it can be considered to be a MTFS interval.

Let us consider a set of polynomials orthonormalized on [0,1]:

$$P = \{P_0(\tau), P_1(\tau), ..., P_{n-1}(\tau)\}^T = colomn\{P_0(\tau), ..., P_{n-1}(\tau)\} \qquad (4)$$

Assume the main peculiarity of these polynomials to be their capability of being presented as the graphs of the independent variable $\tau \in [0, 1]$ functions.

Then each line $V(t_i)$ can be assigned to the function $F_i(\tau) = (V(t_i), P) = \sum q_{i,k} P_k(\tau)$.

Let sequence W assign to sequence $\{F_i(\tau)\}_{i=1}^{i=k}$.

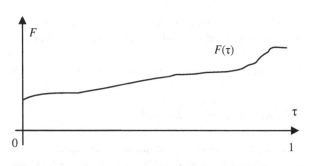

Fig. 1. Function $F(\tau)$ graphical representation

τ in this formula is called formula parameter while it assists defining function $F_i(\tau)$ via vector $V(t_i)$, thus generating visual representation $F_i(\tau)$ of the vector $V(t_i)$. The latter can be seen as a set of values in a spreadsheet and function $F_i(\tau)$ can be presented graphically (Fig.1).

Fuzzy Time Series Visualization. Visual properties of orthonormal polynomials most brightly appear at the interval [0,1], on this account it serves the basis for representing images $F_i(\tau)$ and pre-images $V(t_i)$ [1, 2]. Two spaces appear: pre-images $V(t_i)$ and visual images. These two spaces are interconnected by the condition of isometrics. Objectively, Euclidean norm in the R_n pre-images space

$$\|V(t_i)\|_{R_n} = \sqrt[2]{\sum_{k=1}^{n} q_{ik}^2} \,,$$

and norm of function $F_i(\tau)$ in the space of $L_n(\tau)$ images can be calculated by the formula

$$\|F_i(\tau)\|_{L_n} = \left\|\sum_{k=1}^{n} q_{ik} P_{k-1}(\tau)\right\|_{L_n} = (\int_0^1 (\sum (q_{ik} P_{k-1}(\tau))^2 \, d\tau))^{\frac{1}{2}} = (\sum_{k=1}^{n} q_{ik}^2)^2 \tag{5}$$

The latter equality is attained due to $P(\tau)$ polinomials orthonormalization property. Consequently, the following equality $\|V(t_i)\|_{R_n} = \|F_i(\tau)\|_{L_n}$ is realized; and the isometrics of two spaces follows from it.

The norm function allows defining the metrics function r

$$r(A(\tau), B(\tau)) = \|A(\tau) - B(\tau)\|$$

and observing the difference between two functions – images A(τ) and B(τ).

The resulting relations $A(t_i) \to A(\tau)$ and $B(t_j) \to B(\tau)$ helps to see the difference between images on a computer screen.

Furthermore, analytical abilities of a DT start participating in the scheme of studying images, i.e. pre-images. Human visual system is the fastest system of image analysis and it allows making conclusions about the pre-images sets properties. Thus, functions are distributed between a DT and a computer. Computers deal with a routine spreadsheet processing and preparing images, while a DT processes data in a finer and more analytical way.

If treating $A(t_i)$ and $B(t_j)$ as two points of a multidimensional space, the interval AB can be represented as

$$AB = (1-\lambda)A(t_i) + \lambda B(t_j), \lambda \in [0,1].$$

λ parameter is called sequential, i.e. it is responsible for images sequencing.

Taking three variables (τ composition parameter; variable for F images values; sequential parameter λ) as a basis, visual space $\{\tau, F(\tau, \lambda), \lambda\}$ used for MFSR representation can be formed.

Function of r metrics can be used as an example of λ. In this case, there is a clear pattern of presenting MFSR at a computer screen.

Sequential parameter λ can act as time *t*. Note, that there is the transition from the sequence of pre-images to the sequence of visual representations keeping all characteristics of fuzziness. They are kept in the pre-image spreadsheet and will have no impact on the diagram of images.

From the practical standpoint, all pre-images belong to some universe; at that, each indicator is associated with some property able to generate a fuzzy predicate which can be characterized by a truth value. It is customary to assume that fuzzy predicate can accept [0,1] truth value continuum. Besides, as usually, 0 corresponds to the notion "zero" and number 1 – to the notion "truth". The more the indicator corresponds to the property under consideration, the closer the truth value of a fuzzy predicate must be to 1 [3].

The membership functions can be applied as parameters for defining sequential parameters λ. Consequently, visual representations $F_i(\tau)$ will be ordered with the accordance of membership functions values. One membership function is fixed for all images $F_i(\tau)$; but its values are different values for each of the images according to the data provided.

Visualization enables to research the issue of influencing a certain membership function on the order of images consecution and their relative positions. This information can be received in a form of lists but the visual representation includes the whole images set and allows distinguishing the most significant ones. These images will be grouped closer to the end of sequentiality and the whole images set can be characterized by the points of images condensation. A membership function type will have impact on the images sequence, due to it a membership function can be defined by expertise focusing on the properties which can be measured in one of known quantitative scales. As FTS doesn't require precise membership function defining, it's usually enough to fix the most typical values [4].

Visual data grouping enables a DT to visualize an FTS structure and, what counts most, to precisely define the tendency of this structure. However, it should be taken into account that the indicator $q_k(t)$ is represented as a list of fuzzy values. It means that:

$$q_k(t) = \left\{ \{q_{k1}(t), \mu_{k1}(t)\}, \{q_{k2}(t), \mu_{k2}(t)\}, ..., \{q_{kj}(t), \mu_{kj}(t)\} \right\},$$

where $q_{kj}(t)$ is the value of the indicator, which the value of a membership function is defined for; the membership function assigns some real number from the interval [0,1]. Therefore, $q_k(t)$ indicator is represented as a fuzzy set.

Obviously, having such variety of values visualization, i.e. turning from pre-images to images, poses a problem. There are several solutions of this task; one of them is as follows: the most reliable FTS is chosen from the data represented in **W** FTS. It can be achieved by turning from **W** to **W**$_0$, which presents $q_k(t)$ as a single fuzzy value but not as a multitude, this value is $q^0{}_k(t)$ and it is the most reliable, i.e. it has the maximum value of a membership function in the multitude $q_k(t)$. Thus,

$$q_k^0(t) = \max_{\mu_{ki}}\{q_{ki}, \mu_{ki}\}.$$

Consequently,

$$W_0 = \left\{V^0(t_1), V^0(t_2), ..., V^0(t_k)\right\},$$
$$V^0 = \left\{q_1^0(t_i), q_2^0(t_i), ..., q_{ki}^0(t_i)\right\}.$$

Fuzzy time series W_0 is called a zero basic series and it's possible to draw up the formula $\left\{F_i^0(\tau)\right\}_{i=1}^{i=k}$ using the data mentioned above as a basis. Thereupon, let W_0 get a visual representation marked F_0. Examination of F_0 image shows that this image is a fuzzy one and its properties depend on W_0 properties. On the other hand, there is the possibility of feedback, i.e. W_0 properties can be judged upon F_0 properties.

If TS develops in a rather gradual way, its changes are not significant and the derived image F_0 obtains the properties of W_0. W_0 can be considered as a hard frame of W and, consequently, F_0 will be a more stable construction than F. In the situation of visualization it will lead to the following – in case of changing W a zero time series W_0 will not change if changes of W do not concern W_0 component. This fact will concern image F_0 as well.

If W_0 components are excluded from W, it's possible to get W_1, the first zero basic series, and to assign it to $\left\{F_i^1(i)\right\} = F_1$. Image F_1 will be more adaptable to changes in W and will show a more variable pattern. When analyzing image F_1, it is possible to set a greater image changing range $\left\{F_i^1(\tau)\right\}$. Due to the transformation linearity (5), the additive character of the transition $F_0, F_1, ..., F_{n-1}$ is kept.

We have used this approach dealing with the problems of identifying hidden regularity in medical data [8], particularly analyzing the characteristics of various bronchopulmonary diseases [9].

Background information is data of patients with four types of bronchopulmonary diseases:

- Bronchial asthma non-psychogenic (BANP);
- Bronchial asthma somatic psychogenic (BASP);
- Bronchial asthma psychogenic-induced (BAPI);
- Psychogenic dyspnea (PD).

Let us compare the sample data of all 4 forms of the disease on visual closeness of observations spectra.

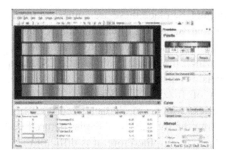

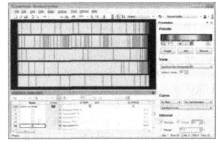

Fig. 2. The spectral representation of the data on patients diagnosed with BAPI

Fig. 3. The spectral representation of the data on patients with a diagnosis of BASP

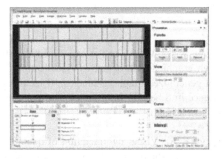

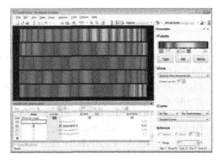

Fig. 4. The spectral representation of the data on patients diagnosed with BANP

Fig. 5. The spectral representation of the data on patients diagnosed with PD

Each color bar in the spectral view corresponds to a certain patient data. In our case in pictures 2-5 each image is represented by five bars respectively representing five members of a certain group. The color scheme of the patients diagnosed with BAPI and patients with a diagnosis of PD are similar. The same is true of patients with a diagnosis of BASP and BANP.

As it can be seen from the Pictures, people with BASP and PD have the closest figures. The most evident differences can be seen in patients with BAPI.

Thus, the use of cognitive graphics has revealed some previously unknown regularity of physiological reactions of the bronchopulmonary system in response to the psycho-physiological effects (similar reactions are observed, on the one hand, in patients with psychogenic dyspnea and psychogenic-induced asthma, on the other hand-in patients with somatic and non-psychogenic and somatic psychogenic asthma).

Conclusion. On the basis of visualization it's possible to solve a number of tasks, which then require finding a similar method of tasks statement. These are such tasks as segmentation, clusterization, prognostication. Users of such tasks will mainly be various decision takers, who will be offered a less complicated process of results achieving, which can have different forms. In the first place these are numerical results which have linguistic description outlining qualitative aspects of various subject areas.

It is essential to mention that the given approach is not connected with the pre-existing mathematical models of the system, which the visual analysis of FTS is conducted for. Due to it there is low forecast precision, insufficiency of fuzzy description quality standards, which leads to limitation of fuzzy TS modelling. This aspect defines a new approach to analyzing time series, which are characterized by a high degree of certainty. It is essential when analyzing the dynamics of semistructured systems when is not possible to identify a model class, and, therefore, it is difficult to get high accuracy models.

The research is conducted with financial support from The Russian Foundation for Basic Research, projects № 14-06-00026.

References

1. Berestneva, O.G., Volovodenko, V.A., Sharopin, K.A.: Visualizatsiya experimentalynyh mnogomernyh dannyh na osnove obobschennyh graphicheskih obrazov (Visualization of experimental multivariable data on the basis of generalized graphical images). (Electronic resourse) Vestnik nauki Sibiri (Bulletin of Science in Siberia) - Information Technologies and control systems, vol. 1, pp. 363–369 (2011) (in Russia),
   http://sjs.tpu.ru/journal/article/view/75
2. Volovodenko, V.A., Berestneva, O.G., Sharopin, K.A.: Visual interpretation of quantitative characteristics of biosystems. In: Fundamental Medicine: From Scalpel Toward Genome, Proteome and Lipidome: Proceedings of I international Conference, pp. 126–129. State Publishing Cente, Kazan (2011)
3. Mnozhestva, N.: Fuzzy sets. In: Pospelov, D.A. (ed.) Science, 32 p. (1986) (in Russia)
4. Leonenko, A.V.: Nechetkoye modelirovanie v srede TLAB and fuzzyTECH (Fuzzy modelling in TLAB and fuzzyTECH environments), p. 736. BHV - Petersburg, Spb (2005) (in Russia)
5. Duke, B., Emanuel, B.: Information technology in biomedical research, p. 528. Piter, St. Peters-burg (2003) (in Russia)
6. Volovodenko, V.A., Berestneva, O.G., Osadchaya, I.A., Nemerov, E.V.: The use of imaging techniques in the study of the multi-dimensional experimental data structure. Proceedings of the Tomsk Polytechnic University 320(5), 125–130 (2012) (in Russia)
7. Berestneva, O.G., Volovodenko, V.A., Gerget, O.M., Sharopin, K.A., Osadchaya, I.A.: Multidimensional Medical Data Visualization Methods Based on Generalized Graphic Images. World Applied Sciences Journal (24), 18–23 (2013)
8. Sharopin, K.A., Berestneva, O.G., Volovodenko, V.: Visualization of medical data based on packet NovoSpark. In: Proceedings of the Southern Federal University. Technical Sciences, vol. 109(8), pp. 242–249.(2010) (in Russia)
9. Nemerov, E.V.: Interrelations of rhinitis, rhinosinusitis and bronchial asthma, associated with stressful life events. In: European Respiratory Journal. Abstracts 22th ERS Annual Congress, Vienna 40(suppl. 56). S.73, 508 p. (2012)

10. Nemerov, E.V., Yazukov, K.G.: On the study of personality traits in psychophysiological reactivity in patients with bronchial asthma on the audio-visual stimulation. Bulletin of the Tomsk State Pedagogical University 6(108), 134–137 (2011), (in Russia)
11. Berestneva, O.G., Volovodenko, V.A., Sharopin, K.A., Gerget, O.M.: Visualization of multidimensional experimental data on the basis of generalized graphic images (electronic resource). Journal of Science of Siberia 1(1), 363–369 (2011) (in Russia), Mode of access: http://sjs.tpu.ru/journal/article/view/75

An Intelligent Medical Differential Diagnosis System Based on Expert Systems

Valeriy A. Kamaev, Dmitriy P. Panchenko, Nguen Vien Le, and Olga A. Trushkina

Volgograd State Technical University, Russia
kamaev@cad.vstu.ru, {panchenkodp,nvien.vstu}@gmail.com,
vamp@volgograd.ru

Abstract. This abstract presents an approach to designing an intelligent medical diagnosis system based on the theory of expert systems. A formal model for a medical expert system on differential diagnosis is proposed. The architecture of the system is also presented.

Keywords: medical diagnosis, expert system, frame system, product system, inference engine.

1   Introduction

Medical diagnostics is one of the most difficult tasks of practical health care. Currently, there is a necessity of application of information-communication technologies in medicine, especially in the problems of creation of the telemedical diagnostics systems. The expert systems of medical diagnostics will execute advisory medical aid to patients in the most remote areas, thereby substantially reduce costs for patients. Of a particular importance is the possibility of creating a common knowledge base on the basis of highly qualified and specialized knowledge and experience of doctors from leading medical centers.

The system does the output of a diagnostic solution to the patient based on a set of incoming symptoms in the real-time mode. On the basis of diagnostic hypotheses, you can define the possible qualification of a physician, who needs to be contacted by the patient. The system must function even when the information is not enough, i.e. to be able to reason under uncertainty. In the case of the patient not accepting the result, he may claim the system solutions from the experts-doctors. The system will establish a dialogue with doctors in delayed mode via e-mail.

2   The Formal Model of the Medical Expert System for Differential Diagnosis

The formal model of the medical expert system for differential diagnosis consists of the following components: medical knowledge base; working memory; output control

A. Kravets et al. (Eds.): JCKBSE 2014, CCIS 466, pp. 576–584, 2014.

diagnostic solution; explanation of effective information; acquisition of medical knowledge; user interface [1, 2, 3].

2.1 Medical Knowledge Base

The base of medical knowledge is a key concept of the system. Expert systems are most effectively characterized based on the combination of fuzzy-production and frame models of knowledge representation. This approach also allows the representation of uncertainty of information in the description of the structure of the symptom. Frames are used for the representation of static knowledge on the current state of the field of diagnostics. The frame is considered as a set of slots, which are defined as structural elements that describe the properties of the frame. Fuzzy model of knowledge representation is recommended for the representation of dynamic knowledge about the transitions between different states of diagnosis.

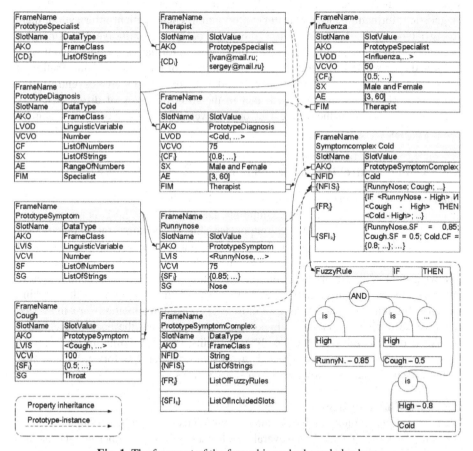

Fig. 1. The fragment of the frame hierarchy knowledge base

As an example, you can define ill-production rules of symptomcomplex cold as follows:

IF   «Runny nose» = «High» (SF=0.85)   AND
       «Cough» = «High» (SF=0.5)   AND
       ...
THE   «Cold» = «High» (CF=0.8)

Here SF – specificity factors of symptoms from symptomcomplex; CF is the certainty factors of the rule. And for the assessment of values of the linguistic variables symptoms and diseases used a single scale qualitative terms: Low; Medium; High. The fragment of the frame hierarchy of the knowledge base is presented in Fig. 1.

2.2   Working Memory

Working memory system is intended to store information of a patient, effective diagnostic information and explanatory information. Under patient information, there are two types: personal information about the patient; quantitative assessment of incoming symptoms. Under effective diagnostic information is the quantitative integrated assessment of each disease. When the facts of receipt of the information of the patient or effective information are updated, the system creates entries (i.e. elements working memory) for each fact in the form of tuples of different length. Each entry can contain the whole fact or vice versa, the fact may be a system of records of fixed length.

2.3   Output Control Diagnostic Solution

Output control diagnostic solution is intended for diagnostic decisions based on quantitative estimates of incoming symptoms. Diagnostic hypothesis is referred to as a disease with the value of the output variable. Depending on a quantitative assessment, the disease is in one of three possible states: inactive candidate, potential candidate and active candidate. Output control diagnostic solution consists of the following four steps: mapping, conflict resolution, activation and action. Before inference engine, it is necessary to enter the facts of the symptoms in the working memory. Inference engine exists as follows [4]: procedures-methods are initialized during specification of diagnostic hypotheses that implement the backward chain to clarify the original values of the possible symptoms; when assigning initial values by slots, proceduresdemons function and are responsible for the forward chain that perform fuzzy output of a target values of slots diseases.

Backward Chain Strategy

Each symptomcomplex includes many symptoms, but some symptoms may simultaneously be included in several syndromes [5]. For further diagnosis, the generation of additional questions, concerning only possible diseases, is required. This provides higher efficiency of diagnosis. Refinement of diagnostic hypotheses consists of the following four steps. The calculation of areas of valid and invalid solutions for each disease is based on the odds of specificity of symptoms of symptom-complexes. To highlight a definite diagnosis for the disease from this set, three main criteria are used: the most minimal reliable solutions; the maximum current integral assessment of the disease; the maximum area of inaccurate decisions. When determining the leading symptom of selected diseases, the leading symptom corresponds with symptom having the maximum coefficient of specificity. At the generation stage of additional question based on the leading symptom, the patient should be asked simultaneous right questions to clarify quantitative estimates of possible symptoms.

Forward Chain Strategy

During literal implementation, the system checks the application of fuzzyproduction rules of each disease to each fact of symptoms in working memory, necessarily executes them and proceeds to the next disease, returns to the beginning after the exhaustion of all diseases.

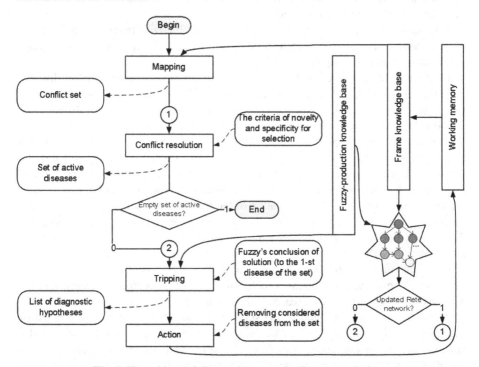

Fig. 2. The scheme of diagnostic output management solutions

Rete algorithm is used to ensure the speed at large knowledge base and a large number of facts in working memory (Fig. 2). When using the Rete algorithm, base of medical knowledge under translation is converted into Rete (or prefix tree) network, in the leaf nodes which are, on the one hand, procedures-demons, attached to the original slots, and on the other - procedures-methods to retrieve the values of the target slots when the truth of the premise of fuzzy-production rules, information which is stored in the intermediate nodes.

At the time of the assignment, all rules are not known under conditions of uncertainty. Therefore, a single network for all rules should not be built. This modification of the algorithm is called the Rete's fast algorithm [4]. In the modified Rete network the following components should be stored: activation list, where parent slots are stored, i.e. frames-prototypes slots; activation context, where links to current frames that caused the activation are stored, i.e. instance frames. When changing the value of some of the original slot located in the premise, all related procedures-demons that are directly trying to calculate the values of the target slot imprisoned are activated. Unification of rules with values in working memory as such is not made, and is replaced with implicit unification of inheritance, which is achieved through the call-demons procedure of all parent frames with the transfer of the current frame (caused by activation) as the calling context. Thus, the network implicitly established is attached to the demons slots, related to rules and fuzzy conclusion, in nodes whose intermediate results are remembered.

Comparison of symptom complexes with the available facts from working memory is performed after approval of incoming symptoms. As a result at this stage conflicting set consists of potential diseases.

Conflict resolution is carried out to select one or several most suitable diseases from the set of conflict. The result is a variety of active diseases, and also determines the order of their execution on the criteria of novelty and specificity. In addition, indistinctly production rules to existing facts should not be used.

Tripping. During tripping of values slots, ill-production rules associated with this slot are triggered, when assigned, i.e. in the left part of which the values for this slot are figured. The application of such rules matches a state change in the field of diagnostics. Fuzzy's conclusion of diagnostic solution on the Mamdani model includes the following steps [6, 7, 8]: fuzzification of the input variables, i.e., the conversion of quantitative estimates of symptoms to fuzziness; prerequisites aggregation, i.e. determining the degrees of truth prerequisites for each rule; conclusion activation, i.e. determining the activated membership function of assessment of the disease to a term of imprisonment for each rule; accumulation of conclusions, i.e. the receipt of the final fuzzy sets of each variable diseases; defuzzification of the output variables, i.e., the conversion of fuzzy variables diseases to the definition.

At the action stage, the update the state of the working memory is the result of triggering of ill-production rules. The composition of effective information includes not only the list of diagnostic hypotheses but also the list of active rules, and also possible medical specialists, to which the patient needs to contact. In addition, it ensures the possibility of the formation of questionnaires with responses to questions if the patient consents or waivers with diagnostic decision before exiting the system.

2.4   Explanation of Effective Information

Explanation of effective information is intended for storage of protocol output log, i.e. information about the behavior of the system of diagnostics of diseases. State memory is used to store log, each entry of which corresponds to one diagnostic solution based on previous symptoms.

2.5 Acquisition of Medical Knowledge

The acquisition of medical knowledge consists of the following 4 steps.

Building a Knowledge Base

At the stage of building a doctor's knowledge base, with the participation of an engineer by field knowledge, the area of medical diagnostic and state diagnostic are described in the form of a hybrid model of knowledge representation. Formalization of hybrid model of knowledge representation is a preparatory stage. Knowledge engineer creates the frame and ill-production model of knowledge representation. At the stage of forming the frame hierarchy, doctors describe the current state of the field of diagnostics as follows: definition of specialties, diseases, groups of symptoms, symptoms; creation of interactions between objects region; display of quantitative estimates of incoming symptoms and quantitative integral evaluation of each disease. At the stage of formation of fuzzy-production rules, doctors describe transitions between the states of the diagnosis as follows: description of input and output variables (symptoms and diseases); the work of membership functions for the generated variables; creation of a vaguely-production rules.

Knowledge Extraction from the Sent Questionnaires

This approach is based on the formation of responses to an email sent by the patient, according to the prepared questionnaire, and the extraction of new knowledge from them, describing its contents. In the capacity of knowledge source, diagnostic solution is formed by doctors for medical consultations, in which the system could not deliver the final diagnosis. The formation of the prepared questionnaire is the preparatory stage. To do this, select the list of the concepts necessary to describe the structure of the questionnaire (possible specialty; questions-answers; and others) then the hierarchy of concepts are formed based on their connections. At the stage of filling out the questionnaire and sending to doctors, all fields of questionnaire are filled in with the information of medical diagnostics. Later the questionnaire in the letter is sent to physicians on possible specialty. At the stage of receiving the letter and response to questions, the doctor decides to accept the letter and answer questions. The answered letter is sent to the patient's email address. At the stage of forming new fuzzyproduction rules, answered questionnaires with a knowledge base to retrieve new facts are compared, which are stored in the form of rules.

Learning of Fuzzy Knowledge Bases

To increase the effectiveness of learning ill-production model of knowledge representation, solving the task of forming a knowledge base, using genetic algorithm is recommended [9]. To do this, first you need to set the encoding/decoding illproduction model of knowledge representation that defines some parameters (membership function parameters; the coefficients of specificity and confidence), which are reduced in a single vector. The value of one parameter lies in a specific surrounding area, which can be broken into 2^16 intervals. Then to encode non interval, the 16-bit value in the code warming can be used, in which adjacent numbers are characterized by a lower number of positions. To create the initial population of chromosomes randomly, generation 100 chromosomes with the initial initialization values genes in a given area performed. Then use the operation of composition to combine a set of genes in a single chromosome for assessing the fitness of chromosomes. Each chromosome of the population is put in conformity assessment of its suitability chromosomes in the population, the calculation of which is based on the training sample and vectors of the model parameters. The learning process is considered as complete if the condition that the estimate is greater than the threshold value. In the selection process, based on the principle of the roulette wheel, the more sectors on the roulette wheel (i.e. corresponding assessment of fitness chromosomes), the more the chance that this chromosome is selected, which in the future after the decomposition operation genetic operators are applied to create descendants for the next population. Application of genetic operators in chromosomes. In genetic algorithms for the transfer of genes of the parents to descendants the crossing operator is responsible. Operators of mutation and inversion are designed to support a variety of chromosomes in the population. The formation of a new population. Effective chromosomes should be placed in the population after the composition operation. To reduce the population to its original number of chromosomes, the operator reduction is applied. After shutdown of the genetic algorithm, a trained model is obtained, which is approximated to a given accuracy data from the learning sample and forming knowledge base, consisting of a system of fuzzy-production rules.

Testing of the Knowledge Base
Testing of the knowledge base is designed to assess the completeness and integrity of the knowledge base by test sample [10].

2.6   User Interface

The user interface handles all messages exchanged between users and the system, and also performs roles of participants of the dialogue between them and the organization of their interaction in the process of medical consultations, and the acquisition of medical knowledge.

3   Information Structures of Medical Expert System for Differential Diagnosis

When designing the system, it is necessary to clearly distinguish the following levels: the presentation layer is intended for user interaction, information display and controls; logic layer is intended to implement the functionality of the kernel; the data access layer is designed to communicate with the data source used by the business logic layer. The system kernel is implemented as software modules. In Fig. 3, the structural scheme of the system kernel is represented.

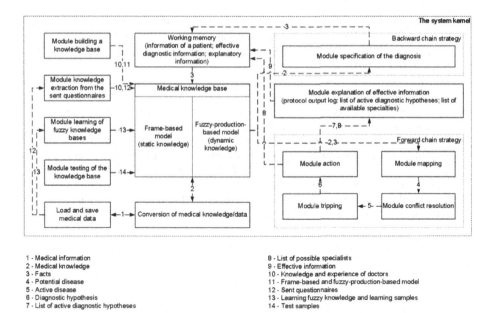

Fig. 3. The structural scheme of the system kernel

4   Conclusion

As an example of practical use of the developed model of the system, the process of medical differential diagnosis is described. Identification of quantitative expert evaluation of diseases and specialties on the basis of incoming signs of disease is needed. As evidence of diseases, 68 independent symptoms are applied, and the output - 89 diseases and 21 specialties. The developed system allows to increase the efficiency of medical diagnosis that she must not stop because of the fact that no part of the input information of the symptoms. Through a combination of ill-production and frame models of knowledge representation the problem of management of medical knowledge from different sources, having fuzzy, blurry structure is avoided.

References

1. Dvoryankin, A.M., Kizim, A.V., Jukova, I.G., Siplivaya, M.B.: Iskusstvennyy intellekt. Bazy znaniy i ekspertnye sistemy. VolgGTU. RPK "Politehnik", Volgograd (2002)
2. Djekson Piter Vvedenie v ekspertnye sistemy. Per. s angl. Izdatelskiy dom "Vilyams", M. (2001)
3. Djarratano Djozef, Rayli Gari Ekspertnye sistemy principy razrabotki i programmirovanie. Per. s angl. OOO "I.D. Vilyams", M. (2007)
4. Soshnikov, D.V.: Metody i sredstva postroeniya raspredelennyh intellektualnyh sistem na osnove produkcionno-freymovogo predstavleniya znaniy: dis. kand. fiz.-mat. nauk. MAI, Moskva (2001)

5. Povoroznyuk, A.I.: Konceptualnaya model obekta diagnostiki v kompyuternyh sistemah medicinskoy diagnostiki. Sistemi obrob. informaciї. Vip. 9, pp. 133–136 (2007)
6. Demenkov, N.P.: Nechetkoe upravlenie v tehnicheskih sistemah. Izd-vo MGGU im, M., N.E. Baumana (2005)
7. Lyu, B.: Teoriya i praktika neopredelennogo programmirovaniya. Per. s angl. BINOM. Laboratoriya znaniy, M. (2005)
8. Fomenkov, S.A., Davydov, D.A., Kamaev, V.A.: Matematicheskoe modelirovanie sistemnyh obektov. VolgGTU. RPK "Politehnik", Volgograd (2006)
9. Katasev, A.S., Ahatova, C.F.: Neyronechetkaya model formirovaniya baz znaniy ekspertnyh sistem s geneticheskim algoritmom obucheniya. In: Problemy upravleniya i modelirovaniya v slojnyh sistemah: Trudy XII Mejd. konferencii, pp. 615–621. Samarskiy nauchnyy centr RAN, Samara (2010)
10. Popov, E.V., Fominyh, I.B., Kisel, E.B., Shapot, M.D.: Staticheskie i dinamicheskie ekspertnye sistemy. Finansy i statistika, M. (1996)

Cognitive Activity Efficiency Factors during Investigative Actions, Performed Using Information and Communication Technologies

Evgeniy Kravets, Yulija Steshenko, Aleksandr Likholetov,
Daniyar Kairgaliev, and Dmitriy Vasiliev

Volgograd Academy of the Russian Ministry of Internal Affairs, Volgograd, Russia
bmv-21@inbox.ru

Abstract. In the paper patterns of occurrence and movement of information in the course of investigative actions have been extensively researched. The factors for partial or complete loss of orienting and evidentiary information throughout translational chain have been analyzed. Data is considered from the standpoint of both procedurally fixed and based on the work of forensic tactics representations about the order of investigative actions. While determining the effectiveness of the information processes that occur during the investigation, it is necessary to take into account that the perception of each person depends on observation, the ability to perceive things of the world more or less acute; degree of remembering process effectiveness; attentiveness; prevailing thinking features; emotions that determine the mental state; volitional processes, developing a person's character. On this basis it is concluded that any mental activity moment of investigation participants analyzed reveals characteristic aspects of the psyche, it is always possible to distinguish volitional, emotional and cognitive processes, encouraging certain actions and deeds themselves affect the further course of the activities of the individual.

Keywords: Investigative action, information, information and communication technologies.

1   Introduction

Research goal: defining criteria for the information value of the investigative action.

Methodological basis of research consists of general scientific, academic and partially-academic methods: systematic and structural, comparative and legal, logical, statistical, analysis, observation, measurement, description, comparison and other research methods, as well as provisions of general scientific materialist dialectics as a method of learning.

Investigative action is a way of cognition based on the norms of criminal procedure law. It's fundamental basis is the theory of outward things reflection in the human mind [2], [11]. Note that the subject of the knowledge theory serves as a reflection of the ability to produce a correct image of reality. [13]

A. Kravets et al. (Eds.): JCKBSE 2014, CCIS 466, pp. 585–592, 2014.
© Springer International Publishing Switzerland 2014

Any investigative action "acts as a specific set of cognitive techniques to identify and display a certain type of evidentiary information" [14]. According to numerous studies in recent years, around three quarters of the entire array of evidentiary information is contained in the testimony of participants in criminal proceedings [8]. Therefore, analysis of the investigative actions information nature we are carrying out, based on the study, first of all, questioning and confrontation. In addition, the identifier while producing the identification parade also, in fact, gives testimony, and even warned about the responsibility for perjury and failure to testify.

2   Information Code as a Form of Evidentiary Information

Evidentiary information obtained by an investigative actions cannot exist outside the data signal - some physical process (changing), carrying information about the object, event, phenomenon, ie object model, phenomena, events [9]. With the concept of data signal about the events under investigation coincides display in converted form. The signal is a result of the mutual impact of at least two processes, structures: person and the environment, subject and object, and serves as a link between them [10]. It comes from the perceived events, actions, and directly connected to it. Signal exists independently within a certain organized system. It is fixed there for a long time and is transmitted for a considerable distance in this form.

Under certain conditions, there is a unique relationship, mutual consistency within defined accuracy of the description, between the event and the signal [12]

Information signals system is made up of the following elements:

1.   the source of information (the process of information appearance);
2.   information transmitter (member of the investigative action);
3.   the recipient (the person conducting the investigation) [10].

In addition to the content the signal has a value and its shape, which serves as a kind way of existing information. Data can not be transmitted and processed without possessing a form. That information code to varieties of which various means of communication are related is a form of signal expression.

Investigative action is a process of both informational and mental activity, the mutual influence of the investigator and the person questioned, aimed at restoring the circumstances, the facts relevant for the investigation. The information circulating in the investigative procedure is the members' subject of the exchange, it is quite diverse.

The quality of information deteriorates with repeated transmission. The reduction of the testimony informational value may be the result of perception errors and sensory apparatus defects, its inability to reproduce the perceived errors of interpretation committed by the investigator, not completely correct protocol recording or misunderstanding of the interrogation protocol by judges. Obviously, to equate the amount of information contained in the study fact ideal model and an information message about him is a bad practice. Interrogates pose memories of the event, have already passed through the prism of consciousness, and not what they perceived. The most important is to determine how accurately reflects reality the "output" information, i.e.

how correct it is introduced, transformed and conveyed by interrogates, received, recorded in a protocol by inspector. A video of investigative action can become an invaluable mean of fixing defects compensation.

Partial loss of the information takes place during each act of transmission, but not to the extent that speaking the same language people could not understand each other. Data information loss is inevitable in the investigation in general, and in particular during the interrogation, but they can be filled from new sources due to receipt of other information, combining a number of fractional steps transmitting information. To the forefront here comes the testimony of the first-person, eyewitness of the crime or the relevant circumstances, it is a mean of detecting evidence of the use of direct evidence that stops the loss of information and the probability of its distortion - that is the principle of immediacy. [10] Therefore, in the case of the person involved distance a preferable production of his interrogation directly investigator having a criminal case in its production. At present this is looks like a time consuming and lengthy implementation time, and serves as yet another argument in favor of the introduction of information and communication technologies as a means of providing technical and forensic investigative action. [6]

3   Communication Interaction Structure during the Investigative Procedure

Process of the investigative action production there is always communication, characterized by a high degree of interactivity and intellectual tension of the parties involved. The result - it's not just snapshots of information transmitted by interrogatee as a protocol, but also the result of the integrated activities of the investigator. Communication procedure is directly related to the interrogated' mnemonic abilities. Getting the most objective, complete and comprehensive testimony sealed his memory and perception.

To the characteristics of the interrogation objectively defined by interrogated' behavior in the interrogation and its biological properties are properties of memory, especially endowed with some defect, in particular, the lack of a mechanism to reflect the elements of the offense and the whole event, deviations in mental development and age-specific perception of individual circumstances and facts consisting in susceptibility to suggestion, fantasy, involuntary distortion of reality. Currently available researches proving weighty predetermination perception as psychological, sexual, gender, and social personality traits [4].

Interrogation (confrontation) should be attributed to the investigation activities associated with the extraction of information reflected at the level of the psyche in the form of shaped structures. Interrogation is the process of communicating with the position of psychology, which is subject to such general properties as perceptual, interactivity and sociability.

Communicative component characterizes the process of communication as an information procedure broadcast verbal information between actors; detection of each of the entities objectives, intentions and attitudes; specificity means of communication appears in pantomime, gestures, speech (intonation, pauses), etc.

Interactive component (between subjects) characterize its two types - cooperation and competition, defined as the interaction strategy.

Perceptual component (generating an image of the opponent) defines the communication process from the standpoint of the laws of one person by another perception and image generation, where each participant uses interrogation methods such as identification, casual attribution (psychological mechanism of social interactions responsible for the interpretation of the individual causes of the behavior of others) [1] stereotypification [3].

It is the properties of the psychological structure of human activity in a certain moment of formation material evidence will depend on the structure of interrogated' consciousness. All external influences are refracted through the system due to internal social conditions of human activity, ie through his personality. Examining the work of an expert, the witness, the accused, the suspect, it is easy to identify specific personality traits. This is largely due to the fact that, as we wrote earlier, psychic phenomena are divided into three main types:

- psychic processes: reflex memorization, acoustic perception, concentration, emotional arousal, etc. Each person has all mental processes with varying degrees of intensity quickly come to replace each other, and proceed with some individual characteristics:
- psychic states: involuntarily intrusive recalled image; absent-mindedness, lack of sleep caused by a bad mood; thoughtfulness; tension or confusion when a stressful situation and other psychic states longer in duration compared to the mental processes;
- psychic personality traits, personality constant consciousness, ie ensure a certain level of activity behavior peculiar to particular individual stable mental formations [7].

4   Information Technology as a Means to Improve the Effectiveness of Investigator's Cognitive Activity

Ensuring the investigator's effectiveness, the complex formation of the evidence base in the investigation of crimes is achieved primarily active use of advanced scientific and technological tools, special techniques and methods [15].

The purpose of a specially designed automated system is to conduct investigative actions as videoconference, ensuring mutual visual observation participants of investigatory actions. The system should also provide an exception visual observation of the person conducting identification in the identification process.

There should be more focus on the capabilities of the software - the automated system "investigative actions in videoconference." It implements the possibility of mutual observation of participants in both connection locations. The presence of the "face recognition" function, as well as an option, which provides the ability to disable the image at a point of maintaining voice, allow the person filing for identification under conditions precluding identifier's visual observation. Investigator at the same time has the ability in a text editor to make the report produced by the investigative procedure, which by his decision at any time may be available for perusal in the peripheral point of contact.

At the same time the following tasks are being solved:

- receiving video from the webcam;
- streaming audio and video over a network;
- transfer of investigative actions protocol and other documents;
- encryption of data traffic transmitted - for reasons of security and understanding of the mysteries of providing preliminary investigation; face detection and concealment party investigation if necessary.

The proposed approach is to be implemented a three-tier client-server architecture, which is made up of the following modules:

- general component library implements the functions available to client and server software systems, such as encryption (Fig. 1);
- the server, transmits information between clients;
- client, captures video and audio, face recognition and retouching, transmits audio and video streams, files on the server.

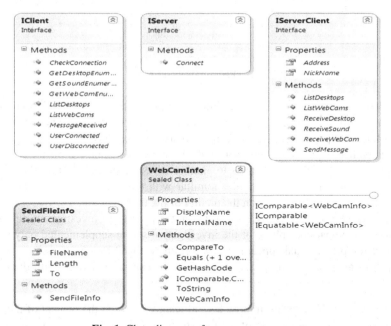

Fig. 1. Class diagram of common components

According to the concept established, the system must perform the following functions (Fig. 2):

- providing interaction between investigation participants: transmission of video, audio files;

- visualization of information transmitted: protocol text, visuals, visuals combined with different clients in one window;
- exclusion of visual observation by one of the parties in the face retouch image;
- providing security of information transmitted;
- video capture from user desktop;
- video capture from Web-camera;
- providing access to the investigation record.

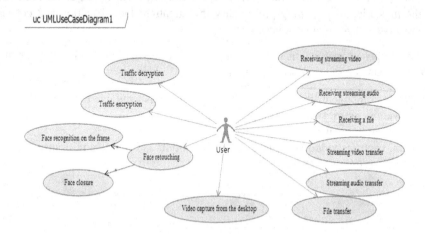

Fig. 2. Diagram of system use

The key advantage of ICT over traditional forms of investigative action is unique opportunities for the conservation of the evidentiary information by reducing the time to consolidate its procedure. Delaying investigative actions involving geographically remote person involved in connection with the need to organize a business trip, as well as order of investigative actions to another investigator, not having in their production of the criminal case, not fully familiar with the circumstances of the crime, can only have a negative impact on the quality of the investigation.

By itself, the use of ICT has little effect on the process of investigative action. In particular, the preparatory phase of the investigative action supplemented only by the need to ensure professional appearance, performing technical support session.

Conclusions of a working phase study of the investigative actions with the use of ICT are:

1. the use of ICT does not impose a significant imprint on the content of the main part of the working phase of the investigative action when it reaches its immediate goal;
2. produced by the prediction of possible losses and distortion of evidentiary information related to the change in the regime of production investigation leads to the conclusion on the admissibility of video conferencing for these purposes.

5   Conclusion

In determining the effectiveness of the information processes that occur during the investigation, it is necessary to take into account that the perception of each person depends on observation, the ability to perceive things of the world more or less acute; degree of effectiveness of the process of remembering; attention; prevailing thinking features; emotions that determine the mental state; volitional processes, developing a person's character.

Proceeding from the above, we can conclude that any analyzed moment of mental activity involved in the investigation reveals characteristic aspects of the psyche, it is always possible to distinguish volitional, emotional and cognitive processes, encouraging certain actions and deeds themselves affect the further course of the individual activities [5].

Reducing the time period between the occurrence of the evidentiary information and procedural fixation will reduce the impact of these negative factors. An innovative way to solve this problem may serve as the introduction of production practices of specific investigative actions by using videoconferencing. It is necessary to pay special attention to the characteristics of the equipment used, as well as facilities for remote sessions, as consequence of non-compliance with certain rules may be the appearance of additional misstatements.

References

1. Antsupov, A.Y., Shipilov, A.I.: Conflictologist dictionary(2009)
2. Belkin, R.S.: Lenin's theory of reflection and methodological problems of Soviet criminology (1970)
3. Bodalev, A.A.: Perception of man by man. Leningrad (1965)
4. Gavrilova, N.I.: Man as an object descriptions testimony. Questions of Crime Fighting (1978)
5. Dospulov, G.G.: Questioning psychology on the preliminary investigation (1976)
6. Kravets, E.G., Popov, E., Yu., K.A.G., Al-Ashval, M.A.S.: The approach to implement an automated system for remote investigative actions. In: VolGTU Proceedings: Interuniversity Collection of Scientific Papers, Volgograd, vol. 4 (91) (2012)
7. Levitov, N.D.: Character psychology (1969)
8. Petukhovsky, A.A., Shurukhnov, N.G.: Proof in criminal proceedings, types and order of investigative actions. Tula, Moscow (2002)
9. Poletaev, I.A.: Signal (1958)
10. Porubov, N.I.: Informational essence of interrogation. Problems of the Preliminary Investigation. Volgograd (1974)
11. Strogovich, M.S.: Material truth and forensic evidence in the Soviet criminal trial (1955)

12. Tekutjev, V.M.: Informational essence of questioning and its importance for the investigation of crimes - D.Sc. of law dissertation (2007)
13. Lektorsky, V.A., Oizerman, T.N. (eds.): Theory of knowledge. T.2: Socio-cultural nature of cognition (1991)
14. Sheifer, S.A.: The nature and methods of gathering evidence in the Soviet criminal trial (1972)
15. Kravets, A.G., Kravets, A.D., Korotkov, A.A.: Intelligent Multi-Agent Systems Generation. World Applied Sciences Journal. Information Technologies in Modern Industry, Education & Society 24, 98–104 (2013)

Retrieval of Drug-Drug Interactions Information from Biomedical Texts: Use of TF-IDF for Classification

Mikhail P. Melnikov and Pavel N. Vorobkalov

Volgograd State Technical University, Volgograd, Russia
{m.p.melnikov,pavor84}@gmail.com

Abstract. Detection of drug-drug interactions (DDIs) is an important practical challenge. Information about DDIs can help doctors to avoid potentially dangerous interactions. Text mining of articles can solve the problem of DDI databases actuality, thus reducing time of detecting new articles related to drug-drug interaction. There are databases containing large amount of biomedical articles, therefore computational performance of classification method used for identification of documents with DDIs become a valuable factor. In this article, we propose a fast text mining approach to DDI articles classification using term frequency–inverse document frequency (tf-idf) statistic. As a result our approach was able to achieve F1 score value 0.69 (precision = 0.89, recall = 0.57) in DDI articles classification while still keeping short run-time.

Keywords: Information retrieval, drug-drug interaction, machine learning.

1 Introduction

Detection of drug-drug interactions (DDIs) is an important practical challenge. One drug can increase, decrease, or change the effect of another drug. Information about DDIs can help doctors to avoid potentially dangerous interactions. Other interactions can be useful and can be used to improve the efficiency of treatment. A common source of DDIs information is commercial databases such as factsandcomparisons.com [1] and reference.medscape.com [2]. Being up-to-date is a crucial quality of such systems. Scientific articles are a common source of new DDIs. Search of such interactions is a difficult task which requires specialists in pharmacology or medicine. Finding new articles, which contain evidences of new DDIs, demands looking through thousands of scientific articles, filtering the articles with DDI evidences, determining which drugs take part in the interaction and what is the type and significance of the described interaction. All these time-consuming steps make almost impossible quick updating of DDI databases. Instant adding of new interactions and their correction remains an unresolved problem, that's why DDIs databases may lack the supporting scientific evidences and different databases can have unmatched DDI information [3]. Text mining of articles can solve this problem reducing time of detecting new articles related to drug-drug interaction and thus giving experts an opportunity to focus more on quality. To use text mining algorithm we need authoritative

A. Kravets et al. (Eds.): JCKBSE 2014, CCIS 466, pp. 593–602, 2014.
© Springer International Publishing Switzerland 2014

and complete source of scientific articles and MEDLINE can be such a source. MEDLINE [4] is the biggest bibliographic database of life sciences and biomedical information. It provides over 13 millions article records with abstracts which are available for free for any users. The abstracts can be used as the main source of texts for DDIs text mining, but for such a large number of articles computational performance of classification method can be still a valuable factor.

In this article we briefly review the recent papers in the area of DDI automated search, which describe different methods used for classification of articles. We highlighted algorithms that demonstrate high precision and recall. Also we describe how we construct a corpus of articles that contains a mixture of DDI evidence articles and randomly selected life science articles. We provide a detailed description of software architecture we designed for testing of developed algorithms. The main purpose of the research is to find an approach for fast retrieval of drug-drug interactions information from large databases of biomedical texts. For this task we consider using different methods and estimate their computational performance. Finally we revise possible approaches to improve the developed algorithm, which can help to increase its precision and recall. After these improvements the software implementation of the algorithm may be used by experts in DDI area to search new DDI evidences in scientific articles.

2   State of the Art

The proven importance of the DDI automated search explains why many scientists investigate this subject.

In [5] the authors construct a corpus from MEDLINE articles, using "Facts & Comparisons" Drug Interaction Facts database and their institution's care provider order entry system as a source of expert-reviewed drug interactions. They applied the LIBSVM implementation of the SVM machine learning algorithm for classifying the articles. They show the advantage of using this method over using simple search queries in the MEDLINE database.

Another approach is described in [6]. The authors discover DDIs through "the integration of 'biological domain knowledge' with 'biological facts' from MEDLINE abstracts and curated sources". They use "parse tree query language" requests for extracting information from natural language texts. After that they use AnsProlog programming language for reasoning. Using this approach over MEDLINE abstracts helped to find several potential DDIs which were not present in DrugBank database.

There are also researches that compare different methods of classification. In [7] authors use variable trigonometric threshold, support vector machine, logistic regression, naive Bayes and linear discriminant analysis (LDA) linear classifiers on articles containing DDIs. The learning and test sets are composed manually classifying articles finding articles with DDIs evidences. With 5 different feature transforms it's shown that all methods except LDA are effective and achieve high quality of classifying.

In 2011 in Huelva the "1st Challenge task on Drug-Drug Interaction Extraction" was held [8]. The corpus of the challenge consists of DDIs marked-up by a researcher with pharmaceutical background and annotated at the sentence level. The challenge organizers assert the advantages of kernel-based methods over classical machine learning classifiers.

Many of methods mentioned above are computationally intensive and require feasible time to perform on large text corpuses. As faster and requiring less computational resources we suggest using of term frequency–inverse document frequency (tf-idf) statistic for classification. Because of its high performance it was used in early search engines and showed its effectiveness on large document sets.

3   Classification Software

To implement and test the classification algorithm we developed the text classification system. This system should meet the following requirements:

— It should be simple to use, it should use text user interface, the user specifies in command prompt which action the system should perform, which file contains the input data and where the system should place the output data.
— It should be able to work with various input data;
— The system should be easily scalable – it should allow adding new algorithms and modifying already implemented algorithms without changing the core and other mechanisms of the system.

To meet these requirements we developed the following system architecture (Fig. 1). Each function of the system corresponds to one command typed in the console. Each command corresponds to the Action – the object which has only two public methods "make" and "setArguments". Every Action has access to the articles corpus via the object of PreprocessingFacade class, which can return learning, test and validation sets of scientific articles' abstracts. Each abstract is stemmed and labeled as DDI_ARTICLE or OTHER_ARTICLE. The object of ProcessingFacade class implements some subsidiary functions such as counting frequencies of stems in abstracts.

Thus adding new algorithm is adding of new class, which implements IAction interface and its registration as a command in the Factory class. We used the following design patterns for implementing the described architecture: Command, Abstract Factory, and Facade.

As programming language for this system we have chosen Java. First of all this decision made because many NLP libraries, including Stanford CoreNLP library, are implemented using this programming language and therefore are easy to integrate. The other reasons are its full cross-platform development support and its popularity among researchers in NLP area.

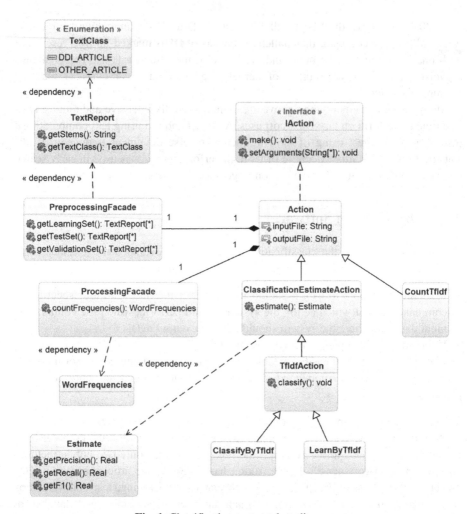

Fig. 1. Classification system class diagram

4   Corpus

We used "Facts & Comparisons" Drug Interaction Facts database for constructing a group of articles, containing DDIs. It's s a reputable and comprehensive source of drug information [5] containing over 1,800 detailed monographs. Each monograph has references to articles containing pharmacokinetics studies in which evidence for DDIs is reported. We randomly selected 186 drug-drug interactions from the database. Most of the reference are listed by URL to article in MEDLINE. For each of the 186 DDIs, we included every reference to MEDLINE. So we identified 483 DDI articles and included their abstracts and bibliographic information to our corpus and labeled them as containing DDI information (DDI articles).

To construct group of articles without DDI information, we randomly selected 532 life science articles from MEDLINE database. It's known there are about 1% prevalence of drug-drug interaction citations in MEDLINE's database [5]. Thus we consider that possible quantity of DDIs articles in this set as insignificant and ignored them. All these article's abstracts were added to the corpus as negative examples and labeled as not containing DDI information (not-DDI articles).

The whole corpus was divided into three parts: training set (60% articles), validation set (20% articles) and test set (20% articles).

5   Classification

We extracted textual features from the abstract texts. Every word was replaced with its stem using Stanford Core NLP library [10]. To ignore numbers we deleted all words, containing numerical symbols, removing the words, matching the following regular expression: "[^0-9a-zA-Z]+". Thus we presented every abstract as a word vector $d = \{w_0, w_1, \ldots, w_n\}$ where w_i is a word's stem.

Tf–idf is a numerical statistic that is intended to reflect how important a word is to a document in a corpus [9]. It helps to determine how unique is the word for the texts from the specified text class. Term frequency is calculated as follows:

$$tf(w,d) = \frac{n_i}{\sum n_k} \tag{1}$$

n_i represents the total number of the word w in the document. $\sum n_k$ represents the total number of the words in the document.

Inverse document frequency is calculated as follows:

$$idf(w,D) = \frac{|D|}{|(d_i \supset w)|} \tag{2}$$

|D| represents the total number of documents among the entire training documents corpus. $|(d_i \supset w)|$ represents the total number of documents containing the word w.

Tf-idf statistic is calculated as follows:

$$tfidf(w,d,D) = tf(w,d) \times idf(w,D) \tag{3}$$

For classification we used terms confidence and support [11]. Confidence is similar with term frequency: if term frequency determines how important the word w is for document, confidence determines how important is document for a class of texts. The value of confidence is calculated as follows:

$$conf\left(w_j, c_m\right) = \frac{N\left(w_j, c_m\right)}{N\left(w_j, all\right)} \tag{4}$$

$N\left(w_j, c_m\right)$ represents the total number of documents containing word w_j among the DDI articles category. $N\left(w_j, all\right)$ represents the total number of documents containing feature word w_j among the entire training documents corpus.

Support is a frequency of documents containing the word w. Thus it's a document frequency. The value of support is calculated as follows:

$$\sup\left(w_j, D\right) = \frac{1}{idf\left(w_j, D\right)} = \frac{N\left(w_j, all\right)}{(D)} \tag{5}$$

We modified the classification method "one-word location" based on presence or absence of "feature" word in the text [11]. In this case, feature word is determined as a word with confidence and support values bigger than some threshold values. Thus the classification works as follows:

$$class = DDI : conf\left(w_j, c_m\right) \geq threshold \wedge \sup\left(w_j\right) \geq threshold \tag{6}$$

$$class \neq DDI : conf\left(w_j, c_m\right) < threshold \vee \sup\left(w_j\right) < threshold \tag{7}$$

Instead we used the following algorithm. Previously we calculate the values of confidence and support for every word in the corpus. Then we count the number of feature words in every abstract for current values of confidence and support thresholds. If the number of characteristic words in the abstracts is bigger than some particular value M, the article is classified into DDI articles as follows:

$$class = DDI : \left|w : conf\left(w_j, c_m\right) \geq Tc \wedge \sup\left(w_j\right) \geq Ts\right| \geq M \tag{8}$$

$$class \neq DDI : \left|w : conf\left(w_j, c_m\right) < Tc \vee \sup\left(w_j\right) < Ts\right| < M \tag{9}$$

Where Tc is confidence threshold and Ts is support threshold.

As can be seen we have three parameters which affect whether abstract is classified as DDI or not. We choose F1-score value as classification quality characteristic. In that way we have three parameters which can be changed for optimization of F1 score. Because of low computational complexity of classification with beforehand calculated confidence and support values, a method of grid search optimization is suitable. It guarantees finding of global maxima in given borders. Appling this method we looped all possible values of optimization parameters with particular steps. Confidence and support thresholds were looped with 0.01 step in borders [0, 1], when M parameter was looped with step 1 in borders [1, 10]. The choice of upper border for M parameter is explained by the length of abstracts and frequency of characteristic words in the texts. We present a part of looped values of thresholds and M in the table.

Table 1. Optimization parameters and classification quality measures

Optimization parameters			Classification quality measures		
Tc	Ts	M	Precision	Recall	F1-score
0.95	0.03	2	1	0.28	0.44
0.85	0.03	2	0.86	0.55	0.67
0.75	0.03	2	0.69	0.60	0.64
0.86	0.02	2	0.89	0.57	0.69

The optimal values for learning set are the following: confidence threshold = 0.86, support threshold = 0.02, M = 2. With these values we achieved F1 score value 0.69 (precision = 0.89, recall = 0.57). Applying these values to test set we get F1 score value 0.68 (precision = 0.80, recall = 0.60). It indicated that learning model is neither under, nor overfitted.

Table 2. Top 15 feature words

Word	Confidence	Support
curve	1.000	0.057
withdrawal	0.950	0.021
volunteer	0.951	0.063
metabolite	0.880	0.026
half	0.882	0.053
elimination	0.941	0.035
ritonavir	1.000	0.021
contraceptive	0.961	0.027
cmax	1.000	0.021
adverse	0.909	0.023
dose	0.883	0.160
randomize	0.896	0.049
coadministration	1.000	0.030
absorption	0.919	0.038
twice	0.905	0.022
life	0.900	0.051

The list of feature words for these thresholds values includes the following: withdrawal, volunteer, elimination, adverse, dose, randomize, pharmacodynamic, pharmacokinetic, mg, and other words. These words are obviously connected to pharmacology and DDI subject.

To check if the method's accuracy depends on the subject of the articles from the negative group at the next we added pharmacology articles to the random MEDLINE articles in the test set. We manually selected 62 abstracts from "British Journal of Pharmacology" not related to DDI. In this case F1 score value still is 0.69 (precision = 0.81, recall = 0.60).

Also we can calculate computational complexity of this algorithm. For that we should consider complexity of different steps of learning and classification stages.

The algorithm for calculating tf-idf values can be divided into the following stages:

1. Create an empty hash table where the key is the word stem and the value is structure containing: a number of DDI abstracts, containing the stem and a total number of documents, containing the stem.
2. For each stem in each abstract: if the hash table doesn't contain the stem, add it to the hash table. Else, if it is the first appearance of this stem in the abstract, increment the total number of documents, containing the stem. If the abstract also contains information about DDI, increment number of DDI abstracts, containing the stem.
3. For each stem in the hash table calculate values of confidence and support.

Because the average time complexity of adding new values and search in hash table is $O(1)$ [12], the complexity of the whole algorithm is $O(n)$, where n is a number of stems in the learning set. After that the values of confidence and support are calculated for each stem. There are 7942 unique stems in our training set. Adding new abstracts into training set can add new words into this dictionary, but this amount can't be considerable, because the vocabulary of scientific articles isn't infinite and is kept within reasonable limits. The counters for each stem should be saved for further use. It simplifies extending of the learning set later.

The next step is the learning. After the values of tf-idf have been calculated the optimal values of thresholds should be found. The time for learning depends on the constant number of iterations we chose before start of learning and the size of the learning set. Thus the complexity of the algorithm we used for learning is $O(n)$, where n is the number of stems in the learning set.

The process of classifying of one abstract doesn't require feasible time for computation. We should count how many feature words the abstract contains to determine whether the abstract describes DDI interaction or not. Using hash table of feature words this algorithm's complexity is $O(m)$, where m is the number of the words in the abstract which is classified.

The next operation which computational complexity should be considered is the extension of the learning set. If we add new abstracts into the learning set, values of confidence and support should be recalculated. The complexity of this operation is $O(kp)$ where k is the number of stems in the new abstracts and p is the number of the words in the dictionary.

As we can see complexity of all steps of the algorithm is low, the algorithm isn't computationally intensive and doesn't require feasible time to perform even on large text corpuses.

6   Conclusions and Further Works

The suggested method of DDI articles classification demonstrates its stability under various conditions, but its accuracy should be significantly improved. If the value of precision is high enough, the value of recall is low. In this case "low" and "high" estimates mean algorithm's applicability to practical tasks. 19% of incorrectly classified DDI articles can be filtered by human editor but 40% of articles with DDIs lost by classification algorithm is still too much. The techniques which can be used for improvement of accuracy can be split into three groups: replacing classification method, changing features and feature values, manipulating with learning sets.

There are several different classification methods that can be used instead of modified "one-word location" method we are using now:

— Logistic regression.
— Linear discriminant analysis.
— Support vector machines (SVM).
— Binomial Naive Bayes.

Still because we target large article corpuses computational performance of these methods should also be considered.

Improvement possibilities that require changing features and feature values are:

— Filtering of drugs names. The list of feature words includes such words as *phenytoin* and *aspirin*, which are named entities and they obviously can't improve the classification accuracy.
— After deleting or replacing named entities, using the dictionary with drug names, the number of drug names in the abstract can be considered as an additional parameter.
— Using bigrams and monograms instead of just unigrams. Using bigram textual features together with unigrams has shown its effectiveness [8]. This improvement can significantly improve classification accuracy.
— Include Medical Subject Heading (MeSH) terms. Every article at MEDLINE has a list of Medical Subject Heading words. These words can be used as textual features too.
— Convert strings with numbers into '#' [7]. This action can help to increase classification's accuracy in case of using bigrams, because in this case, for example, such bigram as "# mg." can become a feature word.
— Delete short textual features (those with a length of less than 2 characters) [7]. It can exclude prepositions and conjunctions from the text features.

— Delete infrequent features (which occurred in less than 2 documents) [7]. It can exclude named entities and other rare words which can't improve classification accuracy.

Improvement techniques that simply changing learning set are:

— Increasing number of DDI articles in learning set. The size of the learning set can influence the method's accuracy [13].
— Including DDI articles from other sources to learning set. To diversify the learning set there may be included articles from the sources besides "Facts & Comparisons" Drug Interaction Facts database.

Acknowledgement. We would like to thank "Facts & Comparisons" for granting us temporary access to their Drug Interaction Facts database.

References

1. Facts & Comparisons,
   http://www.factsandcomparisons.com/facts-comparisons-online/
2. Medscape from WebMD. Drug interaction checker drug-interactionchecker,
   http://reference.medscape.com/
3. Tari, L., Anwar, S., Liang, S., Cai, J., Baral, C.: Discovering drug-drug interactions: A text-mining and reasoning approach based on properties of drug metabolism. In: ECCB 2010, vol. 26, pp. 547–553. Oxford University Press (2010)
4. U.S. National Library of Medicine. MEDLINE,
   http://www.ncbi.nlm.nih.gov/pubmed
5. Duda, S., Aliferis, C., Miller, R., et al.: Extracting drug–drug interaction articles from MEDLINE to improve the content of drug databases. In: AMIA Annu. Symp. Proc., pp. 216–220 (2005)
6. Tari, L., Anwar, S., Liang, S., et al.: Discovering drug–drug interactions: A text-mining and reasoning approach based on properties of drug metabolism. Bioinformatics 26(18), i547–i553 (2010), doi:10.1093/bioinformatics/btq382
7. Kolchinsky, A., Lourenko, A., Li, L., et al.: Evaluation of Linear Classifiers on Articles Containing Pharmacokinetic Evidence of Drug-Drug Interactions. In: Pacific Symposium on Biocomputing (2013)
8. Proceedings of the 1st Challenge task on Drug-Drug Interaction Extraction
9. Rajaraman, A., Ullman, J.D.: Data Mining. Mining of Massive Datasets, 1–17 (2011), doi:10.1017/CBO9781139058452.002, ISBN 9781139058452
10. Stanford CoreNLP, http://nlp.stanford.edu/software/corenlp.shtml
11. Yun-tao, Z., Ling, G., Yong-cheng, W.: An improved TF-IDF approach for text classification. Journal of Zhejiang University Science (2005)
12. Cormen, T.H., Leiserson, C.E., Rivest, R.L., Stein, C.: Introduction to Algorithms, 3rd edn., pp. 253–280. Massachusetts Institute of Technology (2009) ISBN 978-0-262-03384-8
13. Kurczab, R., Ling, S.S., Bojarski, A.: The influence of negative training set size on machine learning-based virtual screening. Journal of Cheminformatics 6 (2014), doi:10.1186/1758-2946-6-32

A Consistency Check of Dependability Case (D-case) Produced from Data Flow Diagram (DFD)

Nada Olayan[1] and Shuichiro Yamamoto[2]

[1] Graduate School of Information Sciences,
Nagoya University, Nagoya, Aichi, 464-8601 Japan
dew2019dew@hotmail.com
[2] Strategy Office of Information and Communications Headquarters,
Nagoya University furocho, Chikusa-ku, Nagoya, Aichi, 464-8601 Japan
yamamotosui@icts.nagoya-u.ac.jp

Abstract. After producing the D-case based on DFD, a question about the consistency of the produced D-case was raised. In this paper we will be discussing consistency checks for the produced D-case according to DFD and D-case rules and propose some approaches based on it . There are some rules used to define and formalize the DFD, in the same manner we will define the syntax and semantics of the produced D-case.

Keywords: DFD, D-case, GSN, Assurance case, Dependability case, consistency.

1   Introduction

Dependability is one of the most important properties in most systems specially the critical ones, the need for dependability has triggered a large growth in demand and has encouraged the seek for more dependability assurance methods.

In this paper and in our previous paper we have used the Dependability Case (Dcase) tool to prove dependability, D-case is a technique and a tool used to help build an agreement with the stakeholders; it is based on the concept of discussing evidence until a claim of system dependability is proven valid to guarantee the dependability.

Based on our previous paper "A dependability assurance method based on Data flow diagram (DFD)"[7], where we have discussed the method and explained our first approach, we are going to continue our research by providing consistency proof for this method.

In the early stages of the system development life cycle, precisely in the system analysis phase, context diagram and Data Flow Diagram (DFD) are produced.

DFD is a graphical representation of the "flow" of data through an information system, modeling its process aspects. Often they are a preliminary step used to create an overview of the system, which can later be elaborated. [6][3]

Starting from the Context diagram, the DFD processes are created according to some rules. Tools to ensure DFD Diagram consistency were produced by defining the following: the produced DFD processes from the context diagram, the set of syntax and semantics, the general meaning and fundamentals of DFD.

A. Kravets et al. (Eds.): JCKBSE 2014, CCIS 466, pp. 603–616, 2014.

The check process can be a manual consistency checks from Context diagram to lower level data flow diagrams using checklist, however this method is time consuming and could be subject to human mistake. So new techniques were introduced by formalizing the rules. Providing a formal model for DFD is helpful while developing the DFD diagrams in the analysis phase of the software development lifecycle.

DFD diagrams are considered important for their essential role in tracing the flow of data in the system, and therefore must be produced in details, which will result in a lot of multi-level processes.

Using the DFD to prove dependability seems simple but with large amount of processes and their sub levels, it is difficult to track the produced D-case and prove its consistency.

Between the Data flow and D-case diagram we will look at the meanings for each, and then come up with the formal rules to define the produced D-case from DFD.

In this paper our goal is to define the general meaning of consistency for the produced D-case from DFD in a clear as possible way, and to elaborate and simplify knowledge concerning D-case. We will be defining the syntax and semantics for the produced D-case from DFD in general. The complete formalized rules will not be introduced mathematically, it should be directly produced since the rules were set already, but it shall be formalized in later work for some automated solutions. This paper begins with words on our research background and related work then proceeds with the fundamental rules of both D-case and DFD independently. Then we present an example, which will be used to explain a new approach (improvement on our first method) to reduce the produced D-case levels in order to simplify the checking process. Finally and based on the previous information we present the map to define and check consistency for the produced D-case from DFD, which includes: the rules and, semantics and check tables.

2   Background and Related Work

In our previous paper, we explained the method of producing D-case from DFD. The method was explained and proven valid and functional by examining the DFD thoroughly, however a question was raised about the consistency of the produced Dcase from DFD.

In classical concept, consistency means the lack of contradiction.it can be defined in either semantic or syntactic terms.

In the case of DFD several approaches and techniques were proposed to prove the diagrams consistency. The important rules of DFD were formalized to address the consistency issues in DFD, the research developed a formal method for consistency check between data flow diagrams based on formal notations [1].

It has been realized that the semantics of D-case need to be defined rigorously so that we can systematically reason about its consistency. [2]

It is difficult to ensure consistency of the D-cases in every detailed document. So the parts that can be checked mechanically were checked by the "D-case in Agda" system developed by the authors of [2].

Agda system is a general-purpose proof-assistant that can be used to support Dcase description.

Using Agda allows the user to build a D-case interactively while incrementally checking the syntax and types. However, Agda does not support consistency checking between D-Case and other types of analysis diagrams such that Data flow Diagrams.

3   Fundamental Rules of D-Case [5]

A graphical notation called D-case diagram based on GSN (goal structuring notation) is used to elaborate dependability [9] [5], using a D-case editor we can prove dependability of the system by setting a top goal for the system "system is dependable".

Various types of documents are associated with D-case such as UML, DFD, risk analysis.... etc. In order to prove D-case consistency we have to mention the set of syntax and semantics that defines the D-case based on DFD.

Unlike GSN, which mainly focuses on the field of safety, D-case handles all the attributes of dependability: availability, safety, integrity, reliability and maintainability.

We will start with the rules and definition of the D-case in general as a graphical structure then we will define the main elements briefly.

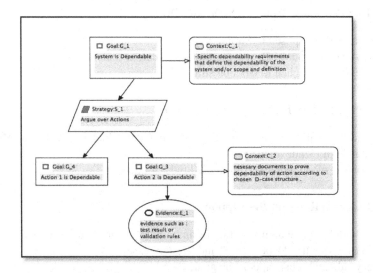

Fig. 1. D-case Diagram example showing node types

D-case diagram nodes normally consist of:

- Goal
- Context
- Strategy
- Evidence
  Where:
- **Goal or claim** is an assertion to be proven, it embodies what we want to show.
- **Context** is the means by which the case references detailed artifacts that have been developed elsewhere.
- **Strategy or argument** is how evidence supports claim There are two types of arguments that support a claim:
  – Arguments that disassemble the claim into several different claims.
  – Argument that confirms the claim by evidence.
- **Evidence** requires document and it supports the argument that may take many forms including test results, formal analyses, simulation results, fault-tree analyses, hazard analyses, modeling, and inspections.

3.1   General Rules of D-Case

- Output data flows usually have different names than input data flows for a process
- The diagram is traced only in one direction (downwards)
- Every context connects to either goal or strategy.

D-Case Diagram Basic Rules on Structure [6]

- A Goal is decomposed to Strategy.
- Every leaf is either evidence, monitor, external, or undeveloped.
- Contexts are attached to Goal or Strategy

Arrows in the D-Case Diagram has Two Types

- Solved By: Goal to Strategy, Strategy to Goal, Goal to Evidence, Monitor, External, and Undeveloped
- In Context of: To context from other kinds of nodes

D-Case Diagram Rules on Description

- Goal should not be an instruction or an opinion, it should be a proposition in the form of "system is Dependable" and "system is safe".
- Every sub goal must support the goal.
- Evidence is not just a sentence but must be a solid detailed proof, such as a document that supports the goal.
- Context associates documents of information, assumptions and definition:

- Such as system environment, identified risk list, system structure, dependability requirements or term definition.
- The scope of the context is only the attached goal or strategy and the child tree.
  - Monitor is a data available from runtime system (runtime log result)
- External is a link to other system's D-case.

4   Fundamental Rules of DFD [1][8]

A Data Flow Diagram consists of Processes, Data Flows, Data Stores and External Entities Where:

- **Process** is an activity to manipulate the incoming input to produce a specific output.
- **Data flow** is the way which data travels within the diagram, it could be from or to a process and another processes, a processes and external entity or process and data stores.
- **Data store** is where the data is stored, created or manipulated in those stores.
- **External entity** is an external entity to the system but interacts with it.

4.1   General Rules of DFD

- For external entity there is at least one input or output data flow.
- For a process there is at least one input data flow and/or at least one output data flow.
- Output data flows usually have different names than
- Input data flows for a process
- Data flows only in one direction
- Every data flow connects to at least one process
- General rules for drawing the data flow diagrams. For each external entity, there should be at least one input or output for data flow coming in or going out from the external entity.
- For every data store, data cannot move directly from one data store to another data store.
- Data must be moved by a process.

Naming, decomposition, balancing and consistency rules are discussed in details by Ibrahim and Yen Yen in [1]. I will not be defining syntax and semantics of the DFD assuming consistency checks have already taken place for the Data Flow Diagram.

4.2   DFD Example

In our previous paper [7] we used an online bookstore system as an example. The online bookstore is a system that offers search, buy and compare capabilities for bookstores.

Figures 2,3and 4 are sub levels of one of the process in the system, which is the search process; The Search process and its sub-processes are one of the simplest processes in the Bookstore system. To define the nature of the produced D-case; lets take a look at the following process and sub processes (Figures 2, 3and 4) to recognize the common rules.

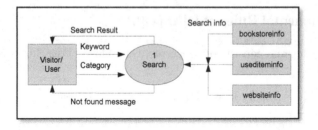

Fig. 2. Level-0 diagram for the process "Search"

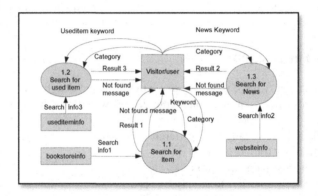

Fig. 3. Level-1 diagram for the process "Search"

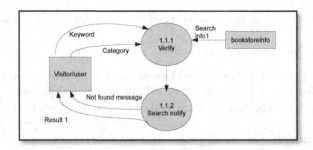

Fig. 4. Level-2 diagram shows the decomposition of the process "Search for Bookstore items"

To apply the concept of dependability to the whole bookstore system, we need to examine all the processes in the system. It is clearly easier to keep track of the system using our method, because as DFD Diagrams are created, each process would be investigated accordingly. The investigation includes every input, output, data store and the process itself.

The Search process allows the user to search for Items, used items or News of the website. We can easily identify the attributes to be checked directly just by looking at the DFD and then argue over their dependability for each process.

To elaborate the above-mentioned point, we will list the attributes to be checked for the Search process, it shows how easy it is to identify the concerned attributes:

- The inputs for the search process are:
  - Search info 1,2 and 3
  - Item keyword (keyword), Used item keyword and News keyword
  - Category
- Outputs are:
  - Result 1, 2 and 3
  - Not found message
- Processes are:
  - Search for item, search for used item and search for news
  - Verify and search notify
- Data Stores are:
  - BookstoreInfo ,UsedItemInfo and WebsiteInfo

5   Constructing the D-Case from DFD (The Bottom Up Oriented Method)

To identify the nature of the produced D-case lets take a look at the following Process decomposition structure for the previously mentioned Bookstore System (Figure.5).

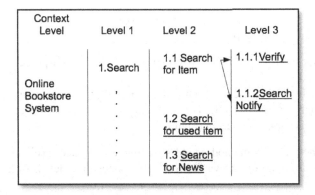

Fig. 5. Online Bookstore System processes (decomposition structure)

Now lets take a look at the produced D-case diagram (Figure.6), as you can see there are three levels that corresponds to the DFD levels.

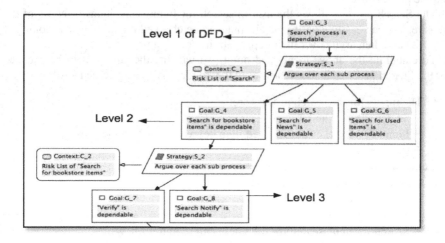

Fig. 6. D-case diagram for "Search" process

Our method was to basically investigate each process and sub process; the checks included the data flows in and out of the process and checks for data stores.

On our previous paper we introduced a method to create a D-case from DFD, the paper explained the usefulness and validity of the method, we have also provided the steps and general rules for construction [7], as we were looking to improve the method gradually, we will introduce and explain this method as a simple addition to flatten the produced D-case and to make the process less time consuming. In this part, a bottom-up approach to produce D-case from DFD is elaborated.

From (Figure.6) we can easily notice that the D-case diagram can grow large to multiple levels.

To avoid such situation, the bottom-up proposes method, flattens the D-case diagram in the following steps:

(a) Check the bottom processes: from (figure.5) the bottom processes have been underlined.
(b) Start off by listing each bottom process and change it to an appropriate Goal name such as: process 1.1.1Verify (Figure.4) changed to > Verify of "Search for item" is dependable as in (Figure.7)

Applying the previous method would save time and reduce levels in the produced Dcase The D-case diagram shown in Fig.6 corresponds the 3 levels of DFD structure in Fig.5

Replacing G_4 with G_7 and G_8 reduces the D-case diagram, as shown in following figure (Fig.7):

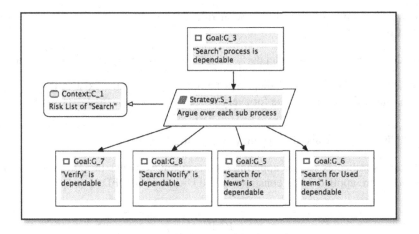

Fig. 7. D-case diagram for "Search" is reduced

6   Rules for Consistency between DFD and D-Case and Semantics of the Produced D-Case from DFD

6.1   General Rules

- Every element that belongs to DFD must exist in the produced D-case.
- Produced D-case will not contain anything that isn't corresponded to the DFD
- Produced D-case should contain the correct element from DFD
- Every process in the DFD must be examined deep down to each sub process on each level.
- Every Process, Input/output and Data store must be examined.
- For every single D-case diagram there is one set data flow diagrams constructed from one context diagram.

6.2   The General Rule of Consistency by Definition of the Used DFD and the Produced D-Case

- Let D mean DFD then D=<DP, DE, DS> where:
  − DP={dp1, dp2...dpm} a finite set of processes;
  − DE={de1, de2...,dem}   a finite set of External entity ;
  − DS = {ds1,ds2..., dsm } a finite set of data stores;

- Let D-c mean D-case then D-c =<D-cg,D-cc,D-cs,D-ce> where:
  − D-Cg={d-cg1,d-cg2...,d-cgm} a finite set of Goals or claims;
  − D-Cmg =main goal
  − D-Cc={d-cc1,d-cc2...,d-ccm} a finite set of Context;
  − D-Cs={d-cs1,d-cs2...,d-csm} a finite set of Strategy;
  − D-Ce={d-ce1,d-ce2...,d-cem} a finite set of Evidence;

Now we can come up with the General rule to prove consistency of the produced Dcase from DFD:

$$\forall \, dpi, dei, dsi \in D \, , \, \exists \, dpj, dej, dsj \in d\text{-}cg \, , dpi, dei, dsi = dpj, dej, dsj \, , \, 1 \leq i, j \leq m$$

Which means that every element that belongs to DFD must exist in the produced D-case. This rule should be true for every process, input/output and data store.

6.3   Checking D-Case Consistency According to Semantics

As Figure 8 indicates we are applying the consistency checks in a one-way manner. The checks are applied while constructing the D-case from DFD.

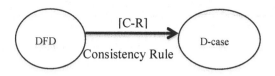

Fig. 8. One-way consistency check

- There must be one main Goal in the D-case, which states System is dependable, the system name is the same as in the context diagram.
- **Context diagram** is level 0 DFD, which is a one process diagram that shows the scope of the system and summarize the inputs and outputs (Figure.9)
- Every top process in level 1 of the DFD is mentioned in a Goal in the produced D-case.

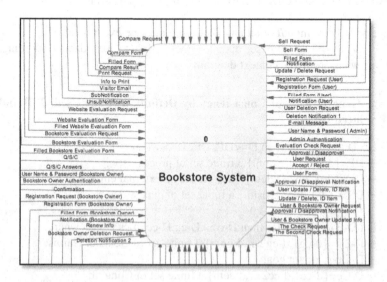

Fig. 9. Part of Context Diagram or Context Model of the Bookstore System (bulk process flow)

- Every leaf process in the DFD with no further sub process in the DFD diagram must be in a sub goal in the D-case (sub goal of the main top goal) and must be proven dependable.
- Main strategy must argue over each Process in the DFD in order to prove the top goal dependable.
- Every Input/output and Data store in the DFD must be checked under a strategy.

6.4   Consistency Check Tables

From the above-mentioned rules in section 6 we can come up with check tables that could facilitate the consistency checks for the main elements to be tested for consistency:

- **DFD:** main process, top process, leaf process, input, output and data stores.
- **D-Case:** Goals and strategies.

As processes are added to the DFD in the early stages of the analysis phase or after the design changes in the design phase, the check tables should be updated and a check should be commenced to determine how many sub process are there for each process. DFD levels and other information such as names are added as context to the D-case.

Note: Context of D-case is the means by which the case references detailed artifacts that have been developed elsewhere. It is attached to a Goal or a strategy in the D-case.

While Context of DFD is a model that represents the whole system from a broad view as level 0.

The check tables are initially empty; it is filled as the D-case diagram is created. Creating the tables should be a prior step to updating the D-case from DFD. It is easier to use the tables than to roughly create the D-case because it organizes while help to keep track of changes.

The check processes is unidirectional, it is used to check the produced D-case from DFD and not the other way around. The tables could also be used as a guide to create the D-case from DFD from scratch for a system after the analysis phase is done or even after the D-case is created.

The Tables:

- **Top Process Table (Table 1):** Top Processes are level 1 DFD processes.
  - o **Check** Column 1 and 2:
    - All the processes must be top processes.
    - There should be one main process.
    - Processes must be correctly named and numbered in ascending order.
  - o **Assignment** of Columns 3 and 4: every top Processes is assigned a Goal and a Strategy (including the main goal)

- **Sub Processes Table (Table2)**
  - o **Check** Columns 1 and 2:
    - ▪ The processes types are either Sub processes or Leaf process.
    - ▪ Processes must be correctly named and numbered in ascending order
  - o **Assignment** Column 3: Assign a Goal only for the Leaf processes.

- **Leaf Processes Table (Table 3):** Leaf processes are the DFD nodes with no further decomposition.
  - o **Check** Column 1:
    - ▪ All the processes in this table must be Leaf processes
    - ▪ Processes must be correctly named and numbered in ascending order
  - o **Assignment** Columns 2, 3,4 and 5: in every Leaf process assign 4 strategies to argue over inputs, outputs, Data stores and the process.

Example: The following figure (Fig.10) shows a system with three main processes and their sub process, we will use this simple example to demonstrate the consistency Check tables. Where: C=Context model of DFD, X=Process, G=Goal of D-case, S=Strategy of D-case

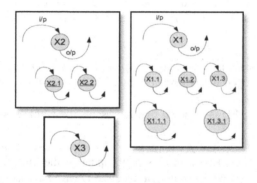

Fig. 10. Process X1, X2 and X3 and their sub processes

The following tables (Tables 1,2and 3) show an example based on Figure 10. The process could also be implemented as an automated solution to save time and effort while keeping in mind that further checks are needed.

Table 1. Top Process consistency check table

Top Process from DFD	Type	Goal from D-case	Strategy
C1	Level 0 main Goal	G1	S1
X1	Level 1 top goal	G2	S2
X2	Level 1 top goal	G3	S3
X3	Level 1 top goal	G4	S4

Table 2. Sub Process consistency check table

Process from DFD	Type	Goal from D-case
X1.1	Sub Process	-
X1.2	Leaf process	G5
X1.3	Sub process	-
X1.1.1	Leaf process	G6
X1.3.1	Leaf process	G7
X2	Sub process	-
X2.1	Leaf process	G8
X2.2	Leaf process	G9
X.3	Leaf process	G10

Table 3. Leaf Process check table

Leaf Process from DFD	Argument by risk for Input	Argument by risk for Output	Argument by risk for Data Store	Argument by risk for Process
X1.2	S5	S6	S7	S8
X1.1.1	S9	S10	S11	S12
X1.3.1	S13	S14	S15	S16
X2.1	S17	S18	S19	S20
X2.2	S21	S22	S23	S24
X3	S25	S26	S27	S28

7   Summary and Future Work

A Consistency check method was proposed in this paper based on DFD and D-case and their definitions .It is easy to check a flatter D-case diagram (less levels) so a bottom-up approach was also proposed. Furthermore, The methods can contribute to risk mitigation by using the DFD functions as mentioned in our previous paper [7].

Defining the syntax and semantics of the D-case produced from DFD will help us set the rules and prove the consistency by checking the produced D-case manually. This can be very useful but time consuming, for future research those rules can be used to facilitate the process of producing the formalized rules by mathematical notation and therefore making it easy to produce an automated solution that could check the consistency automatically for this particular method.

References

1. Ibrahim, R., YenYen, S.: A Formal Model for Data Flow Diagram Rules. International Journal of Software Engineering & Applications 1(2), 60–69 (2010)
2. The Agda Wiki, http://wiki.portal.chalmers.se/agda/pmwiki.php
3. Dependability Case Editor with Pattern LibraryYutaka Matsuno, Hiroki Takamura,Yutaka Ishikawa Information Technology Center/ The University of Tokyo
4. Tong, L., Tang, C.S.: Semantic Specification and Verification of Data Flow Diagrams. Journal of Computer Science and Technology 6(1), 21–31 (1991)
5. Yutaka, M., Takai, T., Yamamoto, S.: D- Case Pocket Book Let's write Dependability Cases! Asset Management Co. Ltd., (2012) ISBN: 978-4-86293-080-4
6. Bruza, P.D., Van der Weide, T.P.: The Semantics of Data Flow Diagrams. University of Nijmegen (1993)
7. Olayan, N., Patu, V., Matsuno, Y., Yamamoto, S.: A Dependability Assurance Method Based on Data Flow Diagram (DFD). In: 2013 European Modeling Symposium (EMS), pp. 113–118 (2013)
8. Dennis, A., Wixom, B.H., Roth, R.M.: System Analysis and Design, 4th edn. John Wiley and sons, USA (2008)
9. Kelly, T., Weaver, R.: The Goal Structuring Notation - A Safety Argument Notation. In: Proceedings of the Dependable Systems and Networks 2004 Workshop on Assurance Cases (July 2004)

The Method of D-Case Development
Using HAZOP Analysis on UML Models

Feng Ding[1], Shuichiro Yamamoto[2], and Nda Abrahim[2]

[1] Nagoya University, Gruduate School of Information Science, Yamamoto Lab.
Furo-cho. Chikusa-ku, Nagoya 464-8601 Japan
[2] Nagoya University, Strategy Office, Information and Communications Headquarters
Furo-cho. Chikusa-ku, Nagoya 464-8601 Japan
ding.feng@i.mbox.nagoya-u.ac.jp,
yamamotosui@icts.nagoya-u.ac.jp

Abstract. As modern systems are becoming complex and large rapidly, the dependability of these systems are important. Standards and regulations for developing software of these systems usually need restricted programming language and formal methods. For reasons of scale and complexities of these large systems it is preferable to use the modern object-oriented technique during the development, such as Unified Modern Language (UML). While using UML models, the notation and associated techniques should ensure to be dependable. We have proposed the method for developing a Dependability-Case (D-case) based on UML models. In this paper, the HAZOP will be used for hazard analysis and presents a systematic way of performing HAZOP on UML models.

Keywords: Dependability case, UML, Sequence diagram, HAZOP.

1 Introduction

As the modern systems are becoming complex and large rapidly, the specification of these systems   not only needs integrity, its reliability, dependability is also needed. Providing dependability to these systems seems be important. This dependability can be implicit through a safety standard. Therefore, the research on D-Case which can verify the safety, reliability, availability, maintainability and integrity of systems has been attracting attention recently. D-Case is a method to verify the dependability of the systems. D-Case presents an argument, supported by the evidence, that the system is acceptably dependable to operate in a given environment. A D-Case should consider technical factors that may contribute to dependability. It should provide dependability for the process of which system is developed , operated and maintained. Therefore, to ensure the dependability of systems, it is necessary to confirm the dependability of each stage of the system development process. A lot of system development processes are based on the Unified Modeling Language(UML) which uses notations to exhibit the system architecture descriptions. To verify the dependability of these systems, we can use the D-Case method based on the UML model to ensure the dependability of the systems.[1][2][3]

A. Kravets et al. (Eds.): JCKBSE 2014, CCIS 466, pp. 617–629, 2014.
© Springer International Publishing Switzerland 2014

In this paper, D-Case can be developed to decide dependability of a system from a functional concept prospective. The object of the dependable concept is to define a set of functional dependable requirements which together satisfy all the dependable goals associated with the hazards determined during hazard analysis and risk assessment. We will also explore about the contact between D-Case and UML models. By using hazard analysis, we propose a method to develop the D-Case based on UML models.[4][5]

The process of developing a system may face a lot challenges like implicit faults, to solve these we use the hazard analysis. There are a lot of techniques that are used for hazard analysis, like Software Failure Modes and Effects Analysis (SFMEA), Requirement Completeness Analysis , and Hazard and Operability Studies (HAZOP Studies). HAZOP can be applied throughout the entire system development , it will be performed during our hazard analysis process. By performing HAZOP Studies on UML models, we will get a lot of evidences which can contribute to the development of the D-Case.[6][7][8][9]

1.1   Related Work

This paper has been inspired by the work of [10][11], in which the authors provided the method about Model-Based assurance for functional safety and HAZOP studies on UML models. However, they did not try to relate them. In our paper, we will provide the method to develop the D-Case by using HAZOP study on one of the UML models. The specifications of systems have no claims and the evidence which support the claims with dependability. We think that it is necessary to introduce the D-Case during the system development to achieve the high dependability. UML is the most-used modeling language to describe of system's specification, it can describe the w application structure, behavior, function, and architecture. Therefore, Introducing the D-Case to present an argument, supported by the evidence to make the description of systems specification acceptably dependable.

In addition, HAZOP analysis technique has been combined with UML-like diagrams, such as Functional Failure Analysis combined with use cases, and UML elements like messages, actors.   D-Case will be build based on the analysis results.

1.2   Contributes

In this paper, we will give a method to develop the D-Case based on sequence diagram. And verifying the applicability of this method.

To build the D-Case based on sequence diagram, we need approach each elements of sequence diagram. The hazard analysis of each element is very important to verify the dependability of sequence diagram. We will lead the HAZOP study to do the hazard analysis of the elements of sequence diagrams.

2   Using UML Model at System Architecture Description

First, we will present the definition of the system architecture as the structure or structures of the system, which comprise software elements, the externally visible properties of those elements, and the relationships between them.[12]

The reasons we focus on the system architecture from the dependability point like:

1 System architecture is at a early stage of the system development and in high abstraction
2 The abstraction of the architecture is from stakeholders[13]

UML is a general-purpose modeling language to describe the system architecture. And it's not a development method by itself. One of the UML diagrams is a partial graphic representation of a system's model.

Figure 1 shows each diagram of UML models.

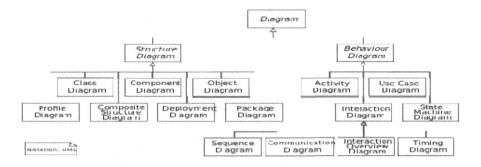

Fig. 1. UML Diagrams

In this paper, we will mainly discuss about the Sequence Diagram. A sequence diagram shows object interactions arranged in time sequence. It depicts the objects and classes involved in the scenario and the sequence of messages exchanged between the objects needed to carry out the functionality of the scenario.[14]

3   D-Case

D-Case which is represented in the Goal Structuring Notation(GSN). GSN represents safety arguments in terms of basic elements such as goals(claims), solutions(evidences), and strategies(Figure 2). [13]Arguments have been created in GSN by linking these elements using two main relationships, 'supported by' and 'in context of' to form a goal structure.[9] The principle of D-Case is to show that goals will be successfully broken down into sub-goals until the last goal which can be supported by the evidence. Then the top goal will be proved dependably. The UML models provide base which bring out the hazard analysis and risk management.(Figure 3) In this paper, we only use GSN to build our D-Case based on Sequence Diagram to show the process.

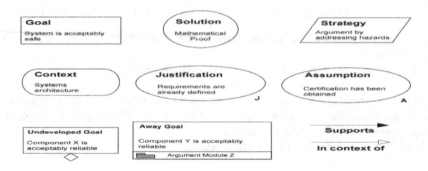

Fig. 2. GSN Elements

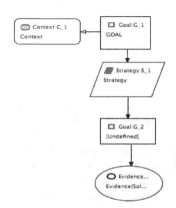

Fig. 3. Example of D-Case

4   HAZOP for UML Models

Each UML model can be considered as a HAZOP entity. The attributes and composed elements of UML model can be considered as HAZOP attributes. In order to do the hazard analysis, each of the elements in a UML model diagram can also be considered as an entity during HAZOP analysis. For example, we may consider Class Diagram as HAZOP entity, and Class diagram's element as HAZOP attribute.

We use the guide words to do the hazard analysis and risk management. Table 1 shows that a list of guide words and interpretation for HAZOP study. This list can be used for different system design, but in UML-based system development, the guide word will be applied when it is necessary. So Not all of the guide words will be used during the HAZOP study on UML models. Table 2 shows that how we use the guide words on the elements of diagrams.

Table 1. Guide word list

Guide word	Interpretation
No	No intention will be achieved
More	More than intention was achieved
Less	Less than intention was achieved
As well as	The intention was achieved together with additions
Part of	Some of intentions were achieved
Reverse	The opposite of intention was achieved
Other than	Complete substitution
Early	Relative to the time clock
Late	Relative to the time clock
Before	Relating to order or sequence
After	Relating to order or sequence

Table 2. Example of guide word using in HAZOP analysis

Entity		
Attribute	Guide word	interpretation
Each	none	The entity contains none of the necessary elements
Element	Part of	The entity contains some, but not all, of elements
	Other than	The entity contains elements, but the elements do not fulfill the design intention
	...	....

4.1   HAZOP Analysis for Sequence Diagram

Implementation of HAZOP analysis on each UML model is a large project. In this paper, we focus on using the HAZOP analysis based on sequence diagram. The Sequence Diagram models the objects based on a time sequence. It shows how the objects interact with others by messages in a particular scenario of a use case. So we can get a lot of information about how a part of a subsystem work from the sequence diagram.

The guide words can help us find whether or not an element of sequence diagram has hazards or risks.

The main entities in a sequence diagram are objects and messages. In this paper, we will focus on using HAZOP analysis based on these two entities. Objects have the following attributes: 1) their classes; 2) their lifetime; 3) source object. Messages have the following attributes: 1) data; 2) time of occurrence; 3) source object; 4) destination object; 5) condition; 6) delay; 7) duration. And for each attribute of the object and messages in the sequence diagram we can be applied for guide words. [15]The work from Lano[15] represents a set of guide words for these two entities. For example, Table 3 present guide words for message conditions of the message entity, and some of the guide works are derived from [15].

Table 3. Guide word for message condition

Guide word	Interpretation
None	Condition is not true
Other than	Condition is unintended truth value
Reverse	Condition is the opposite intended truth value
As well as	An unintended condition in addition is truth value

4.2   Risk Management from HAZOP Study for Sequence Diagram

Through guide words we could get the risk analysis list of the attributes. From the risk analysis list we can build the risk mitigation list. The sequence diagram can be improved through the risk analysis list and mitigation list. Table 4 we will give the example of the risk mitigation list.

Table 4. Example of mitigation list

Message condition	Guide word	Interpretation	Mitigation
Condition 1	None	Condition is not true	Add the right condition
	Other	Condition is unintended truth value	Instead of the Intended value
Condition 2	Reverse	Condition is the opposite intended truth value	Give the right condition
	As well as	An unintended condition in addition is truth value	Eliminate the unintended condition

As in table 4, we should make the list for each attribute of object and message. We can decrease the potential hazard of system by improving the sequence diagram from the risk analysis list and risk mitigation list. Risk analysis list and risk mitigation list provide context and evidence for building a D-Case. Figure 4 shows the process of building D-Case based on sequence diagram.

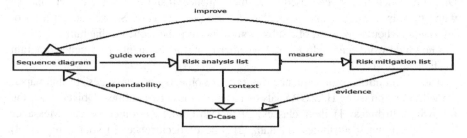

Fig. 4. Process of building D-Case based on sequence diagram

5   The Method of D-Case Development Based on Sequence Diagram

In this section, we will talk about how to develop a D-Case based on the system description of the Sequence diagram . To ensure a sequence diagram is dependable, we need to discuss the dependability about each composed element of a sequence diagram. There may have a lot of sequence diagrams created during the system design process, we should ensure the dependability of each sequence diagram. The process of developing a D-Case based on each sequence diagram is the same, so we introduce the module which contains a set of claims to make top-level D-Case clear. With separating this module, we can get the D-Case from second sequence diagram to nth sequence diagram. Figure 5 shows the top-level dependability argument for a system.

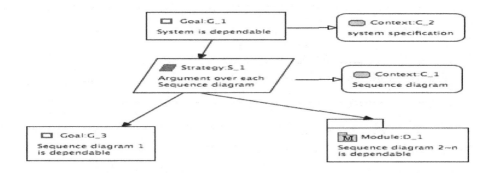

Fig. 5. Top-level D-Case

To make sure each element of a sequence diagram is dependable, we will develop the D-Case on each element to make sure that hazard of the system will not be occurred the risk of each element. In module 1, we talk about dependability of each element.

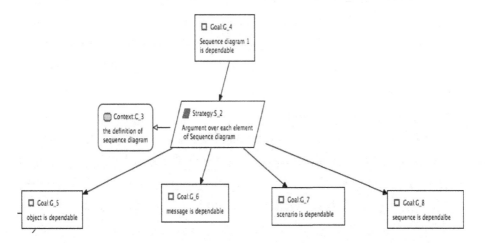

Fig. 6. Argument of the Sequence diagram element

There are four major elements in a sequence diagram. In section 4, we talked about the HAZOP analysis and risk analysis on the attributes of objects and messages. The achievement will be used to develop the D-Case based on object and messages. The risk analysis list can provide the context for the development of D-Case. And the mitigation list of risks can provide the evidence for the D-Case. Figure 6 shows the D-Case of object.

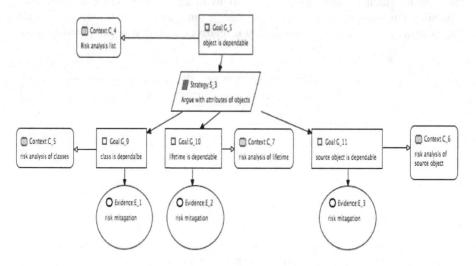

Fig. 7. D-Case of object

The method of developing a D-Case for messages is similar with the D-Case development for object. Figure 7 shows the D-Case of message.

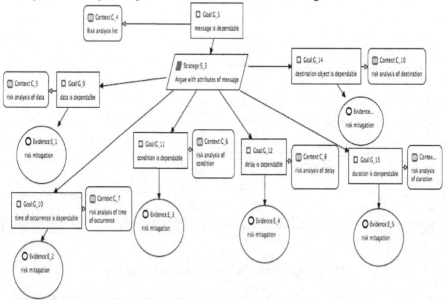

Fig. 8. D-Case of message

Then we need to create D-Case for other elements of sequence diagram. Scenario and sequence represent the use case of system, therefore the dependability of scenario and sequence can be ensured from the use case. Figure 8 shows the D-Case of the two elements.

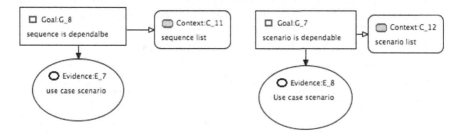

Fig. 9. D-Case of sequence and scenario

So far, we explained the method of developing a D-Case based on sequence diagram. We can employ this method into the system development next section in order to verify its applicability.

6   Application Example

In this section, we will employ this method to a sequence diagram which was drawn based on the process of managing staff's information. Figure 10 shows the UML sequence diagram for this process.

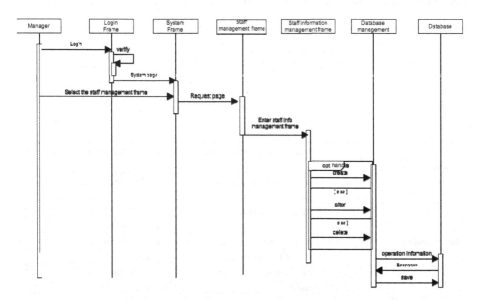

Fig. 10. Example sequence diagram for Staff information management system

In order to ensure the dependability of this process, we will build a D-Case based on the figure 10 through the basis of the presented method. According to the figure 3 process, first we need focus on the HAZOP analysis work. We begin to do the HAZOP analysis on object and messages of this sequence diagram. Table 3 gives us the example which tells us how to apply the guide words for HAZOP attributes. Using table 3, we could have the analysis on manager object given in Table 5.

Table 5. Guide word for Manager object

Entity=object(Manager)		
Attributes	Guide words	Interpretations
Class	None	Manager is not shown in the process
	Reverse	Manager is not shown in the right place which it should be
Lifetime	Part of	Lifetime of manager is not complete
	As well as	A part of the lifetime is uncorrect
Source object	None	Manager's source object is not exist
	Reverse	Manager's source object is not shown in the right place
	As well as	Manager's source object is not correct

Then we need do the HAZOP analysis on the rest of objects of the sequence diagram. When we finish all of these work, we can summary these interpretations of objects as a risk analysis list for the context of the D-Case. Refer to Table 4, the mitigation of each interpretation will be given in the table 6.

Table 6. Manager mitigation list

Entity=object (Manager)		
Attributes	interpretation	mitigation
Class	Manager has no relationship with other object	Add the relationship between manager and other object
	Manager is not shown in the right place which it should be	Move the manager to the right place
Lifetime	Lifetime of manager is not complete	Make the lifetime completed
Lifetime	A part of the lifetime is incorrect	Modify the incorrect part
Source object	Manager's source object is not exist	Check the scenario to find the source object
	Manager's source object is not shown in the right place	Move the source object to the right place
	Manager's source object is not correct	Substitute the right source object

The mitigations of the rest of objects will be made for the evidence of the D-Case. So far, we have given the risk analysis list and mitigation list of each attribute of object for the D-Case development shown in the Figure 7. Next we should do the HAZOP analysis on the message. We picked one of the messages to explain the work of HAZOP analysis on message. In the messages of sequence diagram, they did not involve the attributes like data, delay and duration, so we should do the HAZOP analysis on the rest of attributes. Using the table 4, the interpretation list and mitigation list of the message "login" will be given in table 7.

Table 7. interpretation list and mitigation list of the message "login"

Entity=message(Login)			
Attributes	Guide word	Interpretation	mitigation
Time of occurrence	None	Login is not sent when it should be	To make sure login will be sent in the right time
	Other than	Login sent in the wrong time	To make sure login will be sent in the right time
	More than	Login sent later than intended	To make sure login will be sent in the right time
Source object	None	Login's source object is not exist	Check the scenario to find the source object
	Reverse	Login's source object is not shown in the right place	Move the source object to the right place
	As well as	Login's source object is not correct	Substitute the right source object
Destination	None	Login not sent when indented	Find the right destination of login
	Other than	Login sent to the wrong object	Find the right destination of login
Condition	None	Login's condition is not true	Add the right condition
	Other	Login's condition is unintended truth value	Instead of the Intended value
Data	None	Login's data is null	Add the login data
	Other than	Login's data is wrong	Modify the login data

According to this table 7, we could develop the interpretation list and mitigation list of the rest of messages of sequence diagram. When we finish HAZOP analysis on the objects and messages, these interpretation lists and mitigation lists could be used as contexts and evidences of D-Case which developed based on the presented sequence diagram in order to ensure the dependability of staff information management system. The last work of developing this D-Case is to make the D-Case of sequence and scenario of this sequence diagram. We can read the staff information management sequence from this sequence diagram like this:

a)   Manager send the login data to enter the system
b)   System need verify the data
c)   After entering the system, manager select the staff management frame
d)   Manager select the staff information management frame
e)   Manager choose the operation to the staff information
f)   Send the operation request to the database
g)   Database get the request and save the result

This sequence will be used as one of the contexts of D-Case, its dependability could be verified by the use case scenario. So we need add the use case scenario specification as the evidence of the sequence in the D-Case. So far, we have presented the contexts and evidences to make the complete D-Case based on sequence diagram of staff management system. Through these work, we have verified the applicability of the method of developing a D-Case using HAZOP analysis on sequence diagram.

7   Summary

This paper described the method about developing a D-Case by using HAZOP analysis to one of the UML models. By using guide words applied to parts of entities of the sequence diagram in order to do the risk analysis to discover potential hazards. Based on the risk analysis we can make the risk mitigation. We can improve the dependability of sequence diagram by using the mitigation.

We have used GSN to build the main framework of D-Case based on sequence diagram. The risk analysis list and risk mitigation list help us to develop the complete D-Case. In order to verify the applicability of the method, we applied this method to a sequence diagram of a staff management system.

About the future work, we will apply the HAZOP analysis to other UML models, and give the method of developing D-Case based on each UML model.

References

[1] ISSRE, The 3rd International Workshop on Open Systems Dependability: Adaptation to Changing World (2013),
    http://www.ubicg.ynu.ac.jp/wosd/wosd2013/index.html
[2] 松野裕, 高井利憲,山本修一郎, D-Case 入門―ディペンダビリティ・ケースをかいてもよう！―.株式会社ダイテックホールディング (2012) ISBN978-4-86293-079-8
[3] Matsuno, Y., Yamamoto, S.: Consensus building and in-operation assurance for service dependability. In: Quirchmayr, G., Basl, J., You, I., Xu, L., Weippl, E. (eds.) CD-ARES 2012. LNCS, vol. 7465, pp. 639–653. Springer, Heidelberg (2012)
[4] Matsuno, Y., Nakazawa, J., Takeyama, M., Sugaya, M., Ishikawa, Y.: Toward a language for communication among stakeholders. In: Proc. of the 16th IEEE Pacific Rim International Symposium on Dependable Computing (PRDC 2010), pp. 93–100 (2010)
[5] Object-oriented systems analysis and design using UML, Bennett S, pp.21–50

[6] Leveson, N.G., Heimdahl, M.P.E., Reese, J.D.: Designing specification languages for process control systems: Lessons learned and steps to the future. In: Wang, J., Lemoine, M. (eds.) ESEC/FSE 1999. LNCS, vol. 1687, pp. 127–146. Springer, Heidelberg (1999)

[7] Reifer, D.: Software Failure Modes and Effects Analysis. IEEE Transactions on Reliability R-38(3) (1979)

[8] Ministry of Defence. HAZOP studies on systems containing programmable electronics. Defence Standard 00-58, Parts 1 and 2, Issue 2 (May 2000)

[9] Hansen, K.M., Wells, L., Maier, T.: HAZOP Analysis of UML-Based Software Architecture Descriptions of Safety-Critical Systems

[10] Habli, I., Ibarra, I., Rivett, R., Kelly, T.: Model-Based Assurance for Justifying Automotive Functional Safety

[11] 山本修一郎, 松野裕, ユースケース分析に基づくディペンダビリティケース作成法の提 案, KBSE 研究会,信学技報, BSE2012-61, vol. 112(419), pp. 19-24, (2013); KBSE2012-61, 年 1 月

[12] Bass, L., Clements, P., Kazman, R.: Software Architecture in Practice, 2nd edn. Addison-Wesley (2003)

[13] Hansen, K.M., Wells, L., Maier, T.: HAZOP Analysis of UML-Based Software Architecture Descriptions of Safety-Critical Systems

[14] Sequence Diagram Wikipedia, http://en.wikipedia.org/wiki/Sequence_diagram

[15] Lano, K., Clark, D., Androutsopoulos, K.: Safety and security analysis of object-oriented models. In: Anderson, S., Bologna, S., Felici, M. (eds.) SAFECOMP 2002. LNCS, vol. 2434, pp. 82–93. Springer, Heidelberg (2002)

Means of Computer Modeling
of Microwave Devices and Numerical Methods
as Their Base

Olga A. Astafurova, Nataliya A. Salnikova, and Nikolai V. Lopukhov

Volgograd Branch of the Russian Presidential Academy of National Economy
and Public Administration
olgast@vags.ru, {ns3112,lopuhov_nikolai}@mail.ru

Abstract. This article deals with the issues of modeling in automated design systems of complicated technical devices. Design automation for microwaves devices can be the example. Numerical methods their features and formalization possibilities which are the software basis to design microwaves devices are also represented. The examples of these methods applying in radio-electronic systems design programs are also offered.

Keywords: automated design system, design of ultrahigh frequency devices, modeling methods, numerical methods, the software, programs radio-electronic systems design, microwave devices design, frequency characteristics, electrodynamic modeling.

1   Introduction

Requirements of practice for mass-dimensional parameters lowering, the frequency responses improving, operating frequencies of radio-electronic equipment range extension, of high-speed performance and reliability of information handling systems increase continue to remain actual tasks on enhancement of technique of a very high frequency. Search of new principles and methods of very high frequencies devices design, with the use of modern computing and software is carried along with its theoretical justification. Nowadays there is a heavy demand to lower costs on development, manufacturing and mastering of equipment production, to provide compatibility and eligibility of instrumental decisions in case of simultaneous improving of quality, increase in reliability and service life.

2   Traditional Methods of Simulation in Automated Design Engineering Systems

While designing difficult systems (subsystems) numerous tasks requiring assessment of quantitative and qualitative regularities of functioning processes of such systems, carrying out structural and parametric synthesis arise [1,2,3].

A. Kravets et al. (Eds.): JCKBSE 2014, CCIS 466, pp. 630–642, 2014.

The first automated design engineering systems (CAD) allowed to automate the following stages and operations: execution of engineering calculations in the form of numerous application program packages, search of necessary information in an automated databank, optimization of parameters by means of methods of mathematical simulation, formation of drawings. However tasks of synthesis and choice of improved and new design decisions represent a certain complexity in program implementation because formalization and programming of process of search and synthesis of new technical systems is connected with setting and solution of tasks of technical creativity that causes the considerable difficulties.

According to the experts the cost of operations of preliminary design makes 3 - 5% of a total cost of all operations on object creation, however indexes of the designed technical systems (TS) can be improved in case of the right choice of structure of the hardware for 30 - 50%, and in case of the original decision - several times.

Automated systems of design belong to the class of big systems, which development stages, implementations, maintenance and evolution now are impossible without using different types of simulation [1,2]. At all design stages of difficult technical devices it is necessary to consider the following features:

- complexity of structure and uncertainty of inter-element couplings, ambiguity of algorithms of the solution of an objective;
- large number of variables and incompleteness of the initial information;
- variety of influences of factors of the external environment.

Opportunities limitation of big systems pilot study makes a technique of their simulation actual. This would allow to provide processes of systems functioning in the appropriate form, the description of these processes with the help of mathematical models and to receive necessary estimates of characteristics of researched objects.

The method of simulation and necessary detailing of models significantly depends on a development stage of difficult system. At stages of object survey and development of the specification on design of automated system of model, generally have descriptive character and pursues the aim in the short and simple form most fully to provide information on the object, necessary for the system builder.

At the development stages of technical and working projects of systems, models of separate subsystems are detailed, and simulation serves for the solution of specific objectives of design, i.e. a choice optimum by a certain criterion in case of the given restrictions of option from a set of the admissible ones. Therefore generally at these design stages of difficult systems models for the purposes of synthesis are used.

The analysis of technical systems in CAD is based on mathematical simulation, i.e. on research of designed systems. In CAD tools of the analysis are directly connected to instruments of synthesis. In particular, synthesis tasks often manage to be consolidated to the repeated solution of the appropriate tasks of the analysis. Application of CAD allows to find project solution.

Traditional methods of simulation in automated design engineering systems of difficult technical devices are explained in numerous operations [4,5,6,7]. For example, in the operation [4] the method of synthesis of new technical solutions based on the description of a set of TR with the help And / Or-graph was offered and programmatically implemented. The organization of search of admissible values and their assessment were implemented by means of a matrix of compliances.

Machine orientation of traditional methods of simulation for the purpose of their application in CAD consists of spreading them to multivariate systems of a high order, to determine quality of their design not by one, and by many criteria, having simplified thus procedure of receiving the end result.

For all methods of design of difficult technical systems the following features are characteristic:

- design process structurization, separation of stages and design stages;
- iterative nature of design;
- typification and standardization of project decisions and design tools.

For computer-aided design of difficult technical systems the main question is formalization of formation methods of mathematical models of devices and elements of systems. Efficiency of application of CAD, so and quality of design depends on a level of automation of procedures of obtaining the mathematical description as a whole. It is necessary to remember that the method of receiving the mathematical model, implemented in CAD in many respects defines characteristics of the received model of system as a whole.

3   Design of Devices of Very High Frequency

Intensive development of the radio-electronic systems working in the range of super-high frequencies (very high frequency): radiolocation, wireless data transmission systems, cellular systems, etc. watched in world practice inevitably carry now to intensification of scientific researches in this area.

Design of devices of very high frequency is a rather complex challenge as requirements to the level of transformed power, band width of operating frequencies, reliability and technological effectiveness increase in case of simultaneous reduction of mass-dimensional parameters. Besides, it is necessary to consider the fact that manufacture of physical samples is not cheap and requires big expenses of time. Therefore search of new methods of design of very high frequencies devices, their theoretical reasons, increase of efficiency of these methods due to use of computing means of the modern computers, software development on their basis continue to remain actual tasks on enhancement of technique of a very high frequency.

During designing of very high frequencies devices it is possible to select three main stages. The first stage is constructive or structural synthesis which consists of a choice of different admissible options of the developed device. The second stage is the parametric synthesis specifying parameters of elements for receiving required frequency responses. The third stage arises if the found characteristics don't correspond to beforehand preset values and there is a need of change of construction selected at the first stage or requirements to the designed device. Besides, optimization process consisting of minimization of a deviation of turning-out values from the given ones is selected.

In practice the most widespread method is a heuristic approach, that is at first, the structure (proceeding from the general ideas of the developer of the principle of operation of very high frequencies devices, intuition, a personal experience and use of a reference material about similar devices) is selected, then parameters for the purpose of obtaining required characteristics are specified [8, 9]. This way is labor-consuming and does not always lead to optimum decisions.

At early stages of design engineering constructive and technological characteristics and reliability are estimated, and possibility of obtaining required working (electrodynamic) parameters in system of the given restrictions is evaluated. Considering specifics of very high frequencies devices (complexity of mathematical models in the three-dimensional distributed structures) it is difficult to overestimate automation of development process of very high frequency devices. Use of modern computers gives the chance of continuous monitoring of received parameters for achievement of the given characteristics of a projected node (for example, in case of coordination of antennas, setup of filters etc.), increases informtiveness of experiment. Extension of experiment opportunities especially regarding to increase in volume the accepted, processed and transmitted data leads to increasing of opportunities of means of conjugation, etc.

If automation of each stage is taken to consideration separately, it is possible to say that questions of numerical optimization (including in relation to tasks of radio systems design) are highlighted in the literature. It is difficult to imagine the second stage which is parametric synthesis without the use of modern computers. Algorithms of the parametric synthesis using methods of mathematical programming, include the optimization methods. Formalization and implementation by means of program technical means of search and synthesis of the new technical solutions connected to setting and the solution of the task of automation of retrieval constructioning of difficult technical systems, is considered in many operations of leading experts in this area [1,2,3], [9,10], in which opportunity and prospects of automation of initial stages of design is proved.

In operations [6,7], [11,12] the method of synthesis of the physical principles of action of technical cornerstone was offered which was found of databank use on physics and technology effects and is programmatically implemented.

The advantage of this method is the variety of criteria and valuation methods of design tools of new devices. At the same time the stage of a choice of the physical principle of action is poorly formalized and mathematical models of designer diagrams are insufficiently elaborated.

Thus, at present there is rather developed methodology on the basis of which it is possible to solve problems of creation of automated system of retrieval constructioning of new technical devices successfully.

The methods of structural synthesis are of great interest. Some implementator think that it can't be completely automated as there are cases when the computer isn't able to synthesize the device with the given parameters from the offered Basic Elements. In such cases the interference of the person is necessary. However this defect can be eliminated. Core systems of automated design engineering systems (CAD) of very high frequencies devices is the library of mathematical models of the Basic Elements, containing computing programs for calculation of their scattering matrixes. If to replenish the library with missing Basic Elements, the problem will be removed. One more argument against full automation is complexity of similar systems. Supporters of this approach suggest developing simpler clear dialogue systems. As other tendency devices synthesis methods development it is possible to call search of new approaches to automation of structural and parametric synthesis. Structural and parametric synthesis in addition to the methods used in parametric synthesis, uses methods of the systems concept, knowledge engineering, the theory of machine intelligence. The task of synthesis of structures is difficult formalizable that involves use of methods of the discrete optimization and heuristic morphological methods, and also genetic algorithms.

It is necessary to mark that algorithms of structural and parametric synthesis become more and more universal that expands the range of their applicability.

The numerical analysis and multiple experiences are a way which can confirm good convergence of procedure of synthesis and high performance of an offered technique.

Along with numerical methods of synthesis of devices, it is necessary to recall analytical approaches. In this case the synthesis algorithm of the new device allows to receive both construction of the device and parameters of elements entering, and the device usually turns out optimum. However, such methods are usually narrowly targeted, that is, are applicable to very limited class of the tasks describing rather simple devices.

Efficiency of design in a bigger level depends on level of automation of the standard operations which aren't requiring decision-making. Such standard operations in case of design of a very high frequency of devices are calculation of the frequency responses of the known diagram and in a certain level optimization process. Such method of synthesis shall provide to the developer some versions of the project decisions which are optimum by different criteria, for example on a coordination level on different sections of the frequency range or on convenience of practical implementation.

The method of simulation of new devices shall provide possibility of fast extension of element basis, and also provide the high speed of simulation of a very high frequency of devices at the expense of the multi-level organization of simple analytical models. Thanks to the object-oriented approach it is easily implemented in the form of a program code.

Synthesizable devices often happen to be rather difficult. In this regard there is a problem of simplification of process of release of designer documentation which in a number of CAD is solved by switching on in them of the programs providing communication with designer CAD (in particular, with Auto CAD).

4   Systems of Computer Modeling of a Very High Frequency of Devices

The first systems of design directed on a very high frequency the range, started appearing in the nineties last century. They used rather simple software. Further efforts of software makers were directed on development of more perfect interface of the user which is now graphic, and on transition to the electrodynamic analysis of the device.

First of all it is worth mentioning a packet of Microwave Office of the American company AppliedWaveResearch. Microwave Office - the most integrated packet supporting all design cycle up to manufacture of the diagram. This packet allows to simulate the linear and non-linear circuits. The non-linear analysis here is made by a method of harmonic balance and Voltaire's rows. Electromagnetic simulation of planar microwave devices is executed by a method of the moments of Galerkin. Besides, the packet includes the computing kernel integrating own mathematics and algorithms of HSPICE of the Synopsys company. The module of simulation of the skeleton diagrams, initially developed by the ICUCOM company (www.icucom.com), is successfully integrated into the environment and has the biggest set of libraries of models. The editor of topology represents not simply graphic environment of plotting of topology of microwave devices, but also the powerful instrument of technological preparation for production. In the program there is a convenient system of elimination of the revealed violations, allowing to increase efficiency of work of developers. The competitor the Ansoft company (http://www.ansoft.com/) with the multifunction automated SERENADE system is the next.

Some system modules confirmed the efficiency throughout the long period of maintenance.

The module HSFF is intended for the analysis of three-dimensional electromagnetic fields, the Harmonica module provides design when using the linear models of such devices as coordinating microwave circuits, circuits of communication of the microwave range, filters, and also non-linear devices of the microwave range (power amplifiers, adders, generators, switches), the Trilines module is intended for calculation of transmission lines, the module Synthesis – for synthesis of filters, the Super-Spice module executes simulation of microwave devices in a time domain by means of SPICE system, the Microwave Success module simulates radio telephony systems.

Among the development that solves the problem of full three-dimensional electromagnetic simulation of volume microwave devices, the CST Microwave Studio system of the German company CST (www.cst.de) attracts attention. The program uses different methods of calculation of a field (calculation of transient phenomenon in a time domain, the analysis in the frequency domain, a method of finding of natural frequencies). The main of methods of calculation of transient phenomenon solves problems of excitation of structure radio-frequency pulses that distinguishes this program from the majority of other software products. One more development of this class – the QuickWave-3D program of the Polish company QWED (www.qwed.com.pl). Both programs use the method of finite differences (FDTD) added by a method of conformal conversions. The principal difference of programs consists in completeness of the interface: the German product is the finished graphic environment for a problem definition, Polish in addition to plotting of structure demands from the user of writing of a program code. Both programs have optimization appliances and both show the best results of simulation, than HFSS product from Ansoft.

Simpler and cheaper solution is proposed by the German company – IMST (www.imst.de). Its product of EMPIRE uses classical implementation of the FDTD method therefore receiving exact results for the volume structures of arbitrary form formed by the curvilinear surfaces, requires more time and computational capability. Still here it is possible to receive different frequency responses of microwave devices, and also direction characteristics of antennas.

5   The User of a CAD in the Modern Conditions

Appearance of systems of electrodynamic simulation and design significantly changed requirements to level of training of the user of a CAD. On the one hand, apparently, that these requirements decreased as now the designer of REA isn't obliged to know a detail of the solution of the electrodynamic task. On the other hand, the modern CAD of a very high frequency is the most difficult systems which functioning essentially depends on a set of settings and the parameters set by the user. Thus these settings depend on strategy of the solution of the task and on requirements to quality of the decision which are defined also by the user.

For this reason the user, of course, shan't know all these questions in details, but he shall have high-quality idea of very wide range of problems of application-oriented electrodynamics. Thus it is possible to claim reasonably that absence of knowledge of such character almost with guarantee will bring to incorrect or at best to the nonoptimal decision.

In these conditions employers of the enterprises of the radio engineering and aviation industry speak about the interest in preparation by the higher school of experts in the high-frequency radio engineering making a fundamental principle of all modern radio aids of the most different directions. For increase of this interest and fixing of warranties on demand it is necessary to involve in development of curricula of leading scientists in this direction, and also experts specialists of the branch enterprises and the organizations. Already approved technology of creation of branches of chairs in intersectoral laboratories can become one of forms of education. Such organization of training will allow to implement the address program of target training of required experts.

6   Numerical Methods – A Software Basis

Simulation of difficult electronic devices with use of the computer equipment allows to reduce significantly labor input of their development, and also to fulfill questions of accuracy, reliability and interference free feature, but it should be noted that the end result in many respects depends on quality of mathematical simulation at the initial stages of design. Therefore still interest of the modern science and technique represents — development and deployment to practice of new mathematical methods or enhancement available.

If to speak about devices of super-high frequencies (very high frequency), this direction in which automated design engineering systems develop very intensively.

Integral part of development processes and design of microwave devices are methods of electrodynamic level of severity.

Development of systems of computer-aided design of very high frequencies devices of the range is dictated by need of abbreviation of time and the material inputs on bread-boarding and debug operations. After all the traditional method assumed creation of a set of devices (prototypes) and carrying out with their help of numerous experimental researches [13,14]. The greatest complexity was caused by simulation of very high frequencies devices with difficult geometry [15]. The modern application programs help with research and such tasks [16]. It is at present difficult to provide process of creation and research of difficult microwave devices without application of the electromagnetic simulators reducing the price and reducing on time development process of the new device.

The wide choice of software for simulation of passive and active structures is provided to the modern designers.

Such numerical methods, as becaming a basis of the software for design of a very high frequency of devices: method of finite differences (FDM); finite-element method (FEM); method of matrixes of transmission lines (TLM); method of integrable equations; method of the moments (MoM) and Galerkin's method, and also: method of a cross resonance; method of the generalized scattering matrix; calculation method in spectral area. These methods calculate characteristics of difficult microwave structures.

The greatest distribution in serially let out CAD gained: finite-element method (FEM); method of the moments (MoM); method of finite differences in a time domain (FDTD).

The finite-element method offers rather studied technology of finding of boundary values. The first step of a method is a partition of researched area on not being superimposed zones, usually triangular. The field of each element is represented the member of interpolation polynomials of the low order weighed with function value of a field in nodes of each element. The general field is defined by a way of the linear summing of fields of each element. In a method of a terminal element the variational expressions received from Maxwell's equations are used. The solution of the task can be expressed in members of natural frequency or in members of propagation constant β, depending on different statements. The last case is less preferable as initial approximation for β is required that is difficult to complex value of value β.

For increasing of accuracy of the finite-element method use advanced sampling or apply polynomials of higher order. Both that and another increases labor input. The improved sampling on elements increases the size of matrixes. Application of polynomials of higher order reduces efficiency and leads to additional program efforts.

The method of the moments (Method of Moments, MoM) is applied in case of the solution of tasks in which there are currents at metal or dielectric structures and radiation in the free space. Researched structures shall be electrically small and usually are metallic, however special extensions of a method allow availability of dielectrics in the form of coverings or volume elements of the finite sizes.

The method of the moments executes the solution of Maxwell's equations in the integral form in the frequency domain. The advantage of a method of the moments is that it is "a source method". In this method the interesting structure, instead of the free space, as is sampled only in case of the solution of the equations for finding of a field in volume. Thus boundary conditions aren't required, and used memory is proportional to geometry of the task and frequency.

Method of finite differences in a time domain - one of most widely used numerical methods of technique. It is a universal, methodologically simple and visual teaching method. The wave which is spreading through the waveguide structure, is defined by a way of direct integration in a time domain (Maxwell's equation) in a discrete form. The principal lack of a method of finite differences of a time domain is big time of computation.

In these three methods the same approach to simulation is tracked. Process of simulation can be broken into the following stages:

1. Topology (the description of geometrical parameters of structure, is more often creation of physical model by means of the visualization tools which have been built in the program) and the job of properties of materials.
2. Installation of parameters of electromagnetic simulation (area declaration of simulation and boundary conditions).
3. Simulation (sampling of physical model, partition on cells; field approximation in each cell by means of basis function thus coefficients of function are selected until boundary conditions) will be satisfied.
4. Processing, data retrieveds (calculation of S-parameters, radiation characteristics in a distant zone and so on).

But there are also differences in applicability of the specified methods. The method of the moments is suitable for planar structures whereas the finite-element method and a method of finite differences in a time domain are methods for calculations in volume. The matter is that in case of application in CAD of two last methods volume, and in a method of the moments is only metal parts of construction is sampled (breaks into elements, for example tetrahedrons). It is enough of it as unknown value in a method of the moments is distribution of currents on a metal surface whereas in two other methods define distribution of an electromagnetic field in space. Execution of full three-dimensional calculation of an electromagnetic field often is necessary as not all parts of the real device can be subjected decomposition on the elements which are storing in libraries of models.

Difference of the finite-element method from a method of finite differences is in a time domain that in the first Maxwell's equations are solved indirectly through matrixes whereas in the second it becomes in the explicit form.

As examples of application of the specified methods it is possible to mention the following software:

- finite-element method – Ansoft High Frequency Structure Simulator 8 above, Agilent High Frequency Structure Simulator 5.6;
- method of the moments – IE3D, MWO - Microwave Office, Momentun 2.0;
- Galerkin's method – Microwave Office;
- modified method of the moments – Sonnet;
- method of finite integrals in a time domain – CST Microwave Studio;
- method of finite differences in a time domain – FIDELITY (Zeland firm).

Development of means of computer simulation led to creation of systems working with different computing methods, for example ANSYS company DesignerRF&SI system.

7   Discussion

The vector of development of scientific thought of creation of programs of design of radio-electronic systems tends to integration of different systems of design into the uniform information environment in which there is a possibility of development of various devices from digital circuits of processing and formation of signals to a very high frequency of diagrams and antennas. The uniform information environment is characterized by interpenetration of results of operation of different programs for the purpose of creation of the project of all radio-electronic system as a whole. The full analysis of products of radio-electronic equipment is interesting to ultimate users, since physical prototypes and finishing the analysis of all products taking into account influence on it various factors of maintenance.

The uniform environment of Ansys firm – Ansys Workbench under control of which can work as modules of electromagnetic simulation (HFSS, Q3D, Maxwell), and programs of the analysis of radio-electronic diagrams and systems (Designer RF&SI and Simplorer) can be an example. Any of the specified software products through the environment Ansys Workbench can be also integrated with tools the mechanics and gasdynamic analysis, the thermal analysis. Development of means of computer simulation allowed to make integration of packets of different computing methods in Designer RF&SI system.

An important role is played by questions of integration of systems of different vendors. For example, software products of Cadence firm can be integrated with simulars. For this purpose the Solver on Demand interface simplifying data transfer was jointly developed. That is it is possible to perform tunings for simulation in the environment of Cadence Allegro and to transfer them to Ansys HFSS.

Support of libraries from third-party vendors of radio-electronic components allows developers to design systems taking into account the modern technological norms.

The succes of design automation in areas of simulation and the analysis, parametric and structural synthesis forms basis of further development of information systems and the technologists, used in productions.

The understanding of physical sense of the processes proceeding in the device, competent design both the subsequent constructioning and production is impossible without mathematical models effective, moderately simple and available to the engineer.

With development of the computer equipment a possibility of application of numerical methods with difficult mathematical apparatus appears. For example, finite-element method which is one of direct methods of the solution of boundary tasks. This method involves long ago developers the universality, opportunity to solve problems from the analysis of the waveguide and strip structures before simulation of antennas and the difficult not mutual devices containing the gyrotropic environments. However its application restrained the big time expenditure necessary on sampling of space. After all the first programmes didn't assume automatic partition of area on elements, all of them were brought together to that internal nodes shall be already defined, that is they were set by the user. The modern software contains the special modules solving this problem. For example, in library of the ANSYS company more than 80 types of elements of the partition which application is defined, both geometry of researched object, and physical properties of area of calculations are. Using these elements, the program can independently construct a partition grid. However requirements to level of automation of partition of areas everything increase.

Techniques of sampling or partition of researched area on not being superimposed elements, are discussed by scientific community and at present. Triangular elements (triangulation) consider basic as usual.

There is many different approaching to the solution of the task on an area triangulation:

1. Grid superimposing on implementation area. It is impossible to call this method very effective for areas with rather arbitrary boundary, that is for areas where the boundary is strongly distorted, boundary conditions will be badly considered or it is necessary to apply a large number of small-sized elements of partition (triangles).

2. Area section in nodes straight lines parallel to axes of coordinates, or lines which are continuations of the sides (for the areas having piecewise linear boundary). After section polygons turn out. The positive side of this approach is that circumstance that all polygons convex. It is possible to carry out their triangulation. The negative moment is that, as well as in the first case, elements can be very small. For example, in a Fig. 1 the area sampled in this technique is shown.

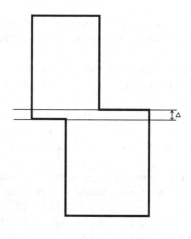

Fig. 1.

A question appears: what size shall be triangles? Certainly with the sides comparable with Δ. Breaking all polygons into elements with the side approximately equal Δ, we will receive big expenses on time as Δ it isn't enough.

3. Grinding by similar figures. Is suitable for convex figures as the nonconvex can have self-intersections.

4. Opposite pairs.

5. The great interest is represented by the idea of quasiconformal mappings using. It is based on theorem and consequence use from it, given in L. Alfors's book "Lectures on quasiconformal mappings" (p. 60). Any figure, which interior angles 60 or 120 degrees are equal, it is possible to break into equilateral triangles. If to

such area to apply the display described in a consequence, it is possible to receive new rather arbitrary area, and the main thing this area will be already triangulated. In other words the purpose of this approach consists in effectively to execute a triangulation of original area by means of kvazikonforny display of this area to another, which partition to triangles doesn't cause difficulties.

In the first works of one of authors of article one more approximation algorithm of area was provided by triangular elements. The entity of a method consisted of the following. The convex area and its boundary undertook it was represented in the form of a broken line. Further there was smaller on length a broken line link. Concerning this link the triangle side (a partition step) was selected, it shall be smaller or equal. Depending on that as this value a grid of partition is set will be larger or more small. Nodes were renumbered. Beginning from a node with the first number, the angle formed by this node and two adjacent on boundary if it more than 90 degrees was carried out a ray at an angle equal to a half calculated (an angle was calculated was postponed from boundary). On a ray the distance equal to a partition step was measured. Coordinates of a new node were calculated. From the constructed node segments to adjacent nodes on boundary were carried out. And so on. The movement happened on a spiral. Process stopped when the current boundary consisted of three elements. On this algorithm the program which showed rather good results for singly connected domains without self-intersections was written. Areas with selfintersections were offered to be broken manually into subareas without selfintersections and to apply the programme for everyone. For not singly connected domains it was offered to make a section, and on it to consider nodes twice, doing bypass so that the area was always, for example, at the left.

8   Conclusion

Thus, a row of approaches and the methods applied in case of electrodynamic simulation in CAD of microwave devices is reflected in the article, examples of their application in programmes of design of radio-electronic systems are reviewed. The majority of them continues to develop, both in theoretical, and in the applicationoriented plan.

In conclusion it is neccesary to emphasize once again the importance of fundamental development, after all theoretical bases found the application in the modern program complexes were supposed 30-40 years ago. Today such researches are financed, as a rule, at the expense of public funds as the specific firm, and all society is interested in the end result not. Therefore attention of a manual of the state is vital for further development of the science. On December 24, 2013 the Government of the Russian Federation approved the Concept of development of mathematical education which represents "a frame of reference on the basic principles, the purposes, tasks and the main directions of development of mathematical education in the Russian Federation".

Implementation of transition to a way of a sustainable development of fundamental science will lead to development of deeper methods of simulation that in turn will give an impetus to a new level of development of automated design engineering systems.

References

1. Kamayev, V.A., Butenko, L.N., Dvoryankin, A.M., Fomenkov, S.A., Butenko, D.V., Davydov, D.A., Zaboleeva-Zotova, A.V., Zhukova, I.G., Kizim, A.V., Kolesnikov, S.G., Kosterin, V.V., Petrukhin, A.V., Naboka, M.V.: Conceptual design. Development and improvement of methods: Monograph (collective). Mechanical Engineering 1, 360 (2005)
2. Kamayev, V.A.: The automated search design. Science Production (1), 3–4 (2000)
3. Kamayev, V.A., Fomenkov, S.A., Petrukhin, A.V., Davydov, D.A.: Architecture of the automated system of conceptual design, SOFIE. Software Products and Systems (2), 30–34 (1999)
4. Fomenkov, S.A., Petrukhin, A.V., Kolesnikov, S.G.: Automation of procedures of formation of information support for the systems of the conceptual design using structured physical knowledge in the form of physical effects. Quality and IPI (CALS) - Technologies (1), 26–29 (2005)
5. Yarovenko, V.A., Fomenkov, S.A.: Formation of the integrated system of processing of the structured physical knowledge with application of multiagentny approach. News of the Volgograd State Technical University 12(7), 126–128 (2009)
6. Davydov, D.A., Fomenkov, S.A.: The automated design of linear structures of the physical principles of action of technical systems. Mechanician (2), 33–35 (2002)
7. Fomenkov, S.A., Korobkin, D.M., Dvoryankin, A.M.: Program complex of representation and use of the structured physical knowledge. Messenger of Computer and Information Technologies (11), 24–28 (2012)
8. Salnikova, N.A.: Structuring of physical knowledge in search designing of tecnical systems. News of the Volgograd State Technical University 17(14), 118–122 (2013)
9. Petrukhin, A.V., Fomenkov, S.A., Kolesnikov, S.G.: Architecture of the automated system of conceptual design of technical objects and technologies with use of the structured description of physical information (SDPI) for network applications. News of Higher Education Institutions. Mechanical Engineering (4-6), 52–56 (1998)
10. Fomenkov, S.A., Kolesnikov, S.G., Dvoryankin, A.M.: Use of the structured physical knowledge for forecasting of new nanotechnical systems. News of the Volgograd State Technical University 13(4(91)), 80–82 (2012)
11. Gopta, E.A., Fomenkov, S.A., Karachunova, G.A.: Automation of process of linear synthesis of the physical principle of action. News of the Volgograd State Technical University 9(11(76)), 116–120 (2010)
12. Fomenkov, S.A., Petrukhin, A.V., Davydov, D.A.: The automated system of conceptual design of technical objects and technologies. Inventors – to Mechanical Engineering (1), 16–20 (2009)
13. Astafurova, O.A.: Travelling-wave antennas on the basis of the edge-dielectric transmission line. Physics of Wave Processes and Radio Systems 10(1), 66–70 (2007)
14. Astafurova, O.A.: Measurement of radiation characteristics of antennas constructed on the basis of edge-line dielectric. Vestnik of Ryazan State Radioengineering University 20, 54–57 (2007)
15. Astafurova, O.A.: Travelling-wave antennas on the basis of the edge-dielectric transmission line. Electromagnetic Waves and Electronic Systems 12(9), 48–53 (2007)
16. Salnikova, N.A., Astafurova, O.A.: Automating exploratory designing complex microwave devices. News of the Volgograd State Technical University, 17(14(117)), 122–126 (2013)

A Study on the OR Decomposition
of Goal-Oriented Analysis Using GSN

Michitaro Okano and Takako Nakatani

Graduate School of Business Sciences, University of Tsukuba,
Otsuka 3-29-1, Bunkyo-ku, Tokyo, Japan

Abstract. In system development, Requirements analysts can apply goal-oriented analysis to requirements elicitation. In goal-oriented analysis, they can apply two types of decomposition: AND decomposition or OR decomposition. In this paper, we study OR decomposition of goal-oriented analysis. In OR decomposition, requirements analysts evaluate sub-goals based on the requirements in order to make their selections. When analysts evaluate sub-goals, they may face two problems. One is the reliability of the evaluation, as it is possible that an analyst might evaluate sub-goals based on sources which are not reliable. The other problem is that the requirements might change after the evaluation.

The purpose of this paper is to propose a method to solve these problems. Our proposed method is that of a visualization method which will establish the reliability of the rationale for the evaluation, and the propose of the visualization method being the re-evaluation and updating of the requirements after evaluation. This proposed method uses KAOS and GSN(Goal Structuring Notation).

In using the proposed method, we discussed "All the people can safely go over road." As a result, we confirmed that the purpose had been accomplished through the utilization of the proposed method.

1 Introduction

In system development, requirements analysts can apply goal-oriented analysis to requirements elicitation. In goal-oriented analysis, the goal of whole system development is a top goal, where the goals are decomposed into sub-goals repeatedly.

When the goal is decomposed, two methods of decomposition can be used: AND decomposition or OR decomposition. In AND decomposition, when all of the sub-goals are achieved, the goal is achieved. In OR decomposition, when one or some of the sub-goals are achieved, the goal is achieved.

For instance, "All the people can safely go over road" is a top goal. At this time, stakeholders are pedestrians, drivers and local government. Each of the stakeholders has requirements. All stakeholder's requirements should be achieved. So it is AND decomposition. Fig. 1 expresses this by using KAOS[1].

On the other hand, there are various means to achieve the goal of "All the people can safely go over road." A crosswalk is set up, a traffic light is set up,

A. Kravets et al. (Eds.): JCKBSE 2014, CCIS 466, pp. 643–657, 2014.

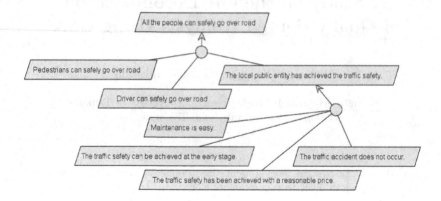

Fig. 1. AND decomposition

a pedestrian bridge is set up and an underpass is set up, and so on. All of the sub-goals do not have to be achieved. Only one or more sub-goals has to be achieved. This is OR decomposition. Fig. 2 expresses this by using KAOS.

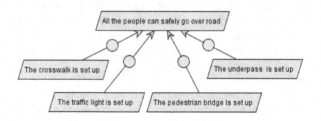

Fig. 2. OR decomposition

If all means are achieved, it becomes safe. However, it contradicts "Traffic safety is achieved at a reasonable price." Those are the requirements of the local government. Therefore, yet if all means are achieved, all requirements are still not satisfied, in which case the means should be evaluated. Table. 1 shows the evaluation of the means.

Table. 1 arranges each stakeholder's requirements within the row, while each means is arranged to the line. Within each cell is shown how much the means contributes to the stakeholder's requirements. For instance, the cell on the left-top of Table. 1shows the evaluation of "Crosswalk" with regard to the requirements "pedestrian safely." The contribution level is described in the cell. The contribution level is as follows. ++: contributes very much. +: contributes. -: obstructs

Table 1. Evaluate requirements and means

	Pedestrian safety	Driver safety	Local government			
			Reasonable price	Easy	Early stage	Not occur
Crosswalk			++	++	+	
Traffic light	+	+	+	+	+	
pedestrian bridge	++	++	-		-	+
underpass	++	++	- -		- -	++

it. - -: obstructs it very much. no filling in: neither the contribution nor the obstruction. The means are selected based on this contribution level. For instance, the traffic light is chosen because there are few obstruction factors.

Thus, the contribution level is important. Therefore, the reliability of the rationale for the evaluation is also important. Because the reliability of the rationale for the evaluation is low, the reliability of the contribution level is low as well. So as a result, the reliability of the selected means also lowers. For instance, if an analist selected options based on hearsay, the evaluation might not be appropriate.

However, when the reliability of the rationale for the evaluation is not described anywhere, we might not notice that the evaluation was undertaken due to an unreliable rationale. In this case, an inappropriate sub-goal might be selected.

In this paper, we propose the application of the visualization method of the reliability of the rationale for the evaluation.

Requirements analysts face with another problem for OR decomposition.

Recently, requirements tend to change frequently, which in turn means that the requirements might be changed after the evaluation. In such cases, consistency is lost between the requirements and the evaluation. So, when the relation between the requirements and the evaluation is not described anywhere, requirements analysts might not notice the loss of consistency.

In this paper, we propose a visualization method to be applied to the re-evaluation step through the updating of requirements after evaluation.

So, our proposed method has the following two focal points:

- Propose a visualization method of the reliability of the rationale for each nodes in a goal model.
- Propose a process of the re-evaluation steps through the updating of requirements after the first evaluation.

We describe the related work in Chapter 2. Then, we propose the method in Chapter 3. The experiment based on the proposed method is conducted in Chapter 4. The experiment is evaluated in Chapter 5. The conclusion is described in Chapter 6.

2   Related Work

2.1   Goal-Oriented Analysis

The goal oriented requirements analysis is the method for analyzing the requirements based on the goal. Famous methods of the goal-oriented requirements analysis are i* and KAOS.

i* [2] is composed of actor, goal, task, soft goal, and resource. The requirements analysis by i* is done based on the dependency.

In KAOS[1], when the goal is decomposed to the sub-goal, the AND decomposition and the OR decomposition are used.

2.2   Owner Partitioned Goal Model (OPGM)

The Owner Partitioned Goal Model[3] is composed of each owner's goal tree. If there are dependencies between the goals within the goal tree, draw a line between the goals, and write a contribution level between these goals.

In this paper, we develop a study that elicits requirements from each owner's goal tree, as well as the means which are evaluated by these requirements.

2.3   Claim in the NFR Framework

L. Chung et al. express the rationale for the evaluation by claim in their NFR framework[4]. They express a contribution level between two goals and the rationale of the contribution level by the claim. In this paper, we write "the reliability" of the rationale of the contribution level, because the reliability of the contribution level is changed by the reliability of the rationale of the contribution level.

For example, the contribution level of "to set up a traffic light" for hreasonable price" is ++, the reliability of this scenario differentiates between a detailed estimate by an expert and a rough estimate by an amateur. The rationale of the contribution level is the same - "by estimate", but they are not the same as "the reliability of the rationale of the contribution level" and "the reliability of the contribution level".

2.4   GSN (Goal Structuring Notation)

GSN[5] is a notation that describes not only goals and other information: i.e. strategy, context and evidence. In the goal structure, GSN can be used to represent the criterion of decomposition using "strategy." The goal and the strategy of its reference to contextual information are described by "context." "evidence" is guaranteed to approve the leaf goal.

Goals are described in the quadrangle. Strategy is described in the diamond. Context is described in a corner round quadrangle, while evidence is described in circle.

3   Proposed Method

The purpose of this study is as follows.

- Propose the visualization method of the reliability of the rationale for the evaluation.
- Propose the visualization method of the re-evaluation step through the updating of requirements after evaluation.

To achieve this purpose, we proposed the following process using GSN.

- Describe the means.
- Describe the stakeholder.
- Describe each stakeholder's requirements.
- Describe the goal tree of whole system with GSN.
- Evaluate and describe "the reliability of the rationale for the evaluation".
- When modifying, paint the modified part in gray.

Using this method, "the reliability of the rationale for the evaluation" is described in the evidence of GSN. And, when the requirements are changed, the changed part becomes gray. The parts of the subordinate position of the gray part should be modified. Hereafter, we explain each procedure in detail.

3.1   Describe the Means

Describe the top goal, and, describe the means under the top goal. A template of the model with KAOS is shown in Fig. 3.

Fig. 3. The goal model of the means with KAOS

3.2   Describe the Stakeholder

Describe the top goal beside Fig. 3, and, describe the stakeholder concerning the top goal under it. Fig. 4 is shown the template of the model with KAOS.

Fig. 4. The goal model of the stakeholders with KAOS

3.3   Describe Each Stakeholder's Requirements

Describe each stakeholder's requirements as a sub-goal of the goal model of the stakeholder. A template for this process with KAOS is shown in Fig. 5.

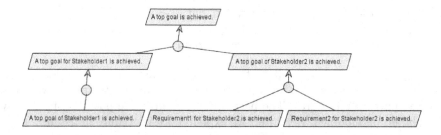

Fig. 5. The goal model of the requirements with KAOS

When the stakeholder has only one requirement, the stakeholder's goal and requirements (i.e. sub-goal) are the same sentences. In this case, the goal of the requirement is repeatedly described in order to associate the goal tree of whole system with GSN and the goal model of the requirements with KAOS. Stakeholder1 in Fig. 5 is in this case.

3.4   Describe the Goal Tree of Whole System Using GSN

Describe the top goal, the means, the stakeholder, and the requirements in one goal tree using GSN. "The goal model of the means with KAOS"(Fig. 3), "The goal model of the stakeholders with KAOS" (Fig. 4), and "The goal model of the requirements with KAOS" (Fig. 5) are described as the GSN's context of each goal. In detail, as follows:

- Describe the strategy "Discussed each means" under the top goal, and the strategy connects the top goal by an arrow. Describe " the goal model of the means with KAOS " (shown in Fig. 3) as a context of the strategy. Describe the means written in Fig. 3 as sub-goals of the strategy.
- Describe the strategy "Discussed each stakeholder" under the goal of the means, and the strategy connects the goal of means by an arrow. Describe " the goal model of the stakeholders with KAOS " (shown in Fig. 4) as a

context of the strategy. Describe the stakeholders written in Fig. 4 as sub-goals of the strategy.

- Strategy "Discussed each requirements" under the goal of the stakeholders, and the strategy connects the goal of the stakeholders by an arrow. Describe " the goal model of the requirements with KAOS " (shown in Fig. 5) as a context of the strategy. Describe the requirements in Fig. 5 as sub-goals of the strategy.
- Describe the evidence in the goal tree of whole system with GSN for each requirement.

Each requirement of each stakeholder of each means corresponds to the evidence in the goal tree of whole system with GSN, and, the cell of the contribution level of Table. 1 corresponds to the evidence in the goal tree of whole system of GSN one by one. Fig. 6 shows this.

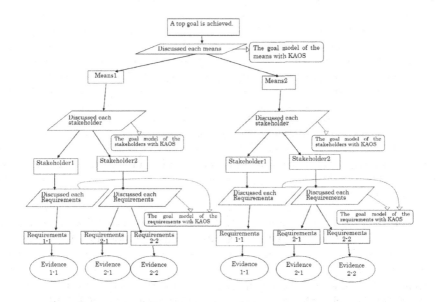

Fig. 6. The goal tree of whole system with GSN

3.5   Evaluate and Describe "the Reliability of the Rationale for the Evaluation"

Fill the reliability of the rationale for the evaluation as the evidence in the goal tree of whole system with GSN. The example of the model is shown in Fig. 6. Each cell of the contribution level in Table. 1 corresponds to an evidence in the goal tree of which the example is shown in Fig. 6.

3.6   When Modifying, Paint the Modified Part in Gray

When an analyst modifies (including deleting and adding goals) the goal model in
KAOS (i.e. Fig. 3,Fig. 4,Fig. 5),paints the context in the goal tree of whole system
with GSN corresponding to modified the goal model in gray. Fig. 7 shows the
goal tree of whole system with GSN modified the goal model of the stakeholder's
with KAOS (Means1 only).

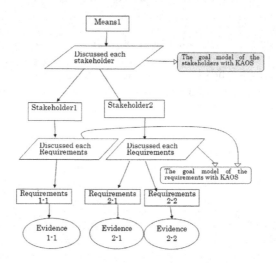

Fig. 7. The goal tree of whole system with GSN modified the goal model of the stakeholder with KAOS (Means1 only)

When the context is painted in gray, look for the strategy corresponding to
it. The sub-goal connected with the strategy must be modified. When the sub-
goal is modified, Change the context from gray to white. and, paint the strategy
connected with the sub-goal in gray.

When the strategy is painted in gray, look for the context corresponding to
it. The goal model with KAOS (i.e. Fig. 3,Fig. 4,Fig. 5) corresponding to the
context must be confirmed and modified if necessary. When the goal model with
KAOS is confirmed, change the strategy from gray to white, and, paint the
context corresponding to the confirmed goal model with KAOS in gray

Fig. 8 is its example. If the goal model of the stakeholders with KAOS is
modified by adding new stakeholder, the goal tree of whole system with GSN is
also modified in order to correspond to the addition of the stakeholder. But still
now, the requirement defined in the goal model of the requirements with KAOS
has not been confirmed yet.

After modified the goal model of the requirements with KAOS, requirements
is modified in the goal tree of whole system with GSN . But still now, The

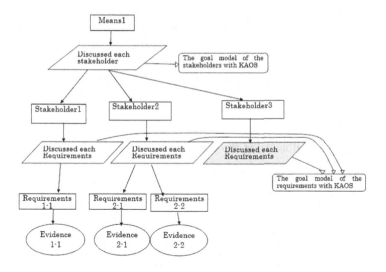

Fig. 8. The goal tree of whole system with GSN added the stakeholder(Means1 only)

requirement does not have yet been evaluated, the icon of an evidence in the goal tree of whole system with GSN is painted in gray.

4   Experimentation

Two experiments were conducted. Experiment 1 assumed "All the people can safely go over road" was a top goal. We applied the proposed method to the goal. In the experiment 2, we added "Neighborhood" as a new stakeholder on the previous experiment.

4.1   Experiment1

The procedure was as follows:

- We described the means.
- We described the stakeholder.
- We described each stakeholder's requirements.
- We described the goal tree of whole system with GSN.
- We evaluated and described "the reliability of the rationale for the evaluation."

First of all, we described the means under the top goal. Fig. 2 shows the result. Next, we described stakeholders. The stakeholders were a pedestrian, a driver, or a local government. Fig. 9 shows the result.

We described requirements for each stakeholder. In Fig. 10, requirements were described as sub-goals of each stakeholder defined in Fig. 9.

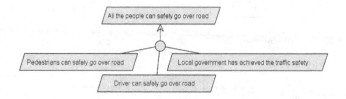

Fig. 9. The goal model of the stakeholders with KAOS in experiment1

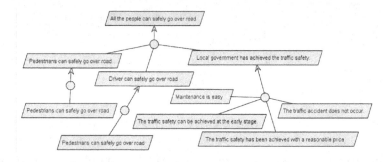

Fig. 10. The goal model of the requirements with KAOS in experiment1

Fig. 10 contains the same content as Fig. 1. However, Fig. 10 describes without omitting requirements even when there is only one requirement of stakeholders such as the pedestrian and/or the driver.

A goal tree of whole system with GSN was developed based on Fig. 2 ,Fig. 9 and Fig. 10. Fig. 11 shows the results. Each evidence in the goal tree corresponds to every leaf goal shown in Fig.11.

We evaluated the reliability of the rationale for the evaluation, we filled the value f the contribution level in Table. 1. Then, the evidence of the reliability of the rationale for the evaluation was filled in the goal tree of whole system with GSN. that is shown in Fig. 12.

Evidence of "Reasonable price", "Easy", and "Early stage" are unreliable rationales, since these nodes have the unreliable words: e.g. "I thinkh, "It seemsh, and so on. The reliability of the contribution level of each node is low and its evaluation is untrustworthy.

4.2   Experiment2

"Neighborhood" was added as a new stakeholder in Fig. 9. The result is shown in Fig. 13.

The context of a requirement of the new stakeholder would be added to the model shown in Fig. 13 and the new icon was painted in gray. The result is shown in Fig. 14.

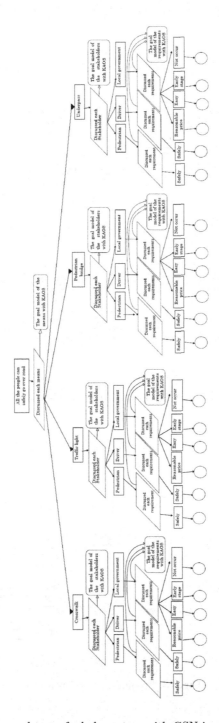

Fig. 11. The goal tree of whole system with GSN in experiment1

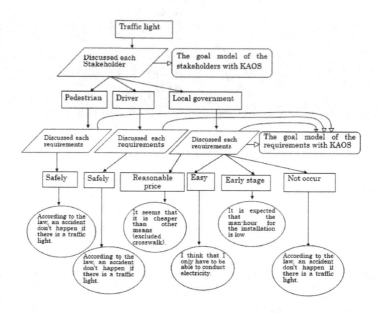

Fig. 12. Filled in the reliability of the rationale (only for the traffic light part)

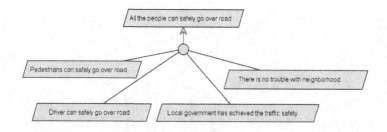

Fig. 13. "Neighborhood" is added

We analyzed the strategy corresponding to the context painted in gray. We could focus on the strategy: "Discussed each stakeholder." Then, we added a sub-goal in the subordinate position of the strategy. Since "Neighborhood" was added as the stakeholder, we added the strategy "Discussed requirements" under the node of "Neighborhood" and painted it in gray. The result is shown in Fig. 15.

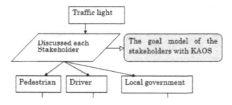

Fig. 14. The goal tree of whole system with GSN (painted gray in stakeholder's context, only different part of Fig. 12)

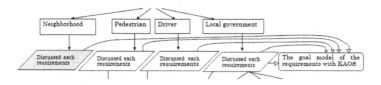

Fig. 15. The goal tree of whole system with GSN (added stakeholder, only different part of Fig.12)

We looked for the context corresponding to the strategy "Discussed requirements" painted in gray and found the context " the goal model of the requirements with KAOS" so, the goal model is modified. The result is shown in Fig. 16. Now, the goal model of the requirements with KAOS was modified, the goal tree of whole system with GSN was modified. The result is shown in Fig. 17.

The context " the goal model of the requirements with KAOS" was painted in gray in Fig. 17. We analyzed the strategy corresponding to the context, we found "Discussed each requirements." As a result, the sub-goal "No trouble" was added at the subordinate position from the strategy. Furthermore, the evidence in the goal tree of whole system with GSN was painted in gray, since it had not yet been evaluated. The result is shown Fig. 18.

Thus, the gray part of GSN shows whether the requirements change is reflected and the necessity of the further analysis.

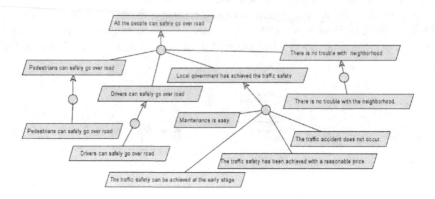

Fig. 16. The goal model of the requirements with that corrected requirements

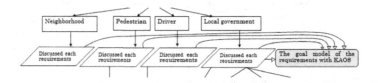

Fig. 17. The goal tree of whole system with GSN that corrected requirements (only different part of Fig.12)

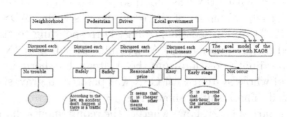

Fig. 18. The goal tree of whole system with GSN of waiting evaluation (only different part of Fig.12)

5   Evaluation

The purpose of our study was as follows:

- Proposal1: Propose a visualization method of the reliability of the rationale for each nodes in a goal model.
- Proposal2: Propose a process of the re-evaluation steps through the updating of requirements after the first evaluation.

As we presented in the experiment1, the reliability of the rationale for the evaluation was visualized by the analysis process of our method. We can conclued that the proposal1 was shown.

Our method shows a process to analyze requirements based on add and/or modified nodes in a goal model. Purpose2 was shown by experiment2. we have to analyze goals correspondent to the gray nodes in the goal tree of whole system with GSN. However, there is a possibility of a mistake or leakage, because our method is performed by manual. In order to avoid these errors, we will develop a tool to support analysts.

6   Conclusion

When evaluating the sub-goals, we face two problems. One is the reliability of the evaluation. The other problem is that the requirements might change after the evaluation. In order to solve the problems we should visualize the reliability of the evaluation with strategy and rationale.

Furthermore, we need to defined the process of the analysis. In this paper, we propose a method to solve these problems. The method had these two focal points. To confirm and to achieve our aim of our proposed method, we applied the method to an example. As a result, we could conclud that the proposed method achieved the purpose.

References

1. van Lamsweerde, A.: Requirements Engineering: From System Goals to UML Models to Software Specifications. Wiley (2009)
2. i* homepage, http://www.cs.toronto.edu/km/istar/
3. Nakatani, T., Fujino, T.: Role and Owner based Business Domain Analysis. In: Proc. of the 12th Asia-Pacific Software Engineering Conference (APSEC 2005), pp. 130–137. IEEE (2005)
4. Chung, L., Nixon, B.A., Yu, E., Mylopoulos, J.: Non– Functional Requirements in Software Engineering. Kluwer Academic Publishers, Boston (1999)
5. Origin Consulting (York) Limited, on behalf of the Contributors "GSN COMMUNITY STANDARD VERSION 1" (2011),
   http://www.goalstructuringnotation.info/documents/GSN_Standard.pdf

Question-Answer Reflections in a Creation of an Experience Base for Conceptual Designing the Family of Software Intensive Systems

Petr Sosnin and Vladimir Maklaev

Ulyanovsk State Technical University, Severny Venetc str. 32,
432027 Ulyanovsk, Russia
sosnin@ulstu.ru

Abstract. This study is bound with a rational management of experience that is used in a design company for developing the software intensive systems (SISs). The approach applied in the study is based on the creation of a precedent-oriented Experience Base the units of which are built by designers when they conceptually solve the project tasks. The specificity of way-of-working used by designers is a reflection of operational space (processes, people and products) on specialized question-answer memory (QA-memory). QA-memory with its cells is intended for registering the conceptual content of reflected units with taking into account the semantics of their textual descriptions. Reflections open the possibility for conceptual experimenting with units of designers' behavior in the instrumental environment based on question-answering. Realization of the approach promotes increasing the efficiency of designing.

Keywords: Conceptual designing, experience base, precedent, question-answering, software intensive system.

1 Introduction

Universally recognized reports [1] of the Standish Group company register very low level of success (about 35%) in designing of software intensive systems (SISs) last twenty years. This problem was one of primary reasons for an attempt of re-founding the software engineering announced in an SEMAT initiative (Software Engineering Methods And Theory initiative) [2].

In normative documents of SEMAT, a way-of-working used by designers is marked as a crucial essence. There, "way-of-working" is defined as "the tailored set of practices and tools used by the team to guide and support their work [2]." Therefore, ways-of-working is very valuable objects of scientific investigations aimed at increasing the successfulness in designing the SISs.

It is our deep belief that investigations of this kind should be fulfilled not only for the subject area of designing the SISs as a whole but in every project of SIS, as well. In the design of a specific SIS, the research of the used way-of-working should be necessarily fulfilled by the team of designers. It should be fulfilled with using of the accessible

A. Kravets et al. (Eds.): JCKBSE 2014, CCIS 466, pp. 658–672, 2014.

experience and can lead to its evolving. Thus, the used way-of-working should include specialized means that support workflows "Interactions with Experience."

Such understanding coordinates with the nature of designing which is impossible without the use of the necessary experience, and it correlates with an empirical tendency in software engineering. The constructive including the real-time works of designers with the necessary experience should facilitate increasing the level of success in designing of SISs.

One direction in the empirical software engineering is bound with a creation and use of Experience Factories and Experience Bases [3]. Our study is aimed at the implementation of such processes in the frame of workflows "Interactions with Experience." The suggested approach is based on reflections of designing the SISs on a question-answer memory that support conceptual experimenting with tasks being solved by designers. Let us notice that question-answer reasoning of designers provides constructive access to their natural experience. The approach is realized in an instrumental environment WIQA (Working In Questions and Answers) [4].

2   Related Works

Mentioned above reports of Standish Group specifies as statistics of successfulness so positive and negative factors that influence on the success of designing. For example, a set of important positive factors includes "Competent Staff" and "Normative Execution." Both of these factors have found their description in standards CMMI-1.3 (Capability Maturity Model Integrated for Development) [5] and P-CMM 2.0 (People Capability Maturity Model) [6] which specify an occupationally mature experience used in software engineering. The first of these standards is focused on specifications of professionally mature processes used in designing the SIS while the second standardizes professional maturity of their developers.

Moreover, called standards specify the continuous improvement of the project activity the importance of which for the success of design companies is declared in ISO/MEK standard 9004-2009: "Managing for the sustained success of an organization – A quality management" [7].

So, processes of successfully designing the SISs should be based on best practices that are specified in standards CMMI-1.3, P-CMM 2.0 and ISO/MEK 9004-2009. These sources of best practices can be extended by a number of publications devoted to specialized areas of the occupational activity. In this set of sources, we mark: Organizational Project Management Maturity Model specifying ways of the perfection of the project management [8]; Business Process Maturity Model opening forms and means of the business-processes perfection (without the accent on the development of the SIS) [9]; Business Intelligence Maturity Model, which focuses on the perfection of practices for intellectual support of the professional activity [10].

The next group of related research includes publications that describe empirical viewpoints on software engineering. In this group, we note the works [11] and [12], which present the domain of empirical software engineering; papers [13] and [2], which define the Goal-Question-Metrics method (GQM-method) and Experience Factory, which includes the Experience Base. All of the indicated studies were taken into account in the offered approach.

One more group of related publications concerns the use of question-answering in computerized mediums, for example, papers [14] and [15]. In this group, the closest research presents experience-based methodology "BORE" [15], in which question-answering is applied as well, but for the other aims, this methodology does not support reflection of operational space on QA-memory.

3   Reflection of Operational Space on Question-Answer Memory

As told above, the proposed approach is aimed at the creation and use of the Experience Base in collective designing of the SIS family. In this case, the designer should operate in operational space the general scheme of which is presented in Fig. 1.

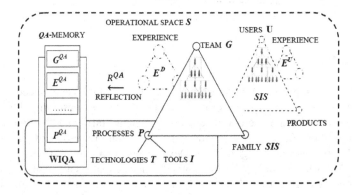

Fig. 1. Operational space

Specificity of named actions is expressed by a reflection R^{QA} of the operational space to QA-memory of the WIQA toolkits. On the scheme, this reflection shows that all what involving in designing of the family of SIS is found their expression as models in the QA-memory. It can be written by the following expression:

$$WW(P, G, E^D, E^{QA}, E^{Pr}, \{SIS_i\}, t) \rightarrow G^{QA}(t+\Delta t) \cup$$
$$\cup E^{QA}(t+\Delta t) \cup P^{QA}(t+\Delta t) \cup SIS^{QA}(t+\Delta t), \tag{1}$$

where WW is a Way-of-Working used by designers and all other symbolic designations corresponds to the names of essences in Fig. 1. Let us additionally note that results of the reflection R^{QA} are dynamic objects, $S^{QA}(t_j)$ models all relations among essences, $E^{QA}(t_j)$ presents models corresponding to the used professional experience E^D which is mastered by members $\{D_k\}$ of the team $G(\{D_k\})$.

At the conceptual stage of designing, means of WIQA are used by designers for the following aims:

- registering of the set of created projects each of which is presented by the tree of its tasks in the real time;

- parallel implementing of the set of workflows $\{W_m\}$ each of which includes subordinated workflows and/or project tasks $\{Z_n\}$;
- pseudo-parallel solving of the project tasks on each workplace in the corporate network;
- simulating the typical units of designers' behavior with using the precedent framework.

These details of operational space are opened on the scheme presented in Fig. 2 where relations with an operational environment are detailed only for one of designers.

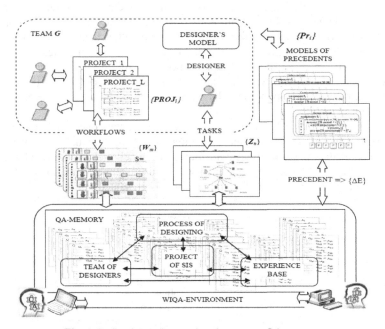

Fig. 2. Reflections of operational space on QA-memory

For the process P_l of designing the project $PROJ_l$, all indicated aims are achieved by the following reflections:

$$WW(P_l)=WW(PROJ_l,\{W_m\}, \{Z_n\}, t)\rightarrow ZP_l^{QA}(t+\Delta t) \cup$$
$$\cup\{ZW_m^{QA}(t+\Delta t)\}\cup\{Z_n^{QA}(t+\Delta t)\}, \tag{2}$$
$$\{Z_n^{QA}(t)\rightarrow Pr_n^{QA}(t+\Delta t)\},$$

where symbol Z underlines that models have a task type, PrQA(t) designates a model of precedent for the corresponding task, RQA(X) indicates that the reflection RQA is applied to the essence or artifact X. For example, RQA(ZQA) designates applying this reflection to the model ZQA of the task Z. In WIQA-environment, the model of such kind is called as "QA-model of the task."

The second scheme includes a designer's model with feedback which shows that, in the proposed approach, a set of precedents mastered by the designer can be used for the creation of the designer model

4   Specificity of QA-memory

QA-memory is specified and materialized for storing the conceptual descriptions of the operational space S in memory cells in the understandable form. For this reason, cells are oriented on registering the textual units in the form of communicative constructions any of which can be divided on "theme" (predictable starting point) and "rheme" (new information) that should receive additional meaning in answering on the corresponding question. Such orientation has led to the solution of using two types of corresponding cells. The cell of the first type is intended for registering the simple question (Q) while the cell of the second type registers the corresponding answer (A). Extracting the theme and rheme from units of the textual description is an important linguistic operation called "actual division." This operation facilitates the process of understanding. Its use corresponds to the dialogic nature of consciousness.

Cells of both types are specified equally because any question includes a part of awaited answer, and any answer includes components of the corresponding question. Therefore, a pair of corresponding cells with a question and answer presents the description unit in details.

QA-memory with its cells is intended for registering the conceptual content of reflected units with taking into account the semantics of their textual descriptions. The necessary semantics is fixed in basic attributes of the cell and in additional attributes which can be added by the individual if it will be useful for a simple object stored in the cell. The potential structure of a simple object is presented in Fig. 3.

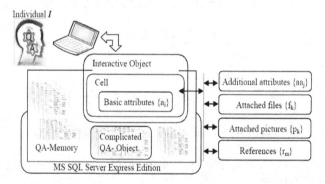

Fig. 3. Specification of the interactive object

A set of basic attributes of the cell helps to register for the stored object its unique identifier (address in QA-memory), type, description, name of the creator, time of storing or last modification, name of the parent object, quantity of "children" and a number of other characteristics. These attributes with their values and the definite subsystem of operations (commands) support interactions of designers with visualized object stored in the corresponding cell.

Additional attributes are attached to the definite simple object for enriching its computerized potential, for example, to enrich semantics of the object representation in QA-memory. It is necessary to note that additional attributes are applied in a number of system processes implemented with the toolkit WIQA. For example, these attributes are applied in following cases:

In workflows that support documenting, one of additional attributes automatically provide replicating the content of "description" in a group of cells marked by this attribute.

The toolkit supports a pseudo-code programming with using the possibilities of QA-memory. More detail, data and operators of such programs are coded in described cells. They found their symbolic expression in attributes "description" of those cells in which the source code of each pseudo-code program is written. Types of data with their features are coded with using the additional attributes. Moreover, basic attributes of cells are inherited by declared data. Operators also inherit features of cells, and their specification can be extended by additional attributes for achieving useful aims. Therefore, pseudo-code programming in the WIQA-environment has differences with other its versions, and our version was called "question-answer programming" (QA-programming) [4].

The designer has the possibility to attach to any cell number of useful files, pictures and references to informational sources for enriching the expressiveness of used cells.

Below, for specifications of question-answer objects (QA-objects) in the QA-memory, a formal grammar GR^{QA} with extended BNF-notations will be used. For example, structures of QA-objects should correspond to the following rules of GR^{QA}:

$$
\left.
\begin{aligned}
&\textit{QA-Memory} = \{QA\text{-}object\}; \\
&\textit{QA-object} = Question,\ ``\leftarrow",\ Answer; \\
&\textit{Question} = Q\,|\,(Q, ``\downarrow", \{Q\}); \\
&\textit{Answer} = A\,|\,(A,\ ``\downarrow",\ \{A\}); \\
&Q = (\{a\},\ \{[aa]\},\ \{[f]\},\ \{[p]\}\ \{[r]\}); \\
&A = (\{a\},\ \{[aa]\},\ \{[f]\})\ \{[p]\}\ \{[r]\}; \\
&a = (address,\ type,\ description,\ time,\ the\ others),
\end{aligned}
\right\} \quad (3)
$$

where "Q" and "A" are typical visualized objects stored in cells of QA-memory, symbol "↓" designates an operation of "subordinating."

Details of the operational space that are presented in Fig. 2 not only indicate reflections of projects on the QA-memory, but it also demonstrates structures which should find their presentations in such memory. For example, structures of objects in QA-memory should correspond to the following rules of GR^{QA}:

$$
\left.
\begin{aligned}
&\textit{PROJ} = ZP; \\
&ZP = (Z,\ ``\downarrow",\ \{Workflows\,\}; \\
&\textit{Workflows} = ZW\,|\,(Workflows,\ ``\downarrow", \{ZW\}); \\
&ZW = \{Task\}; \\
&\textit{Task} = Z\,|\,(Task,\ ``\downarrow",\ \{Z\}); \\
&Z = QA\text{-}model\,|\,(Z,\ ``\downarrow",\ \{QA\text{-}model\}); \\
&\textit{QA-model} = \{QA\}\,|\,(QA\text{-}model,\ ``\downarrow", \{QA\}); \\
&QA = (Question,\ Answer), \\
&\textit{Question} = Q\,|\,(Question,\ ``\downarrow", \{Q\}); \\
&\textit{Answer} = A\,|\,(Answer,\ ``\downarrow", \{A\}),
\end{aligned}
\right\} \quad (4)
$$

where "Z", "Q" and "A" are typical visualized objects stored in cells of QA-memory, symbol "↓" designates an operation of "subordinating." These objects have the richest attribute descriptions [5]. For example, a set of attributes includes the textual description, index label, type of object in the QA-memory, name of a responsible person and the time of last modifying. Any designer can add necessary attributes to the chosen object by the use of the special plug-ins "Additional attributes" (object-relational mapping to C#-classes).

5   Simulation of Project and Practices

As told above, interests of the proposed approach are connected with mastering the professional experience the important part of which is specified in standards CMMI-1.3 and P-CMM 2.0. Therefore, practices of these standards should occupy a central place in the Experience Base. These practices are invariant to their application for designing in definite subject areas consequently they should be adjusted on specificity of definite conditions of designing the SIS. Successful designing demands to widen the invariant practices by practices from the subject area of the designed SIS.

So, the team competence should be enough for the real-time work with following sets of tasks: subject tasks $Z^S = \{Z^S_i\}$ of SIS subject area; normative tasks $Z^N = \{Z^N_j\}$ of technology used by designers; adaptation tasks $Z^A = \{Z^A_j\}$ providing an adjustment of tasks $\{Z^N_j\}$ for solving the tasks $\{Z^S_i\}$; workflow tasks $\{Z^W_m\}$ providing the works with tasks of Z^S-type in workflows $\{W_m\}$ in SIS; workflow tasks $\{Z^W_n\}$ providing the works with tasks of Z^N-type in corresponding workflows $\{W_n\}$ in the used technology; workflow tasks $\{Z^G_p\}$ and $\{Z^G_r\}$ any of which corresponds to the definite group of workflows in SIS or technology.

The indicated diversity of tasks emphasizes that designers should be very qualified specialists in the technology domain, but that is not sufficient for successful designing. Normative tasks are invariant to the SIS domain and, therefore, designers should gain particular experience needed for solving the definite tasks of the SIS subject area. The most part of the additional experience is being acquired by designers in experiential learning when tasks of Z^S-type are being solved. Solving of any task Z^S_i is similar to its expanding into a series on the base of normative tasks. Below, in rules of grammar GR^{QA}, the symbol "Z" will be used in designations for tasks of any kind indicated above.

In conceptual designing the definite SIS, all tasks ZP of its project is divided on two classes. The first class includes the tasks $\{ZPr_s\}$ which are reusable as precedents in the other projects of SISs. The second class ZO comprises the other tasks $\{ZO_v\}$.

For differentiating of these classes in grammar GR^{QA}, the rule for the task

$$
\begin{array}{l}
\textit{Z = QA-model} \mid \textit{(Z, "$\downarrow$", \{QA-model\}),} \\
\textit{should be changed at the following set of rules:} \\
\textit{Z = ZPr} \mid \textit{ZO;} \\
\textit{ZPr = QA-model} \mid \textit{(ZPr, "$\downarrow$", \{QA-model\});} \\
\textit{ZO = QA-model} \mid \textit{(ZO, "$\downarrow$", \{QA-model\}).}
\end{array}
\tag{5}
$$

Implementations of $R^{QA}(Z^{QA})$-reflections are oriented on the use of the framework of the precedent model (FPr), the scheme of which is presented in Fig. 4.

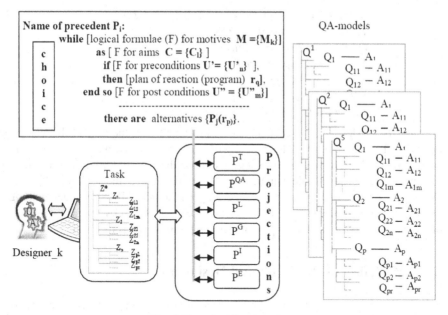

Fig. 4. Precedent framework

The central place in this framework is occupied the logical scheme of the precedent. The scheme explicitly formulates "cause-effect regularity" of the simulated behavior of the designer. The structure of the integrated precedent model FPr is coordinated with the process of task-solving and preparing the solution of the task for the reuse. This structure includes a textual model TPr of the solved task ZPr, its model QAPr in the form of the registered QA-reasoning, the logical formulae LPr of the precedent regularity, a graphical (diagram) representation GPr of the precedent, its pseudo-code model IPr in a form of a pseudo-code program and model which presents its executable code EP.

In the grammar GR^{QA}, the precedent framework is described by the following set of rules:

$$\left. \begin{array}{l} Fpr = \text{``}\rho\text{''}, ZPr; \\ FPr = (Keys, TPr, LPr, QAPr, GPr, IPr, EPr); \\ VFPr = FPr - [QAPr] - [GPr] - [IPr] - [EPr)]; \\ VFPr = \text{``}\pi\text{''}, FPr; \\ Keys = \{Key\}, \end{array} \right\} \quad (6)$$

where "ρ" presents the reflection $R^{QA}(Z^{QA})$ in the operation form, VFP designates a variant or projection of the precedent use, and ⫠ is an operation of the projection. Possibility of projecting is included in the potential of reflections for adjusting the precedent models on conditions of their reuse.

At the level of tasks, the rules of the set (4) can be detailed with the help of the following grammar rules:

$$FPr = ((ZPr, "\downarrow", (TZ, LZ, QAZ, GZ, IZ, EZ)));$$
$$TPr = TZ; \text{ (* specialized Z*)}$$
$$QAPr = QAZ; \text{ (* specialized Z*)}$$
$$LPr = LZ; \text{ (* specialized Z*)} \tag{8}$$
$$GPr = GZ \text{ (* specialized Z*)}$$
$$IPr = IZ \text{ (* specialized Z*)}$$
$$EPr = EZ \text{ (* specialized Z*)}.$$

Thus, the model of any precedent can be presented with the help of the task structure (ZPr, TZ, QAZ, LZ, GZ, IZ, EZ) any unit of which can be detailed in the form of useful QA-model. For the task IZ such model has the type of QA-program written in the specialized pseudo-code language L^{WIQA} embedded to the toolkit WIQA. This language is oriented on QA-memory, and it opens the possibility for understanding of QA-programs of precedents as a kind of their refections on QA-memory. Specificity of the language L^{WIQA} and examples of QA-programs are presented in [4].

6   Modeling of the Team and Designers

As told above, the success of designing the family of SISs depends from occupational maturity of used human resources in the essential measure. Therefore, modeling the team of designers as a whole and members should play an important role in the project activity. In the toolkit WIQA, modeling of the team is supported by the specialized plug-ins "Organizational structure".

First of all, this plug-ins is intended for real-time appointing of tasks to members of the team. This function is demonstrated in general in Fig.5 where one can estimate the scale of the used database.

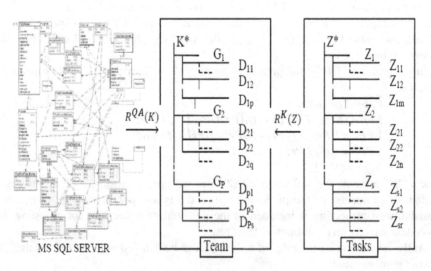

Fig. 5. Organizational structure

The scheme in Fig. 5 also shows the reflection $R^{QA}(K)$ of the team on its question-answer model which opens the possibility for the use of this model in corresponding practices of the standard P-CMM 2.0. The second reflection $R^K(Z)$ presents the distribution of project tasks among designers. In the offered approach, such distribution is implemented with using the personified models of designers (PMD).

As told above, the set of attributes of any Z-object of any tasks' tree includes the personified name of the designer who has been appointed as the solver of the corresponding task. For any designer, it gives the opportunity for extracting from indicated structures following information:

lists of the solved task as for tasks of ZPr-type so for tasks of ZO-type;

- a list of the used precedents models;
- a list of precedents models created by the designer;
- the other professional information reflecting the professional qualification of the designer.

The denoted opportunity is used for creating the PMD framework on the base of precedents' models, which have been successfully applied by the designer in the solved tasks.

The first step of such work is bound with grouping the precedents mastered by the designer. The grouping is oriented on the use of mastered competencies and roles being executed. In the suggested approach, a competency is understood as "a measurable pattern of knowledge, skills, abilities, behaviors, and other characteristics that individual needs to perform work roles or occupational functions successfully" (http://apps. opm.gov/ADT/Content.aspx?page=1-03 &AspxAuto DetectCookie Support=1&JScript=1). The basis of measurability is a set of successfully solved tasks which have been appointed to the designer who used precedents'models.

This understanding has led to the solution of using the precedents' models as units for "measurement" of competencies. Therefore, competencies and roles have been specified in grammar GR^{QA}. Competency K of the designer is expressed structurally by the following grammar rules:

$$
\left.
\begin{array}{l}
K = (Name, Definition, FPr); \\
K = (Name, Definition, \text{``}\gamma 1\text{''}, \{FPr\}); \\
K = (Name, Definition, \text{``}\gamma 2\text{''}, \{K\}); \\
Competencies = \{K\}; \\
Role = (Name, Definition, \text{``}\gamma 2\text{''}, \{K\}); \\
Roles = \{Role\},
\end{array}
\right\} \quad (9)
$$

where **Definition** is a verbal description for the corresponding **Name**, $\gamma 1$ and $\gamma 2$ are operations of grouping.

Rules underline that some competencies can be expressed through a number of subordinated competencies. It helps the use of generalization in brief describing the occupational experience mastered by the designer. The rule for the role fulfills the similar function, but roles are usually used for qualifying the occupational area of designer responsibility, for example, architect, programmer or tester.

Opportunity of the precedent-oriented description of designer competencies opens the question about their systematization. In the management practice of workforces, the job descriptions are widely used. "Job descriptions are written statements that describe the duties, responsibilities, most important contributions and outcomes needed from a position, required qualifications of candidates, and reporting relationship and coworkers of a particular job" (http://humanresources.about.com/od/ jobde-scriptions/ a/develop_job_des.htm).

Documents of this kind can be written as a result of job analysis in different forms. In our case, these documents should be oriented on the personified modeling of any member of the team designing the family of SISs. Furthermore, the personified job description should systematize the measurable competencies of the designer.

Traditionally, a normative text of the job description (JD) includes the following sections: Job title; General summary of job; Key relationships; Education and Experience (Minimum qualifications); Knowledge, skills and abilities; Principal duties and essential functions; Major challenges; Physical, mental, sensory requirements; and Working conditions.

In the section structure, the italic indicates elements the main content of which can be presented by names of competencies and references to models of precedents. For this reason, JD-document has been chosen as a kernel of the PMD. This choice requires the use of reflecting the documents on the QA-memory.

In the WIQA-environment, the work with documents is supported with using their QA-patterns, which should be previously developed and stored in the specialized library. The typical model of each document is presented by two its patterns. The first pattern reflects the document structure and the second defines its printed version. The specialized plug-ins "Documenting" provides adjusting of both patterns on conditions of their use.

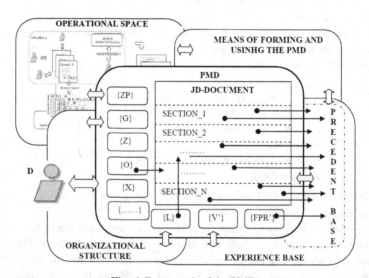

Fig. 6. Framework of the PMD

As told above, the JD-documents are created in the process of the job analysis. In the described case, one stage of this analysis should be aimed at forming the list of competencies. Such work should be implemented with using the generalization for the net of competencies. The net of competencies should be reflected in JD-documents without details.

In the proposed approach, JD is used as a kernel of the personified model of the designer because JD-components have the constructive references on models of precedents stored in the Experience Base. The framework of the PMD with such a kernel is presented in Fig 6.

The scheme generally demonstrates the PMD in the context of its forming and creating. In grammar G^{QA}, the PMD is described by the following rules:

$$
\left.
\begin{array}{l}
PMD = (DName,\ JD,\ \{List\ of\ Features\}); \\
JD = \{Section\}; \\
Section = Text\ \text{-}\{[Role]\}\ \text{-}\{[K]\}\text{-}\ \{[O]\}\ \text{-}\ \{[L]\}; \\
List\ of\ Features = (Type,\ \{F\},\ \{[AF]\}); \\
F = ZP\ |\ G\ |\ Z\ |\ O\ |\ L\ |\ V'\ |\ FPR'; \\
AF = Additional\ Feature,
\end{array}
\right\}
\qquad (10)
$$

where units of O-type present the results of estimating the designer actions, units of L-type registers the results of experiential learning, lists of FPR' indicates the precedents' models built by the designer and V'-units are the references on the other values that are created by one. Lists $\{X\}$ and $\{....\}$ indicate that PMD is opened for the extension.

The PMD is not separated from its use for solving a set of tasks connected with the management of human resources including the management of workforces. The representative system of such tasks is described and specified in the standard P-CMM 2.0. Furthermore, this standard defines the steps of continuous improving the work with human resources. The called standard is aimed at solving the following main classes of tasks:

- rational forming the project team;
- managing the efficient use of workforces;
- continuous improving the project team.

7   Experience Base

In the proposed approach, models of precedents are used for modeling of assets applied by the team in conceptual designing the family of SISs. Any asset is understood from the viewpoint of its application, and; therefore, it binds with the corresponding task of ZPr-type.

Assets are divided on classes of different types the specifications of which are described by a set of attributes including "the name of type", "description", "kind of precedent version VFPr used for its storing in QA-memory" and the others. Some of the types specify the models of precedents for human resources, for example, they should include the type that specifies the personified models of designers.

Potential of L^WIQA is sufficient for QA-modeling and QA-programming the assets of following kinds: previous projects, valuable project solutions, prototypes, documents, interface samples, schemes of reports, standards, frameworks, guides, patterns, samples of different types, schemes of modeling, structure of the software, packages of the source code, tools, platforms, infrastructure and other valuable units.

Models of assets are registered in the catalog of Experience Base and allocated in the specialized area of QA-memory (Fig. 7).

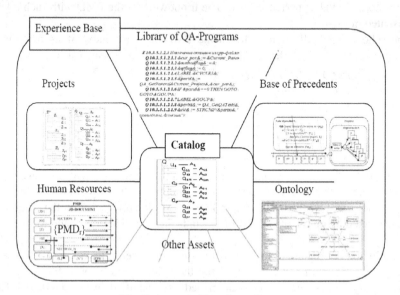

Fig. 7. Assets in Experience Base

It is necessary to notice that only one part of assets is placed in Precedent Base. The greater part of assets are stored in corresponding libraries where they are presented in forms of precedent projections. As told above, components stored in QA-memory can be bound with the attached files which are placed in corresponding libraries too. One of such libraries includes program written in C# that can be used in QA-programming.

The use of a large set of different assets (with orientation on precedents) leads to questioning about means of their systematization. In the describe case, this function is fulfilled by the project ontology, concepts of which are also stotred in QA-memory.

Conclusion

The approach described in this paper is aimed at increasing the level of success in conceptual designing the family of SISs in the project company. Offered means support the constructive work with the occupational maturity of business processes and workforces. It is achieved by the real-time creation and use of Experience Base that accumulate models of assets used in the company.

Specificity of the approach is defined by the reflection of the operational space of conceptual designing on QA-memory. Such reflection opens the possibility for effective modeling the experience used by designers in tasks being solved.

QA-memory opens the opportunity for simulating the using experience in the form of intellectually processed precedents. Such models of precedents are combined in the Experience Base the content of which can be used in the real-time designing. It helps the designer to interact with the used experience and precedents' models in coordination.

Furthermore, reflection of designers' activity on QA-memory allows to conduct conceptual experiments with solutions of tasks. Conceptual experimenting of such type is similar to mental experimenting. Conceptual experiments can be conducted in forms of QA-modeling and QA-programming that are aimed at research of designer actions.

Instrumental conditions of designer actions help to register the used precedents, and that allows revealing the precedents mastered by the designer and estimating the occupational maturity of their implementation. In the proposed approach, such opportunity was used for the choice of precedents' models as units for "measuring" the competencies of the designer.

References

1. El Emam, K., Koru, A.G.: A Replicated Survey of IT Software Project Failures. IEEE Software 25(5), 84–90 (2008)
2. Jacobson, I., Ng, P.-W., McMahon, P., Spence, I., Lidman, S.: The Essence of Software Engineering: The SEMAT Kernel. Queue (10) (2012)
3. Basili, V.R., Lindvall, M., Costa, P.: Implementing the experience factory concepts as a set of experience bases. In: Proc. of SEKE, pp. 102–109 (2001)
4. Sosnin, P.: Scientifically Experimental Way-of-Working in Conceptual Designing of Software Intensive Systems. In: Proc. of the IEEE 12th International Conference on Intelligent Software Methodologies, Tools and Techniques (SoMeT), pp. 43–51 (2013)
5. Capability Maturity Model Integrated for Development, Version 1.3 (2010), http://www.sei.cmu.edu/reports/10tr033.pdf (2014)
6. Curtis, B., Hefley, B., Miller, S.: People Capability Maturity Model (P-CMM) Version 2.0. Technical Report CMU/SEI-2009-TR-003 P (2009)
7. Managing for the sustained success of an organization – A quality management, ISO 9004:2009 (2009), http://www.iso.org/iso/catalogue_detail?csnumber=41014
8. Robertson, K.: Project Management Maturity Model (2014), http://www.klr.com/white_papers/pdfs/pm_maturity_model.pdf
9. Roglinger, M., Poppelbuth, J., Becker, J.: Maturity models in business process management. Business Process Management 18(2), 328–346 (2012)
10. Lahrmann, G., Marx, F., Winter, R., Wortmann, F.: Business Intelligence Maturity Models: An Overview, http://www.alexandria.unisg.ch/Publikationen/72444/L-en
11. Jeffery, D.R., Scott, L.: Has twenty-five years of empirical software engineering made a difference. In: Proc. 2nd Asia-Pacific Software Engineering Conference, pp. 539–549 (2002)
12. Sjoberg, D.I.K., Dyba, T., Jorgensen, M.: The future of empirical methods in software engineering research. In: Proc. of Workshop Future of Software Engineering, pp. 358–378. IEEE, Minneapolis (2007)

13. Southekal, P.H., Levin, G.: Formulation and empirical validation of a GQM-based measurement framework. In: Proc.of the 11th International Symposium on Empirical Software Engineering and Measurement, Banff, Canada, pp. 404–413 (September 2011)
14. Webber, B., Webb, N.: Question answering. In: Clark, F., Lappin (eds.) Handbook of Computational Linguistics and Natural Language Processing, pp. 630–655. Willey-Blackwells, Oxword (2010)
15. Henninger, S.: Tool Support for Experience-based Software Development Methodologies. Advances in Computers 59, 29–82 (2003)

Support Method to Apply User Interface Guidelines to GUIs Using Guideline Templates

Junko Shirogane[1], Kazuya Sugiuchi[2], Hajime Iwata[3], and Yoshiaki Fukazawa[2]

[1] Tokyo Woman's Christian University, Japan
[2] Waseda University, Japan
[3] Kanagawa Institute & Technology, Japan

Abstract. To realize layout consistency and operability of Graphical User Interfaces (GUIs), user interface guidelines (UI guidelines) are common. Currently, UI guidelines vary by platform (e.g., operating systems and desktop systems) and even by company. Although UI guidelines must be applied to GUIs, applying them is burdensome for software developers because UI guidelines contain many detailed guideline elements. To reduce this burden, we previously proposed a method to apply user interface guidelines to GUIs. However, this method targets specific UI guidelines. Hence to apply diverse UI guidelines, unified descriptions of guideline elements and mechanisms to automatically apply guideline elements to GUIs must be developed. In this paper, we propose templates to describe guideline elements of various UI guidelines and a method to automatically apply guideline elements to GUIs. The proposed method can support the development of new guideline elements.

Keywords: GUI, User Interface Guideline, Template, Generation.

1 Introduction

To realize highly usability, the layouts and operability of Graphical User Interfaces (GUIs) must be unified, which is called "consistency" and is an important usability issue [1][2]. Consistency should be realized not only within a software package, but also between software packages because consistency allows end users to operate a software package using their experiences.

To realize consistency, it is effective to develop GUIs along with the user interface guidelines (UI guidelines). UI guidelines have many detailed guideline elements (detailed definitions that should be applied to GUIs) related to consistency issues, such as window layout, usage strategies of widgets (e.g., buttons and text fields) for input/output items, widget size, widget fonts, color usages, terminologies, strategies for shortcut key assignments, etc. In many cases, UI guidelines are developed for platforms (e.g., operating systems and desktop systems) or for companies. Examples of UI guidelines are Windows User Experience Interaction Guidelines [3] (hereafter, Windows guidelines), Mac OS X Human Interface Guidelines [4] (hereafter, Mac guidelines), and GNOME Human Interface Guidelines [5] (hereafter, GNOME guidelines). Windows and Mac guidelines are

A. Kravets et al. (Eds.): JCKBSE 2014, CCIS 466, pp. 673–687, 2014.

for operating systems of Microsoft Windows and Apple Mac OS X, respectively. GNOME guidelines are for the GNOME desktop environment.

Although GUI consistency can be realized by applying these UI guidelines, UI guidelines have numerous and very detailed guideline elements. To apply these guideline elements to GUIs, software developers must confirm the applicability of every guideline element to every widget, which is expensive and burdensome. Additionally, current software packages often must be able to run on several platforms, and it is necessary to develop GUIs for every platform by applying platform-specific UI guidelines. To resolve these issues, we have previously proposed a method to automatically apply UI guidelines to GUIs [6][7] in which guideline elements are prepared for specific formats in advance. Then the elements are analyzed and the source programs of GUIs are generated.

Although we were able to confirm the effectiveness of our method, the target UI guidelines are limited because the describable guideline elements must be prepared in advance. This means that software developers can reduce costs and burdens in applying the prepared UI guidelines, but they cannot apply other UI guidelines.

In this paper, we describe our current method to support various UI guidelines. We define formats to describe guideline elements as "guideline templates". Software developers describe guideline elements using guideline templates. Then the described guideline elements are analyzed and the source programs of GUIs are generated. Using our new method, various UI guidelines can be applied, reducing the costs and burden on software developers.

This paper is organized as follows. Section 2 compares other research on UI guidelines and layout arrangements. UI guidelines are summarized in Section 3. Section 4 describes the contributions of our method, while the proposed templates are detailed in Section 5. Section 6 shows how to generate source programs of GUIs using the proposed templates, and Section 7 evaluates the proposed method. Finally, section 8 concludes this paper.

2   Related Works

Multiple works have investigated UI guidelines and layout arrangements.

Kalawa et al. have proposed a method to reuse user interfaces (UI) across devices [8]. This method consists of six steps. First, the input UIs are described as abstract UI structure models. Second, equivalent widgets in the input UIs are selected from GUI library of the target platform. Third, ranking of the selected widgets are determined based on UI guidelines of the target platform. Fourth, UIs based on the guidelines are proposed as the reused UIs. Then, the proposed UIs are customized by users. Finally, the executable code of reused UIs is generated. Using this method, UIs can be easily ported to other platforms. However, detailed applying guideline strategies and applicable guideline elements are not mentioned.

Feuerstack et al. have proposed a method to generate a GUI layout based on models [9]. Layout information is analyzed using several models, such as existing user interface design models (e.g., task trees, dialog models, abstract user interface models, concrete user interface models, domain models, and context models). In these models, software developers must determine the layout characteristics and specify the layout statement. Then based on the layout statements, the GUI layout is generated as a box-based layout. Widgets are arranged in boxes, which are created by dividing the arrangement area of widgets in a window. Because this method can be used with existing models, software developers do not need to create descriptions and models to arrange the GUI layout. However, layout consistencies realized by UI guidelines are not supported.

Sajedi et al. have surveyed many UI guidelines, analyzed the contributions of guideline elements to usability, and proposed many improvements to GUI guidelines [10], such as color usages. Although color is a powerful tool, its use must be considered strategically because 10% of men and a few percentage of women have color impairments, making it difficult to recognize certain colors. Additionally, monitors may distort the color. When more than five colors are used, end users may have difficultly recognizing differences in colors. Additionally, they discussed user controls, users' memories, error handling, etc. Although this survey and indications are important, concrete strategies to apply UI guidelines to GUIs are not mentioned.

3   User Interface Guidelines

UI guidelines are developed to unify window layout, widget usage, GUI operability, etc. Examples include Windows, Mac, and GNOME guidelines. When developing a software package, the appropriate UI guidelines are selected and applied. For example, when a software package runs on Windows, Windows guidelines are applied.

UI guidelines include numeral elements that define detailed window layouts and operability. Below are some examples.

Shortcut Keys. Shortcut keys are used to operate GUIs via key combinations on a keyboard. Strategies of key assignments and common shortcut keys are defined in UI guidelines.

Widgets. End users operate widgets in a window visually. UI guidelines describe the basic behavior of widgets and define usage strategies, sizes, and arrangements.

Texts. Widgets contain texts, which are defined based on font, color, format, text size, and suggestions of sentences.

Menus. Behaviors, layout, and orders of menus, drop down menus, and popup menus are defined.

Windows. There are different types of windows. The behavior and usage strategy is defined for each type.

4   Features of Our Method

No Limitation of Available UI Guidelines. Our previous method [6][7] was limited to certain UI guidelines, and applying other UI guidelines or adding new guideline elements was difficult. The method proposed here uses templates to describe guideline elements, which are applied automatically to generate GUIs. Hence, the available UI guidelines are limitless, and new guideline elements can be easily added.

Facilitation of Changing UI Guidelines Applied to a Software Package. Because each platform has its own requirements, GUIs of a software package should be developed by applying UI guidelines of the corresponding platforms. When a software package running on a platform is ported to another platform, the applied UI guidelines to GUIs must be changed, which requires major modifications of the source programs.

In our method, the source programs of GUIs and UI guidelines described by the templates are inputted, then GUIs that apply the inputted UI guidelines are generated. Consequently, even if GUIs are developed along with certain UI guidelines, the applied UI guidelines can be easily changed.

Cost Reductions by GUI Generation. UI guidelines include numerous guideline elements, and software developers must confirm whether each guideline element is applicable to each widget, window, etc. This confirmation and modification process of the source programs is extremely burdensome.

Using our method, the confirmations and generation of the source programs are automatic. Although some guideline elements require additional input and confirmations to software developers, the burden of the confirmations and modifications can be substantially reduced.

Clarifications of Guideline Elements. Because UI guidelines are described in a natural language, ambiguous guideline elements exist (e.g., "The label name of a menu item should not be long."). These guideline elements confuse software developers and can be applied by different criteria.

Our method requires that all guideline elements are described by templates. To process guideline elements systematically, guideline elements must be described by clarifying the criteria, resulting in uniform criteria.

5   Templates of Our Method

Our method has three steps: determine the templates, analyze the described guideline elements, and generate the source programs of the GUIs.

5.1   Template Definitions

To apply guideline elements to GUIs automatically, "guideline templates" are developed to describe guideline elements. In addition to generating source programs, widgets associated with the guideline elements must be associated with concrete widgets in the target programming language. Thus, we prepared "programming language templates" for these associations. Guideline templates are independent of the programming language templates. Consequently, when the source programs of GUIs are generated with different programming languages, the guideline templates do not have to be modified.

Guideline Templates. Guideline templates are formats to describe guideline elements. The guideline elements must be classified into categories with regard to the targets, which are called "element categories" (e.g., shortcut keys and menu labels). When guideline elements in an element category are applied, the values of specific methods of widgets associated with the element category are checked. The specific methods are defined using the programming templates. Software developers can define the element categories. Items of the guideline templates include:

ID: The number of identifying each guideline element

Type: The type of the guideline element (There are three types.)

>   **auto:** Guideline elements can be applied automatically
>   **add:** Additional input from software developers is required to apply the guideline element
>   **confirm:** Guideline elements cannot be applied systematically, and the software developers must confirm the results

Windows: The value defined in Windows guidelines

Mac_OS_X: The value defined in Mac guidelines

GNOME: The value defined in GNOME guidelines

Original: The value defined in other UI guidelines (except above three kinds of UI guidelines)

Argument The additional value to compare with the method arguments of widgets (If necessary, plural values can be defined)

The value patterns of "Windows", "Mac OS X", "GNOME", and "Original" are prepared by surveying existing UI guidelines. For example, "n_words" indicates that the number of words in a sentence should be just "n". "not null" indicates that the value should not be empty. "$n-$" indicates that the number of items should be equal to or less than "n".

Tables 1 and 2 show examples of described guideline elements. We prepared the described guideline elements of Windows, Mac, and GNOME guidelines. If necessary, software developers describe the "Original" item.

Table 1 represents a guideline element to suggest the number of words in a menu item. Because this guideline element cannot be applied systematically, the "Type" is "confirm". Words must be modified by considering their meanings when this guideline element is not satisfied. In this case, Windows and Mac guidelines define the number of words in a menu item as one word, while software developers define it as equal to or less than two words.

Table 2 represents guideline elements for shortcut key assignments. The guideline element of ID "1" indicates the undo shortcut and ID "2" indicates the redo shortcut. For the undo shortcut, "Ctrl + Z" is the shortcut key in the Windows guidelines, GNOME guidelines, and the software developers' definitions, while "Command + Z" is in the Mac guidelines. For the redo shortcut, "Ctrl + Y" is the shortcut key in the Windows guidelines, "Command + Shift + Z" is in the Mac guidelines, and "Ctrl + Shift + Y" is in the GNOME guidelines.

Table 1. Example of guideline elements for the number of words in menus (Element category: MenuWord)

ID	Type	Windows	Mac_OS_X	GNOME	Original	Argument
1	confirm	1_words	1_words	1_words	2_words-	

Table 2. Example of guideline elements for shortcut keys (Element category: ShortcutKey)

ID	Type	Windows	Mac_OS_X	GNOME	Original	Argument
1	auto	Ctrl + Z	Command + Z	Ctrl + Z	Ctrl + Z	Undo
2	auto	Ctrl + Y	Command + Shift + Z	Ctrl + Shift + Z	Ctrl + Y	Redo

Programming Language Templates. Programming language templates are used to convert guideline elements described by guideline templates into concrete widgets in a programming language. Details and associations to element categories are described. Items of the programming language templates are described below. Hereafter, each entry described in the programming language templates is called a "programming element".

ID. The number identifying each programming element
Name. The name of each programming element assigned by software developers (This should be assigned so that applied guideline elements can be understood.)
Keyword. The method or class name of a widget applying UI guidelines
Parent. The method or class name that should be checked together with the method or class of "Keyword" item
Relation. The element category applied to the widget

Table 3 shows examples of the described programming elements by the programming language templates. We prepared programming elements of the Swing packages of the Java programming language. When source programs of GUIs for other GUI packages and programming languages must be generated, software developers must describe.

Table 3. Examples of programming elements described by programming language templates

ID	Name	Keyword	Parent	Relation
1	menu_words	JMenuItem		MenuWord
2	shortcut	setAccelerator	JMenuItem	ShortcutKey

The programming elements in this table represent JMenuItem widgets for the Swing packages of the Java programming language. ID "1" is to check the number of words in a menu item. This programming element indicates that number of words can be checked by the constructors of the JMenuItem widgets. ID "2" is to assign shortcut keys. This programming element indicates that shortcut keys can be assigned by modifying the arguments of the "setAccelerator" method in the JMenuItem widgets.

5.2 Target of the Guideline Elements

Our guideline templates cannot describe all guideline elements because our method targets guideline elements that can be checked or applied systematically.

For example, because the guideline element "Number of check boxes in one group should be equal to or less than 10" in the Windows guidelines can be checked systematically, our templates can describe this element. In contrast, the guideline element "A group of check boxes should be reconsidered so that group boxes may be used" in the Windows guidelines is vague, and our template cannot represent the target of this element. Additionally, the guideline element "Check boxes should not be used for running commands" in the Windows guidelines requires that the program logic be checked. Guideline elements that require logic to be checked are not the target of our templates.

6 GUI Generation

In our method, applying UI guidelines generates, analyzes, and modifies the source programs of GUIs. Software developers determine the target UI guidelines ("Windows", "Mac OS X", "GNOME", or "Original" of guideline elements) as well as the source programs. If the specific UI guidelines are applied to the inputted GUIs, software developers specify the UI guidelines. Our method allows some or all of the UI guidelines to be applied. Figure 1 shows the flow of process and data in our method.

In this section, the window in Fig. 2 is used as an illustrative example. Windows guidelines are applied to this example window.

6.1 Source Program Analysis

GUI items used to specify applicable guideline elements are extracted from the inputted source programs. This is performed using JavaCC (Java Compiler Compiler) [11]. Extracted GUI items include:

- Widget types
- Widget variable names
- Method names used by widgets
- Argument values of methods
- Locations of the above GUI items in the source programs

Table 4 shows an example of part of the extracted GUI items from the source programs in Fig. 2.

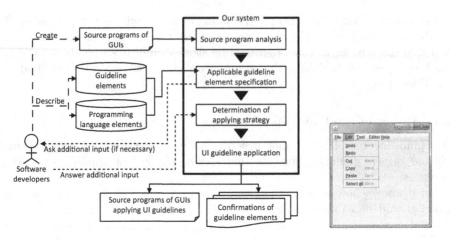

Fig. 1. Process and data flow in our method   **Fig. 2.** Example window

Table 4. Examples of GUI item extraction

Widget variable name	Widget type	Method name	Argument value	Location
	JMenu			6
fileMenu		JMenu	Edit	18
		setMnemonic	E	19
	JMenuItem			6
undoMenuItem		JMenuItem	Undo	22
		setMnemonic	U	23
		setAccelerator	Ctrl + Z	24
	JMenuItem			6
redoMenuItem		JMenuItem	Redo	27
		setMnemonic	R	28
frame		JFrame		8
		JFrame		11

6.2   Applicable Guideline Element Specification

Based on the extracted GUI items, guideline elements applicable to widgets are determined. Widget types in the extracted GUI items are compared to "Keyword" and "Parent" items in the programming elements. The element category of the UI guideline of "Relation" item in the programming elements is applicable to guideline elements for the corresponding widgets.

Figure 3 shows an example of determining applicable guideline elements. The upper table shows example programming elements, while the lower table shows example extracted GUI items. The "Parent" item for ID "2" in the programming elements is "JMenuItem". In the extracted GUI items, the widget types with widget variable names "undoMenuItem" and "redoMenuItem" are "JMenuItem". These two widgets correspond to ID "2" in the programming elements.

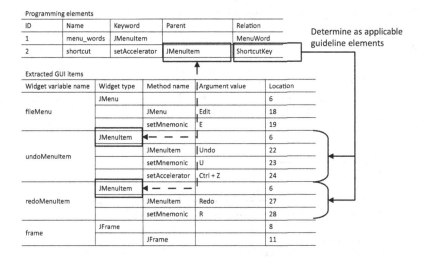

Fig. 3. Example of determining applicable guideline elements

Thus, "ShortcutKey" of the "Relation" item is determined as an applicable guideline element.

6.3   Determination of Applying Strategy

For the guideline elements applied to widgets, concrete strategies are determined. When there are plural guideline elements in an element category of the applicable guideline elements, the values of the specified UI guidelines by software developers and "Argument" in the guideline elements are compared to the values of "Argument value" in the extracted GUI elements. Then concrete guideline elements applied to the target widgets are identified. When there is only one guideline element in an element category, the guideline element is applied to all target widgets.

Figure 4 shows an example with plural guideline elements in an element category. For ID "1" of the guideline elements, the value of "Ctrl + Z" of "Windows" can correspond to the widget variable name "undoMenuItem" in the extracted UI items. For ID "2" in the guideline elements, the argument "Redo" of the argument can correspond to the widget variable name "redoMenuItem" in the extracted GUI items. Thus, ID "1" and "2" of the guideline elements are applied to widgets of "undoMenuItem" and "redoMenuItem", respectively.

After identifying applicable guideline elements, the values of the "Argument value" item in the associated method to the target element categories in the extracted GUIs are compared to the values of the target UI guidelines in the guideline elements. Associations between the methods of widgets and the element categories are defined in the programming elements. If the values do not satisfy the guideline element, whether to apply these values must be determined. Our method uses three strategies: "automatically apply", "require additional input", and "confirm". In the rest of this section, the Mac guidelines are used in the examples.

Automatically Apply. In this strategy, guideline elements are automatically applied and source programs are generated. The type "auto" in the guideline element is associated with this strategy.

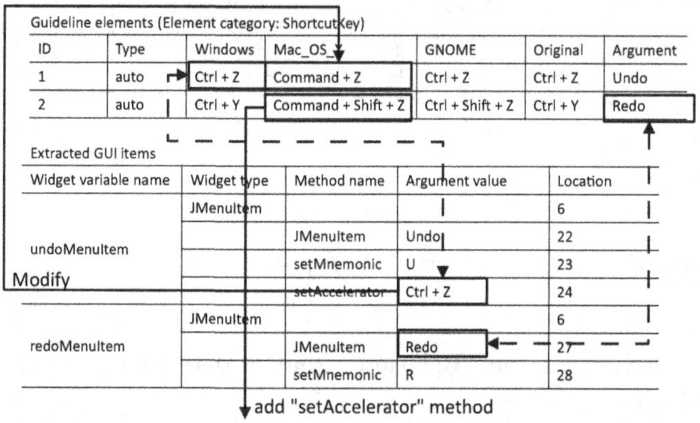

Fig. 4. Example to determine automatic modifications of the source programs

To determine the modification code and the modification line numbers of the source programs, the extracted GUI items are compared to the applicable guideline elements. According to section 6.2, the element category "ShortcutKey" of the guideline elements is applicable to the "undoMenuItem" and "reduMenuItem" widgets. In the element "ShortcutKey" category, the target to apply guideline elements is "setAccelerator" (Table 3). Thus, for the "undoMenuItem" widget, the argument value must be modified because the argument value is already set to the "setAccelerator" method. For the "redoMenuItem" widget, because the "setAccesslerator" method is not used, a method must be added to the source programs. Figure 4 shows an example in which the Mac guidelines are applied.

Require Additional Input. In this strategy, software developers provide additional input, and then guideline elements are automatically applied and the source programs are generated using the additional input. The "add" type in the guideline element is associated with this strategy.

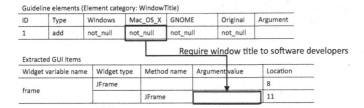

Guideline elements (Element category: WindowTitle)

ID	Type	Windows	Mac_OS_X	GNOME	Original	Argument
1	add	not_null	not_null	not_null	not_null	

Require window title to software developers

Extracted GUI items

Widget variable name	Widget type	Method name	Argument value	Location
frame	JFrame			8
		JFrame		11

Fig. 5. Example of additional input required

Figure 5 shows an example of the guideline element to set window titles. Although the guideline element in the Mac guidelines states that the window titles should not be empty, the window title is not set in the extracted GUI items. Thus, software developers must input the window title as an additional item.

Confirm. In this strategy, source programs are not modified, but confirmations for software developers are generated. The type "confirm" in the guideline elements is associated with this strategy.

Figure 6 shows an example of the guideline element for the number of words in a menu. Although the label names of menus should be just one word according to the guideline element in the Mac guidelines, the number of words in the "helpMenu" widget in the extracted GUI items is two. Thus, software developers must determine and modify the label names.

Guideline elements (Element category: MenuWord)

ID	Type	Windows	Mac_OS_X	GNOME	Original	Argument
1	confirm	1_words	1_words	1_words	2_words-	

Confirm and modify by software developers

Extracted GUI items

Widget variable name	Widget type	Method name	Argument value	Location
helpMenu	JMenu			8
		JMenu	Editor Help	11

Fig. 6. Example of confirmation

6.4   UI Guideline Application

Finally, the source programs of GUIs are generated based on the determined strategies described in section 6.3 by modifying the inputted source programs. For the guideline elements in the "confirm" strategy, concrete confirmations, which include GUI items, line numbers of the target widgets in the source programs, and guideline elements that should be applied, are generated. If necessary, software developers can modify the generated source programs based on these confirmations. Figure 7 shows an example of the modified GUI that applies all modifications mentioned in section 6.3.

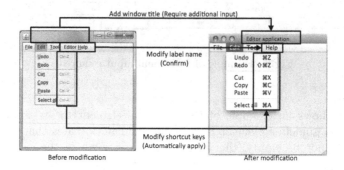

Fig. 7. Example of modified GUI

7   Evaluation

To confirm the effectiveness of our method, two types evaluations are performed. One verifies whether our guideline templates can describe guideline elements and the other assesses the appropriateness of applying guideline elements.

7.1   Capabilities of Describing Guideline Elements

We counted how many guideline elements can be described using the guideline templates for Windows, Mac, and GNOME guidelines. Guideline elements are classified into applying targets (such as widgets, text, etc.). When a guideline element can be classified into plural targets, it is counted as one guideline element.

Table 5. Results of guideline elements described using guideline templates

Applying target	Guideline	Target	Not target	Possible (target)	Possible (not target)
Controls	382	64	318	64	7
Commands	110	26	84	26	2
Messages	84	4	80	4	0
Interaction	172	42	130	42	0
Windows	177	19	158	19	0
Visuals	74	20	54	20	0

Table 5 shows an example using the Windows guideline results. "Applying target" indicates the classifications of the guideline elements in the Windows guidelines. The guideline elements of operations and usage situations for check boxes and buttons are classified into "Controls", while menus and tool bars are classified into "Commands". Errors and warnings are classified into "Messages", operations of a keyboard and a mouse are classified into "Interactions", window managements are classified into "Windows", and visual designs are classified into "Visuals". "Guideline" indicates the number of all guideline element classified into the "Applying target". "Target" indicates the number of guideline elements that are considered as the target guideline elements using guideline templates, while "Not target" indicates the number of guideline elements that are not considered. "Possible (target)" indicates the number of guideline elements of the "Target", which can be described using guideline templates, while "Possible (not target)" indicates the number of non-target guideline elements that can be described.

Most of the "Not target" guideline elements were related to the behavior of the program. An example was "In case that process does not go ahead, the progress bars should be colored yellow". Although the color settings can be described using guideline templates, it is necessary to analyze the program logics to satisfy this guideline element, which is beyond the scope of our method. 44 of the guideline elements of "Controls" were for progress bars, which were similar. As the results, the numbers of "Possible (target)" and "Possible (not target)" were small compared to the number of "Not target". However, logic analysis of programs is without the scope of our method, and numerous guideline elements in "Not target" were related to program logics. Hence, this small number is not a big issue. Note that the guideline templates could describe all guideline elements of "Target" and several guideline elements of "Not target". These results demonstrate the ability of our guideline templates to describe guideline elements.

7.2   Appropriateness of Applying Guideline Elements

We applied guideline elements, which are described using guideline templates, to GUIs and evaluated their appropriateness. We developed GUIs for five software packages, which are browser and editor software packages. Four of which are for windows in actual Windows software packages realized by us strictly using Java and one we developed. The guideline elements of the Mac guidelines were applied to these GUIs, and then we counted the number of guideline elements for "Automatically apply", "Require additional input", and "Confirm".

Table 6 shows the results. "Software" indicates the target software packages, and "A" to "D" are the actual Windows software packages, and "E" is the software package that we developed. "Kind" indicates the kind of software package. "Widget" indicates the total number of widgets in the developed GUIs. "Automatic" indicates the number of guideline elements that could be applied automatically, while "Require" indicates the number of guideline elements that software developers are required to provide additional inputs. "Confirm" indi-

Table 6. Results of applying guideline elements

Software	Kind	Widget	Automatic	Require	Confirm
A	Browser	115	30	0	1
B	Editor	122	48	0	0
C	Browser	10	2	0	0
D	Editor	20	2	0	0
E	Editor	18	30	1	0

cates the number of guideline elements that software developers must confirm how to modify GUIs.

Many of "Automatic" assignments are shortcut keys and locations of buttons. Although the "OK" and "Cancel" buttons differed between Windows and Mac guidelines, these guidelines were automatically modified. There were few "Require" and "Confirm" because the sample GUIs were developed almost simultaneously with the UI guidelines. In particular, most of the guideline elements that required additional inputs were generally satisfied, even if the GUIs were not developed along with UI guidelines. An example of a guideline element was "Window titles should not empty". Additionally, GUIs derived using our method were almost the same as those determined manually. Hence, our method could appropriately apply the guideline elements.

8   Conclusion

This paper proposes a method to automatically apply guideline elements to GUIs. We prepared guideline templates, which are used to describe the guideline elements and to generate the source programs of GUIs. Our method does not limit the available UI guidelines, and UI guidelines can be easily changed when a software package is run on multiple platforms. Additionally, we verified that the guideline elements were sufficiently described and the generated GUIs were appropriate.

However, some future work remains. First, the describable guideline elements using guideline elements should be increased. According to the evaluations (in section 7.1), there were many "Not target" guideline elements. Ideally, there should be few "Not target" guideline elements. Thus, the guideline templates should be further improved. Second, the potential to describe guideline elements using guideline templates for more UI guidelines should be confirmed. Although we demonstrated the applicability of our method using common UI guidelines, software development uses diverse GUI guidelines and new devices (e.g., tablet computers and smart phones) have different strategies for GUI operations than PCs. Consequently, these new GUIs must also be considered.

References

1. Nielsen, J.: Usability Engineering. Morgan Kaufmann (1994)
2. Nielsen, J.: Coordinating User Interfaces for Consistency. Academic Press (1989)

3. Guidelines section, http://msdn.microsoft.com/en-us/library/windows/desktop/aa511440.aspx
4. OS X Human Interface Guidelines, https://developer.apple.com/library/mac/documentation/UserExperience/Conceptual/AppleHIGuidelines/Intro/Intro.html
5. GNOME Human Interface Guidelines 2.2.3, https://developer.gnome.org/hig-book/stable/
6. Shirogane, J., Fukumoto, T., Iwata, H., Fukazawa, Y.: Method of GUI Layout Arrangement along with User Interface Guidelines. In: Proc of 9th Joint Conference on Knowledge-based Software Engineering (JCKBSE 2010) (2010)
7. Sugiuchi, K., Shirogane, J., Iwata, H., Fukazawa, Y.: GUI Generation Based on User Interface Guidelines. In: Procs. of IADIS International Conference Information Systems 2013 (2013)
8. Kalawa, A., Dery-Pinna, A.M., Riveill, M.: Reusing User Interface across Devices with Different Design Guidelines. In: Proc. of 2012 Fourth International Conference on Knowledge and Systems Engineering (KSE 2012) (2012)
9. Feuerstack, S., Blumendorf, M., Schwartze, V., Albayrak, S.: Model-based layout generation. In: The Working Conference on Advanced Visual Interfaces (AVI 2008), pp. 217–224 (2008)
10. Sajedi, A., Mahdavi, M., Pourshirmohammadi, A., Nejad, M.M.: Fundamental Usability Guidelines for User Interface Design. In: Procs. of Computational Sciences and Its Applications (ICCSA 2008), pp. 106–113 (2008)
11. JavaCC Home, https://javacc.java.net/

Method of Software Operation Consistency
for Tablet Devices by Sound Recognition

Hajime Iwata and Kazuhide Koyama

Kanagawa Institute of Technology, Japan

Abstract. Personal computers (PCs) are being replaced by tablet devices. Although end-users mainly use a keyboard and a mouse for PC operations, because tablets lack keyboards, end-users mainly use a touch panel for tablet device operation. Therefore, software developers need to design a user interface for tablet devices as well as realize consistency of software and application operations. By maintaining operation consistency, end-users can use software package by understanding one operation method. However, the guidelines about operation methods for a touch panel are insufficient and consistency via shortcut keys is difficult using tablet devices. Here we propose a method to execute software and application functions via voice commands. If the verbal input matches a keyword for a particular function, then the function is executed. Our method can be incorporated into existing software, allowing operation consistency to be maintained for tablet devices, which makes it is easier for end users to operate new applications.

Keywords: Tablet Device, Operation Consistency, Sound Recognition, Usability.

1   Introduction

Because an application may operate differently on different types of devices (e.g., personal computer (PC), tablet, etc.), end-users must not only learn how to use every application, but also how to use different types of devices. This burden on end users is increasing as the popularity of tablet-type devices (hereafter, referred to as tablets) increases. However, through application consistency, the burden on end users can be reduced because they can use previous experiences to operate unfamiliar software.

Usability is a measure of how easily and effectively an end user can operate an application. [1] If an application is easily learned, then end users can operate immediately. Application developers strive to create usable applications, even if end users are unfamiliar with a specific application. Consistency between applications is one way to realize usability.

Developers can maintain consistency by creating user interfaces that follow conventional guidelines for operation systems, such as Windows User Experience Guidelines [2] or Mac OS X Interface Guidelines [3]. For conventional PCs with a keyboard and a mouse, there are guidelines to create consistency between programs. For example, shortcut keys are the same in different programs, reducing what end users must learn to operate software.

A. Kravets et al. (Eds.): JCKBSE 2014, CCIS 466, pp. 688–696, 2014.

Because the operation methods differ between conventional PCs and tablets, application developers must change how an application functions. Unfortunately, guidelines for tablets are insufficient, and because tablets lack keyboards, PC guidelines are not applicable. Hence, unified operations such as shortcut keys are not possible for tablets. Therefore, end users must learn the operation method for every application. Herein we propose a method to realize consistency via unified operations for different applications, even those on a tablet.

This paper is organized as follows. Section 2 compares our method to related works. Section 3 summarizes tablets, software operation learning support, and software operation consistency. Section 4 describes the features of our works. Section 5 proposes our system architecture and shows how to add our system to existing applications, and Section 6 evaluates our method. Finally, section 7 concludes this paper.

2   Related Work

Other studies have examined how to maintain application operations and user interface consistency.

Motti et al. have proposed a method to ensure a consistent user interface for the any target platforms [4]. This method approach is the use of high level device independent user interface descriptions. This independent user interface is compiled for each target platform, such as smart phones, tablets and so on. This method is developed as a browser based authoring tool. First, developers decide a target device. Second, developers create concrete user interfaces model. Third, developers edit user interfaces model, these models dynamically change by edited models. Finally, these models adjust to reflect the changes accepted.

This method is only supported for user interface design consistency. When end-users cannot find the operation method, this approach is not enough for user support.

Ruiz et al. have proposed the use of motion gestures for smartphones' input tasks [5]. This method approach is using motion sensors to user inputs, end users gesture with the mobile device, in three dimensions, by translating or rotating the device. This method approach use consensus to develop taxonomy for motion gestures and to specify end-users motion gestures.

However, this method supported operations are basic situations, such as "Answer call", "Next", "Previous" and so on. The kind of the motion gesture is limited. These gestures are not enough for support to applications' operations.

3   Operation Learning and Software Operation Consistency for Tablets

3.1   Tablet Characteristics

The input interface of a tablet differs from a conventional PC. On a tablet, the end user employs a touch panel on an LCD screen to operate an application using the most direct passage. Thus, a line can follow an intuitive operation, and a keyboard on the

LCD screen can input letters. Additionally, the LCD screen does not conform to the concepts of top, bottom, right, and left, allowing the screen direction to change freely.

3.2   Support of a Learning Operation Method for End-Users

If end users do not understand the operation method, they cannot operate the application. Consequently, some support methods have been designed for beginning end users. Learning support methods include a tutorial system and a help system. The tutorial system demonstrates how to operate software or an application. Typically software operations are learned via a tutorial system, which displays the sequence of the operation method as operations necessary to use the software. We have proposed a method to generate a tutorial system by UML diagrams [6] and based on end users' operation logs and source programs [7]. Our tutorial system, which is executed as the software is actually used, simulates the software running so that end users can learn to operate it. Our tutorial system displays operation methods by separating each unit, allowing end user to track their progress.

3.3   Consistency of Application Operations

Design consistency allows end users to intuitively understand usability because end users comprehend the user interface and perform appropriate operations. If the same command always results in the same movement, then a user can confidently operate an application. Software or applications with consistency are easier for end users to learn.

A common example of maintaining consistency is assembly operations via shortcut keys. Instead of choosing a function from a menu with the mouse, an operation is performed using a combination of specific key inputs on a keyboard. One shortcut key function in Windows OS is the "Overwrite Save" function, which is executed by simultaneously pushing the Ctrl key and s key. This function is used in a wide range of applications that use the Windows OS.

The user interface, placement, and keyboard operations may vary by OS. Additionally, the operation method may vary according to the type of hardware, and the application must be adapted for different platforms to maintain consistency. For example, Firefox is a web browser available in Windows, Mac OS X, and Android OS. Consistency is maintained because programs use standard shortcut keys for the Windows OS and Mac OS X.

4   Features of Our Work

Developing a method to maintain consistency between different applications should reduce what end users must learn to operate an application. However, tablets applications cannot be prepared using shortcut keys or mouse clicks in menus because they are operated by touch panels. Consequently, new techniques must be devised to maintain operation consistency for tablets, especially for applications adapted from PC software.

Our method uses voice commands (verbal inputs) as a technique to maintain consistency in tablets. Specifically, a database of keywords and the corresponding functions is created. When the verbal input matches a keyword, then corresponding function is executed. Because the OS for the tablet (Android OS) supports voice inputs by default, using a voice input system as an interface can maintain operation consistency. Additionally, implementing our system does not require major modifications of existing applications and has feasibility similar to methods for other OSs.

5   Details of Our Method

To maintain consistency, our method, which is intended for the Android OS, employs voice commands from the user as operation input. Our method supports performing software functions using a voice input for keywords. We assume that end users speak Japanese and English. Figure 1 shows the flowchart for the sound recognition system in our method.

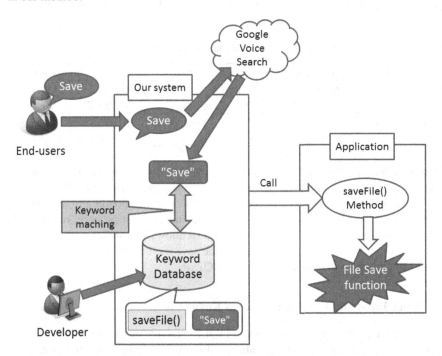

Fig. 1. Flowchart for the sound recognition system in our method

5.1   Voice Input

For a tablet, a function to input text or handle a data operation can be prepared using sound. For example, a tablet using Android OS uses the Google Voice Search, which is a retrieval service using sound recognition technology developed by Google Corporation, as the default [8]. An input sound is transmitted to the server, and then the sound recognition engine converts the voice sound into a text. In our method, we use text converted by this sound recognition function. In order to transmit a message to the server, our method must be connected to the network.

5.2   Keyword Database

In our method, a database is prepared using keywords and the corresponding function names. Application developers create or add keywords and their corresponding functions to the database. Consistency between different applications can be maintained by using the same keyword–function combinations for different applications. Our system support languages are English and Japanese, so the prepared default keyword list is in English and Japanese.

The keyword database uses the CSV format. Developers input the method name of the corresponding function into the first row of the keyword database. An example of the part of keyword database is shown in Table 1, except in the real database, Japanese keywords use Japanese characters.

Table 1. Excerpt of the Keyword Database

Function name	Method name	Keyword (English)	Keyword (Japanese)
Open File	openFile()	"Open", "Load"	"HIRAKU", "YOMU"
Save File	saveFile()	"Save", "Keep"	"HOZON", *"ozone"*
Create New File	newFile()	"New", "Create"	"SHINKI", "SHINKI-SAKUSEI"

In this example, "openFile()", "saveFile()", and "newFile()" are the method name of the list. Developers then register the keyword that is generally used for this method name into a database. One line can contain the keyword corresponding to an application function. However, it is possible that the voice input is not properly recognized. To increase the rate of agreement, our method also allows the similar pronunciations to be entered into the database. For example, the save method also registers the word *"ozone"*, which is pronounced like Japanese "HOZON".

5.3   Voice Input and Correspondence of Keywords

Because the sound recognition may input plural candidates or may return plural output candidates, we compared the agreement between the keyword and the stored sequence for every input candidate. Plural candidates for the output result are returned as character strings. In the comparison, if the keyword in the database does not match the input candidate, then the input candidate is compared with the next word in the database.

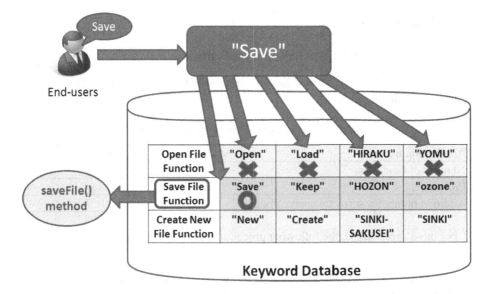

Fig. 2. An example of voice input and correspondence of keywords

An example of voice input and correspondence of keywords is shown in Figure 2. Consider the voice input of the word "Save" as an example. Initially, the database considers "Open File Function", but because "Save" is not registered, this function is not performed. However, the items in the database are sequentially compared, and once the "Save File Function" is reached, this function will be executed because the verbal input of "Save" is associated with "Save File function".

5.4   Evaluation of the Application Function

When the input candidate agrees with a keyword in the database, the application function that corresponds to the keyword is performed. Here we describe the relation between the method name of a function and the keyword database. In our method, a function is performed by verbal input of the calling method on the application side.

The "Save File Function", an example in Figure 2, is allocated the saveFile() method. This function will be executed by saveFile() method in existing application.

5.5   Addition of the Speech Input System into Existing Applications

To add a speech input system into existing applications, the source code of the application must be revised. The procedure includes four steps:

1. Developers import a database management class and create a sound recognition function class.
2. Developers create a keyword database.
3. Developers add the sound operation function to the top menu of the application.
4. Developers connect the corresponding function in the application with a sound recognition function.

6   Evaluation

6.1   Addition of Contents to Existing Applications

Table 2 summarizes the process to add our method to two applications: a media player and a countdown timer.

Table 2. Requirements to add sound recognition

Application name	Media player	Countdown timer
Number of functions	2	2
Procedure	10	11
Addition points for software source codes	6	7

For these applications, the following procedures are implemented.

1. Developers describe a word by creating a raw folder and storing in the database.
2. Developers import the database management class, and then copy and paste the source code of the database management class.
3. The source code of the speech input system in the class calls an application function.
4. Developers change the name of the database from the default to that of created database.
5. Developers describe a class name to accept the input of the speech input system.
6. Developers describe the method to perform the application function.
7. Developers copy and paste the xml file into the menu folder so that the speech input system carries the xml file from the menu.

Because the media player only has one function that is modified, the source code is altered in only three places (import, copy, and paste). Because the remaining source code is not alter, the source code can be easily modified, which reduces the burden on application developers. If the name is unchanged in the database, then the default name is used. However, if the name of the default must be changed, such as for the copy and paste, the database allows the application developer to change and easily manage the changes, which is beneficial as the number of modified functions increases. The keyword database must store the keyword and its corresponding function.

When sound recognition is added to an existing application, the source code for each function must be modified in three places (import, copy, and paste). Our method easily performs these code modifications. However, the burden on application developers increases as the number of functions in the application increases.

For the countdown timer, we used the following procedure. The same procedure as the media player was used for the copy and paste of the source code, except the developer must describe parts that differ from the media player functions, which may be challenging. If a function cannot be described concretely, it does not work properly.

Hence, the ability to use the same method for some of the functions can reduce the burden on developers.

6.2   Recognition Precision

To evaluate sound recognition, we evaluated the accuracy that a verbal input recalled the appropriate keyword in the database. The experiment was conducted using a tablet (Acer ICONIA TAB A500) running an Android OS (Android Honeycomb 3.0). Experiments were conducted using the built-in microphone in quiet room.

The voice input system was successfully incorporated into the media player (section 6.1). The reproduction function for music worked without a problem, but the end user verbal inputs were not recognized while music was playing. However, lowering the music volume resolved this problem, and the verbal inputs properly executed the corresponding function. In the future, how to recognize verbal inputs when other sounds are present must be investigated.

The countdown timer application (section 6.1) confirmed our method worked properly as long as the source code is clearly described. Application functions are executed when the verbal input agrees with a keyword in the database. Additionally, by registering misrecognized keywords into the database increases the execution accuracy.

7   Conclusion

We propose a method that can perform functions via voice input. We then investigated which application functions our method could incorporate. Our method can use voice inputs to realize consistency, even between different applications. Consequently, the proposed method can reduce the time necessary for a user to learn operations in an application. In the future, we intend to work on the following:

- Reduction of the burden on the developer

When functions within application increase, the work load on the application developers also increases. To reduce the burden on developers, we intend to consider a method that can automatically analyze the correspondence between keywords and general functions in the source code.

- Improvement of the keyword judgment precision

It is a possible that the current method may not concretely recognize the correspondence between a voice keyword and one in the database. Hence, we plan to reduce keyword misrecognition by registering similar sounding pronunciations as keyword candidates in the database.

References

1. Nielsen, J.: Usability Engineering. Morgan Kaufmann (1994)
2. Microsoft Windows Develop Center - DesktopGuidelines section,
   http://msdn.microsoft.com/en-us/library/windows/desktop/
   aa511440.aspx
3. Mac OX Human Interface Guidelines, https://developer.apple.com/
   library/mac/documentation/userexperience/conceptual/
   applehiguidelines/
4. Motti, V.G., Raggett, D.: Quill: A Collaborative Design Assistant for Cross Platform Web Application User Interfaces. In: Proceedings of the 22nd International Conference on World Wide Web Companion, WWW 2013 Companion, pp. 3–6 (2013)
5. Ruiz, J., Li, Y., Lank, E.: User-defined Motion Gestures for Mobile Interaction. In: Proceedings of the SIGCHI Conference on Human Factors in Computing Systems, CHI 2011, pp. 197–206 (2011)
6. Iwata, H., Shirogane, J., Fukazawa, Y.: Automatic Generation of Tutorial Systems from Development Specification. In: Baresi, L., Heckel, R. (eds.) FASE 2006. LNCS, vol. 3922, pp. 79–92. Springer, Heidelberg (2006)
7. Iwata, H., Shirogane, J., Fukazawa, Y.: Generation of an Operation Learning Support System by Log Analysis. In: 2nd International Conference on Software Engineering and Data Mining, SEDM 2010 (2010)
8. Google Voice Search,
   http://www.google.com/insidesearch/features/voicesearch/

Lean Mindset in Software Engineering: A Case Study in a Software House in Brazilian State of Santa Catarina

Mehran Misaghi[1] and Ivan Bosnic[2]

[1] UNISOCIESC, Joinville, Brazil
mehran@sociesc.org.br
[2] NeoGrid, Joinville, Brazil
ivan.bosnic@neogrid.com

Abstract. This article presents a literature review whose purpose is to identify the key characteristics of lean software development and its similarities and differences with agile methodologies. For concept proof, a case study conducted in a team of software developers is presented, where lean concepts were applied within the current process, previously based on agile methodologies. It was found at the end of this work that the indicator used by the team, percentage of the time spent on improvements and new features, had a significant increase, causing the team be able to add more value to the product, and to increase the level of quality. This article ends with the presentation of the steps required for the development of lean mindset in software engineering.

Keywords: Lean mindset, Agile methodologies, Scrum, Software.

1 Introduction

Modern societies depend every day more on diverse types of computer programs. Such programs manage our bank accounts, control the supply of water and electricity, monitor our health when admitted to hospitals, entertain us when we play video games, and provide many others critical services to the community. It was expected that, as they are dealing with services so fundamental to our lives, software projects were at a very high level of success.

However, according to [1], the practice of software development has been plagued with critically low success rates for decades. Meanwhile, demand for IT products and services do not stop growing and the situation seems to get into a chaotic situation with no solution. What has brought some optimism is the emergence of agile methodologies, which have shown that it is possible to obtain better success rates. The authors observed that there is a trend of improvement in the quality of the projects, but still the situation requires attention, because the percentage of projects that exceed the costs or terms remains almost as high as before.

[1] also emphasize that lean techniques have been increasingly applied to software development. Ideology and lean techniques to which the authors refer are the same

A. Kravets et al. (Eds.): JCKBSE 2014, CCIS 466, pp. 697–707, 2014.

used in the Toyota Production System and Toyota Product Development. According to [2], the first step in the implementation of the lean software development is to understand these principles, because software development is a form of product development. Applying the concepts of lean manufacturing, used for a long time in traditional industry and especially in the automobile industry, to the process of software development is the challenge behind the lean software development.

This paper presents a case study conducted within a team of experienced software developers that have used agile methodologies in the past decade with great success. Since early 2012 the team has invested in implementing lean concepts in the process of software development, which has had a positive impact on monthly indicators presented to company management [3].

2   Lean Software Development

According to [4], the ideas of lean software have their origin in lean manufacturing and lean product development. These concepts, in turn, had their origins in the Toyota Production System and the Toyota System of Product Development.

According to [2], software development is a form of product development. The authors were first to introduce in 2003 the concept of lean software development. The main focus of their work was to identify lean concepts and how they could be applied to software development.

Although agile and lean software development both have been inspired by the lean concepts, [5] emphasizes that agile methods are applied only to software development, while lean is a much broader concept. According to [6], the lean philosophy is not just a set of tools. It affects all sectors of business, from human resources to marketing. From this work were established seven principles of Lean Software Development [2].

2.1   Principle One: Eliminate Waste

According to [7], the Toyota Production System has as one of its foci the total elimination of waste. The author states that everything that does not add value to the customer must be removed from the process. According to [1], this category includes a number of concepts that must be analyzed so that we can understand how waste indicated in the Toyota Production System can be identified in the process of software development.

- **Defects:** Defects are represented by themselves. Defects cause costly rework, which does not add value to the product. The lean software development has as one of its goals preventing defects.
- **Overproduction:** Unnecessary features. The cost of software is not contained only in writing the source code. This code needs to be maintained, documented, taught to the new team members, etc. For this reason, all the features embedded in the software should come from the real needs of the user, i.e., features that add value to the final product. According to [1], the study 'CHAOS study' Standish Group

showed that 64% of all the features are not used or are rarely used. This is a great waste of resources over time.

- **Stock:** Partially completed tasks. Here we consider requirements analyzed but not implemented, code that has not been tested or errors that have not been corrected. The lean philosophy does not admit the accumulation of uncompleted tasks. Instead, we try to adopt the unit flow that makes the task completed as soon as possible.
- **Transportation:** Switching between tasks. Interruptions and work alternated between very different activities affect productivity. Before starting work on a task, people need time to acclimatize to the problem and to understand the requirements. Any interruption causes this process to be restarted. This is one reason why the flow unit is so productive.
- **Further processing:** Unnecessary processes. This type of process is the most pure waste. It hinders productivity without adding any value to the final product. An example of this process is the creation of documentation that is not used by anyone, or even manual execution of tasks that could be automated.
- **Standby:** Delays. During the process of software development programmers often need to communicate with other project participants to ask questions and clarify certain requirements. If these participants are not available, there will be delays in delivery or implementation will be done without the proper information, which in most cases will generate rework. This rework is one of the most common forms of waste in the process of software development and should be avoided at any cost.

2.2   Principle Two: Integrating Quality

[7] states that it is not possible to inspect the quality of a product at the end of the production line. According to [1], traditional development methodologies make exactly this error: allow defects to be detected later by the team of quality assurance.

Lean software development, moreover, proposes a different philosophy. Instead of creating systems to control defects (nonconformities queues to be resolved), the process should be focused on the total elimination of defects and the consequent elimination of rows control [2]. To achieve such a degree of maturity in the process is only possible with the use of resources such as unit testing and continuous integration, among others.

2.3   Principle Three: Creating Knowledge

According to [2], one of the major flaws that software development plans aimed at is the idea that knowledge in the form of requirements exists separately from coding. Authors emphasize that software development is a process of knowledge creation and the detailed design, although it should be outlined before, it stands only during the implementation of the code.

[1] has put that knowledge should be stored in such a way that it can be easily located the next time it becomes necessary. People should not waste time learning something that has already been studied and put into practice by other team members.

2.4   Principle Four: Postpone Commitments

[1] assert that the best decisions are made when we have as much information as possible. If a particular decision needs not be made immediately, we should wait until we have more knowledge on the subject. According to [2], this item applies mainly to making irreversible decisions. The reversible decisions can be taken before, because they can be easily modified.

2.5   Principle Five: Delivering Fast

[8] teaches that we must begin with a thorough understanding of what adds value to the customer. Once understood the needs of the client, we create a workflow that seeks to make rapid and frequent deliveries of working software. According to [1], the importance of delivering fast is to get customer feedback as soon as possible. Thus, we avoid the requirements change just because they take too much time to be delivered.

2.6   Principle Six: Respect People

According to [2], thinkers and people engaged in the project are the largest and most sustainable competitive advantage that a company can have. This thought defines what people represent in a lean philosophy. Respecting people means trusting that they know the best way to perform a job and enables them to find ways to improve processes.

2.7   Principle Seven: Optimize the Whole

According to [2], improving a local process is usually achieved at the expense of the value stream in the entire process. This occurs when changes are made without considering the whole. This is known as sub-optimization, and an organization that implements lean concepts always tries to avoid it.

3   Case Study

The company chosen for this case study has a long experience in software development. Currently, it is ranked as the leading supplier of systems for the supply chain in Brazil. Furthermore, it has successfully implemented the agile software development, Scrum and XP during the last decade. In the last five years, the company has increased its interest in the concepts of lean software development, with the intention of improving the productivity of its teams [3]. This case study was conducted from September 2011 to August 2012. At this time, we had 12 people on staff. 8 people have had solid experience in software development (levels between full and senior). The rest were younger and some also trainees.

3.1   Lean Concepts in Practice

Several indicators have been used to monitor the productivity of these teams, and goals have been established to evaluate their progress. One of the main indicators evaluates the time that a team invests, during each software version, in improvements and new features. These tasks add value to the product and the increase of this indicator has been one of the goals of the company.

All other activities performed by the team are considered waste, even if some are needed so that the process can be managed correctly. Examples of some activities performed by the team are correction of non-conformities, participation in meetings, planning and others. When the time spent in correction of nonconformities (errors caused during the execution of software) increases, it is an indication that the product quality has worsened. Consequently, the team will have less time to invest in improvements and new features.

In an attempt to improve the indicators and increase the quality of the product, the team that was followed in this case study chose to adopt the concepts of lean software development. Each of the seven concepts explained in section 2 of this paper had a corresponding action based on [9,10,11,12,13].

3.1.1   Eliminate Waste

The problem of multitasking has been identified as a major cause of decreased productivity. People were constantly engaged in more than one activity, which took their concentration of the main tasks (implement improvements and new features). Some multitasking arose by the constant need to provide support to other teams about how the software works, but others were caused by the behavior of the team itself. That is, developers were involved in more than one task at a time, because there were no clear rules within the process about what should be the correct behavior in these cases.

To deal with the problem of multitasking, the team defined two new guidelines in the process of software development:

1. Each version of the software, one developer would be elected to handle support tasks requested by other teams. Thus, the rest of the team would be free to devote to the development of new features and improvements.
2. No developer would be involved in more than one feature at the same time. The aim was to implement the flow unit (continuous). Only after completing an activity the developer would dedicate to another, even if that meant some downtime.

3.1.2   Integrating Quality

The practice of automated tests, i.e., tests that do not depend on human interaction and ensure the correct operation of one or more software features, would be integrated into the process from the beginning. Experience had shown that leaving the development of tests for a later stage caused waste, because it created an inventory of tasks that hardly was handled.

3.1.3 Creating Knowledge

All knowledge about the product should be available to all team members. To achieve this goal, the company implemented a collaborative tool for knowledge management, where everyone could contribute documenting the processes in which they were working. The knowledge could not be restricted to a group of more experienced developers.

3.1.4 Postpone Commitments

Important decisions, especially those involving changes in the architecture of the system, were postponed until such time that the team had more knowledge on the subject and therefore more security in the process of decision-making. This practice proved to be very effective, because it avoided hasty decisions.

3.1.5 Delivering Fast

Divide the project into smaller iterations between three to four weeks, enabled rapid delivery of functionalities, even partially completed. It was thus possible to obtain customer feedback more rapidly, and allow them to have a higher level of involvement in the evolution of the product. This practice is widely used in Scrum, one of the agile methodologies adopted by the team.

3.1.6 Respect People

At all meetings of planning future versions of the software, all team members are heard. The final decisions take into account everyone's opinion and make the team commits to the estimates.

3.1.7 Optimize the Whole

The importance of understanding the processes of the company was highlighted within the team. Workshops were made with other teams to clarify several questions about how the software was used in practice. This knowledge was useful for evaluating the impacts of development of a new feature on internal and external customers. The result of this approach was an improvement in usability and better acceptance by customers.

3.2 Data Collection

The company at which the case study was conducted has several tools to manage the process of software development. All developed requirements are recorded as well as the tasks and corrections of bugs. The data of this case study was obtained from tools used in the process of software development:

1. **Jira:** This tool is provided by the company Atlassian and is used for registration and monitoring of requirements, time recording and graphs tracking progress of versions;

2. **Confluence:** Also provided by Atlassian, tool is used for documenting functional and technical details of systems developed by the company. It is a collaborative software where all team members have access to edit documents.

Every day, the team members record worked hours. Each time recording is obligatorily linked to a task, which can be an improvement, a bug correction, a meeting, etc. Each of these tasks, in turn, is linked to a particular component. Currently the components are divided into:

1. **Product:** Groups all the hours spent on tasks that add value to the product, such as improvements and new features, development of automated tests, etc.
2. **Bugs:** The time spent on correction of nonconformities;
3. **Support:** hours are recorded in support activities provided to other teams;
4. **Management:** all tasks related to project management: meetings, planning, daily meetings, etc.

3.3 Analysis of Results

To analyze the results, we used the one-year period, from September 2011 until August 2012. The actions taken by the team and which were explained in the previous sections had its implementation in February 2012. Thus, it is possible to observe the evolution of the indicators analyzed in this case study, covering the phases before and after the implemented changes. Data were obtained from the BI (Business Intelligence) tool provided by the team of software quality. The percentage of time spent is monitored monthly, and information is divided into three groups [3].

The group "product" covers all the hours spent on improvements and new features. Corrections of bugs are classified as group "bugs", while in the group "others" are inserted all other activities performed by team. Table 1 shows the history of the percentage of time spent in each of the groups defined above.

Table 1. Data collection of time invested by component

Month	9/11	10/11	11/11	12/11	1/12	2/12	3/12	4/12	5/12	6/12	7/12	8/12
Product	50	54.2	51.82	54.4	51.65	60.02	57.37	61.29	65.13	64.21	60.47	61
Bugs	13.9	13.7	10.8	10.2	9.4	8.6	8.5	8.6	7.4	6.7	6.6	5.9
Others	36.1	32.1	37.38	35.4	38.95	31.38	34.13	30.11	27.47	29.09	32.93	33.1

Through the graph shown in Fig. 1 it can be seen more clearly how the tracked indicators evolved during one year.

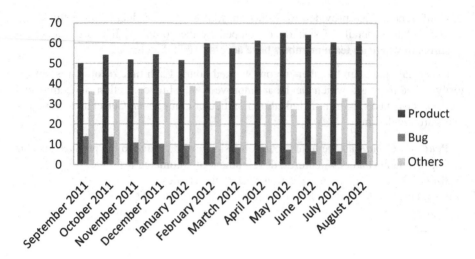

Fig. 1. Evolution of the percentage of time spent per component

3.3.1 Time Invested in Improvements and New Features

Through the collected data, it can be observed the increase of time spent on product relative to other components. While in 2011 the indicator stood at around 50%, from the changes implemented the same shall remain in the range of 60%. Therefore, we conclude that the indicator had an average increase of 20%.

Fig. 2 shows, in isolation, the evolution of the percentage of time spent on product. It is possible to observe that, as of February 2012, the month in which it started implementing lean software development; there was an average increase of 20% in this indicator.

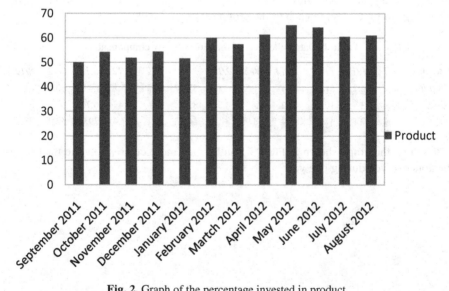

Fig. 2. Graph of the percentage invested in product

3.3.2 Time Spent on Bug Fixing

While there was an increase in the percentage of time spent on improvements and new functionalities, it was observed, on the other hand, a decrease in time spent on correcting bugs. Fig. 3. shows the evolution of this indicator.

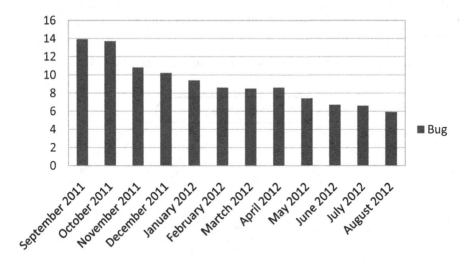

Fig. 3. Graph of percentage spent on bug fixing

It is important to note that the reduction of time spent on bug fixing was achieved with better product quality. That is, since the implementation of automated testing was incorporated into the process of software development, fewer errors were released and hence more time was available for investment in new features and improvements.

4   Lean Mindset in Software Engineering

According to [14], lean is a mental model of how the world works, lean is a mindset. For the impacts generated through implementation of lean principles in fact continue, there is a need to implement lean mindset.

[14] also emphasize that for presenting a mental model, we have to start with two questions: What is a purpose of a business? What kind of work systems are for accomplishing that purpose?

To understand how lean mindset work and how we can implement lean mindset, [14] propose five steps:

1. *The Purpose of Business*: emphasizes the principle Optimize the Whole, taking the Shareholder Value Theory to task for the short-term thinking it produces.
2. *Energized Workers*: is based on the work of Mihaly Csikszentmihalyi, who found that the most energizing human experience is pursuing a well-framed challenge [15].

3. *Delighted Customers*: urges readers to Focus on Customers, understand what they really need, and make sure that the right products and services are developed.
4. *Genuine Efficiency*: starts by emphasizing that authentic, sustainable efficiency does not mean layoffs, low costs, and controlling work systems.
5. *Breakthrough Innovation*: starts with a cautionary tale about how vulnerable businesses are—even simple businesses like newspapers can lose their major source of revenue seemingly overnight.

Fig. 4 shows in detail the various components of each step based on [14].

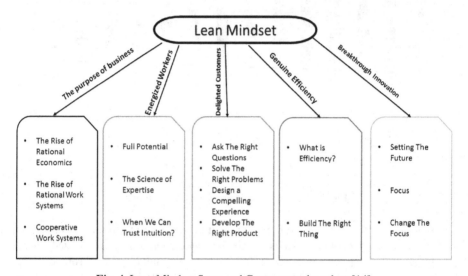

Fig. 4. Lean Mindset Steps and Components based on [14]

For successful implementation of Lean Mindset, there is need for cooperation in various sectors of the whole organization, not just those directly involved with software engineering. We should view the organization as unique unit to ensure this success.

5   Conclusion

During the conduct of the case study and the subsequent analysis of the results, it was observed that the implementation of lean development software had several impacts on the development process adopted by the company. All the impacts were positive as they enabled the company to improve its software development process, adding more productivity and quality.

On the other hand, the specific objectives of this study, analysis of indicators of time invested in improvements and new functionalities and time spent on correcting bugs had their data collected and compared over a period of one year. Both indicators have improved, easily observed by the analysis of the results.

The elimination of waste was achieved with the elimination of multitasking, which had been identified as a major cause of reduced productivity. The practice of automated testing was responsible for integrating more quality to the developed software, while the implementation of a collaborative tool for knowledge management contributed to the creation of a unique knowledge base.

Our challenge is to define the criteria to implement lean mindset in software engineering, in our organization according to our need, with innovative ingredients.

References

1. Hibbs, C., Jewett, S., Sullivan, M.: The art of lean software development. O'Reilly Media, Inc., Sebastopol (2009)
2. Poppendieck, M., Poppendieck, T.: Implementing Lean Software Development: From Concept to Cash. Addison-Wesley, Boston (2007)
3. Bosnic, I., Misaghi, M.: Lean Software Development: A Case Study in a Medium-sized Compnay in Brazilian State of Santa Catarina. In: ADIS-AC Proceedings, USA, pp. 163–170 (2013)
4. Shore, J., Warden, S.: The Art of Agile Development. Reilly Media, Inc., Sebastopol (2008)
5. Gustavsson, H.: Lean thinking applied to system architecting.Thesis. Department of School Of Innovation, Design And Engineering, Mälardalen University, Västerås, Sweden (2011)
6. Petersen, K.: Implementing Lean and Agile Software Development in Industry. Thesis - Department of School Of Computing, Blekinge Institute Of Technology, Karlskrona, Sweden (2010)
7. Ohno, T.: Toyota Production Software: Beyond Large Scale Production. Productivity Press, Oregon (1988)
8. Kniberg, H.: Lean from the Trenches: Managing Large-Scale Projects with Kanban. The Pragmatic Bookshelf, Dallas (2011)
9. Cohn, M.: Succeeding with agile: Software development using scrum. Addison-Wesley, Boston (2010)
10. Dyba, T., Dingsoyr, T.: Empirical studies of agile software development: A systematic review. Information and Software Technology 50, 833–859 (2008)
11. Pressman, R.S.: Software Engineering: A Practitioner's Approach, 6th edn. McGraw-Hill, New York (2004)
12. Sommerville, I.: Software Engineering, 9th edn. Addison-Wesley, Boston (2011)
13. Vlaanderen, K., et al.: The agile requirements refinery: Applying SCRUM principles to software product management. Information And Software Technology 53(1), 58–70 (2011)
14. Poppendieck, M., Poppendieck, T., Kniberg, H.: Lean Mindset – Ask the Right Questions. Addison-Wesley, Boston (2014)
15. Csikszentmihalyi, M.: Flow: The Psychology of Optimal Experience. HarperCollins, New York (1990)

Lean Data Science Research Life Cycle: A Concept for Data Analysis Software Development

Maxim Shcherbakov[*], Nataliya Shcherbakova, Adriaan Brebels,
Timur Janovsky, and Valery Kamaev

Volgograd State Technical University,
Lenin av. 28, 400005 Volgograd, Russia
{maxim.shcherbakov,natalya.shcherbakova}@vstu.ru
http://www.vstu.ru

Abstract. Data Science is a new study that combines computer science, data mining, data engineering and software development. Based on the concept of lean software development we propose an idea of lean data science research as a technology for data analysis software development. This concept includes the mandatory stages of the life cycle that meet the lean manufacturing principles. We have defined the business understanding stage with defining the targeted questions, the set of lean data analysis sprints and a decision support stage. Each lean data analysis sprint contents of the task statement step, a step of data integration, a step of data analysis and the interpretation of the results. This approach allows to build data analysis software with iterative improvement quality of the results. Some case study have been suggested as examples of the proposed concept.

Keywords: data science, software development, data analysis.

1   Introduction

Jim Gray in his visionary speech found the four stages of science evolution and he detected the shift a 'fourth paradigm' [1]. Based on his representation, the first age of science was *experimental* describing natural phenomena. The second was *theoretical* using abstract entities as models and generalizations. The third is *computational* branch allowing to simulate complex phenomena. And the fourth paradigm is called *data exploration* or eScience that unify theory, experiment and simulation. Based on the definition eScience revolves around developing new methods to support scientists in conducting scientific research with the aim of making new scientific discoveries by analyzing vast amounts of data accessible over the internet using vast amounts of computational resources [2]. Another similar term came from data mining domain and it is called Data Science (DS). Data Science is becoming a new study that combines computer science, statistics and machine learning, domain knowledge, data engineering and software development. Drew Conway suggested the representation of

---

[*] Authors would like to thanks RFBR for finacial support in terms of grant # 14-0700945_a.

A. Kravets et al. (Eds.): JCKBSE 2014, CCIS 466, pp. 708–716, 2014.

Data Science using Venn diagram as intersection of the different skills: hacking skills, mathematics and statistics knowledge, and substantive expertise [3].

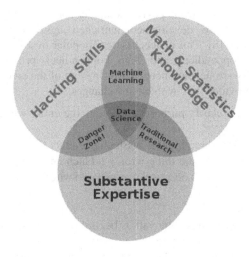

Fig. 1. Data Science Venn Diagram proposed by Drew Conway

Also there are many variations of the Data Science representation based on this diagram. Note, there is no final approved definition of Data Science for common use. Moreover this term still controversial and we can observe a lot of different discussion around this definition.

Another polar meaning in this kind of discussions is that Data Science could force out statistics from data analytics. Vincent Granville response: 'Data science is more than statistics: it also encompasses computer science and business concepts, and it is far more than a set of techniques and principles. I could imagine a data scientist not having a degree - this is not possible for a statistician...' [4].

However it is evident that Data Science is not a subject for ignoring any more. Harvard ran extension course 'CS109 Data Science' [5] focusing on the technique based on IPython Notenook [6]. Springer founded the scientific journal EPJ Data Science [7].

In spite on these even 'buzz- word' and frequent discussions, two main questions are still open:

- how to find the proper and efficient way for carrying out data science research?
- what is the new approaches for building efficient software to support data science research could be?

The main contribution of the paper is the concept of lean data science research life-cycle based on the key principles of lean development. This approach allows to consider data science research in framework of decision support process. The case study shows the way for implementing this method for data science research software development has been proposed here.

2   A Lean Data Science Research and Software Development

2.1   A Key Principles of Lean Development

Lean is the term which came from Toyota company and it already became the most efficient way for software development enriched agile software development paradigm (e.g. SCRUM) [8]. This concept is very popular in software development at the moment. Mary Poppendieck and Tom Poppendieck proposed the following principles of lean software development [9,10]. In spite of the emotional background, these principles are provided here without any changes.

1. *Optimize the Whole*: clarify purpose, appreciate the entire value stream and think long term.
2. *Eliminate Waste*. The three biggest wastes in product development are: building the wrong thing; building the thing wrong; a batch and queue mentality (work in progress hides defects, gets obsolete, causes task switching, and delays realization of value).
3. *Focus on Customers*
   - Ask the right questions. Innovation begins with a fresh perspective, a keen insight, a penetrating question.
   - Solve the right problems. Do not focus on the products you are building, focus on the problems customers are encountering.
   - Design a great experience. It is not enough for customers to be satisfied, they should love your products.
4. *Learn First*
   - The predictability paradox: Predictable organizations do not guess about the future and call it a plan; they develop the capacity to learn quickly and rapidly respond to the future as it unfolds.
   - Integrating events. Knowledge-based development seeks out knowledge gaps, develops multiple options for solutions, and frequently synchronizes all teams developing the system.
   - The last responsible moment. Do not make expensive-to-change decisions before their time and do not make them after their time.
5. *Deliver Fast*: speed, quality and low cost are fully compatible, focus on flow efficiency, not resource efficiency, manage workflow rather than task-based schedules.
6. *Build Quality In* or find and fix defects the moment they occur: mistakeproof the process, integrate early and often, do not tolerate defects.
7. *Empower the team* and energize workers. Purpose: a meaningful purpose inspires and energizes workers. Challenge: provide challenge, feedback, and an environment that enables everyone to become excellent. Responsibility: the most productive groups are semi-autonomous teams with an internal leader that accept end-to-end responsibility for meaningful accomplishments.

2.2   Data Research Life-Cycle: The Background

How to do data analysis is precisely highlighted in the textbooks (e.g. [11]). This approach is well known as Knowledge Discovery in Databases (KDD). KDD is the non-trivial process of identifying valid, novel, potential useful, and ultimately understandable patterns in data [12]. KDD includes *data mining* phase and contains on the following steps:

- data sourcing, selection and sampling
- data preparation
- data transformation
- model building,
- model evaluation
- model visualization
- data scoring.

More advanced technique for KDD is known as CRISP-DM created by consortium of NCR, SPSS, and Daimler-Benz companies. CRISP-DM includes additional phases such as: business understanding, data understanding and deployment phase. It includes the feedback handling stage evaluating the deployment phase's results.

Nowadays a lot of open source software tools and libraries are proposed for data mining process, e.g. IPython and sklearn library [13], Octave, R. That leads to increasing possibilities for research conducting for many people with low computational and statistics expertise. It allows to make some changes in the vision of CRISP-DM life-cycle making the life-cycle more flexible and agile.

Philip Guo in his thesis proposed the typical research programming workflow [14]. The workflows contains the following phases. Preparation phase includes acquire data process, reformat and clean data. Analysis phase contains the internal cycle with operations of (i) edit analysis scripts, (ii) execute scripts, (iii) inspect outputs and (iv) debug. The next phase is reflection with operations of making comparisons, taking notes and holding meetings. This phase creates the feedback for explore alternatives and analysis phase. The final stage is dissemination with writing reports, deploying online, archiving experiments and sharing experiments.

2.3   Lean Data Science Research Life Cycle: A Proposed Concept

Based on (i) the background analysis, (ii) the key lean development principles and (iii) theory of decision support systems [15,16] we propose the two-levels Lean Data Science Research Life Cycle. The life-cycle contains on two levels: external (or macrolevel) and internal (or microlevel). Figure 2 shows the entire scheme for lifecycles.

Problem Understanding is the first step of the external cycle. This is the most essential step is about asking the right questions. The answers these questions should improve decisions and management. As we consider the data science research in the framework of decision support process it is necessary to highlight objectives for research conducting. There are three types of research can be defined.

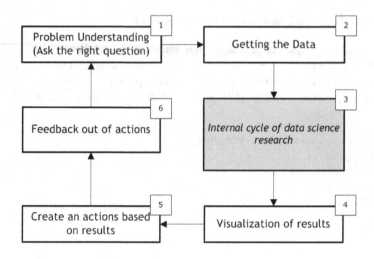

Fig. 2. Levels of lean data science research

Descriptive task (or descriptive modeling) is about finding dependences between variables and finding patterns (or complex events) in the data [11,17]. The data analysis script could contains statistical analysis methods (finding mean, median, standard deviation, range, percentiles, histograms, etc.), correlation analysis (e.g. Pearson, Kendal and Spearman Rank correlations), decision tree approaches [18] and the ways for their visualisation (e.g. Matplotlib [19]) and so on.

Predictive task (or predictive modeling) is finding forecasting models for certain variable based on the historical data and other variables (or features). In many cases this task can be considered as a part of time series analysis problems (TSA). TSA has long history and suggests the formal procedures for analysis and forecasting of time series [20,21].

Prescriptive task is the extension of the precious task which explains the predictive behaviour. It also connected with time series analysis and the techniques of interpreting the models (e.g. whitening methods [22]).

Getting the Data. Since the task statement is clearly defined the next step is to understand what kind of data might be used. Basically, three types of data are defined:

- structured data such as MSDB databases tables, CSV files containing raw data in row-columns format.
- semi-structured data such as log files, tweets that can not fit to the certain structure;
- unstructured data, e.g. video streams, pictures, sounds and so on.
  Also two types of data sources can be identified:

- *internal data sources* as a part of corporative information system and enterprise data warehouses
- *external data* sources provide additional information for research (e.g. NOAA as a weather forecast service can provide data for energy management).

Data collectors or data managers should be implemented for data gathering. In this case data collectors should guarantee the quality of data and freshness of data [23].

Internal Cycle of Data Science Research. The internal cycle contains the procedures of data analysis which is represents a sprint in SCRUM-based approach. The result of the Internal Cycle of Data Science Research is the script (or software) with the sequence of the command from uploading data to getting results.

- Task statement step. This step contains the operation for data exploration and understanding through analysis of accessible variable and features. It includes the procedure to describe format of data, build statistic characteristics (e.g. mean, median, etc), observe missing data and possible outliers. Also it necessary to understand the potential correlation between variables and ways for data aggregation.
- Data integration. This step includes operations for data merging, data preparation and cleaning. The branch of algorithms includes data imputation, outliers detection and handling, do some actions over categorised data and so on. If data is excluded from the consideration, these data might be the additional subject of study.
- Data analysis or data modelling phase includes the following steps: select model (or a set of models) , fitting model to the data and evaluating the models. Since the modern tools and packages allow to include in the script code for usage different models in the easy way (just 3 or 5 lines of code), it leads to possibilities to try different models with the same set of features.
- Interpretation of the results. The goal of this step is understanding: should we use these results for decision making or launch additional internal cycle? Based on 'deliver fast' principle it important to deliver results to the external cycle to get a feedback.

An additional important process is logging that performed in background mode. It can be implemented in the way of laboratory notes (date; time; comments, results).

Visualization of Results. This step includes the different ways for visualization of the results. The are the following types of visualization can be done.

1. Visualization of results as the initial point for decision support. For instancetime series with predicted values across the forecast horizon or scatter plot as the results of visualization of clustering analysis.
2. Visualization the results of comparison with baselines or benchmark models.
3. Visualization the information about modelling phase (e.g. AUC, ROC, forecasting errors, residual analysis, etc.).

Creating Actions Based on Results. There are two main types of action might be performed. The *positive* outcome where we need to find and to perform some actions based on the results (e.g. success of the research phase). And the *negative* outcome, that means we need repeat data analysis cycle and to improve it.

Getting Feedback from Action. This step contains the evaluation how the results of analysis were useful and trustful for end-user and person who makes decision. The quality of decision support can be measured using Key Performance Indexes (KPI). There are three general types of KPI can be defined as

- absolute $kpi_1 = \sum_{i=1}^{h} (w_i \cdot y_i)$, where h — interval of observation, w — weight, y — measured variable;

$$kpi_2 = \left(\frac{\sum_{i=1}^{h} (w_i \cdot y_i)}{|y_{base}|} \right) -$$ relative), where y_{base} — baseline value;

- trade-off function: $kpi_3 = \mu \cdot \sum_{i=1}^{h} (w_i \cdot (y_{i+1} - y_i)) + \lambda \cdot \sum_{i=1}^{h} (w_i \cdot s_i)$, where s_i — measured variable (in contradiction with y), μ, λ — coefficients.

IP[y]: Notebook   ClusterProfiles Last Checkpoint: Apr 17 16 43 (autosaved)

File   Edit   View   Insert   Cell   Kernel   Help

Energy Data Exploring

The task statement. We have observation for more than 1000 buildings including time stamps, gas consumptions, so on and idea to explore the types of daily patterns.

Task 1. Load data from the files

```
In [1]:  %matplotlib inline
         #include libraries
         import pandas as pd
         import numpy as np
         import matplotlib.pyplot as plt
```

```
In [2]:  picture_width = 15
         picture_height = 5
         daily_pattern = 96
```

```
In [3]:  bemtdata = pd.read_csv('c:/datahub/bemt.csv', index_col=False, sep = ';', header=0)
         bemtdata = bemtdata.set_index('ExpectedDateTime')
         list(bemtdata.columns.values)
```

```
Out[3]:  ['Openning_hours',
          'DateTime',
```

Fig. 3. The initial part of IPython script

3   Case Study

This section describes the case study for explanation of the Lean Data Science Life Cycle using IPython:notebook for energy time series analysis. The benefit of IPython:notebook is feature to combine experiment description and Python code. Based on the suggested approach we consider the Python script including two segments: external with steps regarding to external lyfecycle and internal (or iterative internal life cycle)

Figures 3 contains the initial part of the script with task statement and data loading procedure.

Figure 4 contains the results of visualization of time series to understand dependencies of gas consumption and external temperature.

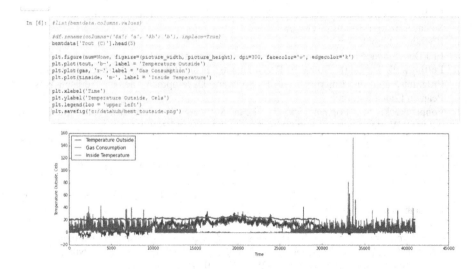

Fig. 4. The results of visualization

4   Conclusion

This paper suggest the overview of lean data science research life cycle based on lean development principles. This concept includes the mandatory stages of the life cycle that meet the lean manufacturing principles e.g. eliminate waste, focus on right questions, iterations based on learning, fast delivery. The life cycle contains on external cycle with the steps: problem understanding, getting the data, iterative internal life cycle, step of results visualisation, creating action and decisions and getting feedback.

Each internal cycle or lean data analysis sprint contents of the task statement step, a step of data integration, a step of data analysis and the interpretation of the results. This approach allows to build data analysis software with iterative improvement quality of the results.

Acknowledgments. Authors would like to thanks RFBR for finacial support in terms of grant # 14-07-00945 a.

References

1. Hey, T., Tansley, S., Tolle, K. (eds.): The Fourth Paradigm: Data-Intensive Scientific Discovery. Microsoft Research, Redmond (2009)
2. eScience Center, http://esciencecenter.nl/
3. Conway, D., The Data Science Venn Diagram,
   http://drewconway.com/zia/2013/3/26/
   the-data-science-venn-diagram
4. Is Data Science The End of Statistics? A Discussion
   http://www.kdnuggets.com/2013/04/
   data-science-end-statistics-discussion.html

5. CS109 Harvard Data Science Course, Harvard School of Engineering and Applied Science, http://cs109.org/
6. IPython:notebook
7. EPJ Data Science http://www.epjdatascience.com/
8. Leffingwell, D.: Agile Software Requirements: Lean Requirements Practices forTeams, Programs, and the Enterprise. Agile Software Development Series. Addison-Wesley, Pearson Education, Inc.
9. Poppendieck, M., Poppendieck, T.: Lean Software Development: An AgileToolkit. Addison-Wesley Longman Publishing Co., Inc., Boston (2003)
10. Poppendieck, M., Poppendieck, T.: The Lean Mindset: Ask the Right Questions. Poppendieck LLC (2013)
11. Nisbet, R., Elder, J., Miner, G.: Handbook of Statistical Analysis andData Mining Applications. Academic Press (2009)
12. Fayyad, U., Piatetsky-shapiro, G., Smyth, P.: From Data Mining toKnowledge Discovery in Databases. AI Magazine 17, 3754 (1996)
13. Pedregosa, F., Varoquaux, G., Gramfort, A., Michel, V., Thirion, B., Grisel, O., Blondel, M., Prettenhofer, P., Weiss, R., Dubourg, V., Vanderplas, J., Passos, A., Cournapeau, D., Brucher, M., Perrot, M., Duchesnay, E.: Scikit-learn: Machine Learning in Python. Journal of Machine Learning Research 12, 2825–2830 (2011)
14. Guo, P.: Software Tools to Facilitate Research Programming, Ph.D. thesis. Stanford University (May 2012), http://purl.stanford.edu/mb510fs4943
15. Burstein, F., Holsapple, C.W.: Handbook on Decision SupportSystems 1: Basic Themes, 1st edn. Springer Publishing Company, Incorporated (2008)
16. Burstein, F., Holsapple, C.W.: Handbook on Decision Support Systems 2: Variations, 1st edn. Springer Publishing Company, Incorporated (2008)
17. Bishop, C.M.: Pattern Recognition and Machine Learning. In: Jordan, M., Kleinberg, J., Schölkopf, B. (eds.) Pattern Recognition, vol. 4, p. 738. Springer (2006), doi:10.1117/1.2819119
18. Williams, G.: Data Science with R Decision Trees (2014), http://onepager.togaware.com/DTreesO.pdf
19. Hunter, J.D.: Matplotlib: A 2D Graphics Environment. Computing in Science& Engineering 9, 90–95 (2007), http://dx.doi.org/10.1109/MCSE.2007.55
20. Gooijer, J.G., De Hyndman, R.J.: 25 years of time series forecasting. International Journal of Forecasting 22(3), 443–473 (2006), http://dx.doi.org/10.1016/j.ijforecast.2006.01.001
21. Goodwin, P., Ord, J.K., Oller, L.-E., Sniezek, J.A., Leonard, M.: In: Scott Armstrong, J. (ed.) Principles of Forecasting: A Handbook for Researchers and Practitioners, p. 849. Kluwer Academic Publishers, Boston (2001, 2002)
22. Bishop, C.M.: Neural Networks for Pattern Recognition. OxfordUniversity Press, Inc., New York (1995)
23. Tyukov, A., Brebels, A., Shcherbakov, M., Kamaev, V.: A concept of web-basedenergy data quality assurance and control system. In: ACM International Conference Proceeding Series, pp. 267–271 (2012), doi:10.1145/2428736.2428779
24. Tyukov, A., Ushakov, A., Shcherbakov, M., Brebels, A., Kamaev, V.: Digital signage based building energy manage-ment system: Solution concept. World Applied Sciences Journal, Information Technologies in Modern Industry, Education and Society (24), 183–190
25. A photovoltaic out put backcast and forecast method based on cloud cover and historical data. In: Owoeye, D., Shcherbakov, M., Kamaev, V. (eds.) Proceedings of the 6th IASTED Asian Conference on Power and Energy Systems, AsiaPES (2013)
26. Kamaev, V.A., Shcherbakov, M.V., Panchenko, D.P., Shcherbakova, N.L., Brebels, A.: Using connectionist systems for electric energy consumption forecasting in shopping centers. Automation and Remote Control (2012)

Argument Algebra:
A Formalization of Assurance Case Development

Shuichiro Yamamoto

Information Strategy Office, Nagoya University, Nagoya, Japan
syamamoto@acm.org

Abstract. Assurance case has been applied to various safety software domains. Many argument patterns approaches were proposed for reusing assurance cases. One of the issues of argument pattern based assurance case development is the application orders of patterns. In this paper, the argument algebra is proposed to define argument expressions for assurance cases. The argument expressions are used to compare different assurance cases. This paper shows the equivalence problem of assurance cases can be solved by using the proposed argument algebra. The freeness of argument pattern application is also shown for assuring the dependability of a sensor device management system.

Keywords: assurance case, dependability case, argument pattern, equivalence.

1   Introduction

The assurance case is currently the focus of considerable attention for assuring that systems are dependable. Methods have thus been proposed for representing assurance case using Goal Structuring Notation (GSN)[1-5]. However, in order to facilitate the creation of assurance cases by engineers during real-world system development, it is not enough to simply provide them with an editor. They also need a more concrete development method for assurance cases that has been adapted to suit the system development process and documentation.

Against this backdrop, a number of methods have been developed for safety cases and dependability cases as part of research in the field of assurance cases: For example, Kelly has proposed the following six-step method for GSN creation: (1) Identify the goals to be supported; (2) define the basis on which the goals are stated, (3) identify a strategy to support the goals, (4) define the basis on which the strategy is stated, (5) evaluate the strategies, and (6) identify the basic solution[1-2]. The Safety Case Development Manual[4] established by the European Organization for the Safety of Air Navigation identifies the establishment of contexts for safety cases as being extremely important. This manual also proposes a checklist for the review of safety cases.

In terms of the development process for a system that itself comprises multiple systems (i.e., a system of systems), a technique involving system analysis, goal elicitation, identification of candidate design alternatives, and resolution of conflicts has been proposed for the creation of assurance cases in a structured fashion[5].

A. Kravets et al. (Eds.): JCKBSE 2014, CCIS 466, pp. 717–725, 2014.

Meanwhile, methods for the decomposition of arguments as required when creating assurance cases have been arranged into categories such as architecture, functional, and set of attributes [15].

The diversity of these techniques is evidence of assurance-case development methods being proposed on an individual basis for a range of different development processes and fields of application. However, in order that the assurance case may be used to validate that real-world systems are dependable, its specific correlation with the system development process and stage deliverables and its mode of use must be clear and consistent. In this regard, many pattern based approaches still be proposed to today's methods for developing assurance cases. Although these pattern based approaches are useful to reuse best practices of assurance cases, there is still an issue during decomposing process for developing assurance cases with argument patterns. The issue is the equivalence problem between two assurance cases that are developed by different application sequences of argument patterns. In the Fig.1, two different argument pattern application sequences create different assurance cases A and B. Argument algebra is used to show the equivalence between assurance cases created by argument patterns.

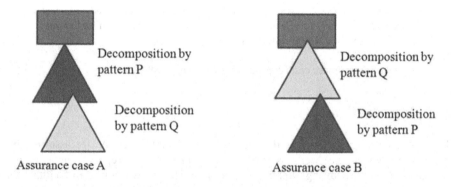

Fig. 1. Equivalence between assurance case with different pattern applications

Section 2 describes related work of argument pattern approaches for assurance cases. Argument algebra is proposed to formalize argument decomposition process in section 3. An example case study of the argument algebra is explained in section 4. Discussions on the effectiveness and appropriateness of argument patterns are shown in section 5. Our conclusions are presented in section 6.

2   Related Work

In the absence of any clearly organized guidelines concerning the approach to be taken in decomposing claims using strategies and the decomposition sequence, engineers has often not known how to develop their arguments. It is against this backdrop that the aforementioned approaches to argument decomposition patterns — architecture, functional, attribute, infinite set, complete (set of risks and requirements), monotonic, and concretion—were identified[15]. When applying the architecture decomposition pattern, a claim of the system is also satisfied for each constituent part of the system based on system architecture. Despotou and Kelly proposed a modular approach to improve clarity of safety case argument [6]. Hauge and Stolen described a pattern based safety case approach for Nuclear Power control domain [11]. Wardzinski proposed an approach for assuring vehicle safety domain based on the assumption that hazardous sequences of events [9]. An experimental result of argument patterns was reported [16]. Argument pattern catalogue was proposed based on the format of design patterns [7] [17]. Graydon and Kelly examined that argument patterns captures a way to argue about interference management [13].Alexander and others showed the safe argument pattern based on failure mode analysis [8]. Ruiz and others proposed an assurance case reuse system using case repository [12].

Denney and Pai proposed a Formal Basis for Safety Case Patterns [14]. They formalized pattern refinement such as (1) Instantiate parameters (2) Resolve choices (3) Resolve multiplicities (4) Unfold loops. These are refinement rules of parameterized argument patterns.

Although these argument pattern approaches were proposed, effects on the application sequences of argument patterns were not analyzed.

3   Argument Algebra

3.1   Definition. Argument Expression

(1) x is an element of a domain set X then [x] is an argument expression.
(2) [x,d] and [y,d] are argument expressions, then [x, y, d] is an argument expression.
(3) [x] and [y] are argument expressions, then [x], [y] is an argument expression.
(4) For any context C and argument expression [x], [x] | (C) is an argument expression.
(5) [x] is argument expression. and e is the evidence to assure x, then [x]/{ x->e} is an argument expression.

3.2   Definition. Argument Expression Transformation Rules

- Rotation [x, y] => [y, x]
- Commutation [x],[y] => [y], [x]
- Dimension extension [x], [y] => [x, y]
- Dimension restriction [x, y] | [x] => [x]
- Context introduction [x] => [x] | (Context)
- Context deletion [x] | (Context) => [x]
- Element decomposition by context [x] | (x->a,b) => [a,b] | (x->a,b) , where context: (x -> a, b) means x is decomposed by a and b
- Element composition by context [a, b] | (x->a,b) => [x] | (x->a,b)
- Evidence introduction [x] => [x]/{ evidence}
- Evidence deletion [x]/{ evidence} =>[x]

Let S, A, and B, mean a system and its two subsystems. IntrOfAandB means interaction between A and B. d means "dependable." For example, [S, d] means that system S is dependable.

Example of Claim transformation is as follows.

[S, d]   ... Top claim
=>[S, d]|(S->A,B, IntrOfAandB)   ... Context introduction
=>[A, d], [B, d], [IntrOfAandB, d]|(S->A,B, IntrOfAandB)
                                                ... Element decomposition

3.3   Argument Interpretation

For claims of assurance cases, argument expressions can be defined. Suppose each claim sentence has a subject, object, and adverb. Argument interpretation τ of a claim is defined as follows.

τ(Claim sentence) = [Subject, Object, Adverb]

If the claim sentence is assigned to context, argument interpretation is as follows.

τ(Claim sentence, Context) = [Subject, Object, Adverb] | (context)

When context is defined as (s-> s1, s2) for subject, the argument interpretation of above claim sentence is as follows.

τ(Claim sentence, (s-> s1, s2)) = [s, Object, Adverb], [s1, Object, Adverb], [s2, Object, Adverb] | (s-> s1, s2)

When context is defined as (o-> o1, o2) for object, the argument interpretation of above claim sentence is as follows.

τ(Claim sentence, (o-> o1, o2)) = [Subject, o, Adverb], [Subject, o1, Adverb], [Subject, o2, Adverb] | (o-> o1, o2)

Argument interpretation of evidence is as follows.

τ(Claim sentence, evidence) / {Evidence}

Example of the argument interpretation of assurance case shown in Fig.2 is as follows.

[A, d], [B, d], [IntrOfAandB, d]|(S->A,B, IntrOfAandB)

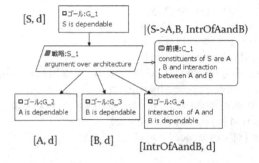

Fig. 2. Argument interpretation of assurance case

3.4   Argument Transformation

Argument expression X is transformed to argument expression Y, if there is a sequence of transformation rules $r_1, \ldots, r_{n-1}$.

$X = X_1$, $X_1 \Rightarrow X_2$, ..., $X_{n-1} \Rightarrow X_n$, $X_n = Y$, where X_k is transformed to X_{k+1} by rule r_k, where X ==> Y if X is transformable to Y.

For assurance cases A, B, and their corresponding argument interpretations $\tau(A)$ and $\tau(B)$, if $\tau(A)$ is transformable to $\tau(B)$ then $\tau(A) \Rightarrow \tau(B)$.

In this sense of transformability, we can clearly define the following equivalence relationship between assurance cases.

For assurance cases A and B, if $\tau(A) \Rightarrow \tau(B)$ then A and B are equivalent by transformation.

4   Example

4.1   Overview of the Target System

The LAN Device Management System (LDMS) consists of manager, sensors, and devices. These components are connected by LAN. The purpose of LDMS is to detect invalid devices connected to LAN by managing appropriate information on valid devices. Devices are monitored by sensors that are controlled by the LDMS manager. The LDMS manager controls approximately 2000 sensors. Each sensor monitors approximately 1000 devices through LAN in each location. The sensors are located in regional and oversea locations through Intranet as well as Internet. Fig.3 shows the configuration of LDMS.

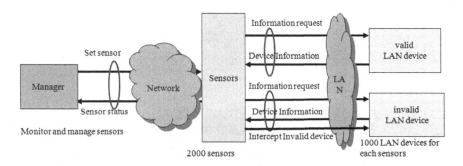

Fig. 3. Configuration of LAN device management system

4.2   Target Processes

Dependability issues shall also be validated for system development and operation processes as well as the target system as shown above. In this case study, O-DA process [18] is used. The process constitutes the change accommodation and failure response cycles as shown in Fig.4.

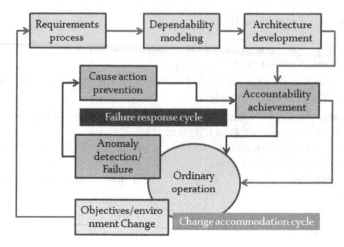

Fig. 4. O-DA Cycles

4.3   Assurance Case Developed by Argument Patterns

By applying process decomposition pattern and then architecture decomposition pattern, the assurance case of Fig. 5 is developed.

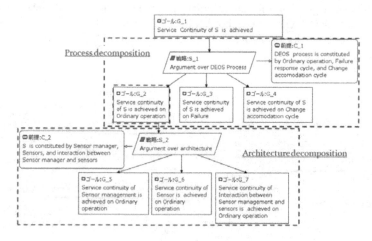

Fig. 5. Assurance case of LDMS

4.4   Equivalence of Pattern Application Sequences

It can be shown that there is no difference between two argument patterns which have different application orders by using the argument expression. First some notations are defined for simplifying expressions. Then argument expressions are transformed reversibly. The transformation shows that there is no difference in the different application orders of process decomposition and architecture decomposition patterns.

Notations

S: LDMS,
T1: Sensor manager,
T2: Sensors,
T3: Interaction between Sensor manager and sensors
C: DEOS process,
C1: Ordinary operation process,
C2: Change accommodation cycle,
C3: Failure response cycle

[S, d]: Argument interpretation of D-Case on LDMS , where S: LDMS, d: "Service continuity is achieved"

The meaning of [S, d] is "Service continuity of LDMS is achieved." [S, C, d] also means that Service continuity of LDMS in DEOS process is achieved.

Reversibility of Decomposition Pattern Application

[S, d]
=> [S, C, d]
=> [S, C, d] | (C->C1, C2, C3) -- by Process decomposition
=> [S, C1,d],[S,C2,d],[S,C3,d] | (C->C1, C2, C3)
=> [S, C1,d],[S,C2,d],[S,C3,d] | (C->C1, C2, C3)| (S->T1, T2, T3)
=> [T1, C1,d], [T2, C1,d], [T3, C1,d],   [S,C2,d],[S,C3,d] | (C->C1, C2, C3) | (S->T1, T2, T3) -- by Architecture decomposition
=>[T1, C1,d], [T2, C1,d], [T3, C1,d],   [T1,C2,d], [T2,C2,d], [T3,C2,d],[S,C3,d] |(C->C1,C2,C3)|(S->T1,T2,T3)
=>[T1,   C1,d],   [T2,   C1,d],   [T3,   C1,d],   [T1,C2,d],   [T2,C2,d], [T3,C2,d],[T1,C3,d] ,[T2,C3,d] ,[T3,C3,d]
   |(C->C1,C2,C3)|(S->T1,T2,T3)
=>[T1, C1,d], [T1,C2,d], [T1,C3,d], [T2, C1,d], [T3, C1,d], [T2,C2,d], [T3,C2,d] ,[T2,C3,d] ,[T3,C3,d]
   |(C->C1,C2,C3)|(S->T1,T2,T3)
=>[T1, C1,d], [T1,C2,d], [T1,C3,d], [T2, C1,d], [T2,C2,d], [T2,C3,d] ,[T3, C1,d], [T3,C2,d] , [T3, C3,d]
|(C->C1,C2,C3)|(S->T1,T2,T3)
=>[T1,C,d], [T2, C1,d], [T2,C2,d], [T2,C3,d] ,[T3, C1,d], [T3,C2,d] , [T3,C3,d]
|(C->C1,C2,C3)|(S->T1,T2,T3)
=>[T1,C,d], [T2, C,d], [T3, C1,d], [T3,C2,d] , [T3,C3,d] |(C->C1,C2,C3)|(S->T1,T2,T3) -- by Process composition
=>[T1,C,d],[T2,C,d],[T3,C,d] | (S->T1,T2,T3) -- by Architecture composition
=>[S, C, d]

4.5   Effectiveness of the Pattern Transformation

For the large scale system development, many engineers will participate. Different engineers tend to develop assurance case by different pattern applications. By using the proposed method, the equivalence check of the assurance cases developed by different engineers is easily confirmed.

5   Summary and Future Issues

In this paper we proposed the Argument algebra to define an equivalence relationship between assurance cases using argument patterns. The transformation rules of argument expressions are effectively used to decide the equivalence of assurance cases. The transformation rules have nice property of reversibility. The running example showed the applicability of the argument algebra for the realistic cases.

Future issues are as follows:

Automatic Tool to automate assurance case comparison

Integration with architecture and process models

Argument expression management with Natural language analysis and Word dictionary

References

1. Kelly, T.P.: A Six-Step Method for the Development of Goal Structures. York Software Engineering (1997)
2. Kelly, T.: Arguing Safety, a Systematic Approach to Managing Safety Cases. PhD Thesis, Department of Computer Science, University of York (1998)
3. McDermid, J.A.: Software safety: Where's the evidence? In: SCS 2001: Proceedings of the Sixth Australian Workshop on Safety Critical Systems and Software, pp. 1–6. Australian Computer Society, Inc., Darlinghurst (2001)
4. Bate, I., Kelly, T.: Architectural considerations in the certification of modular systems. Reliability Engineering and System Safety 81, 303–324 (2003)
5. Kelly, T., Weaver, R.: The Goal Structuring Notation – A Safety Argument Notation. In: Proceedings of the Dependable Systems and Networks 2004 Workshop on Assurance Cases (July 2004)
6. Despotou, G., Kelly, T.: Investigating the use of argument modularity to optimize throughlife system safety assurance. In: Proc. 3rd IET Int. Conf. on System Safety (ICSS). IET (2008)
7. Kelly, T., McDermid, J.: Safety Case Construction and Reuse using Patterns (1998)
8. Alexander, R., Kelly, T., Kurd, Z., McDermid, J.: Safety Cases for Advanced Control Software: Safety Case Patterns (2007)
9. Wardzinski, A.: Safety Argument Strategies for Autonomous Vehicles (2008)
10. Denny, E., Pai, G.: A Lightweight Methodology for Safety Case Assembly (2012)
11. Hauge, A., Stolen, K.: A Pattern-Based Method for Safe Control Systems Exemplified within Nuclear Power Production (2012)
12. Ruiz, A., Habli, I., Espinoza, H.: Towards a Case-Based Reasoning Approach for Safety Assurance Reuse (2012)
13. Graydon, P., Kelly, T.: Assessing Software Interference Management When Modifying Safety-Related Software (2012)
14. Denny, E., Pai, G.: Formal verification of a safety argumentation and application to a complex UAV system AdvoCATE: An Assurance Case Automation Toolset (2012)

15. Bloomfield, R., Bishop, P.: Safety and Assurance Cases: Past. Present and Possible Future – an Adelard Perspective (2010)
16. Yamamoto, S., Matsuno, Y.: An Evaluation of Argument Patterns to Reduce Pitfalls of Applying Assurance Case, pp.12–17, Assure (2013)
17. Hawkins, R., Kelly, T.: A Software Safety Argument Pattern Catalogue, YCS-2013-482 (2013)
18. Open Group Standard, Real-Time and Embedded Systems: Dependability through Assuredness[TM] (O-DA) Framework (2013)

An Environment of Programming
of Strategies on the Base of Knowledge

Valeriy N. Kuchuganov and Denis R. Kasimov

Kalashnikov Izhevsk State Technical University, Izhevsk, Russia
kuchuganov@istu.ru

Abstract. In the paper an environment of programming of strategies is proposed, which can form the basis of new generation intelligent programming tutors. The proposed approach is based on ideas of the situation calculus, involves representation of problem conditions in the form of appropriate knowledge semantic categories and specification of a solving strategy. A user is provided by libraries of term definitions and implementations. Determination of semantics of actions and directives is carried out with help of a process-oriented ontology. On this basis it becomes possible to solve programming problems not at the level of planning actions, but at the level of describing strategies of allocation of resources and works. Examples of formalization of problem statements and solving strategies are provided.

Keywords: programming tutor, combinatorial problems, search methods, situation description, actions, process ontology, strategy description.

1   Introduction

A leap in development of programming tutors, intelligent system development environments is possible at the expense of creation of languages and interpretation methods, which allow a programmer to better focus on the sense of solving a given problem. For this, first of all, it is necessary that an interpreter has and actively uses knowledge.

The need for knowledge-based programming is sharply felt by developers of intelligent agents. An attempt to meet this need is the programming language GOLOG [1] which extends traditional imperative programming by logical reasoning about actions which an agent can perform, on the base of the situation calculus. However, this language requires from a programmer specifics absolutely at all levels: in semantics of predicates and actions, in their arguments etc., Inputting relevant domain knowledge, creation of techniques of it processing are entirely the responsibility of a programmer.

Another example of a knowledge-based language is DECLIMP [2]. A program in it consists of three types of codes: 1) imperative procedures; 2) background knowledge in an expressive logic; 3) structured concrete data. Various methods of reasoning (theorem proving, constraint propagation etc.,) of theories and structures may be initiated in procedures. In general, the language DECLIMP is an environment in

A. Kravets et al. (Eds.): JCKBSE 2014, CCIS 466, pp. 726–734, 2014.

which it is possible to simultaneous use both imperative and declarative programming style, but the intelligence of its interpreter also remains at a primitive level.

Complicated tasks are characterized by the large enumeration problem which is usually solved by means of various strategies and heuristics which *are embedded* in an algorithm. In the theory and practice of programming there are many techniques and strategies to solve problems. Here are some of them:

- *Recursion* is a method of search by analysis of a limited space, for example, the nearest environment of a current state. A recursive procedure achieves a goal due to the fact that (having found a "trace", i.e.) having partially solved a problem calls itself.
- *Iterative method* solves a problem by successive approximations to a goal, checking the distance to the target after each step. Unlike recursion, each iteration finds a solution immediately, but the solution's precision depends on the number of completed steps. For example, digging a ditch by the uniform removal of soil layers throughout the whole length.
- *Methods of the enumeration of variants*: *"greedy" algorithm* – consideration of variants in the order of descending of the estimation of their proximity to a goal; *breadth-first search* – analysis of variants in the order of appearance; *depth-first search* – processing an alternative which appeared most recently; *search by the simulated annealing method* – random selection of a successor state, in which a variant that does not improve the situation is accepted with a probability depending on the degree of the deterioration of the situation and the duration of the search process; *search by priorities*; *search by expert rules*.
- *Pyramidal search in a parameter space* – partition of the space into subspaces and selection of the best initially in each subspace, then among the neighboring etc.,
- *Splitting a goal into subgoals* – movement through control intermediate situations.
- *Genetic algorithms* – successors are generated not from one, but two alternatively considered variants, with elements of randomness.
- *Random search.*

Such techniques often form a frame of a program; therefore it would be nice to make them primitives of the programming language.

The purpose of the study is to transfer the problem solving process from the level of planning actions (commands, operators) to the level of planning strategies of allocation of works and resources given in a problem statement.

We define a problem solving strategy as a complex of actions and criteria of the selection of resources needed for their implementation. Actions which are specified in a strategy are divided into two categories: actions described in a problem statement and the solver's actions. Restrictions are also divided into two categories: restrictions from a problem statement and restrictions that are defined by a user in order to narrow/expand the search space.

The description of a strategy of solving a combinatorial problem consists in specification of criteria (priorities) and restrictions when selecting variants of objects, actions and attributes from ones that are provided according to the problem statement, as well as in specification of follow relationships between actions. Due to this a user can manage the process of solving the problem in a visual mode.

The result of the problem solving is a sequence found of actions that are predefined by the problem statement and results of executing this sequence.

The solver actively uses a process-oriented domain ontology and a knowledge base as a source of background information as well as an ontological explanatory dictionary (OED) that refers to concepts in the ontology in order to determine the sense (interpretation) of terms encountered in a problem statement.

2   Knowledge Ontology of the Solver

The system's knowledge are divided into the following semantic categories: property, object (thing, process), relation, compound object, action, situation and script [3].

A *concept-property* has the form:

<Property> ::= <Name>, [<Comment>], <Value type>, [<Method>],

where the *Method* is a method for measuring the property.

An *object* is described by a function, attributes and a model. Things have a geometric model (cinematic scheme, drawing, map, image, 3D geometric model, printscreen), processes – a computational model (formula, algorithm etc.,)

<Object> ::= <Name>, <Comment>, <Function>, <List of attributes>, [<Model>],

where *<Attribute> ::= <Name>, <Property instance>, [<Range of values>, <Expected value>], [<Measure>], [<Method instance>].*

A process changes a situation; a thing can change a situation only if it is an instrument of a process.

<Relation> ::= <Name>, <Type>, [<Comment>], [<List of attributes>], <List of objects>, <Value type>, [<Expected value>], [<Measure>], <Method instance>.

Here the *Method instance* is a concrete method of calculating the relation's value.

A *compound object* is a thing or a process having a composition (entrance tree) and a connection scheme (spatial graph).

An *action* is an object-process and a system of its relations with objects-participants of the action:

— an agent (executor);
— a beneficiary – a customer in whose interests the action (work) is performed;
— a recipient – a receiver of the action (for example, *"Vasya gives an apple Kate"*, the recipient is *Kate*);
— a subject of the influence: initial/result (in the above example – *an apple*);
— scene of the action;
— an instrument;
— a co-agent (accomplice);
— an effect etc.,

A *situation* is a set of states of things, processes and relations between them, where a *state* is a set of values of parameters of things, processes and relations in some moment or period of time.

A *script* is an ordered in time sequence of situations and a *scenario* (the script's model) – an ordered sequence of actions (digraph, diagram).

A script describes the dynamics of domestic, industrial and other relations between subjects.

3   The Order of the Description of a Problem and a Solving Strategy

The process of programming a problem is as follows:

1. Describe things of the problem (objects on which actions are performed or with respect to which statements are made) in a table.
2. Select appropriate actions in the tree of actions of the OED, wherein at the top level actions are defined in the physical sense and at the bottom one – according to specifics of domains.
3. Bind actions with things (an executor, a receiver etc.,).
4. Add pre- and post-conditions to the actions.
5. Describe explicit and implicit relationships (including rules and restrictions) in the problem.
6. Define arithmetic and logical functions which were required in the previous stages.
7. Specify a solving strategy from the problem's actions and the solver's actions. As the latter quantifiers and variant generators are serve, which are also selected from a library.

A problem's actions are described in a table. Rows correspond to actions, columns – to their attributes: name; properties (priority, duration, speed etc.,); participants (who, where to, whom etc.,); pre-condition; operation (a function which implements an action, i.e. changes a state); post-condition.

The solver's actions:

1. *CreateVariant(Way = <Enumeration kind>, What = <Variant specification>, From = <Object collection specification>, Conditions = <List of conditions>)*.
   The action *CreateVariant* is automatically creates a loop which works until a goal is achieved or until all variants are tested. The loop's body begins and ends with brackets. The positive outcome of the variant research loop is checked by the solver's action *Success*.
2. *Success(Conditions = <List of conditions>, <List of the solver's actions>)*.
   In the list of actions, for example, may be *Stop*, *GiveReport* etc.,
3. *Select(Way = , From = , Conditions =)* – an analogue of a SQL-query.

Just like actions of a problem, the solver's actions contain conditions. The role of a user is to "felicitously" arrange variant generation commands and their conditions.

Actions (commands) of a user, which he creates himself, include *SetPriorities*, *Sort*, *ChangeRestrictions* – on variants or actions.

Many problems contain terms understandable by humans but in order to they will be understandable by a machine it is necessary to define them in the form of functions. For example: on the left, on the right, upward, downward, nearby, adjacently, west, east etc., Also fuzzy or numeric parameters which are evaluated and compared. The solver has a library of functions, but a user can supplement it according to a problem statement.

For example, the function *Nearby(a, b)* will have different implementation depending on the domain of a problem: towns or houses or chessboard cells. In the solver it is implemented as for adjacent elements of a list or a matrix; this gives it some universality.

4   Solving a Problem

The solver acts according to the user-entered system of directives, generates and analyzes alternative solving paths.

On individual steps the solver performs: checking pre- and post-conditions of actions; execution of actions; control of the compliance of states (obtained as a result of the execution of actions) with restrictions; addition of new states to a state tree; assessment of the strategy being implemented.

The analysis of states, finding new facts is carried out by forward and backward logical inference (Prolog). Systems of relations, which are given in a problem, are also solved by numerical methods.

In general, the solver's algorithm is close to approaches based on the situation calculus [4].

5   Examples

Consider the proposed problem programming style on examples.

5.1   Climbers [5]

The representation of the problem includes:

— subjects – Figure 1;
— initial (everyone is on the base with a certain unknown amount of freight), intermediate (at least one on the top) and final (everyone is on the base without freight) situations – Figure 2;
— actions of the problem: *"Go"*, *"GiveAway"* – Figure 3;
— restrictions and rules of the problem.

	Name	Number	Capacity	Consumption	Freight	Place
1	Climber	1	7	1		
2	Climber	2	8	2		
3	Climber	3	12	2		
4	Climber	4	15	3		
5	Climber	5	7	1		

Fig. 1. Description of subjects of the problem

	Name	Number	Freight	Place
1	Climber	1	?	Base
2	Climber	2	?	Base
3	Climber	3	?	Base
4	Climber	4	?	Base
5	Climber	5	?	Base

a)

	Name	Number	Place
1	Climber	?	RelPosition(Base, +N Days)

b)

	Name	Number	Freight	Place
1	Climber	1	0	Base
2	Climber	2	0	Base
3	Climber	3	0	Base
4	Climber	4	0	Base
5	Climber	5	0	Base

c)

Fig. 2. Description of situations: a) initial; b) intermediate; c) final

	Name	Who	WhereTo	Days	Pre-condition
1	Go	Some Climber	Upward ∨ Downward	?	Same(Place, Who)

	Name	Who	What	Whom
2	GiveAway	Climber$A	PartOf(Freight)	Climber$B

Fig. 3. Description of actions of the problem

Regarding actions, typical for problems pre-conditions and implementation algorithms are contained in the knowledge base. Below are some of the knowledge about the action "*Go*":

- *Who.Resource ≥ Who.Consumption * Go.Duration.*
- ***Decrease*** *Who.Resource **By** Who.Consumption * Go.Duration.*
- ***If*** *Go.WhereTo is SpatialObject **Then** Who.Place := Go.WhereTo.*
- ***If*** *Go.WhereTo is PositiveDirection **Then** Who.Place := RelPosition(Who.Place, +Go.Speed * Go.Duration).*
- ***If*** *Go.WhereTo is NegativeDirection **Then** Who.Place := RelPosition(Who.Place, –Go.Speed * Go.Duration).*
- ***Increase*** *Who.Time **By** Go.Duration.*

In the knowledge base there is also the following restriction which is relevant to the considered problem: *Object.Freight ≤ Object.Capacity.*

One of the problem conditions is the rule of prohibiting the re-ascent: *If Performed Go(Who = $X, WhereTo = Downward)* ***Then*** *Disallow Go(Who = $X, WhereTo = Upward).*

Below is the strategy (action plan) of solving the problem.

```
Climbing = CreateVariant(Way = 1, What = Group, From =
Climbers)
{
   Go(Who = Group, WhereTo = Upward, Days = 1);
   CreateVariant(Way = 1, What = (Group1, Group2), From =
Group)
   {
      GiveAway(Who = Group2, Whom = Group1, What = Sur-
plus);
      Go(Who = Group1, WhereTo = Upward, Days = 1);
      Go(Who = Group2, WhereTo = Base);
      Success(Conditions = Achieved ProblemGoal, GiveRe-
port);
      Climbing;
   }
}
```

Here is the recursion since:

— climbing height is replaced by the parameter "*Number of days upward*";
— problem (search space) is narrowed after each pass of 1 day without changing the plan.

Anyway, a good strategy is an author's art.

5.2   A Wolf, A Goat and A Cabbage

The problem's restrictions:

— *(Wolf.Place = Waterman.Place)* ∨ *(Wolf.Place ≠ Goat.Place)*;
— *(Goat.Place = Waterman.Place)* ∨ *(Goat.Place ≠ Cabbage.Place)*.

Below is the main plan of solving this problem:

```
CreateVariant(Way = 2, What = Freight, From = Subjects
Bank[1])
{
   Transport(Who = Waterman, What = Freight, WhereTo =
ThereTo);
   Success(Conditions = Count(Subjects[Place = Bank[1]]) =
0, GiveReport);
   CreateVariant(Way = 2, What = FreightBackward, From =
Subjects Bank[2])
   {
      Transport(Who = Waterman, What = FreightBackward,
WhereTo = Backward);
   }
}
```

This problem can be considered solved only when all subjects have been transported, and there are no priorities. Thus there is no other strategy except the exhaustive search in compliance with the restrictions of the problem.

6   Conclusion

So, the problem solving moves from the level of direct planning actions to the level of selecting a strategy of allocation of resources and works, and the exploratory research – to selecting strategies of performing the work on the search for a solution of a given problem.

References

1. Levesque, H.J., Reiter, R., Lespérance, Y., Lin, F., Scherl, R.B.: GOLOG: A logic programming language for dynamic domains. The Journal of Logic Programming 31(1-3), 59–83 (1997)
2. Pooter, S.D., Wittocx, J., Denecker, M.: A Prototype of a Knowledge-Based Programming Environment. In: Tompits, H., Abreu, S., Oetsch, J., Pührer, J., Seipel, D., Umeda, M., Wolf, A. (eds.) INAP/WLP 2011. LNCS (LNAI), vol. 7773, pp. 279–286. Springer, Heidelberg (2013)
3. Kuchuganov, V.N.: Elements of Associative Semantic Theory. Upravlenie Bolshimi Sistemami (40), 30–48 (2012) (in Russian)
4. Pirri, F., Reiter, R.: Some contributions to the metatheory of the situation calculus. Journal of the ACM 46(3), 261–325 (1999)
5. Heyderhoff, P., Hein, H.-W., Krückeberg, F., Miklitz, G., Widmayer, P.: Final Report International Olympiad in Informatics, Bonn/Germany (1992),
   http://www.ioinformatics.org/locations/ioi92/report.html

Theory of Category Approach
to Knowledge Based Programming[*]

Alexander Zhozhikashvili and Vadim L. Stefanuk

Institute for Information Transmission Problems of Russian Academy of Science,
Moscow, Russia
{zhozhik,stefanuk}@iitp.ru

Abstract. Methods of knowledge based programming for intelligent systems
are demonstrated using the theory of category language developed by the
present authors to describe Production Systems. The methods proposed allow to
separate the process of programming of an abstract intelligent system involving
productions from the process of association (binding) this system to the solution
of a concrete problem. There are examples are given of the use of technology in
real programs.

1   Productions, Patterns and Pattern Matching

A typical knowledge based system acts in the following way. When it meets the situation, where something is to be done, it "recognizes" the situation, i.e. it finds in its
memory the description of the situation and the description of what should be done in
this situation. Such a description allowing to recognize the situation and to remember
what should be done in this situation we call the production. The use of productions
for the design of knowledge base systems is well known practice [1,2]. However we
understand productions slightly different from the traditional one [3]. The main two
parts of a classic production are the conditions of its applicability and the description
of actions, which should be performed if the conditions are valid. The production in
the present paper also contains two sides. Its left side presents the conditions of its
applicability, however its right side the description of the situation, which will be the
result of the application of the production. It means that the left and right sides are
similar. Such productions are similar to rules in Markov algorithm [4] and to the Post
production [5] (who actually proposed the term "production"). With such a general
understanding of productions we may say that the productions is the most important
element of many intelligent knowledge based systems, even those that usually are not
considered as production based.

If one wants that the production should be applicable not only for once concrete
situation, but for the whole class of such situations, which are similar in some sense,
in the left side of a production should stay the description of such a class of situation.
Such a generalized description of similar situations called a pattern. If the situation

---

[*] This work was partially supported by the Russian Fund for Basic Research (RFBR), Grant #12-
07-00209a, and by the Presidium of Russian Academy of Sciences Program #15, Project 211.

A. Kravets et al. (Eds.): JCKBSE 2014, CCIS 466, pp. 735–746, 2014.

corresponds to the generalized description, we say that the situation matches the pattern. The pattern differs from exact description of the situation as some elements of the situation are not having concrete values. These elements may be different for various situations which match the same pattern. The concretization of those elements actually converts the pattern to the situation. Thus, the situation is considered to be matching the pattern, if the pattern maybe concretized in such a way, that in result one obtains the given situation.

As it was mentioned above the production presents the description of two situations: the source situation and the resulting one. It means that the left and right sides are patterns. The production is applicable to the situation if the situation is matching the left side of it. In this case the result of application of the production is the result of concretization of its left side, and it is necessary that the right side must be concretized in some sense in the same way, as was the concretization of its left side needed for obtaining from the left side the source situation.

2   The Use of the Language of Category Theory

In order to give the formal exposition of the concepts described above and to obtain the possibility to describe the algorithms for working with productions, which are not connected with the concrete situations, for which the productions are applicable, we designed a language, based on the tools of theory of category.

Let one have some category. The character of the category is defined with the details of the concrete problem, namely with way how for the given problem various situations are coded and how the generalized description of the situation are constructed, i.e. the pattern. Let be an object of this category. The pattern with the meaning in S will be any morphism $\varphi : X \to S$, where X is the object of the category.

To make the definition more transparent we will give the following construction. Let S be a real set of situations, for formalization of which the category is being built. Let us consider some pattern. There are many ways to concretize this pattern, i.e. to add to it some data needed for the description of a situation. Let X be the set of all possible ways of the pattern concretization. As for each such a concretization we obtain some situation we have a mapping $X \to S$. Such mappings play the role of morphisms of the category.

The set of the situations with meaning in S will be referred to as some subset of the set of patterns with meaning in S. The only requirement imposed to the set of situation is the following one. If $\varphi\psi$ is a composition of morphisms φ and ψ, then the morphism $\varphi\psi$ is a situation only in case, when the morphism ψ is some situation.

The situation $\alpha : U \to S$ is considered as matching the pattern $\varphi : X \to S$ if there is a morphism $\beta : U \to X$ such that $\alpha = \varphi\beta$ is valid. Note this morphism is not uniquely defined by the equation $\alpha = \varphi\beta$.

Production is the pair of patterns with common source. Speaking more precisely, the production from S to T is the pair of morphisms $\varphi : X \to S$ and $\psi : X \to T$. A production is applicable to the situation $\alpha : U \to S$, if this situation is matching the pattern, which left side of the production, i.e. if $\alpha = \varphi \beta$ for some morphism $\beta : U \to X$. In this case the result of the application of the production will be the morphism $\psi \beta : U \to T$. The latter is a situation due to the condition formulated above imposed over the set of situations.

Note that the action of the production is not a uniquely defined as the equality $\alpha = \varphi \beta$ does not uniquely defined the morphism β.

In our previous publications it was shown that many schemes of pattern matching may be presented on the theory of category language with the use of correspondingly chosen category.

3   Program Implementation of the Theory of Category Description of Productions

One of the goals that were defined by the present authors in formulation of theory of category definitions was to provide experts on knowledge based intelligent systems with a possibility to formulate the algorithms involved in the functioning of such systems in the way, which does not depend on the concrete data with which the system operates. Using our language the algorithm should not depend on the manner in which the situation, the pattern and how the process of matching is organized. The rest of our paper intended to describe ways of achieving this goal and to examples of concrete programming systems.

We assume that the program that implements the knowledge based intelligent systems will have two levels. The upper level should be designed by an expert in the area of knowledge based intelligent systems. At this level there are should be found solutions, related to the theory of production systems: should one use the forward or backward inference, or some combination of the techniques, what to do if different productions leads to the contradictive results and etc. This usually referred to as the inference engine.

The bottom level must be written by the designer of the final intelligent system for solution of some concrete task. This level should perform the binding of some algorithms of the operation of the production system to the concrete task. At this level there should be defined the way of situation coding of situations, patterns, and the matching operation should be described.

Note that similar two level approach was used by the authors for Meta Expert System [6] and later for Expert System Shell [7].

In order to organize the interaction of the levels with one another it is expected the development of some standard. This standard must represent some specification of what should be represented with bottom level, what objects, procedures and functions must be defined at this level. However the specification contains no information on the way the objects are designed, or how the procedures and functions actually operate. The programs of the upper level must rely on this standard, i.e. they may use the constructions provide by the bottom level. No other access to the real data the program of upper level should not have. This will insure that the program of upper level, made in accordance with the standard, will be able to cope with any programs of bottom level, which satisfy the standard.

The standard may exist in forms different from its description. It may be implemented with a program as certain generalization of some programming language. This generalization must be abstract ones, i.e. to have some empty fragments, which may be written down by the designer of the bottom level, i.e. the designer of the final intelligent system intended for solution of some concrete problem.

In the object languages the natural way of designing such construction is the use of abstract classes, which contains some operations that are not defined. The designer of a concrete system must use derived classes and define there necessary operations.

There are some other possibilities as well. For example, in the interpreted languages, which do not require the compilation and linking, may exist some functions, which are announced but not defined functions. The definition of such a function is the task for the final designer.

4   The Examples of Program Implementation

The exposed ideas were implemented on the programming level not once, but even three times.

It was done in the frame of a project of natural text analyses [8]. The description of the project is not given here, however the implemented production system is directly related to the present paper. The texts to be analyzed were in Microsoft Word format. For this reason it was decided to write the program to work with production knowledge base using VBA.

In what followed it turned down that the interpretation language VBA is too slow in order to process complicated productions and the same approach was repeated with tools of C++, namely the tools of Borland C++ Builder. The program interacted with MS Word using COM-interface.

At last the same job was implemented on Lisp. It was done because our collective of designers is involved in research on production systems and the language Lisp in these studies is the main language. Common Lisp was used in the version LispWorks. The interaction with MS Word was performed again via COM-interface.

The base for the generalization constitutes three basic elements: morphism, composition operation and the matching operation. As all three mentioned languages supports object programming (in Lisp it was the system CLOS), it was decides to use corresponding tools. The notion of morphism was implemented as the class with this name. The composition operation was claimed as an empty method in VBA, the abstract method in C++ and generic function in Lisp. In C++ we used even the operator overloading, that resulted in the possibility to write in the program as f*g.

Some difficulty appeared in connection with the matching operation. As it was already mentioned this operation is not a single valued operation. It may produce some set of results, or empty set if the matching is impossible. Meanwhile different programming languages use different constructions for coding of sets. In Lisp it was natural to use a list (which is most convenient due to fact that empty list plays the role of logic value false, which means that the empty list of possible ways of matching in the same time speaks in favor of unsuccessful matching). Yet, there no direct analog for lists in VBA. Though Lists are supported in C++, but the difference from list implementation in List is very big. Indeed, our goal was to create the universal specification for theory of category built up over the language that should not depend on the construction implemented in a language to such great extent.

In result the following decision was made. In all three languages there was a class matcher created. During initialization this class was presented a situation and the pattern, which should match. (In our case both are objects in the class morphism.) Two methods have been defined for the class matcher: next and reset. Object next for each call to it returns the next version of the matching. If there no version left, next returns the negative reply, that is 0 in C++, nil in Lisp, and a special object impossible in VBA. A programmer, using some language is free to decide what to do with the obtained value, for example to put it in a list, to put in a set, or to store it somehow else. The method reset returns the object matcher to its original state and then the next again starts to return first version of matching. Expected more productive version C++ next, which is called after reset does not make the matching a new. Instead of it all the previous results of matches are stored and after reset are taken from the memory. Father in our research the scheme has been used on all the other multivalued operations in the following way. An object was created with methods next and reset, and while the next produces next result, the reset, returns the object to the original state.

The supplementary objects, included into our generalization, were production and production base. They were implemented as classes production and production-base[1]. An object of the class production contains left and right parts, which are the objects morphism. The object of the class production-base keeps the list of productions. In case VBA this list was implemented as an array, in case of C++ a class of standard library std::list was used, for Lisp it was a list.

To use these objects there were created classes Production-matcher и Production-base-matcher with the methods next and reset, having the same property as that for the class matcher. The object of the class production-matcher creates the объект matcher on the base of situation and left side of the production, and then sends to its address all the calls of the method next. The result obtained during the call is combined with the right part with using operation composition. Object production-base-matcher creates the object production-matcher based on the situation and the first production from the list and transmits to it all the calls to next, until the reply will be received that there no more matches. Then it creates object production-matcher using a situation and the next production from the list and starts to work with them. It will act this way until the list of production will be exhausted.

All these supplementing objects are being built on the base of three main elements.

---

[1] Syntactic difference in the languages led us to slightly different notations. In the paper the notations from Lisp are used. For instance, in C++ the name *ProductionBase* was used.

It means that in the process of binding the system to another type of situations only method next for the object matcher and the operation composition should be adapted.

5   Production Nets

Production nets differ from common production bases, i.e. the sets of productions in the property that a production may be used recursively, calling other production in the process of activity. It is achieved in the following manner. If in application of productions $\varphi: X \to S$ and $\psi: X \to T$ to the situation $\alpha: U \to S$ a morphism β was found such that $\alpha = \varphi\beta$, and if this situation is matching with pattern, that is the left side of the production, and then this morphism does not used immediately. Instead it considered as a new situation and a production system is applied to it. Note that possibly it may be a different production system. If the transformation of the situation β turns out to be impossible, the situation β is discarded and the system is looking for another way of matching the situation $\alpha: U \to S$ with the pattern. In case the transformation β turned out to be successful and in the result the situation β' was obtained, the result of the production is considered to be $\psi\beta'$.

Production nets allows transit from our two-level scheme ("task" - "single production") to multilevel scheme ("task"- "subtask"- "subtask"- "subtask"- ...)/ where reduction of a task to a subtask is created with the help of productions. This logic is highly useful for solution of linguistic problems, where certain structure very frequently is described as a set of connected in some way substructures, each substructure must have a certain form.

To be able to work with the production nets the method next of the class matcher have been modified. Having obtained the result of matching of the situation with the left part of the production this method should not start immediately to perform operation composition. Instead it crest an object of the class production-base-matcher, which contains the above result as a situation, and calls the method next of this object till it gets a negative reply. To each of the obtained results the operation composition is applied.

What the production base should be included in the object just built production-base-matcher, must be shown somehow in the production itself. In the following chapters of this paper it will be shown how it may be done.

6   The Use of Direct Products

The production nets turnout to be extremely useful in case, when the objects of the category maybe represented as the direct products of more simple objects. This case is rather frequently takes place as it will be demonstrated in the next chapters. Let the object X is presented as a direct product $X = X_1 \times X_2 \times ... \times X_n$. In this case the morphism $\beta : U \to X$ that was found in the process of matching may be represented as set of morphisms $\beta_i : U \to X_i$, $i = 1,2,...,n$. Now each such morphism is independently transformed into β_i' with the help of the production system (for each β_i' it is a corresponding production system). Then from the obtained morphisms β_i' the morphism β' is being built. The use of direct products may be justified in the categories, where each object may be represented as the direct product of the subobjects that may not be decomposed further. In this case the transition from the analyses of the morphism β to the analyses of the morphisms β_i also means the reduction of the complex task to a combination of the simple ones.

For implementation of the direct product our standard was generalized a bit. The operation product was included that allows to build a morphism $\chi : U \to X \times Y$ as the product of two morphisms $\varphi : U \to X$ and $\psi : U \to Y$. To the class morphism the method next-multiplier has been added. If one have $X = X_1 \times X_2 \times ... \times X_n$ and the morphism $\beta : U \to X$ is represented a set of $\beta_i : U \to X_i$, $i = 1,2,...n$, the method next-multiplier, applied to this morphism will give sequentially β_1, β_2,..., β_n, provided that the next call would give a negative result similarly to the cal to next for the matcher.

7 Ω-categories

Ω-categories have been described un our publications [9]. Without going to details we will show for what situations and patterns these categories have been designed. In many problem we have the following relations among situations and patterns. The situation is a certain structure built in accordance some definite syntactic rules. The pattern is the same kind of structure, yet containing beside the elements, from which the situation is built some variables. The pattern concretization consists in the substitution instead the variables some fragments, provided that the fragments are built in accordance with the same syntactic rules as the situations, that mean that the fragments are situations. The examples of the pattern of these kind are the strings, containing variables, which may be substituted with substrings, the lists, containing variables, which may be substituted with sublists, the trees, where some subtrees may be substituted and etc.

Let S be the set of such patterns, i.e. structures, containing variables. For $s \in S$ we will write $s = s(u_1, u_2,..., u_n)$, if the pattern s contains variables u_1, $u_2,..., u_n$. If $s \in S$, $s = s(u_1, u_2,..., u_n)$, we may consider mapping $\varphi : S \times S \times ... \times S \to S$, where $\varphi(a_1, a_2,..., a_n)$ is defined as the result of substitution a_i instead u_i in s.

Let $U = \{u_1, u_2, ..., u_n\}$ is some set of variables. It is convenient instead the sequences $(a_1, a_2, ..., a_n) \in S \times S \times ... \times S$ indexed with natural numbers, to consider sequences $(a_{u_1}, a_{u_2}, ..., a_{u_n})$ indexed with elements of the set U itself. The set of such sequences we will denote with the symbol $\Omega(U)$. If $V = \{v_1, v_2, ..., v_m\}$ and $(s_{v_1}, s_{v_2}, ..., s_{v_m}) \in \Omega(V)$ we will define the mapping $\varphi : \Omega(U) \to \Omega(V)$ assuming that

$$\varphi(a_{u_1}, a_{u_2}, ..., a_{u_n}) = (t_{v_1}, t_{v_2}, ..., t_{v_m}),$$

where t_{v_i} is the result of the substitution of a_{u_j} instead of u_j in s_{v_i}, $j = 1, 2, ..., m$.

Ω-category is the category, where the objects are the sets $\Omega(U)$, and where U are finite sets of variables, and the morphisms are the mapping of described above type. Not one interesting peculiarity, namely that the morphism from $\Omega(U)$ to $\Omega(V)$ is given by the element of the set $\Omega(V)$. Thus, the morphisms to the set are the same as the elements of this set. This fact is the consequence of our definition of the Ω-category. One see that what is inserted has the same syntax as the item where it is inserted.

The Ω-categories permit the usage of all the methods, described in the previous chapters. It is easy to prove that if $V = \{v_1, v_2, ..., v_m\}$, then $\Omega(V) = \Omega\{v_1\} \times \Omega\{v_2\} \times ... \times \Omega\{v_m\}$. It means that is possible using the expansion into direct product to go from the morphism $\Omega(U) \to \Omega(V)$ to the morphisms $\Omega(U) \to \Omega(\{v\})$. With each variable a certain production base is connected. When there is need to reformat the morphism $\Omega(U) \to \Omega(\{v\})$ it is achieved with the help of the production base connected with the variable v.

The last chapter is devoted to an example how the material was used in the research on the mentioned project related to the text analysis.

8   An Example of Use of the Described Methods of Programming

One of the problems of the project that was mentioned in this paper was the decision whether the phrase is the assertion having the property "If-Then", i.e. if this phrase corresponds to some logical implication. An analysis of phrases was performed with the help of our production system. Some professional linguists were invited who prepared a collection of productions. In the present chapter we show some technical details of the work of the production system.

As we already said the study was made separately for each single phrase. It means that the phrases were taken as the situations. The separation of the text into collection of phrases was made by means of MS Word. In turn, each phrase was treated as a sequence of words. Separation into the sequence of words was achieved also by tools of MS Word. The system MS Word has considered as words not only the words but also it treated as words the punctuation signs in a phrase. It was very convenient as it allowed to take the signs into consideration.

The text analysis is provided with help of a set of production bases. Each production base is stored in separate MS Word file, and its name is considered to be the name of production base. Our program loads production bases when there is a need for it, and it is kept in the working space.

The construction of a single production is quite complex. In particular production may contain exceptions. The exception is a pattern and if some situation matches the pattern the production considered as not implacable. Yet, we restrict consideration with simple version of the rule. Such a rule does not modify the situation. It only checks whether the situation matches the pattern, and in the positive case it returns as the result the situation itself. In the production base, i.e. the MS Word file, such a rule is written down as a phrase, where besides common words so-called variables may be used. A variable is the square bracketed name of a variable with the possible name of the production base going after it.

Let us consider the matching of the situation, i.e. phrase, with such a pattern. Remember that we consider simplified version of production, which consists only from one pattern, and the purpose is not the transformation of a phrase, but to make a decision if the phrase does have the requested type.

At the first step for each of the variables there is the search for the sequence of words, than being substituted instead of variable the pattern converts to a given phrase. If it is not possible the phrase considered to be not matching the pattern.

If the suitable sequence of words found for each variable the system goes to the second step. On the second step for each such a sequence a production base is applied, which is shown in the square brackets after the name of the variable. If for each of these sequences the application of the corresponding base was successful, the starting matching also considered being successful. If even in one of cases the application of the production base to sequence of words was unsuccessful, the starting matching is considered also to be unsuccessful. In case for some variable the name of the production base is not shown, the second step is omitted. The procedure is recursive one as on the second step may be found some variables, which would involve into the matching procedure some new production bases.

In order to apply to the problem solution the algorithms described in the chapters 5-7, it is necessary to make programming of the bottom level, i.e. to implement the class morphism, operation composition and to concretize some other abstract concepts of the theory of category programming.

Let us start with the coding of the pattern. In the program using VBA, which is fast but may be not efficient, many constructions repeats the corresponding constructions of MS Word and some more complex functions for their consideration. For example, the pattern represented the line of text, practically repeating the line in the file MS Word. The variables are contained in this line as the name of variables and the name of production base in square brackets. In C++ there was an abstract class Element was created with depended classes ElementWord and ElementVar. The class Element-Word contained a word as a string of symbols yet, the class ElementVar contained the name of variable and the name of connected production base. To code the pattern itself the construction std::list<Element *> was used. In Lisp the pattern was coded as a list with elements either being strings, or being pairs, consisted from the name of the variable and the name of production base.

The main construction of Ω-category is the sequence of strings, indexed with the variables, also is coded differently. In VBA it is again coded with string of a certain format, which is studied with special programs. In C++ a class of standard library std::map? in List it is an associated list. The operation composition performs the substitution of string instead of variables in accordance with the algorithms, described in the chapter 7. For the matching rather simple search algorithms are used.

One can see that the binding of upper level to the concrete structures essentially different in three described examples of computer languages. However the algorithm of the upper level, that implements the run of production net, is the same in all three cases. As an example we show the fragment of program that provides the matching in C++ and in Lisp.

Version in C++:

```
Morphism *Matcher::next() {
  Morphism *result;
  while (true) {
    if (!m_matcherRest)
      m_matcherRest =
              new Matcher (m_patternNext,
m_situationRest);
    result= m_matcherRest ->next();
    if (result) {
      result=
        product(result,
          new Morphism(m_firstVar,
            new Pattern(m_situationStart,
              m_situationRest)));
      return result;
    }
    m_situationRest++;
    delete m_matcherRest;
    m_matcherRest =0;
  }
}
```

Version in Lisp:

```
(defmethod next((m matcher) &aux result)
  (loop
    (unless matcher-rest
```

```
(setf (slot-value matcher-rest)
   (make-instance 'matcher
      (slot-value pattern-next)
      (slot-value situation-rest) ) ) )
(setq result (next matcher-rest))
(when result
   (setq result
      (product result,
         (make-instance 'morphism
            m_firstVar
            (make-instance 'pattern situation-start   sit-
uation-rest) ) ) )
   (return-from next result) )
(setq situation-rest (cdr situation-rest))
(setq matcher-rest) ) )
```

One may see that the differences in the programs are related to the differences in the language syntaxes.

9   Conclusion

In this paper a universal approach to programming of intelligent systems based on the use of productions was introduced. In this paper there is no study of any new inference algorithms for such systems. Instead a certain construction was finally developed that allows to make these algorithms to be independent on the peculiarity of data used in various intelligent systems.

For instance, the replacement of the category part of a program with a bit more complex one, converts the ordinary production system into the dynamic production system as it was described in [10]. It became possible due to the fact that the inference algorithms were not rigidly related to the proposed category construction.

In some sense our ideas are close to the technology of object oriented programming, allowing creation of objects, which may be used in many problems. Then different developers may fill in these objects with a certain functionality needed for the solution of a concrete problem.

However, in our case it is clear that not every production system admits its conversion to the theory of category language shown in this paper. Thus, in this language it is difficult to describe productions with a large procedural part, say, productions intended to perform complex computations. Yet, the generality of our theory of category language makes it applicable to wide area of problems. The preceding research of the present authors has demonstrated that the language is suitable for study of many production systems used in the area of Artificial Intelligence.

References

1. Newell, A., Simon, H.A.: Human Problem Solving. Prentice-Hall, Englewood Cliffs (1972)
2. Nilsson, N.J.: Principles of Artificial Intellijence. Tioga Pub. Co., Springer, Palo Alto, Berlin (1982)
3. Stefanuk, V.L., Zhozhikashvili, A.V.: Productions and rules in artificial intelligence, KYBERNETES. The International Journal of Systems & Cybernetics, 817–826 (2002)
4. Markov, A.: A Theory of Algorithms. National Academy of Sciences, USSR
5. Post, E.: Formal reduction of the general combination problem. American J. Math. 65, 197–628
6. Stefanuk, V.L.: Some aspects of Expert System theory. Soviet J. Comp. Sci. (Tech. Kibernet.) (2), 85–91 (1987)
7. Zhozhikashvili, A.V., Stefanuk, V.L.: Programmable expert system shell ZNATOK and the problems of its theoryof category description. Soviet J. Comp. Sci (Tech. Kibernet.) (5), 134–147 (1990)
8. Savinitch, L.V., Stefanuk, V.L.: Vyrazhenieobuslovlennosti vestesvennom jazyke. Informatsionnye Technologii Ivychislitelnye Sistemy 1, 30–37 (2008)
9. Zhozhikashvili, A.V., Stefanuk, V.L.: Theory of category patterns for AI problems. New Results. Proceedings of RAN: Theory and Control Systems 5, 5–16 (1999)
10. Zhozhikashvili, A.V., Stefanuk, V.L.: Categories for Description of Dynamic Production Systems. In: Tyugu, E., Yamaguchi, T. (eds.) Proceedings of Joint Conference on Knowledge-Based Software Engineering, JCKBSE 2006, pp. 285–293. IOS Press, Amsterdam (2006)

Author Index